FINANCIAL THEORY

Perspectives from China

FINANCIAL THEORY

Perspectives from China

Xingyun PENG
Chinese Academy of Social Sciences, China

World Century

Published by

World Century Publishing Corporation
27 Warren Street, Suite 401-402, Hackensack, NJ 07601

Library of Congress Cataloging-in-Publication Data
Peng, Xingyun.
Financial theory : perspectives from China / by Xingyun Peng.
pages cm
Includes bibliographical references.
ISBN 978-1-938134-31-9
1. Finance. 2. Finance--China. 3. Economics. 4. Economics--China. I. Title.
HG173.P46 2015
332.0951--dc23
2014017824

British Library Cataloguing-in-Publication Data
A catalogue record for this book is available from the British Library.

Originally published in Chinese by Truth & Wisdom Press, 2010

In-house Editors: Dipasri Sardar/Hongyan Li

Typeset by Stallion Press
Email: enquiries@stallionpress.com

Printed in Singapore

Contents

Foreword vii

Acknowledgments xi

Preface xiii

Part I. Introduction **1**

1. Money, Monetary Systems, and Statistics 3
2. Financial System 23
3. Time Value of Money 49
4. Time Allocation of Resources: Whether to Save or Spend 71
5. Asset Selection and Risk Management of Lender–Savers 91
6. Financing Options for Borrower–Spenders 113

Part II. Financial Institutions and Markets **137**

7. Financial Institutions in the Financial System 139
8. Commercial Bank Operations and Management 167
9. Long-Term Capital Markets 205
10. Short-Term Money Markets 235

11. Foreign Exchange Markets 261

12. Financial Derivatives Market 283

Part III. Financial Controls **319**

13. Money Supply 321

14. Demand for Money 359

15. Interest Rate Levels and Interest Rate Structure 383

16. Price Levels: Inflation and Deflation 409

17. Exchange Rate Determination and the Exchange Rate System 429

18. Balance of Payments 453

19. National Income and Output Determination: The *IS–LM* Model 479

20. Monetary Policy Operations of the Central Bank 501

Part IV. Financial Development and Stability **549**

21. Financial Development and Financial Structure 551

22. Financial Deepening and Financial Liberalization 577

23. Financial Crises 603

24. Financial Regulation and Supervision 631

Glossary 653

Index 681

Foreword

Ever since the economic reforms were introduced, the "Western influence" has come in several waves. Each wave has left China with a great deal of things, of which textbooks on a wide range of subjects are most valued, because they have helped reshape the ideas, concepts and knowledge structure of one Chinese generation after another. In the field of finance, the greatest impact came from a number of textbooks, specifically China Financial Publishing House's edition of Chandler's *The Economics of Money and Banking* in the early 1980s, Shanghai Joint Publishing's edition of Thomas Meyer's *Money, Banking and the Economy* by the end of the 1980s as well as Frederic Mishkin's *The Economics of Money, Banking and Financial Markets* (a new edition of this book was translated and published in 1996). These translated works have played an active role in promoting the development of China's study of money and finance as well as the reform of China's financial system.

However, after all, these translated works are "exotic" by nature, and while they can certainly deliver the basic principles of finance, teach Chinese people about the latest developments in this discipline, and let them know about the financial systems in other countries and what is currently happening, if we were to put these theories into practice in China (this is the fundamental purpose for which we study finance), there will always be something that prevents them from fitting well into the Chinese system. With the deepening of reforms to China's financial system and alongside the narrowing gap between the financial studies at home and abroad, this "unfitness" is beginning to be felt by more people. In light of this, Chinese financial researchers have always had a certain wish: to write a number of course books which not only accurately explain the basic principles of finance but also fully reflect the actual situation of China's financial sector.

Why must we instill finance with "Chinese characteristics"? The most direct reason for this is that if financial principles are presented in a pure Chinese language with vivid Chinese examples, they will certainly make more sense to Chinese people. An even more important reason for this that lies below the surface is that having gone through more than 20 years of reform and development, China's financial system and financial structure have undergone considerable changes, and as a result, a new financial system which is in line with the demands of a market economy is beginning to take shape.

At the same time, China's financial system was developed upon the framework of China's historical traditions, cultural background and economic system, and as such, it has given rise to distinct characteristics which differ significantly from other countries. Clearly, examining such changes and distilling them into certain rules governing the development of China's financial sector should be the historic task of China's financial researchers. It should be said that our financial researchers are approaching the new phase which we have yearned to see for quite some time: a summary of China's experience of financial reform and financial development which may benefit development of the entire study of finance.

This work by Dr. Peng Xingyun is a worthy endeavor in the "localization" of finance. After flipping through the pages, I felt that this book has the following four distinct characteristics. First, this book is integrated. For a long period of time, China's macro-economic focus has been on "the economics of money and banking" which is unrelated to the micro-economic focus on elucidating the principles of finance which apply to financial operations. Over the last few years, many domestic scholars, and even some predecessors, have committed themselves to the work of "integrating" the two. This textbook reflects the author's considerations in this push towards convergence. Second, this book highlights the practical aspects of finance. We are all aware that finance is an applied science. It is precisely because of this that whether it be an exposition on the principles set forth or an explanation of reality, everything must be closely integrated with how it has been put into practice in China. In this regard, this book has made an outstanding effort. Third, this book represents the cutting edge of financial researches. While finance certainly has a long history, yet it is still a relatively young discipline. As such, keeping up with the modern pace of theoretical development is a fundamental requirement of any successful teaching material. This textbook has organically integrated some of the most recent developments in financial theory, such as the perspective of functional finance, the principle of asymmetric information, the theory of financial development, financial globalization, financial crises, and the new technology of financial transactions which gives this book its cutting edge. Fourthly, this book is readable. As important as finance may be, it goes without saying that it is a boring subject. As such, a relaxed tone is used to introduce the basic principles of finance in layman's terms, and as far as we can see, one of the basic requirements of a good textbook is to clarify the obscure and boring theories with things that we have come across. In this regard also, the author has made an outstanding effort.

In short, this book is a suitable textbook for university students, financial professionals, postgraduate trainees, and those who want to be financial literates. I would recommend it to everyone.

Li Yang
Vice President, Chinese Academy of Social Sciences

Acknowledgments

Upon the publication of this book, I harbored both joy and apprehension in my heart as I asked for the advice of my seniors in the Chinese financial research community. What brought me the greatest joy was the positive encouragement bestowed upon me by famous experts and scholars such as (arranged according to the strokes in their surname) Professor Wang Chuanlun of Renmin University who is now well into his eighties, Professor Jiang Chun of Wuhan University, Professor Liu Ya of the University of International Business and Economics, Professor Chen Xuebin of Fudan University, Professor Zhang Jie of Renmin University and Professor Jiang Boke of Fudan University. Professor Li Yang, Professor Wang Guogang and Professor Wang Songqi, to whom I have been indebted for their help since I entered the Graduate School of the Chinese Academy of Social Sciences, also provided me with great support throughout the publication and revision of this book, including a favorable environment for my research and other conveniences. I would also like to thank Professor Zhou Maoqing of the CASS Institute of Finance and Banking for improving the revisions to this book and for the various opportunities which were offered to me. Today, it has nearly been 15 years since I left the university halls, and upon the completion of this revised version, I think back to the teachers at Jiangxi University of Finance and Economics who fostered my learning, for it was they who introduced me to the hallowed halls of economics. Here, in particular, I would like to thank Professor Wang Qiushi, Professor Liu Wenjun, and Professor Lv Jianglin for their teachings, support and encouragement.

After the first edition of this book was published in Chinese, it won the favor of a lot of university and college teachers and students, and the book's system, structure, writing style and material all received high ratings. Some colleges, universities and training institutions have adopted this book as a textbook and as a reference book. There are also a number of non-economic students who have picked this book up for self-study out of an interest in finance. These teachers and students have given me a great deal of encouragement. But as I am honored with their encouragement, in my heart, I feel both guilty and unsettled. Although I burned the midnight oil for over two years on the first Chinese edition of this book, and did everything possible to polish it, upon its publication, I still stumbled across errors and omissions. In this regard, I have always felt a great deal of trepidation. I believe that these errors and omissions have brought about a great deal of inconvenience to the teachers and students who use this book. However, they do not demand that this book be perfect, but instead have tolerated the book with all its defects with a generous heart, promptly sending me an e-mail to tell me where it is sorely lacking, and some have even proposed their valuable opinion as to revisions. I sincerely admire their precision. The revised version is saturated with their hard work (of course, the errors are my own). They, at the least, include (arranged according to the strokes in their surname): Wan Zhihong (Nankai University), Bian Zhicun (Nanjing University of Finance and Economics), Sun Fuzhen (Shandong University of Finance), Chi Feng (Anhui Audit College), Li Kening (Beijing Language and Culture University), Li Yanjun (China University of Geosciences), Li Jiming (Zhejiang University), Lu Mingyang (Foshan University), Zheng Minggang (China Foreign Affairs University), Peng Yun (Hubei University of Economics), Hu Junhui (Zhejiang Institute of Finance and Economics), Zhao Xinping (Northwest University), Zhao Hua (Guangdong Polytechnic Normal University), Zeng Gang (Chinese Academy of Social Sciences), Han Guowen (Wuhan University), and Han Jingfang (Wuhan University).

Here, I would like to express my deepest respect for all the teachers and readers who have encouraged me and provided their valuable suggestions for improving the book.

Peng Xingyun
CASS Institute of Finance and Banking
July 2013

Preface

Why study the principles of finance?

In institutions of higher learning, the study of finance has been, is and will be a popular major. Only those students with a high score on the entrance exams can be admitted into the school of finance. Even without entering this major, many students will also select financial college elective as part of their curriculum. The study of finance is not only intended as a means of future employment for undergraduates, but rather it is a powerful weapon that offers bright and broad prospects for us as individuals.

The financial sector is filled with temptations and fraught with challenges. No matter which way you go, the financial sector is a well-paid "white collar" industry. Working in this field tends to yield a high quality of life. It is precisely because of this that there is fierce competition and selection when it comes to finding work in the financial sector, and if you do in fact make it, your heart will be filled with pride. The uncertainty of financial businesses is much higher than any other industry, and success in the field of finance requires adequate wisdom and courage. Success in this field is incredibly rewarding and allows one to truly realize their own value. However, the premise of all this is whether or not you can deeply understand, grasp and flexibly apply the basic principle of finance to seize fleeting opportunities.

In a highly market-oriented society, "if you don't finance, you will have no finances." The study of financial management is becoming increasingly important to individuals, enterprises and even governments. Financial management consists of the following: Determining how much of this month's salary will be spent and how much will be saved for the future, whether to purchase stock, deposit money in a bank or invest in treasury bills, more importantly, how can you use other people's money to finance your desired house and car, and so on and so forth. The key to your financial success is understanding the basic principles of finance.

The study of finance provides a theoretical guideline for a government's macroeconomic policies. Even in countries like America which firmly believe in the free market, governments will often use monetary policies to intervene in macroeconomics. In China where a planned economy had a deep-rooted effect, monetary policy is also playing an increasingly important role. Monetary policy has had a very direct influence on not only overall economic performance but also on our personal interests. For example, monetary policy will directly lead to changes in interest rates, and such changes will influence the price of stock and bonds which will bring about correspondingly profitable opportunities or potential risks to your investments. Having studied finance, you will have a better in-depth understanding of the operation of the economy, the trend of the government's monetary policy and its possible impact, thereby giving you the upper hand for making your choices.

Finally, finance is a serious scholarship, and the research of issues related to finance is a great joy that has brought value to the lives of many economists, as it has brought them a wonderful reputation. Since the 1990s, the Nobel Prize in Economics has tended to be granted to economists who study finance. Domestically, many well-known economists are active in the field of finance, and they have had a major influence on macroeconomic policies and the reforms to the financial system. Meanwhile, as experts and scholars with a rigorous attitude towards research, they have earned respect and admiration.

Words cannot express the attractiveness and joy that comes from the study of finance, and only in the course of your studies and once you grasp the basic principles of finance will you begin to experience such joy. I wish you the best of luck in your study of finance and sincerely hope that it will allow you to achieve your ambitious goals!

Why choose this book for learning the principles of finance?

Compared with other textbooks on the economics of money and banking or the study of finance, this book has the following unique characteristics:

- An innovative system. This book begins from the most primitive functions of finance — the bridge which connects those with a surplus of funds with those with a shortage — and proceeds to analyze the choice between savings and consumption, the asset selection of the surplus sector and the financing options of those with funding shortages, and thus the organic time allocation of resources, asset selections and the financing structure theory which are integrated into the principles of finance. This allows this book to surpass the limitations of previous Chinese textbooks on finance or on the economics of money and banking which, for a long period of time, only dealt with the relation between money and macroeconomy. As such, a logical, progressive new system of financial principles has been established from the micro to the macro. This systematic structure can help you better understand and grasp the basic principles of finance.
- Enlightening and applicable. Whether expounding on the principles or considering the design of the practice questions, this book is closely linked to the

Chinese reality. In this way, while this textbook expounds upon the principles, it pays much more attention to the flexible application of the principles, and as such, the book is relatively more enlightening than similar books at home and abroad. It focuses on training readers to think like an economist, and to understand ever-changing financial phenomenon. However, this book does not rigidly adhere to the facts and simple descriptions of China's specific financial reforms, which gives this textbook a universal application.

- Cutting-edge. This book has included the new developments in financial theory, such as the perspective of functional finance, the principles of asymmetric information, financial development theory, financial globalization, and financial crises, which gives this book its cutting edge relative to other textbooks on finance or the economics of money and banking.
- Easy to understand and fun. In terms of style, this book strives to blend rational knowledge into perceptual knowledge, introduces the basic principles of finance with a relaxed and easy-to-read approach, attempts to illustrate boring and difficult-to-understand theories with interesting examples that readers can understand. With practically no mathematical models, this book is incredibly readable. The entire book is educational and fun, making it easy for you to approach the study of finance.

Based on the features mentioned above, this book is an ideal source for you to study the principles of finance.

What are the benefits of using this book?

More specifically, different people will derive different "benefits" from using this book.

- If you are a professor of the economics of money and banking or a teacher of finance, the unique system of this book and its closeness to reality as well as the highly readable language it uses to explain complex principles will inspire students to grasp and utilize the principles of finance, and thereby reap the fruits of a sound education. This textbook is accompanied by PowerPoint slides for teaching purposes, and educators who use this textbook may visit http://ifb.cass.cn/show_news.asp?id=9873 to download the slides, primary data for the tables and figures in the book as well as exercise answers.
- If you are a student, you can master and flexibly use the basic principles of finance by reading this book, which will undoubtedly give you another winning weapon in your arsenal for the increasingly fierce employment environment.
- If you still plan to continue your education and would like to apply for a postgraduate program in finance, the flexible use of principles which this book focuses on will help you achieve marks.
- If you have already entered into the workforce and would like to prepare for your future life, then reading this book will help you better manage your finances,

better understand the macroeconomic financial environment, and make better investment decisions.

How should you use this book?

Aristotle once said that "Learning is not child's play; we cannot learn without pain". Fear not the sages warning of "pain" nor the high price you may think that you must pay. Note that studying is also a source of unlimited joy and potential wealth. This kind of joy springs forth from your conquest, which is the same joy of success when you beat your opponent in chess or in a ball game.

Although I have made efforts to make this textbook easily comprehensible and easy to understand, learning requires a bit of work after all. In fact, all joy is as such, and if you truly desire such success in chess, you must carefully calculate each and every move. To truly embrace the joy of studying finance, you must put it all together. The joy that comes from studying finance is the new awareness and understanding when you face financial problems. To make this joy last much longer, you must never stop learning new theories and practices and never stop discovering new challenges.

In order to facilitate your learning, this textbook has made the following technical arrangements.

- Each chapter begins with a Learning Objectives which lets you know the important content that you must focus on in that chapter.
- The Summary which appears at the end of each chapter summarizes the content of the chapter, provides a concluding statement on the topics discussed and draws your attention to information that you learned previously, all of which can enhance your ability to remember.
- Critical Thinking Questions appear at the end of each chapter, and if time is available, we recommend that you write out each of the questions because they can help you digest the basics of what you learned. Most importantly, some exercises address real problems, and they can help you flexibly apply these principles rather than simply memorizing boring concepts.

Additionally, the financial newspapers and periodicals can also act as supplementary teaching materials which may be a benefit to your study of finance. The more that you read this type of news, the better you will understand these principles.

Finally, I should also remind you that the study of finance is an applied science, and its greatest value lies in its practicality. Theoretical learning and practical explorations should reinforce each other. Keep in mind that: "Practice Makes Perfect!"

Contact the author

It is in the structure and style of writing where this book differs from a great deal of other textbooks on finance or the economics of money and banking, and coupled with my own limitations, shortcomings are inevitable. Additionally, this book should be continuously improved in the interaction between the author and readers. In order to further improve this book, I have applied for a specialized e-mail address (financepxy@sohu.com) to receive the various feedback and valuable advice of readers.

I look forward to your treasured opinions!

Peng Xingyun
CASS Institute of Finance and Banking

Part I

Introduction

For real power, it's the person who turns the dials of global capital flow more than the guy who can push a button on an atomic bomb.

— David Jones

Remember that money is of the prolific, generating nature. Money can beget money, and its offspring can beget more, and so on.

— Benjamin Franklin

Be not penny-wise. Riches have wings. Sometimes they fly away of themselves, and sometimes they must be set flying to bring in more.

— Sir Francis Bacon

Chapter 1

Money, Monetary Systems, and Statistics

Learning Objectives

After completing this chapter, you will be able to:

- Fully understand what money is
- Understand the functions of money and its impact on economy and society
- Know the forms of money and their development
- Know the monetary standards and the monetary system
- Understand the categorization of monetary aggregates, the basis, and economic significance
- Fully understand what monetary liquidity structure is
- Know the macroeconomic significance of changes in the monetary liquidity structure

Money is an important factor of human life. Its history is as old as civilization itself, and opinions have always varied as to its true value. Those who are overly attached to money see it as the source of power, happiness, and truth. Moralists, however, see money as the root of all evil. In China, most of us take the middle path; "money isn't everything, but without it you can't do anything" seems to strike a chord among most Chinese.

To discuss the topic of money is no easy task, in part because it touches upon the collective knowledge and wisdom of countless disciplines. What we aim to do is to use the system of theoretical knowledge found in Economics to approach monetary phenomena. Within this chapter, we will understand the difference between *money* and *cash* to help you grasp how money affects every aspect of our lives — on the large scale throughout the entire nation and even the global economic system, as well as on the small scale in our daily lives when we take the bus or buy groceries. You will also know why money is the main instrument of commerce and learn about the development of different forms of money. After completing this chapter, you will have a clear understanding of concepts that often appear in financial reports like *broad money* or *narrow money*.

1.1 Definition of Money

Money is something that we see and touch every day. Even toddlers know what money is. To the average person, so-called money is nothing more than the yuan, dollar or pound that you take to the store to buy things with. This kind of money, however, is referred to as *cash*, or coins and currency in circulation. Within Finance or Economics, this is not the standard definition of money. Nowadays, cash is not the only thing we use to buy everything that we need. Checks, credit cards and debit cards all can act as a method of payment when we go shopping. With the rise of the internet, virtual money, such as Tencent Q coins, has become quite fashionable. In fact, in our modern economic life, no matter if it is for goods or services or even financial transactions, cash is only used to pay for a small fraction of things.

We often hear people talking about money as if it were the equivalent of income. For example, people often admire others who "make money hand over fist". This "money" is what we call income. To equate income with money would cause a lot of serious confusion in economic analysis, because money is a stock concept, i.e., at any given time it will be a fixed amount. Income, however, is a flow concept, and represents a numerical relationship for a given time interval.

For example, when you ask your friend for some money, saying, "Hey, how much money do you have with you? Can I borrow a little?" Your buddy might say, "I have got 3000 yuan". This 3000 yuan is the fixed amount of money that your buddy happens to have with him at the moment that you asked him. When your friend finds a new job, you may ask how much he makes per month or per year. It is pretty straightforward that you are asking him how much his salary is each month or each year. As such, this amount often changes.

Many people still consider money to be the same thing as wealth. If someone is really rich, we might say he has a lot of money. If someone is struggling just to get by, we might say he is short of money or cash-strapped. This "money" is referring to wealth rather than cash or income. Wealth, however, refers to much more than just money. The stock, bonds, funds and other financial assets, houses, or cars that people purchase are all listed as wealth, but these certainly cannot be considered money.

So, how exactly does Finance or Economics define money then? Normally, economists will refer to money as anything that is generally accepted and can act as a unit of account, a medium of exchange, a store of value, and a means of payment. According to this kind of definition, money certainly does not merely refer to the cash in our pockets and the spare change in our wallets. It does not simply mean wealth or income either. It could include physical items like gold, silver, etc.; or it could also be a kind of widely accepted symbol. As long as it fulfills the above four functions, it would be termed "money".

1.2 The Functions of Money

We already know that economists define money from its functions. Money has four main functions: a medium of exchange, a unit of account, a means of payment and a store of value.

1.2.1 Medium of Exchange

Before the birth of money, people directly traded one good for another, namely in the form of bartering. For instance, when farmer Wang Er gives farmer Zhao Si 10 eggs for a handful of tea leaves, this is bartering.

Yet bartering is extremely inefficient. As the division of labor became increasingly complex, bartering began to hinder social development. This is because bartering requires a *double coincidence of wants.* A double coincidence of wants can be considered on three levels. First, exchange must be between two people who both require goods. In other words, the good that each person has can satisfy the needs of the other person. For example, Wang Er has eggs and needs tea leaves. Zhao Si has tea leaves and just so happens to need eggs. At this point in time, Wang Er can exchange his eggs for Zhao Si's tea leaves. However, if Zhao Si does not need eggs, but rather needs a tea cup, the needs of Wang Er and Zhao Si are not complementary. So, they cannot barter directly with each other.

Some goods also happen to be indivisible, and because of this, within a barter economy, the needs of both parties not only have to be complimentary, but the value of the goods must be equal. Otherwise, trading is not possible or becomes unfair. If Wang Er owns a head of cattle, although he needs tea leaves, which Zhao Si just so happens to have, and even though Zhao Si needs a head of cattle, he only has a catty of tea. In this case, bartering would be troublesome for both of them. Obviously, Wang Er would be unwilling to trade a head of cattle for a catty of tea.

The third level of the double coincidence of wants is the timing in which both parties want to trade. If Wang Er has eggs and Zhao Si has tea leaves, yet Wang Er will not need tea leaves until much later, while Zhao Si needs eggs immediately for supplemental nutrition, then the two cannot immediately barter.

Thus it can be seen that only when the two people's needs are completely complimentary can they do any real bartering. History has shown that only when the division of labor is relatively straightforward and the geographic scope of trade is very narrow can bartering be done and only to a limited degree. With the increasing complexity of the division of labor and the expansion of trade regions, bartering could no longer satisfy the needs of societies.

As direct bartering is incredibly inefficient, indirect trading is thus made possible. Indirect trading refers to when people do not use their own goods to trade for the goods they need. Furthermore, the goods they use to trade are generally accepted by others. The more times this good is used for indirect trading and the greater its use, the more willing people will be to accept it. This type of good becomes money. Money serves as a medium of exchange and can greatly improve the efficiency of exchange or reduce transaction costs. Money, as a medium of exchange, must be widely accepted. As money separates the transaction process into two independent parts of buying and selling, the condition of "double coincidence of wants" found in bartering is thus removed. Wang Er, who has eggs but would not need tea leaves for at least half a year, can sell his eggs now, wait six months, and then use the money he earns from selling his eggs and exchange it for the tea leaves he needs.

1.2.2 Unit of Account

The second function of money is to serve as a unit of account, namely the use of money as an instrument for comparing value. Using monetary units, such as the yuan or dollar as a means of measuring and expressing the value of goods and services is just like using "meters" to express length or "pounds" and "ounces" for weight. We can use "meters" to compare the lengths of objects and "pounds" and "ounces" to compare the weights of items. Similarly, we can also use "yuan" to compare the value of goods.

Exchanges in the modern economic system are incredibly complex and require the continuous comparison of numerous goods. If the values of goods are expressed in terms of different other goods, then people will find it almost impossible to compare between them. For example, if a supermarket happens to use the price of an ice cream bar for a bottle of cola, while a different convenience store uses the price of the same ice cream bar for a pack of gum, which ice cream bar would be cheaper? There is no way to directly compare these kinds of prices. Alternatively, if the price of the ice cream bar were to be expressed in terms of money, the supermarket would mark the price 1.6 yuan per bar and the convenience store would mark the price 2.5 yuan per bar. Naturally, we can see which is cheaper.

As a unit of account, money greatly simplifies the frequency of trading as well as the pricing system. Suppose that within an economy there were only two tradable goods, and thus only one exchange rate; if there were three tradable goods, there would then need to be three exchange rates; if there were four tradable goods, the amount of exchange rates and frequency of trade would increase to six, and so on.

If an economy has n number of commodities, then, in a barter economy, we can use induction to calculate that there would need to be $\frac{n(n-1)}{2}$ exchange rates. If there are 10 commodities, we would need 45 exchange rates; if there were 1000 commodities, we would need 499,500 exchange rates. Obviously, there are way more than 1000 goods in the average store nowadays. When the amount of commodities is large enough, like our current market economy with all kinds of goods, the amount of exchange rates we would need for bartering would be unimaginable! Alternatively, if some commodity were to act as money, serving as a unit of account, we would need $(n - 1)$ exchange rates. In this way, within an economy characterized by commodity money, markets that sell 1000 kinds of commodities would only need 999 types of exchange rates. Furthermore, in the age of fiat money (i.e., the renminbi) that is far more complex than the commodity money economies, a market selling 1000 kinds of goods would only need to mark 1000 prices.

As a unit of account, money has greatly simplified book-keeping, streamlined financial accounting for businesses and has offered companies a hand in improving managerial efficiency. Large enterprises require a lot of raw materials; take a packet of ramen noodles, for example. Other than flour, the plastic bag, oil, salt, onions, and spices for flavoring, we also need to factor in the labor, equipment and shipping required. If there was no money to standardize the value of these different inputs, it would be difficult for this ramen noodle enterprise to do their accounting, just as it would be hard for others to tell if this company was making a profit or was in the red. We should not even begin to mention what it takes to produce even more complex goods.

Box 1.1 A Day without Money

The 19th century British Economist William Stanley Jevons once told a story about a situation like this. Mademoiselle Zélie, a singer of the Théâtre Lyrique at Paris, gave a concert in the Society Islands. In exchange for her five songs, she was to receive a third of the profits (about what Pavarotti would earn 150 years later). In the Society Islands, however, coins were very scarce, so they could only use goods to compensate her. When counted, Mademoiselle Zélie had three pigs, twenty-three turkeys, forty-four chickens, five hundred cocoa-nuts, besides considerable quantities of bananas, lemons, and oranges. In Paris, this amount of livestock and vegetables might have brought four thousand francs, which would have been good remuneration for five songs. Yet Mademoiselle Zélie could not consume any considerable portion of the receipts herself, and it became necessary in the meantime to feed the pigs and poultry with the fruits.

— See Martin Mayer, *The Bankers*, Hainan Publishing, 2000 Edition

1.2.3 Means of Payment

Within a barter economy, there is no common standard of value for people to accept, and consequently, there is no basis for measuring long-term contracts and borrowing. Try to imagine such a situation: Wang Xiao'er works in a shoe factory. How might the boss go about giving Wang Xiao'er his salary? One possibility is that he could give Wang Xiao'er 10 pairs of shoes every month, but would not this be a bit inconvenient for Wang Xiao'er? Unless these shoes are the worst he is ever seen, there is likely no way for even Wang Xiao'er's entire household to wear out 10 pairs of shoes each month. Also, other than wearing shoes, Wang Xiao'er's family also has other basic necessities to worry about. If the shoe factory does quite well and Wang Xiao'er earns a decent salary, he may even get a wage of 50 pairs of shoes, putting him in the individual income tax bracket. In a world without money, Wang Xiao'er can take two pairs of shoes and send them to the national revenue service, thereby extending his trifling inconvenience to the national scale!

With money, our wages, taxes, borrowing, and lending are all quite convenient. All long-term and short-term contracts can be signed because of money. It is easy to see that the use of money promotes the development of the credit system, and borrowing and lending, which are the very basis of our modern market economy.

1.2.4 Store of Value

Another function of money is to store value. Within a barter economy, one must buy and sell at the same time. That is to say, if one fails to sell anything, neither can he buy anything. On the other hand, whenever someone wants to sell something, he also must buy a different commodity at the same time. After the development of money, buying and selling became two independent ventures. When selling, there is no need to buy another commodity at the same time. The seller can keep on selling until he chooses to buy something. In the time interval from when the merchant sells a commodity and buys another, money serves its function as a store of value, or rather a "temporary dwelling" for purchasing power.

Money is unique when it serves as a store of value, mainly because it requires few, if any, transaction costs. If you decided to use any other asset as a store of wealth, you would have to use your income in the form of money to buy this kind of asset. Afterwards, when you want something else to replace this type of asset, you also must convert it back into money. These two types of transactions, converting money into the asset and converting the asset back into money, both entail certain costs. Additionally, there are costs that come with storage. For example, a farmer who wants to store grain must build a granary, not to mention the fact that rats will steal some of his grain. The stored goods themselves will also lose value and suffer from physical depreciation.

Suppose that quite some years ago you bought a computer to serve as a store of value. At that time, you would need to spend at least 10,000 yuan to buy a desktop (typically with 486 processors then). Now, however, you need to buy an A/C unit and decide to sell this PC that you bought years ago. You cannot make much from selling it, even if you have never used it after purchase. The key here is that the development of computer technology is so fast and new generations come out so quickly that technical progress has eaten away your nest egg that was meant to be a store of value.

Of course, for money to store value there need to be certain conditions. Most importantly, the value of money must be stable. Under conditions of high inflation where the general price of goods spirals upwards, people's hard-earned money constantly loses value. If a certain amount of money could buy 100 catties of rice a month ago but now can only buy 50 catties, people would resort to savings in kind because the role of money as a store of value is greatly impaired.

As a store of value, money plays a significant role in economic development. Without a store of value like money, large-scale capital accumulation and redistribution would never be possible. It is a given in modern society that the distribution of wealth and talent is uneven. Some people have a great deal of money, but lack managerial skill. Others are born with business skills and a knack for innovation, yet they have no capital. Thanks to the stored value of money, those with money to spend can give their financial surplus to someone with managerial skills to use. This is the means by which the level of economic development can be improved.

1.3 Types of Money

Although money is a great invention of mankind, human society was not endowed from the very beginning with our modern paper currency or bank cards such as the Smart Card of China Merchants Bank or Pacific Card of the Bank of Communications (note that is not to say the Smart Card and Pacific Card are money). The forms of money have continuously changed alongside the developments of human society.

1.3.1 Full-Bodied Commodity Money

Any type of money, if its value as a commodity is equal to its value as a medium of exchange, is commodity money. A gold coin is the most obvious example of commodity money. If it is sold on the gold market, its value would be equal to its face value. Generally speaking, for a commodity to serve as commodity money, it must have the following characteristics: general acceptance, a stable value, portability and durability, a unified value, and ease of division.

Over the course of history, various commodities, such as cloth, shells, pearls, and leather have been used as a medium of exchange. These types of commodity money were bulky, difficult to divide, a hassle to carry around, or worn out easily. For these reasons, as economies developed, these types of commodity money were all replaced in the end with metallic money. Due to their stable value, portability and divisibility, copper, silver and gold had all been widely used as a medium of exchange. The knife-shaped and spade-shaped coins of the Warring States Period and the Qin Ban-liang coins are several examples of ancient Chinese metallic money.

1.3.2 Commodity-Backed Money

With the development of the economy and the growth of commercial transactions, metallic money could no longer satisfy the demands of commodity exchange. Thus, economies transitioned from metallic money to commodity-backed money.

Commodity-backed money, or representative money, is the paper note with the standard of a precious metal issued by a government or specified institution that serves in place of the precious metal as a medium of exchange. The value of commodity-backed money is lower than the value of the precious metal it represents, yet someone with commodity-backed money can exchange it for the precious metal that it represents at any time.

1.3.3 Fiat Money

Fiat money is the logical next step after commodity-backed money and the result of crashes in the precious metal market and further developments in the commercial market. Fiat money is backed by a nation's enforcement ability. In fact, its intrinsic value is lower than the value it represents, and it does not represent any precious metal. In general, if the monetary value of money does not equal its value as a commodity, nor can it be exchanged for commodity money, then this is fiat money. Almost all currencies today are fiat money. Thus it can be seen that fiat money is just a symbol or a sign, giving those who hold it the right to exchange it for goods and services. As a symbol, fiat money itself does not need any intrinsic value, it only needs a national force to maintain it and for people to perceive it as generally acceptable. Its intrinsic value is irrelevant. In reality, symbolic money cannot directly give people any added utility or enjoyment. It would be like eating cash to keep from going hungry or putting a wad of dollars on your head to keep you dry when it is raining. The reason we are willing to hold this fiat money, however, is because when we are actually starving, we can use it to buy some fries or when the weather turns cold, we can go to the store and use it to buy a coat. This is why people are so willing to accept fiat money.

Fiat money is the logical next step in the development of a commercial economy because it satisfies the need for large-scale commercial transactions. Regardless of whether it is commodity money, metallic money or commodity-backed money, the supply of money will always be under constraints of natural resources. For instance, if a country is blessed with a large amount of gold deposits and also happens to discover even greater amounts, then this country's money supply will also be quite plentiful. Since fiat money, at most, is only a symbol, governments can avoid natural resource constraints and freely alter their money supply. Of course, uncontrolled monetary expansion by the government would lead to a much weakened economy; unrestrained growth in a money supply can lead to hyperinflation. The public would also quickly lose confidence in this fiat money, which would cause a chaotic economic scenario, or even political turmoil. As Adam Smith wrote in *The Wealth of Nations*, "the judicious operations of banking, by providing, if I may be allowed so violent a metaphor, a sort of wagon-way through the air; enable the country to convert, as it were, a great part of its highways into good pastures and corn-fields, . . . however, it must be acknowledged, though they may be somewhat augmented, cannot be altogether so secure, when they are thus, as it were, suspended upon the wings of paper money, as when they travel about upon the solid ground of gold and silver."

With a sense of humor, a very frugal mother told her daughter, "Dear, take a taxi instead of a bus; it's much cheaper." The girl was dumbfounded, asking, "Why?" Her mother replied, "Inflation is vicious right now. If you take a bus you have to buy a ticket first; if you take a taxi, you pay later. That's why." Under hyperinflation, fiat money can really run an economy off its tracks.

1.3.4 Electronic Money

With the development of computers and information technology, money today is beginning to take the electronic form (e-money). Electronic money usually refers to the use of a computer or smart card for payments and transfers. Holding this debit card is just like holding cash; every time that goods or services are purchased, it can be used for payment. Most banks now have ATMs, providing customers with 24 hours of automatic banking for services where a bank teller is not needed. Additionally, many stores and hotels use POS terminals. As long as they have established a special partnership with any given bank, you can use the bank's card to buy goods or book hotel rooms.

Strictly speaking, electronic money is a type of fiat money, the only difference being that electronic money has no tangible, physical form, making it a symbol in the truest sense. And yet, electronic money still depends on the cardholder's bank account and any changes in his account balance. If the balance runs out in your bank account, and you cannot get a line of credit, regardless of how many cards you may have, you still cannot buy anything. From this perspective, the widespread use of electronic money only changes the proportion of deposits and currency in circulation. For example, if you have 10,000 yuan saved in your bank account, and you go to the store to buy an LED television for 2000 yuan. Without electronic money, you would have had to withdraw 2000 yuan in cash and only 8000 yuan would be left in your account. With a debit card, however, there is no need for a cash withdrawal. Upon purchasing the television, 2000 yuan would be withdrawn directly from your card. In both of these situations, the total amount of money never changes; there is only a change in the monetary structure. Speaking from this perspective, electronic money is merely replacing currency in circulation. It does not, however, replace bank deposits as a form of fiat money. In essence, electronic money is still a kind of fiat money.

1.4 Monetary System

1.4.1 What is the Monetary System?

The monetary system is a legally defined structure and form of organization for the circulation of a country's currency. A typical monetary system will include the following: minting material, monetary unit, minting, issuance and circulation of currency, the reserve system, etc.

(a) *Minting Material*

The basic condition for a monetary system is to have a determined minting material. Many countries often use metals such as copper, silver, or gold as a minting material. Specifically, minting material selection depends on a country's endowment of resources and level of economic development.

(b) *Monetary Unit*

A monetary unit is also one of the fundamental requirements of a monetary system and carries the defined name of a country's currency. With metallic money, the name of currency unit and amount of metal in each must be determined. Once a monetary unit and fractional monetary units are fixed, a price standard is set, and this currency can better exert its functions as a unit of account and medium of exchange.

(c) *Minting, Issuance, and Circulation of Currency*

Money that enters into general circulation (currency in circulation) can be divided into standard money and fractional money. Standard money is the basic currency in circulation of a country's monetary system. It is a country's legal monetary unit for pricing and settlements and is also called the main currency. Standard money acts as a medium of circulation and means of payment. Creditors or sellers cannot refuse to accept it. For these reasons, standard money has unlimited legal tender.

Fractional money comprises the small amounts of currency below the main currency and is used for daily retail trade and giving out change. In the process of circulation and payments, if beyond a certain amount, a creditor can refuse to accept fractional money. Therefore fractional money has also been called "limited legal tender". Under a metallic monetary system, the face value of standard money is consistent with the actual value of the metal. It is a full-bodied currency that is fixed by a country. Fractional money is often minted with base metals, and the actual value of the contents is less than its nominal value. While fractional money is limited legal tender, they can be traded freely for standard money. Since precious metal reserves and corresponding gold and silver currency could not satisfy the needs of a developing commodity economy, banknotes and paper money emerged. Banknotes are fiat money issued by banks. Originally, people who owned banknotes could go to the bank at any time and exchange their banknotes for metallic currency.

Later on, central bankers stopped exchanging banknotes for precious metals. Since their circulation depends on the strength of state power, banknotes have gradually become the paper money that we currently use.

(d) *Reserve System*

When metallic money and banknotes are in circulation at the same time, to avoid issuing too many banknotes and ensure their credibility, the institution that issues banknotes must keep a certain number of precious metals in proportion with banknotes issued so that banknotes can be exchanged for precious metals when the holders so demanded. After paper money issued by central banks replaced banknotes, gold once acted as a reserve currency. However, with gold acting as a reserve, the money supply is constrained by the size of the gold reserve which in turn will constrain the flexibility of the central bank's monetary policies. At present, gold no longer serves as a reserve for any paper money issued by central banks. To ensure a country's sufficient means of payment, when the central banks of some countries or regions issue local currencies, however, they will still use some forms of foreign exchange assets as a reserve currency. For example, as we will see in Chapter 17, when the banks in Hong Kong issue Hong Kong dollars, it must submit to the Hong Kong Monetary Authority at a rate of 1:7.85 foreign exchange assets as a reserve for currency issue. In this sense, Hong Kong implements a dollar standard monetary system.

1.4.2 Types of Monetary Systems

Historically, monetary systems have been divided into four classes.

(a) *Gold Standard*

The gold standard refers to a monetary system in which gold acts as the standard money. This is mainly in the form of gold coin standard, gold bullion standard and gold exchange standard. The **gold coin standard** uses gold as the minting metal and the typical gold standard. Under the gold coin standard, gold coins can be freely minted and melted. Coins in circulation and the symbols of value (i.e., banknotes) can be freely exchanged for gold coins. In other words, gold can be freely imported and exported. When the gold standard is in effect, the exchange rate calculated based on the gold content of two currencies is also known as gold parity.

The **gold bullion standard** refers to a monetary system where a central bank issues and uses paper money as currency in circulation with gold bullion acting as a reserve. It is different from the gold coin standard in several ways. First, the gold bullion standard uses paper money or banknotes, instead of gold coins, as currency in circulation. These notes also have a regulated gold content for which they can be exchanged. Second, the central government manages a gold reserve, allowing residents to exchange a certain amount of paper money above a defined threshold for gold bullion.

The **gold exchange standard** refers to a monetary system that uses banknotes as the currency in circulation which can be converted indirectly into gold via the foreign exchange market. The gold exchange standard and the gold bullion standard are similar in that they make use of a monetary unit with a regulated gold content, circulate banknotes domestically and do not circulate metal coins. However, banknotes regulated by the gold exchange standard can only be exchanged for foreign exchange assets, not gold. The central bank of a given country will deposit gold and foreign exchange in a country that implements the gold standard, allowing indirect exchange for gold via the foreign exchange market. The country will also maintain a fixed exchange rate between their own currency and that of the other country, thereby stabilizing the value of the local currency.

The **Bretton Woods system** is a monetary system in which governments tied their exchange rate to the dollar. Since the dollar traded for gold at a fixed rate, this indirectly linked these currencies to gold. Under the Bretton Woods system, the dollar, which was made equivalent to gold, held a pivotal position relative to the currency of other members. For this reason, the Bretton Woods system has also been called the dollar-based international monetary system.

(b) *Silver Standard*

The silver standard refers to a type of monetary system which uses silver as standard money. In the evolution of the monetary system, the history of the silver standard predates the gold standard. The principles behind the silver standard are similar to those of the gold standard, with the exception that silver is used as the minting material, silver coins are also unlimited legal tender and the nominal value is consistent with the actual value of silver.

(c) *Bimetallic Standard*

The bimetallic standard refers to a monetary system which regulates both gold and silver as standard money. Under the bimetallic standard, gold and silver can be freely bought and sold, freely minted and melted, and can be freely imported and exported. As such, the bimetallic standard is an inherently unstable monetary system.

For example, when France implemented the bimetallic standard, the rate of minting between gold and silver was 15.5:1 — people could either get what contained the equivalent of gold from the mints or they could use a fixed amount of gold to trade it for 15.5 times the amount in silver. If the global price of gold rose above that of silver, there would be an incentive for arbitrage. For example, if the price of gold rose to a level in which 16 ounces of silver could only buy one ounce of gold, a spread trader would import 15.5 ounces of silver, which could be minted into silver coins which could be traded for one ounce gold coins. When he exports, the gold coins would be worth 16 ounces of silver in foreign markets. Without considering transaction costs, through the arbitrage, not only can he recover his investment, but also gain an additional half ounce of silver.

As long as the market ratio is clearly higher than the mint ratio, there will always be an incentive for spread trading. Spread traders add silver to the circulation and take gold out of it, up to point where all of the gold coins in the country have gone abroad. Conversely, if the market rate falls below the mint rate, the spread trader will add gold to the circulation and take silver out of it up until the latter completely disappears from circulation.

Under the bimetallic standard, arbitrage behavior causes gold or silver, whichever has a market value higher than the official fixed rate, to be removed from circulation. This kind of phenomenon is referred to as **Gresham's Law,** commonly known as "bad money driving out good".

(d) *Paper Standard*

With precious metals as a reserve for issuance, the amount of money issued is subject to the quantity of precious metals one has. As the size and volume of commerce evolved, it has been difficult to apply the gold standard to the needs of economic development. Thus, we began using the paper standard.

The paper standard is called the fiat money standard. Paper money does not need any gold reserves, because it relies purely on the strength of a country and the backing of that nation's credibility. People see this paper money as generally acceptable, and can use it as a medium of exchange or a symbol of value. Under the paper standard, functional currency in circulation includes paper money and bank deposits. Through regulating the money supply, governments can use this monetary system to influence economic activity. However, this can also provoke wanton issuance and serious inflation.

1.4.3 The Chinese Monetary System

December 1, 1948 marks the first issuance of the renminbi and the establishment of the Chinese monetary system. China's current monetary system is a special system of "one nation, many currencies", namely the renminbi in the Chinese Mainland and different monetary systems implemented in Hong Kong, Macau, and Taiwan. These different areas also have their own legal tender and limited scope of circulation. Alongside China's economic rise, the Chinese renminbi is becoming more and more common in the Hong Kong SAR.

The renminbi is the legal tender of the Chinese Mainland. According to the Law on the People's Bank of China (PBOC), the basic unit of the renminbi is the "yuan"; the fractional money used is the "jiao" and the "fen". Renminbi is the fiat money that cannot be exchanged for gold. It exists in the form of either cash or deposits. Cash is issued and uniformly managed by the PBOC, while deposit money enters circulation through the commercial bank system via business activity.

The renminbi has a fiat money standard. Yet under China's compulsory exchange settlement and surrender system, the issuance of the renminbi is on the basis of the accumulation of foreign exchange reserves, or it could be said that whenever there is an increase in the foreign exchange reserves, a corresponding amount of Chinese yuan will be issued, which is actually a form of dollar standard in disguise. Only when the growth of China's foreign exchange reserves no longer propels the growth of the renminbi (and vice versa), can the renminbi truly be the fiat money based on the credit of the PBOC.

1.5 Monetary Measurements and Aggregates: Money and Quasi-Money

1.5.1 Different Methods for Defining Money

Economics uses two methods for defining and measuring money, namely the inductive method and the empirical method. When defining what money is by induction, economists focus on the characteristics of money. These unique properties are what make money different from other things. If anything bears these characteristics, then it belongs to the category of money.

What is the most significant characteristic of money? The most significant feature that distinguishes money from all other things is that it has the function of exchange. Other items cannot usually be used as a medium of exchange. In contrast, the function of stored wealth does not belong to money alone. For example, people can use real estate as a wealth storage method. They can also buy stock or gold to accumulate wealth. For this reason, inductive reasoning would define money in the narrow sense as a generally accepted medium of exchange. In addition to the currency in circulation, checkable deposits and demand deposits with electronic payments can also act as mediums of exchange. For example, if you have a China Merchants Bank card with a demand deposit of 5000 yuan, when you go shopping, there is no need to bring cash; you can pay directly with your card. According to the inductive definition, the 5000 yuan demand deposit in your card is money. Time deposits, however, cannot be listed as money, because you cannot use them directly.

The second approach to defining money is through the empirical method. The empirical method emphasizes the effects of money on the economy and monetary policy. First, this is because changes in the money supply have a large influence on the nominal national income. Another reason is that the central bank must control the money supply. Thus, when macroeconomic fluctuations occur, the central bank must use monetary policy to stabilize the economy. In this way, the empirical method does not define money according to its intrinsic qualities that separate it from other things. Instead, money is defined as current assets or set of current assets which bear strong correlation with the nominal national income or the rate of inflation, and which can be controlled by the central bank. According to the empirical definition, besides currency in circulation and demand deposits, money also includes time deposits. Obviously, the empirical definition of money is much wider than the inductive definition.

1.5.2 Monetary Aggregates

Apart from the fundamental differences between the inductive and empirical definitions described above, one is a constituent part of the other. Statistically, each country has its own way of measuring its stock of money. Depending on how they categorize, there may be big differences in the economic impact of each category from country to country. China's money supply is measured based on liquidity and can be divided into three main monetary aggregates:

$$M_0 = \text{Currency in circulation}$$

$$M_1 = M_0 + \text{Demand deposits}$$

$$M_2 = M_1 + \text{Time deposits} + \text{Savings deposits} + \text{Other deposits}$$

Note: Demand deposits refer to demand deposits of organizations; time deposits refer to time deposits of organizations; organizations here include enterprises, government departments, armed forces, and public institutes as opposed to a private individual. Personal demand deposits and time deposits are accounted for under savings deposits. Other deposits refer to customer margins of securities firms, deposits of the housing reserve fund management centers and deposits made by non-depository financial institutions at commercial banks.

Table 1.1 lists the components of China's monetary aggregates in even-numbered years from 2006 to 2012.

From Table 1.1, we can see that from the owner's point of view, all of the components are assets, regardless of their differences or whether they are demand

Table 1.1 2006–2012 Components of Chinese Monetary Aggregates (Unit: 0.1 billion yuan)

Year	2006	2008	2010	2012
M_0 = currency in circulation	27,072.62	34,218.96	44,628.17	54,659.77
+ demand deposits	98,955.43	131,998.20	221,993.37	254,004.46
= M_1	126,028.05	166,217.13	266,621.54	308,664.23
+ time deposits	60,549.93	88,407.88	143,232.08	195,940.13
+ savings deposits	161,587.30	217,885.35	303,093.01	411,362.59
+ other deposits	24,485.25	36,875.20	12,905.15	54,181.86
= M_2	345,577.91	475,166.60	725,851.79	974,148.80

deposits or time deposits. However, not all assets can be listed as money. For example, real estate, vehicles, factories, and other physical assets are not included within the category of money. Stock, corporate bonds, mutual funds, and other standardized financial assets that can be traded on the open market are also not included in the statistical range of money. Why is it that some kinds of asset will be included in the statistical range of money and others will not? This is because different assets have difference liquidities.

Assets that are included in the statistical range of money have high liquidity. This so-called liquidity refers to an asset's ability to be converted into cash and not suffer losses. If an asset is highly liquid, it is very marketable; conversely, if an asset has low liquidity, it is not very marketable. Marketability refers to an asset's ability to carry out the functions of money (especially as a measure of value and a medium of exchange). Since the liquidity of currency in circulation and demand deposits is the highest, you can use cash or checks to pay for goods and services directly. Statistically speaking, these forms of payment are listed as money. On the other hand, the liquidity of time deposits, savings deposits and other deposits that comprise M_2 is relatively low. Since they cannot be used as a direct means of exchange, functioning instead as a store of value, these deposits are only quasi-money.

Naturally, every country accounts for its money supply in a different way, and there is no single custom by which all countries abide by. From one perspective, the financial structures and level of financial development among countries is uneven. Furthermore, there is no uniform definition of monetary aggregates from country to country. From yet another perspective, though, a wide range of new assets have emerged as a result of financial innovations since the 1970s. These assets are not only incredibly profitable but also highly liquid. Additionally, with the development of technology and trading systems, liquidity gaps in various financial instruments are gradually shrinking. With these financial innovations, a country can revise and perfect money supply measurements. Since November 2010, China has included Housing Fund Management Center deposits and the deposits of non-depository financial institutions in commercial banks in the monetary statistics. The specific aggregates of each country's money supply should at least reflect the basic conditions of the country's financial structure. It can certainly be said that with the rapid development of China's capital and money markets, as well as the constant emergence of new financial instruments, the make-up of China's monetary aggregates will also gradually change.

1.5.3 Monetary Structure

The monetary structure, often called the liquidity structure of money, refers to the ratio between high liquidity money and low liquidity money balance. The liquidity structure of money is often measured by two indicators, namely the ratio between M_0 and M_2 and the ratio between M_1 and M_2. It can also be said that the measurement of the liquidity structure via these two indicators is also the ratio between the balances of transaction money and broad money. More specifically, it reflects the ratio between transaction and non-transaction money balances. Transaction money directly acts as a medium of exchange of goods and other assets, while the balance of non-transaction money acts as a store of wealth. Therefore, an increase or decrease in the ratio reflects different changes in the economic environment.

For example, during inflationary periods, we naturally want to hold more cash or demand deposits so that we can conveniently buy various physical assets in order to avoid currency devaluation. During these times, we usually can see the liquidity of money increase. Conversely, during deflationary periods, it makes sense to save. During this time, the liquidity of money will naturally decrease.

Of course, even though changes in liquidity are a natural response to changes in the economic environment, yet these changes may also create new changes within the economic environment; central banks judge direction in which the economy is going, via frequent observation of changes in the monetary liquidity structure. In other words, a rise in the liquidity of money means increasing public expectation of inflation; in turn, a fall in the liquidity of money means diminishing public expectation of inflation, or even suggests a deflationary trend. Figure 1.1 displays China's monetary liquidity structure (M_1/M_2) and consumer price index (CPI). The positive correlation between M_1/M_2 and CPI is obvious. For example, from the beginning of 2004 until the end of 2005, as M_1/M_2 declined, CPI fell as well; from the beginning of 2006 until the beginning of 2008, M_1/M_2 rose as China's CPI rose. Therefore a drop in M_1/M_2 will be accompanied by a declining CPI trend. From early 2009 to 2012, M_1/M_2 and the CPI all experienced this kind of cyclical rise and fall.

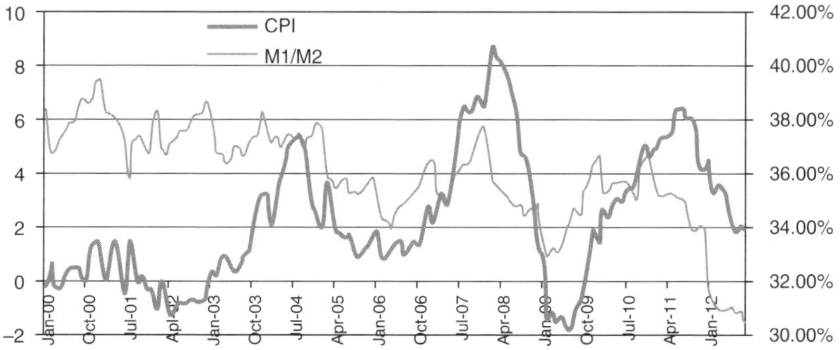

Fig. 1.1 China's Monetary Liquidity Structure and CPI (%)

Source: Periodic data retrieved from *The People's Bank of China Quarterly Statistical Bulletin.*

Summary

Money is not the same as the "cash" we talk about every day, neither is it the "income" or "wealth" that people often refer to. Money can act as a unit of account, a medium of exchange, a store of value, and a generally accepted means of payment. Thus, money has four functions. Money has spurred the division of labor and trade. As a store of value, money has facilitated capital accumulation and reallocation.

Historically, there appeared successively commodity money, commodity-backed money, fiat money, and electronic money. The forms of money have evolved with technological advances.

The money supply of each country is divided into different categories in accordance with liquidity differences, usually M_0, M_1, and M_2. The function of each component varies; M_0 and M_1 primarily act as mediums of exchange, while M_2 primarily acts as a store of value. The ratios between these various categories of monetary aggregates are called the monetary liquidity structure. Changes in the monetary liquidity structure also reflect changes in the macroeconomic conditions. By observing these changes, central banks can adopt corresponding monetary policies.

Key Terms

Money; Unit of Account; Medium of Exchange; Store of Value; Means of Payment; Fiat Money; Electronic Money; Quasi-Money; M_0, M_1 and M_2; Monetary Liquidity Structure

Critical Thinking Questions

1. What is money? What are the differences between this and the cash or income that we use daily?
2. What are the functions of money?
3. What effect does the development of money have on the economic activities of our society?
4. How is money divided into different aggregates? What is each aggregate composed of?
5. Does analysis of the monetary liquidity structure have any macroeconomic significance?
6. In your opinion, is the meal card you use in your dining hall a form of money?
7. Rousseau in *Confessions* wrote that "the money that we possess is the instrument of liberty; that which we lack and strive to obtain is the instrument of slavery." Is "money" that he speaks of in this sentence the same as the "money" of Finance? Please explain.
8. Adam Smith, the founder of economics, wrote in *The Wealth of Nations* that money is the great wheel of circulation, the great instrument of commerce. How should we understand what Adam Smith meant in this phrase?

9. What are your thoughts on current Chinese categorization of monetary aggregates? Or, what are the kind of things you use every day that act as a medium of exchange but are not counted as money? Do you think that they should be?
10. In early April 2013, Nanfang Food (000716), a listed Chinese company, announced that shareholders (except for the Havle Group, one of its major shareholders) who hold more than 1000 shares (including 1000 shares) of the company's stock would receive a dividend gift box (12 cans) of black sesame milk for every 1000 shares. This is known as the marvel of listed Chinese companies — physical dividends — i.e., listed companies distribute their products to shareholders as a kind of dividend. Based on publicly available information, the China AMC Dividend Fund and China AMC Industry Select Fund hold 3.8434 million shares and 1.2952 million shares. Given this calculation, they would receive a total of 61,656 cans of Nanfang Food sesame milk products. If we were to calculate this conversion based on the top ten shareholders, the China Post Fund and the Golden Eagle Fund would also receive over a thousand boxes of sesame milk products. Afterwards, several other companies decided to follow suit. According to the functions of money, how would you evaluate the "physical dividends" of listed Chinese companies?

Chapter 2

Financial System

Learning Objectives

After studying this chapter, you will be able to:

- Understand the definitions of borrower–spenders and lender–savers in the economy
- Understand the mechanism of channeling funds from lender–savers to borrower–spenders
- Understand the basic functions of financial system
- Understand what financial instruments are and the difference between financial instruments and financial assets
- Understand the categories of financial instruments
- Understand the characteristics of financial instruments and their relations
- Understand information asymmetry of financial system and its consequences
- Understand ways to address information asymmetry

Finance has been the core of the modern market economy, and a sound financial system is essential to the normal economic operation of a country. It is fair to say that if the financial system catches a cold, the economic activities of corporations and individuals will suffer from a fever; if the financial system is crippled, corporate and individual economic activities are unlikely to leap forward. This chapter will introduce the rationale behind the operation of the financial system, and clarify why it plays such an important role in economy. Furthermore, this chapter will provide a brief introduction to the financial instruments necessary for normal operation of the financial system. Finally, this chapter will tell you about information asymmetry and its impacts and why it occurs in financial activities and help you understand the methods of addressing information asymmetry in financial activities.

2.1 Lender–Savers and Borrower–Spenders

In economy, some sectors have saved surplus funds by spending less than what they earn; conversely, other sectors have a shortage of funds because they spend more than their income. The same person or corporation may have a surplus or shortage of funds in different periods. As far as we personally are concerned, our expenditure is huge while our income is often limited when we just enter the workforce. At this time, we may live beyond our means and become the borrower–spenders. In contrast, after we have been working for a few years, our income may exceed our expenditure, and thus we become lender–savers.

Generally, governments and corporations are borrower–spenders, and households and individuals are lender–savers. **Net financial investment** is used to tell whether a sector or entity is a lender–saver or a borrower–spender. As viewed from financial transactions, net financial investment is the balance of increase in financial assets in current year less increase in financial liabilities in current year. Therefore, a sector or entity with a positive net financial investment generally has a net lending and is a lender–saver; conversely, a sector or entity with a negative net financial investment has a net borrowing and is a borrower–spender. As shown in Table 2.1, the Chinese government and non-financial sectors recorded negative net financial investment for many of years between 1994 and 2009, suggesting that they are borrower–spenders in the country's economic system; the household sector always has a positive net financial investment, making it the lender–saver.

Since the funding gap of borrower–spenders is made up by lender–savers, the total fund surplus of the household sector and financial sector equals the total fund shortage of the non-financial sector, government sector, and foreign sector. As reflected in Table 2.1, the net financial investment of each sector is zero. So how does the fund flow from lender–savers to borrower–spenders?

Table 2.1 Net Financial Investment by various Sectors in China (Unit: 100 million yuan)

Sectors	Households	Non-financial Businesses	Government	Financial	Foreigners
1994	7499.5	−6683	−49.3	105.23	−662
1997	11,027.1	−8637.4	−744.9	826.2	−2471.1
2000	7898.1	−5269.3	−999.9	66.9	−1695.7
2003	16,122	−14,531	−540	2672	−3726
2006	27,706.0	−9637.0	4687.0	−2454.0	−20,300.0
2007	23,119.0	−11,453.0	−6540.0	20,450.0	−25,575.0
2008	50,290.0	−27,546.0	61.0	8490.0	−31,296.0
2009	35,907.0	−25,326.0	2066	8264.0	−20,911.0

Source: *China Statistical Yearbooks*, website of the China National Bureau of Statistics.

2.2 Mechanism Linking Lender–Savers with Borrower–Spenders

The mechanism of channeling funds from lender–savers to borrower–spenders is also called saving–investment transformation mechanism, namely, which channel is used to allocate surplus funds to the sectors short of funds. Generally, saving–investment transformation mechanism can be categorized into fiscal transformation mechanism and financial transformation mechanism.

Fiscal transformation mechanism means that the government pools the financial surplus funds in society and then allocates them to each business sector. Fiscal mechanism is a national income allocation mechanism related to the state function, and is also an involuntary mechanism backed by the coercive power of the state. In the planned economy, the fiscal transformation mechanism plays a dominant role. Under the fiscal transformation mechanism, the government often leverages its coercive power to control corporations beyond economic powers. What has happened has proved that this type of transformation mechanism is quite inefficient.

Financial transformation mechanism is to manage fund surplus and shortage via the financial system. Funds will flow from the sectors with surplus funds to those short of funds via financial intermediaries in some cases, and via direct financial market in other cases. The former is called **indirect financial transformation mechanism** and the latter, **direct financial transformation mechanism**. In the indirect financial transformation mechanism, lender–savers first deposit their financial surplus in financial intermediaries, which pool the scattered financial surplus to lend to those short of funds. In the indirect financial transformation, there are two independent contracts on deposits and loans. The depositors do not care when and to whom the surplus funds are granted after being pooled by the financial intermediaries. As long as financial intermediaries can repay principal and interests on time, the depositors will not suffer any loss. Though the poor business performance of the borrower–spenders may cause financial intermediaries non-performing assets, depositors will be risk-free inasmuch as it has not threatened the safety of the banking system. Accordingly, in the indirect financial transformation mechanism, there are two independent contracts, serving as a risk buffer between the end lenders and the end borrowers.

Direct financial transformation mechanism means the surplus funds of lender–savers flow to the borrower–spenders through the financial market. The borrower–spenders will raise necessary funds by issuing financial instruments such as stocks and bonds. Different from indirect financial transformation mechanism, the end lenders and the end borrowers in the direct transformation mechanism only have one contract, and thus the end lenders are directly exposed to various business risks faced by the end borrowers. For example, when a company issued new shares at 5 yuan per share, Zhang San purchased 2000 shares for 10,000 yuan. One year

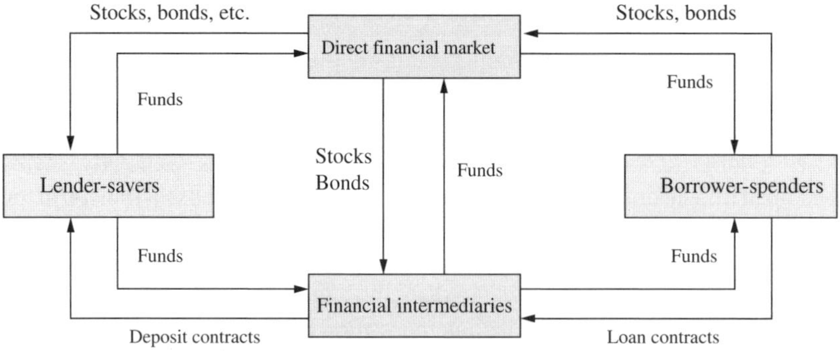

Fig. 2.1 Capital Flow in Financial System

later, the company disclosed that it suffered a huge loss due to wrong decisions, and as a result its stock price dropped to 4 yuan per share. If Zhang San did not sell his shares within the year, it would suffer a loss of 2000 yuan. In the direct transformation mechanism, such losses are not uncommon

In the direct financial transformation mechanism, a majority of financial instruments take the form of stocks and bonds. By reading *China Securities*, *Shanghai Securities*, and *Securities Time*, you will find the prospectuses of some corporations which are about to directly raise capital in the stock market. Moreover, investors may subscribe for their stocks, and will become the shareholders of these listed companies after purchase. Such direct financial transformation mechanism is organized and standardized, and has quite strict procedures.

In the direct financial transformation mechanism, some are largely different from public offering of stocks and bonds, and the agreements on channeling funds from lender–savers to borrower–spenders are reached in private. There is no open market and it is also not standardized. For example, you are out of money at school and borrow some from your friends; or you plan to run a restaurant jointly with several of your friends, and each of you invests in it and receives a return in proportion to your respective investment. Such financial activities are direct and we call them informal finance. Do not underestimate the role of informal finance. Even in highly developed market economies like the UK and the US, informal finance is rather active, and many venture capital corporations and self-employed businesses raise fund mainly through informal finance. In China, the stocks we see today, for example, developed from informal finance.

It is necessary to say a few more words about informal finance here as formal finance will be dealt with in detail in the following chapters. In general, informal finance has the following characteristics:

(1) It involves relatively small amounts, and it is difficult to commit a trans-regional and large-scale transfer of funds through informal financing. (2) Most

of it is financing amongst a "circle of friends". For example, you will not give your surplus funds to someone you do not know. Because both parties of informal financing are relatively close, asymmetric information is not a serious problem in most cases. (3) In these non-standardized financial activities in which no financial institutions are involved, generally just a temporary loan contract has been signed by both parties.

All the direct finance mechanisms mentioned above that link lender–savers and borrower–spenders are all examples of capital market in the financial market. According to the length of time, the market mechanisms linking lender–savers and borrower–spenders are divided into capital market and money market. **Capital market** is the financial market with a maturity of more than one year, the major function of which is to translate savings into investments and promote the formation of physical capital. Money market is the financial market with a maturity of less than one year, which is dedicated to regulating temporary fund surplus and deficit. The reason for the classification is because it is unlikely to change the aggregate amount and structure of existing fixed capital or the existing production technology within one year. Only for a period of more than one year, can the fund raisers utilize the capital raised to construct factory buildings and purchase machines, equipment and other physical capital. Generally, the financing activities with a maturity of less than one year can only generate working capital, and contribute nothing to the formation of physical capital.

2.3 Functions of Financial System

As mentioned above, transfer of surplus funds from lender–savers to borrower–spenders can be made via informal finance such as borrowing money from family and friends. In reality, however, the surplus funds transferred in this way account for a very small proportion, and most of the funds are transferred and regulated by the formal financial system. So what functions and advantages does the formal financial system have in allocating surplus fund and translating savings into investments?

2.3.1 Reduce Transaction Cost

Financial institutions may help reduce information collection and transaction costs for borrowers and lenders. For example, Company A intends to borrow 50 million yuan for a project. If 1000 persons who do not know one another provide loans to the company, before they lend 50,000 yuan respectively, they will have to assess the company and its investment project and collect related information. If the assessment and information collection cost 50 yuan every time, the 1000 lenders will need to spend 50,000 yuan in total. On the contrary, if a financial intermediary pools 5000 yuan from every one of the 1000 investors and then assess the company and collect relevant information instead, all these activities still cost 50 yuan, with a saving of 49,950 yuan.

2.3.2 Time–Space Conversion

The second advantage of leveraging financial intermediaries is to pool short-term funds and translate them into long-term investments. For example, it may take several years to construct a factory and more than 10 years to fully recover investments. Any corporation investing in such a factory will not rely on short-term financing of one or two years, while the deposit term of most families would not exceed 10 years. Besides, if there were no financial intermediaries, people would have to rely on their own resources and would not be able to buy houses before they save enough. That will take a long period of time. The mortgage loans of financial intermediaries can strike a balance between people's income flow and the upfront payment at the time of purchase, and evenly amortize the expenditure on housing purchase over a long period in the future.

The time conversion in the financial system can not only translate short-term funds into long-term investments, but also even out income across their entire lives and allow people to reasonably arrange their income and expenditure in the whole life-cycle. Income and expenditure are not evenly distributed in one's lifetime. Before entering the workforce and after retirement, we generally have no income, but still need to spend on food and other necessities. If there were no financial system, we would have many troubles in our lives before taking up a job and after retirement. If there is no chance to obtain student loans, students from poor backgrounds will have to drop out due to inability to afford various expenses in universities and colleges. Also, if the financial system did not participate in operating pension schemes, life after retirement would be unimaginable.

Apart from term conversion, the financial system may also regulate capital surplus and deficit across regions, by overcoming the restrictions of regional distribution of financial resources. In a certain period, a region may have a surplus of funds, while another region may have a shortage of funds. If there were no financial system, the regions short of funds would not obtain the capital necessary for development, while the capital in the regions with a surplus cannot be fully utilized. The financial system solves this problem. Therefore, Beijing-based investors can buy the stocks issued by a corporation in Guangdong via the financial system. Moreover, people can also make investment in foreign countries via the financial system, for example, Japanese investors may purchase the bonds or stocks issued by American corporations. In China's A-share market, Qualified Foreign Institutional Investors (QFII) can trade stocks listed on the Shanghai and Shenzhen Stock Exchanges (SZESs). China's Qualified Domestic Institutional Investors (QDII) may invest in securities of countries and regions outside of the Chinese mainland.

2.3.3 Liquidity and Investment Continuity

Financial intermediaries may provide liquidity and maintain the continuity of physical capital investment. Without financial intermediaries, investors will face the liquidity problem. Even though Company A can borrow 50 million yuan from 1000 lenders, if some lenders need to withdraw money under urgent circumstances in the second year of the project, and the company has no other financing channels, it will have to suspend its investment. To ensure the continuity of Company A's investment, the investors in the urgent need for withdrawal will face the liquidity problem.

However, financial institutions can solve the problem. The reason financial intermediaries can translate short-term surplus funds into long-term investments is because they have many scattered retail depositors who generally will not withdraw money at the same time. Therefore, financial institutions can meet these withdrawal needs with only a limited amount of reserves. Financial institutions are like buses. As long as it is not the last stop (bankruptcy of financial institutions), there are passengers (withdrawers) getting off and passengers (new depositors) getting on at every stop, thereby ensuring that there are always a certain number of passengers (deposit balance) in the bus thereby avoiding empty run and waste of gasoline.

Liquidity may also be provided by the financial system through the secondary market of direct finance. The secondary market is relative to the primary market. The **primary market**, also known as issue market, is the market for those short of funds to raise capital by issuing various financial instruments. Assume that you bought 5000 shares in China Unicom at 2.3 yuan per share at its initial offering, and the deal was completed in the primary market. However, if you were in urgent need of cash four months later and you had no other cash sources, what would you do? The **secondary market**, the marketplace for negotiation and transfer of various negotiable financial instruments, can meet your need. When you need cash, you may sell your 5000 shares in China Unicom to other people in the secondary market. If the market is bullish, you may sell them at 4 yuan per share, with a gross return of more than 80% in the four-month period. Through negotiation and transfer in the secondary market, you can obtain cash when needed, and meanwhile your share transfer will not affect the continuity of China Unicom's CDMA investment.

2.3.4 Risk Sharing

The financial system makes it easier for families and corporations to cope with risks. With complex financial instruments, private institutions, and government agencies, the financial system provides families and corporations the opportunities of risk pooling and risk sharing. Among the 1000 loans of Company A above, if the consequences unexpected by the lenders occur, and 250,000 yuan of the loans to the Company cannot be repaid, each of the 1000 investors will worry that their

50,000 yuan will not be able to be recovered. However, if all their funds are pooled together, they will each lose merely 0.5%, i.e., 250 yuan. Therefore, pooling the funds of depositors can mitigate loan risks.

Another example for risk sharing is insurance. Insurance provides a sound mechanism for individuals and corporations to manage risks. The rationale of insurance is that you can avoid huge losses in the future by paying a small fee at present. For example, Wang Xiaoer spent 1000 yuan purchasing a 500,000-yuan insurance for his house. If a fire disaster unfortunately occurs during the effective period of the insurance contract, and creates an actual loss of at least 500,000 yuan he may obtain a compensation of 500,000 yuan. If no fire disaster happens, he would lose only 1000 yuan. As the Chinese saying goes, to buy insurance, you are paying for the peace of mind.

2.3.5 Clearing and Payment

In the financial system, financial institutions may provide clearing and payment services for the market traders and thereby improve the efficiency of market transactions. The most obvious example is that banknotes replaced gold as a payment means. Banknotes are easy and convenient to carry and have a production cost far below that of gold mining, selection and smelting. However, most of our actual transactions are not settled by banknotes. Different from cash transactions we use when buying vegetables in the groceries, the transactions between corporations are seldom settled by cash, but by transfer or check. Imagine if all the transactions between corporations were to be settled by cash, how inefficient it would be. Different from trade in consumer goods, the transactions between corporations may involve millions or even billions of yuan. For such big transactions, it is inconvenient to carry and count cash. But you can easily do it by bank transfer with only a check.

Box 2.1 Financial Innovation of Shanxi Exchange Shop and New Means of Payment

In a period before 1857 (the seventh year during the reign of Qing Emperor Xianfeng), China's financial industry was dominated by two groups, namely Shanxi Exchange Shop and Ningshao Money Shop. Shanxi Exchange Shop was founded by Lei Lvtai, a native of Pingyao, Shanxi. He was originally employed by his countryfellow Li who ran a paint shop in Tianjin named "Ri Sheng Chang". Thanks to Lei's meticulous efforts, Ri Sheng Chang became very profitable and rose to fame. Lei also extended his business to Sichuan,

(*Continued*)

Box 2.1 (*Continued*)

and he often went there to buy such paints as verdigris. However, Sichuan had been known for its inaccessibility and poor communications with other parts of the country since ancient times. As Lei had to carry a large amount of cash to purchase paints in Sichuan, it was not only troublesome but also highly risky. If he was robbed on the way, he could hardly keep himself alive. Lei thus innovated an exchange approach, whereby Ri Sheng Chang issued notes upon receipt of silver, and the note holders might exchange notes for silver at the designated sites. Certainly, exchange would be charged a fee called remittance fee. Since silver is exchanged based on notes, it was called exchange shop. Lei effectively improved the payment efficiency and mitigated risks by such a financial innovation as "exchange shop".

— *Source*: Gao Yang, *Hu Xueyan*, Sanlian Bookstore, 2001

At present, we may settle our accounts by the transfer function of the financial system. Credit card and electronic fund transfer may replace traditional cash settlement method. After opening a deposit account with a bank, we can apply for a debit card like All-in-One Card of China Merchants Bank, Great Wall Card of Bank of China, Peony Card of Industrial and Commercial Bank of China and Oriental Card of Shanghai Pudong Development Bank. In a department store or a hotel which is a chartered merchant of these banks, you need not carry cash at all, as you can complete payment by swiping your card at a POS terminal of the chartered merchant and then entering your password.

2.3.6 Supervision and Incentive

Another function of financial system is the supervision and incentive mechanism. Assume that Company A borrowed 50 million yuan from 1000 persons, who will supervise its investment activities thereafter? If there is no supervisor, the company may use the 50 million yuan loans in investment at its sole discretion, and there are even risks of its person-in-charge absconding with the funds. It is presumed that, among the 1000 lenders, one person named Wang Xiaoer was interested in supervising Company A. Thanks to his supervision, the company did not violate any contract. However, Wang Xiaoer bore a cost of 2000 yuan in the supervision. If nobody agrees to share his supervision cost, it will be borne by Wang Xiaoer alone. However, the benefits brought by Wang Xiaoer's supervision should be shared by all these 1000 lenders. Wang Xiaoer assumed the entire supervision cost but enjoyed only one-thousandth of supervision benefits. The other 999 lenders who enjoyed the benefits brought by Wang Xiaoer's supervision without paying for it are called free riders. Because of free ride, none of the 1000 lenders has the incentive for supervision, leading to the lack of supervision over the borrower.

Box 2.2 Boxed Pig Game on the Supervision of Listed Companies

Boxed pig game describes a big pig and a small pig in a pigsty. There is a trough at one end of the pigsty and a button at the other end that controls the supply of hogwash. By pushing the button one time, 10 units of hogwash will flow into the trough. But pushing the button will result in two units of cost. If the big pig reaches the trough earlier than the small pig, the big pig eats nine units, and the small pig eats only one unit; if they arrive at the same time, the big pig eats seven units and the small pig eats three; if the small pig arrives earlier, the big pig eats six units and the small pig eats four. In such a cost and return pattern, if the small pig pushes the button, it has a negative ultimate return of one unit; if neither of the pigs push the button, as far as the small pig is concerned, though it has nothing to eat, it has no cost either. Therefore, whether or not the big pig pushes the button, the best choice for the small pig is to wait by the trough. When the big pig pushes the button, the small pig reaches the trough earlier and eats four units, and the big pig eats six units. In this case, the small pig takes the free ride of the big pig pushing the button.

In a joint-stock company, shareholders undertake the functions of supervising the manager. However, there are majority shareholders and minority shareholders with different benefits from supervision. In the supervision of the manager, it is necessary to spend time on information collection. If the supervision costs are the same, the benefits received by majority shareholders from supervision obviously are more than those by minority shareholders. Here, majority shareholders are analogous to the "big pig", and minority shareholders to the "small pig". The best choice for supervision of the company is that the majority shareholders take the responsibility for information collection and supervision of the manager, and the minority shareholders take the free ride of majority shareholders. Hence, we note that minority shareholders seldom strictly supervise the operation of the company, and most of them "vote with their feet". When they are unsatisfied with the company's performance, they will simply sell off its securities in the market place.

— *Source*: Zhang Weiying, *Game Theory and Information Economics*
Shanghai Sanlian Bookstore, Shanghai People's Publishing House, 1994

Nonetheless, the benefit of supervision is more than its cost. If there is no supervision, it may be hard for them to recover their principal. Therefore, the

1000 lenders have the incentive to entrust their supervisory right to a third party to supervise Company A's investment activities on their behalf. Financial intermediaries play such a role of "supervision agency". Financial institutions have the incentive to supervise because the loans granted by financial intermediaries, especially banks, are not publicly tradable and negotiable, and their activities are generally kept secret from investors. It can effectively solve the problem of free ride, internalize the supervision benefit, and overcome the spillover effect of income growth in supervision activities.

How are the problems of supervision and incentive solved by the direct link mechanism in the financial market? In the stock market also, the problem of free ride exists. In a joint-stock company, shareholders are widely scattered in different regions and the shares held by each shareholder in the same company are also different. A Shanghai-listed company may have tens of thousands of shareholders from across the country. Legally, these scattered shareholders have the right to supervise the listed company. The act that the shareholders participate in the business decisions of a listed company and directly supervise the company is generally referred to as "voting by hand". Because the shares of a listed company are much decentralized, it is quite inconvenient to directly supervise the operating activities of the company. In fact, because there is the problem of free ride of the decentralized shareholders in supervision of the company, every shareholder hopes that the other shareholders will vote in their best interest, and thus he can reap without sowing and take a free ride. Since every shareholder thinks that way, finally none of them directly supervises the listed company.

In fact, the supervision of a joint-stock company is mostly conducted by "voting with feet". "Voting with feet" means shareholders will sell out all their shares in a listed company in the secondary market when they are dissatisfied with the company's operation. If most shareholders did so, the company's stock price would plummet. When the stock price decreased to a certain degree, for example, below net asset per share in an extreme case, investors would heavily buy shares in the company so as to acquire a controlling stake in it. Once the company is controlled by external investors, they will reorganize the company in the capacity of controlling shareholders and replace its original management. Voting with feet and take-over mechanism impose a strong binding force on the management of listed companies.

2.4 Financial Instruments

As the basic architecture guiding the flow of funds, the financial system is generally composed of financial instruments, financial institutions and market participants, trading models and the financial regulatory framework. Here, we first introduce financial instruments in the financial system.

2.4.1 Financial Instruments and Financial Assets

What are the vehicles transferring funds from lender–savers to borrower–spenders? This task falls to financial instruments. The stocks, corporate bonds, Treasury bonds, and certificates of deposits that we are familiar with are all financial instruments serving as the bridge between lender–savers and borrower–spenders. Financial instruments are the contracts bearing the debtor–creditor relationship, generally providing for the amount, terms and duration of transferring financial surplus from lender–savers to borrower–spenders.

Financial assets, when spoken in terms of financial instruments, are a general term used for the financial instruments with present price and future valuation as well as specific ownership. Financial instruments constitute financial assets only in relation to the holders; and for the issuers, they are not financial assets. If you hold a 1000-yuan Treasury bill, it is a financial instrument for both the government as the issuer and you as the holder. It is also a financial asset for you, but not for the government. Similarly, if China Unicom issued 5 billion floating shares, these shares are financial instruments, rather than financial assets, for China Unicom to raise capital. However, if you purchased 100,000 shares in China Unicom, these shares will constitute a part of your financial assets and they are also the financial instruments via which you invest in China Unicom.

2.4.2 Typical Financial Instruments

Generally, financial instruments are divided into equity instruments and debt instruments. Equity instruments are the stocks that we commonly observe; debt instruments are deposits, loans and bonds, etc.

Stock is a certificate of partial ownership of a company. Assume that you hold 100,000 out of the total 20 billion shares in China Unicom, you will hold 1/200,000 of the ownership of the company. Typical ones are common stocks, which represent the residual claim against company assets. The holders of common stocks are entitled to the remaining assets of a company after all its other claims have been satisfied. For example, if a company in which you hold common stocks stopped operation and sold out all its assets, you could obtain a part of the residual assets (if any) in proportion to the shares you hold after all its other claims have been met. Since the holders of common stocks can share the company's residual assets only after all its other claims have been satisfied, they have the highest risk. Meanwhile, holders of common stocks should only undertake limited liability for risks, that is, if the company is liquidated and the proceeds from asset disposal cannot cover all its debts, the creditors should not claim more compensation from the holders of common stocks to make up for the gap. The holders of common stocks are only liable for the company's debts to the extent of their respective capital contributions.

Why do investors take such a high risk to hold common stocks? That is because the holders of common stocks can benefit from the company's growth if it is promising. Many international leading companies like Microsoft, IBM, Apple and Intel have brought about a high return to the holders of their common stocks. Of course, the immediate goal of most investors holding shares in a company is not to share the company's dividends. If the company has a promising prospect and its earnings per share grow fast, it will lead to a surge in the company's share price, and thus bring about a high capital premium to the holders of common stocks, which is far more than the dividends paid out by the company.

Debt instrument is a written certificate issued by the borrower to the lender, indicating a certain amount and repayment period and conditions. Our passbooks, loan contracts signed when a bank grants a loan to a corporation, the Treasury bills issued by the government and the corporate bonds issued by corporations are debt instruments. The issuers of debt instruments generally promise to pay a fixed amount, which is known as interest. Accordingly, they are also called fixed income securities. Some debt instruments are negotiable, while others are not. Generally, the passbooks and bank loan contracts are not negotiable or tradable; Treasury bills and corporate bonds are allowed to be traded and transferred in organized stock exchanges or over-the-counter (OTC) markets. In 2004, Shanghai Stock Exchange (SSE) recorded transactions of spot Treasury bills of 296.15 billion yuan and transactions of repos of 4,408,622 million yuan. With the development of the financial market and financial innovations, some bank loans are also negotiable in the secondary market. Bank loan transfers typically come in two forms, the first is loan sales, in which Bank A will sell the loan contracts of some enterprises to Bank B, thereby transferring the earnings, risks and relative claims and obligations that come with the loans. The other form is securitization. Such a process of re-pooling original non-standardized loan contracts of banks and then subdividing them into standardized financial instruments with the same amount, same term, and same return, and tradable in the secondary market is referred to as securitization. Securitization provides a good channel and mechanism for banks to improve liquidity management.

Stocks, bonds, and certificates of deposits are primary financial instruments, also known as underlying financial instruments, whose main functions are to translate savings into investments or serve as the certificates of debt service. Those corresponding to underlying financial instruments are derivative financial instruments. Derivatives, including futures and options, are the financial products derived from the underlying financial instruments. The value of derivative financial instruments depends on the prices of related underlying products, and their main functions are to deal with the risks related to the underlying instruments, instead of regulating fund surplus and deficit, directly promoting translation of savings into investments and liquidity management. With the intensification of competition among financial institutions and continuous development of trading technique, a growing number of increasingly complex financial products have been developed, which are called structured financial instruments. Structured instruments are the financial products that derive from bundling underlying financial instruments or derivative financial instruments and they are new products with cash flows, income and risk profiles different from the previous ones. Asset securitization products and Liang De Bao as introduced in Box 12.2 in Chapter 12 are structured financial instruments.

2.4.3 Characteristics of Financial Instruments

Financial instruments generally have four characteristics — maturity, liquidity, safety, and profitability.

(a) *Maturity*

Maturity means that the debtor must pay off the balance of debts of a specific financial instrument within a given period. Deposits comprise demand deposits and time deposits of one year, two years, three years or other different periods; the Treasury bonds issued by government have a term of one year, three years, five years, etc. Here, one year, two years and such other periods mean the respective repayment periods of these financial instruments. Therefore, financial instruments have different repayment periods; demand deposits, for example, have short repayment periods. You may withdraw cash with your passbook or bankcard anytime, which actually has a repayment period of zero. Stock is another extreme case with an indefinite and unlimited term of maturity. After purchasing stocks, you cannot ask corporations to refund your principal some time later.

(b) *Liquidity*

Liquidity means the ability to transform financial instruments into cash without suffering loss. Generally, the banknote issued by the government and the demand deposits of banks have the highest liquidity. Essentially, banknote is cash and can be directly used to purchase commodities and services without conversion. You may also convert demand deposits into cash anytime or directly use the bank card with a demand deposit account to go shopping and lose nothing by doing so. However, to convert other financial instruments into cash, you may suffer losses more or less. When you need cash and have to sell your stocks, you should pay a certain amount of handling charge to the business department of the securities companies, in addition to the stamp tax. What is even worse is when share prices dropped drastically after you bought them. If you cash in on the stocks at that time, you will not even recover the principal. Hence, the liquidity of stocks is far worse than that of demand deposits.

The liquidity of a financial instrument is primarily affected by two factors: the credit of issuers and the length of repayment period. Generally, the issuer with a higher credit is more likely to perform the obligations specified in the financial instrument and repay principal and interest as scheduled. The financial instruments of the issuer with a higher credit are easier to be traded. Would you like to buy the bonds issued by a corporation on the verge of bankruptcy and insolvency?

The answer is very probably no. Thus it is evident that the liquidity of a financial instrument is directly proportional to the issuer's credit. Furthermore, the liquidity of a financial instrument is inversely proportional to its repayment period, that is, the longer the repayment period, the lower the liquidity. That is, because the longer the repayment period, the more unforeseeable factors that will be in the future. That also explains why the liquidity of demand deposits is higher than that of stocks.

(c) *Safety*

Safety or risk profile means the probability of the principal of a financial instrument suffering losses. Risks are divided into two categories. One category is the performance risk that the debtor cannot repay principal and interest on schedule, which is also called default risk. Default risk depends on the debtor's ability and will to repay debts. If a borrower cannot recover investment due to poor management, it will be unable to repay debts. Additionally, the default risk will arise sometimes when the debtor is unwilling to repay the debts due, though it has enough cash flows. China's commercial banks have accumulated a great amount of non-performing loans, which may expose the banks to the risk of losing loan principal when corporate borrowers are unable or unwilling to perform their obligations under loan contracts. The other category is market risk, namely the risk of decline in the market price of financial instruments due to various reasons. For instance, securities prices will rise when interest rates go down; conversely, when the interest rates go up, securities prices may drop. Selling securities will incur losses when the securities prices drop.

Generally, safety is inversely proportional to repayment period, that is, the longer the repayment period, the greater risks the principal will have; conversely, the shorter the repayment period, the lower the risks. People generally prefer five-year bonds to 30-year bonds mainly because the former carries much lower risks. Moreover, the financial instrument with a higher liquidity will be safer and thus carry lower risks, and vice versa.

(d) *Profitability*

Profitability refers to the characteristics of financial instruments to regularly or irregularly generate return to holders. Once you hold a financial instrument, you will hope to benefit from it, in the same way as a chicken farmer would expect each of his hens to lay an egg every day and as a fruit grower would expect his trees to bear fruits every year. Whether you make a deposit at a bank or purchase corporate bonds or Treasury bonds, you will earn certain interests; if you hold stocks of Haier, you will receive dividends paid by the company. Both interest and dividends are the benefits you receive by holding these financial instruments.

To compare the profitability of different financial instruments, you should compare their rates of return. **Rate of return** means the ratio of return on a financial instrument to the principal inputted, and it is divided into holding period return and yield to maturity. **Holding period return** means the return that you earn during the period of holding a certain financial instrument; yield to maturity means the annual return you earn until a certain financial instrument you hold becomes due. Holding period return and yield to maturity are often different. Assume that you purchased 10 bonds at a total price of 1000 yuan on October 8, 2001, with a par value of 100 yuan. The bonds have a coupon rate of 10% and a term of three years, and interest is paid annually. Then you sold the 10 bonds to another person at 1050 yuan on October 9, 2002, and earned a total return of 150 yuan. Your holding period return is as follows:

$$(100\text{ yuan} + 50\text{ yuan})/1000\text{ yuan} = 15\%.$$

If you hold a financial instrument from time t to time $t+1$, and assume RET is the rate of return on the financial instrument during the period, P_t is the purchase price of the financial instrument at time t, P_{t+1} is the selling price of the instrument at time $t+1$, and C is the coupon interest or dividend earned from the financial instrument from time t to time $t+1$, then the holding period return from time t to time $t+1$ is calculated as below:

$$RET = \frac{C + P_{t+1} - P_t}{P_t} = \frac{C}{P_t} + \frac{P_{t+1} - P_t}{P_t} = i_c + g. \tag{2.1}$$

Hence, holding period return can be divided into current yield i_c and capital gains yield g. Capital gains yield means the ratio of the difference between the purchase price and selling price of a certain financial instrument to the purchase price.

If you did not sell the bonds but instead held them until October 8, 2004, you would have an interest income of 300 yuan, or have an average yield to maturity of merely 10% over the three years, which is far less than the holding period return of 15% earned by selling the 10 bonds at a total price of 1050 yuan on October 9, 2002. If buyer A purchased the 1000 yuan bonds at a total price of 1050 yuan from you on October 9, 2002 and held them until October 8, 2004, he would receive an interest of 200 yuan. Then, his total yield to maturity was only

$$9.524\% \left(\frac{200}{1050} \div \dot{2} = 9.524\%\right).$$

All the returns calculated above are nominal returns, not the real returns. Nominal return means the ratio of total paper profit to the principal actually paid, without taking into account inflation. However, since the general price level is constantly changing, the real return should be the nominal return minus the inflation rate. If inflation is positive, nominal return will be higher than the real return; conversely, if the price level kept decreasing, nominal return will be lower than the real return. Assume that the inflation rate was 1% during October 8, 2001–October 9, 2002, the real holding period return would be merely 14%.

Is there any relation between the profitability and other characteristics of a financial instrument? Generally, the longer the holding period, the higher the rate of return, that is to say, long-term financial instruments have a higher rate of return than short-term financial instruments. The interest rate of demand deposits is very low. In some countries, it is forbidden to pay interest for demand deposits; the interest rate of one-year deposits is far lower than that of five-year deposits. And so is the interest rate of Treasury bonds. Why the rate of return increases with the term is due to term premium required by investors. Higher liquidity of a financial instrument results in lower rate of return, and vice versa. Demand deposits have the highest liquidity, and therefore their rate of return is the lowest. Why higher rate of return comes with lower liquidity is because investors require a liquidity premium. Generally, higher risk requires higher rate of return. The interest rate of junk bonds is significantly higher than that of the bonds issued by renowned leading corporations such as IBM and Microsoft because investors require a risk premium.

2.5 Information Asymmetry in Financial System

2.5.1 Information Asymmetry and Its Basic Issues: Adverse Selection and Moral Hazard

After the emergence of money, saving and investment become two acts independent of each other. Thus, information asymmetry will inevitably occur between the lender–savers and borrower–spenders. Information asymmetry means one party has more information than the other. The earliest research on information asymmetry was about the used-car market. The sellers of used cars are certainly more familiar with their cars. They know the car performance while the buyers do not know. Since the buyers do not know the quality of used cars, in general, they are only willing to purchase a used car at a price that reflects the average quality of used cars. If the used car turns out to be a lemon, the seller, certainly, is pleased. However, if the price paid by the buyer for a good-quality car is not commensurate with its quality, the seller would not be willing to sell it. Consequently, in the used-car market there are only lemons left.

The lemon problem in the used-car market also exists in the financial sector. In the insurance market, insurance companies had to set a uniform premium standard, for example, 2% of insured amount, for all drivers insured against traffic accidents since they cannot determine the probability of traffic accident occurring to every insured driver. However, the probabilities of accident occurring to every driver are different. Some drivers have a strong awareness of safety, and undoubtedly they have a lower probability of accident. Some drivers are careless and are more prone to drunken or furious driving, and therefore they have a higher probability of traffic accident. Due to information asymmetry, it is difficult for insurance companies to distinguish the two categories of applicants and thus they apply a uniform premium rate. However, the drivers who are more easily exposed to traffic accidents are more likely to purchase traffic accident insurance than those who drive carefully.

Credit market also has the lemon problem. Information asymmetry makes it difficult for the lenders to have a good knowledge of the borrowers and their risk profiles. Therefore, they have to adopt the same interest rate for all the borrowers. The lenders who tend to expect a higher interest rate may help squeeze out borrowers with a relatively low probability of repayment and they can screen borrowers by interest rates. Paradoxically, since the same interest rate is applied to all borrowers, those who are willing to borrow are often high-risk borrowers, while the low-risk borrowers turn out to be squeezed out of the credit market.

Problems like the "lemon car" as a result of information asymmetry are called adverse selection, which occurs before the transaction occurs. Information asymmetry also leads to another problem, i.e., moral hazard, which arises after the transaction occurs. In the context of finance, moral hazard means a borrower, after receiving money, engages in activities that are undesirable from the lender's point of view. In the credit market, after borrowers obtain a loan, they will possibly take a big risk because they are using other people's money. Here is a hypothetical example. A friend of yours borrowed 50,000 yuan from you, which, plus his own fund of 20,000 yuan, makes a total of 70,000 yuan and would be invested in a restaurant. He paid you interest at an annual rate of 5%. If he runs the restaurant well, he will gain a return on investment of 15% annually, that is, he can earn a return of 10,500 yuan in a year; after paying you a return of 2500 yuan, he still has a profit of 8000 yuan, representing a rate of return of up to 40%. Assume, however, that he used the 50,000 yuan borrowed from you to buy sports lotteries instead of running a restaurant, as lured by the grand prize of 5 million yuan. We all know that winning a grand prize has a very low probability. Hence, the moral hazard occurred, that is, the 50,000 yuan you lent him possibly cannot be repaid. After purchasing an insurance policy, the policy holder will possibly exercise less caution because he or she will be indemnified by the insurance company once an accident takes place. That is the moral hazard in insurance.

In joint-stock companies, similar moral hazard is called the principal–agent problem. Here, principals generally refer to shareholders, and agents are the managers who run the company. In a joint-stock company, if the management members hold very few or even no shares in the company, the ownership and control power are separated. The separation of ownership and control right may result in moral hazard to the management, who are likely to act for their own benefits instead of for the benefits of shareholders. Take the 70,000 yuan restaurant investment for example again. Assume that there are 98 investors in addition to you and your friend, and each of you invested 700 yuan and owned certain shares in the restaurant. All of you agreed to have the restaurant run by your friend who, in turn will receive a yearly salary of 8000 yuan. He worked hard and the restaurant's return on investment was still 15% every year. The total return in one year was 10,500 yuan. Because every investor owns 1% stake in the restaurant, everyone can receive a dividend of 105 yuan every year. Your friend who ran the restaurant has a total income of 8105 yuan. However if he loafs on the job, going bowling or visiting cafes now and then during office hours and the restaurant consequently has relatively poor performance with merely a 1% return on investment each year and 700 yuan of annual profit, then each investor can only obtain 7 yuan of dividends per year. Your friend who manages the restaurant has a total annual income of 8007 yuan, only 98 yuan lower than the income he would gain if he works conscientiously. In his mind, this 98 yuan is not enough to compensate for the utility of going bowling or whiling away the time drinking coffee, so he will probably not take good care of your restaurant.

Besides laziness, if this man is not honest, he will not tell you and 98 other investors the true profitability of the restaurant. Even if the restaurant has a profit of 8000 yuan per year, he will say that only 2000 yuan is earned and the rest 6000 yuan will go to his own pocket. This consequently generates the insider control problem in the principal–agent relationship of the stock company. The so-called insider control is that the agent hides the real situation of company operation to maximize his own interests by means of his information advantage. We may look at some listed corporations. The business performance may not be so satisfactory, but the senior executives of these companies still live in spacious and high-end apartments, drive luxurious cars and stay in five-star hotels on business trips. Of course all the expenses are covered by the company budget and the shareholders are the ones who foot the bills.

2.5.2 Solutions to Information Asymmetry

(a) *Private Production and Sale of Information*

Since both the moral hazard problem and adverse selection problem are caused by information asymmetry, the key to solve them is to acquire as much information as possible. We often say that you should "look before you leap". It means that you should collect all kinds of information before you act so as not to make adverse selections. An ancient Chinese fable about a proverbial donkey in the province of Guizhou which has exhausted its tricks vividly describes how to avoid adverse selection through careful and detailed information collection. When the donkey went to Guizhou for the first time, the tiger saw it as a huge monster and did not know how much power the donkey had, therefore the tiger hid behind a tree to observe the donkey secretly. After a while the tiger walked from behind the tree and gradually got closer to the donkey. The donkey brayed loudly and the tiger was frightened and ran away in panic. Later the tiger was accustomed to the cry of the donkey and felt that the donkey did not have marvelous skills, so it offended the donkey intentionally. The donkey was angry and kicked the tiger. The tiger judged that the donkey's ability was nothing more than this and finally it killed and ate the donkey. At first the tiger did not know the ability of the donkey, and in order to avoid the adverse selection of being eaten by the donkey, the tiger collected all kinds of information on the donkey in advance so as to avoid the tragedy of being eaten.

Like the tiger which gathered information on the donkey, the solution to the moral hazard and adverse selection problem in financing lies in providing fund suppliers with detailed information on the individual or company seeking funds. If an insurance company is able to tell the probability of accidents occurring to each driver, it could charge the premium according to the probability. If you had known that the guy would use what he had borrowed from you to buy lottery tickets, you would probably not lend him money in the first place. Likewise, if you and 98 other investors had known that the man who manages the restaurant would not report the operating performance truthfully, you may ask him to make detailed records on the business operation of the restaurant every day.

One way to help money lenders obtain the information on borrowers is to set up private companies which collect and generate corporate information to distinguish good and bad companies, and which would then sell such information to investors. The worldfamous S&P's and Moody's Investors Service are such companies which specialize in the production of information. Before you invest, you can also investigate the company you plan to invest in and obtain relevant information. However the information is a public good to a certain extent and being used by others will not compromise its utility. The marginal cost of the consumption of information products is zero and it is difficult to supervise the use of information. Unlike tangible personal items, the utility of which may be obtained through market exchange it is hard to achieve this for information product because the "free ride" phenomenon widely exists in information consumption. The fact that information is produced and processed by individuals will cause the insufficient supply of such public products.

(b) *Financial Intermediaries*

Financial intermediaries can become the experts of borrower information production, thus distinguishing credit risks to a certain extent. They can obtain funds from savers and then lend them to good companies. Since the majority of bank loans are issued to good companies, through the loans, banks can get profits that are higher than the interests they would pay savers. In this way, banks gain profits, which enable them to engage in information production. Banks have the abilities to profit from information production because they can accumulate special skills on company information production and processing through lending activities over the years. An important factor for banks to collect the information in this aspect is that they mainly issue private loans instead of purchasing securities which are traded in the open market, which effectively avoids the problem of free ride. Furthermore, unlike small loans of individual investors bank loans are usually large in volume. As the costs of information collection, handling and processing do not change significantly with the size of loans, banks are able to effectively reduce the unit cost in collecting and processing corporate information and issuing loans to corporations. This is the economy of scale we talked about earlier. It helps to overcome the problem of free ride in information collection.

However, financial intermediaries only partially solve the problem of information asymmetry. They do not solve all the problems caused by information asymmetry. In fact, as intermediaries, banks also often suffer from the impact of the adverse selection and the moral hazard of borrowers. In order to better obtain the information of borrowers, banks can also adopt other measures, such as loan commitments, collateral and net worth requirements.

(c) *Loan Commitments*

Another way to address information asymmetry is by way of loan commitments and credit limit of financial institutions. Loan commitment is a bank's commitment to provide a firm with loans up to a given amount for a specified future period of time as long as the contract conditions remain unchanged. The credit line is pure revolving loans, which means that within specified time intervals, if a corporation needs funds, it can obtain loans up to a given credit limit from the bank. Therefore, for borrowers, the credit limit has relatively high flexibility and can often be used as the main source of working capital. The loan commitment can be divided into revocable loan commitment and irrevocable loan commitment. In revocable loan commitment, after the bank signs a loan commitment contract with a corporation, if any changes not conducive to the bank occur, such as the deterioration of the macroeconomic environment or significant personnel change of the company which affects its business prospects, the bank can refuse to provide loans to the corporation according to the commitment. In irrevocable loan commitment, the bank must provide the corporation with loans as prescribed in the commitment contract no matter what changes take place in the future.

Loan commitment relieves borrowers from the hardship of credit rationing or credit crunch. It can help solve the problems of adverse selection and moral hazard, but it may also make the problems more serious. In the loan commitment, a variety of conditions will be prescribed for potential borrowers to get the loan commitment, such as front-end charges, user fee and interest rates. The bank may make borrowers show their real types or choose investment projects with higher net present values, which solves the problem of adverse selection to a certain extent. Furthermore, in the loan commitment, the bank has the right to know the actual state of operation of the company and to supervise the operation activities of the company. Especially in the revocable loan commitment, once there is a change of corporate conditions unfavorable to the bank, the bank can refuse to continue to provide the corporation with loans, which not only requires the corporation to exercise more caution to a certain extent, but also partly solves the problem of moral hazard. However, the loan commitment may also make the information problem more serious because the commitment contract is signed earlier and the relevant information of borrowers obtained is inadequate. If so, for those irrevocable loan commitments, the problem of information asymmetry may become worse.

(d) *Collateral and Net Worth*

Only when the borrowers fail to repay the loans which leads to defaultand the lenders suffer losses, will adverse selection and moral hazard hinder the normal operation of the financial market. However most banks have collateral requirements or ask for third-party guarantee when they issue loans. When we apply for the housing mortgage, the bank often requires us to take the houses we buy as collaterals; when the bank issues loans to companies, it often requires companies to mortgage corresponding equipment or plants. The reason is that collateral weakens the adverse consequence of adverse selection and moral hazard because it reduces the lender's losses in the event of a default. Especially when the ratio of the mortgage value to the loan is higher, the possibility of default will be lower. If the default occurs, the lender can sell the collateral and use the proceeds to make up for its losses on the loan. However, the effectiveness of the collateral depends on the maturity of the secondary market for collaterals. If the secondary market for collaterals is relatively active, the bank can successfully liquidate them in the market and thus recover outstanding loan balance in the case of a default. However if the secondary market is underdeveloped and it is difficult for the bank to liquidate the collateral or the cost of liquidation is high, it will reduce the usefulness of collaterals as a means to address adverse selection and moral hazard.

Net worth plays a role similar to collaterals. If the net assets of a company are higher, its dependence on external financing will be reduced. But on the other hand, it also means that it is easier for the company to access external financing. If the net worth of the company is high, even if it engages in investment that leads to losses and thus causes default in loan payment, the lender may still take title to the net worth of the company and sell it off to cover the outstanding loan balance with proceeds obtained this way. In addition, the higher a company's net worth, the smaller the probability of default; this is because the company has the cushion assets to repay loans. The higher an entrepreneur's net wealth investment as a percentage of the total investment in a project, the more cautious the entrepreneur will be in project selection. In this situation, the probability of adverse selection will be reduced and the entrepreneur will be less motivated to change the purpose of the funds and use them to finance some high-risk projects which go against the interests of lenders. If the man who opens the restaurant together with you invests 50,000 yuan out of the total investment of 70,000 yuan, he will probably spend more time on restaurant management rather than going bowling or drinking coffee and will be less likely to conceal the information of true profitability. In extreme cases, if the 70,000 yuan is wholly invested by him, it is totally unnecessary to conceal the profitability unless he tries to avoid tax. Consequently, if a company or an individual who seeks loans has great net worth and the consequence of adverse selection and moral hazard is not significant, the lender will be more willing to grant them a loan.

(e) *Positive Incentive of Contract*

The positive incentive of contract means, when both parties of trade sign a financial contract, the party at a disadvantage in obtaining information agrees that if the party with information advantage has, within a specified period, conducted no activities infringing upon its interests, the party at a disadvantage will provide corresponding financial services with favorable conditions to the party with information advantage. Insurance contracts or loan contracts generally include the clause of positive incentive. For example, in automobile insurance, if no accident occurred to the policy holder within an insurance period, the insurer will give him a policy with higher discount in the next insurance period; if a borrower had no default record in the past, the bank may provide loans to him at a more preferential interest rate. In October 2009, the People's Bank of China (PBOC) adjusted interest rates, expanding the downward floating zone of the interest rate of housing mortgage loans to 30%; that is, the interest rate of the housing mortgage loans granted by commercial banks may enjoy a 30% discount based on the benchmark interest rate promulgated by the PBOC. However, many commercial banks require that the borrowers be entitled to the discount only when they have no previous record of default. As a result, some borrowers could not enjoy the discount because they failed to pay a small amount of interest on their credit cards, and thus had bad track records in the personal creditreporting system.

(f) *Role of External Regulation and Government*

Another way to solve the adverse selection and moral hazard problem is to implement external mandatory regulation. In all countries, financial sector will be subject to the strictest government regulation. Each country has laid down laws requiring companies to adopt the normal accounting standards so that people can easily judge their actual performance; government agencies also require that public companies must regularly make public their operating status, interim statements, and annual reports, and disclose their significant events of operation on designated publications in time. In such newspapers as *China Securities, Shanghai Securities* and *Securities Times*, we can read the announcements published by public companies on the changes in their operating status. These public companies are performing their obligations of information disclosure according to the regulatory requirements of governments. However, some companies may provide false information and conceal their true profit status, which constitutes violation of the regulations and will be subject to legal punishment.

Apart from regulation, the government also made use of modern information technology to provide the credit records of individuals as a quasi-public good to financial institutions. In order to mitigate the adverse impact of information asymmetry on China's banking sector, the PBOC set up the Credit Information System Bureau and developed a corresponding credit-reporting system in 2003. So far, the credit information of all individual borrowers in China (including the student loans you received in school and your housing mortgage loans afterwards as well as repayment of such loans) has been incorporated into the credit-reporting system. Commercial banks may inquire about credit information of those with loan records in the system. For example, if Wang Xiaoer obtained a student loan during his college years, and was unable to pay principal and interest on schedule after graduation, it might be difficult for him to apply for other loans in the future.

Summary

In the economic system, some sectors have surplus funds, while other sectors may be short of funds. There are two channels to transfer the funds from lender–savers to borrower–spenders: fiscal transformation mechanism and financial transformation mechanism. Fiscal transformation mechanism means to transfer the funds from lender–savers to borrower–spenders through government. Financial transformation mechanism, including indirect finance and direct finance, is to transfer funds from lender–savers to borrower–spenders through the financial system. Indirect finance connects borrower–spenders with lender–savers through financial intermediaries; direct finance means the lender–savers directly transfer funds to the borrower–spenders, and there is a one-to-one relationship between them.

The financial system has its unique functions and plays an important role in resources allocation. The major functions of the financial system include: reduction of transaction cost, time–space conversion, improved liquidity and investment continuity, risk sharing, payment and settlement, and supervision and incentives.

Transferring funds from lender–savers to borrower–spenders depends on financial instruments. A financial instrument is a contract that specifies the debtor–creditor relationship. Financial assets, corresponding to the financial instruments, are a general term of the financial instruments with actual price and future valuation. Financial instruments constitute financial assets only relative to the holders; and for the issuers, they are not financial assets. Financial instruments can be divided into equity instruments and debt instruments, primary financial instruments (underlying financial instruments) and derivative financial instruments.

Financial instruments have four characteristics, namely maturity, profitability, liquidity and risk. Generally, the longer the term of a financial instrument, the higher its profitability, the lower its liquidity and the greater the risk; conversely, higher liquidity comes with lower profitability.

There is the problem of information asymmetry in the financial system. Information asymmetry means one party has more information than another in financial activities. Information asymmetry will lead to moral hazard and adverse selection. In finance, moral hazard refers to borrower–spenders engaging in some activities undesirable to investors after receiving funds from them; adverse selection refers to lenders often ending up selecting borrowers with higher risks, and insurance companies often ending up selecting insurance applicants with higher risks, while squeezing low-risk borrowers or insurance applicants out of the market. In joint-stock companies, moral hazard and adverse selection caused by information asymmetry are mainly manifested as the principal–agent problem and insider control.

Moral hazard and adverse selection caused by information asymmetry can be solved by the following channels: private production and sales of information, financial intermediaries, loan commitments, collateral and net worth requirements and external regulation.

Key Terms

Lender–Savers; Indirect Finance; Secondary Market; Primary Financial Instrument; Adverse Selection; Voting by Hand; Nominal Return; Capital Market; Borrower–Spenders; Direct Finance; Financial Instruments; Derivative Financial Instruments; Net Financial Investment; Voting with Feet; Real Return; Money Market; Fiscal Transformation Mechanism; Financial Market; Financial Assets; Information Asymmetry; Loan Commitment; Principal–Agent; Debt Instruments; Securitization; Financial Transformation Mechanism; Primary Market; Fixed Income Securities; Moral Hazard; Net Worth; Insider Control; Equity Instruments.

Critical Thinking Questions

1. What is the mechanism of fund flow?
2. What are financial instruments? What are their characteristics? What are the relationships between them?
3. What are the functions of the financial system?
4. What are the differences between monetary market and capital market in transfer of financial resources?
5. What are moral hazard and adverse selection? Which methods can be used to avoid moral hazard and adverse selection?
6. Why can collaterals and net worth mitigate or prevent moral hazard and adverse selection?
7. Can financial intermediaries completely solve moral hazard and adverse selection problems?
8. What are the primary financial instruments and derivative financial instruments? What are the differences between them?

9. Please illustrate the role that the financial system plays in time–space conversion of resources allocation.
10. Assume that you purchased 1 million shares in a company. What will you do to avoid the moral hazard and adverse selection in this investment? Will you personally supervise the behaviors of the management?
11. Will you collect related information before making a stock investment? What kind of information will you collect and analyze?
12. What role will the government play in the financial system?
13. In response to the rapid growth of fixed asset investments and economic overheating, the Chinese Government usually adopts the following macro-control measures: increasing the proportion of equity capital in fixed asset investments in certain industries, to 35% for example. Analyze how the increase in equity capital will influence the total loans as well as the consequence of information asymmetry.
14. From 2007 to 2008, a crisis broke out in the US, which was triggered by subprime mortgage loans. A subprime mortgage loan is a housing mortgage loan without down payment requirements. It is granted by financial institutions in the US for individuals without income certificates or with a low credit rating. Many mortgage loans in the US have negative amortization as an important feature, that is, in the first several years after obtaining a loan, the borrower only needs to pay part of the interests instead of the principal; the accrued interests unpaid will be automatically included in the principal, leading to an increase in the payable principal in the first couple of years. Please use the theory of information asymmetry to analyze that: (1) in a subprime mortgage loan, what are the main factors affecting the net worth of the borrower in terms of the property? (2) Holding everything else unchanged, how will the net value of the subprime borrower change as a result of negative amortization? (3) Holding everything else unchanged, how will the net worth change if the housing price drops? (4) Based on the analysis above, how differently will the borrower behave when the housing price drops? What implication will it have for the financial system? (5) Based on the analysis above, what do you think will China's financial system learn from the subprime mortgage loans and the subprime crisis?

Chapter 3

Time Value of Money

Learning Objectives

After studying this chapter, you will be able to:

- Understand the time value of money
- Understand simple interest and compound interest
- Understand the nominal interest rate, the Fisher effect and the after-tax real interest rate
- Fully understand future value and present value
- Understand annuity
- Distinguish between the present and future value of annuity
- Learn to calculate monthly mortgage payments
- Understand the influence of inflation and interest taxes on savings plans

When you deposit a sum of money in the bank, how much interest can you expect in the future? Likewise, suppose you take out a loan to buy a house or a car, how much should you pay off per month? Say you wanted to start saving for retirement, how much should you save each month? After you retire, how much can you expect to receive each month? Almost everyone will run into these kinds of questions. To answer these questions, you must first understand the time value of money. When it comes to finance, the time value of money is one of the most fundamental concepts. This chapter will provide a comprehensive introduction to the time value of money and its calculation. From there, we will discuss the effects of inflation and interest taxes on savings plans.

3.1 Time Value of Money and its Calculation

3.1.1 What is Time Value of Money?

The time value of money refers to the fact that a certain amount of money today has a higher value than it will in the future. For instance, one yuan today has a higher value than one yuan would have a year from now. Similarly, one yuan a year from now will also have a higher value than one yuan two years from now, and so on. That is to say, money loses its value over time.

Money has such a time value for the following three reasons:

Today's money can be invested and can generate additional income.

- A change in the price level can affect the purchasing power of money and thus the value of money. When the general price level of goods rises, the purchasing power of money will decline. In this case, one yuan a year from now would not be worth today's yuan. Conversely, when the general price level of goods declines, the purchasing power of money will rise. In this case, one yuan a year from now would be worth more than what it is today.
- In general, there is a degree of uncertainty with expected future income.

3.1.2 Calculating the Time Value of Money

We generally use **interest rates** to display the time value of money. Interest rates are the reason lenders are willing to give money to borrowers. It is also the price that borrowers must pay to use the money. Suppose that you deposit 100 yuan in the bank, and after a year it may be willing to return you your 105 yuan, thus, the annual interest rate on your deposit is 5%; if a bank lends 50 million yuan to Company A, after a year, Company A must pay the principal and total interest of 53 million yuan, thus the annual interest rate on this sum of money is 6%. According to the interest formula, interest rates can be divided into simple interest and compound interest. Based on actual values, interest rates are divided into the nominal interest rate and the real interest rate.

(a) *Simple Interest and Compound Interest*

In our financial life, we have quite different approaches to calculating interest rates. Suppose you went to the bank today to deposit 10,000 yuan. The current interest rate is 10% and this will not change for the next few years. After two years, your principal and interest would be 12,000 yuan and interest on your deposit is calculated according to the simple interest formula. If you make a withdrawal after two years and receive 12,100 yuan for your principal and interest, then your deposit is calculated according to the compound interest formula.

Where exactly did this 12,100 yuan come from? First of all, at the end of the first year, your interest would be 1000 yuan. Including your original 10,000 yuan, your principal and interest would be 11,000 yuan. Beginning at the start of the second year, calculating based on the 10% interest rate on the 10,000 yuan that you originally deposited, at the end of the second year, your interest would still be 1000 yuan. However, in the meantime, a 10% interest is also calculated based on the 1000 yuan of interest that you earned during the first year. The interest earned on this interest would be 100 yuan. In this way, you would have 12,100 yuan in your account at the end of the second year. The specific calculation is as follows:

$$\underbrace{10{,}000}_{\downarrow\atop\text{Principal}} + \underbrace{10{,}000 \times 10\%}_{\substack{\downarrow\\ \text{Interest earned}\\ \text{on principal in}\\ \text{the 1st year}}} + \underbrace{10{,}000 \times 10\%}_{\substack{\downarrow\\ \text{Interest earned}\\ \text{on principal in}\\ \text{the 2nd year}}} + \underbrace{10{,}000 \times 10\% \times 10\%}_{\substack{\downarrow\\ \text{Interest earned}\\ \text{in 2nd year on}\\ \text{1st year interest}}} = 12{,}100.$$

Summarizing the example above, we can begin to see the difference between simple interest and compound interest. Simple interest is only calculated based on the original principal. Compound interest, commonly called "interest-on-interest", is calculated each period with the same interest rate not only on the original principal, but also on all prior interest earned. When simple interest is calculated, the total principal and interest at maturity is equal to the initial principal PV plus the product of the initial principal, the interest rate (i) and the term of the deposit n, or $PV(1 + i \cdot n)$. In the example above, the initial principal is 10,000 yuan, the interest rate is 10%, and interest bearing period is 2. As such, the final principal and interest is 12,000 yuan ($10{,}000(1 + 10\% \times 2)$). We will leave the calculation of the total amount for compound interest rates for the next section.

(b) *Nominal Interest Rates and Real Interest Rates*

The nominal interest rate uses nominal money to express interest rates. The 10% interest rate on the one-year deposit mentioned above is a nominal interest rate. In general, whenever you deposit money in a bank or purchase a government bond or corporate bond, all of these interest rates are nominal interest rates. These rates are not adjusted for inflation. If you adjust the nominal interest rate for the rate of inflation, you get the real interest rate. In other words, the **real interest rate** is the difference between the nominal interest rate and the rate of inflation. It is measured by the goods and services that you are capable of purchasing.

For instance, in our example above, suppose that today your 10,000 yuan could buy 10 T-shirts. If it were not for inflation, and each T-shirt was still 1000 yuan, after a year, your total principal and interest could purchase 11 of the same T-shirts. This extra T-shirt comes from the actual interest you received, namely the real interest rate of $10\%\left(=10\% - 0\% = \frac{1}{10} \times 100\%\right)$.

However, if the rate of inflation was also 10%, and the price of the T-shirt rose by 10%, at the end of the first year, the price of each T-shirt would be 1100 yuan. Then your 11,000 yuan from your principal and interest can only buy 10 T-shirts. That is to say, even though the total capital in your account includes the added 1000 yuan in interest after a year, you cannot buy any extra T-shirts. Hence, the real interest rate is zero. The relationship between the real interest rate, the nominal interest rate and price increases is called the **Fisher effect**.

By using r_r to express the real interest rate, r_n to express the nominal interest rate, and p to express an increase in the average price of goods, the real interest rate would be:

$$r_r = r_n - p. \tag{3.1}$$

If the interest rate on your deposit were 10%, and the current price of goods increased by 10%, then the real interest rate for your deposit is 0. If the price of goods rises at a rate beyond the nominal interest rate, then the real interest rate is negative. This means that if you save money to purchase a house, when the price of goods rises to a rate higher than the interest rate on deposits, people start to pull their hair out. Conversely, if the price level falls, the real rate of interest will be higher than the nominal interest rate. Hence, during high inflation, saving money just is not worth it. During deflation, you cannot lose with a savings account.

In addition to inflation, interest taxes will also affect the actual value of nominal interest rates. For example, there is a 20% interest tax that must be paid on all of the interest accrued in your account. However, the interest tax is collected based on the nominal interest rate and does not adjust for inflation. Hence, an interest tax of 200 yuan must be collected on the 1000 yuan of nominal interest from the 10,000 yuan that you saved. If the rate of inflation is 10%, then the real interest rate after taxes becomes −2%.

If we use r_{at} to express the after-tax real interest rate, t to express the interest tax rate, r_n is still the nominal interest rate, p is still the increase in the average price of goods, then the after-tax real interest rate would be:

$$r_{at} = r_n \cdot (1 - t) - p. \tag{3.2}$$

The effect of this interest tax on the after-tax real interest rate is called the **Darby effect**, because Professor Darby of UCLA was the first to discover this problem.

3.2 Calculating Compound Interest and Future Value

3.2.1 Compound Interest and Future Value

Continuing with the example of the 10,000 yuan that you deposited in the bank as an example, the interest rate is still 10%. Supposing that this interest rate does not change, what would be the total amount of principal and interest after five years? Initially, you deposited 10,000 yuan, and in finance, this is called **present value** and is expressed with the notation *PV*. In finance, the principal and interest after five years, which we want to calculate for the 10,000 yuan that you initially deposited (present value) is called the **future value** and is expressed as *FV*. This so-called future value is the total principal and interest at the end of any given period based on a specific amount of initial investment (present value) calculated with a certain compound interest rate.

We have already worked out the future value of the deposit on the present value of 10,000 yuan at the end of the first year:

$$10{,}000 \times (1 + 10\%) = 11{,}000.$$

The principal and interest, namely the future value at the end of the second year is

$$10{,}000 \times (1 + 10\%) \times (1 + 10\%) = 10{,}000 \times (1 + 10\%)^2 = 12{,}000$$

and so on and so forth, so that for the future value at the end of the fifth year, we would get:

$$10{,}000(1 + 10\%)^5 = 16{,}105.1.$$

The change of future value during these five years is listed in Table 3.1.

For a better understanding of the effects of compound interest on your total interest, we list in Table 3.2 the changes in interest during the first four of these five years:

Table 3.1 Future Value Comparison (Unit: yuan)

Year	Initial Balance	Added Interest	Final Balance
1	10,000	1000	11,000
2	11,000	1100	12,100
3	12,100	1210	13,310
4	13,310	1331	14,641
5	14,641	1464.1	16,105.1

Table 3.2 Changes in Interest (Unit: yuan)

Year	Simple Interest	Compound Interest on 1st Year of Simple Interest	Compound Interest on 2nd Year of Simple Interest	Compound Interest on 3rd Year of Simple Interest	Compound Interest on 4th Year of Simple Interest	Total Simple Interest	Total Compound Interest	Total Interest
1	1000					1000	0	
2	1000	100				2000	100	
3	1000	110	100			3000	310	
4	1000	121	110	100		4000	641	
5	1000	133.1	121	110	100	5000	1105.1	
Total	5000	464.1	331	210	100			6105.1

We can see from Table 3.2 that although the simple interest each year is a fixed 1000 yuan. Compound interest, however, increases. The amount of compound interest in the second year is 100 yuan more than the first year. At the end of the third year, the amount of compound interest is 210 yuan; at the end of the fourth and fifth year, the amount of compound interest is 331 yuan and 464.1 yuan, respectively. This is because the compound interest rate each year is constantly increasing.

More often than not, we set *PV* as present value, *FV* as future value, *r* as the interest rate, and *n* as the number of years. When interest is calculated annually, we can calculate future value based on the following formula:

$$FV = PV \cdot (1 + r)^n. \tag{3.3}$$

For instance, for the 10% interest rate level on the 10,000 yuan that you deposited in the bank, the future value after 10 years is:

$$10{,}000 \times (1 + 10\%)^{10} = 25{,}937.$$

If interest is calculated more than once every year, how would we calculate the compound interest? We suppose that interest on your 10,000 yuan is compounded once annually (the annual interest rate does not change). After six months, the principal and interest would be:

$$10{,}000 + 10{,}000 \times \frac{10\%}{2} = 10{,}000 \times \left(1 + \frac{10\%}{2}\right) = 10{,}500.$$

Total principal and interest after the first year:

$$10{,}000 \times \left(1 + \frac{10\%}{2}\right) \times \left(1 + \frac{10\%}{2}\right) = 10{,}000 \times \left(1 + \frac{10\%}{2}\right)^2 = 11{,}025.$$

Total principal and interest at the middle of the second year:

$$10{,}000 \times \left(1 + \frac{10\%}{2}\right)^2 \times \left(1 + \frac{10\%}{2}\right) = 10{,}000 \times \left(1 + \frac{10\%}{2}\right)^2 = 11{,}576.3.$$

Total principal and interest at the end of the second year:

$$10{,}000 \times \left(1 + \frac{10\%}{2}\right)^3 \times \left(1 + \frac{10\%}{2}\right) = 10{,}000 \times \left(1 + \frac{10\%}{2}\right)^4 = 12{,}155.1.$$

So on and so forth, so that the total principal and interest at the end of the fifth year would be:

$$10{,}000 \times \left(1 + \frac{10\%}{2}\right)^{10} = 16{,}288.9.$$

After a little bit of comparison, you will soon discover that when interest is compounded twice annually, you will earn much more interest than compounded only once. At the end of the fifth year, for instance, an additional 183.8 yuan in interest will be added to your principal when compounded twice annually.

Generally in our calculations, interest is compounded m times annually. So, the formula for the future value at the end of the nth year is:

$$FV = PV \cdot \left(1 + \frac{r}{m}\right)^{m \cdot n}. \tag{3.4}$$

We call $\left(1 + \frac{r}{m}\right)^{m \cdot n}$ the future value interest factor.

According to the above formula, we can work out that when interest is compounded four or five times annually, by the end of the fifth year, the future value of your 10,000 yuan, respectively would be:

$$FV_4 = 10{,}000 \times \left(1 + \frac{10\%}{4}\right)^{4 \times 5} = 16{,}386.2,$$

$$FV_5 = 10{,}000 \times \left(1 + \frac{10\%}{5}\right)^{5 \times 5} = 16{,}406.1.$$

When the interest rate, present value, and the term are fixed, as the number of times that interest is compounded annually increases, future value will also increase. When interest compounds a set number of times annually, future value will rise when interest rates rise. Similarly, the future value will grow exponentially as the duration of savings extends. In Table 3.3, we can use the present value calculation for one yuan to work out the future values under different interest rates and different terms:

In fact, Table 3.3 also displays the future value interest factor under varying interest rates and terms. From this table, we can clearly see that when an interest rate is fixed, the future value increases when the term is extended, as does the future value interest factor. Conversely, when the term is fixed, as interest rate increases, the future value interest factor will also increase.

If you deposit 5000 yuan into an account with an interest rate of 6% that compounds annually, and if you save this principal for a five-year period, what would its future value be? If we look at Table 3.3, we can find that the future value interest factor for an interest rate of 6%, compounded annually, and a five-year period is 1.3382. If we multiply the principal balance of 5000 yuan by the future value interest factor, we can obtain a future value of roughly 6691 yuan.

Whenever investing, we always hope that our investment can grow exponentially or hope that the future value of our capital will be twice its present value. So, when the interest rate is fixed, how much time do you need to double your investment?

Table 3.3 Future Value of One Yuan Under Varying Interest Rates and Terms (Future Value Table)

Year	Interest Rate: r							
n	1%	2%	4%	6%	8%	9%	12%	18%
1	1.0100	1.0200	1.0400	1.0600	1.0800	1.0900	1.1200	1.1800
2	1.0201	1.0404	1.0816	1.1236	1.1664	1.1881	1.2544	1.3924
3	1.0303	1.0612	1.1249	1.1910	1.2597	1.2950	1.4049	1.6430
4	1.0406	1.0824	1.1699	1.2625	1.3605	1.4116	1.5735	1.9388
5	1.0510	1.1041	1.2167	1.3382	1.4693	1.5386	1.7623	2.2878
6	1.0615	1.1262	1.2653	1.4185	1.5869	1.6771	1.9738	2.6996
7	1.0721	1.1487	1.3159	1.5036	1.7138	1.8280	2.2107	3.1855
8	1.0829	1.1717	1.3686	1.5938	1.8509	1.9926	2.4760	3.7589
9	1.0937	1.1951	1.4233	1.6895	1.9990	2.1719	2.7730	4.4355
10	1.1046	1.2190	1.4802	1.7908	2.1589	2.3674	3.1058	5.2338
11	1.1157	1.2434	1.5395	1.8983	2.3316	2.5804	3.4785	6.1759
12	1.1268	1.2682	1.6010	2.0122	2.5182	2.8127	3.8960	7.2876

If we check the future value interest factor table above, you will discover the following pattern:

- When the interest rate is 6%, the future value interest factor in the 12th year is 2.1022.
- When the interest rate is 8%, the future value interest factor in the ninth year is 1.9990.
- When the interest rate is 9%, the future value interest factor in the eighth year is 1.9926.
- When the interest rate is 12%, the future value interest factor in the sixth year is 1.9738.
- When the interest rate is 18%, the future value interest factor in the fourth year is 1.9388.

In all these cases, the future value interest factor is close to 2. In other words, given the corresponding interest rates, your investment needs 12, 9, 8, 6, and 4 years to double respectively. Their common multiple in this case is 72, hence the so-called Rule of 72 in future value calculations. The rule of 72 demonstrates that when interest is compounded annually, the number of years for the present value of an investment to double is roughly 72 divided by the annual interest rate, and then divided by 100:

$$\text{Number of years until investment doubles} = 72/n \div 100.$$

3.2.2 Future Value of Annuity

(a) *What is an Annuity?*

Most banks will offer a wide range of savings accounts, one of which is **deposit in installment with lump sum withdrawal**. It is a savings account into which a person deposits a fixed amount of principal each month. After a few years, the depositor will make a one-time withdrawal of the entire balance. For example, if you deposit 500 yuan each month in your time deposit account for five years, which is to say that you would make 60 monthly deposits of 500 yuan. After five years, your principal would be 30,000 yuan. At the end of the fifth year, you can make a one-time withdrawal of your 30,000 yuan plus any interest that it earned during the five-year period.

In addition to your time deposit, you may also purchase pension insurance. The insurance company has promised that you will receive a fixed amount of pension annually in the future if you set aside a fixed amount to your pension insurance account every month starting from today. Insurance companies also offer **defined contribution pension plans**. For defined contribution pension plans, each employee has their own pension account. The employer agrees to deposit a sum of money each month into the account based on a certain percentage of the employee's salary. Only after the employee retires can this sum of money be withdrawn to be used as the employee sees fit.

Suppose that you earn a salary of 5000 yuan each month. If your company has a defined contribution pension plan, 5% of what you earn must be deducted from your wages and deposited into your pension account. As such, you and your employer will each deposit 250 yuan into your pension account every month, giving a total deposit of 500 yuan. Again, suppose that you work for 30 years and your salary never changes (thankfully this is just a hypothesis) and will have deposited a total sum of 180,000 yuan. You purchased pension insurance and made monthly insurance payments. At 60, you retire and can withdraw a fixed amount from your pension account each month to cover your basic needs and then some.

When purchasing commercial real estate, you may want to apply for a mortgage loan. Most home mortgage loans these days are fixed-rate mortgages. This means that the borrower makes the same payments each month. Say that you are given a 500,000 yuan mortgage loan. The bank requires you to make monthly payments of 3000 yuan at a fixed interest rate and for a fixed period. This fixed amount of monthly payment is often called the **monthly installment**.

For all of these different financial activities, the cash flow has a common characteristic in that the monthly cash flows are equal. In finance, we call this series of equal cash flows or payments **annuities**. Annuities can be divided into immediate annuities and ordinary annuities. **Immediate annuities** are a series of equal cash flows such as time deposits and pension plan payments that are generated immediately. If equal cash flows only begin at the end of the current period, these are **ordinary annuities**. For instance, suppose that today is March 1, and you have just signed off on a home mortgage loan. The bank requires you to make a 2000 yuan repayment on the 25th of each month. This payment is an ordinary annuity.

We can express the difference between immediate annuities and ordinary annuities with a time line, as shown in the figure below:

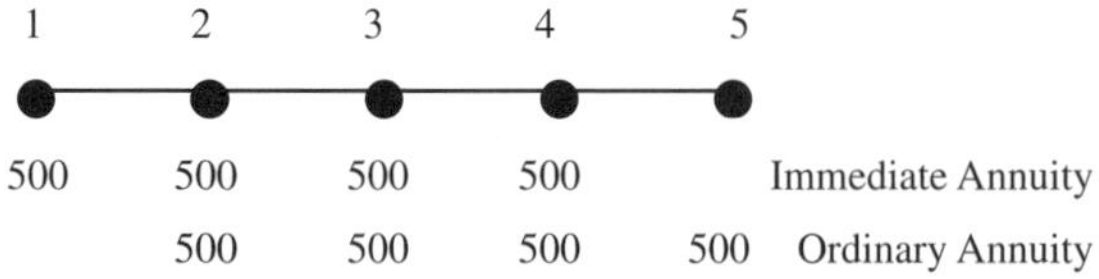

(b) *Future Value of an Annuity*

The future value of an annuity is the principal and interest of a series of cash flows over a period of time in the future. Using your time deposit as an example, suppose that you open a five-year time deposit at China Merchants Bank. You deposit 10,000 yuan annually and interest compounds annually at 6%. How much money will be in your account at the end of the fifth year?

In fact, this is only asking you for the future value of your time deposit annuities which equals the total future value of the 10,000 yuan that you deposit each year. According to the future value formula above, we can get the future value for your account each year as follows:

Year One: $10{,}000 \times (1 + 6\%)^5$,
Year Two: $10{,}000 \times (1 + 6\%)^4$,
Year Three: $10{,}000 \times (1 + 6\%)^3$,
Year Four: $10{,}000 \times (1 + 6\%)^2$,
Year Five: $10{,}000 \times (1 + 6\%)^1$.

If we add up the future value of each year, we can get the balance in your account at the end of the fifth year:

$$10{,}000 \times \left[(1 + 6\%)^1 + (1 + 6\%)^2 + (1 + 6\%)^3 + (1 + 6\%)^4 + (1 + 6\%)^5\right]$$

$$= 10{,}000 \times \frac{1.06 \times (1 - 1.06^5)}{1 - 1.06} = 59{,}753.97.$$

In general, *PMT* stands for immediate annuity, *r* for interest rates, *n* for number of years, and interest compounds once annually. From this, we can put together the future value of annuity formula:

$$FV = PMT \cdot \frac{(1 + r) \cdot [(1 + r)^n - 1]}{r}. \tag{3.5}$$

Say, for instance, that you purchase pension insurance with an annual pension payment of 6000 yuan for a 30-year period with an 8% interest rate. As such, what is the pension that you will receive 30 years later? By using the future value of annuity formula, we can calculate the amount of pension that you will receive after 30 years:

$$FV = 6000 \times \frac{(1 + 0.08) \times [(1 + 0.08)^{30} - 1]}{0.08} = 734{,}075.21.$$

Did your heart skip a beat? If you only pay 6000 yuan each year, after 30 years you would have paid a total of 180,000 yuan, and in the end, the total amount in this account would have reached more than 730,000 yuan!

We have already seen from the time line above that the cash flows from immediate annuity earns an additional one-year interest than ordinary annuity cash flows. As such, the future value of immediate annuity is $(1 + r)$ times greater than the future value of ordinary annuity. For this reason, the future value of ordinary annuity formula is as follows:

$$FV = PMT \cdot \frac{(1 + r)^n - 1}{r}. \tag{3.6}$$

If you purchased pension insurance with an ordinary annuity, then you would only receive the following pension after 30 years:

$$FV = 6000 \times \frac{(1 + 0.08)^{30} - 1}{0.08} = 679{,}699.27.$$

3.3 Present Value and the Present Value of an Annuity

3.3.1 Present Value and Discount

Suppose that you plan to go to Singapore, Malaysia, and Thailand next year and plan to spend 15,000 yuan. If you want to deposit a sum of money for this vacation and the interest rate for a one-year deposit is 5%, how much should you deposit?

With PV standing for the amount that you should deposit, we would have the following equation based on the future value formula:

$$PV \cdot (1 + 5\%) = 15{,}000,$$

giving us: $PV = 14{,}285.71$.

In other words, if you deposit 14,285.71 yuan, you will have enough to pay for your 15,000 yuan vacation.

Assume that you plan to take out a mortgage loan three years later and purchase a 500,000 yuan home. The bank requires a down payment of 20% which means that you must first pay 100,000 yuan in cash and can only borrow 400,000 yuan from the bank. If the interest rate on a three-year deposit is 6%, how much would you need to deposit so that you can pay your down payment in three years.

With *PV* standing for the amount that you should deposit, and since your 100,000 yuan down payment is really nothing more than the future value of your deposit after three years, we would have the following equation based on the future value formula:

$$PV \cdot (1 + 6\%)^3 = 100{,}000,$$

which gives us: $PV = 83{,}961.93$.

In other words, if you deposit 83,961.93 yuan, you will have enough to pay for your required down payment.

It can be seen from the calculations above that we can get the present value when we divide the future value by the future value interest factor. This just means that present value is the inverse calculation of the future value.

In general, r stands for the interest rate, *PV* for present value, *FV* for future value, n for number of years, and m for the frequency that interest compounds annually. Based on this, we have the following equation:

$$PV = \frac{FV}{\left(1 + \frac{r}{m}\right)^{n \cdot m}}.$$

We can call $\frac{1}{(1+\frac{r}{m})^{n \cdot m}}$ the present value interest factor which displays the present value after several years when the future value is set at one yuan, interest compounds m times annually and the interest rate is r.

Table 3.4 shows the present value interest factor under varying interest rates and number of years with an interest that only compounds annually.

By multiplying the future value by the corresponding present value interest factor, we can obtain the present value. Take a look at Table 3.4. At an interest rate of 6% and a term of 3 years, the present value interest factor is 0.8396. Thus, after three years of the required 100,000 yuan payments, there will be 83,960 yuan in the account. This approach is very similar to our previous calculation.

In finance, we often call the calculation of present value discount and call the interest rate used in the present value calculation the **discount rate**.

Now suppose, for example, that your initial down payment on your home was not at a one-time deposit at the start of the first year but at the beginning of each of the three years of equal deposits with an interest rate of 6%. As such, how much will you need to deposit to satisfy this requirement? In fact, this is just a calculation of the present value of your down payment annuities. Suppose that you deposit at the start of each year, each deposit would then be an immediate annuity.

Table 3.4 The Present Value for One Yuan of Future Value under Varying Interest Rates and Terms (Present Value Interest Factor rounded to the nearest ten thousandths)

Year	Interest Rate: r							
n	1%	2%	4%	6%	8%	9%	12%	18%
1	0.9901	0.9804	0.9615	0.9434	0.9259	0.9174	0.8929	0.8475
2	0.9803	0.9612	0.9246	0.8900	0.8573	0.8417	0.7972	0.7182
3	0.9706	0.9423	0.8890	0.8396	0.7938	0.7722	0.7118	0.6086
4	0.9610	0.9239	0.8548	0.7921	0.7350	0.7084	0.6355	0.5158
5	0.9515	0.9057	0.8219	0.7473	0.6806	0.6499	0.5674	0.4371
6	0.9421	0.8879	0.7903	0.7050	0.6302	0.5963	0.5066	0.3704
7	0.9327	0.8705	0.7599	0.6651	0.5835	0.5470	0.4523	0.3139
8	0.9234	0.8535	0.7307	0.6274	0.5403	0.5019	0.4039	0.2660
9	0.9143	0.8366	0.7026	0.5919	0.5003	0.4604	0.3606	0.2255
10	0.9053	0.8203	0.6756	0.5584	0.4632	0.4224	0.3220	0.1911
11	0.8963	0.8042	0.6496	0.5268	0.4289	0.3875	0.2875	0.1619
12	0.8875	0.7885	0.6246	0.4970	0.3971	0.3555	0.2567	0.1372

PVT shall stand for the amount you should deposit at the start of each year. Thus we get the following:

$$PVT \times \left[(1+0.06) + (1+0.06)^2 + (1+0.06)^2\right] = 100{,}000,$$

which gives us: $PVT = 29{,}633.00$

In other words, to make an initial down payment of 100,000 yuan on your home after three years, we now see that you must make three consecutive annual deposits of 29,633 yuan at the start of each year.

3.3.2 Present Value of an Annuity

If you happen to have a certain spending plan, namely that you must make several certain fixed payments of 2000 yuan each year for a period of five years in the future. As such, you decide to begin saving enough money to make those 2000 yuan payments for that five-year period. How much should you save now?

Suppose that the interest rate is 6% and you deposit a sum of money for a full year, after which you will withdraw at the end of each year. Thus, this is an ordinary annuity. Set the present value of the 2000 yuan withdrawn at the end of year i as PV_i. Based on the future value formula, we can obtain the following expressions, respectively:

$$PV_1 \cdot (1 + 6\%) = 2000,$$
$$PV_2 \cdot (1 + 6\%)^2 = 2000,$$
$$PV_3 \cdot (1 + 6\%)^3 = 2000,$$
$$PV_4 \cdot (1 + 6\%)^4 = 2000,$$
$$PV_5 \cdot (1 + 6\%)^5 = 2000.$$

The total amount that you deposit is simply the total present value of the 2000 yuan that you intend to deposit over five years as follows:

$$PV = \sum_{I=1}^{5} PV_1 = 2000 \times \left(\frac{1}{1.06} + \frac{1}{1.06^2} + \frac{1}{1.06^3} + \frac{1}{1.06^4} + \frac{1}{1.06^5}\right)$$
$$= 2000 \times \frac{\frac{1}{1.06} \times \left[1 - \left(\frac{1}{1.06}\right)^5\right]}{1 - \frac{1}{1.06}}$$
$$= 8{,}424.73.$$

In general, we set ordinary annuities as *PMT*, interest as r, number of years as n, the present value for this series of future annuities would be as follows:

$$PV = PMT \cdot \left[\left(\frac{1}{1+r}\right) + \left(\frac{1}{1+r}\right)^2 + \left(\frac{1}{1+r}\right)^3 + \cdots + \left(\frac{1}{1+r}\right)^n\right].$$

Based on the formula for a geometric series, we get the following equation:

$$PV = PMT \cdot \frac{\frac{1}{1+r}\left[1 - \left(\frac{1}{1+r}\right)^n\right]}{1 - \frac{1}{1+r}}. \tag{3.8}$$

After simplifying, we get:

$$PV = PMT \cdot \frac{1 - (1+r)^{-n}}{r}. \tag{3.9}$$

3.3.3 The Present Value of Perpetuity

If n becomes infinitely large, the ordinary annuity above becomes a **perpetuity**. In other words, these are annuities that have an infinite term. In our daily lives, stock is similar to perpetuity in that it does not expire. While we cannot calculate the future value of perpetuity, we can, however, calculate its present value.

What is the present value of a perpetuity? As n approaches infinity in the formula above, we can obtain the present value of a perpetuity, as follows:

$$\text{Present Value of Perpetuity } PV = PMT/r. \tag{3.10}$$

Suppose that you could live forever, and the interest rate at your bank will be 10% forever and ever. Say you want to withdraw 5000 yuan each year to cover your living costs. The bank, however, will not let you have your cake and eat it too. If you were to withdraw a sum of 5000 yuan each month, the bank demands that you deposit a certain initial capital. How much should you deposit? This in fact is nothing more than the present value of the perpetual annuities of your annual 5000 yuan. Based on the formula above, you will need to deposit 50,000 yuan. The reason is quite simple: if you were to deposit 50,000 yuan at the beginning of this year, by the end of the year your balance would be 55,000 yuan. After you withdraw 5000 yuan, you would still have 50,000 yuan remaining in the bank which would last indefinitely. In fact, the 5000 yuan that you withdraw each year is the interest that you deserve. There never was any "cake" coming from the bank after all.

3.3.4 How Much is Your Monthly Mortgage Payment?

Consequently, if the present value of an annuity is known, the annuities of some future period can be calculated based on the formula above, as in the following equation:

$$PMT = \frac{PV}{\frac{1-(1+r)^{-n}}{r}}. \tag{3.11}$$

This is the formula we often use in equated monthly installments.

Suppose that during the next three years you will have saved enough for an initial down payment of 100,000 yuan for a home purchase. You also successfully signed off on a 400,000 yuan mortgage loan from the bank. Assume that the interest rate on the loan is 6%, and the term is 30 years. How much will your monthly installments be? Since the bank requires you to make you installments at the end of each month, this is a type of ordinary annuity.

Because these are monthly installments, we must first convert the annual interest rate into a monthly interest rate of 0.5% ($6\% \div 12 = 0.5\%$). Since the repayment period is 30 years, we can think of it as a 360-month repayment period, that is $r = 0.005$ and $n = 360$. The calculation of the monthly installment is then:

$$\text{Monthly Installment} = \frac{400{,}000}{\frac{1-(1+0.005)^{-360}}{0.005}} = 2398.20.$$

If we know the interest rate and term for a mortgage loan, we can calculate the monthly installment amount based on the calculation for the present value of an annuity. If we set the annual interest rate as r, the term for the mortgage loan as n years, and the mortgage loan as PV, the formula for monthly installment payments is as follows:

$$\text{Monthly Installment} = \frac{PV}{\frac{1-(1+\frac{r}{12})^{-12\times n}}{\frac{r}{12}}} = PV \cdot \frac{\frac{r}{12}\cdot\left(1+\frac{r}{12}\right)^{12\times n}}{\left(1+\frac{r}{12}\right)^{12\times n}-1}. \tag{3.12}$$

We will call $\frac{\frac{r}{12}\cdot(1+\frac{r}{12})^{12\times n}}{(1+\frac{r}{12})^{12\times n}-1}$ the monthly installment coefficient which displays the monthly payment for one yuan of mortgage for the corresponding mortgage rate and term. By multiplying your total mortgage by the monthly installment coefficient, you can know how much your monthly installments will be.

3.4 Combining the Present and Future Value of an Annuity: Pension Plans

For some savings plans, we will calculate the future value as well as the present value. Pension plans are a perfect example of this type of savings plan. Suppose that you are 30 years old and an insurance company pitches their services to you. They promise that once you purchase a pension plan, you will only be required to continue to deposit a certain amount into your pension account for a number of years (e.g., 30 years). At 60, you retire and can continue to receive a monthly pension from the company for 20 years. Let us say that this amount will be 1000 yuan. If we assume that the interest rate will be 6% and the pension that you receive each month will be 1000 yuan, how much will the insurance company require you to pay each month over the next 30 years?

To calculate the amount that you should pay each month, there are two steps. First, calculate the present value of your pension of 1000 yuan received each month after retirement. This present value of annuity is actually the future value of an annuity for your monthly payments. Thus, the second step is to calculate your monthly payments based on this future value.

Step one: Use the formula for the present value of an ordinary annuity to calculate the present value of your pension of 1000 yuan that you will receive each month after retirement. Since you receive your pension on a monthly basis, the annual interest rate must be converted into a monthly interest rate of 0.5%. At the same time, the number of years must also be converted into months, of which we will have a total of 240. With a monthly interest of 0.5% over 240 months, the present value of 1000 yuan is then:

$$PV = 1000 \times \frac{1-(1+0.005)^{-240}}{0.005} = 139{,}581 \text{ yuan.}$$

Step two: Calculate how much money should be deposited each month starting today to obtain 139,581 yuan after a 30-year period. If you purchased an immediate annuity pension, this in fact will determine that the future value of annuity of your purchase must be at least 139,581 yuan. As such, we can use the formula $FV = PMT \cdot \frac{(1+r)\cdot[(1+r)^n-1]}{r}$ to calculate how much you should pay each month. Since you bought 30 years of annuity, the annuity period is 360 months. If the monthly interest rate and the general annuity per month are added to the above equate, then:

$$139{,}581 = PMT \cdot \frac{(1+0.005)\times[(1+0.005)^{360}-1]}{0.005}.$$

Solving for the equation, we get: $PMT = 138.26$.

This means that your monthly payments over 30 years would only need to be 138.26 yuan. Given a 6% interest rate, upon retirement 30 years later, you can make 1000 yuan monthly withdrawals under your pension plan. Your monthly pension upon retirement is nearly seven times the amount of your current monthly payments. Sounds pretty good, does it not?

3.5 Effects of Inflation and the Interest Tax

3.5.1 Inflation, Interest Taxes, Future Value, and Savings Plans

When we calculated the future value of savings above, it was implied that the inflation rate was zero and that the government did not collect an interest tax. However, this was merely an assumption. In reality, not only does the average price level of goods fluctuate, governments also will collect interest taxes on any interest that we earn. The effects of inflation and interest taxes are great.

Continuing the example in which you deposit 10,000 yuan into a bank account, the nominal interest rate is 10% as before, and the period is still five years. Unique to this situation is that we now assume that consumer prices are increasing at a rate of 5% and the interest tax is 20%. After five years, what has been the after-tax real interest rate?

According to our formula for after-tax real interest rates, the calculation for the after-tax real interest rate of this sum of money would be:

$$10\% \times (1 - 20\%) - 5\% = 3\%.$$

Thus, at the end of the fifth year, your real principal and interest is then:

$$10{,}000 \times (1 + 3\%)^5 = 11{,}592.74 \text{ yuan}.$$

This means that the interest you earn actually would only be 1592.74 yuan. Compared to the previous total, this sum is 4512.36 yuan short of the other. That is to say that if you deposit 10,000 yuan today, your total principal and interest can only purchase goods with an actual value of 11,592.74 yuan five years later. If after five years you decide that you want to use this savings to purchase goods with an actual value of 16,000 yuan, your 10,000 yuan deposit is simply not enough. As such, inflation and interest tax force you to deposit a greater portion of money.

If we convert the nominal interest rate into the real interest rate, we can obtain the after-tax future value for the known present value. If we replace r in $FV = PV \cdot (1+r)^n$ with r_r in Eq. (3.2), the after-tax real future value equation is then:

$$FV = PV \cdot [1 + r_n \cdot (1-t) - p]^n. \tag{3.13}$$

In the same fashion, the equation for the after-tax future value of an immediate annuity would be:

$$FV = PMT \cdot \frac{[1 + r_n \cdot (1-t) - p] \cdot \{[1 + r_n \cdot (1-t) - p]^n - 1\}}{r_n \cdot (1-t) - p}. \tag{3.14}$$

The actual after-tax future value of an ordinary annuity equation is then:

$$FV = PMT \cdot \frac{[1 + r_n \cdot (1-t) - p]^n - 1}{r_n \cdot (1-t) - p}. \tag{3.15}$$

Say, for example, that you open a time deposit account at the bank and make monthly deposits of a nominal 1000 yuan. The account has a 6% interest rate and a five-year term. During the next five years, if the general price of goods increases by 0.3%, i.e., inflation stays at an annual rate of 3.6%, and the interest tax rate is 20%, what would be the actual future value of your time deposit account after five years?

This is asking for the actual future value of immediate annuities, and if we convert the annual interest rate into a monthly interest rate of 0.5% and because a five-year term has 60 months, using Formula 3.14 we can work out the actual future value of annuities for your time deposit to be 61,866.52 yuan.

3.5.2 Inflation, Interest Taxes, Present Value, and Savings Plans

Suppose that you plan to purchase a 100 square meter condo three years from now. The current price is 5000 yuan per square meter (in places like Beijing and Shanghai, this is already unrealistic), the down payment is 20%, and the remaining 80% can be covered with a mortgage. If you bought the condo today, you would need to pay 100,000 yuan. The current interest rate of savings deposits is 6%, so you must deposit 29,633 yuan each year. Our calculations again assume that housing prices will not rise.

In reality, however, housing prices could continue to rise. Suppose that the price rose 8% each year. After three years, the price of the condo per square meter would be 6298.56 yuan. In other words, the total price for this 100 square-meter home would be 629,856 yuan after three years. Since the down payment is 20%, you would need to make an initial payment of 125,971.2 yuan. In this way, the 29,633 yuan that you deposited annually would not be enough after all.

How much would you need to save each year to have enough for the down payment then? This requires you to calculate based on the inflated price of the down payment. Multiply 125,971.2 by the present value interest factor:

$$PMT \cdot \frac{1.06 \times (1.06^3 - 1)}{0.06} = 125{,}971.2.$$

Giving us: $PMT = 37{,}329$ yuan.

By comparing the two, you will see that when the housing prices rise by 8% each year, you must save an additional 7696 yuan per year to afford the down payment on your home.

If the government collects 20% on interest, the after-tax nominal interest would only be 4.8%. Given this interest rate, your annual deposit would then be:

$$PMT \cdot \frac{1.048 \times (1.048^3 - 1)}{0.048} = 125{,}971.2.$$

Giving us: $PMT = 38{,}204$ yuan.

Thus it can be seen that for actual fixed payment plans, if you happen to save during inflation and if the government has collected interest taxes, then the nominal savings that you will spend must rise.

Summary

One yuan today is worth much more than one yuan in the future. This speaks of the time value of money.

In general, the time value of money is measured by the interest rate. As far as interest calculations go, there is simple interest and compound interest, as well as nominal interest rates and real interest rates. The nominal interest rate is the stated interest rate of a given financial instrument. The real interest rate is the nominal interest rate after it has been adjusted for inflation.

Future value is the total amount of principal and interest at the end of a certain period in the future, with the interest of a specified amount of initial investment compounded at a certain interest rate. This initial investment is also the present value of the future value. Setting the interest rate as r, the present value as PV, the future value as FV, the number of years as n, and the frequency that interest compounds annually as m, then $FV = PV \cdot \left(1 + \frac{r}{m}\right)^{m \cdot n}$ of which $\frac{1}{(1+\frac{r}{m})^{n \cdot m}}$ is known as the future value interest factor. Present value is the inverse calculation of the future value, thus $PV = \frac{FV}{(1+\frac{r}{m})^{n \cdot m}}$ of which $\frac{1}{(1+\frac{r}{m})^{n \cdot m}}$ is known as the present value interest factor. The process of calculating present value from future value is called discounting, and the interest rate used to discount is called the discount rate.

A stream of equal cash flows or payments is known as an annuity. Annuities are divided into immediate annuity and ordinary annuity. Immediate annuity is a series of cash flows that are generated immediately. If a series of cash flows arise from the end of the current period, it is an ordinary annuity. An annuity with an infinite term is perpetuity.

If immediate annuity is set as *PMT*, interest rates as r, number of years as n, and if interest is calculated once a year, then the formula for the future value of an annuity is $FV = PMT \cdot \frac{(1+r)\cdot[(1+r)^n-1]}{r}$. The formula for the future value of an ordinary annuity is $FV = PMT \cdot \frac{(1+r)^n-1}{r}$. The present value of an annuity is the inverse calculation of the future value of an annuity. The formula for the present value of an ordinary annuity is $PV = PMT \cdot \frac{1-(1+r)^{-n}}{r}$. Perpetuity does not have a future value, yet its present value is annuity divided by the interest rate; in other words, the present value of perpetuity is $PV = \frac{PMT}{r}$.

Monthly mortgage repayments are a type of ordinary annuity. The monthly installment is equal to the initial loan amount multiplied by the monthly installment coefficient.

Inflation and interest taxes have a great effect on people's savings plans. In order to ensure actual future spending, during periods of inflation and when there is interest taxation, nominal savings must be higher than nominal savings in periods without inflation or interest taxation.

Key Terms

Time Value of Money; Simple Interest; Compound Interest; Nominal Interest Rate; Real Interest Rate (The Fisher Effect); After-Tax Real Interest Rate (The Darby Effect); Future Value; Present Value; Annuity; Immediate Annuity; Ordinary Annuity; Perpetuity; Future Value of an Annuity; Present Value of an Annuity; Future Value Interest Factor; Present Value Interest Factor; Actual Future Value; Actual Present Value

Critical Thinking Questions

1. What is the time value of money?
2. What is the difference between simple and compound interest? How do we calculate each of them?
3. What is the difference between the nominal and real interest rates?
4. How do inflation and taxes on interest affect our savings plans?
5. What are present and future values?
6. What are annuities? What are the kinds of annuities and how do we calculate their future and present values?

7. Suppose that you took out a mortgage to purchase a home. How can you figure out how much your monthly payments will be?
8. Suppose that you put 100,000 yuan in a savings account for a five-year period at an annual interest rate of 7.2% which compounds only once a year. How much will be in your account after five years? Suppose that the government takes 20% out of your interest for taxes. For the next five years, inflation will remain at 3% per year. As such, what is your after-tax real interest rate?
9. Suppose that you open a time deposit savings account. Each month you deposit 500 yuan over a period of five years. The monthly interest rate for your account is 5.25‰. What will be the total principal and interest in your account after five years?
10. In the previous question, suppose that during the five-year period of your time deposit inflation happens to be 2.5‰ per month and the government will also take 20% of your interest in taxes. After five years, how much will your actual balance be?
11. Suppose that you use 90 yuan to purchase bonds of par value 100 yuan. After two years, you can be reimbursed 100 yuan for these bonds. As such, what is the annual interest rate for these bonds?
12. Suppose you purchased a home with 200,000 yuan mortgage loan from the bank. With a 20-year repayment term and an annual interest rate of 8.4%, what would your monthly payment be?
13. Imagine that you have an eight-year-old daughter. By the time she is 18, she will go to college and you will have saved enough for her annual tuition which is 5000 yuan at present. Over the next 10 years, however, the cost of tuition will grow an annual 8%. You plan to pay for all four years of tuition at once. Suppose that 10-year time deposits have an annual interest rate of 7.2% and taxes on interest are 20%. To alleviate this added burden, you plan on saving an additional equivalent sum for these 10 years. As such, how much do you need to save each year?
14. Suppose that you are 25 years old and have purchased pension insurance. You must make a monthly payment of 200 yuan to the insurance company until you turn 45. In other words, you must make monthly payments of 200 yuan to the insurance company for 20 years. After you retire at the age of 60, you can withdraw your pension and the insurance company promises that you can enjoy your pension for 20 years. Now, suppose that the interest rate would remain 7.2% for the 55 years from the time you make your monthly pension payments to the time you stop making payments. As such, how much would your monthly pension be when you retire? If the insurance company gives you 1500 yuan each month have you gained or lost?
15. Pigs really can fly! You purchased a lottery ticket and actually won the 5 million yuan reward! (Congrats!) After taking out 1 million in taxes, you still have 4 million yuan. You hold onto 2 million to pay for your future living costs and decide to invest the remaining 2 million. You have two choices: first, you can purchase ten-year government bonds with an 8% interest rate (compounding); secondly, you could invest in industry. The investment also so happens to be 2 million yuan, with a cash flow in the first year of 200,000 yuan. Afterwards, the cash flow increases at a rate of 10% annually. Starting in the eighth year, the cash flow declines by 20% annually. In the 10th year, the project does not bring in any more money. But you still have 200,000 yuan of rejected products. Suppose that at the end of each year you decide to invest the money you recover in a savings account with a 7% interest rate annually. Calculate the following: (1) How much

principal and interest will you accumulate on your government bonds after 10 years? (2) What is the annual recovered amount of cash flow on your industrial investment? (3) After 10 years, what is the balance in your savings account? (4) Which of the two choices would you prefer? Why?

16. In 2006, several banks proposed two-week mortgage loans under the slogan "Save on Interest". Calculating these two-week installments would require roughly three steps: First, use 1/2 of the typical monthly installment as the two-week installment. With a repayment method of equated principal and interest for a 500,000 yuan loan over a 20-year period as an example, and supposing that the annual interest rate is 5.508%, the calculated monthly installment would be 3441.70 yuan. Having determined that the two-week installment is 1/2 of the monthly installment, the installment would be 1720.85 yuan. Secondly, under the circumstances of a 500,000 yuan loan with an annual interest rate of 5.508% (the interest rate for each two-week period is $5.508\% \times \frac{14}{360}$) and an installment of 1720.85 yuan per period, the repayment term will be 455.12 two-week periods. By rounding down to 455 two-week periods, we also adjust each installment to 1721.13 yuan. Given these conditions, the loan can be completely paid off after 455 two-week periods. Third, compare the pros and cons of both repayment methods. Over the entire loan cycle, the total interest on two-week installments calculates out to be $1721.13 \times 455 - 500{,}000 = 283{,}112.39$ yuan. The total interest on monthly installments calculates out to be $3441.70 \times 240 - 500{,}000 = 326{,}007.07$ yuan. Based on these calculations, two-week installments will save you 42,894.68 yuan, saving over 13% compared to typical monthly installments. This truly is a better deal!

    Based on everything you learned in this chapter, comment on whether or not two-week installments can actually let borrowers save on interest. Is the interest rate on borrowing considerably lower? Hint: for traditional monthly installments, banks calculate daily interest as 5.508%/360 and calculate the annual interest based on 360-day years. For two-week installments, banks still calculate daily interest as 5.508%/360, and calculate annual interest based on the actual number of days, namely 365 days (ordinary year) or 366 days (leap year).

Chapter 4

Time Allocation of Resources: Whether to Save or Spend

Learning Objectives

After studying this chapter, you will be able to:

- Understand what it means to save
- Fully understand the different purposes that people have for saving
- Understand the effects of absolute income, permanent income and relative income on savings
- Understand the life-cycle hypothesis of spending and saving as well as the influence of a changing demographic structure on savings
- Understand the effects of changes to interest rates, consumer credit, wealth and institutions on savings
- Learn about life-cycle saving plans

In Chapter 2, we learned that finance is a bridge between the surplus and shortage of funds. As such, capital surplus is the foundation of finance. Savings is the original source of surplus, as well as one of the most important aspects of a rationally allocated lifetime income. After receiving a salary or bonus, the first decision you must make is what to do with this income. In other words, how much can you spend and how much should go towards future savings? This is the time allocation of resources. Savings has a great influence on the macroeconomy and is also an important aspect of our personal finances. This chapter will mainly introduce readers to the factors that motivate people to save and that influence people's decisions to save, as well as the reasons why people decide to spend or save.

4.1 Nature and Forms of Savings

4.1.1 The Nature of Savings

We often hear people say that someone has "put a great deal of money away". When people talk about savings in our daily lives, they are really just referring to savings deposits. This is very different from the concept of savings found in economic analysis. In formal economic analysis, the two cannot be confused for one another. To economists, the part of your current income that you do not spend is called **savings**, regardless of whether or not you plan to spend this income or deposit it in a bank, purchase bonds, purchase any variety of funds or even simply stash it away in your shoebox. Say, for example, that you earned 5000 yuan this month, of which you spent 200 yuan at your friend's party 1200 yuan on basic needs 400 yuan on a T-shirt and 200 yuan that went to your phone bill. At the end of the month, you still have 3000 yuan left over. In economics, this 3000 yuan is called savings. As you can see, savings has a much broader definition in economics than it does in our daily lives.

Savings can be divided into positive and negative savings. If you spend less than what you earn each month, then you are a positive saver. Positive savers are people with surplus funds. Conversely, if you spend more than what you earn, then you are a negative saver. Similarly, you are a negative saver if you purchase a home or an Audi with a mortgage loan from the bank. Negative savers are people with a shortage of funds. As you can see, positive savings is a way of deferring current income for spending in the future, regardless of whether you or someone else will be doing the spending (e.g., Saving for your children's college tuition). Negative savings is in fact a way of spending your future income on current expenses. One of the roles of finance is to transfer the surplus funds of positive savers to negative savers, and then repay the former with the latter's income. Throughout the rest of this book, savings shall always refer to positive savings unless stated otherwise.

Depending on whom the savers are, savings includes household savings, corporate savings and government savings. Just as household savings are the margin between a household's income and spending, so too are corporate savings the margin between a corporation's revenue and its spending on wages, taxes, interest, dividends and so on. Government spending is also the margin between a government's revenue and spending. Household and corporate savings are collectively referred to as private savings. Government savings, in turn, is known as public savings. Of course, savings also includes foreign savings. The Chinese policies aimed at attracting foreign investment since the country's "Reform and Opening-Up" are meant as a way to use foreign savings to compensate for a lack of domestic capital as well as introduce foreign technology and managerial expertise to the Chinese economy (see Figure 4.1).

4.1.2 Forms of Savings

Savings can be divided into financial savings and physical savings. **Financial savings** arise from surcharge in the form of financial assets such as securities, bank deposits, cash, etc. In addition to savings deposits in banks, financial savings can also be cash, national debt Treasury bills, corporate bonds, stocks, insurance, capital mutual funds, etc. **Physical savings** are savings such as in the form of housing,

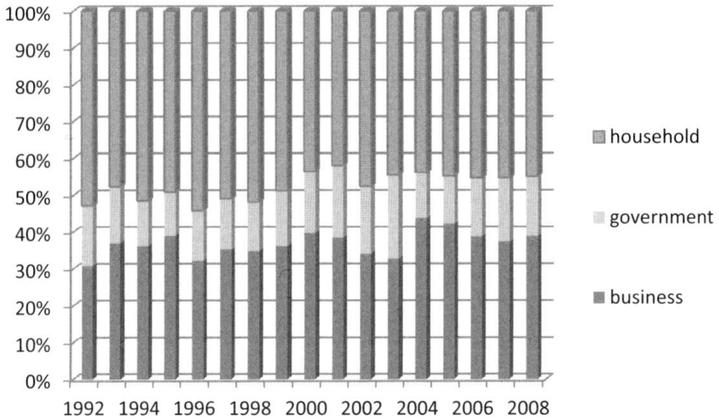

Fig. 4.1 Composition of China's National Savings
Source: *China Statistical Yearbook* and the website of the China National Bureau of Statistics

consumer durables, inventories, etc. A classic example of physical savings is the portion of grain that a farmer would keep in his granary after harvest, rather than selling in the market.

Compared to physical savings, there are many more advantages that come with financial savings. First of all, the cost of financial savings is relatively low; all you need to do is to take the remainder of your income after spending and deposit it into a bank account or purchase bonds or shares. The cost of physical savings, however, is relatively high. Some forms of physical savings are extremely inconvenient. For instance, if a farmer wishes to save his grains, he must first build a granary. If you wished to save meat, you not only need a cold storage facility but will also consume a large amount of energy. Additionally, financial savings can also earn a certain amount of interest. As long as the rate of inflation does not surpass the nominal interest rate, financial savings can also appreciate in value. Physical savings, on the other hand, are affected by the constant depreciation of goods. More importantly and from a wider perspective, financial services are much more conducive to cross-regional reallocation of financial surplus. For instance, when China Merchants Bank issues new shares, investors across the nation can subscribe for them at their local stock exchange. If you succeed in your application, even if you are all the way up north in Harbin, you can still transfer a part of your savings to the headquarters of China Merchant Bank in Shenzhen. If not for financial savings, it would be difficult to imagine how the share issue could be used to raise funds throughout China. Besides, the majority of physical savings is mainly reflected in the form of durable consumer goods and other inventory investments. As such, financial savings is more suited for capital formation and does a better job of propelling the economy forward.

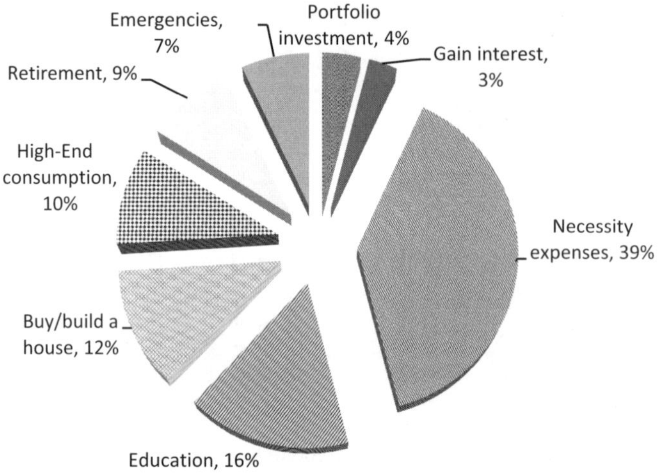

Fig. 4.2 Motivations of Chinese Households for Making a Deposit
Source: *Almanac of China's Finance and Banking* (1998)

4.2 The Motivation to Save

Why do people save? People do not save simply because it can bring them a sense of well-being or innate happiness, in fact, the motivations to save come in all shapes and sizes. According to a survey of the People's Bank of China (shown in Figure 4.2), people save for basic living expenses, when preparing to purchase luxury goods and when people want to purchase or build a home. Also, people save for retirement and for the unexpected. What is more, people will save for their children's education or their own training or even to just gain interest on their savings. Regardless of the different reasons to save, in fact, each individual is likely to have several reasons for saving, yet we still can reduce these various reasons down to a few types, namely transaction, precautionary and investment motives.

4.2.1 Transaction Motive

During a person's life, income may at times be greater than one's spending, at other times, spending may be greater than one's income. During the years before we enter the workforce, when we just enter the workforce and after we retire, we pay for much more than what we make. To balance out the cycle of earning and spending, we must salt away for the future during our prime working years. By the time we want to get married or purchase a home, there must be some savings to help pay for these things. Thus, we save for future transactions, and transaction motives drive us to hold money for future spending. The notion that savings is really just deferred consumption reveals the transaction motives of saving Basic living expenses and high-end consumption as shown in Figure 4.2, are both examples of the transaction motive for our saving. Savings for future transaction can help smooth out the income in our lifetime.

4.2.2 Precautionary Motive

In addition to transaction, there are also precautionary motives for saving. The future is unexpected, and we all know that life has many twists and turns. While we all hope and pray that good things come in pairs, it is always wise to "expect the unexpected". Say that something happens, for example, you may suffer from a serious illness which comes with a price tag. In order to avoid any last-minute need for money in the future, people save for emergencies and precautionary savings occur accordingly.

Box 4.1 The Grasshopper and the Ants: The Importance of Precautionary Savings

One of Aesop's fables is about a grasshopper and an ant. The grasshopper spent the entire summer hopping about, chirping and singing to his heart's content, not once stopping to stash a crumb or two away for the cold winter months. Of course, the grasshopper died at the first cold breeze of winter. The ant, however, spent the same summer toiling away under the sweltering heat, but because he had stored enough away, he spent the winter months quite peacefully. The moral of the story reveals the importance of this precautionary savings that we've been talking about. Noel Whittaker advised us when he said that "Wealth is like a huge tree that grows from a tiny seed. It takes a long time to grow to a great height but, provided it is watered and fertilized regularly, it will slowly but surely grow at a faster and faster rate . . . Our savings are the 'seed corn' for our money tree and compound interest (plus added savings) is the fertilizer that causes the fast, lush growth. If you wish to travel down the path of financial independence, you will need to start, and maintain, a money tree".

Of course, the fate of the grasshopper is a bit extreme, but he is a perfect example of people who "live for today". The consequences of such frivolous consumption seem to fall short of Li Bai's longing to "drown away the woes of ten thousand generations" which is naturally not advisable. Nevertheless, there is yet another type of people in our society who see savings as the only source of happiness. The miser Grandet in Balzac's novel *Eugénie Grandet* is representative of this kind of person.

It's best not to spend so freely, and neither would we recommend that you place all your hopes and joys upon your savings. What's important is that people must learn to find a balance between spending and saving. Only in this way can people be truly happy and truly enjoy their lives.

4.2.3 Investment Motive

Some people save just so that they can consume and earn more in the future. This kind of savings is known as **investment savings**. After all, whether it be money deposited in a bank or the purchase of government bonds, this kind of savings has a specific interest rate. Although the risks that come with stock are admittedly higher, so too are the possible returns that come with them. These are all financial investment savings, and people choose to purchase government bonds or stocks primarily for higher capital gains.

In addition, people may also save for the purpose of investing in human capital. In today's new technology and information era, a person's educational and intellectual level determine their position and income to a great extent. Statistically, the higher one's level of education, the higher is the income. People who are better educated not only have more stable lives but also earn the respect of others. So, people are beginning to take investment in education more and more seriously. As a parent, you will need to save for your children's education. Because "knowledge" changes with each and every passing day, even those with a formal education need to further their learning. We can see in Figure 4.2 that 16% of Chinese savings goes to education, second only to saving for basic living expenses.

4.3 Choice between Consumption, and Savings

Since economics defines savings as the portion of income that has not been used for consumption, any analysis of one (either consumption or savings) must consider the other. The two are in fact two sides of the same coin.

4.3.1 Disposable Income, Consumption and Savings

The main economic determinant for consumption and savings is the disposable income. **Disposable income** is the total balance of income after deducting for taxes. In general, the higher the disposable income, the more that one will spend, and similarly, the more that one will save. Say that a laid-off worker received 300 yuan each month in unemployment benefits. The most that he can spend each month is 300 yuan, and although he can only spend just a little, this does not mean that he can save a lot. Conversely, a white-collar worker with a salary over 10,000 yuan each month can spend over 5000 yuan. Be that as it may, he can still have 5000 yuan left over that he can save.

The ratio of consumption to income in the current period is called the **propensity to consume**. In our above example, the laid-off worker receives barely enough to cover his expenses. Thus, his propensity to consume would be 100%. The white-collar worker only spends half of his income, thus his propensity to consume would be 50%.

Corresponding to the propensity to consume is the **propensity to save** which is the ratio of savings to income in the current period. In the above example, the laid-off worker has a propensity to save of 0; while the white collar worker's savings propensity would be 50%.

In general, we set disposable income as Y, consumption as C savings as S, the propensity to consume as c, and the propensity to save as s. Thus, given the definition:

$$c = \frac{C}{Y}, \tag{4.1}$$

$$s = \frac{S}{Y}. \tag{4.2}$$

Since savings is the part of income not consumed during the current period, the sum of savings and consumption is equal to income in the current period, i.e.,

$$C + S = Y. \tag{4.3}$$

When we divide both sides by Y, we can get the following:

$$\frac{C}{Y} + \frac{S}{Y} = \frac{Y}{Y} \Rightarrow c + s = 1. \tag{4.4}$$

This shows that the sum of the propensity to consume and the propensity to save is equal to 1.

When disposable income increases by an additional unit, the corresponding increase in consumption is the **marginal propensity to consume**. Suppose that you get a raise of 100 yuan and your consumption increases by 60 yuan accordingly, your marginal propensity to consume would thus be 60%. Similarly when disposable income increases by one unit, the increase in savings that results is the **marginal propensity to save**. In this example, the increase in income of 100 yuan allows you to save an extra 40 yuan, which means that your marginal propensity to save is 40%.

In general, the increase in income is set as ΔY, the increase in consumption as ΔC, the increase in savings as ΔS, the marginal propensity to consume as c', and the marginal propensity to save as s', thus:

$$c' = \frac{\Delta C}{\Delta Y}, \tag{4.5}$$

$$s' = \frac{\Delta S}{\Delta Y}. \tag{4.6}$$

Similarly:

$$\Delta C + \Delta S = \Delta Y. \tag{4.7}$$

Dividing both sides by ΔY:

$$\frac{\Delta C}{\Delta Y} + \frac{\Delta S}{\Delta Y} = \frac{\Delta Y}{\Delta Y} \Rightarrow c' + s' = 1. \tag{4.8}$$

That is to say, the sum of the marginal propensity to consume and the marginal propensity to save is equal to 1.

In general, the higher one's disposable income, the lower will be the marginal propensity to consume and the higher the marginal propensity to save. Conversely, the lower one's disposable income, the higher will be the marginal propensity to consume and the lower the marginal propensity to save. Hence, when people's disposable income is relatively high, the share of savings will also rise. This is the absolute income theory of John Maynard Keynes. In other words, our marginal propensity to save depends on our absolute level of disposable income.

4.3.2 Permanent Income and the Life-Cycle Hypothesis

Milton Friedman put forward the permanent income hypothesis which emphasizes that our decision to spend or save is not influenced by our current income so much as it is influenced by a permanent income during one's lifetime. **Permanent income** refers to the average income of an individual at each period of their life. Some unexpected temporary rise in income may not increase a person's consumption expenditure, as people will, more often than not, put their temporary additional income into savings.

Suppose that a laid-off worker purchases a sports lottery ticket and just so happens to win the 5 million yuan lottery. Since the probability of winning is incredibly low, the laid-off worker would not expect to win each month and each year. That is to say, the winning lottery is certainly not his permanent income and is only his temporary income. Albeit this sum of income came out of the blue, yet he most likely will not spend it all at once. He may have plans for the future and may use a part of this 5 million yuan to improve his current living conditions and then save the remainder to cover his future living needs.

The absolute income theory and the permanent income hypothesis have different policy implications. Based on the absolute income theory, tax cuts will cause an increase in disposable income. This, in turn, will result in an increase in spending, as well as a rise in the propensity to save. Conversely, tax hikes will cause a decrease in consumers' disposable income and spending, though consumers' propensity to save will be lowered as well. However, based on the permanent income hypothesis, only when tax cuts are believed to cause an increase in long-term disposable income will spending increase. Conversely, only when tax hikes are believed to cause a drop in long-term disposable income will spending decrease.

Different from both the absolute income theory and the permanent income hypothesis, Franco Modigliani proposed the life-cycle hypothesis of savings. For

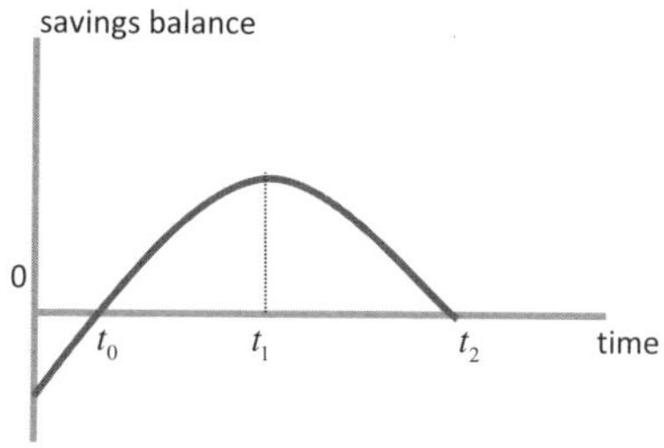

Fig. 4.3 Changes in the Balance of Savings over a Lifetime

most of us, a lifetime of income is rarely if ever distributed evenly. Our earnings before we enter the workforce and after we retire are at or near zero, yet there is never a point in our lives where we do not make any expenditure. Hence, the distribution of income and consumption over time is not consistent. In Figure 4.3 we can see that consumption is greater than income before t_0. As such, this is a period of negative savings. Savings continue to grow from t_0 to t_1 but gradually decrease after t_1 which represents a person's consumption pattern after retirement when dissaving occurs.

However, an individual's consumption or savings behavior is not only related to his or her current income People will always try to direct a lifetime of income towards optimal allocation between consumption and savings. In general, people do not earn much during their youth and old age, while the income that they earn in the middle of their life will be relatively high. To maximize the utility of their lifetime consumption, most people's consumption will stay at a certain level throughout their life, as much as possible. In other words, although income will fluctuate, consumption will remain relatively constant. The propensity to save, accordingly, will fluctuate with an income that constantly changes. More specifically, young people who have joined the workforce should have a relatively high propensity to save. As they grow older and once they retire, the propensity to save will drop. Since the propensity to save changes at different periods of a person's life, the propensity to save in one's youth will be relatively high, while the propensity to save in old age will be relatively low.

In macro terms, changes in a country's demographic structure (such as changes to the ratio of the working-age population *vis-à-vis* the non-working-age population) will have a major influence on the national savings rate. In general, during the thirty odd years after a baby boom, the working-age population will grow and the non-working-age population will decrease, accordingly, thus raising the national savings rate in general terms. An aging population, however, will have a decreasing national savings rate. In fact, economists have coined the term "demographic dividend" to refer to the influence of a growing working-age population on the gross national savings rate.

4.3.3 The Ratchet Effect: The Relative Income Theory of Consumption and Savings

In addition to absolute income and permanent income, our relative income can also affect our consumption and saving habits. American economist James Duesenberry was the first to propose the **relative income hypothesis**. He believed that compared to the absolute level of consumption, people cared much more about comparing their own consumption with others. Only when a person's consumption level rises above the average of those around him or her can their consumption effectively increase. This is what we would call "keeping up with the Joneses".

A person's consumption as a share of his or her income, namely his or her propensity to consume, depends on his or her position in the distribution of income. If one's income is lower than the average, their consumption as a share of their income will be relative high. This is because they are trying to keep up with an average consumption standard with a below-average income. If a person's income exceeds the average level of income, his consumption as a share of his income will be relatively low. This is because he only needs to use a relatively small portion of his income to maintain the average level of consumption. Moreover, current consumption is not only influenced by the relative income of the current period, but also by the maximum level of consumption attained in previous periods.

Duesenberry believed that it is much more difficult to lower one's consumption from the existing level than to lower one's propensity to save. This is known as the irreversibility of consumption. This is really the meaning of the Chinese saying that: it's easier to go from rags to riches than riches to rags. This means that savings as a share of income in the current period depends on the difference between the most that someone has ever earned and what they currently are earning. If income for the current period is a relative increase from the highest that one has earned, savings as a share of income will also rise. Conversely, if income for the current period is a relative decrease from the highest that one has earned, savings as a share of income will also drop. As such, the short-term consumption of the past is capable of, to some extent, preventing long-term consumption from dropping in the future. This is the **ratchet effect**.

4.3.4 Wealth

While wealth may be the fruit of savings, it can also influence our decisions on future consumption and saving. Imagine for a moment the following two situations. In the first case, your monthly salary is 5000 yuan, but you also have a fortune of 500,000 yuan in stocks, bank deposit and other forms of financial savings. In the second case, your monthly income is also 5000 yuan, but you have saved absolutely nothing. Although your monthly income is always 5000 yuan, yet since your accumulated wealth in the former is different than that of the latter, your choice to spend or save will certainly be different. In the first case, since you have a savings of 500,000 yuan, of the 5000 yuan for the current period, you can spend most of it on consumption. In the second case in which you do not have any wealth whatsoever, you must make careful arrangements for the future, such as your marriage, or for purchasing a home or car. You can cut back on your current consumption and add that money to your future consumption.

Typically, when income is the same, but wealth is different, people with a greater amount of wealth will have a higher propensity to consume and a lower propensity to save. Conversely, people with relatively little wealth will have a lower propensity to consume and a higher propensity to save. The phenomenon in which different propensities to consume or save are caused by different levels of wealth is called the **wealth effect**. The principle behind the wealth effect's influence on the propensity to consume is as follows: When holding all else equal, the greater an individual's savings, the lesser his desire to accumulate even more money.

In general, annual changes in wealth are minor, and for this reason, the wealth effect generally does not lead to sharp fluctuations in consumption. On the other hand, changes in capital income and asset price can immediately change the status of a person's wealth. When the price of stock or real estate appreciates, and if people expect this to be a long-term shift, then their consumption will increase. They do this because their aggregate wealth has increased, even though this is just a rise in book value and they may not have realized any immediate gains from the increase of asset prices. Therefore, after China experienced deflation in 1997, many economists proposed raising the price of stocks and other assets, thereby raising the book value of assets to make investors feel richer, causing them to increase their consumption and lower their savings as a means to stimulate the economy. Their proposal was based upon the wealth effect on consumption and savings. After the Wall Street Crash of 1929, the evaporation of wealth previously invested in stocks, forced a lot of rich folks to really tighten their belts.

4.3.5 Consumer Credit and Savings

Consumer credit can also affect our choice to consume or save. Consumer credit is a kind of financial arrangement that allows consumers to spread out their income evenly across their lifetime, known as consumption smoothing, which causes consumers to more reasonably allocate their resources and configure their consumption habits. This is the time transformation that we had emphasized in Chapter 2 when we analyzed the functions of the financial system. The smoothing effect of finance on consumption appears at two levels.

(1) When people expect their future income to be higher than their current income, this requires a financial mechanism allowing them to spend their future

income in advance so that they can evenly arrange their lifetime income. This is the role of consumer credit.

(2) When people expect their future income to be less than their current income, they must save to spread out their lifetime income. After retirement, there will be no source of income which is why we all must save for retirement when we are still young.

Our consumption and saving habits change from one stage of life to the next: in youth, people tend to borrow; at middle age, people tend to be much more eager to save for retirement. This illustrates the different roles of consumer credit and savings in smoothing out a lifetime of income. Nevertheless, since consumer credit and savings depend on different conditions, an incomplete consumer credit market will affect our savings behavior. For example, when consumer credit is constrained, consumers will increase their rate of savings.

There are two sides to consumer credit constraints:

(1) Asymmetric information may produce moral hazards or adverse selection in the credit market. To reduce the resulting credit risk as much as possible, banks will often implement credit rationing, and as such, the demand for credit is only partially satisfied, if at all. This type of incomplete credit is called incomplete consumer credit caused by financial constraints.
(2) Institutional arrangements for consumer credit are insufficient. In other words, the financial policies of some developing countries have not attached enough importance to consumer credit, so much so that consumer credit has not been built into the government's formal financial system. Consumers thus have no hope of obtaining consumer credit from an organized banking system. This type of incomplete consumer credit market is called incomplete consumer credit caused by financial repression.

The inability to obtain consumer credit will greatly impact people's choices. For instance, before the development of home mortgage loans, if you did not have enough in savings, you would have no way of purchasing a home. With the presence of consumer credit quotas, consumption, especially for several particularly valuable durable goods, strictly depends on a person's current income and their accumulated wealth. Consumer credit, however, can change this situation. Increased access to consumer credit often will lower consumers' savings rates.

4.3.6 Institutional Changes, Uncertainty, and Savings

Under a centrally planned economy, the relationships between the government and households, and between businesses and employees can be summarized by the word "guaranteed". In terms of a monetary income, since wages increased at a fixed rate and jobs were always guaranteed (i.e., The Iron Rice Bowl), people could calculate their gross income before and after retirement in advance. According to the housing allocation policy, workers were housed according to their work unit, replacing financial intermediaries with the worker's enterprise, relieving households of the burden and liabilities that come with purchasing a home, nor was there any incentive for workers to save up for home purchase. In terms of education, apart from the college tuition being waived, workers could also receive a fixed "stipend" guarantee to cover their living costs. If the worker got sick, he could be treated at no cost, and he did not need to worry about paying for retirement. Since this institutional system virtually eliminated any uncertainties, it also eliminated any incentive for households to save. As such, before the economic reforms, the average savings rate of Chinese citizens was very low. From 1952 to 1977, the average savings rate of Chinese households was less than 2%.

One aspect of the transition from a planned economy to a market economy is the added diversification of economic decision-making. Another aspect is the shift from centralized risk control to risk diversification, and thus people are faced with greater uncertainty. First and foremost is the added incentive in the distribution of household incomes. Household monetary income not only includes wages but bonuses as well. Thus, people are paid on the basis of the fruits of their labor and the uncertainty of the market. Also, workers must bear the risk of being "laid off" at any time, so households must save for all types of expenditures that may occur from the time they are fired to the time that they find a new job.

Second, as the physical distribution of income becomes smaller and smaller, workers' monetary wages will become bigger and bigger, giving them greater freedom in consumption decisions. Meanwhile, households may have to take on consumer debt or save for certain expenditures. Reforms to the housing system forced households to begin long-term savings for consumption on one of the largest consumer durables, all the more so when down payments for loans were relatively steep.

Third, households had to save for unexpected emergencies and for retirement, which was shown in the growing awareness of households of the need to purchase insurance. Finally, reforms to the educational system forced parents to save for their children's education, a considerable share of household savings. All in all, market reforms forced households to face greater uncertainties, prompting households to increase their precautionary savings.

To save as a way of preparing for future uncertainties is called **precautionary savings**. Precautionary savings refers to when consumers save to adjust for uncertain future income levels that would drastically lower their level of consumption or for large expenses that may arise unexpectedly. If there is a higher balance of savings, it can buffer the shock of such unexpected or unfortunate events.

However, with a well-developed social security and social insurance system, although people are still faced with the uncertainty of a loss in earnings or dramatic consumption increases, this may lower their propensity to save. This is because insurance uses smaller payments to compensate for large future expenditures. If Wang Xiao'er purchases health insurance, only to unfortunately come down with a serious illness, the treatment of which cost 100,000 yuan, he would not be liable to pay this sum in full. America's low savings rate has a lot to do with insurance and social security. According to some American economists, the perfection of social security, such as unemployment insurance and medical services for the poor reduced the need for people to save for retirement. This is one of the main reasons for America's low savings rate since the 1980s.

4.3.7 Will Lower Interest Rates Always Raise Consumption and Lower Savings?

To some extent, the interest rate is the time value of money, and it also reflects the time preference between current and future consumption. In other words, it reflects how willingly people may "give up" and "do without" their current level of consumption to increase their future consumption Given that Wang Xiao'er prefers his current consumption, if you would like to ask him to increase his savings at the expense of current consumption, to do so, a higher interest rate must be offered to him. Interest rates impact consumption and savings mainly through two ways:

- When people spend money through borrowing, the lower the cost of borrowing, the more willing will consumers be to finance their consumption through borrowing.
- Consumer wealth will have a direct impact on consumer spending. Changes in the interest rate will also affect consumers' wealth. This is because the bond price is negatively related to the interest rate. The lower the interest rate, the higher the bond price. Similarly, if interest rates fall, the present value of the assets or the market price will rise. As a result, the lower the market interest rates are, the higher the market value of wealth will be, which will encourage people to spend more. This is the wealth effect.

However, this analysis only solves half of the problem. Will changes in the interest rate actually increase people's propensity to consume? It depends on the relative size of the income effect and substitution effect of interest rate changes If interest rates rise, you may forego part of your current consumption, so that you can consume more in the future. The higher the interest rates are, the more will be the future consumption. This will promote savings, which is the **substitution effect** of higher interest rates. At the same time however, higher interest rates will also increase the future earnings on interest so much so that you only need to deposit a small amount of savings to meet your specific expenditures in the future. Therefore, this will encourage you to increase your current consumption and reduce your savings for the future, which is the **income effect** of higher interest rates In general your propensity to save will highly depend on the relative size of the substitution effect and the income effect when interest rates are changed. If the substitution effect is greater than the income effect, higher interest rates will raise your propensity to save. Conversely, if the substitution effect is smaller than the income effect, higher interest rates will reduce your propensity to save and increase current consumption.

4.3.8 Non-Economic Factors

People do not fully act as "economic animals". In other words, personal values have a very important impact on consumption and savings. People who "live for today" will naturally skimp on savings. Meanwhile people who believe that a "penny saved is a penny earned" prefer saving and shy away from consumption. It is as if saving money is one of their greatest joys. When discussing the driving force behind the classical capitalism in the 19th century, Max Weber and some other scholars argued for the important role of thrift and savings, both highly valued in Protestant work ethic.

Changes in the patterns of civilization reduce the level of savings out of the bequest motive. Since ancient times, Chinese people had always liked to leave a legacy for their children, but changes in the modern society have made the relationship between family members more distant. In addition, with the growing independence of Chinese youth, there are many college students who can pay for part of their tuition through their own labor, so that the parents' incentive to save for education will also be reduced. What's more, rather than relying on their children during their old age, more and more people want to use their own savings from their working years to independently arrange for their own old age, which also reduces the burden on their children. This has become an important reason that causes Chinese people to save even more.

4.4 Life-Cycle Savings Plans

We have already analyzed different factors that may affect savings, such as in Chapter 3 when we analyzed the effects of the interest rate, inflation and taxes on interest and their effects on pension plans and savings. But for different individuals, the main factors affecting their savings will also vary. Some people are simply born pinching pennies, so even if their absolute and relative income is not high, their marginal propensity to save will still be high. Others take delight in a life of ease, always spending on a whim, so that even though they may have a relatively high income, their marginal propensity to save will still be low. In reality, no one should be too frugal or too luxurious, after all, "We came into this world with nothing, and we leave with nothing" and "those who do not plan for the future find trouble at their doorstep". To a rational consumer, it makes sense to come up with a lifetime savings plan.

When working out your own savings plan, you need to consider the following factors,

- Future income.
- Future expenditures, including marriage, purchasing a home, children's education, retirement, purchasing a car, etc. Other than these expenses, one should also make allowances for unexpected needs that may arise from time to time.

Since each and every person lives in different circumstances, when working out a savings plan, one should consider their own individual situation. Some savings may be for the short term, for example, such as for saving up for marriage or purchasing a home. Other savings are determinedly long-term, such as for saving for a child's education or for taking care of oneself after retirement. We will return again to the pension plan below as an example to illustrate how one ought to work out a savings plan.

Suppose that you are 30 years old and plan to retire at 60. Your current salary is 50,000 yuan per year, and the after-tax interest for the years that follow will be 3%. Let us say that you will live until 80, which means that you still have 20 years of life after you retire. As such, how much of your current income can you consume and how much should you save for retirement?

Suppose that your goal after retirement is to consume at least as much as you do during your working years. This means that for the next 50 years you will maintain the same level of consumption. If we use C to indicate your consumption, your savings each year from 30 to 60 is $(50{,}000-C)$. Based on the future value formula of Chapter 3, we can figure out the future value of the annuity of savings for each of your 30 working years.

$$\begin{aligned}&\text{Future Value of annuity for savings during working years}\\&= (50{,}000 - C)\cdot\frac{(1+3\%)\times\left[(1+3\%)^{30}-1\right]}{3\%}\\&= (50{,}000 - C)\times 49.002678.\end{aligned}$$

After 60 years of age, the amount you withdraw from your retirement account is C, which is converted to the present value. Based on the present value formula of Chapter 3, we can get:

$$\begin{aligned}&\text{Present value of annuity for post-retirement consumption}\\&= C\cdot\frac{1-(1+3\%)^{-20}}{3\%} = 14.877\times C.\end{aligned}$$

Therefore: $14.877 \times C = (50{,}000 - C) \times 499.002678$.

Giving us: $C = 38{,}355.45$ yuan.

Hence, your total annual savings would be $S = 11{,}644.55$ yuan. In other words, you will only need to save 11,644.55 yuan to satisfy this requirement.

Obviously, actual savings plans are rarely if ever this precise and also tend to be much more complex. First of all, just as we mentioned above, there are all sorts of reasons for saving, other than retirement, there is also saving to purchase a house, put a child into school, prepare for any unexpected needs, etc. Secondly, the future is highly variable, suppose that your income will grow substantially in the future, so there is little need for you to cut back right now. If you plan to enjoy 20 years of life after retirement but end up living to 100, your savings that was intended for a life expectancy of 80 will not be enough. Additionally, some things are unpredictable and tend to happen out of the blue. For this kind of precautionary savings, there is no way of measuring ahead of time just how much is enough. As such, an individual's savings plan can never be as accurate as knowing your own height and weight, rather you may have as many choices as if you are to paint a picture, of which there are water-color paintings, sketches and oil paintings, etc. It all depends on what you like and what catches your eye.

Summary

Savings refers to the portion of income that has not been consumed and can be divided into financial savings and physical savings. Compared to physical savings, financial savings is far more significant and useful in promoting economic development. Depending on whom the savers are, savings can also be divided into household savings, corporate savings and government savings.

The reasons that motivate people to save are varied, although the fundamental motivation to save is for future transactions, to prepare for the unexpected and for investment.

The major factors that affect a person's propensity to save are as follows: disposable income, permanent income, relative income, wealth, real interest rates, the availability of consumer credit liquidity constraints, culture core values, and so on.

Throughout our lives, we ought to always develop more comprehensive savings plans. When working out a savings plan, we must fully consider future income and consumption. The future, however, is unpredictable, and as such, it is impossible to come up with an absolutely perfect savings plan. No matter what, saving for the future is just the same as buying insurance for oneself.

Key Terms

Savings; Physical Savings; Financial Savings; Propensity to Save; Propensity to Consume; Marginal Propensity to Save; Marginal Propensity to Consume; Permanent Income; Hypothesis of Relative Income; Income Effect; Substitution Effect; Ratchet Effect; Precautionary Savings

Critical Thinking Questions

1. What is savings? What are the basic characteristics of savings?
2. What motivates people to save?
3. What are the different forms of savings? Please summarize the content of Chapter 1 to compare and contrast financial savings and physical savings.
4. What are the different factors that can affect people's saving habits/behavior?
5. Adam Smith once said "every prodigal appears to be a public enemy, and every frugal man a public benefactor" How would you evaluate this sentence?
6. Suppose that you are 25 years old this year and plan to get married when you are 30. You do not own a home and your annual salary is 70,000 yuan. Your girlfriend insists that you buy a home before the two of you get married, the down payment on which you estimate to be 150,000 yuan, the rest of which you can make on installments. You plan to spend 50,000 yuan to feed the wedding guests, take wedding photos and go on your honeymoon. If we can also assume that the real interest rate is 6%, at least how much money will you need to save each year for these two major events?
7. There is a common saying in China "to slap one's face until it's swollen", which means to do something beyond one's means in order to be impressive. This certainly could represent some people's way of thinking about consumption. Is this very rational? For such people, what is the decisive factor in their choice to spend or save? Please use the contents of this chapter to explain your reasoning.
8. Beginning in the second half of 1997, China began to experience deflation. In the years that followed, insufficient aggregate demand became one of the biggest obstacles to Chinese economic growth. So economists recommended giving pay raises to civil servants thus raising their income levels. By imposing an interest tax, people will not be as enthusiastic to save which will encourage more consumption. How would you evaluate these economic policy proposals?
9. In the late 1970s, China implemented the One Child Policy and with it, China's national growth rate has dropped dramatically, effectively controlling China's population growth. Try to analyze what kind of effects the One Child Policy has had on China's population structure over the last several decades. Briefly summarize the life-cycle hypothesis of savings and how it relates to future changes in China's national savings rate. When will China's national savings rate begin to decline? In what ways will this affect China's long-term economic growth?
10. In 2008, the American subprime mortgage crisis was at its height and the American economy suffered a major shock. In February, the Bush administration launched a \$168 billion tax cuts plan to stimulate consumption. By the 4th quarter of 2008, China

had also clearly suffered from the economic crisis; the rate of economic growth as well as the growth rates of exports and imports rapidly declined, and in an attempt to "sustain economic growth", the Chinese government implemented a series of macroeconomic regulations and controls. One of the measures was "household appliances to the countryside", although China was not exactly willing to first directly subsidize farmers who would then go out and purchase home appliances. Rather, the government subsidized 13% of the total cost. Using the absolute income theory and the permanent income hypothesis, briefly analyze the effectiveness of the Bush-era tax cuts and China's "household appliances to the countryside".

Chapter 5

Asset Selection and Risk Management of Lender–Savers

Learning Objectives

After studying this chapter, you will be able to:

- Learn about a wide range of financial assets
- Learn about the factors affecting asset selection
- Understand what are the risk, systematic risk and non-systematic risk
- Understand the advantages of diversified portfolio
- Understand the expected rate of return, variance and standard deviation of rate of return
- Understand optimal investment portfolio and CAPM model
- Understand the role of insurance, hedging and options in risk management

After making the saving or consumption choice, people immediately have to make the second choice — how to allocate savings among various assets. This is called asset selection. In asset selection, people often face the uncertainty of losses which is called risk. Uncertainty has a great impact on people's selection. If people can completely predict or determine the future, they will face fewer options in fact. Although uncertainty brings many pains in that people have to make hard choices, it cannot be avoided in most cases. This chapter mainly introduces the types of assets and the factors that people should consider when they choose an asset for investment. In addition, it will also introduce the nature of risk and methods of risk management.

5.1 "Asset Types and their Respective" Property

Although the forms of assets vary, we still can classify all assets into two categories according to their common property: financial assets and physical assets.

5.1.1 Financial Assets

Financial assets refer to the assets in the form of value, such as stocks, mutual funds, trusts, bonds, deposits and cash. Financial assets can be further divided into:

- Monetary assets
- Credit assets
- Equity assets

(a) *Monetary Assets*

Monetary assets include the cash in hand and deposits in banks. If you have 20,000 yuan of cash and 200,000 yuan of deposits, then you will have 220,000 yuan of monetary assets (thinking about the measurements of monetary aggregates in Chapter 1). Compared with other assets, with relatively stable returns and high liquidity, monetary assets can be predicted and will not suffer from capital losses generally. You can use cash to buy things and others cannot refuse as long as the cash is not counterfeit. Therefore cash asset has the highest liquidity. However if you hold too much cash, you will not gain the interest. Monetary assets are mainly in the form of deposits, while the cash in circulation takes up only a very small portion. Compared with cash assets, deposits have relatively low liquidity. Although you can pay directly through your bank card when you go shopping in some big department stores, you must pay in cash when you go shopping in some of the smaller shops. Unlike cash assets, deposits can bring you some interest returns. If you do not need to use cash urgently, it is cost-effective to hold certain monetary assets in the form of deposits. Of course your deposits in banks are also your debt claims on banks because deposits are credit assets as well.

(b) *Credit Assets*

The credit assets we are talking about here are in a relatively narrow sense. They include corporate bonds and government bonds you hold and in an open economy, you may also purchase bonds issued by a foreign company. Compared with monetary assets, most of the credit assets have less liquidity. If you buy and sell credit assets at the secondary market, your assets may even suffer a partial loss when the market is not good.

Among our investment, bonds which are most likely to become assets are mainly government bonds and corporate bonds. **Government bonds** are debt instruments issued by the government with certain denominations and repayment terms. Treasury bills are government bonds. **Corporate bonds** are debt instruments issued by industrial and commercial corporations with certain denominations and repayment terms. The Three Gorges bonds issued by Three Gorges Construction Corporation and power bonds issued by China Power Group are all corporate bonds. In addition, there are financial bonds. The so-called financial bonds are debt instruments issued by financial institutions. In China, however, financial bonds are generally restricted to financial institutions and the general public cannot invest in financial bonds.

(c) *Equity Assets*

A stock is an instrument issued by a company, which represents partial ownership of the corporate asset. Therefore, stock asset is a form of asset which represents ownership of part of the corporate property and residual claim right. Corresponding to the financing modes of corporations, stock assets can also be called equity assets.

Generally speaking, equity assets have the following characteristics:

- They have no maturity date. If you spend 100,000 yuan to buy the stocks of a company, it is impossible to require the company to return the principal of 100,000 yuan to you. But you can get the profits of the company in corresponding proportion.
- Equity holders are residual claimants in profit distribution. If you buy the stocks of a company which earns a profit of 200 million yuan this year, the company will allocate corresponding profits to you only after it pays the interests of other debts and due taxes.
- Equity holders are residual claimants in case of insolvency. If the company whose stocks you buy has a loss of 200 million yuan and is insolvent, it will be bankrupt. Only after the company pays off all of its debts and still has any assets left, can you obtain the corresponding portion of remaining assets according to the proportion of stocks you hold.
- Equity holders have limited rights and liabilities. Suppose the total equities of the company are 200,000,000 shares and the shares you buy account for only 1/10,000 of the total equities. If there is still a profit of 100 million yuan left for distribution after the company pays the interests of debts and due taxes and draws the accumulation funds from the total profits of 200 million yuan it has earned, you will get a bonus of 10,000 yuan then. In this profit distribution, you can only get so much. But if the company operates poorly and has huge losses, the losses you should bear are limited according to expenses you pay when you buy stocks. Your losses will not exceed 100,000 yuan, i.e., your liabilities are limited.

The standardized credit assets and equity assets can be circulated and transferred in the open market. With the help of modern means of communication, you can easily trade bonds or stocks in the Shanghai Stock Exchange and the Shenzhen Stock Exchange. At present, under normal circumstances, the bonds and stocks traded in these two stock exchanges have a total worth of billions or even tens of billion yuan per trading day. However, you should bear the risk of price fluctuation when you trade these assets in the open market.

(d) *Wealth Management Product Assets*

Even though every item in your portfolio could be a kind of "wealth management", these specific "wealth management products" are a form of asset selection different from your direct purchase of stock, funds, trusts or bank deposits. Nowadays, many financial institutions sell a wide variety of "wealth management products" every single day. These so-called "wealth management products" refer to the financial products issued by banks, securities companies, and other financial institutions to businesses and individuals to invest in particular financial instruments. Wealth management product assets come in many forms: in terms of differences in risk, they are either principal-guaranteed or not guaranteed; in terms of currencies, they include Renminbi products and those in foreign currencies. Compared to other financial assets, wealth management products have their own characteristics. First of all, the rate of return on a wealth management product is usually slightly higher than that of a deposit. For example, in the first half of 2013, China's interest rate on one-year term deposits was 2.85%, while China Construction Bank offers a non-principal-guaranteed wealth management product in Renminbi — the expected rate of return for Lideying is 3.95%. Second, their terms are typically shorter, and wealth management products with terms that exceed three years are rare; the majority of wealth management products have terms of less than one year. The term of the aforementioned Lideying product is less than half a year. Third, there is no negotiable market. Many financial products must be held until the payment of principal and interest at maturity. There are also open-ended wealth management products which you can redeem prior to maturity. Finally, although there is a minimum subscription threshold, the threshold is not too high, which is different from bank deposits with no threshold and trust assets with a higher threshold.

(e) *Trust Assets*

A trust asset is a financial asset which is formed from the purchase of trust products which trust companies issue specifically to invest in a certain project. In recent years, China's trust industry has developed rapidly, and in turn, more and more people are investing in trust assets. Compared to currency assets and bonds, the expected rate of return on trust assets is higher. For example, the expected annual rate of return for a trust product issued by Hunan Trust in 2013 reached 9.5%. Precisely because the expected rate of return on trust assets is higher, many people prefer them. However, risks of trust asset are also higher and there lacks a standardized negotiable market. Also, their terms tend to be longer, and liquidity lower. There is typically a higher threshold for investing in trust assets, which excludes the participation of small investors. For instance, for the above-mentioned trust products issued by Hunan Trust, the starting point for investment is 3 million yuan.

(f) *Securities Investment Fund Assets*

Securities investment fund assets are financial instruments issued by mutual funds to invest in certain securities. Corporations and individuals can purchase mutual funds which would form fund assets within their own asset selection. Based on the different methods of investment, funds can be divided into different categories: stock funds, bond funds, composite funds, ETFs, etc. They can also be divided based on the style of investment: value funds, growth funds, balanced funds, etc. Also, funds can be divided into closed-end funds and open-end funds. In terms of earnings and risks, a large difference exists between different types of funds. In general, the rate of return on bond funds is relatively stable and with lower risks. The rate of return on stock funds tends to fluctuate a lot, and the risks are also higher. As for securities investment funds, we will go into further detail in Chapter 9.

5.1.2 Physical Assets

In addition to cash, deposits, bonds, funds and stocks, people also own houses, large and durable consumption goods, factories and equipment. All of these are physical assets. Different from financial assets, physical assets can bring direct utility or service to us. If you have a TV set, you can watch the football match over the weekend; if you have a computer, you can play chess on the internet, or grow flowers or fruits in your virtual garden; and if you have a villa, you can lie on the balcony and enjoy the baptism of the sun.

Under high inflation circumstances, it is not cost-efficient to hold a large number of cash, deposits or other financial assets, because the physical assets those financial assets can exchange for will become less or you will need to spend more money in the future to buy the same quantity of things at present. In 2004, China's CPI reached 3.9% and the price of real estate rose by 14.4% while the one-year deposit rate was only 2.25%. Under the circumstance of "negative interest rate", namely, the deposit rate is lower than CPI, there has been an upsurge since 2004 in China where people withdrew their bank deposits and invested it in the real estate. Many people regard gold as a product that does a good job of weathering an inflation, and investment in gold has also become an important asset selection. In April 2013, when the international gold futures price fell sharply, many average Chinese people bought in and ransacked each and every shopping mall for gold products, even to the point where "old Chinese aunties" bought up 300 tons of gold in only two days. This rush to buy gold led to a subsequent rebound in gold prices, and some people went on to joke that these "old Chinese aunties" had defeated the Wall Street "vultures". Of course, you cannot help but see the absurdity in all of this, and this rush to buy gold itself illustrates that people still hope that physical assets will do a better job as a store of value when everything else fails. However, under deflation circumstances, it is probably not worthwhile to invest in physical assets. From 1998 to 2002, China was in a deflationary cycle when the price level kept falling. The price of household appliances and cars fell considerably at that time. It would be probably not worthwhile to invest in these physical goods. In addition, compared with financial assets, the biggest deficiency of physical assets is their low liquidity. It is difficult to sell physical assets at once when you need cash badly. On the contrary, if you have deposits in the bank, you can withdraw the money at any time; if you own stocks or bonds which can be traded publicly, you can sell them in a few seconds when Shanghai Stock Exchange and Shenzhen Stock Exchange are open for trading.

5.2 Factors Affecting Asset Portfolio

In the several categories of assets listed above, we can also subdivide a very large number of assets. It is impossible for you to invest in all of them. You must make a choice. Well then which factors will you consider when you are drawing up your asset portfolio? Asset selection depends mainly on the following factors: wealth or income, assets' expected rate of return, risk and liquidity.

5.2.1 Wealth or Income

When our income or wealth increases, we will have more resources to purchase assets. At this time, will our demands towards every type of asset increase in the same proportion? The answer is no. When your income or wealth increases, the growth of your demands on some assets may be greater than the growth of your demands on other assets. The demand of a person with a monthly income of only 500 yuan is relatively small towards stocks or bonds; but if your monthly income reaches 30,000 yuan, in addition to cash, you may use a large portion of your income to purchase stocks, funds, bonds or other wealth management products, even to the point where you get into collecting and invest in precious metals.

We can use income/wealth elasticity of assets to measure the influence of changes of income or wealth on your asset demands. **Income/wealth elasticity of assets** is the percentage of change in asset demands caused by every 1% change in income/wealth. If your income/wealth increases by 1% and your demand on stocks increases by 5%, then your income/wealth elasticity on stocks is 5; likewise, if your income/wealth increases by 1% and your demand on cash increases only by 0.5%, then your income/wealth elasticity on cash demand is 0.5.

According to the income/wealth elasticity on asset demands, we can divide assets into two categories: necessities and luxuries. If the income/wealth elasticity on an asset demand is less than 1, i.e., the growth rate of an asset demand is lower than the income/wealth growth rate, this kind of asset is called **necessities**. In the above example, the cash is a necessity because the income/wealth elasticity on cash demand is only 0.5. On the contrary, if the income/wealth elasticity on an asset demand is more than 1, i.e., the growth rate of an asset demand is higher than the income/wealth growth rate, this kind of asset is called **luxuries**.

We make a distinction between necessities and luxuries because it is very meaningful to our asset selection behavior. It is similar to the necessities and luxuries in your daily consumption. In your consumption life, if the growth rate of your consumption of certain goods is faster than your income growth rate, the goods may be classified as luxuries. High-end cosmetics, designer clothes, and jewelry are all luxuries; on the contrary, if the growth rate of your demand for certain goods is lower than your income growth rate, the goods may be classified as necessities. Cooking oil, salt, soy sauce, and vinegar are all necessities. Unless we are trying to impress others by pretending to be rich, our selection of necessities and luxuries in consumption will strictly depend on our income level. With a low income, we will certainly allocate more income to the consumption of necessities; while with a high income, we will allocate a higher proportion of income to high-end consumption or to the pursuit of a special experience, such as traveling to foreign lands. Similarly, our asset choice between necessities and luxuries also depends on our income. When your income is low, choosing more luxuries may not be a rational allocation of your income.

5.2.2 Expected Rate of Return

When we select assets, our first consideration may be the expected return that the asset generates. We should repeatedly compare the expected rate of return between various kinds of assets. The expected rate of return has a great influence on our selection of assets. To cite an extremely unlikely example, if the expected rate of return of Treasury bonds rises to 10% and the interest rate of deposits is only 5%, which one would you like to hold, Treasury bonds or deposits? Obviously, you are willing to hold Treasury bonds. Similarly, if the expected annual rate of return for investing in stocks or mutual funds is up to 50%, there will probably be nothing appealing about the expected rate of return of only 10% on Treasury bonds.

However, in most cases, an expected rate of return is not "guaranteed" or "iron-clad". When we select assets, if we only look at the expected rate of return, we may often not only get nothing back in return, but may even suffer an unexpected loss. This is because risk is an attribute that comes with each type of asset. When you walk into the business hall of a bank, you may be greeted by a friendly staff member, who may brag about the high expected rate of return for some of their wealth management products, and you have to ask yourself: Where are the risks? How high might the risk be?

5.2.3 Risk

Risk is the probability of an asset suffering potential losses or the uncertainty of future expected return. Suppose the expected rate of return of Treasury bonds is a fixed 10%. And a company's stock price is 10 yuan at present. If the company's operating performance is greatly improved, its stock price may rise to 16 yuan. In this case, its rate of return is 60%; on the contrary, if the company does not operate very well, its stock price may fall to 6 yuan. If you buy in stocks at the current price, you will suffer a loss of 40%. Suppose the probabilities of good operation and bad operation of the company are half and half. Therefore, the expected rate of return of stocks of the company is 10% $\left(\frac{1}{2} \times 60\% - \frac{1}{2} \times 40\% = 10\%\right)$. If you buy the stocks of the company, you will earn a 60% return if you are lucky. It is of course a happy ending; but if some bad things happen, you will lose 40% of your investment. Therefore, although the expected return is still 10%, you are exposed to great uncertainties.

If two kinds of assets have the same expected returns and different risks, which one you choose to invest in depends on your attitude towards risk and your risk tolerance. Generally speaking, people's attitude towards risk can be divided into three types: risk averse, risk neutral and risk seeking. If you only want to get the 10% guaranteed returns and decide to buy Treasury bonds rather than taking risks to pursue the possible 60% returns of stock investment, you are a risk-averse investor. On the contrary, if you are willing to take risks to buy stocks and expect a 60% capital return, you are a risk preferrer. If it does not matter which option you take, you are neutral towards risks. For a risk-averse person, if an asset is more risky than the other, he will reduce his demand on this asset though this asset may have a higher expected payback; on the contrary, for a risk lover, he will increase his demand on this kind of asset.

The most important point is that when we select assets, we should fully consider our risk tolerance which is influenced by many factors, such as age, family status, position, income level, mentality and personal experience. From the aspect of future cash flow, young people's risk tolerance is higher than that of old people, because old people have a shorter period of future cash flow. On the other hand, however, old people, who usually know more about the twists and turns of life and are less mindful of wealth, may be better prepared psychologically to take risks. The risk tolerance of people with high positions and stable incomes is also generally higher because when they need to make cash payment, liquidity will not be a big problem. In a word, in addition to one's own economic conditions, one's own mentality is also an important factor which influences risk tolerance and cannot be ignored.

5.2.4 Liquidity

Another factor affecting the selection of assets is liquidity. Liquidity is the ability of an asset to turn into cash without incurring losses. Suppose you have an asset, yet it is difficult to find buyers when you urgently need to cash it in; or suppose there are potential buyers, but the conditions are very harsh and the selling price is even lower than the purchase price, are you willing to hold such an asset? The answer is no. In the 1980s, for a long time after the reinstatement of Treasury bonds, China lacked a well-organized market for their circulation and transfer and it was difficult for holders to liquidate the bonds. Therefore, the liquidity of Treasury bonds was very low. At that time, people were very reluctant to buy Treasury bonds, so the government had to take compulsive and administrative measures to force people to buy Treasury bonds. Later on, China established a Treasury bond market so that the holders not only had high liquidity, but also had a steady interest income. Also, when Treasury notes were issued, never again would there have to be such a nationwide political mobilization, people would be eager to wait in long lines at the bank to purchase Treasury bonds. Similarly, people are willing to take on the risks of buying stock, corporate bonds or various funds, and apart from the expected earnings, another important reason for them doing so is that they now have access to the stock exchange where transactions are conducted with increased securities liquidity.

All in all, when putting in place an asset portfolio, one should always make careful arrangements according to income, future spending plans, the expected rate of return, liquidity and other such aspects.

5.3 Asset Risks and Risk Management

5.3.1 Introduction to Risks

(a) *What are Risks?*

Risk means the uncertainties in the future. However, uncertainties are the necessary conditions, rather than sufficient conditions, for risks, and not all the uncertainties are risks. After you buy a stock, the stock price may rise or drop. If it rises, you will be pleased; however, if it drops, you will be trapped in the stock market. It is uncertain whether you will make a fortune or be trapped, but it is the possibility of being trapped that we call a "risk". Therefore, people usually regard the probability of increase in losses, rather than in profits, as risk.

(b) *Systematic Risks and Non-Systematic Risks*

Risks are divided into systematic risks and non-systematic risks. **Systematic risk** is the risk triggered by things like currency depreciation, financial crisis, political unrest, etc., which will be incurred by all the assets in an economic system. Some policy factors may also cause systematic risks. When China deliberated on the proposal on reduction of state-owned shares in 2001, it once exacerbated the plummet of the stock market. That is a policy-related systematic risk. After the US subprime mortgage crisis of 2008 (see Chapter 23) which triggered a global stock market crash, not a single country or a single company's shares were spared. This is also a systematic risk. **Non-systematic risk** is the kind of risk peculiar to a single asset, such as lawsuits, failure in development of market and new products, fires, etc., which may impair a company's future cash flow and profitability. Why we distinguish between systematic and non-systematic risks is because it is of great importance to risk management. Non-systematic risks can be diversified by portfolio investment, which, however, does not work for systematic risks. As suggested by the proverb "When a bird's nest is overturned, no egg can remain intact" systematic risks can hardly be diversified.

We usually measure systematic risks by the value of β, an indicator reflecting the sensitivity of the rate of return on an asset to the changes in the value of the market as a whole. It is the percentage change in the value of an asset divided by that of the market as a whole. If you bought a stock, if its price rose 80% within half a year, and the market index only rose 10% in the same period, the β of the stock you purchased would then be 8. Conversely, if the market index rose 10%, and the price of another stock you purchased only rose 5%, its β would then be 0.5.

Generally, we call the assets with β greater than 1 "aggressive" assets, and the assets with β less than 1 "conservative" assets. As for aggressive assets, their profitability will be more volatile than the overall return of an investment portfolio. When the market goes up, it will outperform the market; however, when the market drops, it will be worse. Assume the market index only drops 10%, the stock with a β of 4 will decline 40%. As for conservative assets, their prices will be less volatile than that of the whole market. If an investor purchased a conservative asset, though he may lose the opportunity of earning more when the market index goes up, his loss will be much smaller when the market drops. If the β of an asset is 1, it means the rate of return on the asset will change in the same direction and proportion as the market as a whole.

If investors are risk-averse, there will be a small demand for assets with a big β as they suggest higher systematic risks. In contrast, assets with a small β will have smaller systematic risks, and thus are more popular with investors.

5.3.2 Diversification and Capital Asset Pricing Model

(a) *Benefits of Diversification*

The **expected rate of return** on an asset portfolio is the weighted average return on each asset in the portfolio. Assume that you purchased three stocks, namely stocks A, B, and C, with a total investment of 100,000 yuan, of which 20% was invested in Stock A, 30% in Stock B, and 50% in Stock C. That is, your investment in the three stocks was 20,000, 30,000, and 50,000, respectively. If the expected rates of return on stocks A, B, and C were 10, 30, and 60%, the total expected return on the investment portfolio is calculated as below:

$$\begin{aligned}&\text{Expected rate of return on investment portfolio}\\&\quad = 20\% \times 10\% + 30\% \times 30\% + 50\% \times 60\%\\&\quad = 41\%.\end{aligned}$$

Assume that the weight of investment in A_j in the portfolio is w_j, and the expected rate of return on asset A_j is r_j, the expected rate of return on the portfolio will then be:

$$E(r) = \sum w_j \cdot r_j. \tag{5.1}$$

In the example above, it seems to be most advisable to invest all 100,000 yuan in Stock C because it has an expected rate of return of 60%, far higher than the 41% expected payback for the investment portfolio. However, it is an expected rate of return, rather than the actual rate of return. If all the money was used to buy Stock C, it will be very happy to see a rise of 60% in the expected period, but it may also suffer a loss. After you invested all in Stock C, if its price dropped 2%, and the stocks A and B had a rate of return of 10% and 30%, respectively, you will lose 2% of principal, on top of stamp taxes and handling charges. However, if you invested in Stocks A, B, and C according to the original proportion, the realized rate of return will then be:

$$20\% \times 10\% + 30\% \times 30\% - 50\% \times 2\% = 10\%.$$

In that case, even though Stock C suffered a loss of 2%, due to diversified investment, you will still have a gross rate of return of 10% after offsetting the loss with the profits generated from stocks A and B. The idiom "never put all your eggs in one basket" has demonstrated the benefits of diversification.

Generally speaking, the more categories of assets that are included in an asset portfolio, the more risks that will be diversified. In the meanwhile, the return will become increasingly equalized, that is, you may only achieve the average rate of return in the market but you will lose an opportunity to achieve excess return. But when you invest in portfolio, except the major assets such as cash, deposits, bonds and stocks in which you must have a certain proportion of investment, there is no need for you to invest in every asset. That should be decided by various factors including the income, liquidity and risk tolerance of a person. If you want to have a higher return and are willing to bear higher risks, and if you can raise funds without selling your assets when you or your family are in financial difficulties, it might be advisable to invest more heavily in stocks or other investments with both relatively high expected rate of return and high risks.

(b) *Correlation and Effectiveness of Diversification*

An important principle of risk diversification through portfolio investment is the mutual independence or negative correlation of the rates of return or risks of the assets you choose. The correlation is the level of connectedness between variables of various assets. If your emotion affects how your friend may feel, then there is a correlation between the emotions of both of you. The correlation between various variables can be divided into positive correlation, negative correlation, and mutual independence. Positive correlation means that two variables change in the same direction and the negative correlation means that two variables change in the opposite direction. When we say, "I am happy because you are happy", it suggests a positive correlation and "working hand in glove" also vividly expresses the positive correlation. On the contrary, if your friend is delighted or even takes pleasure in your misfortune when he finds that you are in a bad mood (not exactly "friend" material), then the emotions between you and your friend have a negative correlation. If your friend's emotion is not influenced by your emotion at all, then the emotions between you and your friend are mutually independent.

The correlation between the returns and risks of various assets may also be classified as positive, negative and independent. A positive correlation between assets means that the returns or risks of two kinds of assets change in the same direction; on the contrary, if the returns or risks of two kinds of assets change in the opposite direction, there will be a negative correlation between the two; if the return or risk change of one kind of asset has nothing to do with the other, then the two kinds of assets are mutually independent.

It should be noted that correlation is not a causal relationship, namely, if there is a correlation between two kinds of assets, it does not mean that the return or risk change of one asset is the cause or result of the return or risk change of the other. In econometrics, a famous example is the correlation between the ups and downs of stock market and the rise and fall of the water level of the Ganges River. The ups and downs of the stock market are certainly not the cause or result of the rising and falling water level of the Ganges. Another example is that there is a negative correlation between the economic growth rate and the length of miniskirt, namely, the shorter the miniskirt, the higher the economic growth rate and vice versa. Maybe this is just a joke, but it shows that no matter how short a miniskirt is, it cannot be the reason for a higher economic growth rate, though they have a negative correlation in econometrics. If this were the case, there would be no need to stimulate the economic growth through increasing public investment or expanding the money supply. All we would need is a seamstress who can cut short the shirts.

In portfolio investment, if you choose the assets which have a positive correlation, the purpose of risk diversification will not be achieved. This is because the returns of assets which have a positive correlation will "be bound together for good or ill". The purpose of risk diversification can be better achieved towards assets with negative or mutually independent correlation, because among assets with mutually independent correlation, their returns or risks do not influence each other and among assets with negative correlation, the return of one asset can compensate the loss of another asset. However when you invest, the main goal is the pursuit of returns. The opportunities to gain returns will be reduced greatly if you invest in assets with negative correlation. Especially when you invest in assets with 100% negative correlation, the return of one asset may just be offset by the loss of another, which is a situation investors simply do not want to see. Therefore when you choose the investment portfolio, it is better to choose completely independent assets to gain returns and diversify risks.

(c) *Expected Rate of Return of Investment Portfolio, Variance, Standard Deviation, Covariance, and Correlation Coefficients*

The concept of expected return has been introduced above. With the same expected return, will investment portfolios be exactly the same? Here is a hypothetical example.

Assume there are two stocks, A and B, and the price of Stock A is 10 yuan, which has a probability of 0.25 to rise to 16 yuan, 0.5 to rise to 12 yuan, and 0.25 to remain at 10 yuan. In other words, investing in Stock A will have the probability of 0.25 to achieve a rate of return of 60% within one month, 0.5 to achieve a rate of return of 20% and 0.25 to break even. The expected rate of return for investment in Stock A is:

$$[(0.25 \times 16 + 0.5 \times 12 + 0.25 \times 10) - 10] \div 10 = 25\%.$$

Assume that the price of Stock B is also 10 yuan but the company suffered a loss and is being restructured. If the company succeeds in restructuring in a short time, the probability of its stock price rising to 22 yuan in one month is 0.25; if the restructuring goes ahead slowly, the probability of its stock price rising to 11 yuan in one month is 0.5; if the restructuring fails quickly and if it is impossible for the company to turn around losses, the probability of its stock price dropping to 6 yuan in one month is 0.25. That is to say, if you invest in Stock B now, you will have the probability of 0.25 to achieve a rate of return of 120% in one month, 0.5 to achieve a rate of return of 10% and 0.25 to suffer a loss of 40%. The expected rate of return of Stock B is:

$$[(0.25 \times 22 + 0.5 \times 11 + 0.25 \times 6) - 10] \div 10 = 25\%.$$

Though stocks A and B have the same expected rate of return, their risks differ greatly from each other. Which one has the bigger risk? We usually measure risks by the variance or standard deviation of expected return. Variance is the probability of various possible returns multiplied by the quadratic sum of the difference between possible return and expected return. If σ^2 denotes variance, r_i denotes rate of return, p_i denotes probability of achieving r_i, and $E(r)$ denotes expected return, then according to the definition, variance can be calculated as below:

$$\sigma^2 = \sum p_i \cdot \left[r_i - E(r)\right]^2 \tag{5.2}$$

In the previous example, the variances of expected return of stocks A and B are as follows:

$$\sigma_A^2 = 0.25 \times (0.6 - 0.25)^2 + 0.5 \times (0.2 - 0.25)^2 + 0.25 \times (0 - 0.25)^2 = 0.0475,$$

$$\sigma_B^2 = 0.25 \times (1.2 - 0.25)^2 + 0.5 \times (0.1 - 0.25)^2 + 0.25 \times (-0.4 - 0.25)^2 = 0.3425.$$

Standard deviation is the square root of variance. Using σ to denote standard deviation, it is calculated as below:

$$\sigma = \sqrt{\sum p_i \cdot [r_i - E(r)]^2}. \tag{5.3}$$

The standard deviations of stocks A and B are around 0.2180 and 0.5852, respectively. The standard deviation of Stock B is far bigger than that of Stock A, indicating that the rate of return of Stock B will fluctuate more sharply than that of Stock A. Hence, it is very safe to invest in Stock A. In this case, risk-averse investors will buy Stock A. It follows that the larger the variance/standard deviation of rate of return, the bigger the risks; and the fluctuation of the rate of return will become sharper with the rising of variance/standard deviation. Once the price changes in an undesirable way, you will possibly suffer a huge loss.

However, in portfolio investment, covariance shall be taken into account in order to observe the fluctuation of rate of return.

If there are two risk assets, A and B in an investment portfolio, the expected rate of return of A is $E(r_A)$, and that of B is $E(r_B)$, their covariance is denoted by $\sigma_{A,B}$ and calculated as below:

$$\sigma_{A,B} = \sum_{i=1}^{n} p_i[r_{Ai} - E(r_A)] \cdot [r_{Bi} - E(r_B)]. \tag{5.4}$$

The standard deviations of risk assets A and B are σA and σB, respectively, the correlation coefficient of assets A and B equals their covariance divided by the product of standard deviations of A and B. Correlation coefficient is denoted by ρ and calculated as below:

$$\rho = \frac{\sigma_{A,B}}{\sigma_A \cdot \sigma_B}. \tag{5.5}$$

Correlation coefficient ρ is between 1 and -1. If the correlation coefficient ρ is $+1$, the two assets are fully positively correlated; if ρ is -1, the two assets are fully negatively correlated; if ρ is 0, the two assets are mutually independent of each other, that is, there is no correlation between them (see Table 5.1).

Table 5.1 Calculation of Deviation and Covariance of Stocks A and B in Portfolio Investment

	Stock A		Stock B		
Probability p_i (%)	r_{Ai} (%)	$r_{Ai} - E(r_A)$ (%)	r_{Bi} (%)	$r_{Bi} - E(r_B)$ (%)	Product of Deviations $[r_{Ai} - E(r_A)] \cdot [r_{Bi} - E(r_B)]$
25	60	35	120	95	0.3325
50	20	−5	10	−15	0.0075
25	0	−25	−40	−65	0.1625

The covariance of stocks A and B is calculated as:

$$\sigma_{A,B} = 25\% \times 0.3325 + 50\% \times 0.0075 + 25\% \times 0.1625 = 0.1275.$$

The correlation coefficient ρ between stocks A and B is as:

$$\rho = \frac{0.1275}{0.218 \times 0.5852} = 0.9994.$$

Therefore, stocks A and B are highly correlated.

(d) *Optimal Investment Portfolio and the CAPM Model*

We first study a special circumstance. Assume there are two kinds of assets, namely risk-free assets and risk assets. **Risk-free assets** refer to assets whose rate of return can be predicted within the decision range of an investor, and the variance/standard deviation of their rate of return is zero. **Risk assets** means the assets whose rate of return cannot be predicted within the period of transaction by the investor, and the variance/standard deviation of their rate of return is positive. If you purchased a stock and intended to hold it for half a year, but you are uncertain how much you will earn from it, such stock is a risk asset.

Assume that the rate of return of a risk-free asset is r_f, and the expected rate of return of a risk asset is $E(r_r)$. We further assume that total investment is one yuan, a proportion of a will be invested in risk assets, with the remaining $(1 - a)$ invested in risk-free assets. The expected rate of return of such an investment portfolio is set out below:

$$E(r) = a \cdot E(r_r) + (1 - a) \cdot r_f = r_f + a[E(r_r) - r_f]. \tag{5.6}$$

Assume the standard deviation of risk asset is σr. Since the standard deviation of risk-free asset is zero, the standard deviation σ of the whole investment portfolio equals the product of the standard deviation σr of the risk asset and the proportion

(a) of risk asset in the investment portfolio. The equation is set out below:

$$\sigma = a \cdot \sigma_r. \tag{5.7}$$

If the two sides of the equation are divided by σ_r concurrently, we get:

$$a = \frac{\sigma}{\sigma_r}. \tag{5.8}$$

Substitute the value of a in Eq. (5.6), we get:

$$E(r) = r_f \frac{E(r_r) - r_f}{\sigma_r} \cdot \sigma. \tag{5.9}$$

The formula shows that the expected rate of return on risk assets and risk-free assets equals the linear function of the standard deviation (σ) of the whole investment portfolio, with an intercept of r_f and a straight slope of $\frac{E(r_r)-r_f}{\sigma_r}$. The slope denotes the extra expected return, also known as **risk premium**, provided for every unit of extra risk that the investor is willing to bear. If an asset has a higher risk, we must provide investors with higher expected return in order to encourage people to hold such asset. A Chinese saying goes: "generous rewards rouse one to heroism". We should not blame the bold persons for being attracted by awards regardless of danger. It is perhaps more appropriate to understand it from the theory of modern finance: ancient Chinese generals were actually granting a "risk premium" to the soldiers to encourage them to charge forward for victory.

In order to analyze it more clearly, let us look at a simple example. Assume there is 1 million yuan to be invested in risk-free assets and risk assets. Among them, risk-free assets have a rate of return (r_f) of 8%, and risk assets have an expected rate of return (r_r) of 20%, the standard deviation (σ_r) of risk assets is 0.5. There are several investment plans as explained in Table 5.2.

Table 5.2 Relationship between Expected Rate of Return and Standard Deviation of Investment Portfolio and the Investment Portfolio

Investment Portfolio	Proportion of Investment in Risk Assets (a) (%)	Proportion of Investment in Risk-Free Assets ($1-a$) (%)	Expected Rate of Return (%) $r_f + a[E(r_r) - r_f]$	Standard Deviation of Investment Portfolio $a \cdot \sigma_r$
A	0	100	8	0
B	25	75	11	0.125
C	50	50	14	0.25
D	75	25	17	0.375
E	100	0	20	0.5

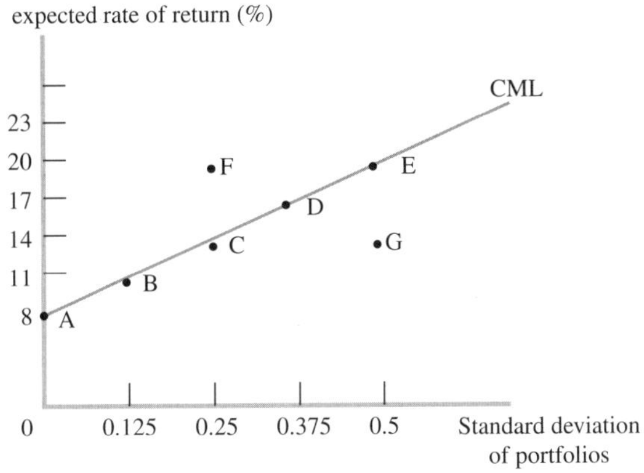

Fig. 5.1 Optimal Investment Portfolios

Figure 5.1 maps out the curve showing the relationship between the expected rate of return and standard deviation of the investment portfolio.

Figure 5.1 shows the curve of relationship between the expected rate of return and standard deviation of the investment portfolio, which is also called capital market line (CML). The intercept of CML is the rate of return (r_f) of risk-free assets, i.e., 8%; the slope is $\frac{20\%-8\%}{0.5} = 0.24$. Only the investment portfolios on CML are optimal, since these investment portfolios can have the largest rate of return when risks are constant; or risks are the lowest when the expected rate of return is constant. If an investment portfolio is above CML, for example, at point F, though the expected rate of return is up to 20%, it is impossible to realize when the risk probability is 0.25. The expected rate of return is only 14% at the risk probability of 0.25. If an investment portfolio is below CML, for example, at point G, the risk probability is 0.5, but the expected rate of return is merely 14%. If the investment portfolio is restructured, at such a risk probability, we may obtain the highest expected rate of return, which can reach as high as point E. At point E, the expected rate of return is 20%, but the risk probability is still 0.5. Therefore, only the investment portfolios on CML are the effective portfolios, because they can provide investors with highest expected rate of return when risk probability is given.

5.4 Other Risk Management Methods

In addition to diversification, there are many other methods to reduce or avoid risks, such as risk evasion, purchase of insurance, hedging, and options.

(a) *Risk Evasion*

One way for us to avoid the tangible damage caused by potential risks is risk evasion, namely, we refrain from participating in any uncertain activities. In order to stay away from the viral influenza, we can avoid contact with patients who suffer from such diseases; many people shun people who suffer from infectious diseases, which is a kind of conscious risk evasion. Similarly, in investment management, we do not invest in projects which we are not 100% sure of. This is a strategy to evade risks.

Although the value of assets can be better preserved through risk evasion, the lower the risk, the lower the return. Therefore risk evasion also means the loss of opportunities to make money. That is what is meant by the idiom of "the only way to catch tiger cubs is to go into tiger's den". We must undertake due risks to gain certain returns.

(b) *Insurance*

Insurance is a risk management measure which transfers the loss caused by a risk to insurance companies through the payment of additional fees. At present there are many types of insurances, such as property insurance, medical insurance, life insurance, and personal accident insurance. The varieties are too many to enumerate. When you purchase insurance, you will turn the uncertain big losses into certain small expenditures, namely, the insurance premiums.

Not all risk losses can be transferred to insurance companies through insurance. Insurance companies will prescribe some insurance conditions for their own interests. Generally speaking, insurance companies will pay compensations only for losses caused under the following situations: (1) Pure risk losses; insurance does not cover risks arising from speculation. For example, insurance companies will not insure the returns on any of your stocks. (2) Accidental instead of inevitable occurrence of risks; for example, insurance companies will not insure the perpetual rejuvenation of Wang Xiaoer. (3) Losses caused deliberately; for example, a man who has purchased insurance for his new car wants to test the performance of the car. So he deliberately drives the car and hits the wall, then the car is crashed. In this case, the insurance companies will not indemnify his losses.

Box 5.1 Role of Insurance in Risk Management: a Story of Shop Owner Wu

At 3 am, August 8, 2002, a mountain flood occurred in Koushui Town, Jianghua County, Yongshou City, south of Hunan Province and the whole Koushui Town instantly turned into a vast expanse of water. Wu Yuping who was in his 40s

(*Continued*)

Box 5.1 (*Continued*)

ran a small shop in this town. When Wu woke up, he found that the flood rose as high as the bed. He, together with his wife and children opened the door and ran to the high buildings in the town for escape. Although their lives were saved, the commodities for sale which were worth 180,000 yuan in the shop were lost. Fortunately, Wu spent 700 yuan per year and bought the insurance in the past five years. After the flood disaster, in less than a week's time, Wu obtained more than 24,000 yuan in cash paid by People's Insurance Company in Jianghua County. Although the payment of the insurance company was just "a drop in the bucket" as compared with the loss of 180,000 yuan, Wu thought this "deal" worthwhile and he was envied by his neighbors who also suffered from heavy losses in the disaster.

— *Source*: *21st Century Business Herald*, September 9, 2002

(c) *Hedging*

Hedging is adopting two opposite trading strategies on the same kind of asset and compensating the losses of one transaction with the returns of the other. The purpose of hedging is purely evading the risk. Hedging is not expected to add value to assets because this kind of transaction evades the risks and also gives the opportunities to gain earnings at the same time.

Assume that your company exports a batch of goods which are worth US$50 million and the payment will be made three months later. Suppose the exchange rate is 6.28 yuan to one US dollar at present and if the exchange rate falls to 6.20 after three months, your company will lose 4 million yuan for its export proceeds of US$50 million three months later if without good risk evasion means.

However as a financial manager, you can avoid such losses if you conduct a hedging transaction, namely, you sell US$50 million in the spot market at present and buy US$50 million in the three-month forward exchange market at the same time. Why? The profit-loss offset process of hedging is as follows:

If you sell US$50 million at present, you can get 314 million yuan according to the current exchange rate.

If you buy US$50 million at the exchange rate of 1:6.20 in the three-month forward exchange market, you should pay a total of 410 million yuan.

In this hedging transaction, your company will gain a profit of 4 million yuan. However US$50 million of payment for goods of your company will turn into 310 million yuan only after they are changed into RMB three months later, which is 4 million yuan less than RMB exchanged at the exchange rate of 1:6.28 at present. Therefore, the previous profit precisely offsets the current loss, which ensures that your company will still have 314 million yuan three months later.

(d) *Purchase of Options*

Suppose you want to rent a house. You just see a house today in a satisfactory location and you think the house is fine. The rent is 1000 yuan per month and the owner requires a payment each six months. However you still want to rent a better house at the same level of rents and you want to have one more week to find a better one. But if you do not decide to rent this house now, the owner may rent it to others. What should you do with this? And if you rent the house through paying a half-year rent and on the third day you find a more desirable one, you will regret you have rushed into the decision. The situation may also be opposite. If you do not find a more satisfactory house at the same level of rents within one week and the previous house has been rented out by the owner, you will regret that you have not rented the house at that time. Therefore, there exists a risk when you rent a house.

How can we evade this kind of risk? The best method is that after inspecting the house, you pay certain deposits to the owner, say, 200 yuan. You make an arrangement with the owner whereby, if you move into the house within one week, you will pay the rent of 1000 yuan per month and if you do not move in after a week, the owner has the right to rent it to others and then you only lose the deposits of 200 yuan. Since you have paid the deposits, the owner has an obligation to hold the house for you for a week. This house is reserved for you for one week. If you do not find a better house in one week, you can rent this one; otherwise, you may give up the deposits of 200 yuan and rent the better house you have found. In this case, your loss is only 200 yuan.

The example of house renting in essence is the risk management by means of options. The so-called option is a future choice, namely, the buyer of options (you, the tenant) has the right to require the seller of options (owner) to sell (rent a house) or buy a primary product at the predetermined price (1000-yuan rent per month) in the coming period of time (one week) after paying a certain option money (that is, deposits). We will discuss about option in detail in Chapter 12.

Summary

Assets include physical assets and financial assets. Financial assets are divided into monetary assets, credit assets, equity assets, wealth management product assets, trust assets, and various securities investment assets. Monetary assets have high liquidity and low risks, but the profitability of monetary assets is the lowest among all financial assets. Credit assets and equity assets have a higher profitability but low liquidity and high risks, and sometimes they may incur capital losses. In the face of inflation, physical assets are an effective means to maintain value. But physical assets have the lowest liquidity and sometimes they may be affected by physical and moral depreciation.

In asset selection, we should first take into account the stability and size of our income flow; second, expected rate of return is a major factor that we should consider. Risks and liquidity, attitude towards risks, and risk tolerance also have significant influence on asset selection.

Risks are divided into systematic and non-systematic risks. Systematic risks are the risks for all the assets in the same group and category, which cannot be diversified by portfolio investment; non-systematic risks are the specific risks facing a certain category of assets, which can be diversified by portfolio investment.

There are many methods that can be used to manage risks. The first one is risk evasion, that is, the decision of consciously evading a specific risk; the second is risk diversification, that is, making portfolio investment; the last one is risk transfer, including purchase of insurance, purchase of options, and hedging. Though risk evasion can minimize risks, it also means giving up the opportunity of making profits. Diversification, insurance, and options can obtain part of the potential return by bearing some risks.

Key Terms

Asset; Monetary assets; Credit assets; Equity assets; Necessities; Luxuries; Systematic risks; Non-systematic risks; Diversification; Expected return; Correlation; Standard deviation; Insurance; Hedging; Options

Critical Thinking Questions

1. What are the assets, asset types, and their respective characteristics?
2. What factors will you consider in asset selection?
3. What are asset risks, systematic risks and non-systematic risks?
4. How can we evade non-systematic risks?
5. Do you have good methods to evade systematic risks?
6. Mr. Wang got a better paid job. How will his job change affect his asset selection?
7. If you have purchased two stocks, one with an expected return of 25% and the other 10%, and you have invested 10,000 yuan in each of them, please calculate the expected rate of return on the investment portfolio.
8. Assume there are two stocks, A and B. If you invest in Stock A, there is a probability of 60% to achieve a return of 15% and a probability of 40% to achieve a return of 5%; if you invest in Stock B, a return of 10% and 8% are both 50% probable. If you have the same investment in the two stocks, what would be the expected rate of return for this portfolio? If you only wanted to invest in one stock, what are the expected rates of return for A and B? Which has a higher risk?
9. In 2008, the Chinese stock market plummeted, many investors were trapped, and the trading volume on the stock market continued to decline. In order to prevent a further decline in the stock market, the authorities reduced the stamp duty on stock transactions. At the same time, various securities companies reduced their commissions in order

to compete for the limited number of investors. Suppose that you were one of these investors and after hearing word of this "good" news, would you throw your money into stocks? Why or why not?

10. Over the past few years, when the Chinese stock market made significant improvements, people have invested in stocks with great enthusiasm, as the saying that has been circulating on the market goes, "people are spending their grocery money on stocks". How would you evaluate this kind of asset selection behavior?

Chapter 6

Financing Options for Borrower–Spenders

Learning Objectives

After studying this chapter, you will be able to:

- Distinguish between **internal** and **external** financing
- Compare debt financing and equity financing
- Know the role of financial leverage
- Understand the Modigliani–Miller Theorem
- Know the impact of taxes and bankruptcy on corporate value
- Understand the pecking order theory
- Fully understand the means of government financing
- Understand the Ricardian Equivalence Theorem

Lender–savers and borrower–spenders are at the two ends of the financial system. Options for lender–savers (those with surplus funds) concern asset allocation; options for borrower–spenders (those in need of funds) involve how to obtain surplus funds from lender–savers. In the previous chapter, we analyzed lender–savers' behaviors. In this chapter, we will go on to analyze the behaviors of borrower–spenders on the other end of the financial system, including personal, corporate, and government financing options.

6.1 Internal and External Financing

6.1.1 What are Internal and External Financing?

Sources of financing for capital shortage can first be divided into **internal** and **external** financing. When the user of capital finances its expenditures by internal accumulation of funds, it is referred to as **internal financing**. Corporations use retained earnings, depreciations, and undistributed profits to build new factories or purchase new machinery and equipment. When consumers accumulate savings for the purchase of commercial housing, this is internal financing. **External**

financing, then, refers to any other means by which those in need of capital finance their spending. Corporate applications for bank loans, stock or bond issue and so on are all external financing. Nowadays, more and more buyers purchase their homes with mortgage, which is a form of external housing financing. When we are short on cash and go to our friends for a small loan, this too is a type of external financing.

Internal and external financing have different effects on the economy. Suppose that your monthly income was 5000 yuan. If we do not consider the time value of money, there is a home available for 600,000 yuan. If you completely rely on your own savings to purchase this home, based on your current level of income, if you never eat and drink, you could buy this home in 10 years. However, if you apply for a mortgage loan from the bank, you could purchase this home right now and then make monthly payments to the bank. As you can see, we can use our future income for current consumption, spread our income across our entire lives, and improve the life-cycle utility through external financing.

To corporations, external financing allows them to start and finish investment programs that cannot be achieved through internal financing alone. The Three Gorges Hydroelectric Power Plant became the world's largest hydroelectric power plant upon its completion. However, construction costs exceeded 200 billion yuan. If the Three Gorges Construction Corporation relied on internal savings alone, this engineering project that brings huge benefits to humanity would have been unimaginable. However, through the offering of Three Gorges Construction securities, bank loans, and a variety of other forms of external financing, a "smooth lake rising in the narrow gorges" is no longer just a pipe dream.

Lastly, only through external financing can we have financial intermediaries, risk management, and a series of other organizations and institutional arrangements. If all sectors or branches of economy completely relied on their own internal financing to meet their spending needs, these financial activities would make little sense. For this reason, substantial development in finance would never be possible but for the advent of external financing. In external financing, the capital providers and users are different organizations and individuals, and because of asymmetric information, moral hazards and adverse selection arise, while in internal financing, these risks may be weakened or eliminated. A large variety of organizations, institutional arrangements, and trading skills have thus come into being to reduce the risks associated with external financing. This is what complicates the financial sector and fills the study and research of finance with an air of "mystery".

6.1.2 Internal Financing

Sometimes, internal financing may be voluntary, and at other times, mandatory. Suppose that your monthly income was 5000 yuan. After an initial calculation as to your future spending, you decided to save 2000 yuan each month for a home purchase. After weighing your income, expenditures, profit and risks, you made this decision, so this would be voluntary. However, governments often will require a deduction of a certain proportion of personal income for specific future spending. Regardless of your willingness, this amount will be deducted each time that you are paid and is deposited into your personal account. To individuals, this type of internal financing includes such things as housing funds and pension insurance. To corporations, this includes risk allowances and a variety of statutory accumulation funds.

Pension insurance can be divided into defined benefit plans and defined contribution plans. For **defined contribution plans**, each employee has their own pension account. The employer agrees to deposit a sum of money each month into the account based on a certain percentage of the employee's salary. Only after the employee retires, can this sum of money be withdrawn to be used as the employee sees fit.

Suppose that you earn a salary of 5000 yuan each month. If your employer has a defined contribution pension plan, 5% of what you earn must be deducted from your wages and deposited into your pension account. As such, both you and your employer will deposit 250 yuan into your pension account every month. In the defined contribution plan, the amount of pension that you can enjoy after retirement depends on what you earn, the percentage of contributions, the term for contributions, and the interest rate.

Defined benefit plans determine in advance the total amount of pension that an employee will receive after working for a certain number of years. Suppose that you are now 25 years old, will retire at the age of 60, and as such, will work for another 35 years. Under a defined benefit plan, it stipulates that you will receive a total pension of 200,000 yuan. So, this 200,000 yuan may be converted into its present value according to a specified discount rate which can be used to calculate the fixed deposit that you and your employer must deposit each year into your pension account. For this type of plan, the fixed amount that you and your employer must deposit each year depends on the fixed amount of benefits that you will receive after retirement, how long you intend to work and the discount rate. Clearly, the most obvious difference between defined contribution plans and defined benefit plans is that the amount of pension received in the former is unclear while it is clear in the latter.

Another type of mandatory internal financing is a housing fund. **Housing reserve funds** are similar to defined contribution pension plans in that employees and their employers must deposit a set sum of money into the employee's housing reserve funds account based on some percentage of the employee's wages. Up until the point that the employee must purchase a home, they can use their own housing funds, while they can also apply for a loan from the public pool of funds for the purchase of a home. Generally speaking, the interest rate on publicly pooled funds is much lower than that of the interest rate on bank loans.

Corporate internal financing mainly comes in the form of retained profits, depreciations, loss provisions, statutory accumulation funds, public welfare funds, etc. At the end of a corporation's fiscal year, aside from paying a certain tax on revenue, loss provisions, depreciation of fixed assets, statutory accumulation funds, and self-directed public welfare funds must also be withheld. Of these different funds, loss provisions, depreciation, and accumulation funds are mandatory according to the accounting standards, and belong to internal financing. Additionally, corporations, in general, will not distribute all of their profits to the owners, but instead will retain a portion of the earnings for refinancing. Retained earnings are also an important form of corporate internal financing.

6.2 External Financing

External financing is divided into debt and equity financing.

6.2.1 Debt Financing

Debt financing is a way of financing in which the borrowers promise to repay lenders at some time in the future under specific conditions, primarily in the form of bank loans, bonds, bills, commercial credit, etc.

(a) *Bank Loans*

Applying for a loan from the bank is one of the primary sources for users of fund to obtain external financing. When a corporation's working capital is insufficient or when it must invest in fixed assets or upgrade equipment, the corporation may apply for a loan. Nowadays, commercial banks offer consumer loans, home mortgages, and student loans. For this reason, whenever we need to purchase a car or a home, we may also apply for a loan from the bank.

Box 6.1 Beware of the Debt-Trap

Going into debt for everyday consumption is becoming more and more common. Home mortgages, auto loans, and so on all allow us to use our unearned money to be consumed ahead of time. Naturally, this has raised our standard of living. However, on the whole, it's best to only borrow for emergencies, not for poverty. When we plan to go into debt for consumption, we must first carefully consider our ability to repay and the risks if we cannot.

In less than two years after graduation, Mr. Luo was earning about 4000 yuan a month, and he decided to buy a flat valued at 700,000 yuan. He and his family scraped together 210,000 yuan for the down payment, and the

(*Continued*)

Box 6.1 (*Continued*)

remaining 490,000 yuan would be paid off through a mortgage loan from the bank. To this end, he had to make monthly repayments of more than 2800 yuan, leaving him with only 1200 yuan to live on. Each day he only managed to get by with what little he had left. His friends jokingly called him "Mr. Can't": can't get sick, can't dine out, can't take a taxi, can't go to the movies, can't decorate his home, can't go on vacation. Mr. Luo was practically drowning in debt.

This is why people need to pay attention to a few things when they want to go into debt: first of all, he or she should consider his or her ability to repay. Generally speaking, going into debt for these kinds of loans means that people need to make sure their repayments would not exceed 40% of their personal income. For Mr. Luo, on the other hand, he was paying more than 70%, which was clearly too much debt for him to bear. Second, one must consider interest rate risks. Interest rates on loans are typically adjusted once a year. If interest rates will increase in the future, interest payments will also increase. This is called the interest rate risk of debt. For Mr. Luo, if interest rates ever happened to rise, his monthly repayments would probably exceed 3000 yuan which is even more overwhelming. Third, we have to leave room for any other future spending. China no longer has the "iron rice bowl" and as the economy changes, future income is uncertain. Similarly, as we grow older, the burden of spending will also likely increase. Since we do not know what tomorrow may bring, it's a good idea to save for a rainy day. Borrowing money really is an acquired skill.

However, when applying for a loan, not all loan applications will be accepted. After a bank issues a loan to a corporation, or an individual, it must assume the risk of borrower default. To reduce loan risks, banks often require borrowers to present all kinds of materials and will then issue the loan based on the results of the credit assessment. Usually, the borrowers will not receive the full amount of the loan they have asked for. Other times, the banks will reject the loan application outright. This is known as **credit rationing**.

(b) *Bond Issue*

Bonds are issued to investors to raise funds and will come with an agreement that after a certain period of time and according to certain conditions, the principal will be repaid with interest. It is the legal certificate proving the debtor–creditor relationship between the bond holder and the issuer. Treasury bonds are a kind of debt instrument issued by the government to raise funds. Apart from Treasury bonds, nowadays more and more corporations will finance through the issuance of corporate bonds. For corporations, bond financing comes in a variety of forms, and we commonly see straight bonds or corporate bonds. Additionally, there are also convertible bonds and bonds with warrants. In order to support small and medium-sized enterprise (SME) financing, China has explored SME collective bonds, SME private placement bond, SME collective notes, and so on. These bond financing instruments will be discussed in further detail in Chapter 9.

Bond issues and bank loans are both debt financing, however, there also exist quite a few differences between them:

(1) Bond issues are direct financing, and the final supplier of funds assumes a variety of risks pertaining to borrowers. Bank loans are indirect financing because depositors do not directly assume the risk of borrower default.
(2) In terms of the creditor, bond holders could be any individual or any corporation. Bank loan originators, on the other hand, are none other than banking and financial institutions.
(3) Bonds are standardized in that for all bond investors, corporate or government bonds issued in the same batch have the same face value, maturity, and interest rate. In general, repayment conditions after bond issuance are unchangeable. Bank loans, on the other hand, do not have the same face value or fixed payback periods, much less are bank loans standardized than bonds.
(4) In general, bonds can be transferred in secondary markets while bank loans cannot, and as such, have different levels of liquidity.
(5) Bond issuers (corporations) shall assume the obligation of information disclosure, while loan applicants are not required to publicly disclose their information. In general, these are privately negotiated.

(c) *Commercial Credit*

Many people have experience buying on credit. Buying on credit is known as commercial credit. Generally speaking, **commercial credit** is the credit provided by way of deferred payment during the sale of goods between corporations. Suppose that your company was in desperate need of a batch of raw materials, yet your cash, deposits, and any other forms of working capital were insufficient. In this case, if the corporation that owns these raw materials requires you to pay in full, your production would be in trouble. However, this problem could easily be solved through commercial credit. You claim that you will pay for this raw material purchase within three months. If the other party can trust your words, they will sell these materials to you on credit. Through this kind of commercial credit, those who are short of funds can meet their turnover. This also allows merchants to sell their products and services right away.

For commercial credit to run smoothly, it all depends on whether or not the debtor strictly abides by the payment terms. If the debtor is unable to pay when payment is due or refuses to pay, it will bring a lot of trouble to the creditor. Finally, it may end up forming a **triangular debt** where you owe me, while I owe someone else. In the early 1990s, triangular debts were a big problem to China's economic development.

(d) *Bill Financing*

In Western countries, some large, well-known corporations can issue bills as a means of financing. These bills are known as **commercial papers** which refer to a promise of payment issued by some large well-known corporations for short-term financing. Although the issuance of commercial papers is a type of debt financing, yet it is different from bank loans and corporate bonds. Compared to bank loans, all kinds of industrial and commercial enterprises and financial institutions can purchase commercial papers. Compared to corporate bonds, commercial papers are not standardized. The face value of each commercial paper can be worth several million yuan. Once someone has purchased commercial papers and is in desperate need of funds, they can sell their commercial paper to a bank at a discount. We will talk about bill discounting in more detail in Chapter 10.

6.2.2 Equity Financing

Wang Xiao'er wants to open a restaurant in which he must make an initial investment of 200,000 yuan. Unfortunately, he only has 100,000 yuan in savings. Zhao Xiaosan also wants to open a restaurant and also has only 100,000 yuan in savings, so neither can meet his funding needs to open a restaurant. Hence, if the two of them can come to an agreement, making a joint contribution, they will just so happen to match their needed 200,000 yuan. The two agree to jointly open this restaurant. Since they both agree to run the business, they split the profits as well as the risk. If they earn 100,000 yuan each year, Wang Xiao'er and Zhao Xiaosan will both earn 50,000 yuan. This partnership between Wang Xiao'er and Zhao Xiaosan fits under the definition of equity financing because they share voting rights and residual profit, as well as risks according to their respective contribution of capital.

Equity financing is not only in the form of partnerships. Very often nowadays there will be a company getting listed on Shanghai or Shenzhen Stock Exchange to publicly offer stocks for trading. This is also equity financing. Through public offerings, centralized, large-scale investments can be raised through pooling together small volumes of funds from all reaches of society. Sinopec, China Unicom, and China Merchants Bank have all raised billions of dollars of external funding through initial public offerings (IPO). In 2009, China set up the Chinese growth enterprise market. For those small businesses in their start-up or growth period, they can get listed in the growth enterprise market and thus have access to external financing. For those small start-ups that cannot meet the strict requirements for a public offering on the stock exchange, their equity financing may take the form of venture capital financing or private equity financing. Within the industry, venture capital is typically simplified as VC, and private equity capital is typically acronymized as PE.

In addition to partnerships and stock offerings, equity financing also includes retained earnings, capital reserve, and other types of internal financing. Nevertheless, external financing, in the form of partnerships, joint ventures or public stock offering, is still the main vehicle of equity financing.

6.2.3 Impact of Debt Financing and Equity Financing on Companies

(a) *Financial Leverage*

If the partnership of Wang Xiao'er and Zhang Xiaosan has earned a payback of 100,000 yuan, the rate of return on total investment would be 50%. Each would earn 50,000 yuan in profit, based on their respective proportion of capital contributions. As such, the rate of return on investment for Wang Xiao'er and Zhao Xiaosan would still be 50%. Now, suppose that Wang Xiao'er did not form a partnership with Zhao Xiaosan, but instead borrowed 100,000 yuan from Zhao Xiaosan as a form of debt financing with an annual interest rate of 10%. As such, Wang Xiao'er must deduct 10% from gross profit each year to pay 10,000 yuan to Zhao Xiaosan. However, after deducting interest, Wang Xiao'er still has a remaining 90,000 yuan, increasing his rate of return from 50% to 90%. This is the purpose of **financial leverage**, namely that through debt financing, borrowers can earn a higher rate of return than what they will earn from equity financing as long as the return on assets is certain.

Using R to represent the total return on investments, A to represent total assets and r_a to represent the rate of return on assets, we can come up with the following equation:

$$r_a = \frac{R}{A}. \tag{6.1}$$

That is, $R = r_a \cdot A$. If we set corporate debt as B and equity as E, then:

$$A = B + E. \tag{6.2}$$

Financial leverage ratio is the ratio between corporate debt and equity. Using l to represent the leverage ratio, by definition:

$$l = \frac{B}{E}. \tag{6.3}$$

Thus, $B = l \cdot E$. Using the accounting identity, we can obtain:

$$A = (1 + l) \cdot E. \tag{6.4}$$

Again suppose that the interest rate on debt is i, thus the interest cost on debt would be:

$$C_b = l \cdot E \cdot i. \tag{6.5}$$

Once we have deducted for the interest cost, the total return on equity investment would be:

$$R_e = R - C_b = r_a \cdot (1 + l) \cdot E - l \cdot E \cdot i. \tag{6.6}$$

The rate of return on equity investment is expressed as r_e, thus:

$$r_e = \frac{R_e}{E} = r_a + l \cdot (r_a - i). \tag{6.7}$$

The above equations illustrate that the rate of return on equity is equal to the rate of return on assets plus the product of leverage ratio and the difference between the interest rate on debt and the rate of return on assets. When the rate of return on assets is greater than the interest rate on debt, debt financing can increase the rate of return on equity. Conversely, when the rate of return on assets is lower than the interest rate on debt, debt financing will lower the rate of return on equity. As you can see, leverage is a double-edged sword; it can let borrowers earn a higher rate of return and can also lower their rate of return. It simply depends on the difference between the rate of return on assets and the interest rate on debt financing. When Wang Xiao'er borrows money from Zhao Xiaosan to open a restaurant, his rate of return on equity is as high as 90%; this is because his 50% rate of return on assets is much higher than the 10% interest rate on debt. However, if Wang Xiao'er's rate of return on assets was only 8%, after one year, he would only earn 16,000 yuan. It would not be worth it to borrow from Zhao Xiaosan the 100,000 yuan on an interest rate of 10%, because, after deducting 10,000 yuan in interest, Wang Xiao'er would actually only have 6000 yuan left at the end of the year, namely his investment return had dropped to 6%.

(b) *Impact on Corporate Governance*

Equity financing and debt financing also have different effects on corporate governance structure. After forming a partnership to open a restaurant, Wang Xiao'er and Zhao Xiaosan would have to select a site for their restaurant, decorate, come up with a business plan and agree on a series of other issues. If any of his proposals on operation meets with strong disapproval from Zhao Xiaosan, Wang Xiao'er would have no way of putting his idea into action. So, as you can see, when Wang Xiao'er uses equity financing by going into a partnership with Zhao Xiaosan, he will have to bear Zhao Xiaosan's restrictions.

Conversely, if Wang Xiao'er were to borrow from Zhao Xiaosan, he would have to promise to pay him a 10% interest. Now, when Wang Xiao'er has enough to pay off the principal with interest, Zhao Xiaosan has no right to question Wang Xiao'er about how he runs his restaurant. For this reason, Wang Xiao'er will not lose any of his control over his business operation through debt financing.

On the other hand, equity financing may lead to extensive insider control. **Insider control** is a corporate manager's use of business information or advantage for their own benefit, while damaging the interests of shareholders. For instance, a manager may embezzle corporate assets or substantially increase the perks of management. In general, this kind of behavior is rarely found in debt financing, especially when the operator also happens to be the owner. If Wang Xiao'er and Zhao Xiaosan run the business together and both of them selfishly cut a bit off the top for their own selves, then Wang Xiao'er could simply tweak purchasing costs up a bit and pocket the difference. However, if they did not go into a partnership together, after Wang Xiao'er had paid Zhao Xiaosan his 10% interest, Wang Xiao'er would be the sole owner and there would be little incentive for him to transfer assets or hide income (apart from tax evasion or to avoid loaning out money to others). From this perspective, debt financing, to a certain extent, can lower insider controls.

6.2.4 External Financing: Private Offering versus Public Offering

When Wang Xiao'er goes into a partnership with Zhao Xiaosan to open a restaurant, this is a type of equity financing. When China Merchants Bank issues an additional 1.5 billion shares of common stock to replenish its capital, this too is equity financing. Although both cases are external equity financing, what is the difference? The difference primarily lies in the fact that the former is a private placement while the latter is a public offering.

Private offering is a method of financing in which securities are issued to a specific minority of investors. Wang Xiao'er's need to go into a partnership with Zhao Xiaosan is specifically with Zhao Xiaosan, rather than with Li Si or Wang Wu or anyone else. Applying for a loan from a bank is also a form of private offering. When you apply for a mortgage loan, it is specifically with banks that offer mortgage loans and only one bank will offer your particular mortgage loan for the purchase of your home.

Unlike private offering, **public offering** is a way of raising funds in which financial instruments are issued to the general public. Regarding the issuance of 1.5 billion shares by China Merchants Bank that we mentioned above, as long as you had an account in the Shanghai Stock Exchange and enough money, you could apply to purchase a stake in China Merchants Bank, regardless of whether you were Li Si or anyone else. When Three Gorges Construction Company issued Three Gorges bonds on the Shanghai Stock Exchange to raise funds for the construction of the Three Gorges Hydroelectric Power Station, this was also external financing via public offering.

Generally, the conditions of a public offering are much stricter than a private offering and not all individuals or companies are eligible for a public offering of securities. So, when you raise funds, you must also consider the availability as well as the costs of financing.

6.2.5 Financing Costs

Although we just analyzed so many forms of financing, however, not every form of financing suits every need for funds. Additionally, when choosing financing options, you absolutely have to consider financing costs. Financing costs are all kinds of expenses that come with acquiring funds, which typically include:

- Dividends paid to shareholders
- Interest payments to creditors
- Underwriting cost and attorney fees in a public offering of bonds
- Spending on credit evaluation, etc.
- Opportunity costs of internal financing. We use bank deposit rates or rates of return of investing in Treasury bonds to calculate opportunity costs

People often tend to divide these costs into debt financing costs and equity financing costs. If we set rate of debt financing costs as r_d, the rate of equity financing costs as r_e, and the rate of opportunity costs of internal financing as r_o, then the weighted average cost of capital is:

$$c = w_d \cdot r_d + w_e \cdot r_e + w_o \cdot r_o. \tag{6.8}$$

Wherein w_d, w_e, and, w_o are the weights of debt financing, equity financing, and internal financing, respectively.

Let us use an example to illustrate. Suppose that the interest rate on debt financing was 8%, the interest rate on deposits was 6% and the dividend rate paid to shareholders was 10%. These three types of financing as a proportion to the total investment are 20%, 50%, and 30%, respectively. Disregarding other financing costs, then, the weighted average costs of capital would be:

$$8\% \times 20\% + 6\% \times 50\% + 30\% \times 10\% = 7.6\%.$$

Namely, the weighted average cost of capital would be 7.6%.

When the rate of return on assets is lower than the cost of financing, this project would not be worth investing in. Conversely, if the rate of return on assets is higher than the cost of financing, this investment would pay off. Keep in mind that financing costs also include your own opportunity costs. In our example of Wang Xiao'er and the restaurant that he wants to open, if the deposit rate at a bank was 10%, then the opportunity cost for his 100,000 yuan investment would be 10%. If the rate of return on assets was 8%, then he should not invest in his restaurant.

6.3 Corporate Financing Structure

6.3.1 M&M Theorem

Since corporations have a wide variety of financing options to choose from, what kind of impact will different corporate financing structures have on corporate value? The **M&M theorem** (also called the Modigliani–Miller Theorem) states that in a frictionless market, the corporation's market value and its financing structure are unrelated. In other words, regardless of whether a corporation chooses to financing through debt or equity, neither will have any impact on the market value of the corporation. Corporate value is determined by its real assets and is not determined by the means by which the acquisition of these real assets was financed.

The following must be true for the frictionless market of the M&M theorem:

- No income taxes.
- No bankruptcy costs.
- Perfect capital market with no transaction costs. Securities are also infinitely divisible.
- Dividend policies of a company have no effect on its value.

Under these assumptions, capital flows freely, perfect competition exists in the capital market, all investment yields are equal, and there is no room for arbitrage. Under this kind of frictionless environment, the market value of corporations is unrelated to its financing structure.

Suppose that the two health care companies Jianqiang and Kangrui had cash flows and earning power that were exactly the same. The difference between these two companies lies in the fact that Jianqiang is completely financed through equity while Kangrui is financed through both equity and debt. Set annual profit as P. In this way, the market value of Jianqiang is V_A which is equivalent to the market value of its equity E_A. The market value of Kangrui, then would be equal to the sum of its market value of debt, D_B, and the market value of its equity, E_B, giving us:

$$V_B = D_B + E_B. \tag{6.9}$$

Suppose that you wanted to invest between these two companies. You have two different options to choose from.

Option 1: If you purchase a 1% stake in Jianqiang, your total investment spending would be $0.01V_A$. Since you hold a 1% stake, you can receive 1% of Jianqiang earnings, namely $0.01P$ which is your investment earnings.

Option 2: You can purchase 1% of Kangrui shares and bonds. Since the market value of the company's shares and bonds is E_B and D_B respectively, you would need to spend $0.01E_B$ and $0.01D_B$ on them, giving a total of:

$$0.01(E_B + D_B) = 0.01V_B. \tag{6.10}$$

Table 6.1 Comparison of Costs and Earnings for Two Investment Options

Investment Project	Option 1 Purchase 1% Stake in Jianqiang	Option 2 Purchase 1% Stake and Bonds in Kangrui
Investment Costs	$0.01V_A$	$0.01V_B$
Investment Earnings		
Bond Interest	0	$0.01i \cdot D_B$
Dividends	$0.01P$	$0.01(P - i \cdot D_B)$
Total Earnings on Investment	$0.01P$	$0.01P$

Again suppose that Kangrui pays an interest rate of i on bonds, thus total interest would be $i \cdot D_B$. Since you own 1% of its bonds, then your total earnings on interest would be $0.01i \cdot D_B$. The distributable profit for shareholders would be $P - i \cdot D_B$. With a 1% stake in the company, you can earn a dividend of $0.01(P - i \cdot D_B)$. Total earnings on bonds and shares would be $0.01P$. A comparison of these two investment options can be seen in Table 6.1.

Your total earnings for both of these options are exactly the same, namely 1% of corporate earnings. Since we assume a perfect market, the investment earnings for these two investment options are the same. As a result, options with the same investment earnings will have the same investment expenses, or:

$$0.01V_A = 0.01V_B. \tag{6.11}$$

Hence,

$$V_A = V_B, \tag{6.12}$$

which gives us: $V_A = V_B$.

This shows that debt-free Jianqiang and Kangrui which is partially financed through debt have exactly the same market value.

Although the market value of Jianqiang and Kangrui are the same, the return on equity and risks of investment are different. We have already pointed out that when the established rate of return on assets is higher than the interest rate on debt, the increase in the leverage ratio will improve the rate of return on equity. With the increase in leverage, however, there will also be an increase in the risks associated with equity investments. In order to more clearly analyze this, we will suppose that the financing structures of Jianqiang and Kangrui are as follows:

Jianqiang: Equity financing of 100%. It issues 10 million shares with a price of 10 yuan per share.

Kangrui: Issues 50 million yuan in bonds at an interest rate of 8%, and 5 million shares with a price of 10 yuan per share. In other words, its leverage ratio is 1.

Suppose that in different macroeconomic scenarios, their total earnings were the same and would fluctuate with the fluctuating macroeconomy. In these different scenarios, their total return on assets, earnings per share, and variance of earnings per share are as shown in Table 6.2.

From Table 6.2 we can clearly see the effect of leverage on the earnings per share of Jianqiang and Kangrui. When the macroeconomy is doing fairly well, Kangrui's earnings per share with a leverage ratio of 1 are 2.2 yuan while Jianqiang's earnings per share are only 1.5 yuan; the former is 147% of the latter. On the other hand, when the macroeconomy is relatively weak, Jianqiang's earnings per share would be 0.5 yuan and Kangrui's earnings per share would be 0.2 yuan, which is only 40% of Jianqiang's earnings per share. As a result, since Jianqiang and Kangrui's financing structure is different, there is considerable gap between the variance and standard deviation of their rates of return on equity. The standard deviation of Kangrui's earnings per share is twice that of Jianqiang. This shows that the shares of the company with the higher debt ratio (higher leverage) will have a higher risk for investors. This is because Jianqiang's total risk is distributed amongst its 10 million shares, while the 8% interest on the 5 million yuan bond of Kangrui is a priority payment and the total risk can only be distributed amongst its 5 million shares. As a result, its EPS volatility is larger.

6.3.2 Corporate Financing Structure and Corporate Value in the Presence of Tax Differences

One of the most important assumptions of the M&M theorem is that there is no income tax. In reality, in addition to the creditors and shareholders that participate in the distribution of profits, governments will typically also impose a tax on companies. The primary taxes that governments will impose on a company are corporate income taxes and personal income taxes. Generally speaking, when the government imposes a tax on a company, interest payments on debt can be counted as costs. Interest payments on debt, tax payments, and the distribution of dividends are usually in the following order:

- Interest payments
- Tax payments
- Distribution of dividends

In other words, companies will first pay the interest on their debt. Profit left after interest payment is used as the tax base. The surplus that remains after paying taxes will finally go to the shareholders' dividends.

Table 6.2 Total Return on Assets, EPS, and EPS Variance Under Different Macroeconomic Conditions

Macroeconomic Conditions	Profit of Jianqiang and Kangrui (10 K yuan)	Jianqiang (100% Equity)			Kangrui Co., Leverage Ratio of 1		
		Shares Outstanding (10 K yuan)	EPS (yuan)	Interest expense (10 K yuan)	Distributable Profit (10 K yuan)	Shares Outstanding (10 K yuan)	EPS (yuan)
Poor	500	1000	0.5	400	100	500	0.2
Average	1000	1000	1.0	400	600	500	1.2
Good	1500	1000	1.5	400	1100	500	2.2
Expected Value	1000		1.0	400	600		1.2
Variance			0.167				0.67
Standard Deviation			0.41				0.82

Table 6.3 Distribution Structure of Jianqiang and Kangrui

Company	Jianqiang (Debt-free)	Kangrui (Amount of Debt Financing Set as D_B)
Pre-Tax Earnings	P	P
Interest Payments	0	$i \cdot D_B$
Tax Base	P	$P - i \cdot D_B$
Tax Payments	$t \cdot P$	$t \cdot (P - i \cdot D_B)$
Distribution of Profits to Shareholders	$(1 - t) \cdot P$	$(1 - t) \cdot P + t \cdot i \cdot D_B - i \cdot D_B$

Table 6.4 Comparison of Costs and Earnings for Two Investment Options

	Option 1	Option 2
Investment Option	Purchase 1% Stake in Jianqiang	Purchase 1% of Kangrui Shares and Bonds
Investment Costs	$0.01V_A$	$0.01V_B$
Investment Earnings		
Bond Interest	0	$0.01i \cdot D_B$
Share Dividends	$0.01(1 - t) \cdot P$	$0.01[(1 - t) \cdot P + t \cdot i \cdot D_B - i \cdot D_B]$
Total Earnings on Investment	$0.01(1 - t) \cdot P$	$0.01[(1 - t) \cdot P + i \cdot t \cdot D_B]$

What effects do government taxes have on the market value of corporations? Setting the rate of corporate income taxes as t, with all other conditions just as they were before, Jianqiang and Kangrui will distribute earnings as shown in Table 6.3.

Again suppose that you still have the original two investment options. Option 1 is still a 1% stake in Jianqiang. Option 2 is still 1% of Kangrui shares and bonds. Since the government will impose a corporate income tax, the earnings from these two investment options will experience the following changes, as shown in Table 6.4.

Now, earnings from option 2 are higher than option 1 by $0.01 \cdot i \cdot t \cdot D_B$. Since this is a perfect market, the rate of return for both options would be the same, thus:

$$\frac{0.01(1 - t)P}{0.01V_A} = \frac{0.01[(1 - t)P + i \cdot t \cdot D_B}{0.01V_B}. \tag{6.13}$$

From which we get:

$$\frac{V_B}{V_A} = 1 + \frac{i \cdot t \cdot D_B}{(1 - t) \cdot P} > 1. \tag{6.14}$$

Table 6.5 Earnings on Investment Options

	Option 1	Option 2
Investment Option	Purchase a 1% Stake in Jianqiang	Purchase 1% of Kangrui Shares and Bonds
Investment Costs	$0.01V_A$	$0.01V_B$
Corporate Pre-Tax Earnings	1000	1000
Bond Interest	0	$0.01 \times 8\% \times 5000 = 4$
Corporate Tax Payments	$30\% \times 1000 = 300$	$(1000 - 400) \times 30\% = 180$
Dividends	$0.01 \times (1 - 30\%) \times 1000 = 7$	$0.01 \times 1000 - 400 - 180) = 4.2$
Total Earnings on Investment = Dividends + Bond Interest	$7 + 0 = 7$	$4.2 + 4 = 8.2$

In other words, the market value of Kangrui with liabilities is higher than the market value of Jianqiang without debt.

For a clearer analysis, let us now suppose that macroeconomy is in the average-case scenario. As such, the pre-tax earnings of both Jianqiang and Kangrui are 10 million yuan. If we set the corporate income tax rate at 30%, the investment return would be 10%. Under these conditions, the investment costs and earnings of both options would be as shown in Table 6.5.

Since the rate of return on both investment options are 10% with respective investment costs of 700,000 yuan and 820,000 yuan. Since your stake in Jianqiang and Kangrui's market value would be 1%, Jianqiang and Kangrui's market value would be 70 million yuan and 82 million yuan respectively. In other words, the market value of debt-financed Kangrui is higher than that of debt-free Jianqiang. As such, in terms of corporate income taxes, when a company raises its leverage ratio, its market value will also increase.

Question: Everything else being equal, what would be the respective market values of these two companies without taxes?

6.3.3 Costs of Bankruptcy

Although an increase in corporate debt can lower taxes, this does not mean that a higher leverage ratio is always a good thing. One of the most important factors constraining debt financing lies in the fact that a company's default risk is higher and higher as the leverage ratio increases. So, the costs of debt financing will also rise with a higher leverage ratio. The higher costs primarily come from the following four aspects:

- As default risks increase, risk premiums will become higher and higher for bond investors, and the marginal rate of interest will rise accordingly.
- When interest rates increase to a certain extent, there will be increasing likelihood of investors' adverse selection due to asymmetric information. That is to say that when the leverage ratio reaches a certain degree, investors will no longer buy bonds issued by the company, or, in order to avoid losses, banks will use credit rationing or reject loan applications outright. Due to the lack of external financing, companies are forced to abandon profitable investment opportunities. Between a rock and a hard place, as the leverage ratio rises, the opportunity costs of a company, too, shall increase.
- With the rising leverage ratio, the risks of insolvency and bankruptcy will increase. When a company files for bankruptcy, they will have to pay lawyer and liquidation fees.
- Since the risk of bankruptcy has increased, investors will gradually lose confidence in the company, share prices will slump, and the chances of a takeover will increase. Existing managers will take various anti-takeover steps, spending a lot of energy that can be otherwise used for the betterment of the company. At the same time, employees will face higher risks of losing their jobs, and will be increasingly concerned with their career prospects. This may well decrease the efficiency of companies and reduce their cash flow.
- As a result, in the initial stages of increasing financial leverage, since the tax evasion effect of debt financing is higher than its cost rise effect, corporate value will rise with an increased financial leverage. Once the ratio surpasses a critical point, debt financing costs and the likelihood of bankruptcy will significantly increase, thus causing a drop in the market value of the company. This can be seen in Figure 6.1.

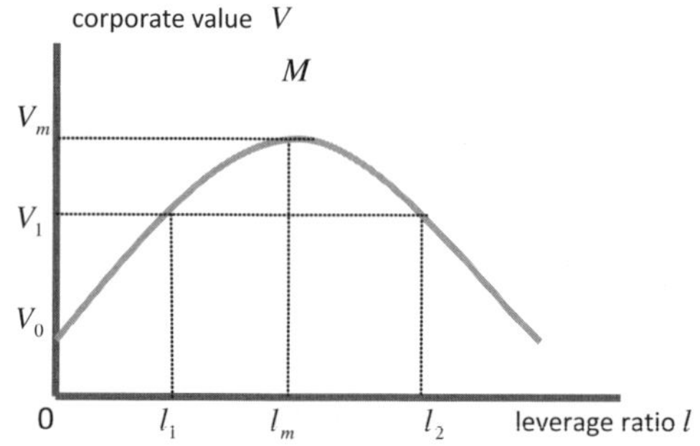

Fig. 6.1 Effects of Financial Leverage on Corporate Value

In Figure 6.1, when the financial leverage ratio is 0, corporate value is V_o. As the financial leverage ratio increases, by avoiding taxes, corporate value will gradually increase. Once financial leverage increases to l_1, corporate value is V_1; when financial leverage is l_m, corporate value reaches the highest at V_m. Beyond this point, when the ratio of financial leverage increases, corporate value begins to decline. When the financial leverage ratio is l_2, corporate value has dropped down to V_1. For this reason point M determines the optimal financial leverage ratio at l_m.

6.3.4 Corporate Pecking Order

The pecking order theory states that corporate executives have a specific preference for certain means of financing. In general, executives will choose financing options in the following order:

- Internal financing
- Debt Financing
- Equity

Managers first opt for internal financing because it avoids the increased costs of external financing. Furthermore, when using a company's internal financing, apart from opportunity costs, there will be no other extra costs. Managers will not choose targeted rate of dividends that matches the long-term investment opportunities to avoid the adverse effects of a sudden change in dividends. For example, if a company were to apply for a loan, they must provide a great deal of information and submit to a bank's credit evaluation. Furthermore, banks will choose credit rationing to avoid moral hazard and the effect of adverse selection. Under this kind of situation, companies will face many obstacles when they use external financing to meet their investment needs. Finally, if a company chooses to issue bonds, it has to pay the attorney fees and underwriting costs. Internal financing has none of these costs. For this reason, generally speaking, the costs of internal financing will be lower than external financing. This is why executives will first opt for internal financing.

When internal financing cannot meet investment needs, companies must use external financing. Of the different types of external financing, executives will first weigh the option of debt financing because debt financing will not cause a loss in their control. Additionally, as long as the leverage ratio is not too high, use of debt financing will not dilute shareholder earnings. If Wang Xiao'er is certain that he will earn 100,000 yuan each year and can secure a loan from Zhao Xiaosan at an interest rate of 10%, he would not even consider going into a partnership with Zhao Xiaosan to open his restaurant. In this case, his rate of return on capital would be 90% while his rate of return on a partnership with Zhao Xiaosan would only be 50%.

Only when debt financing still cannot meet investment needs, will executives consider external equity financing, namely partnerships or stock offerings. Executives would do anything before they have to consider external equity options; this is because with an increase in external equity financing as we analyzed previously, executives will lose a portion of their control. Furthermore, the costs of equity financing are the highest of all of the financing options.

When executives select financing options, they also must consider the kind of signal that financing behavior will send to the market. In an effective capital market, issuing new stock will transmit a negative signal to the market and will always lower the price of shares. On the other hand, a moderate amount of debt financing will only have a marginally negative effect on share prices. The reason lies in the fact that asymmetric information lies between executives and shareholders. Since executives possess inside information on the company and a firm understanding of business operations, external investors can only receive indirect information based on corporate behavior. Executives will determine which financing options to use based on their inside information. If share prices are overvalued, stock offerings will benefit current shareholders and damage the interests of new shareholders. Conversely, if share prices are undervalued, issuing new shares will damage the interests of current shareholders. For this reason and given these conditions, to protect the interests of current shareholders, executives will use debt financing. If investors judge corporate behavior along these lines, when a company issues new shares, external investors will assume that the company's stock is overvalued. As such, issuing new stock will transmit a negative signal to the market and lower stock prices. Conversely, debt financing will transmit a very positive signal to the market and cause the company's share prices to rise.

6.4 Government Financing

We have already seen in Chapter 2 that governments are one of the largest segments short of funds. When government revenue cannot cover spending, it will cause a fiscal deficit. The most common options for dealing with a fiscal deficit are: borrowing or overdrafting from the central bank, raising taxes, or issuing government bonds.

6.4.1 Central Bank Loans and Overdrafts

When governments face a fiscal deficit, they can borrow or overdraft from the central bank. Before 1994, China's fiscal deficit was primarily financed through borrowing and overdrafting from the Central Bank. Borrowing and overdrafting from the central bank will increase the issuance of base money. In other words, the supply of base money is tied to the rise and fall of the fiscal deficit (see Chapter 13). An excessively high fiscal deficit will cause an excessive issuance of base money, thus causing relatively high inflation. So, borrowing and overdrafting from the central bank is not exactly one of the best financing options for fiscal deficits. Developed economies will not use this option. In 1994, China discontinued this practice of borrowing and overdrafting for the fiscal deficit.

6.4.2 Tax Increases

Tax hike is another important way of government financing. Tax revenue is actually a redistribution of revenue enforced by government. To governments, although tax increases are a relatively straightforward means of raising funds, however, tax increases will also bring about several adverse effects. If the tax rate is initially low, when government raises taxes, total tax revenue will increase, yet if a government raises taxes without restraint, total tax revenue will decrease, rather than increase. In extreme cases, if the government's tax rate is 0, the government will have no tax revenue whatsoever. On the other hand, if the tax rate is 100%, every cent you earn will be snatched away by the government; naturally, there is little incentive for you to earn money in the first place. Tax revenue will increase with an increase in tax rates, but beyond a certain degree, increasing tax rates will not raise tax revenue but rather decrease it. This phenomenon is known as the **Laffer Curve**. As displayed in Figure 6.2, when the tax rate ranges from 0 to t, if the government raises the tax rate, tax revenue will increase. Once tax rate surpasses t, however, tax hikes will instead lower tax revenue. Additionally, since taxes are mandatory and have no returnability, tax hikes often come with public backlash.

6.4.3 Issuing Government Bonds

In addition to the two financing options described above, governments can also issue Treasury bonds to the general public as well as to industrial and commercial enterprises as a means of financing the fiscal deficit. Since people voluntarily purchase interest-generating government bonds, these government bonds are deemed a kind of investment. This eliminates the kind of resistance seen with tax hikes. Second, encouraging the general public to purchase government bonds,

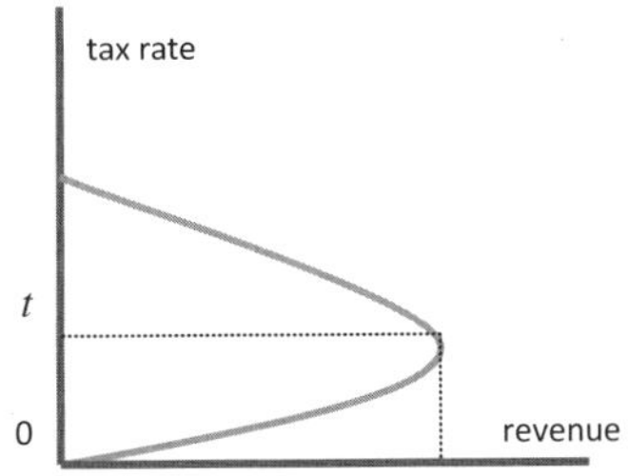

Fig. 6.2 Laffer Curve

rather than mandatorily requiring the central bank to do so, in fact strengthens the central bank's independence in the formulation and implementation of monetary policies which allows the central bank to have more control over monetary supply and stability.

However, there is a cost that comes with issuing government bonds, which includes paying for interest and fees to financial institutions for underwriting service, etc. Naturally, issuing Treasury bonds will also cause crowding-out, i.e., when a government issues Treasury bonds, it will crowd-out private investment. Suppose that you have a savings worth 50,000 yuan which you had originally planned to use to open a cafe. If you used it to purchase Treasury bonds, you could no longer open your cafe; purchasing Treasury bonds like this crowd out your investment in a cafe. Issuing Treasury bonds may produce a strong crowding out effect, which is one of the main arguments that people have against excessive government debt.

So, what kind of impact does issuance of government bonds have on our consumption and savings? The **Ricardian Equivalence Theorem** illustrates that when governments impose taxes or issue bonds, the effect on our choice to save or consume is the same. To clarify, let us use a hypothetical example. Suppose that the government decides to use bonds to replace taxes. Under a set budget, additional government bonds will cut an equivalent amount of taxes. In other words, if the government causes each person who holds government bonds to purchase an additional 100 yuan, its tax revenue will reduce by an equivalent 100 yuan. For the sake of simplicity, assume that the government bonds reach maturity after a year, and the interest rate stands at 5%. Again, assume that within the following year, the population will not change whatsoever. In this case, to repay principal with interest after one year, the government would have to impose taxes of 105 yuan on each citizen in the second year.

Facing changes in tax burden over time, what kind of response will there be from individual consumers? To avoid a reduction in consumption because of an increase in taxes of 105 yuan, individuals must save an additional 100 yuan. In reality, individuals can use the 105 yuan principal and interest they receive in the second year to pay their taxes of 105 yuan. In this way, by the end of the second year, when the government imposes a tax of 105 yuan, households can use their principal of 100 yuan with interest to pay their taxes. After-tax revenue changes (namely a reduction of 100 yuan in taxes in the first year and an increase of 105 yuan in taxes in the second), consumers can spend in accordance with their original budget. You can see that when a government raises funds for some spending program, when choosing whether to raise taxes or issue bonds, this choice will be irrelevant to consumer behavior. Consumer behavior would not change if a government replaced taxes with government bonds.

Summary

Financing can be divided into internal and external financing. When the user of capital finances its expenditures by its internal accumulation of funds, it is referred to as internal financing. External financing is when users obtain capital from lender–savers.

External financing includes debt financing and equity financing. Debt financing primarily comes in the form of bank loans, bond issues, commercial credit, discount notes, leasing, etc. External equity financing includes partnerships, joint ventures, and public offerings. The impact of debt financing on corporations is different from that of equity financing. Debt financing has a leveraging effect. Although equity financing has no term constraints, it can dilute the profits of existing shareholders and dilute the manager's control. Moreover, the problem of insider control may be more significant under equity financing.

External financing mainly comes in two forms, namely private and public offerings. When choosing financing options, the costs of financing must be considered. The weighted average cost of capital is the sum of the products of multiplying the weight of each financing option in total investment and the cost per unit.

The M&M theorem states that corporate value has nothing to do with capital structure. However, given existing corporate taxes on revenue, improving a company's leverage ratio can improve the value of the company accordingly. If the financial crisis is brought about by an increased debt ratio and the bankruptcy costs are considered, an optimal capital structure may exist.

The pecking order theory states that managers will have a certain order of preferences for financing: internal financing, debt financing, and equity financing. Meanwhile, corporate financing options will send different messages to the market. When a company issues bonds, outside investors believe that the company's stock value has been undervalued so the value of stock ought to rise. When companies issue stock, outside investors believe that the stock has been overvalued and the value will likely fall.

There are three kinds of government financing: borrowing or overdrafting from central banks, raising taxes, or issuing government bonds. Borrowing or overdrafting from central banks is not conducive to the central bank's monetary controls. Tax hikes are also widely unpopular. So, the ideal choice is still the issuance of government bonds as a means of financing. However, regardless of whether taxes are raised or government bonds are issued, there is no difference in their impact on consumer behavior: this principle is known as the Ricardian Equivalence Theorem.

Key Terms

Internal Financing; External Financing; Defined Contribution Plan; Defined Benefit Plan; Housing Reserve Fund; Equity Financing; Bills; Commercial Credit; Debt Financing; Financial Leverage; Financing Structure; Insider Control; M&M Theorem; Financing Costs; Ricardian Equivalence Theorem; Laffer Curve

Critical Thinking Questions

1. What is the difference between internal and external financing?
2. Compare debt financing and equity financing.
3. What is the M&M Theorem?
4. What is the impact of taxes and bankruptcy on corporate value?
5. Does the pecking order theory apply to China's corporate financing?
6. What options are available in government financing? What are their strengths and weaknesses?
7. Illustrate the main content of the Ricardian Equivalence Theorem.
8. Suppose that you plan to purchase a home, yet you do not have enough savings on hand for the housing payment. What methods do you have to make this purchase? In raising these funds, which factors should you consider?
9. Suppose you are a fund manager. When selecting a method of corporate finance, what must you consider? Draw up a simple financing plan and calculate the weighted average of the costs.
10. Suppose your company has an investment program. Under the plan, total investment is 50 million yuan. Your company invests 20 million yuan on its own, while the remaining 30 million is loaned from the bank. The interest rate on loans is 7% while the interest rate on savings is 5%. Calculate the leverage ratio and the total financing cost of a year. Suppose that total investment earns a yield of 15%. How much is the return on capital of your company? With an annual return of 6% on total investment, how much is the return on capital of your company? At this time, what is the worth of such an investment project?

Part II

Financial Institutions and Markets

Chapter 7

Financial Institutions in the Financial System

Learning Objectives

After studying this chapter, you will be able to:

- Clearly understand what a commercial bank is
- Understand the organizational pattern of commercial banks
- Understand the Chinese commercial banking system
- Learn what a policy bank is
- Understand the role of insurance companies in the financial system
- Understand insurance services and agencies
- Clearly understand the responsibilities of asset management companies
- Know the financial institutions in the capital market
- Clearly understand the policy and regulatory financial institutions in the financial system

A financial institution is an organization which makes the smooth operation of the financial system possible. Whether it be an individual, an enterprise, or the government, the majority of financial services are provided by financial institutions. In a modern economy, financial institutions have become ever more complex. This chapter will introduce the most basic financial institutions in the financial system and their corresponding functions, primarily: commercial banks, policy banks, insurance agencies, capital market institutions, regulatory institutions, and other such financial institutions.

7.1 Commercial Bank

7.1.1 What is a Commercial Bank?

As for us individuals, of all the financial institutions that we encounter, we work with commercial banks most of the time. With commercial banks, we can deal with things as significant as applying for a home mortgage or as trivial as depositing and withdrawing money or paying for water, electricity, telephone bills, and so on. **Commercial banks** refer to for-profit financial enterprises that primarily provide such services as accepting deposits, providing loans, conducting transfers, and settling accounts. They have an extremely large business scope and are therefore known as "financial department stores". The Industrial and Commercial Bank of China, the Bank of China, China Construction Bank, the Agricultural Bank of China, and China Merchants Bank are well-known commercial banks in China.

Compared to other financial institutions, the most typical features of a commercial bank lies in its ability to take deposits and create money. Other financial institutions such as security companies and insurance companies, on the other hand, cannot take deposits or issue loans. After obtaining a loan from a bank, enterprises usually do not withdraw cash directly from the bank but deposit it into their accounts in the bank. Therefore, the bank can get a deposit after it issues a loan to an enterprise. The deposit created by issuing a loan by a commercial bank is called a **derivative deposit**. As discussed in Chapter 1, deposits are an important component of money supply, so the process by which commercial banks create derivative deposit by issuing loans to enterprises is called **money creation**. It is thus clear that it is wrong for you to think that commercial banks' money creation refers to the release of cash for our small daily spending. Because they create money, commercial banks possess a special function in that their current deposits constitute an important element of the money supply as a medium of exchange. It is also an important source of credit expansion. Therefore, people also regard commercial banks as deposit money banks.

7.1.2 Functions and Roles of Commercial Banks

Commercial banks function as credit intermediaries, payment intermediaries, and financial service providers, and they also play important roles in creating credit, regulating the economy, and so on. As a credit intermediary, a commercial bank acts as a go-between to link those in need of funds with those who have a surplus. This is the most fundamental function of a commercial bank and plays a multi-layered role of regulation in the economy, for example, by transforming idle money into capital, by effectively utilizing idle funds, and by converting short-term funds to long-term funds. As a payment intermediary, commercial banks conduct business such as currency settlements, currency payments, currency exchanges, and deposit transfers by transferring funds from a customers' current deposit account using credit transfer instruments such as checks. By acting as a payment intermediary, commercial banks can save circulation expenses, reduce financial costs, and expand sources of capital. Credit creation means that commercial banks increase their capital and enlarge the economy's money supply by absorbing current deposits and creating loans. By creating means of circulation and payment like deposit money and so on, the role of credit creation mainly lies in saving on cash, reducing economic circulation expenses, and satisfying the demands of circulation and payment means arising from socio-economic development. As financial service providers, commercial banks can, drawing upon their special position and advantages of wide-ranging relations throughout the economy and of well-informed characteristics, provide their clients with various financial services such as financial counseling, financing agencies, trust leases, and collection and payment based on the enormous information obtained from acting as a credit intermediary and payment intermediary and by means of many advanced approaches and instruments such as electronic banking. By providing financial services, commercial banks can improve the practical value of information and information technology and strengthen the relation between banks and society as well as enlarge their market share. Meanwhile, they can obtain quite a bit of fee-based income and thus enhance their profitability.

7.1.3 China's Commercial Banking System

China possesses a relatively unique commercial banking system. It is made up of three different layers:

- State-controlled commercial banks
- Other joint-stock commercial banks
- City commercial banks and other small and medium commercial banks

(a) *State-Controlled Commercial Banks*

State-controlled commercial banks were previously known as state-owned commercial banks, including the Industrial and Commercial Bank of China, the Bank of China, China Construction Bank, and the Agricultural Bank of China. These four banks resumed their operations successively after 1979 and took charge of the banking business in different fields. They were strictly segregated based on establishment over a fairly long period after their foundation. Industrial and Commercial Bank of China concentrated on urban industrial and commercial credit business to satisfy the working capital needs of enterprises. The Bank of China mainly operated business concerning foreign exchange. China Construction Bank was originally targeted at medium and long-term loans to meet the demands of fixed-asset investments. Agricultural Bank of China focused on operating agricultural credit business. Therefore, they were worthy of the name the "Four Largest State-Owned Specialized Banks" as people usually called them. With gradually deepened financial reformation, the traditional business boundaries of the four banks have been broken. At present, these four banks can carry out all banking services in their true sense. Foreign exchange business is not exclusive to the Bank of China anymore and Industrial and Commercial Bank of China is no longer confined to working capital loans. Under the neon city lights, we can also often see striking billboards for the Agricultural Bank of China. By the end of 2008,

China Development Bank, previously a policy bank, also was transformed into a commercial bank. Now, they all possess the common features of commercial banks, that is, they are all driven by profit.

For quite some time after market reforms, the government acted as their sole owner and all their capital was allocated by the Treasury with no capital raised from the general public or from enterprises. Therefore, they were also called solely state-owned commercial banks. As the government was their sole owner, the power of appointment and removal of executives was still firmly controlled by the government. Actually, the government's control of state-owned banks is a kind of administrative control beyond the economic sphere. State-owned commercial banks had to a large extent become the source of government funds, which was detrimental to their development. It constitutes the main objectives for reform of state-owned commercial banks to turn them to enterprises with the capacity for self-management, responsibility for their own profits and losses and a favorable governance structure. The major path of reform was to transform these banks into shareholding companies. At the end of 2003, the government used 45 billion dollars of foreign exchange reserves to inject 22.5 billion dollars of assets each into China Construction Bank and the Bank of China. In June of 2005, the government again injected 15 billion dollars into the Industrial and Commercial Bank of China. By the end of 2008, the government also made a capital injection into the Agricultural Bank of China. After obtaining these capital injections, these commercial banks also introduced strategic investors and changed their organizational structure as a part of the shareholding system reform. China Construction Bank, Bank of China, and Industrial and Commercial Bank of China have become listed joint-stock banks with a diversified equity structure, yet the state still retains its dominant holding position. Central Huijin Investment Ltd. and the Ministry of Finance represent the central government to exercise responsibilities and rights of ownership on them.

Although the monopoly of state-controlled commercial banks has gradually been broken and some joint-stock commercial banks have emerged, state-owned commercial banks are still the main part of China's financial system and take the majority of deposits of urban and rural residents as well as enterprises. For example, in 2005, the proportion of the four state-controlled commercial bank assets in the total of China's banking assets still amounted to 70%.

(b) *Joint-stock Commercial Banks*

Joint-stock commercial banks are the commercial banks founded by raising capital stock. From the very beginning, there have been many investors in these banks, which was fairly different from the solely state-owned commercial banks whose assets used to be allocated by the Treasury without a public offering. Some joint-stock commercial banks are also listed in the Shanghai Stock Exchange or Shenzhen Stock Exchange. For instance, Shenzhen Development Bank, Shanghai

Pudong Development Bank, Minsheng Bank of China, and China Merchants Bank are well-known listed banks. All these joint-stock banks have adopted a headquarters-branch organization structure, that is, they have all established headquarters in a major city and establish branches in other large and medium-sized cities all over the country. You can conveniently enjoy these financial services in their branches. The headquarters of China Merchants Bank is in Shenzhen, but you can withdraw money with your debit card in Wuhan or Chengdu because there are branches available in these cities.

(c) *City Commercial Banks and Other Small and Medium Commercial Banks*

City commercial banks in China were originally founded as city cooperative banks. Although they are called "cooperatives", they are actually joint-stock commercial banks. There were about 5000 urban credit associations in China, quite a number of which have lost their cooperative nature and have practically turned into small-sized commercial banks. In 1995, based on asset and capital verification of urban credit associations, city cooperative banks were set up by absorbing the investment of the local government and enterprises. In 1998, all of the city cooperative banks were renamed as city commercial banks.

City commercial banking reforms are still underway. Some city commercial banks with comparatively good quality of assets have been or are preparing to be listed. Moreover, city commercial banks in some provinces and cities are being (or will be) reconstructed. Anhui Province combined several city commercial banks and credit associations to set up a regional Huishang Bank. To facilitate the development of the banking sector, some regional commercial banks have also been established, such as Bohai Bank.

Joint-stock commercial banks and city commercial banks are in contrast to state-owned banks in the development of China's market economy. Whether it be total assets or total loans and deposits, both joint-stock commercial banks and city commercial banks are far behind state-owned commercial banks. However, they have maintained a momentum of rapid development over the past few years and have become emerging forces in breaking up the state-owned commercial bank monopolies in China's banking system, which is of great benefit for the reformation of China's banking structure and the reinforcement of banking competitiveness.

Corresponding to city commercial banks, there are also rural commercial banks. In the same way that city commercial banks were restructured out of urban credit unions, rural banks were also primarily restructured out of rural credit unions and are local joint-stock financial institutions jointly formed out of the funds of farmers, rural merchants, and enterprises. Even though they are labeled as "rural", Beijing, Shanghai or Shenzhen, and other such modern megacities also have their own rural commercial banks, such as the Beijing Rural Commercial Bank, the Shanghai Rural Commercial Bank, and so on.

In order to strengthen financial support for small and medium-sized enterprises, for agriculture, for rural areas, and for farmers, after 2005, China also established village and township banks. These banking and financial institutions in rural areas are formed by Chinese financial institutions, non-financial enterprises, and individual investors, and are primarily directed at improving financial services to local farmers, for agriculture, and for rural economic development. Village and township banks, while some may say they are the "small potatoes" of the industry, have all the basic features and offer the same major businesses as commercial banks. Similarly, they are also subject to the same regulations of the China Banking Regulatory Commission.

7.2 Policy Banks

7.2.1 What is a Policy Bank?

In addition to commercial banks, there are also policy banks. **Policy banks** mainly refer to the financial institutions that are not profit-driven but are established or guaranteed by the government and targeted at implementing national industrial policy and regional development policy with special financing principles.

In the process of economic development, some areas are of great significance for the national economy and social stability, but they also feature long-term, large-scale investments, low profits, and long period of time for capital recovery, high risk, and low return rates. Therefore, profit-driven commercial banks are usually unwilling to provide loans for such projects, and financing for these areas suffers from market failure. For instance, agricultural development and other important infrastructure projects are of this nature, but in the light of their public benefits, the government often establishes policy banks to specifically provide subsidized financing for them with low interest rates.

Compared with ordinary commercial banks, policy banks possess the following characteristics:

First of all, policy bank capital is mainly allocated through government budget and cannot be raised by issuing stocks. Although the original capital of all the four largest state-owned commercial banks was allocated by government financing, they have been or will be transformed into joint-stock commercial banks to raise stock publicly.

Second, policy banks mainly take the benefits and returns for the entire nation into account and profitability is not their main concern, which is the fundamental difference between policy banks and ordinary commercial banks. However, since the capital of policy banks is not budgetary money of government, they have to consider profits and losses by persisting in the basic principle of banking management, that is, "repay after borrowing", to break even and thereby maintain at least meager profits.

Finally, policy banks have specific sources of funds. They mainly depend on the issuance of special bonds or borrowing from the Central Bank. Generally speaking, they do not take deposits from the public or make loans to ordinary industrial and commercial enterprises. Meanwhile, policy banks will not provide intermediate services like collecting telephone, water, and electricity bills, foreign exchange, etc. In consequence, you can see many branches of commercial banks all over the streets but no savings agencies of the Export–Import Bank of China could be found. Therefore, the business scope of policy banks is far narrower than that of commercial banks.

7.2.2 China's Policy Banking System

Before 1994, there were no specialized policy banks in China. Although the government provided some policy loans with deducted interest for some projects, all of these loans were entrusted to the state-owned commercial banks, referred to, at that time, as the four specialized banks. As the interest rates of policy-related loans were much lower than those of commercial banks and the capital, being mainly from the Treasury, has a lower financing cost, the four largest banks were given an opportunity for interest arbitrage. Meanwhile, the mixture of policy-related operations and commercial business was not conducive to their commercial development, nor could their business performance be accurately assessed, and thus the losses of commercial loans were often said to be caused by policy lending China established the following three policy banks in 1994, China Development Bank, Export–Import Bank of China, and the Agricultural Development Bank of China. Nevertheless, China Development Bank was eventually converted into a commercial bank, and only the Export–Import Bank of China and the Agricultural Development Bank of China remain as policy banks.

(a) *Export–Import Bank of China*

Founded in April 1994, the Export–Import Bank of China carries out autonomous, capital reserved and commercialized management. Its primary task is to implement national industrial policy and foreign trade policy in order to provide financial support for the export of capital goods such as China's mechanical and electrical products, complete sets of equipment, etc.

In accordance with relevant Chinese laws, decrees, foreign policies, industrial policies, and its own policies, the Export–Import Bank of China independently evaluates and appraises loan projects. It raises capital mainly by issuing financial bonds towards domestic or foreign investors with a market-based approach. The Export–Import Bank of China concentrates on providing credit support to both suppliers and buyers in the export of complete sets of equipment, technical services, shipping, project contracts, other mechanical and electrical products and new advanced non-mechanical or non-electrical technology. Meanwhile, this bank also deals with Chinese government loans to aid other countries and transfer loans for foreign governments.

(b) *Agricultural Development Bank of China*

Founded in April of 1994, the primary mission of the Agricultural Development Bank of China is to collect agricultural policy credit funds, undertake the agricultural policy financing business specified by the central government and serve as an agency for the Treasury to allocate the special funds for supporting agriculture on the basis of sovereign credit.

The business scope of the Agricultural Development Bank of China focuses on providing loans for the procurement, storage, mobilization, and marketing of grain, cotton, and vegetable oil for relevant state-owned enterprises as well as cooperatives. Moreover, it acts as an agency to disburse the fiscal funds of the central or provincial government to support agricultural development, and disburse grain risk funds from special accounts opened by the government at all levels. However, the Agricultural Development Bank of China has "closed operation" principles of loan granting and retrieving, requiring the bank to make sure that the stock of grain, cotton, and vegetable oil equal to the amount of loans retrieves all loans in sales proceeds, manages funds truly on the basis of "credit", prevents the procurement funds from becoming misappropriated, ensures on-time and full-amount supply of funds, promotes the production of grain, cotton, and vegetable oil, and facilitates purchasing, marketing, mobilization, and storage.

7.3 Insurance Companies

7.3.1 Insurance Companies and Their Functions

As the old saying goes, "storms can gather without warning, and bad luck can befall overnight", people may encounter natural disasters and accidents and suffer losses. Therefore, we all live in a very uncertain world. This is risk.

One of the ways to manage risks is to purchase insurance. **Insurance** is a kind of financial arrangement to share accidental losses. For example, Mr. Wu in the Box 5.1 of Chapter 5 avoided greater loss from natural disasters by purchasing insurance. Those who apply for insurance are actually attempting to turn uncertain large losses into a definite small expense, that is, an insurance premium. Although there is always uncertainty, yet not all uncertainty will transform into a specific loss. Therefore, insurance companies collect insurance premiums from various applicants and compensate for the unfortunate applicants who have an accident with the money collected from those not who are more fortunate. It is thus clear that the basic feature of insurance is "mutual assistance", which embodies the idea of "one for all, all for one".

Insurance companies are the financial institutions which offer insurance services. They are different from commercial banks and security companies, which have the basic function of transforming savings into investments. The fundamental function of insurance companies lies in the sharing and management of risks. In addition, insurance companies play a more and more important role in evening out our life-cycle income. Some insurance companies also offer their pension schemes, which are called commercial pension insurance. The applicant deposits a certain amount of money into a commercial pension account, so that years later, the beneficiary of the insurance can withdraw a certain amount from this account every month.

Besides commercial pension insurance, there are government pension funds, namely, social security. The national social security fund is amassed by the central government and is mainly used to meet the demands of social security for the aging baby boomers. It is managed by the National Council for Social Security Fund of The People's Republic of China. Therefore, it has a vital function that other financial institutions cannot substitute.

7.3.2 Insurance Services and the System of Insurance Institutions

Based on coverage, the main insurance services offered by insurance companies can be divided into the following four categories:

- Property Insurance
- Liability Insurance
- Guarantee Insurance
- Life Insurance

Property insurance is insurance coverage for property and related interest protecting the insured from economic losses caused by natural hazards or accidents. For example, you purchase insurance for your car to prevent theft or buy insurance to prevent fires from causing corporate property damage, both of which are property insurance. **Liability insurance** is insurance coverage designed to protect the insured from the risk of liabilities for civil damages. For example, a company may purchase insurance for the water heaters that they manufacture because they are worried of the potential hazard it may cause for users. This is liability insurance. **Guarantee insurance** refers to the insurance coverage for the losses caused by the default of a party to a loan or sales contract. For instance, in the export of ornaments, the seller may be worried about timely payments and thus will purchase insurance. Also, when a bank is worried that the borrower cannot fulfill their debt obligations and will purchase insurance because of this worry, these are considered guarantee insurance. In America, there is a special kind of guarantee insurance known as deposit insurance. Deposit insurance arises from a worry that a bank will mismanage funds or encounter liquidity difficulties and cannot meet the withdrawal demands of depositors and thereby such an insurance system was established. In accordance with the provisions of the *Federal Deposit Insurance Law*, deposit insurance must be applied when the deposit amount exceeds $100,000 dollars. In the event of the bank being unable to satisfy withdrawal demands, the federal deposit insurance corporation will pay the corresponding amount to the depositors in lieu of the bank.

Personal insurance includes life insurance, health insurance, accident insurance, etc. Life insurance is a type of insurance coverage for a person's life and body which will determine benefits on the basis of a person's existence or death. Health insurance refers to insurance coverage for illnesses, childbirth as well as injuries, disabilities, or death they may cause, and is also referred to as sickness coverage. Accident insurance refers to provision of benefits in situations where the insured suffers harm from an accident that results in injuries, disabilities, or death. When passengers purchase aviation insurance, this is considered a form of accident insurance.

Another insurance service offered between insurance institutions is known as reinsurance which is also called cession. **Reinsurance** is a type of insurance where the insurer enters into a contract to transfer the risk it has underwritten to one or several other insured parties so as to lower its exposure to risks. For example, China's *Insurance Law* stipulates that for each policy they have sold, unless in the case of life insurance, insurance companies must place reinsurance for at least 20% of the insured amount.

Since different insurance services are associated with different risks, the government typically does not allow certain insurance companies to offer other kinds of insurance services. For instance, a life insurance company cannot offer property insurance, and in this way, the system of insurance institutions is made up of various services. China currently has a system of insurance institutions made up of life insurance, property insurance, and reinsurance.

7.4 Securities and Futures Market Organizations

7.4.1 Securities Companies

If you would like to purchase stocks, then you must open an account in the sales department of a securities company. Securities companies are the necessary organizations through which you can enter the capital market for trading of stocks bonds or mutual funds. Securities companies are also known as brokerage firms and are non-banking financial institutions which operate on the securities market. These companies play a vital role in guaranteeing the issuance and trade of securities. In China, when a company issues shares, they must be underwritten by a securities company. When investors would like to purchase stock, they must open an account or handle designated trading through the sales department of a securities company.

Brokerage, investment banking, and proprietary trading are the three major businesses of Chinese securities companies and their primary sources of income. Investment banking is a means of assistance for the sale of newly issued securities by the government and industrial or commercial enterprises and it provides financial advice to help enterprises carry out asset reorganization and so on. One of the most important features of investment banking is securities underwriting. This process transfers the financial surplus of the society to areas in need of funds and transforms savings into investment. Therefore, underwriting is conducted in the primary market. Securities companies underwrite securities and collect a certain fee based on the amount of money raised through underwriting. Brokerage services are a means by which securities which have already been issued are traded for clients who have entrusted the securities company for ordinary investor behavior. If a securities company earns a financial profit for its client, in addition to the commission that it collects, the additional profit will belong to the investor who entrusted the money with the company. Conversely, if the securities suffer any losses, the losses will also be borne by the investors themselves. Brokerage services are unlike investment banking in that they do not transform savings into investment because their primary business is conducted on the secondary market. Proprietary trading refers to the trading of securities with the securities companies' own account in order to earn a return on investment behavior. Unlike brokerage services, if a securities company earns money through proprietary investment, all of the earnings belong to the company. If losses are suffered, they too must be borne by the company itself.

At present, the securities companies in China are classified by management into comprehensive securities companies and brokerage securities companies. This comprehensive securities firm refers to a securities company which offers brokerage services, proprietary investment, and investment banking. A brokerage securities company, as its name implies, only engages in brokerage services and proprietary services and does not offer investment banking.

7.4.2 Fund Management Companies

In addition to securities companies, another kind of capital market institutions that have become ever more popular are fund management companies. More and more Chinese people have allowed fund management companies to manage their surplus capital to reach an even better balance between earnings and risks. Bosera, Huaxia, and E Fund are examples of fund management companies on the Chinese capital market. Fund management companies serve as institutional investors, and by issuing fund shares, they organize a mass of idle funds and portfolio investments to allow fund investors to share the profits and risks. A fund management company, often composed of many different securities investment funds, can also manage stock funds, bond funds, or money market funds. Fund management companies, through the management of securities investment funds, make an earning from collecting a fee from the fund holders.

7.4.3 Securities Exchange

(a) *Functions of a Stock Exchange*

When you need to invest in stocks or bonds, where exactly would you purchase them? When you need to sell your stock or bonds, where exactly would you sell them? If you were an investor, you could make a phone call to conveniently commission the purchase or sale of stocks and bonds. Additionally, you could also go online on the trading floor of the sales department of a securities company to commission your trading. However, whether you telephone in your trading or go online to commission your securities trading, in the end, you will always pass your request via the sales department of the securities company to the stock exchange for call auctions and trading.

A stock exchange is the place where securities are bought and sold. Well-known international stock exchanges include the New York Stock Exchange, the Tokyo Stock Exchange, the Stock Exchange of Hong Kong and the London Stock Exchange. China currently has two stock exchanges: the Shanghai Stock Exchange and the Shenzhen Stock Exchange. A stock exchange creates an organized, regular, and continuous trading market for the purchase and sale of securities. As a public venue for the trading of securities, it primarily has the following functions:

- It provides a complete public venue for securities purchase and sale, and by organizing a lot of investors, greatly reduces the time and costs for buyers and sellers to look for each other so as to improve the efficiency of securities trading.
- It ensures continuous securities trading, and through call auction and computerized settings, it can achieve uninterrupted, open trading on a large scale. For instance, nowadays, even in a market downturn, the daily trading volume on the Shanghai and Shenzhen Stock Exchanges will be at least several billion yuan. Were it not for stock exchanges which offer an organized trading venue and clearing system, transactions of this magnitude would be impossible to even imagine.
- For convenient investment planning, stock exchanges provide up-to-date information on the volume and prices of trading. For instance, on the trading floor of a securities company you can see all the highest prices, lowest prices, and volume of deals made for all shares, the current buyer's offer and the seller's asking price as well as other information on the display board.
- A stock exchange is a major institution that organizes and controls the securities trading so as to conveniently regulate securities trading behavior and reduce price manipulation and other illegal trading.

(b) *Organization of the Stock Exchange*

The organization of stock exchanges around the world can be roughly divided into the following two categories: a corporate stock exchange and a membership stock exchange.

A corporate stock exchange is a corporation jointly invested and established by banks, securities companies, trust investment companies and other institutions. Corporate stock exchanges bear the responsibilities of their securities traders and usually set up a compensation fund or pay an operating margin to the national Treasury to compensate investors for member default and the relevant losses. Corporate stock exchanges typically forbid brokerage firms and their shareholders or executives to act as directors, supervisors, or managers of the stock exchange so as to ensure the separation of the stock exchange managers and trading participants. At present, the stock exchanges of Canada, Australia, Japan, and Hong Kong adopt the corporate system.

Membership stock exchanges are non-profit organizations that have brokerage firms as their members. In a membership stock exchange, only members and entrusted brokers can engage in securities trading on the exchange. Membership liabilities on the stock exchange are limited to the membership fees they have paid. At present, America and China's Shanghai and Shenzhen Stock Exchanges are membership-based.

7.4.4 Futures Exchange and Futures Brokerage Companies

A futures exchange is a venue that specializes in the buying and selling of futures contracts and is typically membership-based in that it is a joint venture invested by the members in which each member shall have equal rights and obligations, have the right to directly participate in transaction, and must follow the rules of the exchange, pay membership fees and fulfill the obligations. Futures exchanges are not profit-driven but with a mission to provide facilities and services for futures trading. They do not have any commodities nor do they buy and sell future contracts, and are also not involved in futures pricing. All futures exchange members are required to pay margins to guarantee the fulfillment of the futures contract. The Chicago Mercantile Exchange, the New York Futures Exchange, and New York Commodity Exchange are all internationally renowned futures exchanges, providing currency, interest rate, and stock index futures and options as well as other financial futures. In September 2006, the China Financial Futures Exchange was established in Shanghai. Its primary function is the organization of trading, clearing and settlement services of financial futures and other financial derivatives. The Exchange uses electronic transactions, and bids for financial futures transactions all go through the Exchange's computer systems. In accordance with price and time priority principles, transactions are automatically brokered within the trading system.

Since futures exchanges are membership-based, only members have a seat on the trading floor, and for this reason, the majority of futures trading is done through futures brokerage companies. A futures brokerage company refers to a company which represents clients who are not members on futures exchanges but are an intermediary organization between the futures exchange and non-member clientele. Futures brokerage companies are companies that specialize in the business of futures brokerage. Futures brokerage companies can engage in metals futures, such as copper, aluminum and gold futures or in the futures trading of agricultural products such as corn and soybean futures. The company can also engage in the trade of stock index futures, Treasury futures (interest rate futures) and other financial futures on behalf of their clients. Meanwhile, in order to control trading risks, companies will collect a margin from their clients and make an earning primarily from commissions.

7.5 Other Financial Institutions

7.5.1 Financial Asset Management Companies

Financial asset management companies are wholly state-owned non-banking financial institutions that specialize in the acquisition of the non-performing loans (NPLs) of wholly state-owned commercial banks, as well as the management and disposal of assets resulting from such acquisition.

In 1999, China established four financial asset management companies: China Huarong Asset Management Corporation, China Great Wall Asset Management Company, China Orient Asset Management Corporation, and China Cinda Asset Management Corporation, which respectively acquire the non-performing assets of the Industrial and Commercial Bank of China, the Agricultural Bank of China, the Bank of China and the China Construction Bank.

Financial asset management companies, in the scope of their acquisitions of the non-performing loans of wholly state-owned commercial banks and the management and disposal of assets resulting from such acquisition, can engage in the following business activities: (1) recovering debts; (2) leasing the acquired assets of non-performing loans or transferring and restructuring them by other means; (3) making a debt-to-equity swap, and maintaining shareholder status in an enterprise for a period of time; (4) acting as sponsors for the IPO of companies included in the scope of asset management and underwriting stocks and bonds; (5) providing financial and legal consultation, as well as asset and project assessment.

There are two primary means through which financial asset management companies access funds to acquire non-performing loans: one is through transfer of a portion of the People's Bank of China's refinancing issued to the four originally wholly state-owned commercial banks to the financial asset management companies. The other is through financial bonds issued by the financial asset management company to the respective banks.

One of the main means by which financial asset management companies handle the non-performing loan is by transferring creditor's rights to shareholder's rights, which is often called a **debt-to-equity swap** — once a financial asset management company has acquired the non-performing loans of wholly state-owned commercial banks, it will transfer these loans to equities in the corporate borrowers. After the swap, the financial asset management company becomes the shareholder of the corporate borrowers and will enjoy all of the given shareholder's rights. Once financial asset management companies have facilitated the debt-to-equity swap, as a shareholder of the enterprise, it can appoint people to the board of directors and the board of supervisors, and exercise the legal rights of a shareholder. The financial asset management company can, in accordance with relevant national regulations, transfer its holdings in the enterprise to Chinese or foreign investors, and can also allow the enterprise to buy back its shares.

7.5.2 Financial Holding Companies

A financial holding company is a pure holding company with subsidiaries such as banks, securities, insurance, and other financial institutions. This pure holding company refers to the parent company which does not fit into a specific industry and serves solely as the decision-maker of a company in terms of its operation strategy. A different type of holding companies is the industrial holding companies, the parent companies of which have their own field of operation and are also charged with governing the business activities of subsidiaries in other fields. A financial holding company may be classified as a bank holding company, a securities holding company, or an insurance holding company depending on the type of its subsidiaries, or it may be termed "financial services holding company" if it has two or more of these types of subsidiaries. Typical financial holding companies in China include China Everbright Holdings and CITIC Holdings. The former is the controlling shareholder of Everbright Securities and Everbright Bank. The latter is the controlling shareholder of CITIC Securities, CITIC Bank, CITIC Prudential, and CITIC Trust (as shown in Figure 7.1).

Financial holding companies first appeared in developed countries in the West. In order to circumvent the laws that prevent commercial banks from setting up branches in different states of a country or the separated operation rules that prevented banks, securities, and insurance institutions from diversifying their operations into the other two sectors, this financial innovation was adopted. America had originally, for fear of monopolies and in favor of free competition, prevented commercial banks from setting up branches in different states. In order to bypass this regulation, some banks decided to establish holding companies that would fund the establishment of independent commercial banks in different

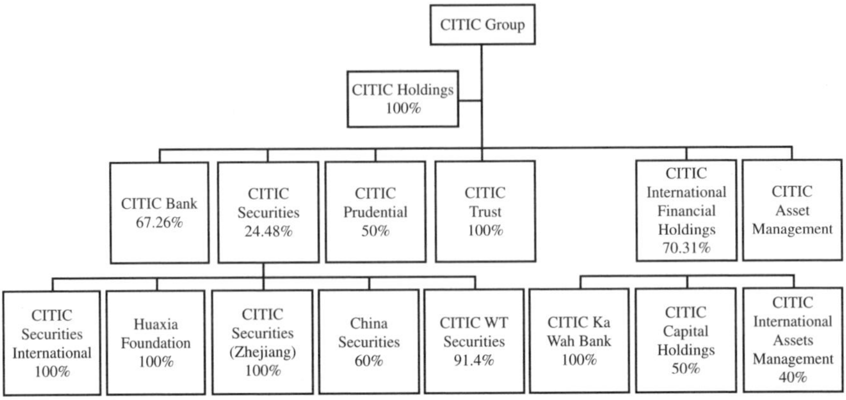

Fig. 7.1 Organizational Structure of CITIC Holdings Group

states. In this way, bank holding companies naturally developed. Afterwards, several other institutions followed this progression and expanded the scope of their business into all or most of the financial sectors in the form of a financial holding company so as to realize mixed operation. Financial holding companies in China are also motivated by separate operation regulations. For instance, CITIC Holdings engages concurrently in the business of banking, securities, and insurance by setting up subsidiaries like CITIC Industrial Bank and CITIC Securities.

Financial holding companies, when compared to a financial institution specialized in a single sector, have the following advantages: (1) A capacity to make full use of limited resources, realize financial economies of scale, lower costs, and raise the level of earnings. (2) Diversification of financial operations is beneficial in risk reduction for the financial businesses themselves. Lower earnings of one operation can be compensated for by another so as to ensure the stability of profits. (3) In a financial holding company, when a commercial bank lends money or an investment bank underwrites securities, it may have an adequate knowledge of the performance of the enterprise so as to lower the rate of bad debts and the underwriting risks of the investment bank. (4) The one-stop financial services give a financial holding company a competitive edge and improve efficiency and promote the improvement of total social utility.

Naturally, financial holding companies also allow risks to be spread more rapidly between the securities market, commercial banks, insurance companies and other financial subsystems, and the risks occurring in a certain aspect may cause greater damage on a much wider scale. For this reason, generally speaking, there is a firewall between the operations of securities, insurance, and banking subsidiaries. For instance, a subsidiary bank cannot provide excessive loans to a subsidiary securities company for securities trading so as to better control risk.

7.5.3 Investment Trusts

For us to understand investment trusts, we should first clarify what trusts are. A trust is a type of property management system where the beneficiaries, based on trust in the trustee, entrust their property to the trustee and the trustee, based on the willingness of the beneficiaries and in the interest of the beneficiaries or out of specific purposes, manages the entrusted property. Modern trusts have already become a property utilization and management system centered on property and based on credit and trusteeship. For this reason, as the name suggests, investment trusts are non-banking financial institutions "entrusted by others to manage property on their behalf".

The primary business of investment trusts consists of trust services, entrusted services, agency services, leasing, and consultation, of which, agency services, leasing, and consultation are essentially the same as what is offered by other financial institutions. Trust services primarily include trust deposits, trust loans, trust investment and property trusts. Entrusted services include entrusted deposits, entrusted loans, and entrusted investment.

7.5.4 Credit Unions

When considering risks and costs, commercial banks are generally unwilling to offer small loans to private enterprises or to small businesses in their start-up phase. As such, these enterprises and individuals cannot access funds on the capital market. When they need these funds, what are they to do? Credit unions can solve their dilemma. Credit unions are cooperative financial organizations that pool together funds of individuals to help one another and provide financial services through simple formalities and at affordable interest rates.

Credit unions are primarily funded by the capital contributed by their members and deposits, and loans are primarily granted to solve the funding needs of members. On a region-by-region basis, credit unions can be divided into rural credit unions and urban credit unions. Rural credit unions have farmers, rural economic collectives, and employees of rural credit unions as their shareholders, while urban credit unions are financial organizations put together by urban citizens, aimed at offering services to small economic collectives and the self-employed to solve their funding difficulties. Although credit unions are rarely seen in major cities, in the vast amount of rural areas, credit unions are practically the only financial organization.

7.5.5 Micro-Credit Companies

Micro-credit companies are established by the investment of individuals, enterprises, and other social organizations, and do not take in public deposits. Micro-credit services are offered by limited liability companies or companies limited by shares. The main source of funds for a micro-credit company will come from the paid-in capital from shareholders, donations as well as the financing of no more than two banking institutions. They can take in the funds of banking institutions, but the amount of financing cannot exceed 50% of the net capital. The range of a micro-credit company's services is very limited, focusing on farmers, agriculture and rural economic development. When loans are issued, they must adhere to the principle of "small and dispersed" and are encouraged to provide credit services to farmers and micro-enterprises. In order to control risk, regulators required that all loans to a single borrower cannot exceed 5% of the net capital. Meanwhile, the interest rate on loans from micro-credit companies is also subject to the interest rate policies of the People's Bank of China. Even though micro-credit companies cannot take in deposits, cannot offer services such as payments and settlements, and do not belong to the scope of the banking sector, yet they are an important initiative in further opening the Chinese financial sector to private capital. Over the last few years since the establishment of micro-credit companies, they have experienced a rapid development and have had a positive effect on promoting competition in China's financial sector.

7.6 Policy and Regulatory Financial Institutions

The responsibility of the central bank and the set-up of regulatory institutions vary among different countries and regions, due to difference in their financial regulation system. Policy and regulatory institutions within China's financial system include the People's Bank of China, the China Banking Regulatory Commission, the China Securities Regulatory Commission, and the China Insurance Regulatory Commission.

7.6.1 People's Bank of China (PBOC): The Central Bank

(a) *Nature of PBOC*

The PBOC is China's central bank. In any given country, the central bank will always enjoy a superior status. The central bank's special status primarily is displayed in the following aspects:

First of all, the central bank enjoys the exclusive right to issue money and is a bank of issue. In this instance, money refers to the cash we often talk about, and is not the deposit which we mentioned previously. As such, when you take out several bills from your wallet, the words imprinted on the front are "PBOC" rather than "Industrial and Commercial Bank of China" or "China Merchants Bank".

Second, the central bank regulates commercial and policy banks throughout the country on behalf of the government, manages the Treasury, and attends meetings and activities organized by international financial institutions, such as Bank for

International Settlements and the International Monetary Fund on behalf of the government. Meanwhile, the central bank will also formulate and implement the government's monetary policy, so it is often referred to as the government's bank.

Finally, the central bank acts as the lender of last resort. When commercial banks run into insufficient funds, especially when a lot of depositors make withdrawals, and there is a chance for serious liquidity difficulties, the central bank will prevent such a crisis by playing the role of the final lender, and thus lends money to the commercial banks. For this reason, it is also referred to as the banks' bank. Naturally, apart from providing refinancing to commercial banks, and for the sake of maintaining financial stability, it may also offer refinancing to non-banking financial institutions. For instance, in 2000, the PBOC injected 550 billion yuan in refinancing to the four large financial asset management companies so that they could acquire the non-performing loans of former state-owned banks. In 2005, to maintain the stability of the securities market, the PBOC again provided tens of billions of yuan in refinancing to Shenyin Wanguo Securities and other securities companies to meet their liquidity needs. From 2007 to 2009, the Central Bank of America, the Federal Reserve, provided a sum of over two trillion dollars in loans and emergency liquidity assistance to several financial institutions and financial markets in difficulties.

(b) *Responsibilities of the PBOC*

The PBOC acts as the central bank of China. It has the following responsibilities:

First of all, it formulates and implements monetary policy and maintains a stable currency. To implement monetary policy, the PBOC can use the required reserve ratio, the benchmark interest rate of the central bank, rediscounts, refinancing to commercial banks, open market operations and other such instruments of monetary policy to adjust money supply in order to maintain a stable currency and promote economy growth. The PBOC is the only Chinese financial institution that can formulate and implement monetary policy.

Second, it maintains the normal operation of the system of payments and settlements. The flow of funds that arises from the complex business conducted between commercial banks will always ultimately be centralized in the PBOC for clearance.

Third, it holds, manages and operates the state's foreign exchange reserves and gold reserves.

Fourth, it manages the Treasury and financial statistics. This includes managing the receipts and payments of the Treasury, as well as making arrangements, on behalf of the financial authorities of the State Council, for the issuance and redemption of Treasury bonds and other government bonds by financial institutions. The central bank is also responsible for financial statistics, surveys, analysis, and forecasting.

For example, the PBOC publishes the *PBOC Statistical Quarterly* to provide information on the money supply, money market rates, deposit bank assets and liabilities, and a range of other information.

Finally, it participates in international financial activities on behalf of the Chinese government. The Chinese government resumed its seat in the International Monetary Fund and the World Bank in 1980, and formally joined the African Development Bank group in 1985, the Asian Development Bank in 1986, the Bank for International Settlements in 1996, and the Caribbean Development Bank in 1998. The PBOC also has its permanent representative in the International Monetary Fund. Additionally, it also has set up representative offices in Tokyo, Europe, and the Americas.

(c) *Organizational Structure and Management of the PBOC*

The PBOC is headquartered in Beijing with a department for each function such as the monetary policy department, the statistics department, the Treasury department, the financial stability bureau, the credit bureau, the anti-money laundering bureau, etc. In 1998, the PBOC, based on regional economic and financial needs, set up nine interprovincial (regional) branches throughout the country to act as its agencies. As illustrated in Appendix A of this chapter, the nine branches are the Tianjin Branch (governing Tianjin, Hebei, Shanxi, and Inner Mongolia), the Shenyang Branch (governing Liaoning, Jilin and Heilongjiang), the Shanghai Branch (governing Shanghai, Zhejiang and Fujian), the Nanjing Branch (governing Jiangsu and Anhui), the Jinan Branch (governing Shandong and Henan), the Wuhan Branch (governing Hubei, Hunan and Jiangxi), the Guangzhou Branch (governing Guangdong, Guangxi and Hainan), the Chengdu Branch (governing Sichuan, Guizhou, Yunnan and Tibet), and the Xi'an Branch (governing Shaanxi, Gansu, Ningxia, Qinghai and Xinjiang). Besides, it has a business management department attached to the head office in Beijing and a business management department in Chongqing.

Apart from these functional departments, the PBOC has a non-permanent organ which is the Monetary Policy Commission. It is the deliberative organ of the PBOC in terms of monetary policy which gathers together to analyze the economy on a macro level, and in accordance with the state's macroeconomic regulatory objectives, discusses the formulation and adjustment of monetary policy, control objectives of monetary policy for a given period of time, uses of monetary policy instruments, and coordination of monetary policies with other economic policies. The Monetary Policy Commission generally meets by the end of the first month of each quarter. The chairman of the commission or more than a third of the members may propose an interim meeting. The Monetary Policy Commission has begun to play an increasingly important role in the formulation and implementation of China's monetary policies.

7.6.2 China Banking Regulatory Commission

Previously, the regulation of China's banks and trust services had always come from the respective departments at the PBOC. To improve the central bank's formulation and implementation of monetary policy, as well as strengthen the regulation and management of commercial banks, in 2003, China implemented major reforms to the banking regulatory system, thereby separating the bank regulatory functions from the PBOC and founding the China Bank Regulatory Commission, known as the CBRC.

The CBRC functions in the following aspects:

First of all, it implements centralized and unified regulation and management of banks and trusts throughout the country, researches and formulates development policies for the banking and trust industries, and develops related laws and regulations.

Second, it reviews and manages the establishment, upgrades and terminations of banks, trusts, and other financial institutions, participates in and organizes bankruptcies and liquidation of banks and trusts.

Third, it regulates and manages the day-to-day business of banks and trusts, promotes their prudent operations, and ensures the health and stability of the financial sector.

Fourth, it performs scheduled and impromptu audits and investigations, reviews the fiscal status of these financial institutions as well as resolves potential risks in a timely manner.

Finally, it investigates the illegal behavior of banks, trusts and other financial institutions in a timely manner.

7.6.3 China Securities Regulatory Commission

The China Securities Regulatory Commission, known as the CSRC, is a financial institution that performs centralized and unified regulation of the Chinese securities market. The China Securities Regulatory Commission regulates and manages the facilitation of securities and futures, and its four responsibilities can be roughly described as follows:

First of all, it researches and formulates policy and development guidelines for securities and futures markets, as well as develops laws and regulations related to securities and futures markets.

Second, it supervises securities and futures institutions, regulates the various securities and futures institutions and the stock exchange, and is responsible for the management of executive management qualifications and employee qualifications for securities and futures institutions as well as the investigation and prosecution of illegal securities and futures behavior.

Third, it is responsible for the regulation and management of the issuance and trade of securities, reviews and monitors the issuance, trade, custody and clearance of stock, convertible securities, securities investment funds, approves and reviews the public offerings of enterprises, regulates the trading activities of listed Treasury bonds and corporate bonds, and regulates trading and clearances on the domestic futures market.

Finally, it takes on responsibilities for the regulation of listed corporations and disclosure of information as well as improves the quality of disclosure.

To fulfill these functions, the CSRC has a public offering supervision department, a market supervision department, an intermediary supervision department a listed company supervision department and a fund supervision department, which are responsible for reviewing, regulating, and managing the issuance of stock, fund, and other securities and companies publicly listed on the Shanghai and Shenzhen Stock Exchanges, and fund management companies as well as supervising illegal behaviors in the secondary market. Additionally, the commission has set up provincial offices across the country so as to realize vertical leadership.

7.6.4 China Insurance Regulatory Commission

With the separate operation of the banking, securities and insurance industries, and to better regulate and manage the insurance industry, on November 18, 1988, China founded the China Insurance Regulatory Commission, known as the CIRC with the function of regulating the nation's commercial insurance market.

The CIRC is the nation's commercial insurance authority, and its six functions are as follows:

First of all, it implements centralized and unified regulation and management of the nation's insurance market; researches and formulates policies, development strategies and industry guidelines specifically for the insurance industry; and develops laws and regulations related to the insurance industry.

Second, it reviews and manages the establishment, change, and termination of insurance companies, insurance agencies, and insurance brokerage institutions; and participates in and organizes the bankruptcy and liquidation of insurance institutions.

Third, it develops basic clauses and rates for main types of insurance coverage; reviews and records the other insurance clauses and rates reported by insurance companies; safeguards the order of the insurance market; establishes insurance risk assessments, forecasts and monitoring systems; and traces analyzes, monitors and estimates insurance market conditions.

Fourth, it regulates and investigates insurance business activities; and conducts scheduled and impromptu on-site and off-site examinations for the business status, fiscal status, and capital use status of insurance companies so as to ensure the adequate solvency of insurance companies.

Fifth, in accordance with the law, it investigates and prosecutes illegal behavior by insurance institutions and personnel; apparent or disguised insurance operations of non-insurance institutions; as well as manages in a centralized and unified manner the international exchanges and partnerships of the insurance industry.

7.6.5 China's State Administration of Foreign Exchange

China's State Administration of Foreign Exchange was founded in 1979. After a series of changes, it is a functional institution currently directly under the State Council and the centralized management of the PBOC for the facilitation of national foreign exchange management. Its primary responsibilities are as follows:

First of all, it is responsible for the statistics and management of international payments; formulation and organization of a system of statistical reports on international payments; data collection for international payments; preparation of the balance of payments; and the policy proposals by which the balance of payments can be maintained.

Second, it is responsible for the management of the foreign exchange market, the regulation of the order of operations on the foreign exchange market, and the development of the foreign exchange market.

Third, it is responsible for the management of foreign exchange and foreign debt; formulation of exchange management measures for current accounts and the regulation of this behavior in accordance with the law; supervision and management of trade; and inward remittance, outward remittance and payment of foreign exchange under the capital account in accordance with the law.

Fourth, it is entrusted by the PBOC to manage the State's foreign exchange reserves.

Summary

Financial institutions within the financial system include indirect financial institutions, risk management financial institutions, direct financial institutions, and policy and regulatory financial institutions.

Indirect financial institutions are primarily commercial banks and policy banks. Commercial banks are intermediary institutions that engage in deposit taking, lending, and off-balance-sheet business and have been considered as "financial department stores". China's commercial banking system consists of the four major state-owned commercial banks, joint-stock commercial banks, city commercial banks, rural commercial banks, village and township commercial banks, and other regional banks.

Policy banks are banks which earn marginal profits in accordance with national industrial policies, although their projects benefit society. The business of policy banks is not profit-driven by nature, although they do operate out of the credit principle of "return after borrowing". China has three policy banks, namely China Development Bank, China Export–Import Bank, and China Agricultural Development Bank.

Insurance companies are financial institutions that primarily engage in insurance. The basic responsibility of an insurance company is to manage risk. Insurance services can be divided into life insurance, property insurance, liability insurance, guarantee insurance, etc. The insurance underwriter will also have to undertake a percentage of reinsurance so as to spread risk.

The direct financing institutions in the capital market consist of securities companies, fund management companies, and the stock exchange. There are three main aspects to the business of a securities company, namely brokerage, investment banking, and proprietary business. China implements categorized management of securities companies in that securities companies are divided into brokerage securities and comprehensive securities companies. Fund management companies are financial institutions operating in the capital market and engaging in securities portfolio investment on behalf of fund holders. A stock exchange is a financial institution that organizes the issuance and transfer of securities and may either take the corporate form or be membership-based. The Chinese securities exchanges currently use the membership-based system.

Additionally, financial asset management companies, financial holding companies, investment trusts, credit unions, and micro-credit companies are other very important financial institutions within the economy.

Apart from the above financial institutions, there are also policy and regulatory financial institutions. These financial institutions are primarily responsible for the formulation and implementation of related laws and regulations as well as the regulatory management of the financial system in accordance with the law. China primarily has five policy and regulatory financial institutions, namely the PBOC, the CBRC, the CSRC, the CIRC and the State Administration of Foreign Exchange.

Key Terms

Commercial Bank; Headquarters-Branch Organization Structure; Deposit Money Banks; Policy Banks; Personal Insurance; Property Insurance; Liability Insurance; Guarantee Insurance; Reinsurance; Securities Company; Brokerage; Investment Banking; Proprietary Business; Comprehensive Securities Company; Brokerage Securities Company; Fund Management Company; Securities Exchange; Central Bank; Financial Holding Companies

Critical Thinking Questions

1. Briefly describe China's commercial banking system and provide your opinion regarding the future of China's commercial banking.
2. What role do policy banks play in a country's economy?
3. What types of insurance services can insurance companies be categorized by?
4. What kind of role do securities companies play? What are the primary services that they offer?
5. What is the role of a securities exchange? What organizational forms may appear on a securities exchange?
6. What are the main differences between a central bank and a commercial bank?
7. What is a financial holding company? What are its kinds? What are the advantages of a financial holding company compared to other financial institutions?
8. What are the duties of the China Banking Regulatory Commission?
9. What are the primary duties of the China Securities Regulatory Commission?
10. What are the primary duties of the China Insurance Regulatory Commission?
11. What are the duties of China's State Administration of Foreign Exchange?
12. Case Analysis: In 2003, China Merchants Bank introduced the Merchants Entrusted Financial Plan for its exclusive "Golden Sunflower" customers (those with deposits greater than 500,000 yuan). This new value-added service for individual assets was similar to a fund for which each unit of investment costs 100,000 yuan and the customer could only purchase in multiples of 100,000 yuan. Once the customer, Merchants Bank, and Merchants Securities signed a contract, the customer would transfer their savings to Merchants Securities through an account the latter has opened with Merchants Bank. Since Merchants Securities was liable for conducting financial transactions, expected profits announced were 1.98–5% and Merchants Bank ensured a payment of at least 1.98%. This product had the dual characteristics of being somewhat similar to a one-year deposit and an open-end fund, yet compared to an open-end fund, the investment costs of this plan were low, had no commission, early termination fees, or any remittance fees for transfers. Because of these advantages, billions of yuan were pooled at a very low cost in as little as 10 days. Merchants Bank and Merchants Security are both subsidiaries of China Merchants Group. Highlight the Merchants Entrusted Financial Plan to explain the kind of benefits offered to customers by financial holding companies. What are the potential risks?

Appendix A: Diagram of China's Financial Structure and Market Organization Structure

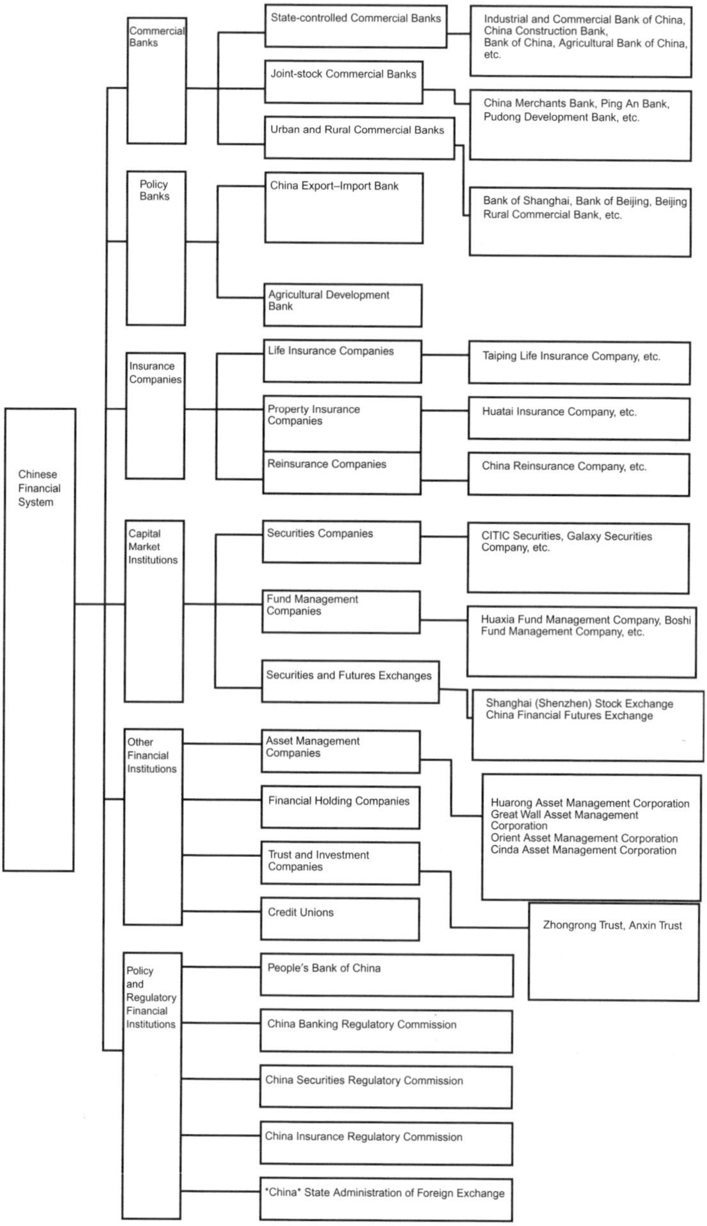

Appendix B: Major International Financial Institutions

Besides the major financial institutions in China mentioned in the main body of this chapter, there are some important international financial institutions worthy of attention. The three most famous among them are the International Monetary Fund (hereinafter referred to as IMF), the World Bank, and Bank for International Settlements.

The IMF was founded in 1947 and is headquartered in Washington, DC. The IMF's business activities concentrate in three areas. First of all, it supervises exchange rates and coordinates policies. The IMF promotes cooperation among its member countries and establishes and maintains a system of exchange rates so as to ensure stable financial order and global economic growth. Second, it creates reserve assets. In 1969, the annual IMF conference decided to establish special drawing rights (hereinafter referred to as SDRs) to supplement the insufficiency of international reserves for its member countries. Special drawing rights denote that the IMF may allocate SDRs to members in proportion to their IMF quotas, which will serve as their reserve assets. When the member countries encounter external deficits, they can resort to SDRs by granting them to another member country so as to compensate payment balances or to repay their loans issued by the IMF. Thirdly, the IMF can provide loans to its member countries. When a member country's international payment is temporarily unbalanced, IMF can provide short-term credit for its governmental agencies like the Ministry of Finance or the Central Bank for current payments for trade or non-trade items. Ever since its foundation, the IMF has made great contributions in maintaining the stability of international exchange rates, eliminating foreign exchange control, balancing international payments and promoting international monetary cooperation.

The World Bank, also called the International Bank for Reconstruction and Development, was established in 1945, with its headquarters located in Washington, DC. Only member countries of the IMF can join the World Bank. At present, the primary mission of the World Bank is to provide developmental loans for developing countries to subsidize developing countries' specific long-term construction projects and promote their economic growth and resource development. These loans are mainly used for investments in public goods such as infrastructure, environmental protection, etc.

There are other two subsidiary institutions of the World Bank, namely, the International Development Association and the International Finance Corporation, both headquartered in Washington, DC. The International Development Association was set up in 1960. As a supplement of the World Bank's activities, the International Development Association provides long-term and low-interest loans for less developed member countries in order to meet their demands in important development areas. Loans of the World Bank and International Development Association are oriented to governments of the member countries. To promote international loans to private enterprises, the World Bank established the International Finance Corporation in 1956, whose mission lies in providing loans for private enterprises of developing member countries in new construction, reconstruction, and expansion so as to promote private economic growth and capital market development in developing countries.

The Bank for International Settlements was established in 1930 and is headquartered in Basel, Switzerland. The original mission of its establishment was to facilitate the payment and transfer of international debts incurred by World War I. Now, it aims to foster international cooperation among central banks in different countries, offer greater settlement convenience for international financial activities and act as an assignee or agent in international financial settlements. In some sense, it is the bank of central banks. Moreover, it serves as an ideal place for collaboration among central banks. It holds an annual conference every year and presidents of central banks in various countries get together in Basel to discuss significant issues of the world economy and the financial situation.

Chapter 8

Commercial Bank Operations and Management

Learning Objectives

After studying this chapter, you will be able to:

- Understand the main balance-sheet business of commercial banks
- Learn about the off-balance-sheet business of commercial banks and its structure
- Understand the asset and liability management of commercial banks
- Clearly understand the liquidity management methods of commercial banks
- Understand the credit risk management measures that commercial banks take
- Grasp the interest rate risk management methods of commercial banks
- Understand the significance of asset securitization on commercial banks' risk management

Commercial banks are the oldest and most important financial institutions within the financial system. As for their impact on the average person and the economy as a whole, to date, there has never been another type of financial institutions that could engage in activities as far-reaching as commercial banking and this is because of the features of commercial bank operations and their determined permeability within the economy. This chapter will provide an in-depth introduction to commercial bank operations and management.

8.1 Commercial Banking

When you go to China Merchants Bank for depositing money, applying for loans, or paying for water, electricity, and telephone bills, China Merchants Bank is conducting its banking business. In fact, commercial banks have various business activities, known as "financial department stores". Their business is far more than just dealing with deposits or collecting utility and telephone bills. In general, all the business of commercial banks can be divided into two basic types: on-balance-sheet and off-balance-sheet business.

8.1.1 On-Balance-Sheet Business

On-balance-sheet business is the business reflected on the balance sheet and which primarily includes the asset business and the liability business.

(a) *Asset Business*

Asset business refers to how commercial banks use the funds obtained by liabilities. The asset business of commercial banks primarily includes: loans, investments, and discounted bills. Discounted bills will be dealt with in Chapter 10.

(i) *Loans*

Providing loans is the most basic asset business of commercial banks. Interest rate spreading between loans and deposits is the basic source of profits of commercial banks in China. Therefore, in order to obtain more profits, they will always be willing to expand lending. However, the loan balance of a commercial bank shall not exceed 75% of its drawn deposits balance. Depending on the borrowers, commercial bank loans are divided into corporate loans and consumer loans. Corporate loans include fixed-asset and working-capital loans. After an enterprise obtains a fixed-asset loan, it will purchase machinery or equipment and construct plants with the funds, which will form physical capital. A fixed-asset loan is an important part of transforming deposits into capital. Enterprises will sometimes encounter seasonal fund shortages. For example, before Christmas or the Spring Festival, some business enterprises will prepare goods in advance to meet holiday spending. However, there are stock constraints on these goods depending on the company's own remaining idle funds. At that time, they will apply to the bank for working capital loans. For example, suppose your company sold a batch of goods worth 50 million yuan, but you have to wait three months before receiving payment. In addition, your company now needs to buy raw material inputs; otherwise, you will face the risk of shutdown. One solution to this problem is to apply for a working capital loan. When commercial banks issue a particularly large loan to an enterprise or project that is in great demand of capital, they often organize a syndicated loan. Namely, one commercial bank acts as the lead bank which works together with several other commercial banks to issue loans for the enterprise or project. Syndicated loans can effectively spread the credit risk of the project or enterprise between several banks. In addition, due to regulatory requirements, a business loan cannot exceed 10% of the commercial bank's capital funds. This tends to limit the ability of small and medium-sized commercial banks whose capital funds are limited to provide credit business for large enterprises. Through syndicated lending, they overcome this barrier.

Corporate loans can be divided, in terms of the size of the businesses, into two categories: loans for large and medium enterprises and loans for micro, small and medium enterprises (MSMEs). Compared with their larger counterparts, micro and small enterprises are faced with more serious asymmetric information problems. Therefore, they are more risky, and thus have to pay a higher rate in an environment where interest rates are market-driven. In China, these companies have great difficulties in obtaining bank loans, and they are often faced with credit rationing. However, with the development of the corporate bond market, an increasing number of large enterprises have begun to raise capital by issuing bonds, and their demand for bank loan financing has begun to shrink. As a result, commercial banks tend to compete for the credit loans of MSMEs. In China, there is a special kind of corporate loan, namely the **local government financing vehicle** (LGFV) loan. An LGFV is a special kind of enterprise set up by local governments by transferring assets such as land and stock equities, and even fiscal subsidies, as a promise to pay, if necessary, to make these companies qualified to meet credit standards. These companies primarily come in the form of a local government's municipal construction investment company and the fund raised is used for city infrastructure and utility projects. Now that we realize what LGFVs are, we can define what an LGFV loan is. These loans are given by commercial banks to financing vehicles that have been set up by local governments such as municipal construction investment companies. LGFV loans are a product of China's characteristic institutional system in a particular period.

Consumer loans, just as their name implies, are mainly issued for the purchase of consumer goods. Home mortgage and auto loans are the most common consumer loans. If you obtain definite credit lines of the Industrial and Commercial Bank of China and have the Peony Credit Card, you can go shopping at designated merchants of the Industrial and Commercial Bank of China, or stay at luxury hotels, even if you do not have the full specified amount of deposits in your card. This is the consumer loan of credit cards. Different from the home and automobile consumer loans, consumer loans of credit cards do not have specific purposes, but mainly meet sporadic consumer spending. By obtaining consumer loans, we do not have to wait for enough savings to purchase our own homes and cars. With consumer credit, we can spend our future income in advance.

For quite some time since market reforms, China has always been a country with a shortage of capital. Therefore, with regard to the allocation of financial surplus, China has always focused on capital formation and production, and the main part of bank loans is productive loans. However, due to the unreasonable enterprise governance structure, a majority of commercial bank loans to enterprises have become non-performing assets. Along with the increasing emphasis that commercial banks have placed on their own interests as a business entity, as well as the reform of the risk management system on commercial bank loans, commercial banks have become more cautious in issuing loans, and they have begun to seek lower-risk loan opportunities. Consumer loans have become a good channel for commercial banks to develop low-risk loans. Under the effects of these two factors, after 1997, the proportion of individual consumer loans as a proportion of new loans has increased rapidly. Presently, its proportion of all-new loans accounts for more than 20%.

Apart from the productive and consumer loans, there is a special kind of loan business, which is not directly used for fixed-asset investment, or cash flow, nor is it used for the purchase of high-value consumer goods. This is known as the interbank loan business. Within one business day, a commercial bank's capital inflows may exceed its capital outflows. At this time, it has a liquidity surplus. Conversely, when the inflows of other commercial banks are not sufficient to cover their outflows, they are in a liquidity shortage. In order to balance the liquidity between commercial banks, the commercial banks with a liquidity surplus will issue loans to others who are in a liquidity shortage, thus making full use of their cash through the interbank loan business so as to obtain the corresponding interest income.

(ii) *Investment*

Investment business is the business activity in which commercial banks buy securities or invest in other physical capital, such as buying stocks, government bonds, or investing in real estate or industrial undertakings. However, there are some legal restrictions as to a commercial bank's participation in the investment business. Not all commercial banks can engage in these investments. In general, there are fewer limits when commercial banks invest in government bonds. However, there are large differences among different countries, for investing in stocks, funds, or not-for-self-use real estate. In countries with **separate operation**, laws ban commercial banks from buying shares or corporate bonds, or investing in real estate. However, in countries with **mixed operations** of banking and securities industry, there are fewer restrictions on commercial banks in investing in these assets. In Germany, with a universal banking system, in addition to drawing deposits and issuing loans, their banks can directly invest in newly rising enterprises with large holdings of corporate stocks and underwriting securities. Therefore, banks like these are commercial banks and investment banks all in one. Currently, the world is shifting towards mixed operation. The operation barriers between banking and the securities industry are gradually breaking down. Commercial banks have a larger space in the direct capital market for investment activities. China still implements a relatively strict separate operation system at present. Commercial banks shall neither engage in securities business such as shares, nor invest in not-for-self-use real estate. However, China's commercial banks are not restricted to the purchase of government bonds. At present, in China's commercial banking, nearly 20% of the asset business is investments in government bonds, central bank bills, and policy-based financial bonds issued by policy banks.

Even in countries which require separate operation, though commercial banks are not allowed to hold and/or underwrite stock and other high-risk securities, they may hold some low-risk securities like Treasury bonds. In fact, securities are an important asset of commercial banks. The securities held by commercial banks include government bonds issued by the Ministry of Finance, bonds issued by the central bank, and financial bonds issued by policy banks. They not only bring certain benefits to banks, but also bring high liquidity. In particular, commercial banks can easily sell them in the open market when in need of cash. Therefore, these low-risk bonds constitute the **secondary reserve** of commercial banks. This differs from the **primary reserve** which consists of the required reserve and excess reserve.

Compared to loans, the risk of a bank holding securities, such as government bonds, is much lower. There are several reasons for this. First, the issuer of these securities can be the Ministry of Finance, or the central bank or policy banks supported by the state Treasury whose credit risk is very low. Second, there usually is a market for the standardized securities to circulate and transfer. When commercial banks do not want to hold these securities, they can easily sell them in the secondary market and do not have to hold them until maturity. Because of the lower risk of holding securities and higher risk of credit, increasing holdings of securities has become a main measure for China's commercial banks to optimize their asset structure, improve the quality of assets, and reduce the risks of their portfolio. At the same time, commercial banks with certain securities can facilitate the central bank to improve the control of the base money through open-market operations.

(b) *Liability Business*

Liability business is when commercial banks obtain surplus capital from others through certain channels. The liability business of commercial banks has the following categories: drawing deposits, borrowing money, issuing financial bonds, and raising capital.

(i) *Drawing deposits*

Drawing deposits is the most basic form of liability business. The proportion of deposits in terms of capital sources for a commercial bank in general is above 80%. Without deposits, the loan business of commercial banks will be like going upriver without a paddle. To some extent, the business of drawing deposits is like laying eggs with borrowed chickens. Although the capital cannot be replaced, borrowing money and issuing financial bonds are the supplements to this kind of liability business.

(ii) *Borrowing money*

When commercial banks are in a shortage of cash or liquidity and cannot make up for the shortage because of deposits, they can borrow cash to cover the gap. Commercial banks borrow from both interbank lending market and from the central bank. Interbank borrowing is the activity in which a commercial bank with a liquidity shortage borrows from other commercial banks with a liquidity surplus. This is the opposite of interbank lending. Sometimes, commercial banks can also directly borrow money from the central bank to cover their liquidity gap. From the perspective of the central bank, this is called **refinancing**. Whether through interbank borrowing or borrowing from the central bank, commercial banks will pay a certain interest. Sometimes, commercial bank borrowing from the central bank will also be affected by certain limits, because the increase of refinancing will also increase the base money supply (see Chapter 13) which must respect the objectives of the central bank currency controls.

(iii) *Issuing financial bonds*

Another source by which commercial banks obtain funds is to issue financial bonds. Financial bonds are the bonds issued by financial institutions in order to raise funds or in order to replenish capital. The difference between the issuance of financial bonds and deposits drawing is that the financial bonds are standardized, which means that they are issued at the same time and shall have the same amount, term, and interest rate. In comparison, drawing deposits tends to be more flexible with relatively low interest costs. Another advantage that comes from the issuance of financial bonds is that they are not considered deposits, and for this reason, there is no need to deposit funds in the reserve at the People's Bank of China, though there are more limits on issuing financial bonds, such as information disclosure and supervision by securities regulators. However, very few commercial banks issue bonds as a means of raising funds for loans, yet on the contrary, issuing financial bonds to replenish capital is becoming more and more common.

(iv) *Raising and supplementing capital*

In order to properly carry out various business activities, commercial banks also need a certain amount of capital. *The Basel Agreement* also requires that the risk-weighted capital adequacy ratio of commercial banks shall not be less than 8%. Previously, all the capital funds of Chinese state-owned commercial banks were allocated by the Treasury or injected by the state, with no capital raised from the capital market. Now, they have been or are about to become publicly traded stock companies. Public offerings are an important channel of raising and supplementing capital. Similarly, for other small and medium-sized joint-stock commercial banks, the initial public offering (IPO) or public/private issuance of additional stock is one of the most important ways to raise and supplement funds. Apart from issuing stock, commercial banks can also issue subordinated debt, hybrid capital bonds and convertible bonds as supplementary capital (see 8.2.2).

The major factors to be considered in capital decisions are the size of the bank, the diversification of assets and asset risks. The higher the bank's assets, the more capital it requires. The bank's capital also depends on the diversification of assets. If the loans are highly concentrated in a few enterprises, then, even if only one enterprise goes bankrupt, it is likely to bring a large proportion of non-performing assets to the bank. In this case, the bank needs more capital as a buffer of loan losses. The third factor affecting the bank's capital is its asset risks. The higher the risk, the more the capital that the bank will need so as to buffer losses from risk exposure. If the bank mainly holds government bonds, it would need less capital than a bank that holds corporate bonds.

8.1.2 Off-Balance-Sheet Business

Off-balance-sheet business refers to business which is not reflected in a bank balance sheet but will affect the revenue and profit of the bank. In developed countries, the contribution of off-balance-sheet business to bank profit is up to 40% to 50% or even higher, while off-balance-sheet business revenue of Chinese commercial banks accounts for only about 10% of their operating income. Off-balance-sheet business will be the focus of competition in China's banking future. It may be defined in either the broad or narrow sense. Broad off-balance-sheet business includes intermediate business and narrow off-balance-sheet business.

(a) *Intermediate Business*

Intermediate business refers to the services that a bank uses at their own convenience to handle customers without the utilization of their own assets, including foreign exchange business, trust business, agency business, leasing and credit card business, etc. When handling intermediary business, banks may charge handling fees.

(i) *Remittance and cashing*

Remittance and cashing is that banks, on behalf of the customer, remit cash to the payee in another place. This kind of business should use special remittance certificates: bank drafts or payment orders. These certificates are commands issued by the remitting bank to another bank or branch banks, commanding the latter to pay a certain amount of money to a third party. The bank gives the bank draft to the customer, and the customer sends it to the payee. The payee draws money from the bank designated by the draft. In the case of payment order, the accepting bank will, by telegram or by wire, notify another bank that will then notify the third party for withdrawal. Therefore, remittance and cashing business contains two-phase behaviors: the first is remittance, and then is cashing a draft. When a bank handles remittances for customers, they will typically charge a certain fee. Remittance and cashing business creates risk-free revenue opportunities for commercial banks. Moreover, banks can also use the business to utilize a portion of customer capital. With the development of electronic information technology, even though remitting banks do not hold the remittance funds for such a long period of time as they did in the past, in terms of receiving banks, from the point in which payments are received to the time when the customers receive their funds, there will always be a certain time interval, and in this period of time, the receiving banks can use these payments for other purposes.

(ii) *Trust and agency business*

Trust business is business in which the bank that is entrusted by a customer manages, operates, and handles business on behalf of the client, including trust business to individuals and enterprises. Personal trust business mainly includes holding property, securities, and valuables, and handling life insurance for customers. The trust business to enterprises mainly includes investing and raising capital, on behalf of enterprises, such as the issuance of stocks or bonds, the distribution of stocks or dividends, the repayment of principal and interest on debts, the merger with or takeover of other enterprises, the management of employee welfare accounts, the grant of retirement pensions, business consultation services, the issuance of Treasury bonds, and the repayment of principal with interest. When you deposit or withdraw money from a bank, you can often see advertisements saying the bank sells products such as insurance, funds on behalf of other institutions. In general, commercial banks only charge fees or commission on trust business according to a certain ratio. As for operation earnings, they shall be owned by the principal. At the same time, when the bank handles this business, similar to remittance and cashing business, it can also use a portion of trust funds for investment business or temporary liquidity management.

For many individual investors, the main commercial bank trust business that they may come in contact with is wealth management that is now gaining in popularity. This so-called **wealth management** refers to specialized services such as financial analysis, financial planning, investment advice and asset management which commercial banks offer to enterprises and individuals, taking advantage of their own strengths. Depending on the ways of management and operation, commercial banks' wealth management services may be classified under wealth management consultancy and integrated wealth management. The former involves financial analysis and planning, investment advice, recommendations on personal investment products and other specialized services, while in the case of the latter, commercial banks, on the basis of wealth management consultancy, are authrozied to invest and manage assets on behalf of the customer and in accordance with investment plans and strategies as specified in the contract between them, and the earning and risk of investment is borne by the customer or jointly by the customer and bank in the pre-defined way.

Private banking is also one of the most important trust businesses of commercial banking. Just as people have different levels of income and wealth, there also exists a difference in their needs for commercial banking service. Private banking, then, is differentiated financial services which commercial banks offer specifically for the segment of the population that is affluent and with a high net worth (total assets less total liabilities). It includes personal investment and more importantly, asset management which stands at its core. With economic development, the growth of social wealth, and the growing need for specialized and professional asset management of the affluent, commercial banks have begun to expand their private banking services in order to meet their asset management needs. Of course, different banks offer significantly diverse private banking services.

(iii) *Credit card business*

A credit card is a kind of consumer credit. The cardholder can use the card to pay for goods or services. Merchants will send a copy of the invoice issued and signed by the cardholder to the issuing bank each day. Then the issuing bank collects debts from the cardholder each month. Credit cards, in fact, combine the two basic functions of banks — payments and credit.

The issuance of various credit cards provides convenience not only for banks, but also for consumers and merchants. For banks, it can draw the deposits of merchants in the bank and can charge a commission or default interest for non-punctual repayments, at the same time strengthening the cooperation between banks and their customers. For customers with credit cards, they can obtain the convenience of enjoying shopping without carrying any cash, and can often use their credit, which frees them from the trouble of application formalities and credit investigation when each time they borrow money from banks. For merchants, after selling on credit, they can immediately recover payments from the bank, which frees money up from backlogging. In addition, they do not need to investigate the cardholder's credit at each and every store; it is guaranteed by the issuing bank, which makes it unnecessary for merchants to bear the cost of investigation while also expanding their sales market.

(b) *Narrow Off-Balance-Sheet Business*

Narrow off-balance-sheet business includes the four major categories of loan commitment, guarantees, derivative financial instruments, and investment banking business.

(i) *Loan commitment*

Loan commitment is a commitment to issuing a certain amount of loans to bank customers in the future within a specific period according to the conditions previously agreed upon, which is divided into revocable commitment and irrevocable commitment. Revocable loan commitment is attached with specific terms that the customer must fulfill before they can obtain a loan. As soon as the credit ratings of the customer have decreased or the customer does not fulfill the specific terms during the bank commitment and the actual loan period, the bank can revoke its commitment to provide loans. Irrevocable loan commitment is a legally binding commitment, which the bank shall not revoke without the customer's permission.

(ii) *Guarantee*

A guarantee is a business of commercial banks to be entrusted by the customer to provide, as certifier or guarantor, credit guarantee services for domestic and foreign enterprises, in that the commercial bank issues a written guarantee for one party (the principal) of trading activities to another party to ensure that the principal fulfills the contractual obligations at the appointed time. If the principal fails to fulfill the contractual obligations, the bank bears joint and several liabilities. Therefore, guarantee business forms a contingent liability of banks. The guarantee business includes bank acceptance bills, letters of credit, and so on.

(iii) *Derivative financial instruments*

Derivative financial instruments refer to those derived from base assets such as stocks, bonds, or currencies, which are attached to the transactions of primary financial instruments. Derivative financial instruments include forward exchange contracts, currency and interest rate swaps, financial futures, and financial options. With the growing volatility of the financial market, commercial banks must use derivative financial instruments to avoid and manage risk, and through this, help customers to achieve a better balance of benefit and risk. Derivative financial instruments will be introduced in detail in Chapter 12.

(iv) *Investment banking*

Investment banking can be defined as various businesses operated by investment banks and securities companies, including underwriting, agency services and securities market operations. Since the late 1970s, Western financial regulatory authorities have gradually relaxed or canceled limitations on the business scope of financial institutions. There is a growing tendency for commercial banks, investment banks and other financial institutions to diversify their operations into the other sectors, which results in the blurring of the boundaries between them. At present, China's commercial banks can not only underwrite government bonds but also monopolize the underwriting of short-term corporate financing bonds. Along with the development of the financial market, more and more enterprises will rely on the issuance of stocks and bonds to raise cash, and will decrease their dependence on bank credit. Investment banking will gradually become an important avenue of commercial bank competition to win large corporate clients.

8.2 Asset and Liability Management

8.2.1 Asset Management

(a) *Three Principles of Asset Management*

Asset business is the primary source of profits for any bank. When developing asset business, banks are in an effort to promote the consolidation of profitability, liquidity and safety, which are known as the three principles of asset management.

To raise earnings, and earn a higher profit, a bank will search for borrowers who are willing to pay a relatively high interest rate, and grant loans of higher earnings and lower risks. Second, this entails the purchase of high-earning and low-risk securities, striking a balance between profit and risk. By minimalizing the risks of every asset that comes into the bank, the bank must search for an optimal set of assets. Finally, banks must also pay attention to the liquidity of assets and avoid costly acquisition of funds to satisfy the central bank's required reserve or to meet the withdrawal needs of depositors. For this reason, a bank must hold a certain amount of vault cash or excess reserves. However, contradictions exist amongst profitability, liquidity, and safety (recall the characteristics of financial instruments and the relationship between them discussed in Chapter 2), and if profits are relatively high, risks will be higher and liquidity will thus be lower. Conversely, if a bank wants to minimize risks and maximize liquidity, yet this will come at the expense of low profits. For instance, if a bank mainly wants its assets to consist of vault cash or excess reserves, its liquidity will naturally be very high and will not run into any risks of default, yet the bank will also lose its opportunities to earn a higher profit through issued loans or the purchase of securities. For this reason, the asset management of banks is an art of striking a balance amongst profitability, liquidity, and safety.

(b) *Loan Quality Management in Asset Management*

Additionally, another important aspect of asset management is loan quality management. Bank loans can be categorized into normal loans and non-performing loans. When borrowers fully fulfill their borrowing contract obligations by paying the initial principal with interest back in full, it is referred to as a normal loan. Otherwise, it would become a non-performing loan.

To differentiate between normal and non-performing loans, banks will implement the **five-tier loan classification system** based on risk as a means of loan quality management, that is, banks will classify loans as normal, special-mention, substandard, doubtful, and loss. The latter three categories are considered non-performing. The loan is "normal" when borrowers are capable of fulfilling their obligations without enough reason to doubt their ability to repay the principal and interest on time and in full. The loan is a "special-mention" category when the borrower is currently capable of repaying the principal and interests, although there are factors which may adversely affect the repayment. The loan is called "substandard" when a borrower's ability to repay exhibits obvious issues, and the borrower is unable to repay the loan principal and interest by means of its normal operating revenue, and even with the guarantee executed, this type of loan will cause a certain loss. Loans are said to be "doubtful" when the borrowers have no means of repaying the loan principal and interest and even with the guarantee executed, it will certainly result in a major loss. Loss refers to the point when, even with all possible measures or all the necessary legal procedures being taken, the

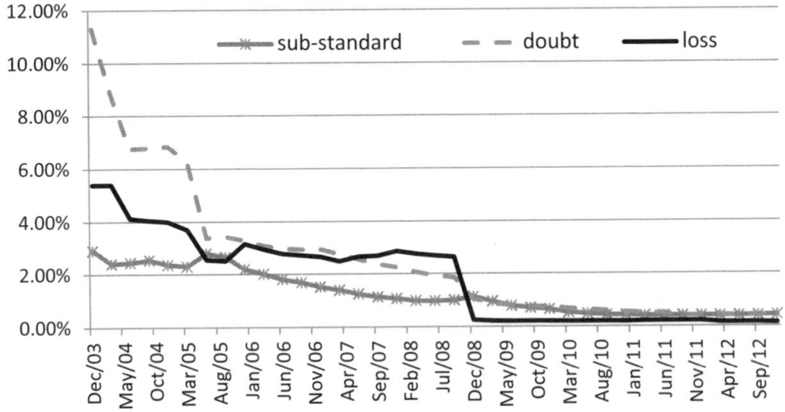

Fig. 8.1 NPL (Non-Performing Loans) Ratio under China's Five-Tier Classification System

Source: The CBRC website

principal and interest cannot be retrieved or the bank can only retrieve a small portion of the original. As illustrated in Figure 8.1, since the dawn of the 21st century, the ratio of non-performing loans of Chinese banking has dropped significantly, and asset quality has also noticeably improved.

After classification of loans, banks shall, in accordance with prudent accounting principles, reasonably estimate possible loan loss, and provide timely provisions for loan loss, which is commonly known as "provisions". The percentage of loan loss provisions to non-performing loans is called **provision coverage**, which is an indicator of a bank's ability to cope with loan losses. Provisions of 2% are required for special-mention loans, 25% for substandard loans, 50% for doubtful loans and 100% for loss loans. The loss provisions for substandard and doubtful loans can rise or fall by 20%. Loan loss provisions are set aside by a bank's headquarters and loss loans or the loss portion of a loan needs to be written off in a timely manner. As required by the regulator, loan loss provisions must be set aside in full, depending on the risk of the loan, and after-tax profit distribution is not allowed if the provision is not adequately set aside. Inadequate provisions for commercial bank loan losses, on one hand may lead to an overestimation of bank profits on the other. In the event of a borrower default or other asset loss, banks will consume their own capital, directly impacting their stability. As depicted in Figure 8.2, since 2008, provision coverage has significantly increased in the Chinese banking sector, and banks themselves have significantly enhanced their ability to resolve asset losses.

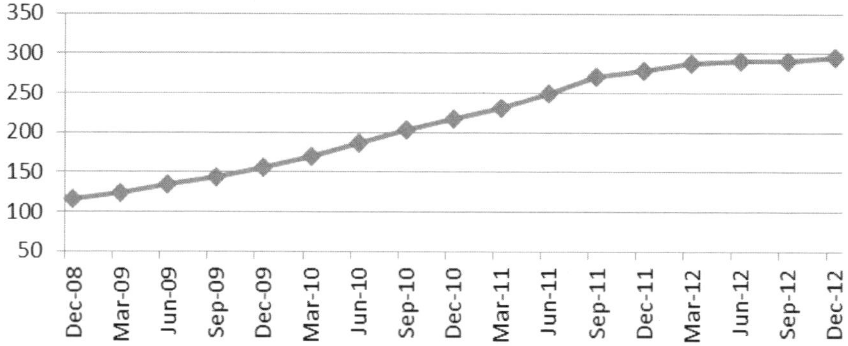

Fig. 8.2 Provision Coverage of Chinese Banking %

Source: Website of the China Banking Regulatory Commission.

(c) *Theory of Commercial Banking Asset Management*

The real-bills doctrine is also known as the theory of commercial loans which developed out of the experiences of 17th century English banks. In accordance with this doctrine, commercial banks are not suitable for issuing security loans, real estate loans, consumer and personal loans, and long-term agricultural loans. In other words, the issuance of these loans should be limited to the bank's own capital and existing savings. This doctrine states that when a bank distributes funds during its initial stage of development, it should take into consideration the ability to maintain a high degree of liquidity because the primary source of the bank funds arise from highly liquid current deposits. Since deposits are determined exogenously, commercial bank asset business should primarily focus on short-term self-liquidating loans and should not issue long-term loans or consumer loans. This is why this doctrine has also been known as the theory of self-liquidating loans.

The banking crisis illustrated that liquidity certainly does not depend on the type of loans but rather depends on the convertibility or saleability of assets held by banks. Based on a new understanding of bank liquidity, the theory of convertibility states that commercial banks are not necessarily limited to short-term self-liquidating loans. A significant portion can also go towards investing in securities assets that can be quickly sold. This expands the scope of commercial bank assets and increases the profitbiliy of commercial banks with liquidity and safety guaranteed.

The basic idea behind the theory of expected income is that the liquidity status of commercial banks is, in the final analysis, based on future income and is positively related to the income. As long as future income is guaranteed, long-term project loans and consumer loans can ensure bank liquidity so long as they are repaid in installments. Conversely, if future income cannot be guaranteed, even short-term loans run the risk of default. Therefore, this theory states that commercial banks should use the future income of borrowers as a standard measurement of their ability to repay loans so as to coordinate profitability with liquidity and safety. The expected income theory also states that the time and amount of borrower income can be expected if a portion of income is used to repay the loans each period, it will not only guarantee loan repayment, but also ensure the amount and time of repayment. If the payment is made in installments, even a long-term loan will often be accompanied with liquidity during the duration of the loan.

8.2.2 Liability Management

(a) *Main Contents of Liability Management*

Liability business is the basis of bank assets. For this reason, liability management is much more important to banks than it is to industrial and commercial enterprises. The basic content of bank management of liability business is to find a stable source of financing at a low cost. Drawing deposits, borrowing from the central bank, borrowing from the interbank lending market and issuing financing bonds are the primary means by which banks obtain funding, although the majority of bank liability funds come from deposits. For this reason, the key to bank liability business management is the means by which more deposits can be drawn.

Capital management is a major element of modern bank liability management. There are three primary uses for bank capital: absorbing operating losses including risk losses, ensuring normal bank operations, allowing some time for the bank management to resolve existing issues, and providing a buffer to avoid bankruptcy. Adequate capital will assist in boosting public confidence in the banks and displaying the strength of the bank to its creditors. The more the bank capital, the more confident will depositors become. The capital adequacy ratio calculated on the basis of regulatory capital is an important tool for regulatory authorities to control banks' risk-taking behaviors and guarantee the stable operation of the market. Therefore, the higher the risk the bank capital is exposed to, the higher is the capital requirement the regulators demand. The capital adequacy requirement may, to some extent, prevent commercial banks from taking excessively risky behaviors in their portfolio choices.

Bank management can be categorized into three levels, namely:

- **Equity Capital:** Bank financial statements display ownership equity which includes the paid-in capital, capital reserves, surplus reserves and undistributed profit, etc.

- **Regulatory Capital:** It is calculated according to the capital requirements of regulatory authorities, including core capital and supplementary capital.
- **Economic Capital:** Economic capital is the amount of capital needed to cover all bank risks, and for this reason it is also known as risk capital.

Economic capital is a fictitious capital that is equal to the amount of the unexpected risk losses of the bank. Economic capital is not true bank capital; it is a "calculated" number. The quantity is equal to unexpected losses, that is, the sum of unexpected losses of credit risk, market risk, and operating risks. Expected loss is calculated into bank operating costs based on the reserve. As its compensation is provided for in the price of products such as bank loan interest rates, it does not constitute a real risk. Unexpected losses are a real risk and must be covered by bank capital. This is determined by the function of capital and volatility of unexpected losses. Economic capital is a determining factor of the boundaries of a bank's risk controls: economic capital is a virtual capital, and when the amount of economic capital comes close to or exceeds the bank's real capital (regulatory capital), it illustrates that the bank's level of risk is near or has exceeded its practical capacity. At this time, the bank must control or shrink its risky behavior through various measures or increase its real capital. Otherwise it will sacrifice its safety. If the risks of certain operations are too large, these operations will need a greater amount of capital to cover the risk they are running. Even if these operations will earn a high profit, given the amount of capital they will occupy, the real profitability may not be high. As such, banks should keep their risks at an appropriate level to maximize shareholder value.

Regulatory capital is capital requirements imposed by the Banking Regulatory Commission in order to improve the robustness of bank operations. It includes core capital and supplementary capital. Core capital consists of paid-in capital and disclosed reserves. Paid-in capital includes issued and fully paid common stock and permanent non-cumulative preferred stock. Disclosed reserves refer to reserves reflected clearly on a balance sheet as retained earnings or other surpluses such as share premiums and undistributed profit.

Supplementary capital includes: (1) Non-disclosed reserves which are also known as hidden reserves. Hidden reserves have approximately the same composition as disclosed reserves but lack their transparency. (2) General reserve or general loan loss provisions. (3) Subordinated debt refers to commercial banks' long-term debt that has a duration of five years or more and which is not used to cover day-to-day operating losses unless the bank faces bankruptcy or liquidation and ranks below deposits and other liabilities with regard to claim for repayment. (4) Hybrid capital bonds refer to bonds with a term of no less than 15 years which cannot be redeemed within 10 years and can be used to compensate for the operating losses of commercial banks and which allow for the suspension of the right of claim and can absorb losses. In terms of repayment, they are located after subordinated debt and before equity capital. (5) Convertible bonds, as in bonds that can be converted to common shares given a certain time period and certain conditions.

The risk-weighted capital adequacy ratio of the commercial bank cannot be less than 8%, of which, the core capital adequacy ratio cannot be less than 4%, while the supplementary capital adequacy ratio cannot exceed 4%. When the commercial bank's capital adequacy ratio comes near to or drops below 8%, it must draw in new capital (government capital injections, IPOs, and additional issuances) or issue subordinated debt, hybrid capital bond, or convertible debt to replenish capital and thereby meet regulatory demands and improve the bank's capacity to take on risk.

(b) *Theory of Liability Management*

The oldest form of liability management theory is the "bank note theory". In the early stages of banking development, bank notes were the fundamental bank liability, yet when they were issued, precious metals served as the reserve for payment. Bankers realized, however, that those who held bank notes would rarely demand their conversion into precious metals at the same time. For this reason, the issuance of bank notes did not necessarily mean that they need to be fully backed by precious metal reserves. Given a fixed amount of precious metals, the banks could issue as many notes as possible as their primary method of earning. Excess bank note issuance would bring about inflation, and after the establishment of central banks, commercial banks could no longer issue bank notes. As such, drawing deposits became the most basic liability of commercial banks which thus brought about "deposit theory".

Deposit theory states that deposits are the primary source of funding for banks and a passive bank liability with the cost of deposit taking as a major item of expenditure for the banks. To depositors, the ability of deposits to be exchanged for cash and their ability to hold value are of utmost importance. To banks, the stability and liquidity of deposits are of utmost importance. For this reason, commercial banks should give safety and liquidity sufficient consideration, arrange deposits in accordance with the willingness of customers, arrange commercial bank loans and other asset operations based on the conditions of deposits, maintain relatively high-liquidity assets, and prevent bank runs, and cannot blindly expand lending and pay excessive interest. Deposit theory is based on the premise of maintaining asset liquidity but sacrifices asset profitability. In the early 1960s, the ability of commercial banks to draw deposits was significantly weakened as a result of interest rate regulation and financial innovations, which added a great deal of pressure on liquidity and as a result, a new theory of liquidity management was developed, dealing with commercial banking operational management. This new theory claims that commercial banks have shifted from a reliance on deposits to external borrowers and from passive liabilities to active liabilities. In this way, commercial banks found a new method of maintaining liquidity to improve their competitiveness. The largest impact on this development is the buying theory and sales theory.

Buying theory states that banks are not passive and helpless when it comes to liabilities. Though through strengthening asset management, banks can improve liquidity, they can also use active liabilities and the active purchase of external funds to achieve liquidity. For this reason, banks do not necessarily need to ensure a large amount of high liquidity assets, but should rather invest funds in highly profitable loans or other such investments. When liquidity is required, banks can use management of fund acquisition to provide the necessary liquidity. Through the active purchase of liability to obtain liquidity, asset business of commercial banks is freed from the constraints of deposit amounts. Traditional liability management theory focuses on fund sources; sales theory focuses on the variety of financial innovations which provide customers with a variety of financial services. This theory states that banks are companies which create financial products, and their primary responsibility is to push these products to earn necessary funds and required profits while designing their overall asset and liability business. From the perspective of liability management, the bank will make overall arrangement for asset distribution and absorb and use the target funds through financial product design.

8.3 Liquidity Management

8.3.1 Commercial Bank Reserves

Liquidity is the basis of all bank management. To understand commercial bank liquidity management, we must first clearly understand commercial bank reserves which are the portion of assets the bank keeps back to cope with the need of depositors to withdraw. They include required reserves, deposits at the central bank, and vault cash. The sum of central bank deposits and vault cash are considered excess reserves. Required reserves are the reserve fund that commercial banks are required to hold on deposit with the central bank as required by the latter. If the percentage of required reserves is 10%, then for each 100 yuan deposited with the commercial bank, the bank is required to deposit 10 yuan at the central bank. Excess reserves are total reserve assets of the commercial bank minus the required reserves. Its proportion to total deposits is the excess reserve ratio.

The more assets that commercial banks hold as reserves, the fewer assets that are available for them to purchase securities or issue loans. Moreover, these reserves commonly have a very low earning. The majority of central banks do not pay interest on the commercial bank reserves deposited with them. Why would commercial banks then be willing to hold onto reserves? One reason is that required reserves are required by law to be deposited in the central bank. Another reason is that excess reserves have a high liquidity. Holding a certain amount of excess reserves allows banks to cope well with potential liquidity difficulties that arise when depositors withdraw cash. Apart from commercial bank deposits and vault cash, we also have introduced above that commercial banks may invest in government bonds and other securities assets that are highly liquid and with a low risk. Since a secondary market exists for these bonds, when banks require cash, they can conveniently sell a portion of their securities. In comparison to the primary reserve of required reserves and excess reserves, government bonds held by the bank become a secondary reserve.

8.3.2 Methods of Commercial Bank Liquidity Management

Having clarified what a reserve is, we can now look at the methods of commercial bank liquidity management.

Generally speaking, banks can manage liquidity from both the asset and liability side. Suppose that a commercial bank's initial balance sheet is as follows:

Commercial Bank's Initial Balance Sheet

Assets (10,000 yuan)		Liabilities (10,000 yuan)	
Reserves	2000	Deposits	18,000
Securities	5000	Central Bank Loans	1000
Loans	15,000	Interbank Loans	1000
		Owner Equity	2000
Total Assets	22,000	Total Liabilities	22,000

Again suppose that the required reserve ratio is 10%. Since this bank has drawn 180 million yuan in deposits, it must deposit 18 million yuan into the required reserve in accordance with the required reserve ratio. Since the actual reserve is 20 million yuan, excess reserves are thus worth 2 million yuan.

Now suppose that a customer wanted to withdraw 10 million yuan from his or her deposit. At this time, the bank's balance sheet would make the following adjustments:

Bank Balance Sheet After a Customer Withdraws 10 Million Yuan

Assets (10,000 yuan)		Liabilities (10,000 yuan)	
Reserves	1000	Deposits	17,000
Securities	5000	Central Bank Loans	1000
Loans	15,000	Interbank Loans	1000
		Owner Equity	2000
Total Assets	21,000	Total Liabilities	21,000

Since the customer withdrew 10 million yuan, this would have the following impact on the bank's balance sheet: on the asset side, reserves would decrease from 20 million yuan to 10 million yuan. On the liabilities side, deposits would decrease from 180 million yuan to 170 million yuan. Since the required reserve ratio is 10%, and deposits of 170 million yuan should have a required reserve of 17 million yuan, the bank's required reserve is 7 million yuan short. How can they compensate for this difference? They can address the issue from either the asset or liability side of the balance sheet.

(a) *Assets* 1: *Sale of Securities*

Since the bank holds 50 million yuan in securities, when the depositor needs to withdraw cash, the bank can make a public offering of 7 million yuan in securities to compensate for the reserve gap. Once the bank has sold 7 million yuan in securities, the balance sheet would display the following adjustments:

Bank Balance Sheet After Securities are Sold

Assets (10,000 yuan)		Liabilities (10,000 yuan)	
Reserves	1700	Deposits	17,000
Securities	4300	Central Bank Loans	1000
Loans	15,000	Interbank Loans	1000
		Owner Equity	2000
Total Assets	21,000	Total Liabilities	21,000

Selling securities to compensate for the gap in the required reserve only impacts the structure of the bank assets and has no effect on its liabilities. In other words, while the reserve increases to 17 million yuan, there is a decrease in securities from 50 million yuan down to 43 million. Commercial banks often hold a certain amount of government bonds and securities, quite a few of which are traded on the market every day. As such, when a bank faces a liquidity shock, it can sell a portion of its held securities to adjust the asset side of its balance sheet and obtain a corresponding liquidity. Meanwhile, the holdings of securities can earn a corresponding profit, thereby replenishing the secondary reserve.

(b) *Assets* 2: *Loan Recovery*

Loans are the largest item on the asset side of a bank's balance sheet. For instance, of the 210 million yuan in assets of this bank, 150 million is in the form of loans. If the bank could successfully recover loans to compensate for the 7 million yuan gap in the reserve, its balance sheet would adjust as follows:

Bank Balance Sheet After Recovery of 7 Million Yuan Loan

Assets (10,000 yuan)		Liabilities (10,000 yuan)	
Reserves	1700	Deposits	17,000
Securities	5000	Central Bank Loans	1000
Loans	14,300	Interbank Loans	1000
		Owner Equity	2000
Total Assets	21,000	Total Liabilities	21,000

As you can see, the recovery of loans to compensate for the gap in the reserve would be the same as that when the bank sold its securities. There is only a change to the asset structure and no effect whatsoever upon the liabilities. This adjusts the reserve to 17 million yuan, satisfying the 10% demand of the required reserve ratio and lowering the total amount of loans to 143 million. In this example, adjustments to the bank's asset structure to meet liquidity demand are simple and easy. In reality, however, when banks truly do face a liquidity shock, most of the time, loan recovery to compensate for a gap in reserves is difficult. Banks would have to recover loans before the agreed expiration which would ruin the borrower's original payment plan and may even suspend the original investment project causing the bank to lose its function of maintaining liquidity as well as investment continuity in the financial system.

Apart from the sale of securities and the recovery of loans to adjust the asset structure, commercial banks can also implement liquidity management on the liabilities side.

(c) *Liabilities 1*: *Draw Cash Deposits*

If the bank drew 8 million yuan in cash deposits, it would deposit this cash into the vault. At this time, the balance sheet would be as follows:

Bank Balance Sheet with New Deposit of 8 Million Yuan as Reserve

Assets (10,000 yuan)		Liabilities (10,000 yuan)	
Reserves	1800	Deposits	17,800
Securities	5000	Central Bank Loans	1000
Loans	15,000	Interbank Loans	1000
		Owner Equity	2000
Total Assets	21,800	Total Liabilities	21,800

Due to the addition of 8 million yuan in cash deposits, the total of assets and liabilities would increase to 218 million yuan. On the asset side, the reserve would increase from 10 million yuan to 18 million yuan. On the liabilities side, deposits would increase from 170 million yuan to 178 million yuan. In accordance with the required reserve ratio of 10%, it would withhold 17.8 million yuan in required reserves. Since the real reserves are a total of 18 million yuan, apart from its ability to meet the demands of the required reserve ratio, it would also have an excess reserve of 200,000 yuan. However, if the bank were to rely on the inflow of cash deposits alone to implement liquidity management, it would be very dangerous and when large amount of deposits are withdrawn, it would be impossible to meet liquidity demand with this method of management.

(d) *Liabilities 2*: *Central Bank Loans*

Suppose that once a depositor withdrew 10 million yuan in cash, the bank was not willing to sell securities nor was it willing to attempt to recover loans to compensate for the gap in the reserve. Meanwhile, the inflow of cash deposits was too low. The bank would also have the option of borrowing from the central bank. The central bank's role as the final lender can provide refinancing to commercial banks when they face liquidity difficulties so as to meet its liquidity demands. China's central bank provides loans to commercial banks and other institutions, and it is collectively referred to as **refinancing**. If this bank borrowed 7 million yuan from the central bank, its balance sheet would adjust as follows:

Bank Balance Sheet After the Central Bank Loan of 7 Million Yuan

Assets (10,000 yuan)		Liabilities (10,000 yuan)	
Reserves	1700	Deposits	17,000
Securities	5000	Central Bank Loans	1700
Loans	15,000	Interbank Loans	1000
		Owner Equity	2000
Total Assets	21,700	Total Liabilities	21,700

The impact on the bank's balance sheet of borrowing 7 million yuan from the central bank would be an addition of 7 million yuan to the bank's total assets and liabilities. On the asset side, the bank's reserves would increase from 10 million yuan to 17 million yuan. On the liabilities side, deposits would remain at 170 million yuan, but the central bank loans would increase from 10 million yuan to 17 million yuan. The reserve of 17 million yuan meets the required reserve ratio demand of 10% for deposits of 170 million yuan.

(e) *Liabilities 3*: *Interbank Loans*

The third method of obtaining liquidity on the liabilities side is to borrow 7 million yuan in funds from the interbank lending market. The interbank lending market is a short-term money market allowing for adjustment of fund surplus and deficiency between banks, providing an extremely efficient method of managing a bank's liquidity. Meanwhile, it also provides a profitable opportunity to those banks with a surplus. After the bank borrows 7 million yuan on the interbank lending market, its balance sheet would be adjusted as follows:

Balance Sheet After Borrowing 7 Million Yuan from the Interbank Lending Market

Assets (10,000 yuan)		Liabilities (10,000 yuan)	
Reserves	1700	Deposits	17,000
Securities	5000	Central Bank Loans	1000
Loans	15,000	Interbank Loans	1700
		Owner Equity	2000
Total Assets	21,700	Total Liabilities	21,700

As you can see, borrowing 7 million yuan from the interbank lending market is the same as when the bank were to borrow 7 million yuan from the central bank; both increase the total assets and liabilities by 7 million yuan. On the assets side, the reserve would similarly increase from 10 million yuan to 17 million yuan. On the liabilities side, interbank loans would increase from 10 million yuan to 17 million yuan with no effect whatsoever on other liability items. The reserve of 17 million yuan just so happens to meet the required reserve demand of 10% for the 170 million deposits.

Commercial bank funds borrowed from the central bank or the interbank lending market makes the reserve a **borrowed reserve**. After deducting the borrowed reserve from the total reserve, the remaining amount is the commercial bank's **own reserve**. When a borrowed reserve expires, it must be repaid, and as such, banks cannot use borrowed reserves to expand lending. In fact, the amount of reserves available for expanding lending is the balance of excess reserves minus borrowed reserves. This amount is the commercial bank's **free reserve**.

The aforementioned, whether it be the sale of securities or recovered loans on the asset side or the drawing of cash deposits or borrowing from the central bank or the interbank lending market on the liabilities side to manage liquidities, all of these methods will inconvenience the bank. So, generally speaking, banks will often hold an excess reserve in addition to the required reserve to meet depositor withdrawal demands.

(f) *Liabilities 4: Excess Reserves*

Suppose that in the very beginning, the bank's asset structure is such: a reserve of 30 million yuan, held securities of 45 million yuan, and loans of 145 million yuan. Its liabilities structure remains the same. As such, its balance sheet would be as follows:

Bank Balance Sheet When Holding 12 Million Yuan in Excess Reserves

Assets (10,000 yuan)		Liabilities (10,000 yuan)	
Reserves	3000	Deposits	18,000
Securities	4500	Central Bank Loans	1000
Loans	14,500	Interbank Loans	1000
		Owner Equity	2000
Total Assets	22,000	Total Liabilities	22,000

After a depositor withdraws 10 million yuan, its balance sheet would adjust as follows:

Bank Balance Sheet After Depositor Withdraws 10 Million Yuan

Assets (10,000 yuan)		Liabilities (10,000 yuan)	
Reserves	2000	Deposits	17,000
Securities	4500	Central Bank Loans	1000
Loans	14,500	Interbank Loans	1000
		Owner Equity	2000
Total Assets	21,000	Total Liabilities	21,000

After 10 million yuan in cash has been withdrawn, the bank's total assets and total liabilities would decrease to 210 million yuan. On the assets side, the reserve would decrease from 30 million yuan to 20 million yuan. On the liabilities side, apart from the decrease of 10 million yuan in deposits, other parts of the liability structure would remain unchanged. As you can see, as soon as 10 million yuan in cash has been withdrawn, the total 20 million yuan in reserves can still satisfy the 10% required reserve demand of 17 million yuan for 170 million yuan in deposits.

However, while holding this amount of excess reserves can conveniently meet liquidity demand, it is not without expense. Since the bank increases excess reserves by 10 million yuan, it causes both securities and loans to decrease by a corresponding 5 million yuan and therefore the holding of excess reserves will decrease the amount of the bank's earning assets. For this reason, regardless of which method is chosen to manage liquidity, each has its own strengths and weaknesses. As the saying goes, you cannot burn the candle at both ends.

8.4 Credit Risk Management

8.4.1 A Real Case of Student Loans

In 1999, Chinese commercial banks began to explore the student loan market. One bank had prepared to offer a student loan plan to all of the students at my university, with a maximum loan of 50,000 yuan. Subsequently, some of my classmates submitted an application to the bank for this loan. To apply for the student loan, the students had to wade through a range of trivial matters; the bank required not only a guarantor for the loan application, but also that the students submit their field of study, scores, academic achievements, and other proof. This bank, based on the evaluation of the applicant's materials and a credit scoring system, determined the amount of loan to the student. If the guarantor was a professor or a researcher, the rating would be higher than that when the guarantor was only a teaching or research assistant. The better the academic performance or achievements, the higher the credit score would be. After examining these various aspects, a considerable portion of loan applications were rejected by the bank. Although the line of credit was 50,000 yuan, the most that a student could obtain was only 20,000 yuan.

8.4.2 Credit Risk Management Strategies

The above example of student loans illustrates measures that commercial banks will take to manage credit risk. The primary means of managing credit risk used by commercial banks are: screening and monitoring, establishing a long-term relationship with customers, loan commitments, mortgages, compensating balances, credit rationing, and self-liquidating loans. As for mortgages and loan commitments, we have already introduced them in Chapter 2. Here, we will only look at the other credit risk management strategies.

(a) *Screening*

Before a bank grants a loan, it must evaluate a variety of aspects regarding the borrower so as to judge the borrower's willingness and ability to repay the loan and thereby distinguish the risk. Banks will not provide credit to every loan applicant. In the student loan example already discussed, before the bank would issue a student loan, it needed to evaluate the student's transcript, academic achievements, etc. These were all methods of examining the student's ability to repay the loan, by which the bank screened student loan applications.

Specifically speaking, bank credit reviews are in terms of 5C or 5P. 5C refers to: (1) Capacity to borrow. When banks issue loans, they will pay attention not only to the borrower's capacity to repay, but also to their legal capacity to borrow, such as when a bank lends to a partnership business, the consent of all partners is typically required. (2) Character which refers to the borrower's honesty, accountability and credibility as well as their strong desire to repay the loan. (3) Capital, the larger the amount of equity capital, the lower the likelihood of adverse selection and moral hazard as a result of borrowing when banks lend. (4) Collateral during loan issuance which reduces the risk of adverse selection, moral hazard, and their consequences. (5) Conditions of business, which refer to the borrower's operational management and profitability. In our example of student loans, banks examined the students' "operational" performance — grades and academic achievements. When examining an enterprise, banks will typically conduct a series of financial index analyses of the borrower, which is necessary to compare the borrower's financial indicators with other enterprises in the industry.

The so-called 5P includes: (1) Personal factor, as in the borrower's reputation and ability to repay the loan. (2) Purpose factor, as in whether or not the borrower's loan can be used to increase production. If the borrower's loan is used to purchase a lottery ticket or for gambling, the bank will not issue the loan. (3) Payment factor, as in whether or not the borrower's funds are self-liquidating by nature and how best to arrange the optimal repayment period. (4) Protect factor, as in loan collateral and safeguard measures for recovery of loans, such as requiring borrowers to provide a third-party guarantee. (5) Prospective factor, as in the evaluation of profits and risks in which the bank will require borrowers to analyze the project's goals and provide an estimate of future cash flows. As in the case of the student loan examination, the better that one's grades are, the better are their chances of finding a good job and the less likely that repayments will run into problems. This is the analysis of the prospective factor.

5C and 5P do not bear any significant differences and many of the factors which they examine are in fact the same. For example, the 5C capacity to borrow and character are in fact the personal factors of 5P. Similarly, the 5C conditions of business are the same as the 5P prospective factor.

(b) *Loan Specialization*

Loan specialization refers to when a bank offers loans mainly to local enterprises or enterprises within a certain industry. From the perspective of risk management, specialization goes against the principle of diversification. If a bank specializes in loans to petroleum enterprises, and the international price of petroleum so happens to take a nosedive, these loans will face a major risk. However, from another perspective, loan specialization is also very beneficial, because banks can utilize the advantages of specialization. When a bank offers these loans to a certain industry, they can better analyze enterprises within that industry, and thereby screen their credit better.

(c) *Credit Rationing*

Credit rationing refers to when a bank will reject a loan application entirely or partially and only meet a portion of the loan required by the borrower or not meet their needs whatsoever. In the student loan example, the applications of a large number of students were rejected by the bank. For those who received loans, even those with the highest credibility, the highest amount was only 20,000 yuan. This is the classical idea of credit rationing. The purpose of this rationing was to prevent adverse selection. The riskiest borrowers usually seek loans with higher interest rates more actively. For banks, despite the higher contract interest rate, these borrowers are high-risk and banks will not only receive no interest, but it may even be difficult for them to recover their principal. For this reason, banks must refuse the temptation of higher interest rates and not offer these kinds of loans.

(d) *Compensating Balance*

Compensating balances refer to when a borrower must keep an account at the lending bank with a percentage of the total loan capital, say, 10% of the total. If a bank issues a loan of 50 million yuan to some enterprises, it may require that they deposit a compensating balance of 5 million yuan in an account at the bank. As soon as the borrower defaults, the bank can utilize this 5 million yuan to compensate a portion of the loan loss.

Compensating balances function partially as a mortgage. Also, they help banks monitor their borrowers, especially when the bank can observe the changes in the borrower's cash flow to be aware of their payment activities and financial status. If the balance gradually drops, the bank can be alerted of the borrower's financial condition as well as any risks to the bank. Banks can then, according to this information, immediately further their understanding of the enterprise's information and avoid any larger losses.

Compensating balances, to some extent, raise loan interest rates. Suppose the loan interest rate is 8%, and a compensating balance is a current deposit account, and the interest rates drop, say, to zero. Since only 5 million yuan of the 50 million is a compensating balance, the enterprise only actually has 45 million, yet annual loan payments are still based on the 50 million yuan. So, in fact, the borrower pays 4 million yuan in interest, and as such, the actual loan interest rate is 8.89%.

(e) *Down-Payment Requirements*

When individuals apply for a home mortgage loan, banks typically will require a certain percentage for down-payment. If the down-payment percentage is 20%, when Wang Xiao'er applies for a home mortgage loan for a home valued at 500,000 yuan, the bank will require that he first pay 100,000 yuan. Afterwards, they will provide a loan of 400,000 yuan. In this way, if he happens to default, the bank will still have room to sell the mortgage and compensate for the amount of the loan outstanding. The higher the requirement for the down-payment, the weaker the adverse selection and moral hazard. If Wang Xiao'er purchases this home valued at 500,000 yuan, and his down-payment is 200,000 yuan, he will probably not default in the first year. This is because the bank has a lot of room to sell the balance of his home mortgage, and he may lose his 200,000 yuan. Apart from weakening a borrower's moral hazard, down-payment requirements will also automatically screen out those borrowers who do not have a certain income, because they have no means by which they can pay the down-payment, and thereby will naturally exclude them from the bank credit market.

(f) *Establishing a Long-term Relationship with Customers*

Banks can establish a long-term credit relationship with enterprises to obtain their related information and thereby benefit from the strengthened borrow monitoring and credit risk management of the enterprise. Say that an enterprise opens a current deposit account at China Merchants Bank and a fixed deposit account. China Merchants Bank can then examine changes to their cash flows, and through their settlements and loan payments, can understand their upstream suppliers and downstream distributors. If the company had previously borrowed from China

Merchants Bank, the bank would have a better understanding of the enterprise's ability to make payments as well as their credit standing. For this reason, establishing a long-term relationship with customers can reduce the costs of the bank to collect the enterprise's information.

If the enterprise ever happens to develop moral hazards after a long-term relationship has been established with the bank, the bank can stop issuing loans, and it may be very expensive for them to find new loans, even to the point where they have no means of getting loans when funds are short. For this reason, borrowers can lower their loan application costs if they establish a long-term relationship with a bank. To banks, maintaining a long-term relationship with customers can improve the opportunity costs of borrower default and will automatically lower the borrower's unexpected moral hazards.

(g) *Self-Liquidating Loans*

Another option for banks when controlling loan risks is self-liquidating loans on the trade chain. **Self-liquidating loans** are loans which are based on business activities and can be automatically paid off, and in which the bank controls the corporate cash flow and logistics of the borrower and the borrower's sales income serves as the first source of repayment. When borrowers receive payment for goods, it will automatically go towards paying off the loan. The duration of self-liquidating trade loans is short, they are highly liquid and the flow of cash and chain of trade are controlled by the bank. To the bank, this is a relatively safe way of issuing loans.

Although self-liquidating trade finance plays the important role of reducing credit risks for individual banks, it also has quite a few shortcomings which prevent it from becoming the banks' main form of credit. First, since the short-term credit of self-liquidating trade finance is based on actual transactions, if commercial banks were to blindly insist on self-liquidating trades as the only form of short-term business loan, then there would be no long-term loans available as they are not based on actual transactions, and self-liquidating trade loans would thus greatly limit the formation of capital to propel economic growth. Second, since consumer credit is not characteristically self-liquidating, based on the principle of self-liquidation, consumer credit would also have no room to develop which would truly weaken finance's ability to smooth consumers' life-cycle income. Third, in accordance with the self-liquidation principle, banks could only provide loans to enterprises with real sales. Those enterprises which primarily make purchases could not get loans. Because of this, the financeial system would lose its ability to adjust fund surplus and deficiency. Fourth, self-liquidating trade loans have a "fallacy of composition" which means that to the individual bank, self-liquidating loans are low-risk on paper, but to the entire bank, things are not quite what they seem. For instance, during recessions, if such banks insist that these loans must be repaid on time, borrowers may be unable to repay and will declare bankruptcy. In this sense, short-term assets or loans are not necessarily safer than long-term assets or loans. Fifth, although self-liquidating loans do expand or shrink depending on the needs of transactions, thus automatically adjusting money and credit, this kind of adjustment is pro-cyclic and may exacerbate cyclical economic fluctuations. If banks issue loans in accordance with business needs on an automatic scale, when the economy booms and trade increases, according to the self-liquidating principle, the credit that banks issue will automatically expand, which will stimulate the economy to the point of overheating and inflation. Conversely, when the situation worsens, in accordance with the self-liquidation principle, the amount of credit offered will automatically shrink, which may accelerate deflation and push the economy into a recession. Finally, self-liquidating trade finance also will exclude medium, small-scale, and high-tech enterprises from the credit market during their start-up. Since these enterprises do not have a real trading base in their start-up period, they have a larger uncertainty of business prospect, higher risks, and obviously do not meet the principles of a self-liquidating loan.

8.5 Interest Rate Risk Management

Commercial banks also face interest rate risks. **Interest rate risk** refers to a bank's potential losses that arise from market rate fluctuations. To manage interest rate risks, banks need to analyze them first of all. Analysis of interest rate risks is primarily in the form of sensitivity, gap, and duration analyses.

8.5.1 Sensitivity Analysis

Sensitivity analysis is when a bank's assets and liabilities are categorized into interest-rate-sensitive assets and interest-rate-sensitive liabilities, that is, assets or liabilities that are more likely to be affected by interest rate fluctuations in terms of their revenue or cost.

Suppose that a bank balance sheet is as follows:

Banks Balance Sheet

Assets (100 million yuan)		Liabilities (100 million yuan)	
Rate-Sensitive Assets	1500	Rate-Sensitive Liabilities	3500
Floating Rate Loans		Floating Rate Deposits	
Securities			
Fixed-Rate Assets	6500	Fixed-Rate Liabilities	4500
Reserves		Savings Deposits	
Long-Term Loans		Equity Capital	
Long-Term Securities			

This bank has 150 billion yuan of assets considered as interest-rate-sensitive because their rates will continuously change. The remaining 650 billion yuan are fixed-rate assets, because regardless of any changes to the economy, their interest rates will remain the same. On the liabilities side, the bank has 350 billion yuan in rate-sensitive liabilities, or rather floating-rate liabilities. The remaining 450 billion yuan is thus fixed-rate liabilities. Now suppose that the original annual interest rate on sensitive- and fixed-rate assets was 5% and the annual interest rate for sensitive- and fixed-rate liabilities was 4%, so that there is a one percentage point difference. If the interest rates on sensitive assets and liabilities both increase by two percentage points, how would this affect bank profits?

Before rates increase, the bank's profit would be as follows:

$$(150 + 650) \times 5\% - (350 + 450) = 8 \text{ billion yuan.}$$

Now that rates have changed, however, the bank's asset returns would adjust to:

$$650 \times 5\% + 150 \times 7\% = 32.5 + 10.5 = 43 \text{ billion yuan.}$$

After rates change, liability costs would be:

$$45 \times 4\% + 350 \times 6\% = 18 + 21 = 39 \text{ billion yuan.}$$

Profits after rates increase are then:

$$43 \text{ billion} - 39 \text{ billion} = 4 \text{ billion yuan.}$$

Due to a change in interest rates, the bank's profits drop from an original 8 billion yuan to 4 billion yuan.

Conversely, if the interest rates on sensitive assets and liabilities decrease by two percentage points, in that the rates drop from 5% to 3%, how would this then affect bank profits?

Given these conditions, asset returns after rates change would be:

$$650 \times 5\% + 150 \times 3\% = 32.5 + 4.5 = 37 \text{ billion yuan.}$$

Liability costs after rates change would be:

$$450 \times 4\% + 350 \times 2\% = 18 + 7 = 25 \text{ billion yuan.}$$

Profits after interest rates fall would then be:

$$37 \text{ billion} - 25 \text{ billion} = 12 \text{ billion yuan.}$$

In other words, after interest rates fall, profits would instead increase by 4 billion yuan.

As you can see, when interest-rate-sensitive liabilities are greater than interest-rate-sensitive assets, a lower interest rate will raise bank profits. Conversely, when interest rates rise, bank profits will fall.

On the other hand, when interest-rate-sensitive assets are greater than interest-rate-sensitive liabilities, what effect will rate changes have on a bank's profitability? Suppose that the abovementioned bank's balance sheet structure was as follows:

Bank Balance Sheet (Simplified)

Assets (100 million yuan)		Liabilities (100 million yuan)	
Rate-Sensitive Assets	3500	Rate-Sensitive Liabilities	1500
Floating Rate Loans		Floating Rate Deposits	
Securities			
Fixed-Rate Assets	4500	Fixed-Rate Liabilities	6500
Reserves		Savings Deposits	
Long-Term Loans		Equity Capital	
Long-Term Securities			

In this kind of balance sheet structure, if the interest rate does not change, the bank's profit will be 8 billion yuan.

If the interest rate on sensitive assets and liabilities rises by 2 percentage points, the bank's respective earnings on assets and liability costs will change as follows:

$$350 \times 75\% + 450 \times 5\% = 24.5 + 22.5 = 47 \text{ billion yuan.}$$

$$\text{and } 150 \times 6\% + 650 \times 4\% = 9 + 26 = 35 \text{ billion yuan.}$$

At this time, the profit would be $47 - 35 = 12$ billion yuan, an increase of 4 billion yuan when compared to the original amount.

Conversely, if the interest rates drop by 2% points, the bank's respective earnings on assets and liability costs will change as follows:

$$350 \times 3\% + 450 \times 5\% = 10.5 + 22.5 = 33 \text{ billion yuan.}$$

$$\text{and } 150 \times 2\% + 650 \times 4\% = 3 + 26 = 29 \text{ billion yuan.}$$

At this time, the profit would be $33 - 29 = 4$ billion yuan, a decrease of 4 billion yuan when compared to the original amount.

As you can see, when the interest-rate-sensitive assets are greater than the interest-rate-sensitive liabilities, if the market interest rate rises, bank profits will increase, and vice versa. When the interest-rate-sensitive assets are less than the interest-rate-sensitive liabilities, if the interest rates rise, it will lower bank profits, and vice versa.

8.5.2 Gap Analysis

A **gap** is the difference between interest-rate-sensitive assets and interest-rate-sensitive liabilities. In the first example above, interest-rate-sensitive assets are worth 150 billion yuan, interest-rate-sensitive liabilities are worth 350 billion yuan with a total gap of −200 billion yuan. By multiplying the gap by the variations in the interest rate, we can know the impact of interest variations to bank profits. If interest rates on assets and liabilities both increase by two percentage points, this bank's profit will decrease by 4 billion yuan, that is $-2000 \times 2\% = -40$. Conversely, if interest rates drop by two percentage points, we also can immediately know that the profits of this bank will increase by a corresponding 4 billion yuan.

8.5.3 Duration Analysis

Another method of measuring interest rate risk is the **duration analysis** of assets and liabilities. Duration analysis is a consideration of the impact on bank profits of the average duration of assets and liabilities when interest rates change. **Duration** is in fact the average time required for investors to recover their bond investment funds. It must be noted that duration and bond maturity are completely different concepts. To illustrate this concept of duration, we must first consider an example. Suppose that a bank issues a loan with a duration of five years with an annual interest rate of 8% paid once a year, and the face value of the loan is 1000 yuan. Upon maturity, one-off payment of principal and interest is required. The market value and face value of this loan are currently equal, and for this reason, the market interest rate is also 8%. Based on these conditions, we can come up with a future cash flow for this loan, as follows:

Nature of Cash Flow	Period (1)	Expected Cash Flow of Loans (2)	Present Value PV_t of (2) with 8% Market Interest Rate (3)	Period n when Cash Flow Received (4)	Present Value of Expected Cash Flow × Period (5)
Interest	1	80	74.07	1	74.07
	2	80	69.58	2	139.16
	3	80	63.51	3	190.53
	4	80	58.80	4	235.2
	5	80	54.44	5	272.2
Principal	5	1000	680.58	5	3402.9
Subtotal	—		≈1000		4314.06

Since the market value of this loan is 1000 yuan, the average time to recover this investment would be 4.314 years $\left(=\frac{4314}{1000}\right)$.

Even more generally, the market value of this bond (loans and deposits can also be seen as bonds) is P, the duration is D and the number of future cash flow periods is $t(t = 1, 2, \ldots, n)$, and the present value of each period of cash flow is PV_n. Based on the preceding table, we can come up with the general formula of duration:

$$D = \frac{\sum_{t=1}^{n} PV_n \cdot t}{P}. \tag{8.1}$$

This is Macaulay Duration. If we take this one step further, setting the nominal interest rate as r, the market interest rate as i, and the face value as V, and based on what we learned in Chapter 3, the above formula can be changed into:

$$D = \frac{\sum_{t=1}^{n} \frac{V\cdot r}{(1+i)^t} \cdot t + \frac{V}{(1+i)^n} \cdot n}{P}. \tag{8.2}$$

In fact, based on the bond value evaluations in Chapter 9, for interest-bearing debt, its price is P, thus:

$$P = \sum_{t=1}^{n} \frac{V \cdot r}{(1+i)^t} + \frac{V}{(1+i)^n}. \tag{8.3}$$

When the market interest rate changes by 1%, how much will the bond price change? In other words, what is the interest rate elasticity of bond price?

Interest rate elasticity of bond price is

$$\varepsilon = \frac{\mathrm{d}P}{\mathrm{d}i} \cdot \frac{i}{P}, \tag{8.4}$$

$$\frac{\mathrm{d}P}{\mathrm{d}i} = -\left[\sum_{t=1}^{n} \frac{V \cdot r}{(1+i)^{t+1}} \cdot t \frac{V}{(1+i)^{n+1}} \cdot n\right] = -D \cdot \frac{P}{1+i}, \tag{8.5}$$

$$\varepsilon = \frac{\mathrm{d}P}{\mathrm{d}i} \cdot \frac{i}{P} = -D \cdot \frac{i}{1+i}. \tag{8.6}$$

The next step is to find the percentage of bond price change:

$$\frac{\mathrm{d}P}{P} = -D \cdot \frac{\mathrm{d}i}{1+i}, \tag{8.7}$$

$\frac{\mathrm{d}P}{P}$ expresses the percentage change in the market price of the bond, $\frac{\mathrm{d}i}{1+i}$ expresses the rate of relative change in the market interest rate. This equation illustrates the negative correlation of bond price changes and interest rate changes after the market interest rate has changed. Percentage changes are equal to the duration multiplied by the rate of relative change in the interest rate. Furthermore, the longer the duration, the more sensitive the bond price is to interest rate changes, and bond prices fluctuations will grow exponentially with changes to the market interest rate.

Example: If the average duration of a certain bond is five years, and the market interest rate rises from 5% to 6%, what will be the percentage change in the market price of this bond?

$$\text{Based on the formula above: } \frac{\mathrm{d}P}{P} = -5 \cdot \frac{(6\% - 5\%)}{1 + 5\%} \approx -4.762\%.$$

Based on what we have learned, we know that we can put together this bank's assets and liabilities and consider what sort of impact interest rate changes will have on the net worth of this bank. Suppose that the assets of this bank were worth 100 billion yuan and the average duration was 5 years. Total liabilities were worth 90 billion yuan and the average duration was 3 years. And suppose that the initial market interest rate for their assets was 5%, and the initial market interest rate for their liabilities was 4.5%. Now, the market interest rate on assets has risen to 7% while the market interest rate on liabilities has risen to 6%. How will this affect the bank's net worth?

Net Worth of the Bank = Market Value of Assets − Market Value of Liabilities.

We know from this equation that before interest rates change, the bank's net worth is 10 billion yuan.

Based on how the changes to the price of bonds are related to changes in duration and interest rate, we can know that once the market interest has risen from 5% to 7%, the asset value has changed by:

$$-5 \cdot \frac{(7\% - 5\%)}{1 + 5\%} \approx -9.5238\%.$$

The market value of liabilities has changed by:

$$-3 \cdot \frac{(6\% - 4.5\%)}{1 + 4.5\%} \approx -4.3062\%.$$

As such, after the interest rates have changed, the total market value of this bank's assets is 90.4762 billion yuan, total market value of liabilities is 86.12442 billion yuan, and the bank's net worth is 4.35178 billion yuan, 5.7 billion yuan less than its original net worth.

Duration analysis illustrates that interest rate changes have a major effect on a bank's net worth.

8.5.4 Commercial Banks' Interest Rate Risk Management Strategies

After conducting sensitivity, gap and duration analyses, when expected interest rate changes may potentially bring losses to a bank, the bank manager will use corresponding strategies to manage or avoid interest rate risks. One interest rate risk management strategy is to adjust the duration of sensitive assets and liabilities. In our above example, since the average duration of interest-rate-sensitive liabilities dropped from four years to only one, the bank's profits thus change from a decrease of 13 billion yuan to a net increase of 8 billion yuan. The second option for interest rate risk management is interest rate hedging. Interest rate hedging is a payment flow swap arrangement between commercial banks whose interest-rate-sensitive assets are greater than interest-rate-sensitive liabilities and commercial banks whose interest-rate-sensitive liabilities are greater than interest-rate-sensitive assets, thereby reducing interest rate risks. This, in fact, is just another form of interest rate swaps. A third option for interest rate risk management is swap transactions on forward market or other options hedging arrangements. The advantage of these options is that transaction costs are lower than that of interest rate hedging, and their relative disadvantage is that these contracts are typically standardized and are difficult to be accurately divided or combined to meet the needs of the bank. As for swaps, hedging, and options, we will discuss these topics in detail when we discuss the derivatives market.

8.6 Asset Securitization and Bank Risk Management

Asset securitization is when a commercial bank will pool non-standardized loan assets together and subdivide them into standardized, negotiable securities assets. For example, a bank issues a large sum of home mortgages, each with a different maturity, amount and interest rate, and decides to collect them together into a standard securities asset with a duration of 10 years, each with a face value of 100 yuan and an interest rate of 6%. Then, the bank would sell these individual, standardized loans. In this way, banks can recover their principal in advance through loan asset securitization. Through transfer of the creditor's right, the risks of borrower default and interest rate volatility have also been transferred to the holders of the securitized assets.

Asset securitization first originated in America's securitization of home mortgages in the 1970s. By the 1980s, auto loans, credit card receivables, commercial leases and computer leases were all becoming securitized. China's asset securitization has also made important progress. In 2005, China Construction Bank branches in Shanghai, Jiangsu, and Fujian created an asset pool of 15,162 home mortgage loans and issued 3.017 billion yuan worth of mortgage-backed securities. China Development Bank created an asset pool of 51 loans from 12 industries and

19 regions for a public offering of 4.177 billion yuan in asset-backed securities. By the end of 2008, China had issued 55.1 billion yuan worth of asset-backed securities.

Summary

Commercial bank operations include balance-sheet business and off-balance-sheet business. Balance-sheet business includes asset and liability business. Commercial bank asset business primarily includes loans, investment, the purchase of foreign currency, etc. Liability business is primarily drawing deposits, borrowing from the central bank or other banks, issuing financial bonds or increasing capital. Off-balance-sheet business is primarily constituted by intermediary business and special off-balance-sheet business, which includes currency exchange, leasing, trusts, investment banking, derivatives, loan commitments, and so on.

Operational management of commercial banks primarily consists of asset management, liability management, liquidity management, and credit and interest rate risk management. Asset management finds a balance amongst profitability, liquidity, and safety. Liability management is when a bank must immediately and conveniently retrieve necessary funds and primarily consists of capital adequacy management. Commercial banks can meet liquidity needs through the recovery of loans, the sale of securities, central bank lending, interbank lending, drawing deposits or maintaining a certain amount of excess reserves, although the best methods are interbank lending, and holding a certain amount of excess reserves and government securities as a secondary reserve.

Commercial banks can adopt the following measures to control credit risk: screening and monitoring, establishing a long-term relationship with customers, loan commitments, mortgages and collateral, compensating balances, credit rationing, and self-liquidating loans. There are two basic methods of managing interest rate risks, namely gap analysis and duration analysis. For the transfer of credit risk and interest rate risk, loan securitization is a relatively useful method. Credit asset securitization is now growing in popularity in China.

Key Terms

Reserves; Excess Reserves; Securitization; Interest Rate Swap; Duration Analysis; Gap Analysis; Loan Commitment; 5C and 5P; Compensating Balance; Loan Specialization; Credit Rationing; Secondary Reserve; Borrowed Reserve; Off-Balance-Sheet Business; Intermediary Business; Self-Liquidating Loans; Borrowed Reserves; Refinancing; Primary Reserves; Free Reserve; Five-Tier Loan Classification System; Equity Capital; Regulatory Capital; Economic Capital

Critical Thinking Questions

1. What is the balance-sheet business of commercial banks?
2. What is the off-balance-sheet business of commercial banks?
3. What is the main content of a commercial bank's balance sheet? How can a balance sheet be used to analyze the activities of a commercial bank?
4. Explain the content of a commercial bank asset and liability management.
5. How do commercial banks conduct liquidity management?
6. What are credit risks? How do commercial banks manage credit risks?
7. What are interest rate risks? What methods and channels do commercial banks use to manage interest rate risks? What is the significance of loan securitization on commercial banks?
8. Suppose that a bank had 50 million yuan in fixed-interest-rate assets and 30 million yuan in interest-rate-sensitive assets, as well as 45 million yuan in fixed-interest-rate liabilities and 35 million yuan in interest-rate-sensitive liabilities. Use the gap analysis and explain how interest rates that have risen 3 percentage points will impact the earnings of this bank. What can the bank do to lower its interest rate risks?
9. Suppose that a bank has assets of 80 million yuan with an average duration of five years and liabilities of 70 million yuan with an average duration of four years. When the interest rate rises by 3% (the interest rate is the same for assets and liabilities), how will this impact the net worth of the bank?
10. Over the past 10 years, China's commercial bank holdings of Treasury bonds have never ceased growing. Why would this happen? With all else equal, suppose that the interest rates in the Treasury bond market face a declining trend. What would this do to commercial bank earnings? If all Treasury bond interest rates rise, what sort of risks would commercial banks run into? How could they manage these risks?
11. Go to any listed commercial bank's website and download their annual report. Look for a description of related risks and their management and provide a brief summary.
12. In 2005, China launched a series of short-term financing bonds (short-term bonds with a duration of less than one year). The interest rate on these bonds was much lower than that of bank loans. Briefly analyze the possible effect of the development of these short-term financing bonds on Chinese commercial banks. What should commercial banks do in response to them?

Chapter 9

Long-Term Capital Markets

Learning Objectives

After studying this chapter, you will be able to:

- Understand the role of long-term capital markets
- Understand financial instruments in long-term capital markets
- Understand various types of securities investment funds
- Clearly understand how stocks and bonds are issued
- Understand stock price indices and their types
- Understand yield to maturity and its calculation
- Understand the impact of dividends on stock prices
- Understand the efficient market hypothesis
- Understand securities market overreactions

The majority of those with surplus fund will purchase stocks or bonds on the capital market, while those with a shortage of funds will issue bonds or stocks on the capital market to raise funds. Thus, capital market is one of the most important parts of a modern financial system, and it relates to individuals, enterprises, and governments closely. In this chapter, we will introduce capital market fundamentals.

9.1 Long-term Capital Markets

Capital markets refer to financial markets in which the maturity of financial instruments is at least one year. Stock markets and medium- and long-term government bond markets are all long-term capital markets. Why are markets with more-than-one-year financial instruments called capital markets? This is because, generally speaking, in the space of one year, it is difficult for those with a shortage of funds to change the aggregate amount and structure of their fixed capital, and they cannot possibly change their production technology, so it is difficult to form an effective supply capacity. Only with more-than-one-year can enterprises use capital raised in financial markets to build new plants or to purchase new machinery.

Long-term capital markets are divided into primary markets and secondary markets. The **primary market** is the issuing market, the most basic function of which is to transfer capital from those with a surplus to those with a shortage in order to convert savings into investment. The issuance of stocks and corporate bonds by companies and Treasury bonds by the government are all completed on the primary market. The **secondary market** is the market for the circulation and transfer of financial instruments after their initial offering on the primary market. Since the secondary market improves the liquidity of these financial instruments, they greatly enhance people's willingness to hold these assets. If there is no highly liquid secondary market, primary market offerings would be very difficult. In the 1980s, because there was no secondary market in China, the liquidity of government bonds was poor, and there was little enthusiasm for the purchase of government bonds. In order to fulfill the government bond program, the Chinese government had no choice but to resort to compulsory allocation, which was an inefficient means of issuance. Meanwhile, the primary market is the basis of the secondary market; if there is no primary market for the issuance of financial instruments, the secondary market would be a fish out of water. The secondary market may also, in turn, affect the offering price in the primary market. For instance, when stock markets are acting rather bullish (a bull market), offering prices on new shares in the primary market will be higher. Conversely, when prices are expected to fall, enterprises have to offer new shares at a lower price.

Long-term capital markets, of course, can also be divided into stock and medium- and long-term bond markets. Stock markets are further divided into main board markets and growth enterprise markets (GEMs). Main board markets are markets for the issuance and trading of stocks of relatively large and well-established enterprises. GEMs are designed specifically for the issuance and trading of stocks of relatively small enterprises in their initial stage of development. The most famous GEM in the world is none other than the NASDAQ, through which countless enterprises have raised capital and gradually grown into large well-known companies. For instance, companies such as America's Microsoft and IBM or China's Sina, Sohu, Baidu, and so on have all been listed on the NASDAQ and are publicly traded. In 2009, China established its own GEM to promote the development of multi-level capital market. In addition, China also has a "Third Market", which stands for the "Agency Share Transfer System", providing a venue for circulation of stocks which cannot be listed on the Shanghai and Shenzhen Stock Exchanges. China's "Third Market" can also be divided into the "Old Third Market" and the "New Third Market". The Old Third Market is a venue for the trading of stocks issued by those companies which suffered losses for years and have been delisted from the Shanghai and Shenzhen Stock Exchanges. The New Third Market is established to provide stock market liquidity to more high-tech growth enterprises. Nowadays, the New Third

Market is primarily a share transfer system for the 2006 Beijing Zhongguancun Technology Park.

Medium- and long-term bond markets are also major capital markets, and as such, when we discuss the coordinated development of direct and indirect financing, do not narrowly understand this as simply the vigorous development of stock markets. In fact, the development of medium and long-term bond markets and stock markets are the necessary conditions for a sound financial system. Based on the different types of bond issuers, medium and long term bond markets can be divided into long-term government bonds market, corporate bonds markets, financial bonds markets, and so on. In accordance with the different terms of bond contracts, bond markets can be divided into common bond markets, convertible bond markets, hybrid capital bond markets, and so on.

9.2 Long-Term Capital Market Instruments

The primary instruments traded in the long-term capital market include: bonds, corporate stocks, securities, investment funds, etc.

9.2.1 Bonds

Bonds are certificates representing creditor–debtor relationship. Those who hold bonds are creditors while those who issue bonds are known as debtors. Suppose that you purchase 100,000 yuan worth of government bonds. In this case, you are the government's creditor, and the government is your debtor.

Based on different bond issuers, bonds on capital markets primarily include medium- and long-term bonds issued by the government, financial bonds issued by financial institutions, and corporate bonds issued by enterprises. As for individuals, people tend to be most familiar with government bonds. Governments, from time to time, issue a certain amount of government bonds, which can be divided into central government bonds (including bookentry government bonds and certificate government bonds) and local government bonds. At present, China's financial bonds are primarily issued by the policy banks and China Development Bank to commercial banks and institutional investors, which, in general, are not offered to individual investors. Besides, commercial banks often issue convertible bonds, subordinate bonds, or hybrid capital bonds (see Chapter 8) to meet the regulatory requirements on capital adequacy ratio. Those bonds can also be classified under financial bonds. Some of the large enterprises, such as China Three Gorges Corporation, Baoshan Iron & Steel Co., Ltd., China Power Investment Corporation, and China Unicom, have issued corporate bonds. In order to promote SME financing, China has also implemented a major innovation in terms of small- and medium-bond financing, such as the SME collective bonds, SME collective bills, SME private placement bonds, etc. SME collective bonds are issued by a collective of SMEs (usually 10 or more) and traded on the Shanghai (or Shenzhen) Stock Exchange. Such bonds have a single name and unified coupon rate, and each of the issuer respectively bears repayment obligations. SME collective bills are very similar to SME collective bonds in that they are issued by two or more SMEs and have a single name and coupon rate. These bills are traded on the Chinese interbank bond market and are paid out by each respective enterprise. SME private placement bonds are issued by SMEs to specific investors.

There is a special kind of corporate bonds known as convertible bonds. **Convertible bonds** can be converted into common corporate shares within a given period of time, in accordance with certain conditions and on a certain scale. The difference between convertible bonds and common bonds is that if investors think that corporate prospects are good, they do not require the issuer to pay principal upon maturity, but instead, the original cost of the bond will be converted into common corporate shares based on a certain percentage. Once convertible bonds are converted into common shares, original bond holders become shareholders of the company. Thus, convertible bonds are a way of providing investors with a right to choose.

Another special kind of bond is known as **corporate bond with attached warrant** (commonly referred to as **warrant bonds**). When bonds are issued, warrants are also provided to the holders, which entitle the holders with a right to subscribe to corporate stocks at an agreed price (strike price) within a certain period. Thus, warrant bond is a combination of bonds and warrants. Warrant bonds and convertible bonds are hybrid securities, and are a type of financing instrument somewhere in-between stocks and bonds, with the characteristics of both debt and equity financing. These warrant bonds can be divided into detachable and undetachable corporate bonds. As to detachable warrant bonds, warrants can be separated from corporate bonds, and thus can be traded independently in the market. As to undetachable warrant bonds, warrants cannot be separated from corporate bonds, have the same maturity as those bonds, and must be traded together. From the moment they are offered to the moment they are transferred, they shall not be separated. Unlike convertible corporate bonds, warrant bonds have the function of secondary financing, in that when a company issues these bonds, primary debt financing is achieved, and if later, the warrant holder subscribes to the company's stocks at an agreed price, the company achieves secondary equity financing. Jiangxi Copper Company once issued warrant bonds and raised 6.8 billion yuan from the issuance of bonds. At the same time, they gave bond holders a total of 1.7612 billion warrants, fixing that every four warrants could be converted into one share at 15.44 yuan. Upon the maturity of these warrants, their holders had mostly exercised their subscription rights, in that they purchased Jiangxi Copper stock at the agreed price, and Jiangxi Copper thereby raised another 6.743 billion yuan from the warrant financing.

9.2.2 Stocks and Depositary Receipts

Stock is a form of securities which is issued by limited joint-stock companies and held by investors and which represents owners' interests of the companies. Shares issued by Chinese enterprises can be divided into A-shares, B-shares, H-shares and N-shares. A-shares are issued by Chinese companies in the Chinese mainland, held by Chinese citizens, and traded on the Shanghai or Shenzhen stock exchange. B-shares are issued to foreign investors and traded on the Shanghai and Shenzhen stock exchanges. H-shares are issued by Mainland companies in Hong Kong and traded on the Hong Kong Stock Exchange. Finally, N-shares are issued by Chinese enterprises on the New York Stock Exchange. By buying B-shares, H-shares and N-shares, non-Chinese citizens outside of mainland China can directly invest in Chinese enterprises.

Suppose that a listed Chinese company wants to have a public offering on the New York Stock Exchange. In addition to N-shares, this company could also issue depositary receipts. **Depositary receipts** refer to the shares of a foreign company in a local stock market. In order to raise funds, most developing countries wish that their domestic companies can issue shares on the stock markets of developed countries. However, some developed countries, in order to protect the interests of domestic investor as well as the normal operation of their stock markets, regulate the listing of foreign companies. These companies must first deposit their shares into a bank or trust company of the country in which they wish to list their shares (this bank or trust company is a depositary institution). The depositary institution would then issue depositary receipts equivalent to the face value. In this way, depositary receipts are then traded on the stock exchanges of the given country. The world's most well-known depositary receipts are ADRs or American Depositary Receipts.

9.2.3 Securities Investment Funds

Securities investment funds are funds which are formed through pooling small amounts of money and are then used to invest in securities on a larger scale. Their most significant characteristic is revenue-sharing and risk-sharing. Revenue-sharing means that profits earned on the securities investment fund are shared by all fund holders. Risk-sharing means that losses on the securities investment fund are borne by all fund holders.

Based on whether or not fund shares can change during its duration, securities investment shares are divided into: closed-end securities investment funds and open-end securities investment funds.

Closed-end funds are securities investment funds which cannot be expanded or downsized during its duration. For instance, China Asset Management Co., Ltd. offered 3 billion shares of Kaiyuan Closed-end Fund with a duration of 15 years. During this 15-year period, fund holders could only trade shares of Kaiyuan Fund on the stock exchange during the trading hours, though the total number of shares of Kaiyuan Fund over the 15 years would remain at 3 billion. Over its duration, fund holders cannot redeem their shares and thus fund management companies are faced with very limited pressure of liquidity.

Open-end funds are investment securities funds which can change in scale during its duration. Suppose that you have purchased shares of Southern Growth Open-end Fund. You can visit the custodian bank to redeem your shares whenever you want. If you redeemed 100,000 shares, the fund would be reduced by 100,000 shares. In contrast, if you did not purchase shares, you can also go to the custodian bank to buy the shares of the fund. If you purchase 100,000 shares, the fund would increase by 100,000 shares. Open-end funds are different from closed-end funds in that the vast majority of open-end fund are not traded on the stock exchange. When cashing is needed, fund holders must go to the counter of the custodian bank to redeem the shares based on the net asset value for that given day. There is one kind of special open-end fund which can be traded like a closed-end fund and can also be purchased or redeemed at a fund management company. This is an **Exchange-Traded Fund**, or ETF for short. ETF is an indexation of investment instruments and invests in the constituent stocks of an index. For instance, the corresponding portfolio of the SSE 50 ETF is the component stocks of the SSE 50 Index, and the proportion of each stock is the same as their weight in the index. Relatively speaking, ETF investment portfolios are relatively transparent. Another type of open-end fund is the Listed Open-ended Fund, or LOF, which investors can either purchase or redeem shares at a designated outlet or they can also trade on the stock exchange.

Based on their various objectives, securities investment funds can also be divided into equity funds, bond funds, and hybrid funds.

Equity funds refer to the funds that invest the proceeds raised through the issuance of fund units into corporate stocks. **Bond funds** are funds which invest the proceeds raised through the issuance of fund units into corporate or government bonds. **Hybrid funds** are funds which invest in both stocks and bonds. The risks of hybrid fund are lower than those of equity funds, and their earnings are higher than bond funds. Relatively speaking, bond funds have steady earnings and low risks. The return on equity funds tends to fluctuate and the risks are higher, so when the stock market takes a downturn, many equity fund investors will suffer a huge loss of principal.

Based on the differences in the risks of fund investments, mutual funds are divided into growth funds, income funds and balanced funds.

Growth funds are mutual funds which pursue long-term capital gains. In order to achieve this objective, they mainly invest in corporate stocks with potential high-speed growth. Because these companies are in a period of rapid development, they rarely pay dividends. Meanwhile, their future is also incredibly uncertain and it is difficult to judge the sustainability of their rapid growth. As such, the risks of such funds are relatively high. **Income funds** are mutual funds which seek a fixed income, and as such, stress sustainability and a stable income. Thus, these funds primarily invest in government bonds, corporate bonds, and financial bonds. The greatest advantage of such a fund is the low risk of principal loss with a return slightly higher than term deposits. **Balanced funds** diversify their investments in equities and bonds in the hope of striking a balance between capital growth and a fixed income. More often than not, when an investment manager has a bearish outlook, it will lead to a strong bond investment ratio. When the market is relatively bullish, the fund will increase its investment in stocks. In theory, these funds should perform much better than growth funds during a stock market crash. On the other end, these funds will not perform as effectively as growth funds in a bull market.

9.3 Issuance and Trading of Long-Term Capital Market Instruments

9.3.1 Issuance of Long-Term Capital Market Instruments: Stocks and Bonds

If an enterprise wants to raise medium and long-term capital on stock or bond markets, they will need to issue stocks or medium- and long-term bonds. Enterprises primarily issue stocks through initial public offerings (IPOs) and seasoned equity offerings. Seasoned equity offerings, thus, are stock issuance by listed companies to raise capital. The issuance of long-term capital market instruments are organized by underwriters. In China, underwriting is carried out by securities companies providing investment banking services. Not all securities companies can carry out investment banking; only all-license securities companies can engage in securities underwriting.

Based on the different degrees of delegation and underwriters' responsibilities, underwriting can be divided into traditional underwriting, standby underwriting, and distribution.

Traditional underwriting is the most common form of underwriting for capital market issuance. The underwriters accept the issuer's full authorization, and bear the responsibility of selling all the financial instruments to the investors. Generally, underwriters buy all the issued stocks or bonds from the issuer in their name, and then sell them to the general public. If the quantity bought by the public is less than the issued, the remaining will be held by the underwriters.

In traditional underwriting, the price at which the capital market financial instruments are purchased by underwriters is typically lower than the price of public offering. The difference represents the fee paid by the issuer to the underwriter. In traditional underwriting, underwriters actually pay the issuers in advance all of the capital to be raised. As for the issuer, this can be a timely manner of raising funds. As for underwriters, the potential earnings on traditional underwriting are relatively high, yet if there is a loss upon issuance, they must bear the entire risk of such a loss.

In **standby underwriting,** the underwriters, who issue relevant financial instruments on behalf of the issuer, shall subscribe for all the remaining instruments if they are unsold within the specified period. The difference between standby underwriting and traditional underwriting is that under standby underwriting, underwriters are not required to advance their own funds to purchase stocks or bonds from the issuer all at once, instead, the issuer will only obtain the required capital after a stipulated time from the public offering. If there is an excess amount after the public offering, only then will the underwriter purchase the stocks or bonds that have yet to be sold. As such, to underwriters, they are not required to pay in advance the amount to be raised as they would have to for traditional underwriting.

Distribution refers to the situation in which the underwriter accepts the commission to undertake the duties of issuing bonds or stocks. In this way, underwriters will only issue bonds or stocks in the name of the issuer at an established price and do not commit to risks of losses during issuance. In case of a failed issue, the issuer cannot raise the needed capital in full. To the underwriter, the risks associated with this method of underwriting are relatively low.

In order to control the risk of failure, when one issues above a certain threshold, it is necessary to organize a syndicate for underwriting. An **underwriting syndicate** is composed of several securities companies and investment banks qualified for underwriting, which work as a group to underwrite a particular stock or bond. When an underwriting syndicate commits to underwriting stocks or bonds, there will also be a lead underwriter. The **lead underwriter** is responsible for the organization of other securities companies and investment banks involved in underwriting, as well as, in the issuance of stocks or bonds, information services, financial consultation, and other services for the issuer. An underwriting syndicate is a very loose organization, and when the issuance of a stock or bond is completed, the syndicate is automatically dissolved. When the underwriting syndicate needs to offer a different stock or bond, a different securities company will act as lead underwriter to organize the underwriting syndicate.

When underwriters or underwriting syndicates issue a company's stock or bond, it will be subscribed to by investors. Subscription indicates an investor's willingness to purchase a newly offered capital market instrument. When Bank of China issues new shares, if you do not participate in subscription, then you will not be able to purchase shares when the bank offers them. In this way, if you still intend to hold stocks of the bank, you must buy at the secondary market. When investors purchase from an initial offering, it is known as "shooting at the new shares".

Public bidding is often used for issuing bonds. When a bond is issued via public bidding, issuers notify the public about the period and volume of the bonds and invite qualified institutions to bid. Investors bid on the price or the rate. Issuers will then rank the investors in a certain sequence (from the higher price to the lower price or from the lower rate to the higher rate), until the bonds are sold out. During bidding, institutions do not know other bid prices and bid rates, and they offer their own prices and rates based on their market judgments, which ensures adequate competition between them. Public bidding is not only a good way to reduce the issuing costs and improve efficiency and shorten the issue time; more importantly, it forms the market rate for bonds, which is a very important step in improving the efficiency of the bond market.

Public bidding mainly includes American auction and Dutch auction. In **American auction**, issuers will give a bidding notice one week prior to issuing date and invite securities dealers, financial institutions, non-financial companies and other medium and small investors to submit their bids. There are two kinds of bids: competitive bids and non-competitive bids. Bidders shall state both the volume desired and price in competitive bids, while only volume in non-competitive bids. Large institutional investors, such as securities dealers and financial institutions, engage in competitive bids to sell the bonds at a higher price in the secondary market to earn a premium. Competitive bidders can offer several bids with different prices. However, to prevent monopoly by a few institutions, the volume which each competitive bidder applies for should be less than 35% of the total volume. A bid exceeding one million US dollars is competitive, otherwise it is non-competitive.

After receiving all sealed bids, issuers will accept all non-competitive bids first. The total volume, minus the non-competitive volume, will be distributed amongst competitive bidders. Issuers will rank the investors in sequence from the higher price to the lower price or from lower rates of yields to higher rates. Bidders with the highest price or the lowest rate win the bids. This continues until the bonds have been sold out. Thus, the highest priced bids will be accepted, and in accordance with the quoted prices, bidders will purchase the bonds. In this case, lower-priced bids will not be accepted. As for non-competitive bids, bidders will buy the newly issued bonds at the weighted average price of all the competitive bids.

The above is called American auction, the main feature of which is that the one who pays the highest price is the winner and different winners offer different prices.

In addition to American auction, there is also **Dutch auction**. In Dutch auction, although winners are still the bidders with the highest price, they pay the same weighted average price of the competitive bids. Therefore, all the winners pay the same price, which can encourage bidders to offer higher prices, and avoid the adverse effects of discriminatory pricing. But the problem is, bidding financial institutions, in order to win the tender, will compete to offer the lowest interest rate or the highest price, which might distort the market interest rate.

9.3.2 Secondary Market Trading of Stocks and Bonds

When an investor needs to convert their stocks or bonds to cash, or when they need to purchase other stocks or bonds, they must do so through transactions on the secondary market. Secondary market trading includes exchange transactions and over-the-counter (OTC) transactions. Exchange transactions are the purchase and sale of stocks or bonds on the Shanghai and Shenzhen Stock Exchanges. Chinese stocks are mainly traded on stock exchanges. In an exchange transaction, investors cannot only use their own capital to buy or sell securities, but also conduct **margin trading and short selling**. Margin trading and short selling is the trading of securities in the form of credit, that is, the buying or selling of securities is based on the credit granted by securities companies where the investor's credit trading account is opened. The **margin trading** refers to the borrowing of funds to buy securities when an investor believes that securities prices will rise but does not have enough money on hand and thus borrows from the Shanghai or Shenzhen Stock Exchange member securities companies by providing collaterals. **Short selling** refers to the activity that investors believe the prices of securities will drop and then borrow such securities from the securities companies at which their credit trading accounts are opened and then sell them. Margin trading and short selling are the equivalents of long position and short position abroad.

In addition to exchange transactions, there are also many **OTC transactions**. OTC trading is a general term for various securities trading activities that are not conducted on the floor of the stock exchange. Prior to the establishment of the Shanghai and Shenzhen Stock Exchanges, the trading of stocks issued by several Chinese companies was in the form of OTC transactions. In fact, the aforementioned "Third Market" for Chinese stocks is also an OTC market. OTC transactions resolve the liquidity problems of those investors who purchase stocks of companies not listed on the stock exchange, and because they greatly improve the liquidity of these securities, they facilitate the issuance and exchange of shares of those companies which cannot meet the requirements to be listed on the stock exchange but need to raise capital. Nowadays, the world's most famous OTC market is the NASDAQ. Many companies which were still in their start-up phase have been listed on the NASDAQ. Since these companies are only in their start-up, their prospects for development are uncertain and the scale of their assets is relatively small, so they naturally cannot meet the requirements to be listed on the stock exchange. However, through listing on the NASDAQ, the capital requirements of these start-up companies can be met. Of these companies, many have developed into some of the world's most famous enterprises. For example, Microsoft, Intel and others are all listed on the NASDAQ.

China's bond trading is also divided into exchange transactions and OTC transactions. The exchange trading of bonds refers to the purchase and sale of government bonds and corporate bonds on the Shanghai and Shenzhen Stock Exchanges.

While the market is open, investors can purchase and sell exchange-traded bonds on the stock exchange. China's OTC bond market can also be divided into the interbank bond market and the OTC market. The interbank bond market refers to a market in which only participating financial institutions can make transactions. Initially, this market was completely as its name would suggest, and only commercial banks could participate. However, nowadays even though it is still called an "interbank" market, since 2000, securities companies, fund management companies, and insurance companies can participate in bond trading on the interbank market as long as they meet the requirements. The volume of interbank bond market transactions is much larger than that of exchange transactions. Of course, not all bonds are traded on the stock exchange or on the interbank market. Some bonds can only be traded through OTC transactions. **OTC transactions** refer to securities trading that occurs on the counter of a securities company or at a bank. These securities which are traded on the OTC market are issued in compliance with the Securities Trading Law but are not listed at the stock exchanges, and their trading price is determined through bargaining. Also, transactions are limited to spot transactions. Since banks and securities companies have many branches, all you have to do is to walk over to your closest savings office or the business department of a securities company qualified for OTC trading, and you can engage in OTC transactions of certain bonds.

9.3.3 Capital Market Price Index

Within a single trading day, capital market transactions of various financial instruments will raise some prices and lower others, while others will be unchanged (in which the current trading price is the same as the previous day's closing price). So, how does one determine a rise or decline in the stock or bond market on the whole? The capital market price index provides a convenient basis for such an assessment. A capital market price index is a statistical indicator which reflects the overall secondary market price changes of capital market instruments, including stock price indices, bond price indices, and fund indices. These indices can be further subdivided. For instance, a bond index can be divided into government bond indices, corporate bond indices, etc. At this point, we will introduce stock price indices to illustrate a capital market price index.

A stock price index refers to either a composite index or a component index. A composite index refers to an index that covers all the shares of listed companies. In China, this would be the Shanghai Stock Exchange (SSE) Composite Index and the Shenzhen Stock Exchange (SZSE) Composite Index (Figure 9.1). A component index is on a selective basis and is calculated based on a sample of selected stock prices. The Shanghai and Shenzhen stock exchanges both have component indices. The SSE 180 launched by the Shanghai Stock Exchange in 2002 is a typical component index, which selects the stock prices of 180 representative companies listed

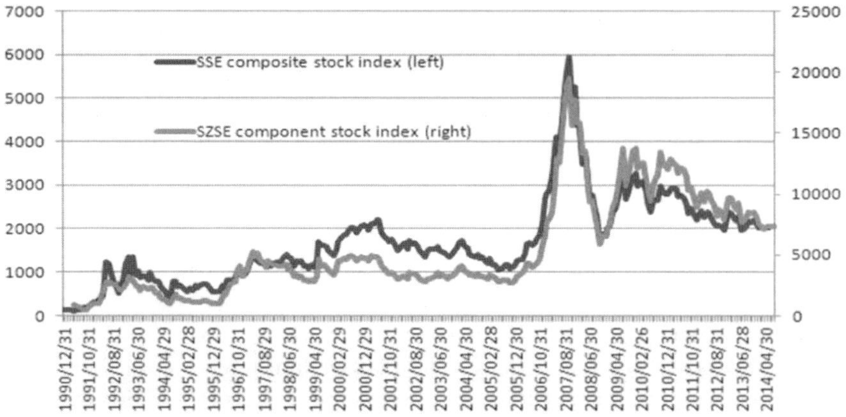

Fig. 9.1 SSE Composite Index and SZSE Component Index

Source: *The People's Bank of China Quarterly Statistical Bulletin*, and the website of the China Securities Regulatory Commission

on the Shanghai Stock Exchange. In addition, there are also a number of industrial stock price indices, such as real estate stock index, commercial retail index, and manufacturing industry stock index.

Stock price indices are of great significance to investors and governments alike, as they are a "barometer" of the economy. In general, when the macroeconomic situation is good, stock price indices will rise, and vice versa. Changes in a stock price index are known as a "trend", that is, the overall trend of the stock market. If stock price indices continue to decline, and the trading volume is gradually declining, then it is a "bear market". A bear market is a very undesirable trend for any market. In a bear market, it is quite difficult for investors to realize spread gains from spot trading in the secondary market. On the other hand, if stock price indices continue to rise, and the trading volume is growing, it is a "bull market". If stock price indices rise quickly and significantly, with very active turnovers, this kind of market condition is known as a "big bull market". Whether you are an investor or a manager, bull markets are always a great thing.

9.3.4 Mutual Fund Purchases and Cashing

Suppose that you have 100,000 yuan of spare cash to purchase a fund, and go to "financial experts" in hopes of getting some earnings. How can you convert your cash into a mutual fund? Or, conversely, if you hold 100,000 shares of a mutual fund, how can you convert it into cash?

The answer depends on what you would like to purchase or hold, a closed-end fund or an open-end fund. Closed-end funds are similar to stocks and are traded on the stock exchange. As long as the Shanghai or Shenzhen Stock Exchange is open, you can use your 100,000 yuan to purchase a closed-end fund, or you can exchange your 100,000 shares of a closed-end fund for cash.

Open-end funds, however, are different. In addition to listed open-end funds, most open-end funds cannot be traded on the market. When you need to invest your 100,000 yuan in a particular open-end fund, you can go to the distribution outlet to purchase, or on the contrary, if you want to have your 100,000 shares of the open-end fund converted into cash, you can also go to the distribution outlet for redemption. In general, open-end funds are subscribed based on the amount of money and are redeemed based on the number of shares. Amount subscription refers to the amount of money which investors have applied for, rather than the number of shares. For example, when you offer to buy 100,000 yuan of an open-end fund, you have not actually purchased 100,000 shares of the open-end fund. If, at the close of a stock or bond market, you would like to purchase funds at a net asset value of 2 yuan per share, not taking into account subscription fees, you can purchase 50,000 shares of an open-end fund. Share redemptions, however, are based on the number of shares at the time investors sell their funds and not based on the amount. For instance, you may plan to sell 100,000 shares of an open-end fund and not sell 100,000 yuan worth of an open-end fund. Similarly, if the stock exchange has already closed, and say you hold open-end shares at a net asset value of 2 yuan per share, then, not taking into account redemption fees, you could have 200,000 yuan in funds. But in fact, whether or not you purchase funds or redeem them, there will generally be a fee that must be paid.

Since open-end funds use amount subscriptions and share redemptions, the amount of subscriptions and the shares of redemptions are typically determined based on the unknown net asset value of the fund for the current day. Why is trading based on the current unknown net asset value rather than the known net asset value of the previous day of trading? The main reason for this approach is in the principle of fairness. Assume that the net asset value of the fund you subscribe for or redeem is 2 yuan on December 1. Suppose again that the stock market soars on December 2, and as such, the net asset value of the fund also rises so that each share is worth 2.2 yuan. If an investor purchases a unit of the fund on December 2 in accordance with the net asset value of 2 yuan on December 1, and perhaps sells that unit on December 3 based on the net asset value of 2.2 yuan on December 2, he could earn a gross profit rate of 10%. Similarly, if the market crashes on December 2, and the net asset value of each share is 1.8 yuan, investors would flock to the fund management company and request for redemption based on the net asset value of December 1, or 2 yuan per share. This would push the fund management company into immediate liquidity difficulties. However, if subscriptions and redemptions are based on a yet unknown net asset value, fund management companies can avoid this kind of arbitrary behavior.

As for listed, open-end funds, investors can either choose to purchase or redeem at a bank or other distributors based on the net asset value of the fund at the close of the current day or choose to trade these fund shares on the stock exchange based on a matchmaking price. As for ETFs, investors can either trade these fund shares on the secondary market or purchase or redeem funds from the fund management company. It must be noted that the purchase and redemption of ETFs is the transactions between fund shares and a basket of stocks, which is very different from LOFs, the purchase and redemption of which is a transaction between fund shares and cash.

9.4 Capital Market Bond Valuation

9.4.1 Discount Bonds and Coupon Bonds

Based on the different means by which interest is paid, bonds can be divided into discount bonds and coupon bonds. **Discount bonds** are honored by the issuer based on the face value of the bond upon maturity, yet prior to its maturity, the market price is lower than its face value. If two-year discount bonds with a face value of 100 yuan were issued at a price of 90 yuan, then, upon maturity, the issuer would pay 100 yuan. The difference between the face value of the bond and its market price is the interest paid to investors by the bond issuer.

Coupon bonds are the bonds for which the issuer promises, at the time of issuing bonds, to pay interest at a certain rate and repay principal to the bond holder in the future. Coupon bonds provide a coupon rate and interest is typically paid annually. If a company issues five-year coupon bonds at a face value of 100 yuan and at a coupon rate of 5%, then, during these five years, bondholders can earn 5 yuan of interest each year. After 5 years, these bonds reach maturity and bondholders can receive a principal repayment of 100 yuan.

Over these five years, cash flows for those who hold this coupon bond would be as follows:

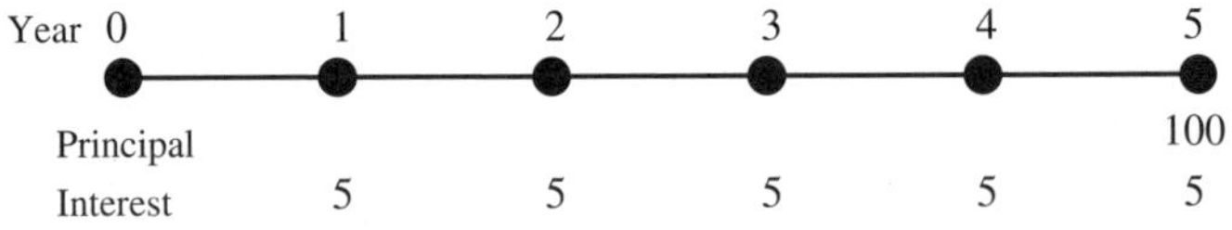

9.4.2 Valuation of Discount Bonds

Discount bond prices are determined by market competition. In general, the market price of a discount bond will be lower than its face value, and the portion below the face value is interest. For this reason, bond investors can calculate annual interest rates of a discount bond based on the market price, remaining time to maturity and face value of the bond.

First, we will look at the following two examples.

Example 1: Suppose that a company has issued a one-year discount bond with a face value of 100 yuan and an issue price of 95 yuan. What is the interest rate?

The interest rate of this discount bond is calculated as follows:

Annual interest rate of one-year discount bond
$$= (\text{the face value} - \text{price})/\text{price} = (100 - 95)/95 = 0.0526.$$

That is, the annual interest rate is 5.26%.

Example 2: Suppose that a company has issued a three-year discount bond with a face value of 100 yuan and an issue price of 80 yuan. What is the annual interest rate?

If we set the rate at i, cash flows of the bond over the three years would be as follows:

Total principal with interest at the end of the first year: $80 \times (1 + i)$.

Total principal with interest at the end of the second year: $80 \times (1 + i)^2$.

Total principal with interest at the end of the third year: $80 \times (1 + i)^3$.

Discount bonds are repaid at face value, and as such, after three years, the total principal with interest would be equal to the face value:

$$80 \times (1 + i)^3 = 100.$$

Giving us: $i = 7.72\%$.

More generally, if we set P as the current market price for discount bonds, V for its face value, n as the remaining years before maturity, and i as the annual interest rate prior to maturity, then:

$$i = \sqrt[n]{\frac{V}{P}} - 1. \tag{9.1}$$

9.4.3 Valuation of Coupon Bonds

In general, market prices for discount bonds are lower than their face value, and if its market value is higher than its face value, bond holders would not have interest but may have to pay the issuer a certain sum. However, the market price of coupon bonds may be equal to their face value, then again, they may be higher or lower than their face value. When the face value of an coupon bond is the same as its market price, this is what we call a **par bond**; when the market price of an coupon bond is higher than its face value, we call it a **premium bond**; conversely, when the market price of a bond is less than its face value, we call it a **discount bond**.

Why is there such a relationship between the market price of a coupon bond and its face value? This is determined by the relationship between the coupon rate and the market rate. When the market interest rate is equal to the coupon rate, the market price will be equal to its face value; and when the market rate is higher than the coupon rate, the market price will be lower than its face value. Conversely, when the market rate is lower than the coupon rate, the market price will be higher than its face value.

Let us cite a simple example. Suppose that a company has issued a one-year coupon bond at face value of 100 yuan and a coupon rate of 6%. In other words, one year after you purchase such a bond, you can convert it for 106 yuan. Now suppose that the market interest rate is 5%. In this case, what should the price be? As we learned in Chapter 3, with interest rate of 5%, the total principal and interest should be 106 yuan. Thus, if we set the bond price as P:

$$P(1 + 5\%) = 106.$$

Which gives us: $P \approx 100.95$ yuan.

Question: When the market interest rates are 6% and 8%, what should the price of these bonds be, respectively?

However, in most cases, we will calculate a bond's yield to see if it is good investment. If a company issued a five-year coupon bond last year with a face value of 100 yuan and a coupon rate of 6%, and its current market price is 102 yuan, how would you calculate its value and yield?

When assessing the value of coupon bonds, there are primarily two indicators, namely:

- Current Yield
- Yield to Maturity

The current yield is the interest paid each year to bondholders divided by the current market price of the bond. The current yield for the above coupon bond would be:

$$\text{Current yield} = \text{Amount of interest/current market price}$$
$$= 6/102 \times 100\% = 5.88\%.$$

The **yield to maturity** is the annual discount rate at which the present value of interest paid in each year of the remaining period of bonds and face value of bonds equal the current market price. The remaining period is the time interval between the current period and the maturity of the bond, which is typically expressed in years. In the example above, the remaining period for the bond is 4 years.

How would you calculate the yield to maturity for such a coupon bond?

If we set the yield to maturity of this bond as r, the amount of interest earned over the next 4 years is 6 yuan and the face value is 100 yuan. As such, when the discount rate is r, the present value of future interest and the face value will be:

$$\frac{6}{1+r}+\frac{6}{(1+r)^2}+\frac{6}{(1+r)^3}+\frac{6}{(1+r)^4}+\frac{100}{(1+r)^4}=\sum_{t=1}^{4}\frac{6}{(1+r)^t}+\frac{100}{(1+r)^4}.$$

In accordance with the definition of yield to maturity:

$$102=\sum_{t=1}^{4}\frac{6}{(1+r)^t}+\frac{100}{(1+r)^4}.$$

Thus, the yield to maturity r for this bond is 5.85%.

In general:

n is the remaining period of the bond.
r is yield to maturity for the coupon bond.
V is the face value of the coupon bond.
i is the coupon rate of the coupon bond.
P is the current market price of the coupon bond.

Thus, we can calculate yield to maturity for this bond based on the following formula:

$$\sum_{t=1}^{n}\frac{V\cdot i}{(1+r)^t}+\frac{V}{(1+r)^n}=P. \tag{9.2}$$

The coupon rate, current yield, and yield to maturity for the coupon bond in the example above have the following relationship:

Yield to maturity (5.85%) $<$ Current yield (5.88%) $<$ Coupon rate (6%).

Is this an accident? Not so; the yield to maturity, current yield and coupon rate of any premium coupon bond will bear this relationship.

Question: What is the relationship between the yield to maturity, current yield, and coupon rate of discount bonds and par bonds?

When the same bond issuer issues bonds with different maturities and the yield to maturity is plotted along the same axis, we can obtain the **yield to maturity curve**. Of these two axes, the vertical axis represents the yield to maturity for the various remaining periods prior to maturity while the horizontal axis represents the remaining periods prior to maturity. Figure 9.2 is a yield to maturity curve for Chinese government bonds with 12 periods.

In general, yield to maturity curves are upward sloping, indicating that the longer the remaining period, the higher the yield to maturity. For bond investments, yield to maturity curves can be a very useful tool for analysis. If a yield to maturity curve is fairly smooth, and investors want to take on even a slight increase in

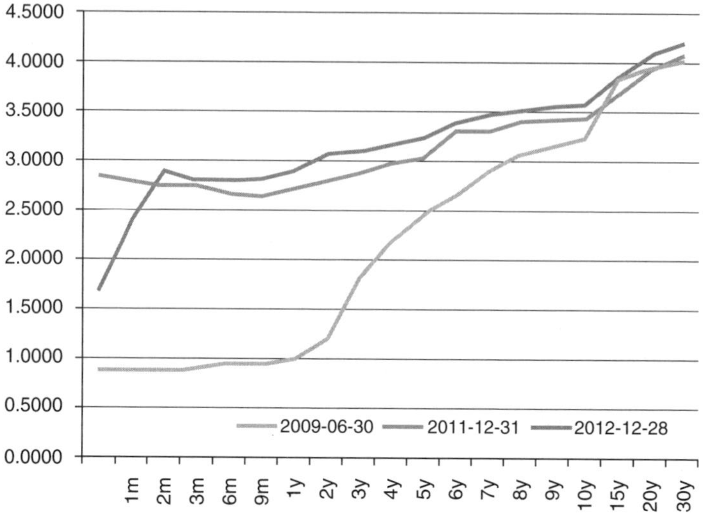

Fig. 9.2 Yield to Maturity Curve of Chinese Government Bonds with Selected 12 Maturities
Source: Wind

their yield, they must take on a large risk. In accordance with the "expectation theory" of interest rate structures in Chapter 15, a flat yield curve suggests that short-term interest rates may fall. On the other hand, a steep yield curve suggests that short-term interest rates are likely to rise.

9.5 Stock Valuation

9.5.1 Price–Earnings Ratio and Price-to-Book Ratio

The **price–earnings ratio** is an indicator often used in stock valuation and refers to the ratio of the market price of stock to the earnings per share in the current period. For example, on June 3, 2002, the closing price of a stock was 12 yuan and the earnings per share was 0.4 yuan. Thus, the current price–earnings ratio was 30.

The reason as to why the price–earnings ratio is such an important indicator in stock valuation lies in the fact that when earnings per share remain the same, the ratio represents the time it takes for the investors to recover their investment by completely relying on cash dividends. The higher the price–earnings ratio, the longer it will take for investors to recover their invested capital. Conversely, the lower the price–earnings ratio, the sooner will investors be able to recover their investment.

By adding up the market price and earnings per share of each stock in the market according to their weights, you can calculate the average price–earnings ratio of the market. The level of the average price–earnings ratio is a key direct indicator of the soundness of market. A high price–earnings ratio indicates that stock prices have seriously deviated from their intrinsic value, which will result in a bubble. When earnings per share of listed companies cannot rise any further to remove the bubble in the stock market, the only way is through a compulsory downward adjustment of the stock prices. The cost of such adjustments is high for both investors and the national economy. For market participants, the wealth redistribution function of market price will cause a continuous depreciation of wealth through stocks. Such microstructural changes, in turn, may affect the macroeconomy.

Another important indicator which corresponds to price–earnings ratio is the **price-to-book ratio**, which is the ratio of stock price to the net assets per share. If a company's stock price is 10 yuan, and book value per share is 5 yuan, then the price-to-book ratio is 2. Sometimes, the price-to-book ratio can serve as an important benchmark for investment analysis. In general, stocks with a relatively low price-to-book ratio will have a relatively higher investment value, with smaller price fluctuation and lower risks correspondingly, and vice versa. In the extreme case, if a company's stock price is lower than the net assets per share, this means that the company's higher valued net assets can be purchased at a relatively low cost. In this case, there is a high likelihood for an external acquisition. If the market makes a prediction based on this, the stock price of the company with extremely low (even less than 1) price-to-book ratio will rise, thereby indicating a profitable opportunity for potential investors.

9.5.2 Dividend Discount Model

Another method of assessing stock prices is the dividend discount model. This stock valuation model is, in fact, none other than the present value formula which we learned in Chapter 3.

(a) *Zero Growth Dividend Discount Model*

P is the price at which stock is purchased;
n is the period for holding stocks, expressed in years;
$E_1, E_2, \ldots, E_n$ are the future earnings per share in different periods;
P_n is the price at which stock is sold after n years;
i is the market interest rate, greater than zero.

In accordance with the analysis in Chapter 3, the current purchase price of stock is the present value of the selling price of the stock in year n and the earnings per share during each of the upcoming years, that is:

$$P = \frac{E_1}{(1+i)} + \frac{E_2}{(1+i)^2} + \cdots + \frac{E_n}{(1+i)^n} + \frac{P_n}{(1+i)^n}. \tag{9.3}$$

For convenience, we assume that the annual earnings per share are all the same:

$$E_1 = E_2 = \cdots = E_n.$$

Thus:

$$P = \frac{E}{(1+i)} + \frac{E}{(1+i)^2} + \cdots + \frac{E}{(1+i)^n} + \frac{P_n}{(1+i)^n}. \tag{9.4}$$

The first half of Equation (9.4) is based on $\frac{1}{1+i}$ as a common ratio of a geometric progression. Based on the summation formula for geometric progression, then:

$$P = \frac{E}{i} \cdot \left[1 - \frac{1}{(1+i)^n}\right] + \frac{P_n}{(1+i)^n}. \tag{9.5}$$

If n is infinite, we would reach the following limit:

$$P = \frac{E}{i}. \tag{9.6}$$

In other words, the stock price is equal to the company's earnings per share divided by the market interest rate. This is the zero growth dividend discount model.

We can use specific examples to illustrate. Suppose that the current earnings per share of the company Heaven Creation are one yuan and the future earnings per share will be maintained at this level. The current market interest rate is 8%. What is the market price of their stocks?

We can take advantage of the zero growth dividend discount model to calculate their stock price:

$$P = \frac{1}{8\%} = 12.5.$$

That is, the stock price of Heaven Creation should be 12.5 yuan.

(b) *Constant Growth Dividend Discount Model*

Now assume that a company's earnings per share grow by a certain percentage each year. The annual growth rate of earnings per share is g, and the stock price when the earnings per share keeps growing is P_g, giving us:

$$P_g = \frac{E}{(1+i)} + \frac{E(1+g)}{(1+i)^2} + \cdots + \frac{E(1+g)^{n-1}}{(1+i)^n} + \frac{P_n}{(1+i)^n}. \tag{9.7}$$

Based on the geometric progression summation formula:

$$P_g = E \cdot \frac{1 - \left(\frac{1+g}{1+i}\right)^n}{i - g} + \frac{P_n}{(1+i)^n}. \tag{9.8}$$

If $g > i$, that is, the growth rate of earnings per share is higher than the market rate, then $\frac{1+g}{1+i} > 1$ so that when n is infinite, $\left(\frac{1+g}{1+i}\right)^n$ would be approaching infinity, and stock prices would also move towards infinity. If this is indeed the case, even if your initial investment was only 1 cent, because the stock price keeps rising, you too will become one of the super-rich. Unfortunately, such an opportunity is like looking for a needle in a haystack.

When $g < i$, that is, the growth rate of earnings per share is below the market interest rate, and when n is infinite:

$$P_g = \frac{E}{i - g}. \tag{9.9}$$

That is, the stock price is equal to the earnings per share divided by the difference between the market interest rate and the earnings per share growth rate.

After a brief comparison, you will find that when the earnings per share grows, so too shall the stock price. How much will it rise?

$$\frac{P_g - P}{P} = \frac{\frac{E}{i-g} - \frac{E}{i}}{\frac{E}{i}} = \frac{g}{i - g}. \tag{9.10}$$

Equation (9.10) shows that even if the growth rate of earnings per share is below the market rate, as long as g gradually approaches the market interest rate i, stock price growth is unlimited. This is why the stock price of businesses under restructuring will double, because one would expect that corporate restructuring will cause an improvement in the earnings per share.

Let us look again at several examples. Heaven Creation's current earnings per share is one yuan, and it is expected that the company's annual growth rate for future earnings per share will be 6%. The current market rate is 8%. What should the stock price be?

We can take advantage of the constant growth dividend discount model to calculate their stock price:

$$P_{\substack{\text{Heaven}\\\text{Creation}}} = \frac{1}{8\% - 6\%} = 50 \text{ yuan}.$$

(c) *Stock Price when the Company Uses Surplus for Reinvestment*

Not all profits of listed companies are distributed to shareholders. Prior to the payment of dividend, the management may set aside a portion of profits to expand the company's production. If we set the earnings per share as E, and the portion of retained profits which the company sets aside for reinvestment as h, then the actual earnings per share for shareholders is $E \cdot (1 - h)$. The expected return on reinvestment is r, and the market interest rate is i. Under these conditions:

The initial earnings per share distributed to shareholders is then:

$$E \cdot (1 - h). \tag{9.11}$$

The growth rate of earnings per share:

$$g = h \cdot r. \tag{9.12}$$

These variables are substituted into the growth dividend discount model to find the market price when listed companies retain a portion of profit for reinvestment:

$$P_h = \frac{E \cdot (1 - h)}{i - h \cdot r}. \tag{9.13}$$

Assume the management of Heaven Creation decides to retain 30% of earnings per share for business expansion, and the remaining 70% are distributed to shareholders. The return on reinvested capital is 20%, and the market interest rate is 8%. Then,

The earnings per share distributed to shareholders for the first year:

$E = 1 \times 0.7 = 0.7.$

The growth rate of dividend: $g = 0.3 \times 20\% = 6\%$.

Therefore, in this case the company's stock price is:

$$P_h = \frac{0.7}{8\% - 6\%} = 35.$$

In other words, based on the given conditions, the company's stock price should be 35 yuan. When a portion of the company's earnings per share are used for re-investment purposes and the company gains a certain return on the reinvestment, its stock price will be higher than that in the first case when all profits are distributed to shareholders, although, in this case, Heaven Creation had originally only distributed 0.7 yuan of earnings per share to its shareholders. The reason why the stock price is higher in this case is not simply the growth in Heaven Creation's future earnings per share but also the return on the re-investment which is higher than the market interest rate.

(d) *How useful is the dividend discount model for calculating the future value of stocks?*

In reality, we can learn a lot when we make decisions for investment. For example, you can know the current market interest rate and the earnings per share for listed companies as well as their current stock prices. We will consider this current market price as a real price. In turn, the market price which we obtain from the dividend discount model is a theoretical price. Since you know these variables, you have already been provided with convenient tools for your investment decisions. For example, if you divide the current earnings per share of a listed company by current market rate, you can obtain the theoretical price of their stocks. Then, you can compare this price with the real price. For example, Heaven Creation's earnings per share is one yuan, and the current market interest rate is 8%. Thus, the stock price calculated by the dividend discount model should be 12.5 yuan. However, if you observe that the current price is actually only 10 yuan, can you come to the conclusion that if you purchase the company's stocks at the real price, as long as you wait until a certain date, you will earn 2.5 yuan?

The answer is: investment decision-making is not as simple as this. In fact, when calculating stock prices, the constant growth dividend discount model is the most appropriate one, rather than the zero growth dividend discount model. There are three fundamental factors which affect stock prices in the constant growth dividend discount model: the growth rate of future earnings per share g, market rate i, and the current earnings per share E. Of these three basic factors, only the current earnings per share is known for sure, while the other two factors are uncertain. Will Heaven Creation's future earnings per share maintain a growth rate of 6%? Will future market rate remain at 8%? There is no way to know.

So, any factors which affect Heaven Creation's future earnings per share growth rate and market rate will impact its stock price. The macroeconomic environment, the demand for Heaven Creation's products, Heaven Creation's suppliers and distributors, its capacity for developing new products, industrial, monetary, and fiscal policies and the market rate of investment itself will all influence the future earnings per share growth of Heaven Creation. The macroeconomic environment, the government's various economic policies, the return on these investment projects, and the entrepreneur's expectations for the future will affect future interest rate trends. With so many uncertain factors, it is nearly impossible for investors to expect and assess their possible impact on earnings per share and market interest rates. That is why Fisher once said: "Valuation is a human process in which foresight enters. Coming events cast their shadows before. Our valuations are always anticipations".

9.6 Market Efficiency and Market Overreactions

9.6.1 Market Efficiency

Capital market efficiency can be divided into internal efficiency and external efficiency. Internal efficiency refers to the trading efficiency of securities market, namely whether or not transactions can be completed in a short period of time and at a low cost relatively, which reflects the efficiency of securities market organizations and services. External efficiency refers to the efficiency of fund allocation in securities market, namely whether or not relevant price can respond on time and quickly to relevant information, reflecting the efficiency of securities market in funds allocation. An efficient stock market can fully reflect all relevant information for stock prices and quickly respond to new information, and as such, can accurately signal the prices for securities transactions.

Eugene F. Fama was the first to judge a market's efficiency based on the volume of information available and proposed three types of efficiency: weak efficiency, semi-strong form, and strong-form.

In general, the prices of a company's securities will be affected by investors' expectations about its future. For instance, if investors believe that a company has good prospects for development in the coming years and that it would provide investors with higher returns than the market average, then, the company would be favored by investors. Conversely, if investors believe that a company has bleak prospects in the coming years, they will sell off the company's securities, resulting in a falling price.

Investors' expectations are influenced by all information related to the company. For instance, a large-scale reorganization may lead to a significant increase in the company's stock price. If the company announces huge losses, the price of its securities will nosedive. Therefore, people would always find ways to access information about the companies they have invested in. So, when you meet with a group of securities investors, the first question everyone asks is "Any information?"

However, is this sort of information always useful for securities investment? In fact, it really depends on the efficiency of the securities market. If historical information has little impact on changes in the securities price, then the market is of weak efficiency. Otherwise, the market has yet to reach such a level of efficiency. For example, assume that a company announced restructuring on June 6, 2002. If securities price is still affected by this information two months later, then the market has not reached the level of weak efficiency. Why is it that when a market is not affected by historical announcements it becomes weak efficient? This is due to the fact that old news has nothing to do with future securities prices or earnings, illustrating that old news has already been used by investors and has already been fully disclosed.

If relevant publicly disclosed securities information has little impact on prices, or in other words, the disclosed information has been fully reflected in a price change, then the market has reached a level of semi-strong-form efficiency. On the other hand, if relevant information which has been released still has an impact on securities prices, then the information has not been used to its full and has not been fully reflected, as such, the securities market has yet to reach a level of semi-strong-form efficiency. For example, suppose that the company in our example above has just announced reorganization, and its stock price rises on the same day, and as such, the stock market has yet to achieve a level of semi-strong-form efficiency.

Strong-form efficiency is the highest form of efficiency. If all relevant information about stock prices, including publicly disclosed information and internal information, does not have any impact whatsoever on securities prices, which indicates that the securities prices have already fully reflected such changes, then the market has reached a level of strong-form efficiency. Thus, for efficient markets, the best indicator of investors' predictions as to a company's prospects is the securities price.

In an efficient market, investors cannot earn a return beyond the equilibrium return. Newspapers, magazines and even bloggers will provide their customers with analytical reports which all investors can quickly get hold of. Thus, if you, as an investor, have made your investment decisions based on public information, you will hardly get the return you want. And so the saying goes: "Buy the rumor, sell the fact."

The efficiency of a securities market is affected by the trading system, trading technology, and information communication technology. Nathan Rothschild was the first to hear of Napoleon's defeat at Waterloo via carrier pigeon. Once he had received this information and before word of Napoleon's defeat had reached England, Rothschild bought shares on London's stock market on a large scale. Once the information was known far and wide, prices soared and Rothschild had made a fortune. However, in today's world, it is difficult to have such an advantage because of the Internet and electronic communication technology.

9.6.2 Securities Market Overreaction

Securities market overreaction refers to the phenomenon in which securities price fluctuates drastically as a result of an event and beyond the expected theoretical level, and then returns to the level that it would have reached by way of reverse correction. Chinese philosophy states that "things will develop in the opposite direction when they become extreme." To a certain extent, this describes market overreaction. This phenomenon is due to the fact that investors cannot reasonably or properly evaluate the impact of such events. In the securities market, the majority of investors may be overly optimistic as to the price of securities after a particular event, which will result in a securities price shooting beyond the theoretical level. On the other hand, investors may also be overly pessimistic when securities price which drops below the theoretical price. After a period of time, investors will be able to reasonably evaluate and adjust for the event, thereby reversing prices towards the original theoretical price. In other words, an overextension or an oversell will fall or rise back to the original theoretical level.

When markets overreact, the following two phenomena will occur: (1) abnormal fluctuations in the price of securities will be accompanied by a subsequent reversal, namely, overextended securities will be oversold and oversold securities will be overextended; and (2) if abnormal fluctuations in the price of securities are rather large, then corrections will also be large.

From this perspective, overreactions are caused by investors' overestimates or underestimations as to the intrinsic value of the securities. Overreactions not only stress an overextension of a price increase or oversell of a fall in prices, but more importantly, it will be accompanied by an oversell after an overextension or a rebound after an oversell. Only when both features exist can it be called an overreaction.

Securities markets are often subject to the impact of various political and economic events, and when the event occurs, most investors will be affected psychologically, either becoming overly optimistic or overly pessimistic and will buy or sell either too high or too low, thus resulting in a market overreaction. It is only after a period of time that people can digest the information and adjust their expectations. When this happens, securities prices return to a reasonable level. Thus it can be seen that, on the surface, overreactions reflect a type of reverse correction which will return securities prices to a level of reasonable expectations. Essentially, though, they reflect the psychological condition of investors at large, and this inherent psychological behavior will affect the movement of securities market prices.

Summary

Capital markets are financial markets in which financial instruments have a maturity of at least one year and can be divided into primary and secondary markets. Primary market is the place where financial instruments are issued, and it is the main venue where savings are converted into investment. Secondary market is the place where financial instruments issued on the primary market are cashed so as to improve their liquidity.

Capital market instruments include bonds, stocks, and securities investment funds. Securities investment funds can be classified into different types based on different criteria.

One of the most important capital market organizations are stock exchanges. In addition, OTC markets are also very important capital market organizations. Capital market instruments are issued primarily through traditional underwriting, standby underwriting, and distribution. When underwriters issue a company's stock or bond, it will be subscribed to by investors.

The present value of discount bonds and coupon bonds refers to their value calculated through discounting the future value with market interest rate. In fact, yield is actually calculated to assess the value of a bond. Bond yields are divided into current yield, holding period yield, and yield to maturity. As for premium bonds, their coupon rate is higher than the current yield while the current yield is higher than the yield to maturity. The yield to maturity curve is a useful tool for investment analysis.

The value of stocks is assessed in two ways: price–earnings ratio and dividend discount models. Price–earnings ratio is the market price of stock divided by the earnings per share. The divided discount model is used to discount earnings per share over the next several years to present value at market rates. In the growth dividend discount model, the primary factors which affect stock prices include market interest rates, earnings per share, and dividend growth rates. Any factors which affect the market interest rate and dividend growth rate will affect the stock price.

Based on information contained in the price of securities, the efficiency of securities market can be divided into weak efficiency, semi-strong form, and strong form. Overreaction also occurs in securities markets.

Key Terms

Capital Market; Primary Market; Secondary Market Convertible Bond; Securities Investment Fund; Closed-End Fund; Open-End Fund; Depositary Receipt; OTC Market; Discount Bond; Coupon Bond; Current Yield; Yield to Maturity; Yield to Maturity Curve; Dividend Discount Model; Weak-Form Efficiency Market; Semi-Strong-Form Efficiency Market; Strong-Form Efficiency Market; Market Overreaction; Par Bond; Discount Bond Premium Bond; Equity Fund; Bond Fund; Balanced Fund; ETF

Critical Thinking Questions

1. What is the capital market? What role do they play?
2. What are the financial instruments in a capital market?
3. What is the difference between open-end funds and closed-end funds?
4. What are the differences between discount bonds and coupon bonds? What are the fundamental differences between their valuation principles?
5. In terms of responsibilities and obligations of underwriters, what are the main ways of stock or bond issuance?

6. During the days of the dot-com bubble, why were many Internet companies at a loss even though their stock prices were surprisingly high?
7. What is an effective market? How can it be categorized?
8. What are market overreactions?
9. A company has issued two-year coupon bonds with a face value of 100 yuan and a coupon rate of 4%. With a remaining period of one year, the current price is 98 yuan. What are the current yield and the yield to maturity respectively? Compare the current yield, the yield to maturity, and the coupon rate.
10. A company has issued five-year discount bonds with a face value of 100 yuan and an issue price of 80 yuan. The current price is 85 yuan with a remaining period of 4 years. (1) Calculate the annual interest rate at the time of issuance; (2) Calculate the future annual interest rate based on the current market price. If all else is held equal, the company now intends to issue four-year coupon bonds with a face value of 100 yuan and a coupon rate of 5.25%. Which is more cost-effective, to buy the discount bonds issued a year ago, or to buy these newly issued coupon bonds?
11. A company's current earning per share is one yuan. The board of directors decides to allocate 60% of the earnings per share to the shareholders and invest the remaining 40%. The expected return on reinvestment is 15% and the current market interest rate is 6.75%. If these conditions remain the same, what should the current stock price be? If the current market price of the company's stocks is 18 yuan, what is the price–earnings ratio? In this case, if you were to make an investment decision, what would you do?
12. There goes a story thus: in order to compare the guiding factor of stock analyst selections over investors, people came up with a plan in which they asked eight stock analysts to select five stocks. Meanwhile, they also had chimpanzees select five. By the end of the year, the return on shares selected by the stock analysts was about the same as those selected by the chimpanzees. It would appear that, in terms of investment, the stock analysts were no smarter than their distant cousins. Based on this chapter, briefly assess this story.
13. Assume that you are a stock investor, and having studied the relevant stock market overreaction theory, how would you use it for short-term operations?
14. How would you make investment decisions based on the stock or bond prices calculated in accordance with the model?
15. Case Study 1: In 2012, Jiu Gui Liquor (000799) was a listed company on the Shenzhen Stock Exchange which specialized in the sale of Chinese spirits, and in the second half of October 2012, its stock prices had risen to about 62 yuan. In November of the same year, media reported that there was an excessive amount of plasticizer in Jiu Gui liquor. Additionally, after the 18th National Congress in November 2012, the Chinese government conveyed a determination to punish corruption and put a strict limit on the spending of public funds. Based on the above information, analyze the impact of plasticizer report on Jiu Gui Liquor's market demand and future earnings expectations. How would the stock price respond? How would the government's push to punish corruption and the limit to public consumption have an impact on the stock prices of high-end liquor companies?
16. Case Study 2: Wuxi Suntech is a PV industry enterprise and was listed in New York in 2005. From 2005 to 2007, its sales revenue increased from 226 million dollars to 1.348 billion dollars, a compound annual growth rate of 144.2%. Its net profits also

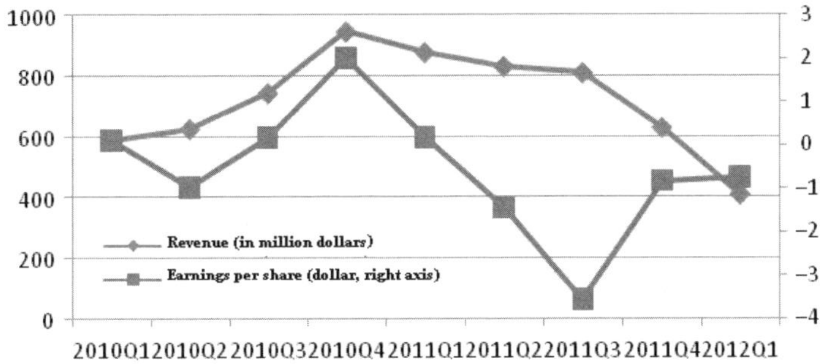

Fig. 9.3 Wuxi Suntech's Revenue and Earnings Per Share

grew from 30.60 million dollars to 171 million dollars, a compound annual growth rate of 136.5%. Over those years, Suntech expanded across the world and rapidly earned large local market shares. However, with the spread of the European debt crisis and its deterioration, the external operating environment of the PV industry rapidly changed. The figure above reflects the change in Suntech's operating revenue and (quarterly) earnings per share from 2010 to 2012. Based on the above information, what kind of change would Suntech's stock prices have experienced from 2005 to 2012?

Chapter 10

Short-Term Money Markets

Learning Objectives

After studying this chapter, you will be able to:

- Understand money markets and their functions
- Clearly understand the interbank lending market and its role
- Understand the interbank lending rate
- Clearly understand the bill market and its role
- Learn the difference between a discounted bill and a bank loan
- Understand the short-term bond market
- Clearly understand bond repo markets and the various types of repo transactions
- Learn about money market funds

A **money market** is a financial market for financing with a maturity of less than one year. Compared to capital markets, the term for money market transactions is much shorter, and for this reason, the financial instruments of a money market have a higher liquidity and lower level risk than those of a capital market. Also, most of the financial instruments of a money market are fundamentally "quasi-money". Another unique feature of money markets is that they are primarily wholesale markets in that the amount of each transaction is incredibly large, and it is precisely because of this that, unlike the majority of individual investors within stock and other long-term capital markets, money market participants are primarily financial institutions or industrial and commercial enterprises. Also, when the central bank engages in monetary policy operations, they will often participate in the money market, and for this reason, the money market plays an irreplaceable role in the monetary policy operations and the monetary policy transmission mechanism. Typically, the central bank will not directly participate in capital market transactions.

Money markets primarily consist of the following: interbank lending markets, Treasury bill markets, and their repurchase markets, and bill markets.

10.1 Interbank Lending Market

10.1.1 What is an Interbank Lending Market?

An **interbank lending market** is a market for short-term credits extended by financial institutions to each other to regulate their temporary positions and meet liquidity needs. It originated from the needs of commercial banks to meet the central bank's demand for required reserve. Nowadays, many countries throughout the world have introduced their own reserve requirements for deposits. In these countries, all commercial banks must deposit a required reserve in accordance with the requirements into the central bank. At the end of each and every business day, commercial banks must deposit the mandatory proportion of their funds into the required reserve account. If the reserve ratio is 8%, for every 100 million yuan in deposits, a commercial bank must make sure there is a balance of 8 million yuan in its required reserve account.

However, due to settlements and daily changes in the amount of receipts and payments, some commercial banks will acquire excess reserves, and other banks will instead lack adequate reserves. For instance, on a given day, some commercial banks will have a capital outflow greater than the amount of funds deposited, and in this case, they may carry a short position. Conversely, another commercial bank, on a given day, may take in more deposits than their capital outflow, and in this case, they will carry a long position. Banks with excess reserves and banks with insufficient reserves can adjust between each other. Commercial banks with insufficient liquidity and short positions can borrow funds from commercial banks with excess liquidity and long positions to compensate for their insufficiency. Commercial banks with excess liquidity and long positions can, in turn, lend funds to reduce their idle position and obtain a corresponding income on interest.

With a highly liquid interbank market, banks can reduce their liquidity position as necessary and can invest their funds in profitable loans, and in turn, can cover funding gaps through the interbank market. Furthermore, commercial banks can also effectively convert short-term interbank lending into long-term loans to improve capital efficiency.

Although interbank lending markets were established out of a necessity to meet the deposit reserve requirements for commercial banks and to adjust commercial bank liquidity and positions, nowadays, in addition to commercial banks, securities companies, fund management companies, financial companies, and insurance companies, as long as they meet a certain set of conditions, can also enter China's national interbank lending market for the financing of short-term funds. Due to the participation of some of these non-banking institutions, China's interbank lending demand is not completely based on a shortfall in required deposit reserves. For instance, when the stock market is bullish, securities companies and fund companies can borrow more funds from the interbank lending market so as to take hold of market opportunities. Through their participation in interbank lending market activities, these institutions form a link between capital markets and money markets, thereby effectively facilitating flows of funds between them. It is precisely for this reason that the interest rates and transaction volume of the interbank lending market and capital market price fluctuations will have a mutual effect on each other.

10.1.2 Characteristics of an Interbank Lending Market

In general, an interbank lending market has the following characteristics:

First is short-term money lending. All financial transactions on interbank lending markets are short-term, to the point where some transactions will begin at the start of one business day only to be repaid at the beginning of the next. This is known as overnight interbank lending. Although there are also interbank lending terms of one month, two months, and beyond, in reality, transactions of greater than a month only account for a fraction of all transactions.

Second, the primary function of interbank lending is to provide commercial banks with liquidity and temporary position adjustments, rather than facilitate the conversion of savings into investment or promote physical capital formation. It is precisely because of this that interbank lending terms are very short.

Third are the unsecured credit loans. When commercial banks that carry a short position borrow funds from commercial banks that carry a long position, they typically do not need to provide collateral, nor do they need third-party guarantees. This is the major difference between interbank lending and lending to a business or individuals which require stringent screening procedures, collateral, and so on. In this regard, the procedure of interbank lending is much more straightforward (Figure 10.1).

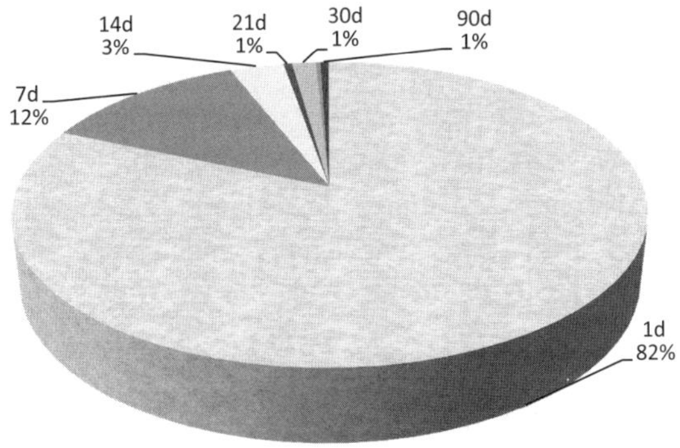

Fig. 10.1 Term Structure of China's Interbank Lending Market in 2013
Source: Website of the People's Bank of China

10.1.3 Types of Interbank Lending

Interbank lending market transactions can be divided into two categories: borrowing positions and interbank lending.

(a) *Position Lending*

Position lending refers to the transfer of short-term funds among financial institutions in the interbank market in order to clear positions and supplement required reserves and funds for bill clearing. When position lending is used to complement deposit reserves, it is typically in the form of overnight lending, that is, a loan is placed on a given day and returned on the next business day.

Compared to position lending for the purpose of replenishing the required reserve, that conducted for the purpose of adjusting the position for clearance is much more common. Banks need to clear their accounts at the end of each business day. The capital inflow of some banks, on a given day, will be greater than their capital outflow, and in this case, these banks carry a long position. Conversely, the capital outflow of other banks, on a given day, will be greater than their capital inflow, and in this case, these banks carry a short position. In order to compensate for a short position, banks which carry a short position can borrow funds from banks which carry a long position, thereby making up for their position in a timely manner and ensuring a smooth clearance. This type of borrowing is much more convenient and much faster than central bank rediscounts and refinancing, and for this reason, it is the primary method by which commercial banks manage their positions.

(b) *Interbank Loans*

An interbank loan is placed to address the temporary or seasonal needs for funds, and its use is not for making up deficiency in reserves or positions, but rather it is a means of obtaining additional short-term liabilities. For financial institutions which borrow funds, the interbank loan allows for the timely acquisition of adequate short-term funds to expand their liability businesses. For financial institutions which lend funds, the interbank loan can stimulate idle short-term funds and increase revenue. Since the purpose of financing in these two cases differs from that of position lending, their terms tend to be longer. For example, the financing activities of the securities, funds, insurance, or financial companies mentioned above in the interbank market are mostly interbank loans.

10.1.4 Interbank Settlements

Whenever ad financial institution engages in interbank lending, funds will need to be settled. There are generally two means by which interbank lending is settled:

(a) *Real-time Gross Settlements*

Real-time gross settlement is a timely settlement of interbank lending transactions, settled one after another. Real-time gross settlements are carried out by the central bank of each country. Their timely settlement is therefore guaranteed by the central bank. The greatest advantage of real-time gross settlements is their security and speed. Since payments are guaranteed by the central bank, even if a bank enters bankruptcy, the payment of funds will not be affected. This is equivalent to transferring settlement risks to the central bank. In order to control risk, the central bank uses the following two measures: first, queue management, that is, to regulate the timing of settlements so that the payments of those banks without adequate reserve will be delayed until reserves have been replenished. Second, granting banks with the convenience of overdrafting on reserves during the day, which allows banks to have "daylight overdrafts", yet banks are also required to make up for the overdraft before the end of the banking day.

(b) *Net Settlement*

A **net settlement**, unlike a real-time gross settlement, settles what remains after the participants have offset claims and liabilities against each other. The most unique feature of a net settlement lies in the fact that only the remaining balance is settled after all else has been offset, and as such, large funds will not be transferred between banks, and net settlements will only have a small impact on a bank's reserve position. However, unlike a real-time gross settlement, a net settlement is just a commitment to pay, and without the guarantee of a central bank, if a bank cannot honor its commitments at the end of a banking day, it will result in a chain reaction, disrupting the entire chain of capital and lead to systematic risks.

10.1.5 Interest Rates on the Interbank Lending Market

Interbank lending rates act as the price of capital on the interbank market and are the core interest rates of the money market. Depending on the country, interbank lending rates go by different names. For instance: in America, it is called the federal funds rate; in England, it is called the London Interbank Offer Rate (LIBOR); in Singapore, it is called the Singapore Interbank Offered Rate (SIBOR). The list goes on.

Interbank lending rates are representative rates of the entire financial market, and for this reason, they play a major role within the financial system. For instance, changes in LIBOR will give rise to corresponding changes in other international financial market rates. The U.S. federal funds rate is the benchmark interest rate of money market operations by the U.S. central bank — the Federal Reserve. The Federal Reserve, through monetary policy operations, influences the federal funds rate and thereby other medium and long-term interest rates and even the dollar exchange rates, ultimately affecting the economic activities of U.S. businesses and households, the level of employment and economic growth.

Interbank lending rates constitute the cost of funds for banks with insufficient liquidity and short positions. However, the interest rates for different banks which borrow short-term funds on the interbank lending market will differ. This is primarily due to the fact that the credit conditions of each and every bank are not exactly the same. Commercial banks with somewhat less-than-ideal credit will naturally pay a higher interest rate. Similarly, commercial banks with better credit will pay somewhat lower interest rates. In addition, interest rates will also differ for different terms. In general, the longer the term of the loan, the higher the rate of interest, and vice versa.

An interbank lending rate includes the rate applied in real transactions and the interest rate quoted by the group of banks. The interbank lending rate in real transactions is the interest rate agreed to by both the debtor and creditor for short-term loan transactions. Furthermore, there is also a quoted rate. The Shanghai Interbank Offered Rate (referred to as the SHIBOR), for example, is a quoted interest rate. SHIBOR is an arithmetic average of the RMB interbank lending rate autonomously quoted by a group of banks with high credit ratings. It is an unsecured and wholesale simple interest rate, and it is not an interest rate used in real transactions. Currently, the eight SHIBOR rates include overnights, 1-week, 2-week, 1-month, 3-month, 6-month, 9-month and 1-year, thereby consisting of an interest rate system from overnight to 1-year, rather than a single interest rate with the largest transaction volume (Figure 10.2).

The SHIBOR quoting group is formed out of 16 commercial banks who are primary dealers on the open market or market makers on the foreign exchange market. The National Interbank Funding Center is responsible for calculating

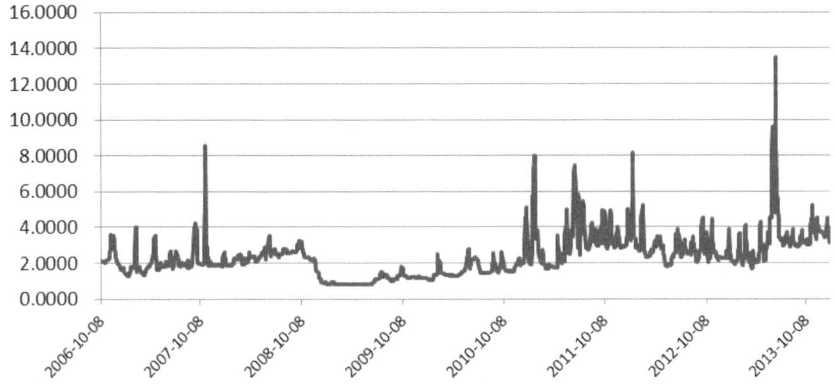

Fig. 10.2 Overnight and 2-Week SHIBOR (End of the Month) Rates
Source: The China Money Website

SHIBOR quotes and issuing information. The quote for each SHIBOR rate on each trading day is based on the arithmetic average of each bank's quote, excluding the highest and lowest quotes, and then released to the public at 11:30 through the Shanghai Interbank Offer Rate website (www.shibor.org).

In China, the interbank lending rate is one of the interest rates with the highest degree of marketization, in that the basis of the interbank lending rate is determined by the lending market supply and demand. For this reason, changes in the interbank lending rate have a greater capacity for reflecting bank liquidity and the supply and demand of funds throughout the entire society in a timely manner. In this way, interbank lending rates are a leading indicator for the central bank when it formulates and conducts monetary policies. For instance, if interbank lending rates continue to rise, it indicates that there is tension in the market supply of funds, and this tension may arise from a substantial increase in investment demand. This may imply demand-pull inflation. Conversely, if the interbank lending rates continue to fall, it indicates that bank liquidity is sufficient, and there may be idle funds. If banks have excess liquidity, investment demand is insufficient, enterprises are not optimistic about their prospects for development, and banks will tend to be "credit grudging", which means that there may be a slowdown in economic growth and signs of deflation.

However, since the People's Bank of China has to pay an interest on commercial bank reserves, the interest rate on the reserves constitutes the floor rate for the interbank lending. For instance, if the central bank's interest rate on commercial bank reserves is 1.89%, the interbank lending rate will not drop below this level. This is the result of arbitrage. When the interbank lending rate is below this level, commercial banks with excess liquidity and long positions will deposit their remaining funds into their reserve account at the central bank. In order for interbank lending rates to better reflect the supply and demand in the money market and the macroeconomic situation, China should gradually phase out this practice of paying interests on commercial bank reserves.

10.2 Bill Markets

10.2.1 What is a Bill?

Another segment of a money market is the bill market. To understand what a bill market is, we should first clearly understand what bills are. A **bill** is a credit instrument that reflects the establishment of debtor-creditor relationship in the course of commodity or fund circulation. Bills can be divided into promissory notes, checks and bills of exchange.

A **promissory note** is a negotiable instrument signed and issued by the maker promising to pay unconditionally the payee or bearer a specified sum of money on demand. A **check** is a negotiable instrument signed and issued by a drawer, entrusting a bank or any other financial institution qualified for check deposit business to unconditionally pay a specified amount of money to the payee or bearer. Checks can be divided into cash checks and transfer checks. Cash checks can only draw cash and cannot be used for transfers; transfer check can only be used for a transfer of funds and cannot draw cash. A **bill of exchange** is a negotiable instrument signed and issued by a drawer to unconditionally pay a specified amount of money to the payee or bearer on demand or at a specified date. Based on different drawers, bills of exchange can be divided into bank bills and commercial bills. Bank bills are a written payment order issued and signed by one bank to another; its drawer and drawee are both banks. Commercial bills, thus are bills issued and signed by companies, enterprises, or individuals.

After commercial bills have been accepted, they are called acceptance bills. This so-called **acceptance** is a promise of payment. Based on different acceptors, commercial bills can also be divided into commercial acceptance bills and bankers' acceptance bills. **Commercial acceptance bills** are notes issued by the payee or payer and honored by the payer enterprise. **Bankers' acceptance bills**, thus, are notes drawn by the payee or payer and honored by the payer's depository bank according to the payer's authorization, and it does a better job of overcoming asymmetric information present in the sale and purchase of goods. Assuming that Jianqiang and Kangrui would like to make a deal, and Jianqiang is to sell goods at a value of 50 million yuan to Kangrui, however, corporate deals are not like the purchases we make at the supermarket where one person hands over the money and the other person hands over the goods. Instead, Jianqiang will first send the goods and only after Kangrui has received them will they make a payment. Other times, Kangrui will first make a payment, and only afterwards will Jianqiang send the goods. During deals between Jianqiang and Kangrui, one party will always assume a certain degree of risk. If Jianqiang first sends the goods, they will assume the risk of Kangrui not paying for the goods upon receipt. On the other hand, there is also possibility that Jianqiang does not ship on time but has already received payment from Kangrui. If this is the case, and if no third party is involved to resolve these risks, Jianqiang and Kangrui may be at a loss for this deal. In fact, this problem can be solved by means of bankers' acceptances.

Briefly put, bankers' acceptances are processed as follows: Kangrui requests its bank (typically a depository bank), such as CITIC Bank, to arrange acceptance bills of 50 million yuan. After Kangrui has received the acceptance bills which were arranged by CITIC, it will transfer them to Jianqiang. Since the bills were accepted by CITIC Bank, if Kangrui is unable to pay, the bank will bear joint liability, and even then, if Kangrui cannot make repayments, CITIC Bank is also required to reimburse the bearer. With CITIC Bank's acceptance guarantee, the risks between Jianqiang and Kangrui will be alleviated.

On the basis of when they are issued, bills can be divided into real bills and financing bills.

A **real bill** refers to bills which are used for trade settlements and arise from commodity circulation. The aforementioned bill of exchange belongs to the category of real bills. A **financing bill** refers to bills which are not based on real commodity trading and are issued specifically for financing. Financing bills are also known as commercial paper. For instance, a large enterprise with a high credibility may issue 50 million yuan in commercial paper for short-term financing. In essence, commercial paper is also a form of creditor–debtor obligations. Unlike the similar creditor–debtor obligations of a bond which are standardized, commercial paper is not standardized and its face value is extremely large, so individuals or enterprises with a limited amount of idle funds cannot purchase commercial paper. However, bonds can be purchased by any individual, as long as they are publicly offered and publicly traded. Generally speaking, commercial paper is unsecured, in that if the drawer cannot make payments upon maturity, there will rarely be asset-backed collateral to redeem the principal. This suggests that investors must make their investment decisions on the issuers credibility alone. In fact, not all companies can issue commercial paper, and usually only those large enterprises with high credibility can issue commercial paper. For instance, while there are approximately 20,000 companies in the US, only 1500 companies have issued commercial paper. Conversely, any company, either big or small, can obtain real bills as long as it really trades goods or services.

Since there exists asymmetric information between the issuer and the bearer, commercial paper bearers must undertake credit risks. Since there are credit risks, commercial paper issuers must pay a higher interest rate to compensate. In order to lower commercial paper financing costs, commercial banks, subsequently, also entered into the commercial paper business of large enterprises. For instance, in the United States, enterprises can issue what is called credit-backed commercial paper, that is, when an enterprise issues commercial paper, it can obtain a specific line of credit from a bank, and in the event that the issuer of the commercial paper cannot make repayments upon the maturity of its commercial paper, the commercial bank will issue a loan to the enterprise within their line of credit so as to settle matured commercial paper. This is, in fact, a guarantee of a commercial bank's line of credit which can improve the ability of a commercial paper issuer's ability to handle maturity settlements and lower the credit risks of the commercial paper bearer.

10.2.2 Bill Discounts, Interbank Discounts, Rediscounts, and Bill Repos

A **bill discount** is the remaining sum which a bank pays to a bill holder after the deduction of the interest when the bill holder transfers acceptance bills or commercial bills which have not yet reached maturity. Since the ownership of discounted bills is often transferred, they are also called a bill buyout or bill sellout.

We can use the example of the CITIC Bank's bankers' acceptance bills of 50 million yuan which were arranged for Kangrui. If Jianqiang, after having received CITIC Bank's acceptance bills given to it by Kangrui, is in desperate need of funds, what can it do? One solution is for Jianqiang to take these acceptance bills to a different commercial bank, such as China Merchants Bank, for a discount. When China Merchant's Bank discounts their acceptance bills, after deducting a corresponding amount of interest, it will transfer the remaining funds to Jianqiang. As you can see, before the invention of bill discounts, bills reflect the creditor–debtor relationship of the two legal persons of the drawee and bearer. After the invention of bill discounts, however, bills reflect the creditor–debtor relationship between the drawee and the discounting bank.

Depending on the process involved, bill discounts include discounts, interbank discounts and rediscounts. The process in which most industrial and commercial enterprises cash their bills at a bank is a **discount**. So-called **interbank discounts** refer to situations in which a discounting bank is in need of funds and will transfer the discounted bills to a different bank at a discount. For instance, in the example above, if after China Merchants Bank has given Jianqiang a discount, because of liquidity management demands and a need for funds, China Merchants Bank will take the acceptance bills to a different commercial bank, such as the Bank of Communications, for a discount. **Rediscounts**, then, are situations in which a discounting commercial bank is in need of funds and will transfer bills to the central bank, before they reach maturity, for a discount. In the above example, if China Merchants Bank does not choose to take the bills to the Bank of Communications for a discount, but instead takes them to the People's Bank of China acting as a central bank, for a discount, and thus, for financing, then this is a rediscount.

Corresponding to bill discounts, there is also a type of bill transaction behavior, which is the repo or reverse repo of bills. Bill repos refer to situations in which a discounting bank has pledged its outstanding commercial bills to another bank and will earn the amount of the bills after deducting for repo interest while also agreeing to buy back the bills at a certain future date. Bill reverse repos, thus, are the opposite process of bill repos. Bill repos and reverse repos are similar to bond repos and reverse repos described below.

At the time of bill discount, discounting banks will deduct a corresponding amount of interest in accordance with the prevailing discount interest. The discount interest rate is typically referred to as the **discount rate**. When commercial banks take the bills which they hold to the central bank for a rediscount, the interest rate which the central bank charges is called the **rediscount rate**. As a general rule, over the same period of time, the rediscount rate of a certain type of bill will be lower than its discount rate.

10.2.3 The Comparison between Bill Discount and Loan

As we have seen, once the bearer of a bill receives a discount, they obtain a corresponding fund from the commercial bank. The discounting bank will then issue funds to bill holders, and as such, bill discounts are one of the most important asset-side services which banks offer. Although discounted bills and loans both belong to the asset business of commercial banks, they differ significantly in the following ways:

(i) *Different objects of credit*: A loan's object of credit is the borrower and embodies a relationship between the lending bank and the borrower. A bill discount's object, then, is the bill and embodies the transactions in claims over the bill. If you go to CITIC Bank to discount TICO bills, this would be equivalent to transferring creditor's rights as to TICO to CITIC Bank, and in this way, your company would not be held jointly liable for the obligations.

(ii) *Different liquidity*: Bank loans must be recovered upon maturity. Discounted bills, on the other hand, can also be transferred or rediscounted prior to maturity to promptly acquire necessary funding.

(iii) *Different terms*: Bill discount terms are relatively short, the majority of which are between three and six months. Typical bank loan terms are relatively longer. Short-term loans are less than a year, medium- and long-term loans are greater than a year. Some loans, such as home mortgages, may have a term of up to 35 years. The difference of term is also one of the factors which determine the liquidity of loans and bill discounts.

(iv) *Different risks*: Discounted bills are usually bills based on real commodity trading or commercial paper issued by large enterprises with high credibility. Upon maturity, automatic payments are made and default is unlikely. Typical bank loans, however, may have a large risk of loan losses due to poor business performance and borrower default.

(v) *Different time and rate of interest*: Interest on bill discounts is first deducted from the amount of bills while interest on bank loans is collected after a certain period of time has passed since the issuance of the loan. Because the time in which interest is collected amongst the two differs, this lowers the risk of bill discounts compared to loans, and for this reason, their interest rates will be lower than interest rates on loans with a similar term.

(vi) *Different ownership of funds*: Bank loans only temporarily transfer the right to use funds to the borrower, in that the ownership of funds is never transferred. What this means is that after a bank has lent you money, upon maturity, you must return those funds to the bank. On the other hand, when a discounting bank purchases bills, it also obtains the creditor's right while fund ownership is attributable to the discount applicant, and for this reason, when you are in the position of a financial manager and discount Tian Chuang bills to CITIC Bank, CITIC Bank cannot demand that you repay this fund.

10.2.4 Functions of a Bill Market

Having clarified what bills and bill discounts are, we can clarify what bill market and bill discount markets are. This so-called bill market refers to a market in which bills are signed, issued and transferred. Similar to all financial instrument markets, bill markets can also be divided into primary and secondary markets. Primary bill markets are markets in which bills are signed, issued, and accepted. If CITIC Bank decides to not sign and issue acceptance bills to Kangrui, Jianqiang cannot take them to China Merchants Bank for a discount and earn discount funds. Thus, if there are no signed, issued, and accepted bills, it would be impossible to circulate and transfer them. The secondary bill market is the **bill discount market**, that is, it provides a market for bill transactions between bill holders and discounting banks. It is unlike stock and other financial markets in that it is an OTC market and its transactions are not conducted on the Shanghai and Shenzhen stock exchanges.

Bill markets have the following roles:

First of all, for sales enterprises, creditor's rights over product buyers can be obtained by accepting real bills on the basis of real commodity transactions in order to reduce inventory and sell products in a timely manner. Prior to the maturity of real bills, if there is an urgent need, discounts can be used to meet short-term liquidity needs and recover funds in a timely manner.

Second, if a large enterprise issues commercial paper, it means that, other than issuing standardized stock and bonds, there is also a channel for raising short-term funds. Thus, in general, bill markets are conducive to the diversification of large-scale corporate financing structures and the diversification of credit risk throughout society.

Third, for commercial banks, when processing bankers' acceptances, a certain fee can be charged based on an enterprise's credit risk rating, resulting in certain earnings. As for acceptances from commercial banks, even though a contingent liability has been formed, so long as an enterprise is capable of repaying the principal in a timely manner, commercial banks will not suffer any losses. As for bill discounts, they are an important form of asset business for commercial banks. Compared to typical loans, the risks of bill discounting are slim, and in this way, they are fairly apt at adjusting a commercial bank's asset structure and can also open up new channels of profit and increase bank revenue.

For China's commercial banks, bill discounting is an effective means of circumventing various regulations. Since 1997, China's amount of bill discounting has risen sharply (as seen in Figure 10.3), one of the primary reasons for which is that by adding a certain percentage point on the central bank's rediscount rate,

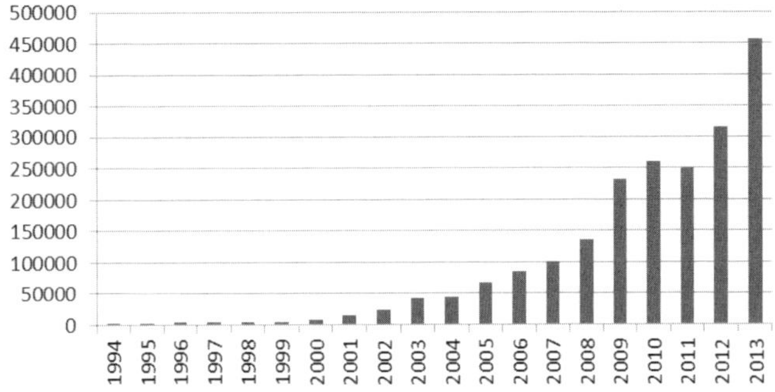

Fig. 10.3 Amount of Discounted Commercial Bank Bills (100 million yuan)
Source: People's Bank of China's Monetary Policy Report

commercial banks can flexibly determine discount rates in accordance with the supply and demand of market funds and the credit risks of enterprises. Meanwhile, commercial bank lending rates are regulated by the central bank. In order to circumvent the central bank's lending rate regulations, commercial banks can compete by increasing discounted loans with discount rates that are far lower than loan interest rates.

Finally, the bill discount market is an important form and mechanism for the implementation of the central bank's monetary policies. Because the central bank uses rediscounted bills for commercial banks to increase the supply of base money and reduces the amount of rediscounted bills to lower the amount of base money, thus, the central bank can use rediscounted bills to control the base money. The volume of rediscounted bills is affected by the rediscount rate because the rediscount rate is the cost of financing for commercial banks to discount bills at the central bank. The higher the rediscount rate, the higher will be the cost for commercial banks, which would thereby lower the willingness of commercial banks to rediscount at the central bank. In this way, the bill rediscount market not only allows bill holders a means for meeting liquidity demands, it also has become an important mechanism for central banks to control the money supply; rediscounting policy is one of the central bank's "three weapons" of monetary control.

10.2.5 Commercial Paper Assessments

If you hold commercial paper at a face value of 10 million yuan and there are three months before they mature, when you discount them at a commercial bank for cash, you will not receive 10 million yuan but will receive less. When the commercial bank takes the bills worth 10 million yuan to the central bank for a rediscount, it also will not receive 10 million yuan. Why is this so? This is because of the time value of money. Since the face value of bills is settled in the future, the 10 million yuan three months from now is not worth the 10 million yuan that you hold today.

When you go to the bank to discount your bills worth 10 million yuan, how much cash can you receive? This depends on the discount rate and the remaining term.

Suppose i is the discount rate, n is the remaining term (in days), F is the face value of bills, B is the annual basis, as in whether years are based on 365 days or 360 days, and P is the amount which can be earned for discounting bills, then:

$$F = P \times \left(1 + \frac{n}{B} \cdot i\right).$$

Thus,

$$P = F \times \frac{B}{B + n \cdot i}.$$

If we suppose that the discount rate for the bills above is 6%, the remaining term is 90 days, the annual basis is 360 days, then the amount which can be earned for discounting bills would be:

$$P = 1000 \times \frac{360}{360 + 90 \times 6\%} = 9{,}852{,}217 \text{ yuan}.$$

In general, the longer the remaining term, the higher the discount rate and the lower the amount which can be earned after the bills have been discounted. Conversely, the shorter the term, the lower the discount rate and the higher the amount which can be earned for bill discounting which would be closer to the face value of the bills.

10.3 Short-term Bond and Repo Market

10.3.1 Short-term Bond Market

Short-term bonds refer to bonds with a term of less than one year which are important instruments in the money market. In accordance with the different issuers, short-term bonds primarily include Treasury bills, short-term financing bills, and central bank bills.

Short-term financing bills are negotiable standardized bonds which are issued by relatively large industrial and commercial enterprises, securities companies, and other financial institutions with a term of less than one year. Furthermore, short-term financing bills can be further divided into super and short-term commercial paper (SCP), which is issued by non-financial institutions with a relatively high credit rating (typically AAA-rated central enterprises) in the interbank bond market and which has a maturity ranging within 270 days (including 7, 14, and 21 days). To reduce the risk of over-borrowing, China requires that the balance of bonds issued by an enterprise shall not exceed 40% of its net asset, which, however, does not apply to SCP. Short-term financing bills are a primary means for these enterprises or financial institutions to have access to short-term liquidity. As opposed to bank loans over the same period, short-term financing bills are flexible, have low interest rates and other such advantages. The development of the short-term bill market has further diversified the financing channels of enterprises and has also contributed to a more comprehensive corporate bond yield curve. Since China began to allow enterprises to issue short-term financing bills in 2005, more and more enterprises have come to rely on short-term financing bills, instead of bank loans, for financing.

Central bank bills are a type of bond issued by the People's Bank of China for withdrawing base money. Their terms range from 3 months, 6 months, 1 year to 3 years. 3-month and 1-year central bank bills are the most common. Central bank bills are the most important segment of China's short-term bond market which far exceeds the issuance of corporate short-term bonds. The purpose of central bank bills issued by the People's Bank of China is clearly different from that of short-term financing bills issued by enterprises. The central bank bills issued by the People's Bank of China are for adjusting the money supply, and the issued volume is determined by the changes in the factors that lead to monetary expansions and the application of other monetary policy tools (such as the required deposit reserve ratio). However, short-term financing bills and central bank bills are issued and traded on the interbank bond market and do not enter the trading system of the Shanghai or Shenzhen Stock Exchanges.

Treasury bills are negotiable securities issued by the government to meet demands for short-term financing and typically have a term of less than one year. Although many bonds are issued by the government, their terms are relatively long, and government bonds which exceed a year are simply referred to as Treasury bonds. Treasury bonds are capital market instruments. Only Treasury bills are money market instruments. For instance, in the United Kingdom and the United States, Treasury bill terms are typically 91 days and 182 days.

There is a special kind of Treasury bill known as a **benchmark bond**. In highly developed market economies like the United States, governments often issue 7-day Treasury bills. This type of Treasury bill is issued by the government not because of a fiscal deficit, but out of necessity of the financial system. There are at least two characteristics of benchmarked bonds: first, they are very short-term, and second, they have no credit risks. Since they are incredibly short-term, there is no term agio on the interest rate for this type of bond, and since there are no credit risks, there is no risk premium either. In this way, benchmark bond rates are risk-free rates. Since these benchmark bonds do not have term agio or risk premiums, they are the benchmark for other bond rates. Treasury bills are issued by the central government with low credit risks and high liquidity and are most suited to the two qualifications of benchmark bonds, and for this reason, Treasury bill rates can play the role of benchmark rates.

Commercial banks will often hold Treasury bills as a secondary reserve. When commercial banks lack sufficient liquidity, they can sell Treasury bills on the secondary market to meet liquidity and reserve requirements. When there is sufficient liquidity and reserves, Treasury bill holders can also earn a certain amount of interest income, which is obviously better than holding cash assets alone.

The development of the short-term Treasury bill market has been significantly influenced by the government bond management structure. Countries which implement **government bond balance management** put a ceiling on the balance of the government debt at the end of each fiscal year and are not as concerned with the volume of government bonds issued during the current year. Under this management structure, as long as the issued Treasury bills are short-term, they will not significantly increase the balance of government debt at the year end. Government bond balance management is thus conducive to the development of short-term Treasury bill markets. Conversely, if there is a ceiling on the aggregate amount of Treasury bills issued in a fiscal year, frequent short-term Treasury bill issuances will easily break those limits, and in such a government bond management system, governments will tend to issue relatively long-term bonds which are not conducive to short-term government bond market. For the 20 years following the restoration of Chinese Treasury bill issuances in 1981, an aggregate amount of Treasury bills that could be issued was determined each year and balance management was not implemented, and for this reason, in the context of the incredible development of China's financial markets, China's short-term government bond market lagged far behind. In 2006, China began to implement government bond balance management in order to provide a legal guarantee for the growth of the government bond market. However, China still regards government bonds as a means for compensating for fiscal deficits and a measure for long-term public financing, and the importance of short-term government bonds within the financial system has been overlooked. Even though China has implemented government bond balance management, the growth of the short-term government bond market is still slow.

10.3.2 Repo Market

(a) *What is a Repo?*

Bond transactions can be divided into spot transactions and repo transactions. **Spot transaction** is the purchase and sale of bonds in the means of payment specified in the contract that has been agreed upon by both parties to be delivered within a certain period with a transfer of the bond ownership. **Repo transactions** refer to a contract promising that one party will sell securities to the other at a specified price and will repurchase these securities from the counterparty at a specified price on a given date in the future.

Suppose that Kangrui currently has 50 million yuan in bonds with a remaining term of one and a half years. Jianqiang has 50 million yuan in cash. Kangrui is now in urgent need of 50 million yuan of working capital and can earn this cash after six months. For simplicity's sake, we will not take into account interest rates, and thus, Kangrui and Jianqiang can conduct this kind of bond repo transaction:

Step 1: Kangrui and Jianqiang will both sign a repo agreement. Kangrui will transfer 50 million yuan in bonds to Jianqiang while Jianqiang will transfer 50 million yuan in cash to Kangrui.

Step 2: In six months, Kangrui and Jianqiang will take the second step of the repo transaction, namely the repo/resell stage. Kangrui will return the 50 million yuan of cash to Jianqiang and will obtain their 50 million yuan in bonds which they had originally sold to Jianqiang. To Kangrui, this is a repo. At the same time, Jianqiang will return the original 50 million yuan in bonds in accordance with the price agreed by both parties and will receive the 50 million yuan in cash that it had loaned to Kangrui. To Jianqiang, this is a bond resell to Kangrui. In fact, in terms of the same bond, repos and resells are carried out simultaneously. It is as if you were to look at the back and the palm of your hand. If there is a repo, there must also be a resell. From this it is clear that bond repo transactions are essentially the use of a bond as a collateral for lending.

From Figure 10.4, we can see that the same repo transaction involves both the bond seller and fund borrower as well as the bond buyer and fund lender. In accordance with the different direction of bonds and cash flows, repo transactions can be divided into repos and reverse repos. **Repos** refer to situations such as when Kangrui sold bonds to Jianqiang and received cash from Jianqiang, and as both parties agreed, on a certain date in the future, Kangrui could repurchase those bonds from Jianqiang at a certain price. **Reverse repos** refer to the simultaneous purchase of bonds and the signed agreement that on a certain date in the future, the bonds will be resold to the original seller at a stipulated price. As you can see, to both parties of the same repo transaction, one party must conduct a repo while the other party must conduct a reverse repo. The party which conducts a repo is the

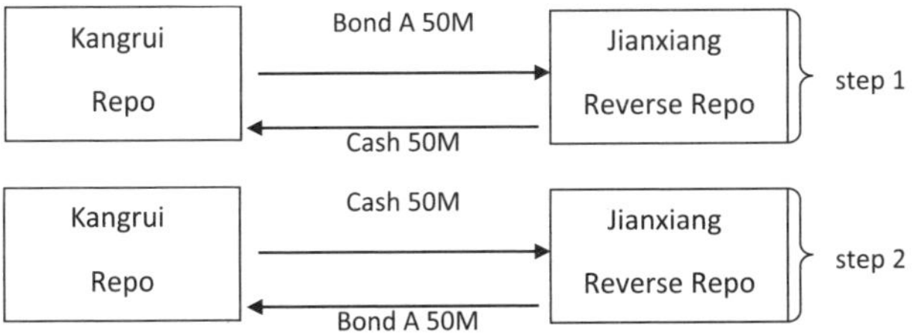

Fig. 10.4 Bond and Fund Flow in Repo Transaction

fund borrower and bond seller. The party which conducts a reverse repo, then, is the bond buyer and fund lender, or you could say that the party which conducts a repo is short of funds while the reverse repo is conducted by the party with excess funds.

In accordance with the different bond disposal rights within validity period of a repo contract, repo transactions can be divided into open-end repos and closed-end repos. If Kangrui and Jianqiang sign a **closed-end repo**, then within the validity period of the repo agreement, Jianqiang as the temporary transferee will hold Kangrui's frozen bonds and cannot dispose of them at its own discretion. **Open-end repos** are different. The following two characteristics embody their "openness": first, the frozen bonds allow for free replacement. If Kangrui needs to use bond A which it has transferred to Jianqiang as a collateral during the validity period of the repo agreement, for open-end repos, Kangrui can negotiate with Jianqiang and replace it with bond B, even to the point where they can re-negotiate the term and price of the repo. Second, once Kangrui has given bond A to Jianqiang, bond A is not frozen, and Jianqiang, during the validity period of the repo agreement, has the right to dispose of bond A, as long as it can be repurchased and repaid to Kangrui upon maturity. In this case, Jianqiang could use the bonds for other repo transactions. As you can see, open-end repos are much more flexible and are an effective way of adjusting fund surplus and shortfall or managing liquidity. They also provide both parties with additional opportunities for profit. For instance, if Jianqiang predicts that the price of bond A will fall, it can first sell off the bonds, and buy them later so as to access market spreads.

(b) *Characteristics of the Repo Market*

Repo markets have the following characteristics:

First of all, similar to the interbank lending market, bond repo market terms are very short, and even though the government permits six month or one year bond repo transactions, those repo transactions longer than a month only account for a minute fraction of all repo transactions. The majority of these short-term transactions are less than a month, and thus, the repo transaction market is highly liquid (Figure 10.5).

Second, unlike the credit transactions on the interbank lending market, repo transactions are in fact the use of bonds as collateral for lending, and therefore the risk of repo transactions is much lower than the credit risk of interbank lending.

Third, it is precisely because of the two characteristics above that repo rates are typically lower than interbank lending rates for the same term. For instance, as can be seen in Figure 10.6, the interbank lending rate volatility curve is almost always above the repo rate curve.

Finally, as with all money markets, the fundamental function of the repo market is to meet the liquidity management needs of market participants and is not meant for raising long-term capital.

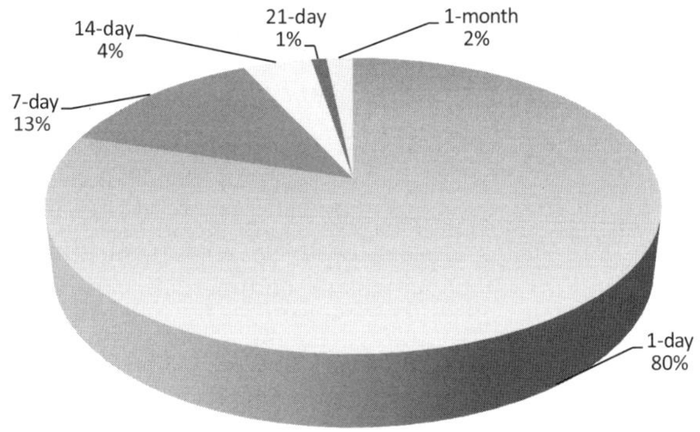

Fig. 10.5 Term Structure of China's Interbank Bond Repo Transaction in 2013

Notes: There are also 3-month, 6-month, 9-month and 1-year bond repo terms, although they only account for an extremely small proportion of bonds, and for this reason, they have been ignored

Source: Website of the People's Bank of China

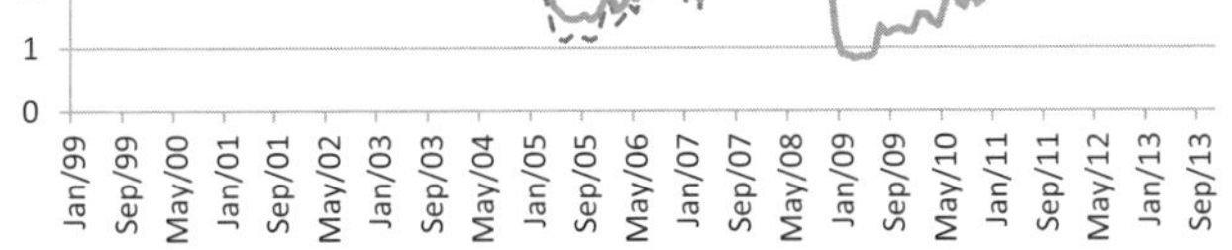

Fig. 10.6 China's Bond Repo and Interbank Lending Rates (%)

Source: Website of the People's Bank of China

(c) *Functions of the Repo Market*

From the analysis above, we can already see that repo markets are in fact lending activities that use bonds as collateral. Sellers in a repo contract can obtain all of the funds they need, and after the repo transaction expires, if they have sufficient funds, they can also buy back the original bonds so that they can continue to earn the interest income on the bonds. To the buyers in a repo contract, during the repo period, they can earn the corresponding interest income on the bonds and upon the expiration of the bond repo, they can resell the bonds and take back their cash. To financial institutions, repo transactions can be used to maximize the liquidity, profitability and safety of their assets all at once, thereby allowing them to achieve diversification and rationalization of their portfolio. For various non-financial institutions (mainly enterprises), this market is the best place for them to make the most of their own short-term funds.

Additionally, repo transactions not only solve liquidity problems for enterprises and financial institutions, since repo rates are relatively low, compared to other options, they also offer a comprehensively lower cost for solving liquidity problems. To the liquidity management of commercial banks, this is of great importance.

Finally, repo transactions are one of the central bank's primary means of open market operations. When the central bank hopes to expand the supply of base money, it can sign reverse repo agreements with commercial banks. Commercial banks can take the government bonds that they possess and transfer them to the central bank. This will increase government bonds on the asset side of the central bank's balance sheet and will also increase commercial bank reserves on the liabilities side. Conversely, when the central bank conducts a repo, the central bank will first transfer its bonds to commercial banks so as to reduce commercial bank reserves and thus decrease the supply of base money.

(d) *Pricing Methods of Repo Transactions: Net Price Transactions and Gross Price Transactions*

Repo transaction pricing occurs in two ways: net price and gross price. Net price transactions refer to when the price is broken down into the transaction price and the accrued interest. Prices reflect the market conditions, and the accrued interest is calculated on the nominal interest per day, making it easy for bondholders to enjoy their interest income for the holding period. Gross price, then, in determining the price of securities will take into consideration interest within repo agreements. In spot bond transaction, the gross price method is typically used. Compared to gross price transactions, the benefit of net price transactions lies in the fact that it clearly outlines the seller's return and the buyer's costs within the bond transaction. In addition, it also conveniently reflects the actual price of bonds, which can allow investors to make a timely and more direct judgment of market prices.

Since the net price transaction of repos differs from the gross price transactions of the spot bond market, there is room for significant arbitrage opportunities. For example, some securities dealers would sign a reverse repo agreement with their counterparties and buy, at the net price, securities with a higher coupon rate and an approaching date for next payment. The dealers can then sell these securities on the spot bond market at the gross price. In this way, a profit can be earned. However, this kind of arbitrage is not risk-free. On the date in which the repo agreement matures, these securities dealers must buy the same type and quantities of securities on the spot market at the gross price. They also must settle this transaction with the same original counterparty. When market rates continue to rise and the security prices fall, this type of arbitrage allows securities dealers to not only sell these securities and invest in markets with higher rates of return, but also purchase them back at a lower price upon the date of maturity and earn a hefty profit. However, when market rates begin to fall and security prices rise, securities dealers who engage in this kind of arbitrage cannot help but buy the original securities in the spot market at a higher gross price, and after-profits arising from the original repo agreement are offset by the purchase cost, and losses are inevitable.

(e) *Repo Rates*

A repo rate is a measure of remuneration paid by a repo agreement's borrower (securities seller) to the lender (securities buyer). Since the repo rate reflects the various types of risks borne during the transaction by the bond reseller, for this reason, it is primarily determined by the type of securities, the credibility of the counterparty and the term for the repo agreement. The higher the credit risk of securities, the higher the interest rate for a repo agreement. Similarly, the term for a repo agreement is positively correlated to its interest rate, in that the longer the term, the higher the interest rate, and vice versa.

In general, with the same term, repo rates will be lower than interbank lending rates. The reason for this is mainly because repos are in fact bonds-backed loans. Interbank lending, on the other hand, is primarily credit lending and is not backed by collaterals. Also, bonds are issued by the government, and the credit risks of government bonds are relatively low. The credit ratings of interbank borrowers are not as good as that of the government. As such, bond repo rates will be typically lower than that of interbank lending.

The difference between repo rates and interbank lending market rates can range from several basis points to over a hundred. This depends on supply and demand in the securities market. When there is a supply shortage in the securities market, the rate difference between repo agreements and the interbank lending market will increase. Conversely, when supply is adequate (for example, if the central bank sells government securities), the rate difference between repo agreements and interbank lending market will decrease.

Similar to the interbank lending market, although current Chinese rates for the bond repo market are one of the most market-based, they also are constrained by the central bank interest rate on commercial banks' required reserve. The required reserve rate is a minimum rate, and this is because when repo market rates are lower than required reserve rates, room exists for risk-free arbitrage. At this time, commercial banks would rather deposit their remaining funds in the central bank's reserve account instead of using it for repo transactions. Thus, whether it be the interbank lending market or the bond repo market, both require a reform on the interest rate on China's required reserve.

10.4 Money Market Funds

10.4.1 What is a Money Market Fund?

A money market is a wholesale market, and the volume of single transactions is very large, on the scale of tens of millions of yuan, or even transactions worth over 100 million yuan. For instance, a single transaction of interbank bond repo in China reached a scale of 170 million yuan. With transactions of such a large volume, personal savings of individual depositors of only tens or hundreds of thousand yuan pale in comparison. Even if you were a wealthy tycoon with a net worth of over 100 million yuan, because some money markets only allow financial institutions to participate, you would still be unable to directly conduct money market transactions. However, the interest rate on money market transactions is often higher than bank deposit rates for the same period. Must we simply sit and wonder what life would be like with the higher earnings from the money market?

Money market funds may be able to help individual investors solve this problem. Money market funds are open-end funds, the shares of which are issued by fund management companies, and the sum of such shares are pooled together to invest in the money market.

The scope of money market fund investments primarily includes money market instruments such as bonds with a remaining maturity of 397 days or less, repos with a maturity of one year or less, central bank bills, bank-endorsed commercial paper, bankers' acceptance bills, time certificates and large negotiable certificates of deposits as well as repos with a maturity of less than one year. However, money market funds cannot be invested in stock, convertible bonds, bonds with a remaining maturity of greater than one year, and bonds of enterprises with a credit rating below AAA.

If we compare this to the investment of securities investment funds in stocks, corporate bonds and long-term bonds that we have dealt with in Chapter 9, we will see that the scope of money market fund investment is very secure with low risks and steady earnings. For enterprises and individuals who wish to avoid the risks of the securities market, money market funds are a must, and under normal circumstances, money market funds allow access to earnings on interest higher than that of bank deposits while also protecting principal. Chinese people prefer bank deposits, but if deposit rates continue to decline and if the risks of investing in stocks are too high, money market funds open up a good investment channel for most Chinese people.

10.4.2 Characteristics of a Money Market Fund

Money market funds are a new type of wealth management tool and differ from bank deposits, stocks, and bonds.

- A unit of the fund is worth one yuan. The net value of each unit of a money market fund is fixed and typically set at one yuan per unit. After having invested in this fund, investors can reinvest their earnings which will continue to accumulate and increase their shares of the fund. For example, some investors will invest 100 yuan into a money market fund and will possess 100 fund units. If the rate of return on investment is 8%, the value of this investor's shares would be 108 yuan one year later.

- Liquidity and safety. The primary characteristic of money markets is that they are low-risk, high-liquidity markets. Additionally, investors are not limited to maturities and can redeem funds as needed.
- Low risks. Money market instruments usually have short terms. For instance, the average term for money market fund portfolios is 4 to 6 months, and for this reason, risks are low and prices are only affected by market rates.
- Investment costs are low. Money market funds typically do not charge redemption fees, and administrative costs are lower. For instance, the annual management fee for money market funds is only 0.25% of the net asset value of the funds which is lower than the 1% annual management fee for traditional funds.
- Most are open-ended funds. Money market funds are typically open-end, which means that as long as you have spare cash, you can invest in a money market fund. Similarly, when you need cash, you can redeem the money market funds that you hold. Money market funds are open-end and thus have higher liquidity.
- Tax incentives. China's deposit interest income used to be subject to a 20% tax. Capital gain taxes must be paid on the dividends earned from investing in stock and the interest earned from investing in corporate bonds, although income earned on money market funds enjoy tax exemptions.

10.4.3 Money Market Fund Returns and Risks

Money market funds can provide investors with a stable investment income, and investment in a money market instrument is typically very short-term. Also, these instruments typically do not have credit risks of default. However, compared with equity-based capital market securities investments funds, advantages of the money market funds can also be seen as their disadvantages. Since money market funds primarily invest in money market instruments with short terms and low risks, their overall level of earnings is also quite low. If the stock market is bullish, money market fund holders will earn less than what they could earn from stock or bond funds. Conversely, the absolute yield of money market instruments is low, their terms are fairly short, and a fall in their prices is also very limited. Compared to stock and bond funds, when the macroeconomic conditions are poor, and the stock and bond markets crash, money market funds will be a safe haven in which earnings are fairly steady. On the whole, money market funds are undoubtedly a better choice for those investors who seek relatively steady earnings and relatively low risks.

Lower risks for money market funds do not mean that no risks exist. First of all, since money market funds primarily invest in short-term instruments such as short-term government bonds, central bank bills and bankers' acceptance bills, money market fund earnings will be affected by fluctuations in the interest rates of these money market instruments. Second, money market funds are operated by fund companies. This does not rule out the possibility of longer term and higher risk securities that the fund manager may choose to invest in for higher earnings. When the stock market is in a downturn, and a majority of fund holders will demand a redemption of funds, the liquidity of the holdings will also decline which will expose money market funds to liquidity risks.

Finally, even though money market funds do not pay taxes on interest income, and typically do not have redemption fees, fund management companies will still deduct management fees. This is the primary cost of investing in money market funds and will lower our actual rate of return for investing in money market funds. The higher the management fees, the lower the potential expected returns for investing in money market funds.

Summary

A money market is a financial market for short-term transactions. Unlike capital markets, the primary function of which is to facilitate the conversion of savings into investment, the primary function of money markets is to provide liquidity to financial institutions and enterprises. Additionally, money market rates play a leading role for the interest rates of the entire financial market, and the central bank's indirect monetary controls are largely accomplished through the money market.

Money markets are primarily categorized into interbank lending markets, bill discount markets, Treasury bill markets and their repo markets. An interbank lending market is a financial market for short-term lending between financial institutions to regulate their temporary positions and meet liquidity needs. Interbank lending is typically short-term, and lending is on the basis of credit. The two methods of settlement are real-time gross settlements and net settlements. Interbank lending rates are influenced by many factors, and different lending terms will have different rates. SHIBOR is an important indicator of China's interbank lending rates.

Bills are credit instruments that reflect the establishment of debtor-creditor relationships, transfers, and repayments in the course of commodity circulation. Additionally, bills are divided into real bills and financing bills. A bill discount is when a bill holder demands for fund, it transfers a bill not yet matured to a bank, and the bank pays the remaining sum to the bill holder after deducting interest. Depending on the process involved, bill discounts include discounts, interbank discounts, and rediscounts. The bill discount market is a venue by which bill discount holders and discounting banks can conduct transactions. Bill discounts reflect transactions with a creditor–debtor relationship. Additionally, bill repos are also an important method of bill transactions.

Short-term bonds are bonds with a term of less than one year and include short-term financing bonds, central bank bills, and Treasury bills. Treasury bills are short-term bonds issued by the government. Secondary markets for Treasury bills are markets which provide Treasury bills with convertibility, and primarily include exchange-traded markets, interbank bond markets and over-the-counter markets. Based on the delivery process, the secondary market for Treasury bills can also be divided into spot markets and repo markets. In essence, repo markets use government bonds as collateral for short-term lending, and repo transactions are of a short duration. Compared to credit-based interbank lending rates, repo rates are relatively low. Repo transactions include repos and reverse repos and can also be divided into open-end repos and closed-end repos.

Money market funds are open-end funds, the shares of which are issued by fund management companies and are pooled together to be exclusively used as a money market instrument of investment. These funds are quite advantageous in that they are fairly secure and bring in fairly stable revenue. However there are also certain risks, such as interest rate risks.

Key Terms

Money Market; Bill; Bill of Exchange; Promissory Note; Check; Discount; Rediscount; Interbank Discount; Treasury bill; Central Bank Bill; Interbank Lending; Bill Market; Net Price Transactions; Real-Time Gross Settlements; Net settlements; Real Bill; Short-Term Financing Bill; Open-End Repo; Closed-End Repo; Repo; Reverse Repo; Money Market Fund

Critical Thinking Questions

1. What is a Money Market Fund? What are the differences between a money market and a capital market in terms of their different functions?
2. Who participates in a money market? Why do they participate in the money market?
3. What is an interbank lending market? What is the economic significance of an interbank lending market?
4. What is a bill market? What is the difference between a discounted bill and a bank loan?
5. What is a Treasury bill market? What is the role of a Treasury bill market?
6. What is a repo market? What is the role of a repo market?
7. What is a net price transaction? What are the strengths and weaknesses of a net price transaction?
8. What are the differences between American auction and Dutch auction?
9. What is a money market fund, and what are its characteristics?
10. Suppose that the government issues a type of short-term bond with a maturity of one year, and a nominal interest rate of 3% with a remaining term of one year. Upon

maturity, an one-off interest payment will be made. The current market interest rate is 2.5%. Summarize the content of Chapter 3 and calculate the expected market price for the government bill.

11. A company's financial manager discounts a set of bills with a face value of 20 million yuan with a remaining term of three months, the proceeds of the discounts amount to 19.75 million yuan. What is the annual discount rate?

Chapter 11

Foreign Exchange Markets

Learning Objectives

After studying this chapter, you will be able to:

- Understand foreign exchange and foreign exchange markets
- Clearly understand exchange rate quotations
- Clearly understand the buying rate and selling rate
- Understand the spot rate and forward rate
- Understand the basic rate and cross rate
- Clearly understand the spot transaction and forward transaction

Understand the methods of currency arbitrage and interest arbitrage

- Clearly understand exchange rate risks
- Understand the measures for managing foreign exchange risks

One of the functions of money is to act as a medium of exchange. However, since the emergence of trade between countries with different sovereign currencies, currency itself has become an object of trade, and transactions in different currencies have shaped the foreign exchange market. If you want to travel to a foreign country or go abroad for further study, you will participate in foreign exchange market trading. Foreign exchange markets facilitate not only the normal operations of import and export enterprises, but also the travel of residents to foreign lands for leisure or learning. At the same time, since there are fluctuations in the exchange rates, there is a chance for returns and risks, and some enterprises, institutions and individuals will often become extensively involved in foreign exchange market trading to reap the benefits of exchange rate fluctuations. From a broader perspective, the development of a country's (region's) foreign exchange market reflects the degree of the country's (region's) financial development, financial openness, and the domestic financial market's position in the global financial system. After introducing capital markets and money markets, this chapter will introduce the foreign exchange market.

11.1 Foreign Exchange and the Exchange Rate

11.1.1 What is Foreign Exchange and Foreign Exchange Market?

(a) *Foreign Exchange*

Forex is short for foreign exchange, which can be divided into dynamic forex and static forex. The concept of static forex can be further analyzed in the broad sense and narrow sense. Dynamic forex refers to currency conversion, that is, the behavior in which people convert one currency into another. For instance, you will be traveling to Europe, and you would like to convert a portion of your yuan into euros, this is dynamic forex.

The broad-sense static forex refers to all assets denominated in foreign currencies, including:

- Foreign cash, such as holding dollars or euros.
- Securities in foreign currency, like foreign government bonds, corporate bonds, stocks denominated in foreign currency, etc.
- Payment documents denominated in foreign currency, such as bills, bank deposit certificates, etc.

Foreign exchange in the narrow sense refers to the means of payment denominated in a foreign currency which can be used for international settlements. According to this definition, the securities denominated in a foreign currency cannot be used to make international payment directly, and thus are not classified as foreign currency. In this sense, is the foreign cash that we hold a kind of foreign exchange? Because the foreign cash we have in our hands cannot be used as a means of international payment, it is not considered a foreign exchange in its narrow sense. In the narrow sense, only the foreign currency deposited in banks and foreign currency bills are deemed foreign exchange, which includes, more specifically, bank drafts, checks, promissory notes, and foreign currency deposits.

But in our daily life, what we call foreign exchange is much more general. For example, when you convert dollars into yuan at the Bank of China, most people would call this foreign currency exchange.

(b) *Foreign Exchange Markets*

The foreign exchange market is the venue for foreign exchange transactions. Even the mention of this venue may bring to mind organized visible markets, like wholesale markets, farmer's markets, etc. In these markets, there are all kinds of shouts and bargaining that can be heard all day long. You may also immediately think of investors in the trading halls of securities companies, staring at computer monitors and worrying over stock trends. In the trading hall, it is utter madness and investors shout in joy when the stock prices are good and nearly tear their hair out whenever the market slumps. This, however, is not the case for the foreign exchange market as it is mainly an invisible market, which means it is an organized over-the-counter (OTC) market rather than a centralized trading market. Foreign-exchange traders do business over the phone or on the computer.

Foreign exchange trading is not like shopping at the mall where people pay their dues immediately. In fact, when banks, companies, and governments, etc. trade on the foreign exchange market, it is not anything like the currency exchanges you do at the bank when you exchange dollars for yuan. In most cases, the deals in foreign exchange markets are just transactions between banks deposits denominated in different currencies. In addition, the foreign exchange market is a wholesale market, and the amount of a single transaction is generally rather large. There is a slight difference between an individual's foreign currency exchange for traveling abroad, studying abroad, or visiting relatives and foreign exchange trading between companies and banks. In the wholesale trading of foreign exchange, the exchange rate will be lower than our individual retail trading.

China's foreign exchange market consists primarily of the foreign exchange center established in 1994 which offered online transactions through computer networks, sub-centers, and swap centers, and designated foreign exchange banks had to send designated traders who had been authorized by the foreign exchange trading center to enter trading venues to conduct transactions. As for the structure of China's foreign exchange market, the Chinese foreign exchange market has two layers: a market between customers and designated foreign exchange banks and an interbank foreign exchange market, as in the foreign exchange transactions between designated foreign exchange banks and between these banks and the Central Bank. China's interbank foreign exchange center is membership-based, and any designated banks and their authorized affiliates which have been approved by the People's Bank of China to operate foreign exchange business can become members of the foreign exchange market. In terms of transaction modes, transactions are organized through an electronic auction trading system. Trading members make autonomous quotes through on-site or remote trading terminals, and the trading system brokers transactions according to "price priorities and time priorities". Foreign exchange transactions on the Chinese foreign exchange market include renminbi to foreign currency transactions and currency pair transactions. Renminbi to foreign currency transactions are transactions between renminbi and foreign currencies; currency pair transactions refer to transactions between two certain foreign currencies, such as trading dollars for euros on the Chinese foreign exchange market or trading euros for pounds. Of course, a wide variety of transactions occur on the Chinese foreign exchange market, such as spot transaction of the renminbi for foreign currencies, forward transaction of the renminbi for foreign currencies, swap trading of the renminbi for foreign currencies, options trading of the renminbi for foreign currencies, etc.

At present, London, New York, Singapore, and Tokyo are the largest foreign exchange trading centers in the world. China also has the Shanghai foreign exchange trading center, but it is not a global foreign exchange trading center. Although these foreign exchange centers are located in different areas, due to the development of communication technology, the foreign exchange markets today are global, and the foreign exchange markets in various areas of the world can join each other regardless of the time zone differences, from Monday to Friday, 24 hours a day and can achieve uninterrupted transactions around the world. When Asian foreign exchange trading centers close, the London foreign exchange trading center has just opened; when the London trading center closes, the New York center is just opening. If you have a friend who is engaged in foreign exchange transactions, and you give him a call in the middle of the night, it shouldn't surprise you if he says he's busy making a transaction.

11.1.2 Quotation of Exchange Rate

(a) *What is exchange rate?*

If you want to go to the United States, you cannot use your renminbi and must convert a portion of the yuan you have on hand into US dollars. How much will you receive if you want to convert 100,000 yuan into dollars? That would depend on the exchange rate between the yuan and the US dollar.

The exchange rate is a price relation in which one currency is converted into another, that is using one country's currency to indicate another country's currency price. It is also known as the conversion rate, foreign exchange rate, and forex rate. For instance, suppose that the exchange rate between US dollars and Chinese yuan is 1:6.28; in other words, one dollar can exchange for 6.28 yuan. If the exchange rate between euros and US dollars is 1:1.35 it means that one euro can buy 1.35 dollars.

(b) *Exchange Rate Quotations*

If you want to know the rate between two currencies, you should first make sure which country's currency is the standard, that is, the exchange rate quotation. Generally speaking, there are two different methods of quotation: direct quotations and indirect quotations.

Direct quotation refers to a certain unit of foreign currency as a standard, converted into a number of units of the domestic currency to show the exchange rate between two currencies. It means that, under the direct quotation, the price of each unit of foreign currency is represented in the domestic currency. In the above example in which the exchange rate between US dollars and Chinese yuan is 1:6.28, Chinese yuan is used to represent the exchange rate between US dollars and Chinese yuan. Therefore, for direct quotation, we are using the Chinese yuan. In direct quotation, a higher exchange rate indicates a larger amount of domestic currency you can convert with a single unit of foreign currency. So, the more expensive that foreign currency may be, the cheaper its domestic counterpart. Conversely, as the exchange rate lowers, the foreign currency is devalued, while the domestic currency appreciates. For instance, if the exchange rate between US dollars and Chinese yuan is 1:6.20 it means that one dollar can be converted into 6.20 yuan. In other words, your 100,000 Chinese yuan can be converted into 16,129 US dollars. When the exchange rate is 1:6.28, you can convert your yuan for about 15,924 dollars. As you can see, relative to the rate of 1:6.28, at the rate of 1:6.20, the Chinese yuan has appreciated.

Indirect quotation refers to a certain unit of domestic currency as a standard, converted into several units of foreign currency to show the exchange rate. Under indirect quotation, the exchange rate uses foreign currency to represent the price of per unit domestic currency. For example, the exchange rate between US dollars and Chinese yuan is 1:6.28, which is the indirect quotation for the US dollar. In contrast to direct quotation, with indirect quotations, when the exchange rate is higher, it shows a larger amount of foreign currency that can be converted for a single unit of domestic currency. Conversely, when the exchange rate is lower, it indicates that the domestic currency can be converted into less foreign currency. As a result, in indirect quotation, when the exchange rate rises, the domestic currency appreciates and vice versa.

If you want to use indirect quotation to represent the exchange rate between Chinese yuan and US dollars, you would convert one Chinese yuan into several units of US dollars. Therefore, with indirect quotation, the exchange rate between the Chinese yuan and US dollar is the reciprocal of the exchange rate of direct quotation. With direct quotation, if the exchange rate between Chinese yuan and US dollars is 1:6.20, the exchange rate between Chinese yuan and US dollars for indirect quotation would be 1:0.16129.

The differences between direct and indirect quotations are listed in Table 11.1.

Table 11.1 Exchange Rate Quotations

Quotations	Direct	Indirect
Definition	Certain units of foreign currency are converted into certain units of domestic currency.	Certain units of domestic currency are converted into certain units of foreign currency.
A rising rate shows	Foreign currency becomes more expensive while domestic currency becomes cheaper.	Foreign currency is devalued while domestic currency appreciates.
A falling rate shows	Foreign currency is devalued while domestic currency appreciates.	Foreign currency appreciates, and domestic currency is devalued.

11.1.3 Types of Exchange Rate

Exchange rates can be divided into the following types based on certain criteria:

- Buying rate and selling rate
- Spot rate and forward rate
- Basic rate and cross rate
- Nominal rate and real rate

(a) *Buying Rate and Selling Rate*

The buying rate and selling rate involve banks. The buying rate refers to the exchange rate with which banks buy foreign currency. For example, when you go to a bank to exchange 1000 euros, even though you are selling euros, the bank will give you the buying rate. Because only a small amount of currency is sold by individuals while a large amount is sold by export merchants, the selling rate is also called the export rate. The selling rate refers to the exchange rate used by the bank which sells foreign currencies. For example, if you want to travel to Europe, you can buy euros with Chinese yuan. The exchange rate when the bank sells these euros would be the selling rate. The exchange rate spread is the difference between the selling rate and the buying rate and is the profit that banks make in the course of trading foreign currencies. We can clarify with the following examples. If you sell 1000 euros at the rate of 1:8.50, you can receive 8500 yuan. However you buy euros at the rate of 1:8.60 and can buy 1000 euros with 8600 yuan. So the exchange rate spread of 0.1 is the bank's profit and the bank can earn 100 yuan in total (Table 11.2).

When the buying rate and selling rate are quoted by banks on the foreign exchange market, this is a two-way quotation. The quotation is shown on the banks' display monitor regarding the exchange rate:

$$1 \text{ USD} = 6.2550 - 6.2560 \text{ CNY},$$

$$1 \text{ GBP} = 12.5560 - 12.6660 \text{ CNY}.$$

The former exchange rate is lower than the latter in a two-way quotation. So the former exchange rate is the buying rate and the latter is the selling rate under direct quotation. For instance, suppose that the exchange rate between dollars and Chinese yuan quoted by banks is US$1 exchanging for 6.2550 Chinese yuan or

Table 11.2 Difference in Exchange Rates

Two-Way Quotation	Direct Quotation	Indirect Quotation
Former Rate	Buying Rate	Selling Rate
Latter Rate	Selling Rate	Buying Rate

6.2560 yuan. We would know that 6.2550 represents the buying rate while 6.2560 the selling rate in direct quotation.

But in indirect quotation, the former rate is selling rate and the latter, which is higher, is the buying rate. For example, the exchange rate between dollars and Japanese Yen was quoted at the New York foreign exchange trading center on April 20, 2002. It was:

$$1\text{ USD} = 125.5000 - 125.9000\text{ JPY}.$$

So in the former formula, 125.5000 is the selling rate while 125.9000 is the buying rate.

The average value between the buying rate and selling rate is the middle rate. The calculation: medium-range rate = (buying rate + selling rate) ÷ 2. For instance, when banks give the exchange rate between yuan and dollars, it is 1:6.2550 – 6.2560. The middle rate is 1 dollar exchanging for 6.2555 yuan.

(b) *Spot Rate and Forward Rate*

The exchange rate is divided into the spot rate and forward rate according to the date of delivery. Delivery is the act of giving and receiving in which the buyer and the seller fulfill their contractual obligation and complete the delivery of goods and payment. Whether it be a commercial transaction or a financial transaction, all transactions must go through a delivery phase. Delivery on the foreign exchange market means that the buyer pays out domestic currency and receives the foreign exchange that he wants to buy and meanwhile, the seller pays the foreign currencies and receives the domestic currency. The date of delivery in foreign exchange transactions may be either spot or forward delivery. A spot delivery means the trading parties are going to complete the delivery within two trading days after the conclusion of the contract. A forward delivery, on the other hand, refers to completion of the delivery more than two trading days after the conclusion of the contract.

Since delivery dates differ, there will be a difference in the exchange rate. The exchange rate used in spot delivery is the spot rate, that is, the exchange rate used within two trading days, which is also known as spot exchange rate. The forward rate is determined by both parties for foreign exchange trade at some point in the future and is also known as the forward exchange rate or forward price.

When you go to the bank to exchange foreign currency, the exchange rate shown on the digital monitor is the spot rate and not the forward rate. Generally speaking, there are two ways to quote the forward rate: direct quotations and forward margins.

A direct quotation refers to the buying rate and selling rate for different delivery times but both appear directly on the bank's monitor, quoted in the same way as that of the spot rate. For instance, Table 11.3 shows the renminbi forward exchange rate quoted by the Bank of China on April 3, 2013. At a glance, you can see the

Table 11.3 The Bank of China's Renminbi Forward Exchange Rates on April 3, 2013

		USD	EUR	JPY	HKD	GBP	SF	AUD	CAD
7-day	Buying Rate	618.19	789.94	6.5969	79.54	931.32	649.78	644.87	608.47
	Selling Rate	622.32	798.47	6.6647	80.26	940.13	655.97	651.24	613.89
1-month	Buying Rate	618.82	790.95	6.6060	79.63	932.15	650.53	644.30	608.69
	Selling Rate	623.15	799.57	6.6733	80.38	941.30	657.18	651.08	614.49
3-month	Buying Rate	620.89	793.99	6.6306	79.93	935.07	653.21	643.47	609.89
	Selling Rate	625.26	802.59	6.6992	80.66	944.14	659.84	650.20	615.68
6-month	Buying Rate	623.06	797.82	6.6633	80.28	938.52	656.72	641.47	611.04
	Selling Rate	627.94	806.29	6.7305	81.00	947.51	663.43	648.07	616.73
9-month	Buying Rate	625.05	801.42	6.6954	80.59	941.78	660.11	639.31	611.93
	Selling Rate	630.43	809.98	6.7626	81.32	950.90	667.11	646.03	617.75
12-month	Buying Rate	627.41	805.47	6.7321	80.95	945.58	664.01	637.43	613.12
	Selling Rate	633.09	814.02	6.7996	81.67	954.82	671.12	644.10	618.99

Table 11.4 Spot Rates and Forward Rates

Quotation Method	Direct	Indirect
If the forward margin is a premium, the forward rate is equal to the spot rate	Plus the premium	Minus the premium
If the forward margin is a discount, the forward rate is equal to the spot rate	Minus the discount	Plus the discount

same-day transaction rates for the renminbi and several other currencies (such as the US dollar) and the forward rate for a delivery several months later. For example, the same day rate for renminbi–dollar transactions and the buying rate for a delivery three months later is 620.89 CNY/100 USD, while the selling rate for a delivery three months later is 625.26 CNY/100 USD.

The forward margin is how much the forward rate is higher or lower than the spot rate. 1 point is one ten-thousandths or 0.0001.

The margin between the forward rate and the spot rate is the forward margin (Table 11.4). The forward margin is equal to the forward exchange rate minus the spot rate. Three things can occur between the forward rate and spot rate:

- The forward rate is higher than the spot rate, so the amount of the forward margin is positive and is called the forward premium.
- The forward rate is lower than the spot rate, so the amount is negative and is called the forward discount.

- The forward rate is equal to the spot rate and the forward margin is zero, so this is called the parity.

If the bank offers the forward margin, how would you calculate the forward rate based on the spot rate? Maybe you blurted it out: the spot rate plus the forward margin. Actually it is not as simple because it depends on how the exchange rate is offered. Under different exchange rate quotations, the forward exchange rate calculated by the forward margin will also be different.

Under direct quotation, if the forward margin is a premium, the forward rate is equal to the amount of the spot rate plus the premium. If the forward margin is a discount, the forward rate is the amount of the spot rate minus the discount. For instance, let us suppose that the following exchange rate between dollars and yuan is offered by a bank:

The spot rate is 1 USD = 6.2710 – 20.

The three-month forward rate is "Discount 80–60".

Because China uses direct quotations, the three-month forward rate is calculated with the following formula:

$$\begin{array}{l} \$1 = ¥6.2710 - 20 \\ \underline{-)\qquad\quad 80 - 60\quad} \\ \$1 = ¥6.2630 - 60 \end{array}.$$

Under indirect quotations, if the forward margin is a premium, the forward rate is equal to the amount of the forward rate minus the premium. If the forward margin is a discount, the forward rate is the amount of the spot rate plus the discount. For example, the exchange rate is also offered by Citibank at the same time as in the former example:

The spot rate is $1 = ¥6.2710 – 20.

The three-month forward rate is "Premium 80 – 60".

Since America uses indirect quotations for all currencies except the British pound, the three-month forward rate is the amount of the spot rate minus the premium, namely:

$$\begin{array}{l} \$1 = ¥6.2710 - 20 \\ \underline{-)\qquad\quad 80 - 60\quad} \\ \$1 = ¥6.2630 - 60 \end{array}.$$

If you need to calculate the forward rate based on the quoted spot rate and forward margin, how would you know if the computation was accurate? Here we have a simple and practical criterion: The buying and selling spread of the forward rate is greater than that of the spot rate. For instance, in the above example, the buying and selling spread of the forward rate in both calculations is 30 points, and the buying and selling spread of the spot rate is only 10 points. As such, we can assume that our calculation is accurate.

(c) *Basic Rates and Cross Rates*

There are more than 200 countries and regions throughout the world, and each country has its own currency, except for those within the European Union. Is it necessary to indicate all the exchange rates between domestic currency and every foreign currency? This would be overly troublesome and is unnecessary. Generally speaking, a country will choose the most traded currency in its international economic activities as the basic currency and use the exchange rate between the domestic currency and the basic currency as the basic exchange rate. Most countries will typically use the US dollar as the basic currency in the exchange rates for their domestic currency. This is because USD is the world's most important reserve currency and is a key currency. As such, the exchange rate between the domestic currency and USD is the basic rate. For the foreign exchange market of each country, only the basic rate is quoted while the exchange rate between the domestic currency and other foreign currencies can be calculated via the basic rate. The exchange rate we obtain through this calculation is known as the cross rate.

For instance, suppose that the exchange rate (the middle rate) between USD and JPY is offered by Citibank as $1 = 120 JPY, that is, one dollar can be exchanged for 120 Japanese Yen. The exchange rate (the middle rate) between USD and EUR is $1 = €0.7550. What is the exchange rate between EUR and JPY?

The exchange rate between EUR and JPY is calculated as follows:

$$\frac{\$1}{\$1} = \frac{120\text{ JYP}}{€0.7550},$$

$$\$1/\$1 = 120\text{ JPY}/€1.0550.$$

In other words, the exchange rate between EUR and JPY is:

$$€1 = 132.4503\text{ JPY}.$$

(d) *Nominal Rates and Real Rates+*

The publicly announced exchange rate which is used in our social and economic lives to reflect the price relations between the currencies of two countries is known as the nominal rate. The various exchange rates between different currencies that we see displayed on monitors in banks, airports, hotels, and foreign exchange markets are nominal rates. Nominal rates change with the fluctuations of supply and demand on the foreign exchange market and cannot completely reflect the actual purchasing power of the two country's currencies.

The real rate is the nominal interest rate adjusted for the price level of the two countries. If we set e for the directly quoted nominal exchange rate, in other words, we use the domestic currency to represent the price of the foreign currency, use e_r for the real exchange rate, p^* for the price level of the foreign country as expressed in their currency and p for the domestic price level expressed in the domestic currency, and we can obtain the following formula for the real rate:

$$e_r = \frac{e \cdot p^*}{p}.$$

The real rate reflects the relative price level of the two countries expressed in the same currency, and in this way, the competitiveness of domestic products. If the inflation rate is higher than it is in America, the real rate between CNY and USD would fall and vice versa.

11.2 Foreign Exchange Trading

11.2.1 Spot Transaction and Forward Transaction

Based on the different delivery time after a transaction, foreign exchange trading can be divided into:

- Spot transaction
- Forward transaction

Spot transaction refers to the delivery within two trading days. In spot transaction, the delivery typically occurs on the next trading day after the conclusion of a contract. For instance, if today is Monday and, as a financial manager, you conclude a spot contract with a bank, the delivery date for this transaction would be tomorrow. If a public holiday occurs immediately after the deal has been concluded, the delivery date should be delayed to the first business day after the public holiday.

Forward transaction refers to the foreign exchange transaction delivered on a future date as stipulated in the forward contract. Generally speaking, any transaction delivered after two trading days is known as a forward transaction. The delivery period of forward transaction is often one month, two months, three months, and six months. Of course, the time limit of delivery can be as short as several days and as long as a year.

People typically use forward transaction for the following two purposes:

- Hedging
- Speculation

Hedging refers to buying or selling a foreign exchange asset or indebted foreign exchange with an equal amount to protect the buyer or seller from exchange rate fluctuations. Suppose that an American importer signs a purchasing contract with a German exporter, which amounts to 50 million euros and promises to deliver the payment three months later. The current exchange rate between EUR and USD is €1 = $1.3500. According to the current exchange rate, this American importer needs to pay 67.5 million dollars. However, after three months, the exchange rate between EUR and USD has risen, say, to €1 = $1.5000, this importer now must pay 75 million dollars. To avoid losses that arise from such a EUR exchange rate, this American importer can buy EUR from the three-month forward market and fulfill their obligation three months later with the purchased EUR. In this way, losses from a rising EUR rate can be avoided. If the premium for a three-month forward rate between EUR and USD is 0.0050, this importer actually only pays 250 thousand dollars to avoid a 7.5 million dollar loss.

Unlike hedging, foreign exchange speculation refers to holding long positions or short positions based on the predicted rate of fluctuation so as to benefit from the exchange rate volatility. It includes spot speculation and forward speculation. Spot speculation refers to buying or selling a certain currency according to the speculator's own prediction of rate fluctuation so that this currency's rate will rise or fall at the expected time. For example, if you have one million dollars and the exchange rate between EUR and USD is €1 = 1.3500 and you predict that this rate will rise sharply in the coming three months, you may convert this one million dollars into 740.8 thousand euros. Three months later, if this rate does indeed rise sharply, for instance, to €1 = 1.6500, you can convert 740.8 thousand Euros into approximately 1.2223 million dollars and earn 222.3 thousand dollars. In fact, this kind of speculation is exactly the same as individual invest in the stock market.

Forward speculation is different from spot speculation. It can give full play to the effect of leverage, that is, to conduct a large deal with a small amount of money. In spot speculation, the transaction amount depends on how much cash you have available. For example, if you predict that the rate between euros and dollars will rise sharply after three months, you can buy three-month euros for forward speculation and sell these euros after three months. If the exchange rate of euros does rise sharply, you make a fortune. Conversely, if the rate drops, you lose out.

There is a special kind of hedging called swap trading. Swap trading refers to buying and selling the same foreign currency at the same time, for the same amount but with different delivery dates for buying and selling. The purpose of such a trade is also to avoid the risks of exchange rate fluctuations. Nowadays, there are three kinds of swap trades:

- Spot to forward, that is to buy or sell a sum of spot exchanges while also selling or buying the same amount of forward exchanges.

- Second day to third day, that is a kind of foreign exchange transaction in which the delivery is made on the second day after the completed transaction and reversed on the third.
- Forward to forward in which both parties of a forward transaction with different delivery periods conduct two reversing transactions with the same currency and amounts.

We will go into further detail on swap trading in the next chapter.

11.2.2 Interest Arbitrage and Currency Arbitrage

(a) *Interest Arbitrage* (*Carry Trade*)

Imagine that the three-month interest rate in America is 2% and that of the China is 4%. If you have some money (and you can choose to deposit it in the form of yuan or dollars), what would you choose, yuan or dollars? You may choose the yuan without hesitation, because the CNY rate is higher. In fact, when there is a large discrepancy between the interest rates of two countries over the same period, there will be room for currency interest arbitrage. Interest arbitrage means that when the interest rates of two countries differ from each other, investors obtain the interest spread by moving money from the low-interest-rate country to the high-interest-rate country.

For instance, suppose that the three-month interest rate in America is 2% at present and that of the euro in the EU is 3%. In such a situation, American investors will transfer their money to the EU. If you have one million dollars in America and deposit it into an American bank for three months, you can earn the following interest:

$$1{,}000{,}000 \times 2\% \times \frac{3}{12} = 5000 \text{ USD.}$$

Suppose that the exchange rate between euros and dollars both at present and three months later are 1:1.3500. If you convert 1 million dollars into 740740.7 euros and deposit it into a commercial bank in the EU for three months, you can earn the following interest:

$$740740.7 \times 3\% \times \frac{3}{12} = 5555.56 \text{ EUR.}$$

Because the exchange rate between dollars and Euros remains unchanged, you can change the principal capital and interest into dollars according to the rate of 1:1.3500 three months later, earning altogether:

$$746296.26 \times 1.3500 = 1007499.95 \text{ USD.}$$

The interest therein is 7499.95 dollars, which is 2499.95 dollars more than if the money had been deposited in America.

When we figure out how much interest you can earn from a certain kind of interest arbitrage, it is based on the precondition that there is no change in the exchange rate between dollars and euros over these three months. If the exchange rate changes, however, it is uncertain whether or not you can benefit from such interest arbitrage. If the dollar depreciates compared to the euro over the next three months, you can earn more than 2499.95 dollars in interest. For instance, suppose that the exchange rate between EUR and USD rises to 1:1.65 three months later. If you change the principal and interest into dollars, or 7,462,962,600 dollars, you have made a serious killing!

On the other hand, if the rate between EUR and USD is not 1:1.65 but 1:1.2000, what about then? To take a brief consideration, if you change the principal and interest of 0.7463 million euros into dollars, you can only earn 895.6 thousand dollars, almost 109.4 thousand dollars less than the 1.005 million dollars of principal and interest you would have earned having deposited the money in America. It is certainly not a good deal.

When you are conducting interest arbitrage, how can you avoid such losses from exchange rate fluctuation? One of the best methods is to combine interest arbitrage and swap trading. For instance, say you buy 0.7408 million euros with 1 million dollars and deposit them in a commercial bank in the EU. Meanwhile, you sell euros in a three-month forward market. This kind of interest arbitrage is called covered interest arbitrage. Conversely, pure interest arbitrage without selling in the forward market is called uncovered interest arbitrage.

(b) *Currency Arbitrage*

Currency arbitrage occurs when the exchange rate for a currency is different in different foreign exchange markets. Arbitrage can come through the foreign exchange rate differences at the different foreign exchange markets at the same time and can also earn a profit. Currency arbitrage comes in the following forms:

- Direct Arbitrage
- Indirect Arbitrage

Direct arbitrage occurs when a difference exists in the exchange rate of the same currency in two different foreign exchange markets, and people will purchase this currency in one market and at the same time sell the same currency in the other market to earn a profit. This is the simplest form of currency arbitrage.

For instance, suppose that the exchange rate between USD and EUR on the New York foreign exchange market is:

$$\$1 = €1.1500.$$

On the Frankfurt exchange market, however, the exchange rate between EUR and USD is:

$$€1 = \$0.9500.$$

We would then convert this for the direct quotation of EUR, which can be represented in the following formula:

$$\$1 = €1.05263.$$

In contrast to the Frankfurt rate, the exchange rate of USD to EUR on the New York market is higher. Why so? This is because one dollar can be exchanged for 1.1500 euros here, while one dollar in Frankfurt can purchase only 1.05263 euros. Herein lies the profitable opportunity of currency arbitrage.

Suppose that you have 1 million dollars on hand. Currency arbitrage can be achieved along the following processes:

1. All the dollars you have can be exchanged into euros on the New York market. This would bring you 1.15 million euros according to the existing exchange rate at New York, or 1 million $\times$ 1.1500 = 1.15 million.
2. 1.15 million euros can be exchanged for dollars in Frankfurt with the exchange rate of 1 USD = 1.05263 EUR, so the total would be 1.092512 million USD dollars.

Now, let us add up the total amount of profit that you can earn: Deducting your principal of one million, you can earn a total of 92,512 dollars in profit. Not too bad, right?

However, the actual direct arbitrage rarely shows up on foreign exchange markets, while indirect arbitrage is an everyday occurrence. Indirect arbitrage can be achieved through exchange rate differences in three different exchange markets, while we can earn profits through buying low and selling high.

For instance, let us suppose that on the New York foreign exchange market, the exchange rate between USD and EUR is:

$$\$1 = €1.1500.$$

On the London market, the exchange rate between GBP and USD is:

$$£1 = \$1.4120.$$

Meanwhile, the exchange rate in Frankfurt between EUR and GBP is:

$$€1 = £0.5000.$$

Can we find an opportunity for currency arbitrage under these exchange rates? If you have 1 million dollars, can you earn profit with the following steps?

1. Exchange one million dollars for euros on the New York foreign exchange market at a rate of $1 = €1.1500 for a total of 1.15 million euros.
2. Exchange 1.15 million euros for pounds in Frankfurt at a rate of €1 = £0.5000 for a total of 575,000 pounds.
3. Exchange 575,000 pounds for dollars on the London market at a rate of £1 = 1.4120 for a total of 811,900 dollars.

This is a rather depressing result that we have come to because, in the end, you will have burned about 190,000 dollars. Does it mean that there is no opportunity for currency arbitrage?

Now, you try out the following steps to buy and sell foreign currencies instead of the former method:

1. Exchange one million dollars for pounds on the London foreign exchange market at a rate of £1 = 1.4120 for a total of 708,215 pounds.
2. Exchange 708,215 pounds for euros in Frankfurt at a rate of €1 = £0.5000 for a total of 1.416431 million euros.
3. Exchange 1.416431 million euros for dollars in New York at a rate of $1 = €1.1500 for a total of 1.231679 million dollars.

Your original one million in principal has become 1.231679 million dollars, earning you a net income of 231,679 dollars. With this kind of method, you can really earn good money.

How can we know whether or not there is an opportunity for currency arbitrage? In direct arbitrage, we can simply compare the exchange rate in the various foreign exchange markets. Indirect arbitrage is a little bit more complicated, but we can use a very practical standard here. We use the same method (either direct quotations or indirect quotations) for the exchange rates of the three currencies at three different foreign exchange markets, and then we multiply these rates; if the product is 1, there is no opportunity for arbitrage at all. On the other hand, if the product is not equal to 1, there is room for arbitrage. Just as we displayed in the above cases, indirect quotation is employed on the New York, London, and Frankfurt markets. The formula for which would be:

$$1.1500 \times 1.4120 \times 0.5000 = 0.8119.$$

The product is not equal to 1, so there is in fact an opportunity for arbitrage.

So we can come to the conclusion that how you choose the arbitrage procedure will greatly affect what you can get. In the first form of arbitrage, a loss of 190,000 dollars was not your set goal because you cannot earn money but instead incur a loss. How, then, do we select an accurate arbitrage procedure?

Note that buying low and selling high is the fundamental principle of arbitrage, and we should always adhere to it. When conducting arbitrage, we must first compare the exchange rates of two currencies in different markets. Under indirect arbitrage, you must first determine the exchange rate between two other currencies. For example, in the former case we multiply the exchange rate of £1 = 1.4120 between pounds and dollars in London with the other exchange rate of €1 = £0.50000 between euros and pounds in Frankfurt, and finally, we arrived at the exchange rate between euros and dollars, that is:

$$€1 = \$0.7060 \quad \text{or} \quad \$1 = €1.4164.$$

Obviously, the price of dollars is lower on the New York exchange market. Hence, the final step of our arbitrage procedure is to buy dollars on the New York foreign exchange market, and the other arbitrage steps would come from determining this final step. Since euros are needed to make the purchase in New York, the penultimate step is to buy euros which can be done by selling pounds in Frankfurt. How would we sell pounds in Frankfurt? We would first need to purchase pounds on the London market. In this way, we have determined the first step of arbitrage in which we can exchange dollars into pounds on the London foreign exchange market.

11.3 Foreign Exchange Risks and Management

11.3.1 What is Foreign Exchange Risk?

With globalization, growing international competition and international flow of capital, enterprises and banks with big volumes of international trade, investments and loan business will receive and pay a great amount of foreign exchange or have claims and debts in foreign currencies. When the exchange rate fluctuates, the amounts of some foreign currencies for exchange or conversion into domestic currency or another foreign currency will change. Just as the previous example shows, after the contract was signed between the American company and the German partner, if the euro's exchange rate abruptly rose, the American company would have to pay an additional 10 million dollars for the goods. This is the exchange rate risk, which is the possibility of incurring loss with the change of exchange rates in the course of an enterprise's operations and an individual's economical activities, such as holding or utilizing foreign currencies.

For some enterprises and financial institutions, the majority of their assets may be denominated in the domestic currency, while their liabilities are mainly denominated in a foreign currency. Conversely, others may have assets which are mainly denominated in a foreign currency while their liabilities are denominated in the domestic currency. This phenomenon is called **currency mismatch**. Since there is a currency mismatch of assets and liabilities, the balance sheet may be very sensitive to changes in the exchange rate. If a large number of enterprises and institutions of a certain country all have severe currency mismatches, the risk of exchange rate fluctuations will not only have an effect on the stability of their operations, but may possibly even have an adverse effect on the domestic currency's exchange rate and the stability of the entire financial system.

11.3.2 Managing Exchange Rate Risks

When there is an exchange rate risk, we must try our best to avoid or reduce it. In fact, some of the strategies to manage exchange rate risks have already been introduced such as hedging and swap trading, and so on. Now, let us introduce the fundamental strategies of managing exchange risks in detail. In short, the dominant strategies are as follows:

- In the course of signing a contract, the strategies can be further divided into the following:
  - Choice of currency for the contract/the denominated currency
  - Hedge Clause
- Financial market operations

(a) *Management Strategies in Contract Signing*

When signing contracts, it is crucial to choose the contract/denominated currency for exchange rate risk management. Several principles can be observed as follows:

First of all, try to make the domestic currency as the contract or denominated currency. In this way, the foreign exchange risk will be avoided for there is no need to convert between domestic and foreign currencies. However, the risk will be transferred to your contractual counterparty. In the above example, the American firm must pay an additional 10 million dollars after import when the exchange rate between the euro and US Dollar rises, because we suppose the euro is the strong currency while the US Dollar is relatively weak. However, if it is stipulated in the contract that the contract currency is the US dollar, then there will be no such risk for this American firm. This strategy is not suitable for all firms, organizations, or individuals, for it requires domestic currency to be freely exchangeable. In fact, currency in many countries cannot be exchanged freely.

Secondly, adopt a strong currency in commercial or capital exports, and a weak currency for imports. A strong currency refers to a currency with an exchange rate that is likely to rise in the foreign exchange market, yet weak currency refers to a currency with an exchange rate that will likely fall. In commercial or capital exports, if a strong currency is used as the contract currency, more domestic currency or other currencies can be converted for the same amount when the strong currency's exchange rate rises. However, if a weak currency is chosen as the contract currency by import merchants or debtors, less domestic or other currencies shall be paid when the exchange rate falls. Just like the first principle, the risk of exchange rate fluctuation is shifted to your counterparty.

As different contract currencies will shift the risk to the counterparty who is absolutely not a fool, choosing the contract currency to avoid risk of exchange rate fluctuation is unrealistic. Nowadays, financial market operations are more frequently used to avoid exchange rate risks.

(b) *Financial Market Operations*

Besides hedging and swap trading mentioned above, we can also choose spot transaction, options, swaps, loans–investments, and loans–spot-transaction–investments to avoid or reduce exchange rate fluctuation risks. In Chapter 12, we will elaborate on foreign exchange options and swaps. Here we have only presented two management strategies to avoid foreign exchange risk, that is, spot transaction and loans–investments.

Spot transaction is when foreign exchange banks conduct foreign exchange buying and selling on spot markets to balance long or short exchange positions caused by foreign exchange buying and selling with customers so as to avoid risk from foreign exchange rate fluctuations.

The loan–investment method avoids the exchange rate fluctuation risk by creating claims and debts with the same currency, amount, and duration as future foreign exchange earnings and payments. For instance, imagine that you are a finance manager and your firm exports a batch of goods worth 10 million US dollars. The exchange rate between the US dollar and the Chinese yuan is $1 = 6.2500, but the goods will be paid for after three months. If after three months, the Chinese yuan has devalued and the exchange rate has dropped to 1 = 6.5000, then you will earn an additional 2.5 million yuan when you convert the 10 million US dollars into Chinese yuan. Of course, it is of great advantage to your firm. However, if the yuan appreciates and the exchange rate becomes $1 = 6.0000, then you will lose 2.5 million yuan. To avoid losses from such kinds of fluctuation, as a finance manager, you can borrow 10 million dollars for three months and immediately change them into 62.5 million yuan at the rate of $1 = 6.2500 in the spot market. When your firm receives 10 million dollars for the goods three months later, you can meet previous liabilities. In this way, your firm bears no other loss apart from the interest of the loan.

On the other hand, if your company imports a set of equipment valued at 10 million dollars and the exchange rate between the US dollar and the Chinese yuan turns out to be $1 = 6.0000 three months later, you can pay 2.5 million yuan less than before. However, if the yuan is devalued and the rate drops to $1 = 6.5000, your payment will amount to 65 million yuan, which is 2.5 million yuan more than before. To avoid such kinds of losses, as the finance manager, you can pay 62.5 million yuan to buy the 10 million dollars in the spot market and pay off the equipment with this sum. In this way, you can fix the export earnings and import costs at a level you expect. Nevertheless, you should pay attention to the different operating directions. Otherwise, you will not fix the export earnings and import cost, but will instead lead the company to a greater loss.

Summary

Forex is short for foreign exchange, which can be divided into dynamic forex and static forex. The foreign exchange market is the venue in which foreign exchange transactions occur and is mainly an invisible market. Foreign exchange markets today are worldwide and round-the-clock markets for non-stop transactions.

The exchange rate is a price relation between one currency and another. Exchange rate quotations can be divided into direct quotations and indirect quotations. Exchange rates can be divided into the following types: buying rates and selling rates, spot rates and forward rates, as well as basic rates and cross rates.

Spot rates are exchange rates that are used in foreign currency delivery within two days of the completion of a transaction. Forward rates are determined by both trading parties beforehand to conduct foreign exchange transactions in the future. There are two ways of quoting the forward rate: direct quotations and forward margins. Forward margin refers to the margin between the forward rate and the spot rate. There could be a forward premium, discount, or parity.

With respect to direct quotations, if the forward margin is a premium, the forward rate is equal to the amount of the spot rate plus the premium; if the forward margin is a discount, the forward rate is the amount of the spot rate minus the discount. In indirect quotation, if the forward margin is the premium, the forward rate is equal to the amount of the forward rate minus the premium; if the forward margin is the discount, the forward rate is the amount of the spot rate plus the discount.

The basic rate is the exchange rate between the domestic currency and the basic currency. The exchange rate between the currency of other countries and the domestic currency can be calculated according to basic rate, and the calculated exchange rate is known as the cross rate.

In light of different delivery times, foreign exchange transactions can be divided into spot transactions and forward transactions. Spot transaction means that both trading parties carry out the delivery within two business days after the deal is made. On the other hand, forward transaction refers to the foreign exchange transaction conducted at some time in the future as stipulated in the forward contract. The purposes of forward foreign exchange transaction are often for hedging or speculation.

In foreign exchange markets, there may also be interest arbitrage and currency arbitrage. Interest arbitrage means that when the interest rate between two countries differs from each other, investors obtain the interest spread by moving money from the low-interest-rate country to the high-interest-rate country. Currency arbitrage refers to the transaction that takes advantage of different exchange rates for the same currency in different foreign exchange markets. It can be divided into direct and indirect arbitrage.

In foreign exchange markets, the exchange rate will fluctuate and hence there is an exchange rate risk. When enterprises and financial institutions exhibit a significant currency mismatch, the risks of exchange rate fluctuations are even more significant. To prevent and avoid risks, investors can carefully select the contract currency or denominated currency. Moreover, financial market operations can be adopted, such as spot transaction, loan–investment, hedging, swaps, and so on.

Key Terms

Foreign Exchange; Foreign Exchange Market; Exchange rate; Direct Quotation; Indirect Quotation; Buying Rate; Selling Rate; Spot Rate; Forward Rate; Basic Rate; Cross Rate; Spot Transaction; Forward Transaction; Hedging; Forward Margin; Forward Premium; Forward Discount; Forward Parity; Interest Arbitrage; Covered Interest Arbitrage; Uncovered Interest Arbitrage; Foreign Exchange Speculation; Spot Speculation; Forward Speculation; Exchange Rate Risk; Currency Mismatch

Critical Thinking Questions

1. What is foreign exchange?
2. What is the foreign exchange market?
3. What is the foreign exchange rate?
4. What kinds of quotations are there in foreign exchange rates?
5. What is the spot rate and forward rate?
6. What is the basic rate and cross rate?
7. What is interest arbitrage and currency arbitrage?
8. Who participates in the foreign exchange market? What are their respective purposes?
9. What is a forward foreign exchange transaction? Why do people conduct forward foreign exchange transactions?
10. What is the exchange rate risk? What are the basic measures to manage rate risk?
11. Suppose you are a finance manager of a firm. Your firm signs an import contract of equipment amounting to 25 million dollars with an American firm and will pay on delivery three months later. At present, the exchange rate between yuan and dollars is \$1 = 6.2550. In order to avoid financial loss from rate fluctuation, what should you do?
12. Suppose the foreign exchange quotations in the Tokyo, New York and London foreign exchange markets (Figure 11.1) are as follows:

    In the Tokyo foreign exchange market, \$1 = 120.0000 Japanese Yen.
    In the New York foreign exchange market, \$1 = £0.7500
    In the London foreign exchange market, £1 = 160.0000 Japanese Yen.

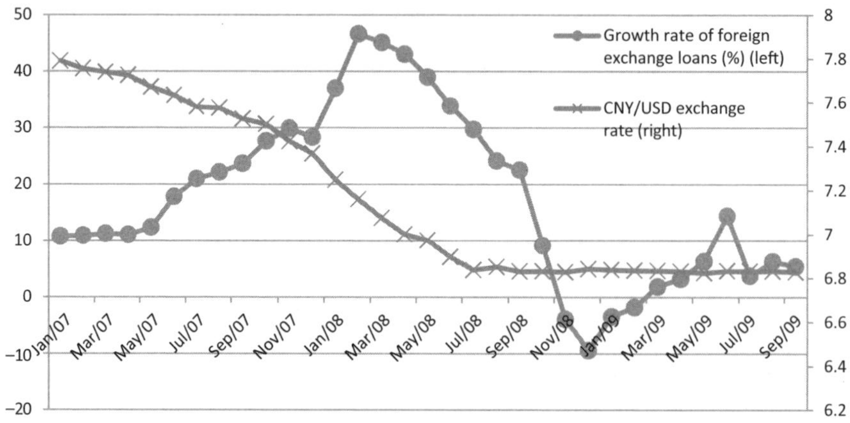

Fig. 11.1 Growth Rate of China's Foreign Exchange Loans and Chinese Yuan-To-Dollars Rate (January 2007 to September 2009)

Source: Based on data from the People's Bank of China and China Foreign Exchange Trade Center

Are there any currency arbitrage opportunities in these three markets? If there are, how would you carry out arbitrage if you had 1 million pounds? How much can you benefit from the arbitrage? If you have 1 million dollars, how can you carry out arbitrage?

13. Suppose there is a wonderful opportunity for currency arbitrage in the boundary areas of Southern America and Northern Mexico. In America, the exchange rate between dollars and Mexican pesos is $1 = 1.1 peso, while, in Mexico, the rate is $1 = 1.0 peso. There is an impoverished Mexican drunkard who only has 1.1 peso. A bottle of beer costs 0.1 peso in Mexico. If there is no other transaction cost and this drunkard can freely move between the two countries and exchange his money, how many bottles of beer can he buy with the original 1.1 pesos? Who pays for his beer?
14. Suppose the American semi-annual Treasury bond rate is 2.5% and England's rate is 3.5%. Currently, the rate between pounds and dollars is £1 = $1.2000. How can you carry out interest arbitrage with 1 million pounds? If the rate between pounds and dollars shifts to £1 = $1.2200 three months later, is it still profitable for arbitrage? If not, how can you avoid such a risk?
15. Suppose that the spot exchange rate between pounds and dollars in the London foreign exchange market is £1 = $1.2000 and the premium for a three-month forward rate is 0.0100. Calculate the three-month forward rate. If the discount is 0.0100, what would the three-month forward rate be?
16. Case analysis. The following figure shows the growth rate of China's foreign exchange loans from January 2007 to September 2009 and Chinese yuan-to-dollars rate change. Analyze: (1) The variation tendency of the CNY/USD exchange rate over this period. (2) The growth trend of foreign exchange loans. (3) What rate risk and currency arbitrage opportunities are brought about by changes to the CNY exchange rate? (4) What is the relationship between the growth rate of foreign exchange loans and changes to the exchange rate? (5) Based on this chapter, what are the main economic factors contributing to changes to the growth rate of foreign exchange loans?

Chapter 12

Financial Derivatives Market

Learning Objectives

After studying this chapter, you will be able to:

- Understand underlying financial products and derivative products
- Clearly understand forward agreements on interest rate
- Understand forward exchange transactions
- Understand futures transactions and their main functions
- Clearly understand the basic principles of hedging transactions with futures
- Understand options and their types
- Clearly understand the role of options in risk management
- Understand the value of options
- Understand swap, their types and the role of swap in risk management

Stock, bonds, deposits, and other such items which we have already discussed are all **underlying financial products**, which are also called primary financial instruments, and they primarily function as a medium for transferring savings into investment, or as a certificate for credit–debt settlements. Correspondingly, there are also derivative financial instruments. **Derivative financial instruments** are financial products, including futures and options, which are derived from underlying financial instruments, the main function of which is not to regulate a shortage or surplus of funds or directly facilitate the transfer of savings to investment, but instead is to manage the risk exposure that arises in connection with the underlying instruments. Similar to stock, bond, and other underlying financial instruments which can be traded on a secondary market, the prices of derivatives in a transaction are determined by supply and demand on the market, and fluctuate with changes in the market environment, which provide profit-making opportunity for speculators. However, it is important to note that the improper use of derivative financial instruments will lead to unbearable losses. Unlike the transaction of underlying financial products, where the buyer and seller will exchange monetary and equivalent financial assets at a certain time after the transaction and in accordance with the full amount of the transaction, some of the financial derivative contracts do not involve the delivery of the principal and are often called non-deliverable derivative transactions.

Derivatives can be divided into the categories of forward, futures, options and swaps. This chapter will provide a fundamental knowledge of various types of financial derivatives.

12.1 Forward Transactions

A **forward transaction** is a hedging instrument which came out in the early 1980s. It is a contract in which both parties agree to trade a certain product at a specific future date and according to predefined terms and conditions, such as the transaction assets, date, and price.

Forward agreements primarily cover interest rate, bonds, and currency.

12.1.1 Forward Agreements on Interest Rate

(a) *What are Forward Agreements on Interest Rate?*

Suppose that you are the financial manager of some company, and on March 30 you expect that starting from June 1, your company will need a total of 100 million yuan in forward funds with a three-month term. Meanwhile, you also believe that interest rates may rise in the future, and thus, you intend to save the company a sum of financial costs, and hedge against the risk of rising interest rates. Thus, on April 1, you purchase a 2×5 forward agreement on interest rate from a bank and agree that the bank will lend 100 million yuan to your company at 4.75%. The contract will use the Shanghai Interbank Offered Rate (Shibor) as a reference rate. The contract is valid until August 31 and will be calculated based on a 360 day year. If, on June 1, the Shibor does in fact rise to 5.25%, since you preemptively agreed to the forward rate agreement with this bank, your company can borrow 100 million yuan at a rate of 4.75%, and as such, you have successfully used a forward agreement to avoid the risk of rising interest rates. On the other hand, if the market rate doesn't rise as you had expected, but rather falls to 4%, your company still must borrow 100 million yuan at the rate of 4.75%. From this it can be seen that banks can use forward agreements to avoid the risk of falling interest rates.

As you can see in this example, a **forward agreement on interest rate, or a forward rate agreement** (FRA) is a fixed interest rate contract of a certain term concluded by both parties of a transaction, and regardless of the future market rate, interests will be paid in accordance with the contractually agreed rate. If the reference rate rises above the contractually agreed interest rate, the seller will pay a sum of cash to the buyer. If borrowers' borrowing costs are expected to rise, they can buy into forward rate agreements in order to avoid this risk. If the reference rates fall below the contractually agreed interest rate, the buyer will pay a sum of cash to the seller so as to compensate for this difference, and for this reason, if lenders hope to avoid the risk of a fall in future interest rates, they can sell forward rate agreements. Forward rate agreements can keep interest rates at a set level. However, forward rate transactions are not without risk. In the above example, after the Shibor rate rises to 5.25%, your company will earn a certain amount in compensation, but if the future rate falls, the buyer must compensate the seller, and thus, the buyer will not receive any benefit from the lower interest rates. As in the above example, after the Shibor rate falls to 4%, your company must pay the relatively higher interest than the market rate.

(b) *The Basic Elements of a Forward Rate Agreement*

Forward rate agreements primarily consist of the following elements:

(i) *Notional principal*: As a matter of fact, the traders within a real forward rate agreement do not necessarily need to borrow or lend funds like the example above, and a portion of traders enter into forward rate agreements purely based on the future movements of interest rates in order to gain access to the profits of rate fluctuations. Within a real forward rate agreement, there is no exchange of principal, and loans or deposits are only nominal, in that the buyer/seller is not obligated to actually lend or borrow these funds on the market. In the absence of the exchange of principal, forward rate agreements are an off-balance-sheet instrument, and the risks involved are only interest rate risks, which will not pose any threat to principal security. In the example above, the notional principal is 100 million yuan.

(ii) *Forward term*: Forward rate agreements often use $m \times n$ to indicate their start and end time: m represents the number of months after which the contract will enter into force, and n represents the number of months after which the contract will expire. For example, a 1×4 forward rate agreement indicates that the contract will enter into force after one month and will expire in four months, which in fact has a term of three months. In the example above, the forward term is 2×5, in that the contract will enter into force in two months, on June 1, and will expire after five months. Typical forward terms are as follows:

	Three-Month Series			Six-Month Series	
	Start Date	End Date		Start Date	End Date
1×4	1 month	4 months	1×7	1 month	7 months
2×5	2 months	5 months	2×8	2 months	8 months
3×6	3 months	6 months	3×9	3 months	9 months
6×9	6 months	9 months	6×12	6 months	12 months

(iii) *Contractual rate*: This is the interest rate which both parties of the transaction agree to in a forward rate agreement. In the previous example, the contract rate is 4.75%.
(iv) *Reference rate*: The interest rate which is used as a reference by both parties during the delivery of the contract. The reference rate is typically a money market rate, such as the London Interbank Offer Rate (LIBOR). In the example above, the reference rate is the Shibor. The reference rate for a Chinese forward rate agreement can be the Shibor, which is released by the National Interbank Funding Center and can also be a benchmark rate announced by the People's Bank of China. The role of a reference rate is to compare the reference rate and contract rate on the maturity date of the contract, in order to determine interest compensation by the transaction parties. In general, if the interest rate is higher than the contract rate, the seller of the forward rate agreement will pay the difference between the reference rate and contract rate in a certain interest compensation in accordance with the notional principal. On the other hand, the buyer will pay a corresponding sum in interest compensation to the seller.
(v) *Year basis*: Whether the calculation is based on a year of 365 days or 360 days. In the example above, the year basis is 360 days.
(vi) *Fixing date*: The date on which the contract enters into force. In the example above, the contract entered into force on June 1.
(vii) *Maturity date*: The date on which the contract is terminated. In the example above, the contract expired on August 31.

(c) *Forward Rate Agreement Settlements and Payments*

If the Shibor rate rises to 5.25% on June 1, the reference rate would be higher than the contract rate of 4.75%. Although you purchased a 2×5 forward rate agreement from the bank, they must raise your funds based on the market rate of 5.25% so as to meet production and circulation demands. Since the reference rate rose above the contract rate, this bank must pay your company the difference, so as to compensate for the additional interest loss of borrowing the 100 million yuan on June 1.

How much should the bank pay your company then? It should be noted that during a forward rate agreement, the payment is settled at the start of the contract rather than its expiration, and thus, the actual payments should be based on the present value converted in accordance with the reference rate when the contract enters into force. There are 92 days between June 1 and August 31. Combined with what we learned in Chapter 3, the bank should pay x amount on June 1, and should make their calculation based on the market rate of 5.25% so that the future value after 92 days would be $x \times (1 + 5.25\% \times 92/360)$, which should be equal to

$$(5.25\% - 4.75\%) \times 92/360 \times 100{,}000{,}000.$$

That is:

$$x \times (1 + 5.25\% \times 92/360) = (5.25\% - 4.75\%) \times 92/360 \times 100{,}000{,}000.$$

So that we have:

$$x = (5.25\% - 4.75\%) \times 92 \times 100{,}000{,}000/360 + 5.25\% \times 92 = 125453.4 \text{ yuan}.$$

Based on the calculation above, we can generalize about the amount to be paid under forward rate agreements. We shall set L as the settlement rate, R as the contract rate, B as the year basis, D as the number of days in the contract, and P as the notional principal of the contract. If the settlement rate is higher than the contract rate, then the seller of the forward rate agreement must pay the corresponding interest difference to the buyer, and the amount to be paid is

$$A = \frac{(L - R) \times D \times P}{B + L \times D}.$$

Question: If the reference rate is only 4% at the time in which the contract enters into force, how much should your company pay to the bank? Conversely, if the settlement rate is lower than the contract rate, the buyer of the forward rate agreement will pay the corresponding interest difference to the seller, and the amount to be paid is:

$$A = \frac{(R - L) \times D \times P}{B + L \times D}.$$

12.1.2 Forward Bond Transactions

Another forward rate transaction for managing interest rate risks is the **bond forward transaction**, which is a financial contract to purchase a certain amount of the underlying bond at a future date and at an agreed price, as determined by both parties of the transaction. For example, suppose that a certain amount of Treasury bills have a coupon rate of 6% per annum, paid semi-annually, and the interest payment date is May 20. Suppose Party A believes that the market rate will fall to 4% after three months and the market price of these bonds will rise. Therefore, on the date on which Party A and Party B reach a transaction, the interest accrued on these bonds has been paid in full. We shall further assume that the market interest rate on May 20 is 6%, and the market price of these bonds at that time is the same as their nominal value, in that the price of each bond is 100 yuan. However, Party A expects the market rate to fall to 4% after three months. Parties A and B come to a forward rate agreement on May 20 in which they both agree that after three months, or on August 20, Party A will purchase Party B's total of 1 million Treasury bonds at the nominal value of 100 yuan per bond, so that the total nominal value of the forward purchase of bonds is 100 million yuan. If the agreed price (net worth) is 100.5 yuan/bond, then on August 20, regardless of whether or not the bond (net) market price is higher or lower than 100.5 yuan, Party A will pay Party B the corresponding amount, and Party B will agree to transfer the agreed one million bonds.

If the market rate does in fact fall to 4% after half a year, based on what we learned in Chapter 9, the price of this bond (excluding accrued interest) will be 101.9231 yuan. For Party A, a corresponding profit can be earned from this kind of forward bond transaction.

Bond forward contracts usually include the following:

(a) *Underlying Bond*

The object of the forward bond transaction. For example, the Treasury bills, central bank bonds, or financial bonds on which a forward transaction is conducted.

(b) *Quantity of Underlying bonds*

The total nominal value of the underlying bonds of a forward transaction, in units of 10,000 yuan.

(c) *Transaction Date*

The date by which both parties of the transaction enter into a contract. In the example above, the transaction date is May 20.

(d) *Settlement Date*

The date by which both parties of the transaction agree to the conduct the bond delivery and payment of funds. In the example above, the settlement date is November 20 of the given year.

(e) *Duration of Forward Transaction*

The actual number of days between the transaction date and the settlement date, including the transaction date but excluding the settlement date. In China, bond forward transactions are limited to a minimum duration of two days and a maximum duration of 365 days. Both parties of the transaction can freely select a duration of transaction within this range, though extension of the term is not allowed.

(f) *Minimum Transaction Amount*

The starting amount of each bond forward contract, with a minimum nominal value of 100,000 yuan and a trading unit of 10,000 yuan in bonds.

(g) *Net Forward Price*

The net price of the underlying bonds in units of yuan/100 yuan par value which are to be delivered on the settlement date as agreed by both parties on the transaction date. The net price is the difference between the market price then and the interest payable. This net price exists because, prior to delivery and settlement, the bond of the forward transaction is held by the seller, and the accrued interest is vested in the seller.

(h) *Accrued Interest*

The total interest to be paid by bond issuers to bond holders between the last interest payment date (or value date) and the settlement date (excluding the settlement date). It is calculated in units of yuan for each 100-yuan-par-value bond.

(i) *Settlement Amount*

The amount of funds paid by the buyer to the seller when the forward transaction is settled. The settlement amount should include accrued interest. In the example above, there are three months of accrued interest between May 20 and August 20, and the accrued interest for each 100-yuan-par-value bond is 1.5 yuan. Thus, the total accrued interest on 1 million bonds would be 1.5 million yuan which should be vested to the seller B. Therefore, the total amount which Party A should pay to Party B is 102 million yuan [$(100.5 + 1.5) \times 1$ million].

(j) *Settlement Method*

The method by which the parties of the transaction clear the bonds and pay funds, including delivery versus payments, payments after delivery, and delivery after payments. "Delivery versus payments" refers to a bond settlement method in which the delivery of bond and payment of fund are made simultaneously on the settlement date with each serving as a binding condition for the other. "Payments after delivery" refers to a settlement method for forward bond transactions in which the buyer, knowing the seller has the required amount of bonds for the fulfillment of the contract, makes payment to the seller and confirms such payment on the settlement date. "Delivery after payments" is the opposite of payments after delivery, and it refers to the settlement method in which the seller (bond seller) in a forward bond transaction requests the delivery of bonds by the Central Clearing Company once it has confirmed the receipt of payment due from the buyer (bond buyer or payer).

In order to control the liquidity risks and market risks of forward bond transactions, the balance of sale and purchase of a single bond in forward transactions cannot exceed 20% of the outstanding amount of the bond. Meanwhile, the total balance of sales by market participants in forward transactions cannot exceed 200% of the total balance of their own available bonds, while the net total balance of purchase by market participants in forward transactions cannot exceed 100% of their paid-in capital (net assets, net value of fund assets, and working capital in renminbi). In order to ensure the fulfillment of the forward transaction contract, both parties of the transaction may negotiate a security deposit or security bonds based on the credit status of their counterparty.

12.1.3 Forward Exchange Transactions

Forward exchange transactions are foreign exchange agreements which are based on a currently agreed exchange rate and a future date of delivery as agreed-upon.

For instance, on July 10 of a particular year, a German company imports a batch of machine parts from America and will pay for them in US dollars after three months. The company currently only has euros and does not have any dollars. However, after three months, the exchange rate between the dollar and the euro may change, which will raise the import costs of this company. Thus, the company's finance manager conducts a forward exchange transaction, and on July 10 purchases three month forward dollars and sells euros based on an agreed exchange rate. On October 10 of that year, the transaction is settled, and regardless of the dollar–euro exchange rate on that date, the conversion of dollars and euros must be in accordance with the forward exchange rate as initially agreed-upon. As you can see, in pure forward exchange transactions, the future exchange rate that may otherwise be uncertain is fixed at a level as agreed-upon, thereby avoiding exchange rate risks.

During a forward exchange transaction, how are forward exchange rates determined? To answer this question, we must first look at an example. Suppose that over a three month period dollar and euro deposit rates are 5.5% and 3.5%, respectively. The current exchange rate between the dollar and the euro is 1:1.1220, in that 1 dollar can be exchanged for 1.1220 euros. Again, suppose that you have 1000 dollars. You now have two choices:

Option 1: If you deposit 1000 dollars with a term of three months and an interest rate of 5.5%, upon maturity, your total amount of interest would be:

$$1000 \times \frac{5.5}{100} \times \frac{90}{360} = 13.75 \text{ dollars.}$$

Thus, your total amount of principal with interest after three months would be 1013.75 dollars.

Option 2: You convert your 1000 dollars into euros and then deposit them for three months. Based on the current spot exchange rate, you could convert your dollars for 1120 euros. After three months, the principal and interest on your euro deposit would be:

$$1120 \times \left(1 + \frac{3.5}{100} \times \frac{90}{360}\right) = 1129.8 \text{ euros.}$$

If the forward exchange rate after three months is the same as the current exchange rate, if you were to convert your euros back into dollars after three months, you could earn 1008.75 dollars, which is 5 dollars less than if you were to directly deposit dollars. This indicates that there is room for arbitrage.

However, arbitrageurs take full advantage of this opportunity, regardless of whether they deposit euros or dollars, and when denominated in the same currency after three months, the total principal and interest of the deposit should be the same. If we set the forward exchange rate as e, then:

$$1013.75 = \frac{1129.8}{e}.$$

Which gives us a forward exchange rate of 1.1145.

China's forward exchange transactions primarily refer to **RMB/FX forward transactions**, in which both parties agree to the foreign currency, amount, and exchange rate and agree to deliver foreign currency for renminbi on a certain date in the future (more than two working days from the transaction date). Forward exchange transactions are one of the basic means of managing exchange rate risks. China's current forward exchange settlement and sale contract is in fact a very unique type of forward exchange transaction. Suppose an enterprise has just signed an export contract worth 20 million dollars, but will have to wait six months before they can receive this payment. The current dollar–yuan exchange rate is 1:6.25. However, if after six months, the exchange rate has depreciated to 1:6.0000, this company's earnings of 20 million dollars can only be converted into 120 million yuan. Hence, when compared to the original exchange rate of 6.2500, they will earn approximately 5 million yuan less in export revenue. In order to avoid this risk, this company can go to a bank, such as the Bank of China, and sign a forward exchange settlement and sale contract. The two parties agree that Company A will sell 20 million dollars to the Bank of China after 6 months based on the 1:6.2500 exchange rate, whether or not the dollar to yuan exchange rate has changed, and both parties will settle the contract based on the pre-determined exchange rate. Conversely, if Company A signs a 20 million dollars import contract and shall pay after six months, and if they are worried that the exchange rate will appreciate after 6 months to 1:6.5000, the company could also sign a forward exchange transaction contract with the Bank of China, in which both parties agree to the purchase of 20 million dollars from the Bank of China based on the exchange rate of 1:6.2500 after 6 months. To the Bank of China, this is a forward exchange sale. As you can see, the exchange rate of foreign exchange transactions can be locked through forward exchange settlement and sales, in order to avoid the risks of exchange rate fluctuations.

12.2 Futures

12.2.1 What are Futures and Futures Transactions?

Futures are one of the derivative products that have been developed from forward transactions. Futures are a standardized contract in which both parties agree to purchase or sell a particular commodity on a certain date in the future, with the contractually agreed price and quantity. Futures transactions are thus, the behavior of trading various standardized commodity contracts on the futures market.

Based on their various underlying products, futures can be categorized into commodity futures and financial futures. Commodity futures are futures transactions with physical commodities as their underlying products, such as copper, mung beans, corn, wheat, oil, etc. Financial futures, as their name implies, are futures transactions in which the object of the transaction is the underlying financial products. Financial futures primarily include interest rate futures, stock index futures, and currency futures.

Interest rate futures refer to standardized futures contracts on the futures market in which the underlying product is bond rates. Since the price of bonds is closely related to the interest rates, they are thus called interest rate futures. From 1994 to 1995, the Treasury bill futures introduced in China were in fact a kind of interest rate future. As a result of the development of China's bond market, the expansion of trade and the increasingly market-oriented interest rates, China will re-introduce interest rate futures contracts.

Stock index futures, short for stock price index futures, are standardized futures contracts for transactions which are based on stock price indices. Since stock price indices are the ratio between the current stock price average and the base period price average, and they are not actual financial assets which in itself cannot be settled, this transaction is thus often delivered through cash. The emergence of stock index futures allowed investors to invest in the entire stock market rather than individual stocks, thereby avoiding the troubles of portfolio investment. The SHSZ300 Stock Index Futures contracts of the China Financial Futures Exchange are a type of standardized financial futures which are delivered in cash.

Foreign exchange futures are a type of standardized futures contract, and the object of these transactions is a variety of freely convertible foreign currencies. On the final trading day, this futures contract allows for the conversion of one type of currency for another based on the exchange rate then. Foreign exchange futures are in fact the oldest type of financial futures in the world. At present, the relatively more active currency futures are primarily that of dollars, pounds, euros, yen, and so on.

The futures trading process can be roughly summarized as opening a position, holding a position, closing a position or physical settlement. Opening a position, also called taking a position, refers to purchasing or selling a certain amount of futures contracts. When a futures contract expires, one would begin to close a position. There are typically two methods for closing a position: physical (or cash) settlement or hedging a position. **Physical (or cash) settlement** is the delivery of the underlying asset (or cash) in order to fulfill the obligations of a futures transaction. For this reason, when their contracts have reached maturity but the positions have not yet been closed, the buyer and seller will fulfill their delivery obligations as stipulated to consummate the futures transaction. However, physical settlement only occurs on a minority of contracts, and in general, prior to the end of the last trading day, there is the option to sell the purchased futures contracts or to repurchase the sold futures contracts. In other words, a futures transaction of the same quantity but in the opposite direction is used to offset the original futures contract, thereby consummating the futures transaction and terminating the obligation of physical settlement upon maturity. Buying back sold contracts or selling purchased contracts is called **hedging a position**. The contracts that are not yet closed are called open contracts or open positions, which is also known as holding a position.

12.2.2 Features of Futures Transactions and Functions of the Futures Market

Futures transactions have the following basic characteristics:

(a) *On-Exchange Transactions*

Futures transactions belong to on-exchange transactions as they are conducted in the exchanges. For example, China has the Dalian Commodity Exchange, the Zhengzhou Futures Exchange, the Shanghai Futures Exchange, and the China Financial Futures Exchange. Each exchange allows for different commodity futures contracts. For instance, futures contracts for gold, silver, copper, and other such metals are traded on the Shanghai Futures Exchange. Stock index futures contracts are traded on the China Financial Futures Exchange.

(b) *Open Bidding*

Transactions are conducted through concentrated open bidding on the futures exchange, rather than through one-on-one privately negotiated contracts. Only exchange members or their authorized representatives are qualified to engage in futures transactions on the trading floor of the exchange. Other investors will have to appoint a brokerage firm to buy or sell on their behalf, which is no different from stock transactions in the stock exchange.

(c) *Standardized Contracts*

Futures contracts are standardized. Each futures contract will have a fixed amount, a delivery time, a delivery deadline, and so on, and futures investors cannot have full discretion. The following section will provide a detailed introduction to the primary content of futures contracts.

(d) *Risk Management or Spread Gains*

The purpose of these transactions is not for acquiring physical commodities but rather for transferring the price risks of commodities or for earning income on futures contract spreads. For example, even though a number of international financial institutions do not need a large volume of crude oil, copper, gold or other such physical commodities, yet the majority of international commodity transactions are purchased and sold by them, the purpose of which is to profit from the price volatility of commodity futures.

(e) *Margin Transactions*

As long as they pay a small margin and commissions, investors can enter into futures transactions. By using a small amount of capital, investors can complete large-amount transactions, which is one of the major features of futures transactions. In general, the margin amount will be approximately 5–18% of the price of the contract, and the majority of margins on futures transactions will not even reach 15%. If a margin is 5%, it means that someone could use 50,000 yuan to complete a futures transaction worth 1 million yuan. Thus, futures transactions are a "small is big" leverage. Futures margins can be divided into initial margins and additional margins, and the margin ratio will adjust with changes in risk. The higher the risk, the higher the required margin ratio. An initial margin is the margin paid in accordance with the required margin ratio of the transaction at the start of the purchase or sale of a futures contract. However, futures market prices change from day to day, and in order to guarantee that both the buyer and seller will fulfill their contractual obligations, the contracts are marked to market, day to day, and a zero debt system is implemented. Specifically, the margin amount will be adjusted based on daily transactions, closed positions, held positions and profits and losses, which is known as margin calls. If changes in the price of futures is completely opposite of the original expectations of traders, after the marked to market settlement, the margin accounts of traders will appear negative, which is known as **"blow-up"**.

In general, there are primarily two functions of the futures market.

(a) *Price Discovery*

On the futures transaction, buyers and sellers trade through an open, fair and just competition process which constantly updates the future price of futures commodities and causes prices to approach a level of equilibrium, thereby providing sufficient information to determine the spot prices in the future.

(b) *Risk Aversion*

This refers to the process in which holders of a certain product purchase or sell a futures contract for the specified product, which is of the same quantity but is traded in the opposite direction in order to offset the risk arising from fluctuations in spot prices. This process is known as hedging or swap transaction.

12.2.3 Hedging and Speculation on the Futures Market

There are two purposes for purchased futures, namely: hedging and futures speculation.

(a) *Hedging*

Hedging refers to when a trader purchases or sells a certain amount of underlying products on the spot market while also taking an opposite position from the spot market on the futures market, thereby transferring the risk of price volatility on the spot market to third parties on the futures market.

Hedging transactions can lower the financial risk of enterprises, although to engage in effective hedging, they must adhere to the following four principles:

(i) Trading in the opposite direction, namely that the trader will purchase or sell simultaneously or successively on the futures market in the opposite direction of the spot market, thereby establishing a mechanism to mutually offset each other. Specifically, when the trader buys into (or sells out of) the spot market, they will also sell out of (or buy into) a futures contract of the underlying product on the futures market. Only in this way can hedging lead to losses in one market and certain profits in the other, and with the losses and gains offsetting each other, the purpose of hedging will be achieved.

(ii) The same underlying product. This means that the futures product which the traders select for hedging must be the same underlying product which they have purchased or sold on the spot market. For instance, if you purchase stock on the spot market, yet sell foreign currency on the futures market, or if you purchase A shares on the spot market, yet sell B shares on the futures market, you cannot achieve the purpose of hedging.

(iii) The transaction amounts must be equal. This means that when hedging, the amount specified in the selected futures contracts must be equal to the actual amount of the product which is purchased or sold on the spot market, and only in this way can the effect of hedging be achieved.

(iv) The same month. This refers to the fact that the delivery month of the selected futures contract must ultimately be the same or near to that of the spot commodity which is actually purchased or sold on the spot market. This is because the futures price and the price of the underlying cash commodity will tend to converge and only in this way can a hedging transaction be consummated in the delivery month.

(b) *Futures Speculation*

Unlike hedging, the purpose of futures speculation is not to offset risks but is rather to allow speculators to use expected changes in future prices and their own funds to purchase and sell futures contracts, thereby profiting from hedging their positions when beneficial price changes. Hedging the positions refers to the settlement of futures transactions in which futures traders purchase or sell futures contracts with the same products, quantities and delivery months as the initial futures contracts, but in the opposite direction of transaction.

Simply put, futures speculation is to seek profit from going long or going short, and the purchase and sale of futures contracts does not actually require ownership of the underlying products. When speculators expect an increase in the price of futures, they will go long by purchasing futures contracts and then sell these contracts at an appropriate time during the rally, thereby earning a profit spread. When they believe that prices will fall, they will go short by selling futures and then repurchase the same amount of futures when prices really go down, thereby earning a profit spread from selling high and buying low.

12.2.4 The Main Content of Futures Contracts

Futures contracts are highly standardized and legally binding transaction contracts that are established by a futures exchange, specifying both the time and place for the delivery of a certain underlying product. Before we introduce the main content of futures contracts, we will first look at the standard terms and conditions for gold futures contracts on the Shanghai Futures Exchange listed in Tables 12.1 and 12.2.

The futures contracts of each and every futures exchange will have content similar to that of the Shanghai Futures Exchange gold futures contract (Table 12.1). Here are a few of the main futures contract terms:

(a) *Trading Unit*

The delivery quantity for the same futures product of a futures exchange will be the same for each contract, however during a single transaction, a number of futures contracts can be purchased. For example, the trading unit for the Shanghai Futures Exchange gold futures is 1000 grams/hand, and each transaction is based on the total number of hands that are purchased or sold. Thus, the total value of the contract is equal to the product of the current futures price, the total number of hands, and the trading unit. In futures transactions, trading units are standardized in order to simplify the overall process of futures transactions so that only the number of futures contracts purchased or sold needs to be recorded.

(b) *Minimum Price Change*

The minimum price change, also called the minimum fluctuation, refers to the smallest change in the quoted price of commodity or financial futures during a futures exchange open bidding or through an automated brokerage system. The minimum unit of change for Shanghai gold futures prices is 0.01 yuan/gram. The minimum unit of change for SHSZ300 Stock Index futures contracts is 0.2 points. The minimum amount of change is calculated as follows:

$$\text{Minimum Amount of Change} = \text{Minimum Price Change} \times \text{Contract Trading Unit.}$$

As a general rule, the minimum price change will differ for different types of futures contract. For instance, the minimum price change for British pound

Table 12.1 Main Content of a Standard Gold Futures Contract of Shanghai Futures Exchange

Trading Product	Gold
Trading Unit	1000 grams/hand
Quoting Unit	yuan (renminbi)/gram
Minimum Price Change	0.01 yuan/gram
Maximum Daily Price Fluctuation	Shall not exceed ±5% of the settlement price of the previous day
Contract Delivery Month	January–December
Trading Hours	9:00–11:30 am, 1:30–3:00 pm
Final Trading Day	The 15th day of the contract delivery month (extended in case of a legal holiday)
Delivery Date	The five consecutive business days after the final trading day
Deliverable Grade	Domestic bullion with the gold content no less than 99.95% and standard gold bullion from qualified suppliers or refiners which are recognized by the London Bullion Market Association (See annex for specific quality requirements)
Delivery Venue	Vault designated by the Exchange for delivery
Minimum Trading Margin	7% of the value of the contract
Transaction Fees	No greater than two ten-thousandth of the transaction amount (including the risk reserve)
Delivery Method	Physical settlement
Transaction Code	Au
Stock Exchange	Shanghai Futures Exchange

Source: Website of the Shanghai Futures Exchange

futures is 0.0005 USD while the minimum price change for Canadian dollar futures is 0.0001 USD. The minimum unit of change for Chinese Gold Futures and SHSZ300 stock index futures are very different, which is determined by the properties of the underlying instruments.

(c) *Maximum Daily Fluctuation*

Maximum daily fluctuations, which are also known as price limits, refer to the highest degree of fluctuation in the price of futures for the given trading day as specified by the exchange. This is exactly the same as the price limits within the stock market. The maximum daily fluctuation of Shanghai gold futures prices is no greater than ±5% of the settlement price of the previous trading day. If the daily price fluctuation exceeds this limit, the exchange will halt trading on that day and trading will begin anew on the second day, based on the given price limit. The main purpose of futures price limits is to control the fluctuation in the price of futures

Table 12.2 Main Content of a SHSZ300 Stock Index Futures Contract of China Financial Futures Exchange

Subject Matter of Contract	Shanghai and Shenzhen CSI 300 Index
Contract Multiplier	300 yuan per point
Quoting Unit	Index points
Minimum Price Fluctuation	0.2 points
Contract Months	The current month, the next month and the next two quarter-months (i.e., the final month of a quarter)
Maximum Daily Price Fluctuation	±10% of the settlement price of the previous day
Minimum Trading Margin	12% of the value of the contract
Final Trading Day	The third Friday in the month in which the contract expires, postponed in case of legal holidays
Delivery Date	The last trading day
Delivery method	Cash delivery
Stock Exchange	China Financial Futures Exchange

transactions, thereby limiting risk and prompting futures investors to adjust their behavior so as to avoid significant losses when futures prices soar or plummet.

(d) *Standard Delivery Time*

The standard delivery time includes the standard delivery month and the standard delivery date. The standard delivery month, also called the contract month, refers to the future month in which a futures contract will be delivered, as determined by each various futures exchange. The standard delivery date refers to the specific delivery date of the futures delivery month. For example, the London International Financial Futures Exchange specifies the second Wednesday of the delivery month as the delivery date. The Chicago IMM (International Monetary Market) specifies the third Wednesday of the delivery month as the delivery date. The delivery month for gold futures on the Shanghai Futures Exchange is from January to December, and the delivery date is five consecutive trading days from the last trading day. The delivery time for SHSZ300 stock index futures is the third Friday in the month in which the contract expires.

(e) *Margin*

The margin refers to the deposited margin which must be given by the investor to a clearing member (a broker or a brokerage firm) to ensure the fulfillment of a securities contract and to ensure the timely payment by loss-making party in the event of changes in the price of futures. The margin is set for three reasons: to effectively control futures market risks, to provide a performance guarantee for futures transactions on the exchange, and to ensure the financial security, integrity and soundness of the exchange. As mentioned above, some futures exchanges may require a margin due to the volatility of the price of futures. The minimum transaction margin ratio of Shanghai gold futures is 7%, while the minimum transaction margin ratio of SHSZ300 stock index futures contracts on the China Financial Futures Exchange is 12%. This margin ratio primarily depends on the extent and severity of price fluctuations in the futures market. Excessively high margin ratios will limit the use of the futures market as a leverage, thereby lowering its liquidity and influencing the level of activity on the futures market. Conversely, an excessively low margin ratio is not conducive to controlling the risks of futures transactions.

Box 12.1 Buried Beneath Derivatives — Barings Bank

Barings Bank was originally a veteran British commercial bank, founded in London by Sir Francis Baring in 1763. It is the world's first "commercial bank". Because of its versatility and innovation, Barings Bank soon achieved great success in the field of international finance.

Later, Barings Bank principally engaged in investment banking and securities trading. Their investment banking was primarily concentrated in Europe while their securities business was concentrated in Asia and South America. Its 17 affiliated securities companies focused their business in Japan, Hong Kong, Singapore, and the Philippines, of which the Singapore branch was particularly impressive. Nick Leeson, the manager who was responsible for futures transactions, was only 28 at that time, and because of his outstanding achievements, he was not only appointed as the general manager of Barings Futures Singapore, but he also became extremely powerful, with only the slightest amount of oversight.

Leeson traded Nikkei 225 stock index futures on both the Osaka Securities Exchange and the Singapore Exchange, short straddling the two exchanges and profiting from the difference. If he was just buying and selling the same amount, there would be little risk involved. However, futures are "derivative securities"; investors are required to pay only a small margin of the contract amount to purchase futures contracts, and only deliver the contract based on the full amount of the contract upon its maturity. In this way, there is a great deal of profit to be gained from this kind of derivative transaction, but associated risks are also great. In 1993, Leeson earned Barings Bank a total of 14 million dollars, thereby earning himself 1 million dollars in prize money. Leeson was overwhelmed with praise from his superiors and counterparts. Beginning in the fall of 1994, he began to wantonly speculate, and it was getting out of control. As a result, Leeson suffered a crippling loss in a Japanese stock and interest rate futures transaction in February 1995, and the preliminary

(*Continued*)

Box 12.1 (*Continued*)

estimate was a whopping sum of 400 million pounds. In that critical moment Leeson fled, and Barings Bank heard too little too late. After more than two sleepless nights of effort, they threw in the towel and filed for bankruptcy.

So it was that a titan of British banking with a history of more than 233 years was thus destroyed. This indeed was a costly, painful lesson.

— See Martin Mayer, The Bankers, Hainan Publishing, 2000 Edition

12.2.5 Risks of Futures Transactions

Although futures markets were originally designed to avoid the risk of price fluctuations of underlying products, however, because of the unique arrangement of the futures trading system, futures transactions themselves are very risky. The risks of futures transactions are primarily as follows:

(a) *Market Risk*

The largest risk in a futures transaction arises from market price fluctuations. The price fluctuation of futures can lead to trading profits or losses. Because futures are traded on a margin, they have a leverage effect, and the profits and losses of futures traders will also be amplified by this margin ratio. When futures prices are contrary to what is expected, because of their leverage effect, they may result in huge losses. The institutions which incur such major losses due to market price volatility are not in the minority, and some of them may even suffer disastrous ruins, such as Baring Bank in the special feature above.

(b) *Liquidity Risk*

This refers to the difficulty of quickly, promptly, and conveniently completing futures transactions and the risk thereof. This liquidity risk is particularly prominent when opening and closing positions. If it is difficult for a trader to open a position at an ideal time and price, it will be difficult to trade futures based on their expectations. Similarly, it will be difficult for them to hedge their way out of short positions, especially when futures prices move in a single direction. Similarly, when approaching the delivery period, market liquidity may decline and if traders cannot quickly close their positions, they will then suffer heavy losses.

(c) *Forced Liquidation Risk*

In general, futures transactions will have a daily settlement system. A futures exchange will settle a trader's bottom line on each and every day, and based on the results of this settlement, will determine whether or not to call for a margin. When the futures price fluctuation is relatively large and margins cannot be met within a specified time frame, traders may face a forced liquidation risk. In addition to the forced liquidation caused by an inadequate margin, if the total amount of positions held is beyond a certain limit, they will also be forced into liquidation. Thus, traders should always pay attention to their finances during a transaction, so as to avoid a forced liquidation due to an insufficient margin.

(d) *Delivery Risk*

All futures contracts have a time limit, and when the contract matures, all open position contracts must undergo a physical settlement. If the traders are not prepared for such a physical settlement, they must close these open positions prior to maturity, thereby avoiding the burden of delivery. At the time of delivery, if there is an inconsistency between the price in the spot market and the original futures price, there will be a delivery risk.

12.3 Options

12.3.1 What is an Option?

Our rental example from Chapter 5 is the closest example of options in our everyday lives. In the financial sector, there is a similar range of options trading, but they tend to be much more formal than our general trading options which involve the payment of a deposit. **Options** are the rights acquired at a small cost which allows the option buyer to purchase or sell a certain financial instrument within a certain specified time in the future and at a specified price. The price which has been paid for these rights is the premium and the price of the future purchase or sale of a certain financial instrument is the strike price.

Recall the rental example in Chapter 5. When you rented this home in the example, your 200 yuan deposit was in fact the entitlement of the option you purchased when you rented your home. If you did not find a cheaper or better home in a week, you would pay 1000 yuan a month to rent the house, and this 1000 yuan of rental fees was the strike price of your option transaction.

Based on the different time for performance, options can be divided into American options and European options. **American options** refer to options in which the option buyer can execute their option rights on the maturity date of the option as well as any time prior to its maturity. Unlike American options, **European options** are options which can only be exercised upon its maturity. In fact, the difference between American options and European options has nothing to do with their geographical names. Amongst the option transactions on the American market, there are more than just a few European options, and on the European option market, there are also a significant number of American options.

Option transactions are also good for risk management. Even if an unexpected change occurs in future spot market prices, and if the trader does not exercise their option rights, the only loss incurred would be the premium. However, option sellers must assume higher risks.

12.3.2 Call Options and Put Options

In accordance with the buyer's right, options can be divided into two types: call options and put options.

(a) *Call Option*

A **call option**, also simply known as a call, refers to the situation in which the option buyer, who expects a rise in the price of a certain product, pays a premium for the right to purchase this product within a stipulated period of time and at a stipulated price.

For instance, suppose that the prevailing price of Yizhi stock is 15 yuan, and you expect the price to rise to 22 yuan after six months, but you are not so sure. Thus, if you purchase a call option from Wang Xiao'er at a price of one yuan per share, you have the right to purchase 10,000 shares of Yizhi stock in six months from Wang Xiao'er at 17 yuan per share. If, after six months, the price does in fact rise to 22 yuan, you can exercise your Yizhi stock rights and purchase 10,000 shares of Yizhi stock from Wang Xiao'er at 17 yuan per share, only to then sell these shares at 22 yuan per share on the spot market. Having executed this right and thereby selling Yizhi stock on the spot market, your income statement will be as follows:

Total revenue from selling 10,000 shares of Yizhi stock	10,000 shares × 22 yuan = 220,000 yuan
Less: Cost of purchasing 10,000 Yizhi shares	10,000 shares × 17 yuan = 170,000 yuan
Less: Total premium on the purchase of call options	10,000 shares × 1 yuan = 10,000 yuan
Total Profit	= 40,000 yuan

For this reason, you can earn back a gross profit of 40,000 yuan from executing your option.

As long as the market price of Yizhi stock is higher than the price which you had previously agreed to with Wang Xiao'er, executing your call option will always be beneficial. When the market price of Yizhi stock is higher than 18 yuan (strike price + premium), you will earn a certain profit from executing your call option. The higher the price of Yizhi stock rises, the more you will earn as an options buyer, and the more Wang Xiao'er will lose as the seller of call options.

If the market price of Yizhi stock after six months is not what you expected, and is instead lower than 17 yuan, say, for example, it has fallen to 15 yuan a share, you do not need to exercise your call option, and at this time, you would only lose the 10,000 yuan which you paid for the call option.

(b) *Put Option*

A **put option**, also simply known as a put, refers to the situation in which the option buyer, who expects a fall in the price of a certain product, pays a premium for the right to sell a certain product within a stipulated period of time and at a stipulated price.

In the example above, if you believed that the price of Yizhi stock would not rise to 22 yuan after six months but would instead fall to 13 yuan, then you could purchase put options. Suppose that the main provisions of your options contract with Wang Xiao'er are as follows: The premium on your put option purchase is one yuan per share, and the strike price which you agree to is 15 yuan, which has a term of six months. In other words, after you have paid Wang Xiao'er a premium of 10,000 yuan, you can sell 10,000 shares of Yizhi stock to Wang Xiao'er at 15 yuan per share at some time in the next six months. If after six months, as you had expected, the price of Yizhi stock does indeed fall to 13 yuan, then you can exercise your put option, thereby purchasing 10,000 yuan of Yizhi stock on the spot market, only to then sell these shares to Wang Xiao'er at the agreed price of 15 yuan per share. Having exercised your put option, your income statement would be as follows:

Total revenue from exercising your put option and selling 10,000 shares of Yizhi stock	10,000 shares × 15 yuan = 150,000 yuan
Less: Cost of purchasing 10,000 Yizhi shares	10,000 shares × 13 yuan = 130,000 yuan
Less: Total premium on purchase of put options	10,000 shares × 1 yuan = 10,000 yuan
Total Profit	10,000 yuan

Since the price of Yizhi stock fell to 13 yuan after six months, you will earn 10,000 yuan from exercising your put option. In fact, as long as the price of Yizhi stock falls below the agreed strike price of 15 yuan, it will always make sense for you to exercise your put option. The lower that Yizhi stock prices fall, the more the money you can earn as the buyer of put options, and the more that Wang Xiao'er will lose as the seller of put options.

From the two examples above, we can see that the primary function of options is to mitigate risks at a relatively small cost. However, unlike forward transactions, options do not "lock" a future price, but through the choice of whether or not to exercise one's rights, risks can be averted. If future changes in the market are beneficial to one party, that party can choose to exercise their options. Thus, this person can earn a certain amount of revenue. However, if market changes are contrary to expectations, the person who holds the rights can also waive them.

12.3.3 The Break-Even Point of Options Transactions

At what point do people neither gain nor lose from an options transaction? Or, at what market price does the underlying product need to be, so that the call option buyer doesn't suffer a loss? For this, we will need to calculate the break-even point. The calculation for the call option break-even point is different than that for put options.

The break-even point of a call option:

$$\text{Break-even point} = \text{strike price} + \text{premium}.$$

When the future market price of the underlying product of the call option is higher than the break-even point, the option buyers will earn a profit. Conversely, when the future market price of the underlying product is lower than the break-even point, if the option buyers were to exercise their rights, they would suffer a loss, and thus, the buyers will waive their options. In the Yizhi stock call option above, the break-even point is 18 yuan, which is the sum of the strike price of 17 yuan and the premium of one yuan, and as such, when the future price of Yizhi stock is higher than 18 yuan, the option buyer can exercise his or her option, not only recovering the cost of the premium but also earning a certain amount of profit (Figure 12.1).

The break-even point of a put option:

$$\text{Break-even point} = \text{strike price} - \text{premium}$$

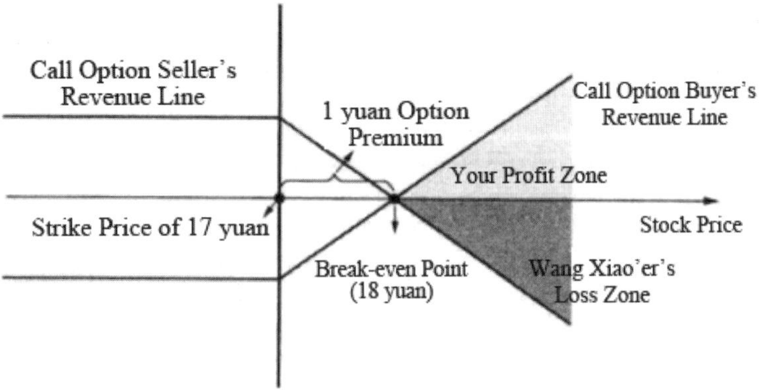

Fig. 12.1 Call Option Buyer's Break-Even Point

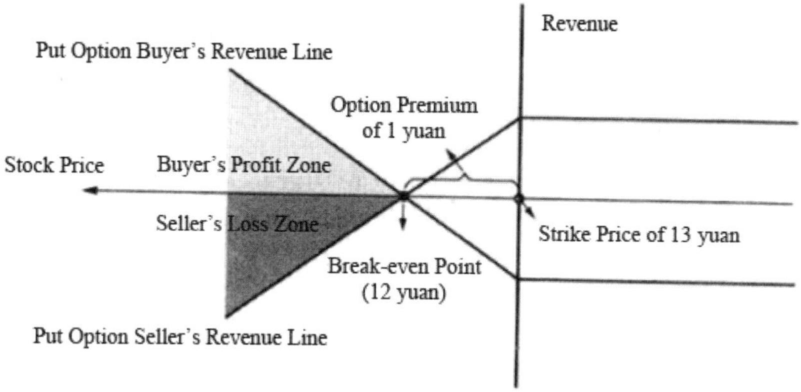

Fig. 12.2 Put Option Buyer's Break-even Point

When the future market price of the underlying product of the put option is lower than the break-even point, the option buyer will earn a profit. Conversely, if the future market price of the underlying product is higher than the break-even point, the option buyers would suffer a loss if they were to exercise their put option, and as such, they will waive their option. The break-even point of the Yizhi stock put option above is 12 yuan, which is the difference of the strike price of 13 yuan and the premium of 1 yuan. As long as the market price of Yizhi stock is below 12 yuan, the put option buyers will not only recover their premium by exercising their option, but will also earn a certain amount of profit (Figure 12.2).

12.3.4 The Value of Options

In general, options are equal to the sum of the intrinsic value and time value of the option. The intrinsic value of the option refers to the difference between the market price of the underlying financial instrument (or basic financial instruments) and the strike price. For call options, the intrinsic value is equal to the market price minus the strike price. For instance, in the example above, when you purchase the call option from Wang Xiao'er, since the market price of Yizhi stock (the underlying instrument) is 15 yuan and the strike price is 17 yuan, then the intrinsic value of each call option is −2 yuan. As for put options, the intrinsic value is equal to the strike price minus the market price. According to this calculation, in the example above, the strike price of the put option is 15 yuan and the prevailing market price of Yizhi stock is 15 yuan, and as such, the intrinsic value of the put option would be zero.

The intrinsic value of an option can be greater than, less than or equal to zero. When the intrinsic value of an option is greater than zero, it is called an

Table 12.3 Different Values for Call Options and Put Options

Intrinsic Value of the Option	Call Options	Put Options
In-the-Money	Futures price > Strike Price of the Option	Futures Price < Strike Price of the Option
Out-of-the-Money	Futures Price < Strike Price of the Option	Futures price > Strike Price of the Option
At-the-Money	Futures Price = Strike Price of the Option	Futures Price = Strike Price of the Option

in-the-money option. When the intrinsic value of an option is less than zero, it is called an out-of-the-money option. Finally, when the intrinsic value of an option is equal to zero, it is called an at-the-money option.

Table 12.3 summarizes the different values for call options and put options:

In options trading, theoretically speaking, the sale price of an option will never be less than its intrinsic value. If the sale price is less than the intrinsic value, arbitrageurs will immediately purchase all of the options that they can buy and then exercise their rights. Their profit is derived from the difference between the intrinsic value and the option price. The result of this arbitrage will frequently shift the intrinsic value of the option to zero.

The time value of an option refers to the total premium a buyer would like to pay for the option when future changes in the price of the underlying product may cause an increase in the value of the option over time. We have already pointed out above that an option buyer will receive the right to purchase or sell the underlying financial instrument at an agreed price after they pay the option premium, and to the options buyer the maximum possible loss incurred would be the option premium, and yet there is a high potential for profits. Thus, the value of the option will be disproportionately influenced by the price fluctuations of the underlying financial instrument, which will cause the total value of the option to exceed its intrinsic value, which is the fundamental source of the time value of options. Unlike its intrinsic value, the time value of an option is difficult to calculate directly, and as such, the time value of an option is typically the difference between its total value and its intrinsic value. Let us look again at the example above in which you purchase call options. When the prevailing market price of Yizhi stock is 15 yuan and the strike price is 17 yuan, the intrinsic value of the option is −2 yuan, and in this case, if you were still willing to purchase the option at a price of 1 yuan, then its time value would be 3 yuan.

In general, there are many factors which will affect the time value of an option. First of all, the time value of an option depends on the remaining validity period of the option. The longer the validity period, the greater the time value. To the buyer, a longer validity period means greater profit-making opportunity, while to the seller, it means greater risk for compliance, and thus a higher sale price of the option. Approaching maturity, the time value of an option will decrease, and upon maturity, the time value will be zero. Secondly, the time value depends on the price volatility of the underlying financial instrument. Since the loss an options buyer may incur is limited to the price of the option, the maximum amount of profit depends on the difference between the market price of the underlying financial instrument and the strike price, and as such, the greater the volatility of the underlying financial instrument, the greater the corresponding time value of a call or a put option. Third, the time value of an option is also affected by the intrinsic value of the option. This can easily be seen from the example above, and there is no need to elaborate.

12.3.5 Financial Options

The stock option above is, in fact, a kind of financial option. In addition, there are also the following financial options: index options, currency options, interest rate options, and futures options.

(a) *Stock Index Options*

Stock index options refer to the right to choose whether or not to require that an options seller will pay with cash, the difference between the actual stock index and the agreed-upon stock index within a certain period of time or on a certain date after the index option buyer has paid a certain premium. Stock index options can be used to better manage stock price fluctuations, and they are a special kind of financial option.

The typical financial option is based on a specific underlying financial product, while stock index options are based on stock price index. The stock index, in itself, is not an actual asset, and similar to stock futures, its delivery will be made in cash.

(b) *Interest Rate Options*

Interest rate options are the right, but not the obligation, of a buyer, having paid a premium to the seller, to purchase or sell a certain quantity of interest rate futures before or on a certain date and at a previously agreed price. In general, the underlying product of an interest rate option is a Treasury bill, or a medium to long-term government bond, and interest rate options are an effective means of avoiding interest rate risks.

Interest rate options include call options and put options. An interest rate call option is the right to borrow at a certain predetermined interest rate after the option buyer has paid a certain premium. An interest rate put option is the right to lend money at a certain predetermined interest rate after the option buyer has paid a certain premium.

Suppose, again, that you are the financial manager of your company and you know that your company will need to borrow 50 million yuan in working capital after three months, and the current market rate is 5.25%. Also, you expect that the market rate will rise to 5.75% after three months. In order to avoid the risk of rising interest rates, you can sign a forward rate agreement with a bank and agree to borrow 50 million yuan from the bank at 5.25% after three months. If the interest rate does in fact rise as you had expected, you have effectively avoided the interest rate risk through a forward rate agreement. If, however, the interest rate falls to 5.00%, the forward rate agreement is irrevocable and you will still have to borrow at the agreed-upon interest rate, and your company will thus pay an additional 0.25% in interest.

In order to more effectively mitigate the risk of interest rate fluctuations, it would be best for you to purchase an interest rate call option. Because a call option is a right to choose, when the interest rate fluctuates contrary to your expectations, you can waive your right to exercise the option, and in turn, go to the market for financing at a lower rate. Conversely, if the market rate changes as you had expected, you can exercise your call option and borrow funds for the company at a rate of 5.25%. Even with the addition of the call option premium, the actual financing cost will be lower than the financing cost of borrowing at the market rate.

(c) *Currency Options*

A **currency option** is the option buyer's right to purchase or sell currency to the option seller at a predetermined exchange rate and within a certain period of time in the future after the buyer has paid a premium to the seller. Currency options are one of the most effective means for managing exchange rate risks and locking in financial costs. Currency options which are traded on China's foreign exchange market are called **RMB/FX options** and refer to the right to use renminbi to purchase or sell a certain amount of foreign currency on a certain trading day in the future based on an agreed-upon exchange rate. In an RMB/FX option transaction, the option buyer has gained the right through the payment of a premium, and the option seller, having received this premium, has to perform the obligation to purchase or sell the foreign currency based on an agreed price when the buyer chooses to exercise the option.

For instance, a certain enterprise needs to import raw materials which will be paid for in six months at a total of 20 million dollars, yet the enterprise is not willing to purchase and hold a six-month dollar position. However, if they purchase 20 million dollars on the foreign exchange market after six months for import of raw materials, they may face the risk of a higher dollar exchange rate.

What should they do? One approach is to purchase from a bank a dollar call/ renminbi put option with a term of six months and a strike price of 6.2500, and pay a certain premium. If, after six months, the spot price is higher than 6.5500, then the enterprise must pay 131 million yuan to purchase 20 million dollars on the foreign exchange spot market. However, if they have arranged a RMB/FX option with the bank in which they can purchase 20 million dollars at an exchange rate of 6.2500 yuan/dollar, the ideal choice for this enterprise would be to purchase 20 million dollars from the bank at the price of 6.2500, in which they will only pay 125 million yuan, which would save them 6 million yuan when compared to directly buying from the spot market. If the spot price is less than 6.2500, say 6.1500, they can waive their option and purchase dollars based on the spot price, which would be 2 million yuan cheaper than exercising their option. Through this renminbi-dollar option transaction, this enterprise can use a relatively lower cost (premium) to obtain the benefits of a rising dollar and avoid the losses from a falling dollar exchange rate, thereby locking in its interest rate risks and thus mitigating them.

Box 12.2 Chinese Options: Currency Options — "Liangdebao"

In fact, currency options already exist in China. At the end of 2002, the Shanghai branch of the Bank of China launched the personal FX investment product, "Liangdebao", which was actually a currency option. Afterwards, several other banks also launched similar currency option investment products. Through a closer look at this financial product, we can come to a clear understanding of currency options.

Suppose that you purchased "Liangdebao" with a 100,000 dollar deposit on June 1, 2003 and chose Japanese yen as the pegged currency. Suppose this is a one-month option with a premium of 0.5% (or a rate of 6% per annum), an agreed-upon exchange rate (strike price) of 120 JPY/USD, and a maturity date of July 1, 2003. You can receive the premium of 500 dollars (100,000 × 0.5%) from the bank two trading days after you complete the transaction, or on June 3, 2003. The bank will then deposit this premium into your account. Suppose that the annual interest rate on a dollar deposit is 6%. Thus, during this one month, the interest on your principal deposit and premium would be:

$$\text{Interest} = (100{,}000 + 500) \times 6\% \div 12 = 502.50 \text{ dollars.}$$

(*Continued*)

Box 12.2 (*Continued*)

+ Premium	500 dollars
Total earnings	1002.50 dollars
+ Principal	100,000 dollars
Total Principal and Interest:	101,002.50 dollars

On July 1, 2003, the "Liangdebao" maturity date, the bank will compare the prevailing dollar–yen exchange rate on the international market with the agreed exchange rate of 120, and thus decide whether or not to pay your deposit principal with dollars or yen.

If the dollar–yen exchange rate on July 1, 2003 is higher than 120, say, it has risen to 125 yen, then the bank will use Japanese yen to pay your principal, in that your account will change to:

$$101{,}002.5 \times 120 = 12{,}120{,}300 \text{ yen.}$$

Because the bank will exchange 12,120,300 yen for your 101,002.50 dollars, based on the conversion rate of one dollar for 125 yen, the bank will obtain:

$$101{,}002.5 \times 125 = 12{,}625{,}312.5 \text{ yen.}$$

The Bank's Gross Profit: $12{,}625{,}312.5 - 12{,}120{,}300 = 505{,}012.5$ yen.

Or rather: $505{,}012.5 \div 125 = 4{,}040.10$ dollars.

Net Profit: – Premium: 500 dollars/3540.10 dollars.

If the dollar–yen exchange rate falls below 120, the bank will pay your principal with dollars, and you will thus earn 100,000 dollars plus the premium of 500 dollars and the interest of 502.50 dollars:

Interest: $(100{,}000 + 500) \times 6\% \div 12 = 502.50$ dollars

$$\frac{+\text{Premium: 500 dollars}}{= 1002.50 \text{ dollars}}.$$

In this case, the bank's loss would be the premium of 500 dollars it has paid to you.

From this it can be seen that within the foreign currency options of "Liangdebao" or "Liangtouli", once the change in the exchange rate is contrary to the bank's expectations, it will incur a certain loss. However, as soon as the exchange rate shifts in favor of the bank, the "Liangdebao" buyer will incur a significant loss, yet the bank's potential profits are also quite substantial (Figure 12.3).

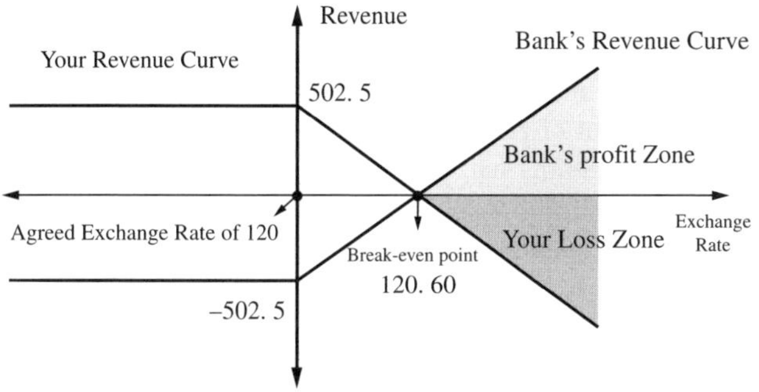

Fig. 12.3 The "Break-Even" Point of "Liangdebao"

12.4 Swap

Swap* refers to a transaction in which upon the purchase or sale of a certain financial instrument, the trader agrees to sell or purchase the identical amount of the same financial instrument at an agreed date in the future. Based on the financial instrument in question, swap transactions include foreign exchange swap, interest rate swap, and commodity swap. A **foreign exchange swap** is the agreement to sell or purchase an identical amount of a certain foreign currency at a certain date in the future when a trader purchases or sells that foreign currency.

Based on the terms, swap transactions can be divided into: spot-forward swap, forward-forward swap, and one-day swap. We can use foreign exchange swap as an example. A spot-forward swap refers to the purchase or sale of a foreign currency on the spot market and the simultaneous sale or purchase of the same amount of the currency on the forward market. A forward–forward swap refers to the purchase or sale of a certain currency on the forward market and the simultaneous sale or purchase of the currency with a later term on the forward market. A one-day swap can be divided into today/tomorrow swap, tomorrow/next day swap and spot/next day swap. The first maturity date of a today/tomorrow swap is the current day, and the second swap date is the next day, and so on and so forth.

For instance, a bank will take in a revenue of 10 million pounds after one month, yet will make a payment of 10 million pounds after three months. Suppose that the current foreign exchange market rate is as follows:

Spot Rate: £1 = US$1.2960/1.2970,

One-Month Forward Rate: £1 = US$1.2868/1.2880,

Three-Month Forward Rate: £1 = US$1.2729/1.2742.

Given these conditions, the bank can make the following choices:

First of all, they can perform two spot-forward swap. In other words, they can first purchase 10 million pounds on the forward market so as to meet the demand for the payment of pounds after three months. In this case, the forward term would be three months with an exchange rate of 1.2742. Meanwhile, the bank would also sell 10 million pounds on the spot market at an exchange rate of 1.2960. Through these transactions, the bank will earn 0.0218 dollars for each pound. Meanwhile, the bank would sell the 10 million pounds, they will receive one month later, on the forward market with a forward term of one month and an exchange rate of 1.2868 dollars/pound. At the same time, they will also purchase 10 million pounds on the spot market at an exchange rate of 1.2970 dollars/pound. At this time, they will lose 0.0102 dollars for each pound. Taken together, the bank can earn 0.0116 dollars for each pound when these transactions are concluded.

They can also directly conduct a forward-forward transaction. In other words, they can purchase a three-month forward worth 10 million pounds at an exchange rate of 1.2742 and again sell a one-month forward with an exchange rate of 1.2868. Through this transaction, they will earn 0.0126 dollars for each pound. After comparing the two, we can see that it would be more favorable to directly perform a forward-forward transaction.

In China, swap transactions between the renminbi and foreign currencies are called **RMB/FX swap**, which refer to an exchange between the two currencies at two different delivery dates and in opposite directions. For example, Enterprises A and B sign a **RMB/FX** swap contract. In the first transaction, A will convert a foreign currency for Enterprise B's renminbi based on the agreed upon exchange rate. In the second transaction, Enterprise A will use the renminbi to buy back the same amount of the foreign currency based on a different agreed-upon exchange rate.

Suppose that Enterprise A is an exporter, and they have received a payment of 10 million dollars from a foreign importer, which they need to convert into renminbi to be able to use this revenue for domestic expenditures. However, Enterprise A also needs to import raw materials for production and will have to make a payment of 10 million dollars after six months. At this point, Enterprise A could enter into a RMB–dollar spot to six-month forward swap agreement with a bank. Enterprise A would first sell 10 million dollars on the spot market to obtain the corresponding amount of renminbi and then purchase a six-month forward of 10 million dollars using renminbi. Through these transactions, the enterprise can close the funding gap and mitigate the risk. If the bank is not willing to bear the exchange rate risk, it can then go to the interbank foreign exchange market and enter into another swap transaction with the same term, amount, and currency, but in the opposite direction to level out their swap position and disperse the exchange rate risk of the swap transaction.

They could also use a **RMB/FX currency swap** to save on financial costs. This refers to an exchange of RMB and FX principal within an agreed-upon time period and at an agreed quantity as well as a scheduled transaction of the interest on the two currencies. The principal transaction is conducted in the following forms: (1) the counterparties exchange the principal in renminbi and the foreign currency based on an agreed exchange rate on the date when the agreement is in force and then reverse the swap at the same exchange rate and with the same amount of principal upon the maturity of the agreement. (2) The renminbi and foreign currency principals are not actually swapped on the dates in which the agreement enters into force and matures. An interest rate swap refers to scheduled interest payments made to the other party which can be calculated based on either a fixed or a floating interest rate.

Let us cite a simple example. Company A requires 10 million dollars to finance their overseas subsidiary for a period of three years, however the subsidiary's offshore financing costs are relatively high and Company A can obtain renminbi financing at a relatively low cost in China. Thus, the company would need to raise 10 million dollars based on the current yuan–dollar exchange rate and for a period of three years. If the current yuan–dollar exchange rate is 6.2500, then the company would need to collect 62.5 million yuan. Then, Company A would use this sum of money for a RMB/FX currency swap and would transfer 62.5 million yuan to a bank and receive 10 million dollars from this designated bank. Afterwards, Company A could make interest payments in dollars to the bank within the agreed interest period based on either the dollar LIBOR plus or minus a spread or at a fixed interest rate. Meanwhile, they can also receive renminbi interest based on the renminbi Shibor plus or minus a spread or at a fixed interest rate. This kind of transaction is equivalent to financing in a certain foreign currency, although the financing costs would be lower than that of direct financing abroad.

A swap is an agreement between two parties to exchange different liabilities, liabilities with different rates or with different delivery times within an agreed-upon period of time and based on certain market conditions and to make a series of payments. It primarily consists of currency and interest rate swap.

(a) *Currency Swap*

A currency swap is a financial transaction in which the two parties of a transaction, in accordance with their complimentary needs, agree to a principal swap and interest settlement on liabilities or investments on the basis of an agreed principal amount or interest rate. In a currency swap, two separate borrowers need to borrow different currencies and are both willing to be responsible for the other party's borrowed principal and interest for an agreed period of time in the future, based on an agreed set of rules.

For instance, suppose that the current foreign exchange market pound–dollar rate is 1.3500, and Company A who operates in one country borrows one million pounds in Europe while another company in a different country borrows 1.35 million dollars. Both sides agree that, within the term of the debt, Company B will provide Company A with pounds to pay Company A's loan interest. Meanwhile, Company A will provide Company B with dollars to pay Company B's loan interest. Upon the maturity of the debt of both parties, they will then pay the principal of the other party's debt and thereby terminate the swap agreement.

Swap transactions not only lower the fund-raising costs of both parties but they also allow relevant enterprises and government agencies to use foreign capital markets to get foreign currency funds which would have originally been difficult to obtain. Additionally, they are also conducive to the mitigation of foreign exchange risks.

(b) *Interest Rate Swap*

An interest rate swap is a financial transaction in which both parties agree to mutually exchange interest rates on the assets or liabilities with the same currency, the same amount, and the same term, but with different interest payment methods. The interest is calculated on the basis of the principal agreed-upon by both parties. The interest rate swap involves the exchange between a fixed rate and a floating rate, a fixed rate and a fixed rate, or a floating rate and a floating rate in the same currency. In the transaction, the parties will only settle the interest rate difference of the swap, and in the overall transaction, there is never any actual transfer of funds.

For instance, suppose that Company A can obtain a US dollar loan at a fixed interest rate of 5% or a floating interest rate of 4%, while Company B can obtain a loan at a fixed interest rate of 7% or a floating interest rate of 4.5%. If Company A obtains a loan with a fixed interest rate of 5%, Company B would then obtain a loan with a floating interest rate of 4.5%. Both companies agree that after Company B agrees to assume a 1% interest rate from Company A, both parties will be obligated to make interest payments for the other company, in that Company A will make Company B's floating interest rate payments and Party B will pay a fixed interest for Party A. In this way, the total interest rate paid by Company B would be $1\% + 5\% = 6\%$, and Company A would pay a floating interest rate of 4.5% for Company B, or 3.5% considering the 1% interest rate Company B would first pay Company A. Through this interest rate swap, Company A has in fact obtained a loan at a floating interest rate of 3.5%, while Company B has obtained a loan at a fixed interest rate of 6%. As you can see, Company A and B have effectively lowered their interest rate costs through an interest rate swap.

Summary

Derivative financial instruments are financial products which are derived from underlying financial instruments. Their values depend on the price of the underlying products and their main function is to manage the relevant risk exposure that arises from the underlying financial instruments. Derivatives can be divided into the four categories of forward transactions, futures, options, and swap.

Forward transactions are a transaction agreement in which both parties have signed a contract agreeing to the transaction of certain products at a specific future date, and primarily include forward rate agreements, forward bond transactions, and forward exchange transactions. The role of forward transactions lies in locking future prices and effectively mitigating risks.

A futures transaction is a transaction in which the buyer and seller agree to a certain predetermined commodity quantity, quality grade, price, time, and place for future delivery. Financial futures primarily include stock index futures, interest rate futures, and currency futures. The basic function of a futures transaction is price discovery and risk aversion. People engage in futures transactions on the futures market for the purpose of hedging and futures speculation. For effective hedging, the traders must perform transactions in the opposite direction, but with the same term, underlying product, and quantity. The main content of a futures contract includes: the trading unit, trading price, a delivery period, the minimum price fluctuation, and the initial margin. Financial futures include stock index futures, interest rate futures, and foreign exchange futures.

An option is the right acquired at a small cost which allows the option buyer to purchase or sell a certain financial instrument within a certain specified time in the future and at a specified price. Options can be used to better mitigate risks. Based on the different time for performance, options can be divided into American options and European options. In accordance with the direction of the transaction, options can be divided into call and put options. Financial options are primarily divided into index options, interest rate options, and foreign currency options.

A swap is an agreement between two parties to exchange different liabilities, liabilities with different rates or with different delivery times within an agreed-upon period of time and based on certain market conditions and to make a series of payments. Swap is primarily divided into interest rate swap and currency swap, and they can be used to effectively avoid the risk of interest rate or exchange rate fluctuations and can also be used to gain necessary financial support.

Key Terms

Futures; Options; Swap; Currency Swap; Interest Rate Swap; American Options; European Options; Forward Transactions; Forward Exchange Settlement and Sale; Derivative

Financial Instruments; Underlying Financial Instruments; Call Options; Put Options; Interest Rate Options; Foreign Currency Options; Financial Futures; Swaps; Forward Bond Transaction; RMB/FX Currency Swap; RMB/FX Swap; RMB/FX Forward Transaction

Critical Thinking Questions

1. What is the difference between underlying financial products and derivative products?
2. What is the role of forward transactions within risk management?
3. Compare the difference of forward transactions and options transactions within risk management?
4. What are future transactions, and what are their functions?
5. What are the basic principles of hedging with futures?
6. Describe the value of options.
7. Describe the basic principles of swap transactions.
8. Suppose that your company will borrow a sum of money after three months. Briefly describe how you would avoid the risk of interest rate fluctuations through forward rate agreements and interest rate options, respectively.
9. Currently, China has no stock index futures. Use the principles of futures transactions to analyze what sort of impact futures transactions will have on investor transactions. If the stock market continues to decline and investors still want to earn a profit, how could they use the futures market? Are there other transaction instruments which can achieve the same purpose?
10. Suppose that some company will import a set of equipment with a contract amount of 10 million dollars to be paid after six months. The current dollar–yuan exchange rate is 1:8.2700. This company is concerned about the risk of fluctuations in dollar–yuan exchange rate after six months; they decide to use forward exchange settlement and sale to lock the exchange rate risk. Suppose they sign a six-month forward exchange settlement and sale contract with a bank, specifying an exchange rate of 1:8.2700. If after six months the dollar–yuan exchange rate is 1:8.3000, then what will the import enterprise gain from this forward exchange settlement and sale arrangement? What would happen if after six months, the dollar–yuan exchange rate is 1:8.2000?
11. In the example above, if the company purchases a foreign currency call option after six months, the agreed-upon exchange rate would be 1:8.2700, and the total premium paid would be 500,000 yuan. Calculate what the break-even point of the exchange rate should be. If the dollar-yuan exchange rate is 1:8.3000, should the company exercise the call option? Suppose that after six months, the dollar-yuan exchange rate is 1:8.2000 or 1:8.2710. What would happen then?
12. In 2008, the international price of crude oil rose, and at one point reached a maximum of 147 dollars/barrel. In this context, several domestic airlines, such as Air China International and Shanghai Eastern Airlines, sought to use options as a means of avoiding the risk of a price increase in crude oil. One airline signed crude oil option agreements with the domestic branches of international investment banks, including Goldman Sachs: This airline purchased call options from these international investment banks and the content of this contract was typically a premium amount of 14 dollars per barrel option.

The highest strike price was 150 dollars/barrel, and the largest contract volume was approximately 10 million barrels. When this contract was signed, the price of crude oil was approximately 120 dollars/barrel. However, this airline was worried that if they couldn't exercise the call options that they had purchased, they would suffer a loss of 140 million dollars in premiums. So, the airline also signed put option contracts with these investment banks. In the put option contracts, the airline is the seller, and the buyer of the put options are investment banks, including Goldman Sachs, and the strike price is 62.5 dollars/barrel, with the same contract quantity of 10 million barrels, and a premium of 14 dollars/barrel. The company believes that the price cannot fall below 60 dollars, based on the prevailing price of oil, and through this purchase of call options and sale of put options, they can avoid the risk of a rise in crude oil prices and would not bear any financial expenses for risk management. It is really a good approach to risk management. However, the airline never imagined that due to the international financial crisis, the international price of crude oil fell significantly in the fourth quarter of 2008; within a short period of time, the price dropped from its highest point at 147 dollars/barrel to 35 dollars/barrel. Analyze the results that this company was faced with when crude oil dropped to 35 dollars/barrel. Do you think that the option combination that this airline took was a good method for avoiding crude oil price fluctuations? If this company's strategy failed, why did it fail?

Part III

Financial Controls

As men advance in life, all passions resolve themselves into money. Love, ambition, even poetry, end in this.

— Benjamin Disraeli

Suppose a yard were defined to be the length of the king's girdle, and suppose the king to be a child. Everybody would then know that the "yard" would increase with age.

— Irving Fisher

The first priority of central banks is to achieve steady, maximum economic growth, without letting the inflation genie out of the bottle.

— Alan Greenspan

Chapter 13

Money Supply

Learning Objectives

After studying this chapter, you will be able to:

- Understand what a base money is
- Clearly understand the base money equation and the supply channels of base money
- Know how changes to the assets and liabilities of central banks will affect the base money
- Understand how the commercial banking system creates deposit money
- Understand what money multipliers are and the main factors influencing them
- Know the main factors influencing the currency deposit ratio
- Clearly understand the factors influencing commercial banks' excess reserve ratios

When reading all kinds of financial or economic papers, you often will come across reports about the money supply. So, how is money supplied in the economic system? Or, does the entire money supply come from the central bank's printing press? What kind of role do individuals and businesses have in the money supply of the entire society? After studying this chapter, you will have a clear understanding of these different issues.

13.1 The Base Money and the Base Money Equation

13.1.1 What is the Base Money?

The base money is also known as high powered money because it refers to the fact that under a fractional reserve system, it can create, via the banking system, deposits that are multiple times the original amount. It equals cash in circulation C plus the total reserves of the banking system R. If MB stands for the base money, then:

$$MB = C + R. \tag{13.1}$$

Having clarified what the base money is, we may then proceed to discuss how it is supplied and what are the primary factors influencing the supply of base money. We can begin to answer these questions by talking about the base money equation.

13.1.2 The Base Money Equation

To observe the base money equation, we must first begin with the balance sheets of central banks. As the contents of a central bank balance sheet will vary from country to country, so too will the factors affecting the supply of base money. Below is the simplified balance sheet of a central bank, which reflects the main items on the People's Bank of China's balance sheet. The items on the asset side are primarily foreign assets, financial claims on the government and on financial institutions. Among them, foreign assets also include funds outstanding for foreign exchange and gold, financial claims on the government include outstanding central government debts to the central bank and government bonds purchased by the central bank, and finally, claims on financial institutions also include claims on depository financial institutions and claims on other financial institutions. On the liabilities side, there are such items as cash in circulation, deposits of financial institutions (reserves), central bank bonds, government deposits, foreign deposits, and beside them, a small portion of equity capital. For our purposes, liabilities will only cover central bank bonds and government deposits.

By finding the equilibrium, we would have:

$$A_1 + A_2 + A_3 = C + R + L_1 + L_2, \tag{13.2}$$

$$\text{which gives us: } C + R = A_1 + A_2 + A_3 - (L_1 + L_2). \tag{13.3}$$

The Central Bank's Balance Sheet

Assets	Liabilities
A_1: Foreign assets	C: Cash in circulation
A_2: Loans to government	R: Deposits of financial institutions (reserves)
A_3: Refinancing to financial institutions	L_1: Central bank bonds
	L_2: Government deposits

Both sides of the equation will affect the supply of the base money. In this regard, additions on the asset side of the central bank's balance sheet, i.e., refinancing to financial institutions (claims), financial claims on government, foreign assets, will also expand the base money by an equal amount. Conversely, reductions in these assets will also cause a reduction in the supply of base money. Additions to central bank bonds, government deposits, foreign deposits, and other items on the right side of the equation will cause a reduction in the supply of base money. Conversely, their reductions will add to the supply of base money.

13.1.3 Influence of Central Bank Assets on the Base Money

Below is an in-depth analysis of the factors that influence the base money.

(a) *Foreign Assets*

Foreign assets refer to foreign currency reserves, gold and the IMF Special Drawing Rights that are held by the central bank. Since gold reserves and special drawing rights are stable (see Chapter 18), they have a minimal effect on base money. Of all foreign assets, foreign currency reserves are the only ones that tend to have any effect on base money.

Because China uses a FX settlement and sale system, the base money is affected by foreign currency reserves. Under this system, enterprises are required to sell their foreign exchange earned through exports to a designated bank. This is called an exchange settlement. When an enterprise requires foreign exchange to import commercial products or equipment, they can apply to purchase foreign exchange. To the bank, this is called an exchange sale. After the settlement of exchange by the designated exchange bank, the foreign exchange will then be sold to the central bank which will directly affect the central bank's balance sheet. Suppose that an enterprise earns an income of 10 million dollars on a certain export. After the enterprise receives this sum of foreign exchange, they must sell this currency to the bank, such as the Bank of China. Suppose that at that time the exchange rate is 1 dollar to 6.28 yuan. After Bank of China receives the 10 million dollars in foreign exchange, its T-account would look like this:

Assets (yuan)		Liabilities (yuan)	
Foreign Exchange	62.8 million	Deposits	62.8 million

After the Bank of China's exchange settlement, it will also make a sale to the central bank (the People's Bank of China). For convenience, we will still suppose that the exchange rate is 1 dollar to 6.28 yuan. At this time, the central bank and Bank of China's T-accounts are as follows, respectively:

Central Bank's T-Account

Assets (yuan)		Liabilities (yuan)	
Foreign Exchange	62.8 million	Bank of China's Deposit in the Central Bank	62.8 million

Bank of China's T-Account

Assets (yuan)		Liabilities (yuan)	
Deposit in the People's Bank of China	62.8 million		
Foreign Exchange	−62.8 million		

As such, after the Bank of China has sold its 62.8 million yuan of foreign exchange assets to the central bank, foreign exchange has been reduced by 62.8 million yuan from the asset side of the balance sheet, which, however, has been added to the central bank's reserve assets. Thus, the base money has expanded by 62.8 million yuan.

(b) *Government Bond Purchases by the Central Bank*

"Financial claims on the government" on the central bank's balance sheet includes previous borrowing from the central bank by the government and government bonds purchased by the central bank. Since 1994, the Chinese government can no longer borrow or get an overdraft from the central bank, so we will only analyze government bonds purchased by the central bank.

To analyze the central bank's government bond purchases, we must look at two different situations: first, the central bank purchases government bonds from commercial banks; second, the central bank purchases government bonds from the public.

In the first scenario, suppose that the central bank purchased from the Bank of China government bonds worth 10 million yuan and paid with a check worth 10 million yuan. After the Bank of China receives this 10 million yuan check, they can save it in their central bank account or exchange it for cash and deposit it into their vault. Regardless of whether or not this sum has been deposited into the central bank or exchanged for cash, the Bank of China's reserve assets have increased by 10 million yuan. After this transaction has been completed, the central bank and the Bank of China's T-accounts would look like this:

Central Bank's T-Account After Purchasing Government Bonds Worth 10 million Yuan

Assets (yuan)		Liabilities (yuan)	
Government Bonds	+10 million	Bank of China's Deposits in the Central Bank	+10 million

Or, alternatively:

Central Bank's T-Account When the Bank of China Makes a Withdrawal

Assets (yuan)		Liabilities (yuan)	
Government Bonds	+10 million	Currency	+10 million

In other words, after the central bank purchases government bonds worth 10 million yuan from the Bank of China, the asset side of the central bank's balance sheet has increased by 10 million yuan. The liabilities side has also increased by the Bank of China's 10 million yuan deposit in the central bank, or the currency, or more specifically, the base money has increased by 10 million yuan.

In the second scenario, the central bank purchases government bonds from the public. Imagine that you were a millionaire, and other than all of the stock you own, you also possess government bonds worth tens of millions. If the central bank purchases 10 million yuan worth of your bonds, what would happen? After you have sold these government bonds to the central bank, the central bank would then give you a check which you could deposit into your China Merchants Bank account. So, at this time, your T-account would be adjusted as follows:

Your T-Account When You Sell 10 million Yuan Worth of Government Bonds and Deposit a Check at China Merchants Bank

Assets (yuan)		Liabilities (yuan)	
Government Bonds	−10 million		
Deposits	+10 million		

After you deposit this check at China Merchants Bank, China Merchants Bank's T-account would be adjusted as follows:

China Merchants Bank's T-Account

Assets (yuan)		Liabilities	
Reserves	+10 million	Deposits	+10 million

In other words, China Merchants Bank's reserves on the asset side and deposits on the liabilities side would both increase by 10 million yuan.

The effect on the central bank's balance sheets would be an increase of 10 million yuan in government bonds on the asset side as well as a 10 million yuan increase in reserves on the liabilities side, as such:

Central Bank's T-Account

Assets (yuan)		Liabilities (yuan)	
Government Bonds	+10 million	Reserves	+10 million

In this way, since China Merchants Bank's reserves increased by 10 million yuan, the base money also expanded by a corresponding 10 million yuan.

Once you receive the check from the central bank for their purchase of 10 million yuan in government bonds, instead of depositing this sum in China Merchants Bank, you decide to exchange it for cash. Then, your account balance remains the same, yet your money on hand increases by 10 million yuan. Your T-account would look like this:

T-Account after You Withdraw Cash

Assets (yuan)		Liabilities (yuan)	
Government Bonds	−10 million		
Cash	+10 million		

The effect on the central bank's balance sheets would be an increase of 10 million yuan in government bonds on the asset side as well as a 10 million yuan increase in cash in circulation on the liabilities side, as such:

Central Bank's T-Account after You Withdraw Cash

Assets (yuan)		Liabilities (yuan)	
Government Bonds	+10 million	Cash in Circulation	+10 million

As a result, if you decided to take the check that you received for selling 10 million yuan worth of government bonds and converted it into cash, this would not affect the reserves of the commercial banking system, yet it would still add 10 million yuan to the cash in circulation. Thus, the central bank's purchase of government bonds will either add to the reserves of the commercial banking system or to the cash in circulation. This simply depends on whether the bond seller decides to deposit the check in a bank account or decides to convert it into cash. If the check is deposited, this will cause an increase in the reserves of the banking system. If the check is converted into cash, the reserves will remain unchanged, yet there will be an increase in the amount of cash in circulation. Even though there may be such a difference, in either case the base money expands.

(c) *Refinancing to Financial Institutions*

Refinancing to banks and other financial institutions is the main channel through which China injects base money into circulation. Suppose that within the above example, the central bank did not purchase bonds with 10 million yuan from the Bank of China, but instead lent 10 million yuan to the Bank of China. After receiving this sum of money, the Bank of China would then deposit it into an account at the central bank. At this time, the central bank and the Bank of China's T-account would be as follows:

Central Bank's T-Account When Refinancing 10 million Yuan to the Bank of China

Assets (yuan)		Liabilities (yuan)	
Refinancing to Financial Institutions	+10 million	Reserves	+10 million

Bank of China's T-Account

Assets (yuan)		Liabilities (yuan)	
Reserve	+10 million	Loans from the Central Bank	+10 million

The result of this action is that the Bank of China has added 10 million yuan to their reserves. If the Bank of China were to convert this 10 million yuan to cash, it would be the same as if they were to sell government bonds and convert the check from those proceeds into cash. In both cases, 10 million yuan would have been added to the cash in vault and there would be no change to the liabilities side of the Bank of China's balance sheet. The effect that this action would have on the central bank is that cash in circulation would increase by 10 million yuan on the liabilities side. On the assets side of the balance sheet, refinancing to financial institutions would increase by 10 million yuan. The central bank and Bank of China's T-accounts would be as follows:

Central Bank's T-Account

Assets (yuan)		Liabilities (yuan)	
Refinancing to financial institutions	+10 million	Cash in Circulation	+10 million

Bank of China's T-Account

Assets (yuan)		Liabilities (yuan)	
Vault Cash	+10 million	Loans from the Central Bank	+10 million

Regardless of the differences that exist, and regardless of whether money is added to Bank of China's reserves or to the Bank of China's cash in vault, the base money has still expanded by 10 million yuan.

13.1.4 The Influence of Central Bank Liabilities on the Base Money

From the balance sheet of the central bank and from the base money equation, we can see that additions on the liabilities side of the central bank's balance sheet will reduce the base money. Here, we will primarily discuss the influence of government deposits and central bank bills on the base money.

(a) *Government Deposits*

All capital that the government raises from taxes or the sale of bonds must first be deposited into an account in a commercial bank. The commercial bank will then transfer the funds to an account in the central bank. Now suppose that the Ministry of Finance issues 100 million yuan in Treasury bills. After these securities have been issued, funds will be deposited in a commercial bank that will then transfer them to an account in the central bank. At this time, the Ministry of Finance's T-account would be adjusted as follows:

Ministry of Finance's T-Account

Assets (yuan)		Liabilities (yuan)
Deposits in Commercial Banks	−100 million	
Deposits in Central Bank	+100 million	

Now that the commercial bank loses the 100 million yuan savings deposit and 100 million yuan are deducted from their reserve, the commercial bank's T-account would be adjusted as follows:

Commercial Bank's T-Account

Assets (yuan)		Liabilities (yuan)	
Reserves	−100 million	Ministry of Finance's Deposits	−100 million

Since the T-accounts of the Ministry of Finance and the commercial bank were adjusted, the central bank's T-account will also change as follows:

Central Bank's T-Account

Assets (yuan)	Liabilities (yuan)	
	Commercial Bank Reserves	−100 million
	Government Deposits	+100 million

As you can see, this government deposit will cause a reduction of 100 million yuan from the reserves of the commercial banking system, and similarly, a reduction of 100 million yuan from the base money.

(b) *Central Bank Bills: Liabilities Created by the Central Bank*

Aside from government deposits and postal savings, the central bank can also create its own liabilities, namely the central bank can issue bank bills to adjust the base money. Central bank bills are debt certificates issued by the central bank as a means of making necessary adjustments to the base money and are presented as central bank bonds on the central bank's balance sheet. Suppose the People's Bank of China issues central bank bills worth 10 billion yuan of which Commercial Bank A chooses to purchase all. In this scenario, Bank A and the central bank's T-accounts would be affected as follows:

Bank A's T-Account

Assets	Liabilities
Central Bank Bonds	
Reserves	

Central Bank's T-Account

Assets	Liabilities	
	Commercial Bank Reserves	−10 billion
	Central Bank Bills	+10 billion

In other words, the central bank's issuance of 10 billion yuan worth of central bank bills has caused a 10 billion yuan reduction on the liabilities side of the central bank's balance sheet in the form of commercial bank reserves. Meanwhile, the liabilities side has also increased by 10 billion yuan in the form of central bank bills. On the asset side of Bank A's balance sheet, 10 billion yuan have been added in the form of central bank bills while 10 billion yuan in reserve deposits has been deducted, also from the assets side of Bank A's balance sheet. Thus, the issue of central bank bills will cause an equivalent decrease in the supply of base money. Conversely, if the central bank were to redeem these central bank bills, this would cause an equivalent increase in the supply of base money.

13.1.5 The Supply and Control of China's Base Money

We have approached changes in the base money from the assets and liabilities side of the central bank in the paragraphs above. We will now take a detailed look at the impact that changes in the People's Bank of China's assets and liabilities have on the base money, and the basis of our analysis is still the base money equation.

First, we will take a look at changes in the People's Bank of China's assets.

(a) *Foreign Assets*

The foreign assets on the People's Bank of China's balance sheet are primarily funds outstanding for foreign exchanges. After reforms to China's foreign exchange management system in 1994, China implemented a mandatory settlement and sale system. In that same year, China also introduced a single, managed floating exchange rate regime for the Chinese yuan. With the unification of the exchange rate, the rate for the Chinese yuan depreciated by approximately 60%, which led to China's massive trade surplus. From then on, the funds outstanding for foreign exchanges have always been a primary channel for injecting China's base money into circulation. After 2000, new changes took place in the way that the funds outstanding for foreign exchange affected the supply of base money. Since the deposit rate for the Chinese yuan had been higher than foreign deposit rates for a long period of time and because of strong expectations for the appreciation of the Chinese yuan, there was a large-scale inflow of hot money into China in order to take advantage of the risk-free interest rate spread and gain from the exchange rate difference, which, in turn, caused a steady increase in the amount of China's funds outstanding for foreign exchange. After the finance ministers of seven different western countries met in 2002, the financial ministers of the United States, Japan and other countries put pressure on China to appreciate the Chinese yuan, which further led to the market's unprecedented expectations for the appreciation of the Chinese yuan. This, coupled with the influx of international speculative capital and China's growing trade surplus, led to the dramatic expansion of China's funds outstanding for foreign exchange after 2003 (as shown in Figure 13.1(a)). Foreign assets held by the People's Bank of China directly led to the passive expansion of the Chinese base money. Foreign assets held by the People's Bank of China as a

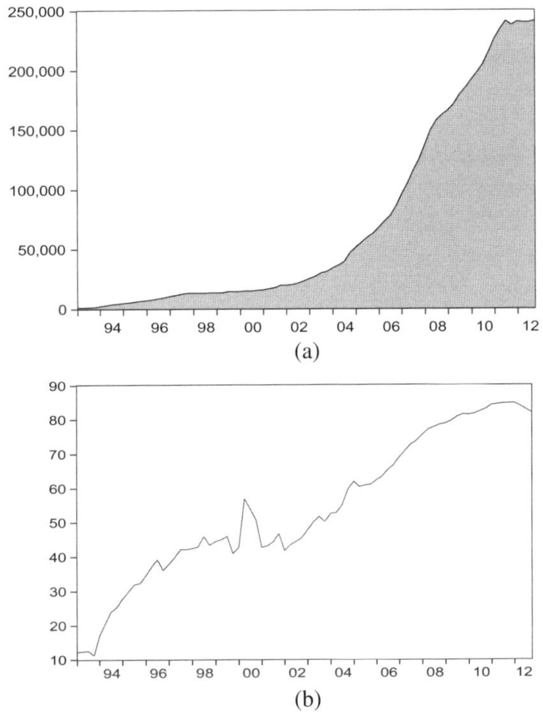

Fig. 13.1 (a) Foreign Assets Held by the Central Bank (Unit: 100 million yuan) and (b) Foreign Assets as a Percentage of Total Central Bank Assets (Unit: %)
Source: *The People's Bank of China Quarterly Statistical Bulletin*

portion of all assets, as can be seen in Figure 13.1(b), increased to approximately 80% by 2012, having only been at 12% in 1994. As you can see, after 1994, the increase in foreign assets has become the primary channel for injecting base money into the Chinese economy, and thus, the settlement and sale system has exposed the People's Bank of China's assets and the supply of base money to the greater risk of external shocks.

(b) *Refinancing to Financial Institutions*

The People's Bank of China's refinancing to financial institutions is reflected in the claims on depository financial institutions and the claims on non-depository financial institutions on the balance sheet. Claims on non-depository financial institutions include refinancing to financial asset management companies, securities companies and other financial institutions (Figure 13.2). First of all, we will discuss the claims on depository financial institutions. Unlike the constant growth of funds outstanding for foreign exchange after 1993, refinancing to these institutions has

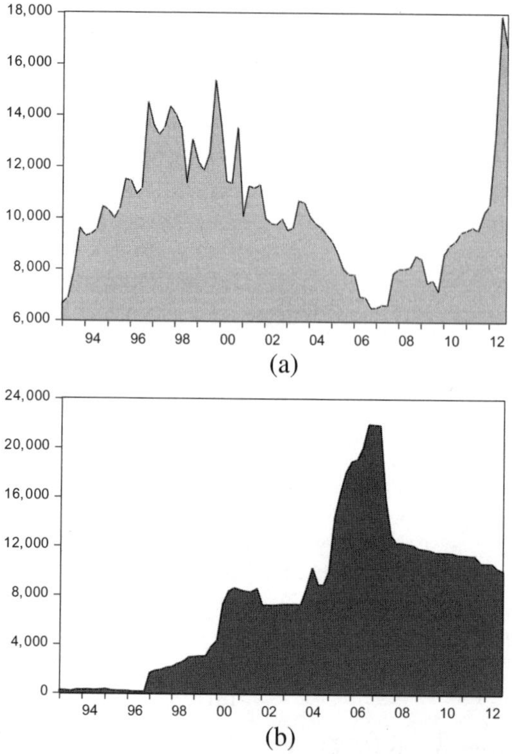

Fig. 13.2 (a) Central Bank Claims on Depository Financial Institutions and (b) Central Bank Claims on Non-Depository Financial Institutions (Unit: 100 million yuan)

Source: *The People's Bank of China Quarterly Statistical Bulletin*

experienced both rises and falls. In 1999, the balance of refinancing to commercial banks reached 1.53739 trillion yuan, which illustrates that within this period of time, claims on depository financial institutions similarly grew as an important channel for the supply of the base money. However, from 2000 to 2007, claims on depository financial institutions continued to decline, which constrained the supply of the base money. Funds outstanding for foreign exchange caused a rigid expansion in the supply of base money, and refinancing to financial asset management companies produced a one-off impact on the supply as well. Adjusting refinancing to commercial banks became a powerful instrument for coping with such shocks to the base money. From 2009 to 2012, claims on depository financial institutions experienced another significant increase, and thus spurred an expansion in the base money, which illustrates that over this period of time, the central bank's money supply policy was expansionary. Second, we will discuss claims on non-depository financial institutions. Of these claims, there are two primary changes that occurred. First, in 2000, in order for financial asset management companies to acquire the non-performing loans of state-owned commercial banks, the People's Bank of China increased their refinancing (claims on other financial institutions) by 476.73 billion yuan which was the main channel of the supply of base money for that year. After 2000, there were no significant changes to claims on non-monetary financial institutions, and this factor had a much weaker impact on the base money. Second, from 2005 to 2006, claims on non-depository financial institutions increased by leaps and bounds, reaching a maximum of approximately 2.2 trillion yuan at one point, which was primarily a result of liquidity assistance to a number of financial institutions including securities companies. For this reason, the central bank's liquidity assistance to financial institutions led to an expansion of the base money.

(c) *Financial Claims on the Government*

Prior to 1994, the fiscal deficit of the central government was basically compensated for through borrowing or getting an overdraft from the central bank (Figure 13.3). After 1994, the fiscal deficit could only be compensated for through government bond issuances, which thereby cut the ties between the fiscal deficit and the issuance of base money. It is precisely this change that strengthened the corresponding independence of the central bank's control over the base money. Nowadays, changes to government bonds within the central bank's assets are primarily through the central bank's bond transactions on the open market. When the central bank needs to withdraw base money from circulation, it can sell government bonds from the central bank's assets which will reduce the financial claims on the government. Conversely, when the central bank needs to inject base money into circulation, it can purchase government bonds through open market operations, which will increase the central bank's claims on the government. In 2001, the central bank's

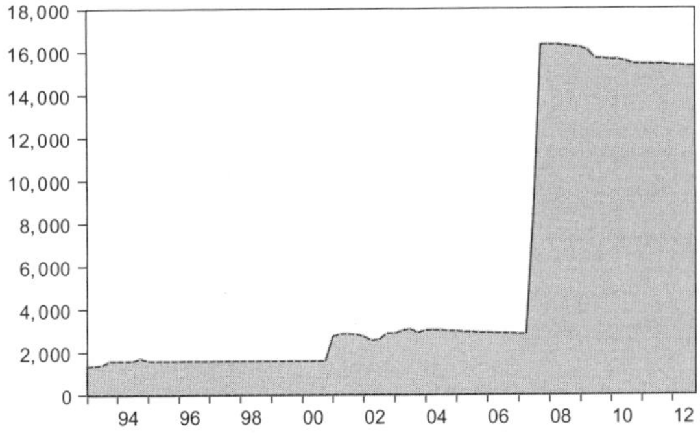

Fig. 13.3 Central Bank Claims on the Government (Unit: 100 million yuan)
Source: *The People's Bank of China Quarterly Statistical Bulletin*

claims on the government increased by 123.85 billion yuan which led to a corresponding increase in the base money of 123.85 billion yuan. After 2002, the central bank's claims on the government remained fairly stable as the central bank actively restructured its liabilities to control base money growth. In 2007, claims on the government again grew by leaps and bounds, primarily because of the establishment of the State Foreign Exchange Investment Corporation in that year and the Ministry of Finance's issuance of approximately 1.55 trillion yuan in bonds to raise capital for the new corporation. This issuance was first purchased by the Agricultural Bank of China. In order to avoid major adverse effects on the market supply of capital, the central bank then purchased these bonds, in full, from the Agricultural Bank of China.

Next, we will look at changes in the People's Bank of China's liabilities, focusing particularly on changes to central bank bonds and government deposits.

(d) *Central Bank Bonds*

Central bank bonds are also called central bank bills, and in China's financial media, they are often referred to as "central bank bills" rather than "central bank bonds". As you can see in Figure 13.4, from 1993 to 2001, central bank bonds were negligible as they did not play a role in the regulation and control of the base money. In 2002, the central bank began a large-scale issuance of central bank bills to withdraw base money as a response to the expansion in the base money caused by funds outstanding for foreign exchange. Over the next few years, the issuance of central bank bills became a basic means for offsetting funds outstanding for foreign exchange (foreign assets). Because of the increase in funds outstanding for foreign exchange, the central bank could not help but issue a large volume of central bank bills in order to stabilize the supply of base money. From 2002 to 2009, the amount of central bank bonds increased significantly, reaching a maximum, at one point, of approximately 4.7 trillion yuan. Central bank bills are a type of liabilities

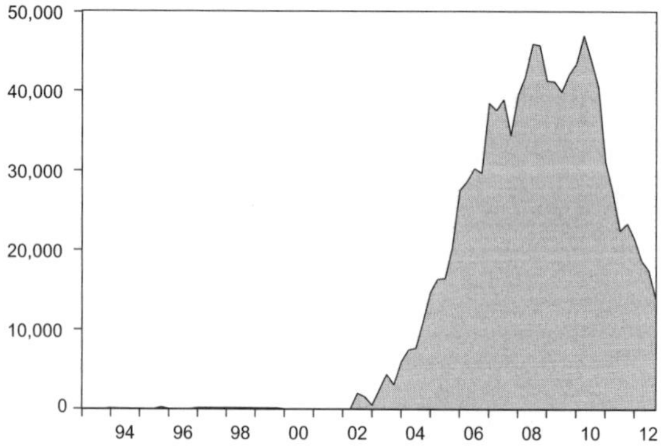

Fig. 13.4 Balance of Central Bank Bonds/Bills (100 million yuan)
Source: *The People's Bank of China Quarterly Statistical Bulletin*

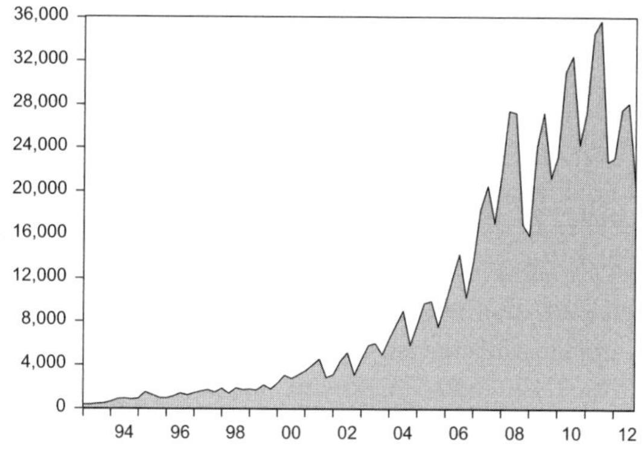

Fig. 13.5 Balance of Government Deposits (100 million yuan)
Source: *The People's Bank of China Quarterly Statistical Bulletin*

actively created by the central bank and used as a means of adjusting the base money, in which the central bank is fairly active and can determine the size of bill issue as necessary. However, after 2010, the balance of central bank bonds has been declining, which illustrates that the role of central bank bonds as a means of offsetting the expansion in foreign assets has been weakened.

(e) *Government Deposits*

An increase in government deposits will tighten the base money, and conversely, a reduction in government deposits will increase the base money. As can be seen in Figure 13.5, since 1994, government deposits have experienced an overall increase and have played an active role in the central bank's withdrawal of base money Changes in the balance of government deposits have had a significant characteristic in that they have fluctuated in a jagged manner and generally speaking, the balance of government deposits will decline significantly in the fourth quarter of each year. Thus, at the end of each year, the change in government deposits will often increase the base money. As you can also see from the figure, after 2010, the balance of government deposits has been declining. In fact, this change is inextricably linked to Treasury cash management. This so-called **Treasury cash management** refers to the process in which the Ministry of Finance entrusts the Yreasury funds, which were previously managed by the central bank, to the People's Bank of China for a rate tender and then have them deposited into the commercial bank with the highest bid (interest rate). Therefore, Treasury cash management will reduce the amount of government deposits from the central bank's liabilities. Even though an increase in government deposits play a role in the withdrawal of base money, changes in government deposits primarily depend on changes in fiscal revenues and expenditures. Systematic reforms to Treasury cash management also have an impact on government deposits on the central bank's balance sheet, and as such, the central bank cannot control government deposits. More precisely, the balance of government deposits within the central bank's liabilities reflects the passive injection or withdrawal of base money and is not one of the central bank's instruments for regulating and controlling the base money.

13.2 The Creation of Derivative Deposits by the Banking System

When you deposit 100 yuan at the bank, would you expect it to grow by several hundred? At first glance, this may seem a little absurd. When I deposit 100 yuan in the bank, by the time I withdraw it next year it would still only be 100 with a little interest at best. There is no way I can earn several hundred yuan on my account. If that were true, would not this be the proverbial money tree?

It is true. The 100 yuan you deposit today cannot become 500 yuan within a single year. However, if you understand the functions of the interbank lending system as well as its method of loans and settlements, you may see the light: my deposit of 100 yuan, within the entire banking system, can become several hundred yuan after all, although the amount in my account does not change. This process is called the creation of deposit money or derivative deposits. These derivative deposits refer to the deposits that are created through the loans of the commercial banking system. We will now analyze this process of creating derivative deposits.

13.2.1 100% Required Deposit Reserves and 100% Cash Withdrawals

We will first look at two special situations. First, when the central bank requires 100% reserve of commercial banks, namely that all commercial bank deposits must be deposited in full to each bank's central bank reserve account. If you deposit 100 yuan at some bank, then at this time, this bank's T-account would be:

Assets (yuan)		Liabilities (yuan)	
Cash in Vault	100	Deposits	100

After this bank receives your 100 yuan deposit, it must hold a 100% reserve. As a result, this bank's T-account would be as follows once it had made a deposit to its central bank reserve account.

Assets (yuan)		Liabilities (yuan)	
Cash in Vault	0	Deposits	100
Required Reserve	100		

After this bank has made a deposit into its reserve account as required by the central bank, it has no funds by which it can offer loans. As a result, derivative deposits cannot be created under this kind of situation.

The second case is when 100% cash is withdrawn. Now suppose that the required deposit reserve rate was 10% yet borrowers withdrew cash in full after they received their loans. After you had deposited 100 yuan in this bank, the bank would be required to deposit 10 yuan to the required reserve. Afterwards, its original balance sheet would be as follows:

Assets (yuan)		Liabilities (yuan)	
Cash in Vault	90	Deposits	100
Required Reserve	10		

After this bank withholds 10 yuan as the required reserve, there would still be 90 yuan remaining. Unlike the 100% reserve requirement, it can still use this 90 yuan in cash to offer loans. Suppose that Borrower A received a loan of 90 yuan from this bank and withdrew the cash in full. At this time, the bank's T-account would be as follows:

Assets (yuan)		Liabilities (yuan)	
Cash in Vault	0	Deposits	100
Required Reserve	10		
Loans	90		

Once Borrower A withdraws cash and does not deposit it into his bank account, then the 100 yuan that you had initially deposited will only be worth 100 yuan throughout the entire banking system.

13.2.2 Fractional Reserves and Deposit Creation When No Cash is Withdrawn

100% required deposit reserves and 100% withdrawn cash are both unrealistic assumptions. In many cases, borrowers will use checks to transfer and settle their loans. After borrowers take out a loan from a bank, the lender will give him a check. Afterwards, the borrower will deposit this check in his correspondent bank.

Once this bank has taken your 100 yuan deposit, and once it has withheld the 10 yuan of required deposit reserves, the remaining 90 yuan can be used to offer loans. Once Borrower A receives a loan from the bank, the bank will give him a check. Once he receives this check, he will likely deposit it in his correspondent bank, say Bank A. After Bank A receives this check, its T-account would be as

Assets (yuan)		Liabilities (yuan)	
Reserve	90	Deposits	90

Bank A must also withhold a required reserve of 9 yuan based on the 10% rate of required deposit reserves. After withholding the required reserve, Bank A's T-account would adjust as follows:

Assets (yuan)		Liabilities (yuan)	
Reserve	81	Deposits	90
Required Reserve	9		

Thus, after withholding 9 yuan in required reserve, Bank A still can use 81 yuan for loan offers. Suppose that this 81 yuan was given in full to Borrower B. At this time, Bank A's T-account would again adjust, as follows:

Assets (yuan)		Liabilities (yuan)	
Required Deposit Reserve	9	Deposits	90
Credit	81		
Loans	81		

Borrower B would then take his loan of 81 yuan from Bank A and deposit it in his correspondent bank, say Bank B. Once Bank B receives this deposit of 81 yuan, it too must withhold a required reserve of 8.1 yuan based on the 10% required reserve rate, which would leave 72.9 yuan remaining for loan offers. If this process continues throughout the entire banking system, we would eventually come up with the following situation:

Bank	Deposits (yuan)	Required Reserve (yuan)
Some Bank	100	10
Bank A	90	9
Bank B	81	8.1
Bank C	72.9	7.29
Bank D	65.61	6.651
⋮	⋮	⋮
Total Banking System	1000	100

In this way, your initial deposit of 100 yuan at some bank, after withholding a required reserve of 10%, the bank system had created 1000 yuan. This is 10 times your original 100 yuan. This is a deposit multiplier. It equals the reciprocal of the ratio of required deposit reserves. Since we have not considered other factors, this is known as the simple deposit multiplier. Conversely, if you withdraw your 100 yuan deposit from the bank, you will also cause a contraction, which happens to be the reciprocal of required deposit reserve ratio.

13.2.3 Leakage during the Creation of Money

(a) *One Form of Leakage during the Creation of Money: Excess Reserves*

In general, aside from the requirements of required deposit reserves, in order to cope with the depositors' withdrawal and liquidity management, commercial banks will also withhold excess reserves. Once commercial banks have withheld for excess reserves, their ability to create deposit money is thereby weakened. Suppose, for example, the commercial banking system withholds excess reserves at a rate of 10%. Now let us have a look at the effect this would have on the commercial banking system's money creation.

After you deposit 100 yuan in the bank, this bank must first withhold 10 yuan in required reserves based on the 10% ratio of required reserves. Afterwards, the bank would again withhold 10 yuan in excess reserves based on liquidity needs. Finally, there would be 80 yuan remaining which is given to Enterprise A. In this way, the bank's T-account would be as follows:

Some Bank's T-Account with Excess Reserves

Assets (yuan)		Liabilities (yuan)	
Required Reserves	10	Deposits	100
Excess Reserves	10		
Loans	80		

Once Enterprise A has received its loan from the bank, this check will again be deposited in its correspondent bank, say Bank A. Once Bank A receives the check for 80 yuan, it will withdraw 8 yuan for required reserves. Similarly, the bank will also withhold 8 yuan to meet the 10% excess reserves requirement. Finally, the remaining 64 yuan will be given to Enterprise B as a loan. At this time, the

T-account of Bank A would look like this:

T-Account of Bank A with Excess Reserves

Assets (yuan)		Liabilities (yuan)	
Required Reserves	8	Deposits	80
Excess Reserves	8		
Loans	64		

In this way, we arrive at the following money creation process:

Deposit Creation with Excess Reserves

Bank	Deposits (yuan)	Required Reserves (yuan)	Excess Reserves (yuan)	Total Reserves (yuan)
Some Bank	100	10	10	20
Bank A	80	8	8	16
Bank B	64	6.4	6.4	12.8
Bank C	51.2	5.12	5.12	10.24
⋮	⋮	⋮	⋮	⋮
Total Banking System	500	50	50	100

As such, since the commercial banking system has held excess reserves, the ability of the banking system to create deposit money has been weakened. After the commercial banking system has drawn 10% in excess reserves, the final deposit created by your initial deposit of 100 yuan will be reduced from 1000 yuan to 500 yuan.

(b) *Another Form of Leakage during the Creation of Money: Cash Leakage*

Once an enterprise receives a loan from a bank, not all of the loan will be deposited in the bank in the form of a check, and a portion will be withdrawn as cash, while the remaining portion will be deposited in the bank. Now, suppose that the required deposit reserve and excess reserve ratios are still 10%, however Enterprise A withdraws 10% in cash, or rather 8 yuan in cash, and then deposits the remaining 72 yuan in a bank. Once the bank receives the enterprise's deposit, it will also withhold 10% for both the required reserve and the excess reserve. The remaining 57.6 yuan will be lent to Enterprise B, and the T-account of the bank will change as follows:

Assets (yuan)		Liabilities (yuan)	
Required Reserve	7.2	Deposits	72
Excess Reserve	7.2		
Loans	57.6		

After Enterprise B receives the loan of 57.6 yuan from Bank A, it also withdraws 10% in cash, and then deposits the remaining in Bank B. Once Bank B receives the enterprise's deposit, it will also withdraw 10% for both the required reserve and the excess reserve, and then lend the remaining to Enterprise C. If this process continues throughout the entire economy and the banking system, we would eventually come up with the following money creation situation:

Money Creation with Excess Reserves and Cash Leakage

Bank	Deposits (yuan)	Required Reserves (yuan)	Excess Reserves (yuan)	Total Reserves (yuan)
Some Bank	100	10	10	20
Bank A	72	7.2	7.2	14.4
Bank B	51.84	5.184	5.184	10.368
⋮	⋮	⋮	⋮	⋮
Total of the Banking System	333	33.3	33.3	66.6

Thus, when cash leakage exists, money creation will be further weakened.

13.3 Money Multipliers

13.3.1 Deriving Money Multipliers Model

Now that we understand the creation of deposit money, we can use a mathematical formula to express the relationship between base money and the money supply, namely:

$$M = k \cdot MB, \tag{13.4}$$

k is the money multiplier by which money supply changes as a result of base money change. So how much is this multiplier? It depends on what we are talking about is M_1 or M_2.

Setting cash in circulation as C, the total amount of reserves as R, the required deposit reserve as Rr and the excess reserve as Re, which gives us:

$$R = Rr + Re, \tag{13.5}$$

$$MB = C + R = C + Rr + Re. \tag{13.6}$$

If we then set the required deposit reserve ratio as r, the ratio of excess reserves as e, the total amount of demand deposits as Dd and time deposits as Dt, we can obtain:

$$D = Dd + Dt, \tag{13.7}$$

$$Rr + Re = D \cdot r + D \cdot e = D(r + e). \tag{13.8}$$

The ratio of cash in circulation is c, thus:

$$C = c \cdot D, \tag{13.9}$$

so that:

$$MB = D(c + r + e). \tag{13.10}$$

According to the structure of monetary aggregates, M_1 is equal to the sum of cash in circulation and bank deposits, such that:

$$M_1 = C + Dd = D \cdot c + Dd. \tag{13.11}$$

Again set that time deposits as a ratio of total deposits t, thus

$$Dd = D \cdot (1 - t). \tag{13.12}$$

$$\text{Thus: } M_1 = C + Dd = D(1 + c - t) = k_1 \cdot D(c + r + e). \tag{13.13}$$

From this, the money multiplier for M_1 is $k_1 = \dfrac{1 + c - t}{c + r + e}$, (13.14)

$$M_2 = M_1 + Dt = D(1 + c) = k_2 \cdot D(c + r + e). \tag{13.15}$$

From this we can get the money multiplier for M_2 is $k_2 = \dfrac{1 + c}{c + r + e}$. (13.16)

We can use a specific example to illustrate. Suppose that the ratio of required reserves is 8%; the total amount of cash in circulation is 200 billion yuan; and the total amount of deposits is 1 trillion yuan of which demand and time deposits are 500 billion yuan each. Commercial banks hold excess reserves of 100 billion yuan.

Based on the data above, we can calculate the following:

Ratio of currency in circulation $c = \frac{2000}{10000} = 0.2$,

Ratio of commercial bank excess reserves $e = \frac{1000}{10000} = 0.1$,

Ratio of time deposits to total deposits $t = \frac{5000}{10000} = 0.5$.

As such, the multiplier of M_1 and M_2 can be calculated as follows:

$$k_1 = \frac{1 + 0.2 - 0.5}{0.2 + 0.08 + 0.1} \approx 1.84,$$

$$k_2 = \frac{1 + 0.2}{0.2 + 0.08 + 0.1} \approx 3.16.$$

13.3.2 Factors that Affect Money Multipliers

Now with all else remaining equal, we will analyze how changes in each of the factors will affect the value of money multipliers.

(a) *Changes in the Required Reserve Ratio r*

Assume that all else remains equal, if we raise the required reserve ratio of commercial banks, it will reduce the funds for loans and reduce the creation of deposit money, causing a decline in the money multiplier. If the base money does not change, then the total money supply will be reduced. Conversely, if the central bank reduces the required reserve ratio, commercial banks will have more reserves available for loans, therefore their capability of creating deposit money will be improved and the money multiplier will rise.

Suppose that in the above example, the central bank raises the required deposit reserve from 8% to 10%, then with all else equal, the money multipliers for M_1 and M_2 would be:

$$k_1 = \frac{1 + 0.2 - 0.5}{0.2 + 0.1 + 0.1} = 1.75,$$

$$k_2 = \frac{1 + 0.2}{0.2 + 0.1 + 0.1} = 3.0.$$

After the central bank raises the ratio of required deposit reserves, M_1 and M_2 money multipliers would drop to 1.75 and 3.0, respectively.

If the central bank reduces the required deposit reserve ratio from 8% to 6%, then with all else equal, M_1 and M_2 money multipliers would change as

$$k_1 = \frac{1 + 0.2 - 0.5}{0.2 + 0.6 + 0.1} \approx 1.94,$$

$$k_2 = \frac{1 + 0.2}{0.2 + 0.6 + 0.1} \approx 3.33.$$

This means that once the central bank reduces the required deposit reserve ratio, M_1 and M_2 money multipliers would increase to 1.94 and 3.33, respectively.

We have reached a conclusion from this analysis: when the central bank raises the required reserve ratio, the money multiplier will decrease; conversely, if the central bank lowers the required deposit reserve ratio, the money multiplier will increase.

(b) *Changes in the Currency Ratio c*

We already analyzed the creation of deposit money previously. If at each link of the creation process, borrowers must withdraw a certain percentage of cash, then the commercial banking system's ability to create deposit money will be reduced, which in turn will further affect the money multiplier values.

If in the above example, the total amount of cash in circulation is not 200 billion yuan, but instead 300 billion yuan, then the required deposit reserve ratio and excess reserve ratio still remain 0.08 and 0.1 respectively. The value of the money multipliers M_1 and M_2 would be as follows:

$$k_1 = \frac{1 + 0.3 - 0.5}{0.3 + 0.08 + 0.1} = 1.67,$$

$$k_2 = \frac{1 + 0.3}{0.3 + 0.08 + 0.1} = 2.71.$$

Once the ratio of cash in circulation rises to 0.3, the money multipliers for M_1 and M_2 decreases to 1.67 and 2.71, respectively. Conversely, if the cash in circulation is reduced from an original 200 billion yuan to 100 billion yuan, we can calculate the multipliers for M_1 and M_2, respectively:

$$k_1 = \frac{1 + 0.1 - 0.5}{0.1 + 0.08 + 0.1} = 2.14,$$

$$k_2 = \frac{1 + 0.1}{0.1 + 0.08 + 0.1} \approx 3.93.$$

In other words, once the currency ratio dropped to 0.1, the value of the money multipliers for M_1 and M_2 will increase to 2.14 and 3.93, respectively.

Thus, we again can reach another conclusion: the money multiplier increases when the currency ratio decreases, and falls while the currency ratio rises.

(c) *Changes in the Ratio of Excess Reserves*

An increase in the ratio of excess reserves causes a reduction in the reserves that can be used to create loans, thus weakening the banking system's ability to create deposit money. This, like an increasing ratio of cash in circulation, will lower the value of the money multiplier, so that when the base money remains constant, the total money supply will still be reduced. Conversely, if the commercial banking system lowers its ratio of excess reserves, then its reserves that can be used to create loans will increase, thereby improving the ability of the banking system to create deposit money, and in turn, improving the value of the money multipliers. When the base money remains constant, the total amount of money supply will increase.

If all else remains constant, the commercial banking system's excess reserves will increase from the original 100 billion yuan to 200 billion yuan. Now, if the ratio of excess reserves e becomes 0.2, at this time, money multipliers for M_1 and M_2 will be as follows:

$$k_1 = \frac{1 + 0.2 - 0.5}{0.2 + 0.08 + 0.2} \approx 1.46,$$

$$k_2 = \frac{1 + 0.2}{0.2 + 0.08 + 0.2} = 2.5.$$

As you can see, once the ratio of excess reserves increases from 0.1 to 0.2, money multipliers for M_1 and M_2 will decrease to 1.46 and 2.5, respectively.

In contrast, if the ratio of excess reserves drops from 0.1 to 0.05, we can calculate that the money multipliers for M_1 and M_2 will increase to 2.12 and 3.64, respectively.

Thus, the money multiplier will fall as the excess reserve ratio of the banking system increases, and it will increase with any decline in the ratio of excess reserves.

13.4 Determinants of Money Multiplier Factors

Previously, we analyzed the impact of changes in the currency ratio and excess reserve ratio on the money multiplier. Now we will further analyze the many factors that influence the currency ratio and excess reserve ratio. Before our in-depth analysis, let us first take a look at the fluctuations of the money multiplier in China over recent years.

We can see from Figure 13.6 that since China's market reforms, the money multiplier has not been constant, and is constantly fluctuating. Of course, the money multiplier around the world is not a constant amount. There are some variations between years. This is because, in addition to changes in the required deposit reserve ratio, more importantly, the currency ratio and the ratio of excess reserves

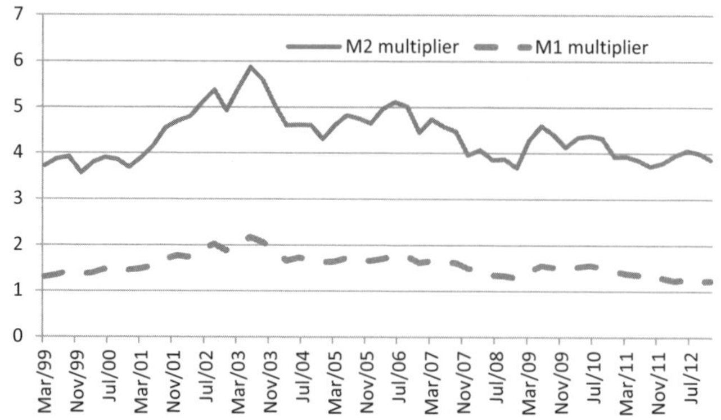

Fig. 13.6 Changes in the Money Multipliers in China
Source: Calculation of the author based on *The People's Bank of China Quarterly Statistical Bulletin* and data on the Website of the People's Bank of China

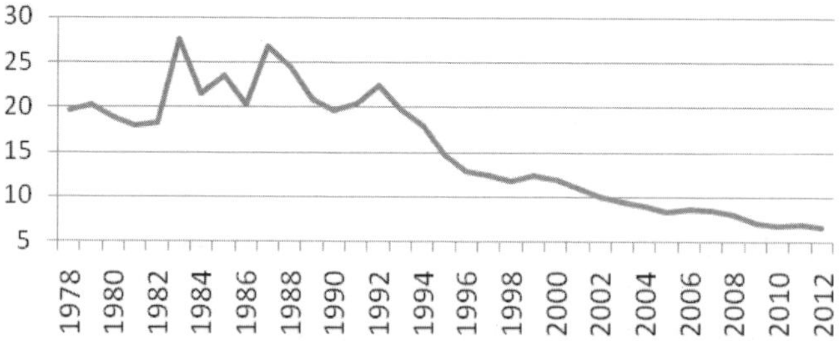

Fig. 13.7 Changes in China's Currency Ratio since Market Reforms were Introduced (Unit: %)
Source: Calculation of the author based on *The People's Bank of China Quarterly Statistical Bulletin* and data on the Website of the People's Bank of China

that commercial banks hold, are also changing and the determining factors of the currency ratio and the excess reserve ratio are countless and complex.

13.4.1 Factors that Affect the Currency Ratio

Is the ratio of cash in circulation a constant? The answer is no. This ratio constantly changes. As displayed in Figure 13.7, in the beginning of the 1980s, the ratio between China's cash in circulation and deposits slightly decreased. From 1983 to 1988, this ratio began to rise. In 1988, this currency deposit ratio had reached above 25%. From 1989 to 1992 the ratio again declined. However, in 1993 and 1994 there was a significant increase. After 1994, this number continued to decrease until it had fallen below 15% in 1999. Over the last ten years of the new century, the ratio between the cash in circulation and deposits has further dropped below

10%. As you can see, the currency deposit ratio is incredibly fluctuant over the last 30 years, generally speaking. What factors cause these changes to the currency ratio and cause such fluctuations?

(a) *Level of Income or Wealth*

Generally speaking, as the level of income and wealth grows, although the total demand for money will increase, the ratio between currency and deposits will decline. If your monthly income is 10,000 yuan, then you might deposit 7000 yuan of your monthly income, while you would probably hold on to the remaining 3000 yuan left in your pocket for normal spending. Your currency deposit ratio is approximately 42.86%. On the other extreme, a laid-off worker can only receive 300 yuan per month in unemployment benefits. This income of 300 yuan will barely stretch to cover his monthly spending, and there is no surplus to deposit and the currency deposit ratio would be nearly infinite. As income levels increase and people accumulate wealth, the currency deposit ratio will tend to fall. When the level of national income rises and the economy becomes developed, the currency deposit ratio will drop, and, the money multipliers will grow and improve.

(b) *Rate of Inflation*

Inflation is equivalent to a tax on your deposit. If the inflation rate each year was 10% and you had deposited 10,000 yuan at the beginning of the year, you would only be able to purchase 9000 yuan worth of goods at the start of next year. This means that 1000 yuan disappeared because of inflation. So the higher the rate of inflation, the less cost-effective a bank deposit will become. During times of high-inflation, people will withdraw their cash and purchase physical assets as a hedge. This would raise the currency deposit ratio. Conversely, during deflationary periods, the stored value of currency comes into full use and people will agree that deposits are a wise choice which would lower the currency deposit ratio. In 1993 and 1994, the sharp rise in the currency ratio and the high inflation rate of these two years were related. The decrease in the currency ratio after 1994 was related in a large part to the deflationary trend that began in China at that point.

(c) *Nominal Yield of Deposits*

Savings deposits are a type of financial investment and a means by which people can earn a set profit. The nominal yield on a deposit is the interest rate that a bank will pay. On January 1, 2009, the interest rate on a one-year term was 2.25%. This is the nominal yield of a one-year time deposit. Suppose that on that day you deposited 10,000 yuan. On January 1, 2010, your principal and interest would be 10,225 yuan. Suppose that the bank did not pay 2.25%, but rather paid −2.25% instead. In other words, you would owe the bank. So the 10,000 yuan that you now deposit into the bank would only be worth 9775 yuan one year from now. You might even think to yourself that stashing this money under your pillow might be a smarter option, and you would not want to deposit this sum of money in the bank. Obviously, the higher the interest rate, the more motivated we are to make a deposit. Conversely, the lower the interest rate, the less motivated we are to deposit.

Naturally, the nominal interest rate on bank deposits is only one of the factors that determine our willingness to make a deposit. Can a drop in the nominal interest rate reduce the amount of savings deposits? Not necessarily. For example, starting from September 2008, in the fourth quarter, the government lowered interest rates in response to the financial crisis. By October 2009, however, the gross savings in financial institutions had reached a whopping 58 trillion yuan, an increase of more than 10 trillion yuan compared to the end of 2008. By the end of 2012, the balance of deposits in China reached 91 trillion yuan. This illustrates the fact that a drop in interest rates, even a zero interest rate, will not necessarily mean that we do not need bank deposit services. If you had several million yuan in cash, for example, and happened to have it stored away somewhere in your home, you would certainly be on the edge. You would feel so much better if it was socked away within a thick safe at a bank. So, the greater the wealth, the lower the currency ratio and vice versa.

(d) *Convenience of Banking Services*

The level of convenience that banking services offer can influence people's willingness to hold onto cash. In our modern city lives, bank branches always seem to be just within arm's reach, not to mention the many 24-hour ATMs, which make depositing and withdrawing easy and convenient. This is not the case for remote rural areas though. In a township that measures tens of kilometers across, there may exist only one rural credit cooperative. Transportation is anything but convenient. In these sorts of extremely inconvenient mountain regions, the demand for cash is a bit higher, and naturally, the currency deposit ratio would also be higher. Therefore, urbanization tends to lower currency ratios.

A more obvious example is the way that bank cards have greatly reduced our demand for cash. Nowadays, from shopping at the mall to enjoying accommodation services at hotels, many places accept the use of bank cards instead of the traditional method of payment with cash. This has drastically reduced the currency deposit ratio. China's inflation rate in 1994 was much higher than that of 1988, yet the currency deposit ratio still decreased. This was largely due to a big push for bank cards that occurred after 1988.

(e) *Banking Panic*

Banking panic refers to a moment when depositors lose confidence in their bank, run to the bank one after another to withdraw their funds, causing an ever more serious lack of liquidity, thereby leading to a series of failed banks. When banking panic occurs, people worry that their deposits will go down the drain, so everyone will stand in long lines outside of banks waiting to withdraw their cash. This leads to a sharp decline in bank deposits and a sharp rise in the currency deposit ratio. Imagine for a moment that some banks were on the brink of failure. People lined up outside the bank to get their money out. You also happen to have a ton of money in one of these banks. Upon hearing the rumors, would you still peacefully type away at your business reports? It is not likely. At the outbreak of the Great Depression of 1930–1933, banking panic caused the American currency deposit ratio in this period to skyrocket.

(f) *The Underground Economy*

Around us there exist a great deal of underground economic activities. This refers to any transactions that violate current laws, rules or regulations such as drug trafficking, pornography, gambling, black market trading, or human trafficking. In these economic activities, cash is used to settle transactions. Moreover, underground dealers use cash payments and will not take checks so as to avoid tax obligations. If checks were used to settle transactions of these underground economic activities, it would be incredibly easy for regulators to monitor, thereby greatly increasing the risk of the dealers. Therefore, as underground economic activities become more rampant, the demand for cash increases, thereby raising the currency deposit ratio.

13.4.2 Factors that Affect Excess Reserves Ratios of Commercial Banks

Figure 13.8 reflects the changing ratio of excess reserves of China's commercial banks since 1993, including the ratio of primary excess reserves and secondary excess reserves. The ratio of total excess reserves is the sum of the two. Although the ratio of excess reserves fluctuates when examined from the three angles, we can still find some of the basic rules and trends from Figure 13.8: (1) there are jagged fluctuations in excess reserve ratios, and within a year, the fourth quarter primary excess reserve ratio will be at its maximum. (2) Since 1996, the fluctuations in the

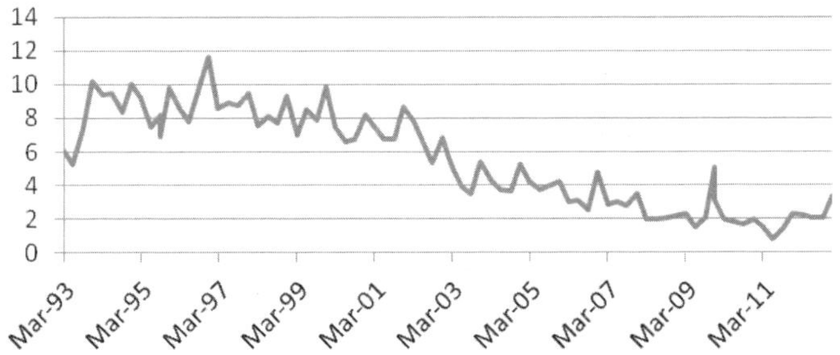

Fig. 13.8 Ratio of Excess Reserves of China's Banking Institutions (Unit: %)
Source: *The People's Bank of China Quarterly Statistical Bulletin;* The People's Bank of China's *Monetary Policy Implementation Report*

excess reserve ratio have been less than they were before 1996, showing a clear downward trend.

Commercial banks can adjust the ratio of excess reserves appropriately, which differs from the ratio of required reserves. What factors affect the ratio of excess reserves of commercial banks? These factors mainly include: the profitability of investment instruments, credit risks, expected outflows of deposits, the stability of deposit flows, and the complexity of borrowing reserves.

(a) *Profitability of Investment Instruments*

The more excess reserves that are available, the less that can be used for loans or the purchase of other income securities. Therefore, in addition to the interest paid to depositors, commercial banks hold excess reserves and opportunity costs. The higher the opportunity cost, the greater the revenue loss that arises from commercial banks' excess reserves. For example, if a bank loan's rate of return is 5% per year, the 10 million yuan of excess reserves that commercial banks hold means the loss of the opportunity to earn 500,000 yuan a year. Therefore, the higher the profitability of investment instruments, the higher the opportunity cost of holding excess reserves will be. Moreover, commercial banks will then be less willing to hold excess reserves. Conversely, the lower the yield on investment instruments, the smaller the revenue loss of holding excess reserves will be, and the lower the opportunity cost. In this case, the motivation to hold excess reserves may be stronger.

(b) *Credit Risks*

Bank loans face a lot of risk, the greatest of which is the borrower's credit risk. If a loan cannot be repaid punctually, the principal amount that the bank loaned out will most likely be lost. Therefore, the higher the credit risk, the less willing banks will be to lend money. When granting loans to risky borrowers, banks will not only potentially lose their interest, even their original capital is uncertain. During economic recessions, business will generally hold onto their inventory for longer. When capital turnover is slow, the credit risk of commercial banks increases as will the excess reserve rates. Conversely, when the economy is in a period of prosperity and when asset prices increase and enterprises have a promising outlook, the adverse selection and moral hazards due to temporarily asymmetric information will not have such a strong impact on the lending activity of banks, thereby lowering credit risks, and thus, will activate bank lending. At this time, banks will reduce their excess reserves.

(c) *Expected Deposit Outflows*

One of the main functions of excess reserves is to facilitate the liquidity management of banks. When facing large withdrawal demands from depositors, commercial banks do not have to sell securities, recall loans, or borrow funds from the central bank and the interbank lending market to meet these demands.

If commercial banks foresee a massive outflow of deposits, they must increase their excess reserves to meet the withdrawal demands of depositors. For example, as we saw in Figure 13.8, the ratio of excess reserves of commercial banks in the fourth quarter of each year was higher than the other three quarters. This is mainly due to the fact that the fourth quarter includes the National Holiday, Christmas, and is close to the traditional Chinese festival — the Spring Festival. Every Chinese company will issue an annual bonus at the end of a year, and holiday spending is always much higher than typical spending. At this time of the year, people will need to withdraw more money, so the fourth quarter exhibits the highest rate of excess reserves.

(d) *Stability of Deposit Flows*

If changes in deposits and withdrawals do not display statistical regularity over a period of time, commercial banks will not be able to predict the statistical range of balances for any given day. In order to cope with sudden outflows, the bank must also hold a greater amount of excess reserves. Imagine if your monthly income was a stable 10,000 yuan. Since your income flow is very stable, you can arrange how much cash to hold and how much stock or government bonds to buy. If your income flow, however, was not very stable, for example, you may have an income of 15,000 yuan a month during on good days and less than 1000 yuan a month on the other days. Because your income is unstable, you may hold onto 6000 yuan in cash, your remaining 9000 yuan can be used for financial investment when your income is higher. The same principle applies to the bank's choice for an excess reserves ratio. The more stable the flow of deposits and withdrawals, the smaller the possibility of sudden liquidity shocks, and therefore the lower the ratio of excess reserves.

(e) *Complexity of Borrowing Reserves*

As we analyzed earlier, banks can implement liquidity management through borrowed reserves. When a commercial bank faces a liquidity shock, if it can easily borrow money from the central bank or the interbank lending market at a low cost, the bank will not need much excess reserves. Conversely, if it is difficult and costly for the bank to obtain reserves by borrowing from the central bank or the interbank lending market, the bank must hold more excess reserves. Therefore, for commercial banks, there lies an inverse association between the demand for excess reserves and the complexity of borrowed reserves. This also explains the third aspect of changing excess reserve rates of commercial banks in China. In 1996, a national interbank lending market was established by the Chinese central bank. Since then, commercial banks have been able to borrow money freely in the market to meet liquidity demands, thus they are able to effectively handle liquidity shocks caused by temporary withdrawal demands. With the help of the market, the ratio of primary excess reserves of commercial banks is relatively stable, and more funds can be used for secondary excess reserves, such as the purchase of government bonds, which can earn a return on investment.

13.5 Endogenous and Exogenous Money Supply

13.5.1 What are the Endogenous and Exogenous Money Supply?

Is it possible for the central bank to independently control the money supply? To answer this, we must consider the concepts of endogenous and exogenous money supply. If the central bank can control the money supply independently, then the money supply is exogenous. Conversely, if money supply is determined by the economy rather than controlled by the central bank, then the money supply is endogenous.

In fact, in discussing whether the money supply is endogenous and exogenous, we can develop our answer from two different aspects: the base money and the money multiplier. As we analyzed earlier, the supply of base money is determined by the central bank's assets and liabilities, and the central bank can only control its own bonds as seen from the multiple items in its balance sheet. Under the exchange settlement and sale system, foreign exchange assets held by the central bank are the result of the trade surplus and capital inflows and outflows. Government debts held by the central bank, mainly the result of open market trading of government bonds, can generally be controlled by the central bank. It may seem that the central bank can determine its lending to financial institutions, including how much it will lend and to which of them it will lend. However, that is not the case. In the face of a financial crisis, for example, the central bank must provide loans to financial institutions when they have liquidity difficulties. At this time, the central bank's lending to financial institutions, to a considerable extent, relies on the robustness of the financial system. On the liabilities side, government deposits cannot be decided by the central bank either, for it depends on the change of financial revenue and expenditures and the Treasury management system. In terms of factors that influence the money multiplier, we can see from the above paragraphs that only the required reserve ratio can be decided or adjusted by the central bank. The ratio of excess reserves and ratio of cash in circulation, which are the results of economic operations and which in turn, can influence these operations, are determined by a variety of factors. From this point of view, we can see that the money supply is very endogenous.

There are two different theoretical propositions on whether money supply is endogenous or exogenous.

13.5.2 Exogenous Money Supply Theories

Keynes regarded the exogenous money supply as an important premise of macro-economic study, namely that the central bank can fully control money supply.

The central bank can change money supply and adjust interest rates in accordance with the changes in economic operations, and the liquidity of money supply would never change without a change in the central bank's policy. Therefore, in this sense, money supply is an exogenous variable independent from the real economy.

The theory of an exogenous money supply, on the other hand, has been highly praised by the Monetarists. Milton Friedman holds that money supply is exogenous because it is mainly determined by the monetary authority which can control the money supply by issuing money or regulating deposit reserve ratios. In Friedman's money supply model, the base money, reserve ratio, and currency ratio are the main determinants of money supply. As for the three determinants, the base money reflects the behavior of the central bank, ratio of reserves reflects the behavior of commercial banks, and the currency ratio reflects the behavior of non-bank sectors. Assuming that both the ratio of reserves and the currency ratio are constant, or change steadily, then the money supply totally depends on changes in the base money; the base money itself is under the control of the central bank, thus the central bank can control the money supply. As such, we can say that the money supply, which is not determined within the economy and monetary system by the monetary authorities, is exogenous and controllable. In the next chapter, monetarism provides that the money demand function is extremely stable over long periods, and the change of nominal income is mainly caused by changes in the money supply. The currency directly controlled by the monetary authorities is an exogenous variable, thus the changes in the money supply become the primary cause for changes in economic activity. Monetary authorities can thus control the output and price volatility completely by controlling the money supply.

13.5.3 Endogenous Money Supply Theories

(a) *New Money Supply Perspectives*

The central argument in the *Radcliffe Report* (Britain, 1959) is that it is the liquidity of the society as a whole, instead of the money supply in the traditional sense that has a real impact on the economy. In other words, the entire financial system, including commercial banks and non-bank financial institutions, determines the money supply. As such, monetary authorities should control the liquidity of the whole society, including the money supply. Some time later, Gray and Shaw, two American economists, drew these two conclusions supporting the endogeneity of the money supply: first, that *primary securities* issued by the private sector can be exchanged into *indirect securities*, such as deposit slips and fund shares with financial institutions, and most of these *indirect securities* circulate as a means of payment as currency in developed financial markets. Secondly, when the monetary authorities assume the obligation to buy some kind of private primary securities, the primary securities issued directly lead to the increase in the money supply.

Commercial banks face competition with other financial institutions during the process of money creation. Therefore, the money supply is determined not only by the commercial banks themselves, but also by the actions of other financial institutions and the public. The larger the statistical coverage of money, the greater the endogeneity of the money supply.

Tobin believed that central banks and banks in general cannot arbitrarily create money and credit, and any new increase in reserves is not necessarily accompanied by a growth in loans. The creation of credit is conditioned by the marginal revenue for loans and the marginal cost of deposits. The supply and demand of currency depends on the price and earnings of all other assets, in addition to that of itself. The interest rate will increase when various economic entities increase the demand for currency due to their own choice of asset structures according to income, interest rates, risk, etc. Then, banks will do everything possible to solve the problem of excess reserves, expanding the money supply to meet that extra demand. The surplus currency will also return to banks in the way of paying off debts by the public, if the demand for it decreases. Therefore, the money supply, subject to the constraints of demand, is endogenous. At the same time, with the rapidly developing and highly competitive financial system, financial institutions intersect and harmonize in terms of assets and liabilities, diluting the traditional distinction between monetary and other financial assets, commercial banks and other financial institutions. In consequence, the assets the public can choose become increasingly diversified and interchangeable. On the one hand, the amount of commercial banks' assets and deposits is constrained by holders' asset preferences, bank loans, and investment opportunities. The deposit-taking capabilities of other non-bank financial institutions will be improved when their lending and financing activities are increasing. Thus, as for the ability of money creation, they differ only in degree, but not in kind. The structural adjustment of public assets comes in the wake of changes in the real economy. Therefore, the fluctuation of money supply is endogenous, not detached from the real economy, and money supply is decided by monetary authorities, commercial banks, and non-bank sectors within the economy.

Although Tobin advocates the endogeneity of money supply, he does not deny the validity of control over the money supply exercised by monetary authorities. He points out that the presence of commercial banks, even if uncontrolled, does not mean that the currency controls, achieved through regulating base money supply, have no effect on the economy. The existence of non-bank financial institutions does not illustrate that the currency control over commercial banks is useless either. The control over the money supply exerted by monetary authorities still takes effect, even though the increase or decrease of the assets and liabilities of the uncontrolled non-bank financial institutions can be fully offset by the reverse fluctuation of monetary assets of the controlled commercial banks. However, the effect will be greatly minimized due to the substitute relation between monetary assets and other financial assets, as well as between the money creation capacity of non-bank financial institutions and that of commercial banks.

(b) *Other Endogenous Money Supply Theories*

Weintraub holds that assuming labor productivity is comparatively stable, if the growth rate of nominal wages exceeds that of average labor productivity, prices will rise as along with the nominal income within the society. As a result, the demand for currency will grow as well. If the central bank refuses to increase the money supply accordingly, interest rates will trend higher and conversely investment, real income, and employment will decline, which, of course, the central bank and the administration would hope to avoid. Consequently, as long as the deals for money wages are negotiated exogenously, monetary authorities will have to guarantee the adequacy of money supply, in order to eliminate the barriers to full employment and economic growth. Therefore, the money supply is endogenous. Kaldor believes that acting as the last lender is the basic function of the central bank, through discount windows to ensure the solvency of the financial sectors. In order to prevent credit crunches which lead to catastrophic debt deflations, the central bank should enlarge the money supply. Otherwise, the entire financial system will be trapped in inadequate liquidity. In other words, the instability of the whole financial system will compel the growth of money supply. In this way, money supply is endogenous.

Mohr furthers the theories above into the following aspects to explore the endogeneity of the currency supply.

First, the endogeneity of the supply of fiat money. In Mohr's theories, money can be divided into three types, the commodity money, the government money, and the fiat money. Commodity money evolved from a variety of physical commodities and was finally reflected in the form of gold. Government money is money put into circulation as a result of bonds issued by the government. Mohr deems that these two kinds of money are exogenous, while fiat money, issued by commercial banks are certificates of deposit and circulation. They result from loans granted by commercial banks, which in turn depend on public demand and loan terms. Fiat money supply cannot exist without the demand for loan, thus it is endogenous.

Second, the endogeneity of the base money. The central bank's trading partners for buying and selling securities are none other than the commercial banks. However, commercial banks generally have already used their own assets for securities or commercial loans which are difficult to recover before their fixed repayment dates. Whether commercial banks sell the securities they hold onto also depends on a cost-benefit comparison. Therefore, the central bank cannot arbitrarily set the amount of base money through open market operations. With reference to rediscounts, the central bank will be in an even more passive position. Raising the rediscount rate may dampen the demand of commercial banks for credit, but it cannot prevent them from obtaining reserves through a discount window. While the central bank may have the power to refuse discounts, this refusal will not only bring about a great deal of political pressure, but it may also endanger the liquidity of the banking system. Conversely, when the central bank intends to increase the money supply by reducing the discount rate, whether commercial banks are willing to receive more of a rediscount depends on their judgment regarding cost, profit, and the risk of the loan or investment.

Third, endogeneity of money supply due to liability management. Mohr points out that because of financial innovations, commercial banks can raise funds directly from financial markets without waiting for base money injections by the central bank. Commercial banks are moving away from asset management towards liability management. Their main source of funding has also shifted from mainly attracting deposits into directly issuing financing instruments in the financial markets. Nearly all the listed financial instruments are not subject to the direct control of the central bank, which weakens the dependence of commercial banks on it. So the change of commercial banks' liability management causes the money supply to be endogenous.

Finally, endogeneity due to the changing role of banks. Mohr divides financial markets into wholesale and retail markets. The former is the market where commercial banks raise funds and the latter is their lending market. In the wholesale market, commercial banks are the recipients of loan conditions and they themselves decide the loan amount. In the retail market, they act as the deciders of loan conditions and the recipients of loan amounts. This means that the public demand for funds in the retail market will be met after direct transmission through commercial banks to the wholesale market including the central bank. Accordingly, the money supply is conditioned by the demand for money. Furthermore, Mohr also refutes the significance of the money multiplier, for it fails to explain the factors and the process of money creation, arguing that the earlier money supply equation of the base money multiplied by the multiplier only describes, rather than explains, this phenomenon. Therefore, the government cannot control the supply of fiat money.

Summary

The base money refers to currency under a fractional reserve system that can create, through the banking system, deposit money that is multiple times the original amount. It is equivalent to the total amount of cash in circulation in addition to the total amount of reserves within the banking system. Factors that increase the base money include foreign assets, government bonds purchased by the central bank, and refinancing for financial institutions. Factors that decrease the base money include government deposits and an increase in central bank bills.

Under a fractional reserve system, commercial banks can multiply the amount of deposit money available through settlement by transfer of accounts; however, excess reserves and cash withdrawals will weaken the ability of commercial banks to create deposit money.

The total money supply is equal to the product of the base money and the money multipliers. The main factors that influence the money multipliers include the ratio of required reserves, the ratio of excess reserves held by commercial banks and the currency deposit ratio. When these three rates rise, it will cause a decrease in the money multipliers. Conversely, any reductions will raise the money multipliers.

Income or wealth, inflation, the nominal yield on deposits, the convenience of banking services, banking panics, underground business, and many other factors can influence the currency deposit ratio and will directly affect money multipliers.

The return on commercial bank investments, credit risk, expected deposit outflows, the stability of deposit flows, and the complexity of borrowing reserves all affect the ratio of excess reserves that a commercial bank will hold, and because of this, directly affect money multipliers.

Key Terms

Base Money; Money Multiplier; Currency Ratio; Excess Reserves Ratio; Underground Economy; Derivative Deposit; Banking Panic

Critical Thinking Questions

1. What is base money?
2. Using the base money equation, explain what factors will increase or decrease the base money.
3. Briefly explain how the commercial banking system creates deposit money under a fractional reserve system.
4. What are the factors that influence money multipliers?
5. Based on what you learned in Chapter 4, explain why people call residents' deposits in a bank savings deposits, yet when companies save money in a bank, it's not usually called a savings deposit.
6. In 1999, China began to levy an interest tax on deposits. Please analyze what effects this policy would have had on the currency ratio.
7. After the Asian financial crisis of 1997, China made it one of its financial priorities to guard itself against and defuse any potential financial risks. What sort of influence would this have had on the ratio of excess reserves in Chinese commercial banks and money multipliers?

8. Beginning in 1994, the Chinese government could no longer borrow or get an overdraft from the central bank. Only by issuing bonds could the government compensate for deficits. What sort of influence would this change have had on the central bank's control of the base money?
9. In 1994, China began to implement a mandatory exchange settlement and sale system. Under this mandatory system, when a company earned foreign exchange income on exported goods, they were required to sell that foreign exchange in full to a designated bank. After the exchange settlement, the designated exchange bank was then required to sell the amount to the central bank. What effect did this policy have on China's supply of base money? If trade surplus was substantial for successive years, how would this affect the central bank's control of the base money?
10. Analyze the role of industry and individuals within the money supply process. Given that these roles exist, how do they affect the central bank's monetary controls?
11. In 2008, China implemented a series of reforms to the foreign exchange system. According to new foreign exchange regulations, foreign exchange income of organizations and individuals can now be transferred abroad or saved abroad, a major change from the original mandatory repatriation requirements. Attempt to analyze the possible effects of this change on the supply of China's base money.
12. In 2007, China began to push for Treasury cash management. The Ministry of Finance entrusted the People's Bank of China with open market operations. Through a public bidding, the Ministry of Finance transfers a certain amount of Treasury funds that had originally been deposited in the People's Bank of China to commercial banks which offer higher interest rates. Attempt to analyze the effect of this push for Treasury cash management on the government deposits on the People's Bank of China's balance sheet as well as its effect on China's supply of base money.

Reference

Maynard Keynes, *The General Theory of Employment, Interest and Money*, Chinese edition, Commercial Press, 1999.

Chapter 14

Demand for Money

Learning Objectives

After studying this chapter, you will be able to:

- Clearly understand the Fisher Equation
- Clearly understand the Cambridge Equation
- Understand the main ideas behind Keynes' theory of demand for money
- Understand the Keynesianism's developments to Keynes' theory of demand for money
- Understand the modern quantity theory of money demand
- Clearly understand the differences between Keynes' theory of demand for money and the modern quantity theory of money
- Understand currency substitution and asset substitution under the conditions of an open economy
- Understand the presence of *missing money* and the reasons for *missing money*

The demand for money corresponds to the money supply. There are many different factors that impact the demand for money within an economy, and the impact of the demand for money on prices, interest rates, and the overall economy itself is also significant. This chapter will provide a comprehensive introduction to the fundamentals of the demand for money.

14.1 Classical Quantity Theory of Money

14.1.1 The Fisher Equation

In the 1911 Publication of *The Purchasing Power of Money*, Irving Fisher proposes the Fisher Equation of demand for money. If P is used to express the price level, T is used to express total real output, V is used to express the velocity of money and M is the quantity of money, then the equation would be as follows:

$$M \cdot V = P \cdot T. \tag{14.1}$$

This is the famous **Fisher Equation**. In this equation, $P \cdot T$ represents the gross nominal income, commonly referred to as the nominal GDP, and velocity of money V is the frequency of exchange of goods with the same unit of money within a given period, or rather, the turnover rate of currency. For example, when the same unit of money is traded for goods three times within a year, then the velocity of money within this year is three. Naturally, the velocity of money V in the Fisher Equation is the average value of the money quantity within the entire society. The Fisher Equation illustrates that the product of the velocity of money times the money quantity is equal to the gross nominal income.

However, the Fisher Equation is only an identity relation and does not explain whether or not the changes in money quantity M will cause an equal change in nominal income in the same direction, nor does it explain whether or not the velocity of money V falls when the money quantity increases, which causes the nominal income to remain the same. For example, suppose the money quantity is originally 500 billion yuan and the velocity of money is four, the price level is two and real output is one trillion yuan, then the identity relation of the Fisher Equation would be: $5000(M) \times 4(V) = 2(P) \times 10{,}000(T)$. When the money quantity has reached one trillion yuan, will the nominal income increase to four trillion yuan or will it still be two trillion yuan? Yet the velocity of money instead falls to two. The above equation, on its own, cannot answer this kind of question.

Fisher states that the velocity of money V is determined by factors such as habits, institutions, and technology, yet as changes to institutions and technology are slow, they will only affect the velocity of money over the long term. In the short term, the velocity of money can be considered as a constant. In other words, in our example above, the velocity of money cannot fall from four to two in such a short period of time.

Since the velocity of money V does not experience any major changes over a short period of time, once the money quantity M changes, the nominal income $P \times T$ will also experience a proportional change in the same direction. In other words, when the money quantity doubles, the nominal income will double; when the money quantity drops by half, so too will the nominal income. In our example above, when the money quantity increases from an original 500 billion yuan to a total of one trillion yuan, the nominal income will increase to four trillion yuan and will not remain at the original two trillion.

However, is an increase in nominal income $P \times T$ due to a doubling in the average price level P or a doubling in the real output T? Classical economists believe that wages and prices are completely flexible, and only because of surplus labor would wages decrease, causing an increase in the demand for labor and thereby reducing the unemployment rate to the point of full employment. In this way, when prices and wages have complete flexibility, the total economy can maintain a perpetual state of full employment; in other words, there would be no surplus labor (unemployment) and there would be no excess demand for labor.

Since the economy is always at full employment, changes to total output T would be minimal. In this way, when the money quantity increases from 500 billion yuan to one trillion, real output T cannot soar from one trillion yuan to two trillion. Could you actually imagine for a moment that the simple double of money could cause a double production of TVs, computers, cars, clothing, food, etc., in only such a short period of time? Impossible! Naturally, neither the velocity of money V nor the real output T can experience major changes over a short period of time, and as such, to balance the equation, we can only rely on a change in the price level P. This is to say that in the above example, when the money quantity increases from 500 billion to one trillion yuan, the price level will increase from an original two to four. In this way, when looking at the Fisher Equation, a change in the money quantity will cause a proportional change in the average price level.

14.1.2 The Cambridge Equation

Cambridge University economists Alfred Marshall, Pigou, and others believe that people's willingness to hold onto money is due to the function of money as a medium of exchange and a store of value. When people exchange goods and services, they must rely on money as a medium. Similar to Fisher and Marshall, other economists also believe that the demand for money and the level of trading are positively correlated. In other words, the greater the amount of traded goods and services, the higher the demand for money. Conversely, the less the amount of traded goods and services, the lower the demand for money. Furthermore, Marshall and others also believe that the level of wealth also has an effect on people's demand for money. The greater the wealth accumulation, the greater the demand for money to store such wealth. As such, with increases in wealth, there will also be an increase in the demand for money. Meanwhile, they also believe that there is a positive correlation between the level of wealth and the nominal income, and therefore there also exists a positive, proportional correlation between the demand for money and nominal income.

If M_d is used to express the amount of money demanded, P and T express the average price level and real output, respectively, and K is the proportional demand for money, then the **Cambridge Equation** can be expressed as follows:

$$M_d = K \cdot P \cdot T. \tag{14.2}$$

If we divide both sides of the above equation by K, then we can come up with an equation quite similar to the Fisher Equation:

$$\frac{M_d}{K} = P \cdot T. \tag{14.3}$$

It is fairly obvious that the inverse of the demand for money coefficient K in the Cambridge Equation is the same as the velocity of money in the Fisher Equation.

Although the forms of both equations are very similar, their economic significance varies greatly. In the Cambridge Equation, the demand for money coefficient K is not assumed to be stable as the velocity of money V in the Fisher Equation. Marshall and others believe that the amount of money that people store as wealth is affected by the absolute level of expected return on money as well as the relative return compared with the expected returns on other forms of wealth storage. If the expected returns on other assets rise while the expected return on money as a store of wealth has not changed, then the demand for money as a store of wealth will decrease, and vice versa. As such, the coefficient of money holding in the Cambridge Equation is in fact also the coefficient of people's asset choice, which means that people are free to choose the amount of money.

14.2 Keynes' Theory of Demand for Money

14.2.1 The Motives for Money Demand

Alfred Marshall and other economists at Cambridge University emphasize the functions of money as a medium of exchange and a store of value in the Cambridge Equation. They also point out that demand for money as a means of value storage depends on its implicit return and relative return. However, they make no further analysis.

After the Great Depression from 1929 to 1933, Keynes published *The General Theory of Employment, Interest, and Money* in 1936, in which he put forward a theory of demand for money called liquidity preference and explored deeper into the motives for an individual's demand for money. He deems that there are three motives for which people hold money, which are as follows:

- Transaction motives
- Precautionary motives
- Speculative motives

(a) *Transaction Motives*

Both the Fisher Equation and the Cambridge Equation hold that people possess money because money can help them buy the goods and services that they need. In other words, people possess money due to the motives to trade. Keynes adopts this viewpoint. Moreover, he divides people's motives to trade into an individual's income motive and an enterprise's business motive. There is always a time lag either between obtaining income and spending it or between earning sales revenue and paying for production and expenses. To cope with such daily transactions, people have to possess a certain amount of money in such a period. In accord with classical economists, Keynes also deems that money demand for trading presents a positive correlation with income level, which means that the higher the income level, the higher the money demand for trading, and vice versa.

(b) *Precautionary Motives*

Precautionary motives refer to the fact that people hold a certain amount of money to cope with unforeseen expenses or seize unexpected opportunities. For instance, you accidentally meet an old friend whom you have not seen for years. "To have friends come to you from afar" is surely "after all, delightful". Hence, you want to find an upscale coffee house to chat with him over some coffee and get reacquainted. You are pleasantly surprised to meet your friend but meanwhile this brings you some unexpected spending. Again suppose that as the seasons begin to change, you unfortunately catch a cold that makes you cough and have a fever. You are absolutely miserable. In order to get better soon, you go to the hospital; this expenditure is unforeseen as well. On this occasion, precautionary money holding comes in handy.

Keynes holds that precautionary money demand is in positive proportion to a person's income level; the higher the income level, the higher the precautionary money demand. Otherwise, the demand is less. This makes sense. To take the above example of meeting a friend as an instance, if your income level is very high, apart from the coffee and chatting, you may also treat him with a golf game together or even readily pay for his return ticket. Therefore, your unforeseen expenses may amount to several thousand. However, if your income is not that high, you can invite your friend to your house and have some casual drink there. In this way, you can also have a good time, but your unexpected spending will be only a few dozen yuan.

Money demands based on both motives to trade and precautionary motives are transactional money demands, which exhibit a positive correlation with income level. If M_t is transactional money demand and Y is income level, then transactional money demand can be described as:

$$M_t = f(Y). \tag{14.4}$$

(c) *Speculative Motives*

Speculative motives refer to the fact that people hold a certain amount of money in order to conduct speculation at appropriate times in the future. The most typical speculation is trading in bonds. Bonds can benefit their holders with not only a certain amount of interest but also capital gains due to bond price fluctuation. However, bond price fluctuation depends on the fluctuation of market interest rates. If the interest rate rises, bond prices will drop and vice versa. If interest rates rise significantly and bond prices drop sharply, this bond investment will lose more than the income from interest. In this case, investments in bonds do not appreciate in value but cause the holder to suffer a loss of principal. Therefore, people might not hold bonds. Although holding money in hand cannot bring them added value or interest income, the principal is at least preserved.

Keynes states that there is a normal interest rate level in the mind of every individual. If the actual interest rate is lower than this normal value, expected interest rates will rise and bond prices will fall. To prevent loss from the drop in bond prices, people will be willing to hold more money and sell off some of their bonds. Therefore, the demand for money will increase. Conversely, when the actual interest rate is higher than this normal value, expected interest rates will fall while bond prices will rise. In this case, people can gain by buying bonds. The higher the interest rate, the greater the expected capital gains from bonds. People will be ready to hold more bonds and reduce their money demands. Therefore, speculative demand for money presents a negative correlation with the level of interest rates. The higher the interest rate, the less the speculative demand for money, and vice versa.

If M_s is the speculative demand for money, i is the interest rate, then the equation for the speculative demand for money can be described as follows:

$$M_s = f(i). \tag{14.5}$$

14.2.2 The Complete Keynes Function of the Demand for Money

By combining the transactional demand for money with the speculative demand for money, the complete Keynes money demand function can be obtained as follows:

$$M_d = M_s + M_t = f(Y, i). \tag{14.6}$$

This is Keynes' money demand function with liquidity preference. It indicates that the demand for money negatively correlates to interest rates and positively to income levels. It can be seen that Keynes' demand for money theory based on liquidity preference greatly differs from the viewpoint of Fisher and that there is no relevance between the demand for money and interest rates.

According to Keynes' function of demand for money, the velocity of money is not a constant. Even though there is no change in the technical conditions over a short period, the velocity of money is still unstable. To make this point easy to understand, we can obtain the following equation by substituting Keynes' money demand function into the Fisher Equation:

$$f(Y, i) \cdot V = P \cdot Y. \tag{14.7}$$

From the equation above, we can obtain the currency circulation formula:

$$V = \frac{P \cdot Y}{f(Y, i)}. \tag{14.8}$$

When interest rates rise, speculative money demand will decrease and $f(Y, i)$ will fall, and then the velocity of money will accelerate. Conversely, if interest rates fall, speculative money demand will increase, and consequently, the velocity of money will be slower. Since interest rates are constantly changing, the velocity of money will also change constantly. Obviously, this differs greatly from Fisher's viewpoint that the velocity of money is stable over a short period of time.

Moreover, Keynes maintains that whether to hold more money or to hold more bonds depends on the difference between actual interest rates and the normal interest rate in the mind of people. If the actual rate is lower than the normal one, expected interest rates will rise and bond price will fall. Therefore, people will hold more money and vice versa. Hence, whenever the normal interest rate in the minds of people changes, the difference between the actual interest rate and the subjective "normal" interest rate will also change, which will in turn change expectation in regards to actual interest rates in the future. If the normal interest rate in the mind of people falls, the expected interest rate will also fall while bond prices will rise. In this case, people will hold more bonds and the speculative demand for money will fall, which means that $f(Y, i)$ will decrease, and the velocity of money will accelerate. Conversely, if the normal interest rate rises, the expected interest rate will rise and bond price will fall. To avoid capital loss, people will hold more money and less bonds. In other words, $f(Y, i)$ will rise, and the velocity of money will slow down. Since the velocity of money also depends on normal interest rates in people's mind and changes with expectations, the speculative demand for money is also unstable, which leads to fluctuations in the velocity of money.

14.3 Keynesianism's Developments to Keynes' Theory of Demand for Money

Keynes' liquidity preference theory of money demand holds that the transactional demand for money is impervious to interest rates and only demonstrates positive correlation with income levels, while speculative money demand only depends on the relative return of money and bonds. These arguments were questioned by economists such as William Baumol and James Tobin who developed and improved Keynes' theory of demand for money.

14.3.1 Transactional Demand

Baumol holds that the transactional demand for money is not only related to income levels but is also affected by the interest rate and transaction costs. Suppose you earn 2000 yuan per month and withdraw this salary on the first day of each month. You think that you should enjoy life and spend all the 2000 yuan in bars or coffee houses or go to concerts with your friends, and so on. Imagine that the 2000 yuan is a necessary expense each month and remains the same amount for every month. Therefore, you have 2000 yuan in sum when you withdraw your salary on the first

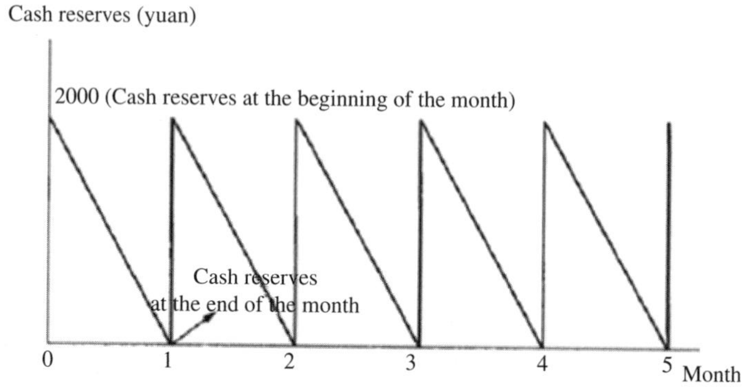

Fig. 14.1 Variation of Cash Reserves for Even Spending

day of a month and spend every last cent by the last day just to wait for next month's salary. In this case, your average holding per month is 1000 yuan. Variation in your cash reserve per month can be shown as in Figure 14.1.

Now suppose that the monthly interest rate for deposits is 1%. Also assume that you deposit 1000 yuan and leave 1000 yuan for daily expenses when you withdraw your salary of 2000 yuan at the beginning of each month. Your spending habit is as usual and your cash reserve is zero in the middle of the month. To cope with the expenditures in the remaining half of the month, you have to withdraw the 1000 yuan from the bank. By the end of this month, you run out of money. This continues once you receive your salary on the first day of the next month. In this case, your average cash reserve per month is 500 yuan. How can you benefit? You can earn 5 yuan of interest from the 1000 yuan that you deposit at the beginning of each month ($1000 \times 1\% \div 2 = 5$).

However, suppose that you instead deposit 1500 yuan in a bank and only keep 500 yuan on hand. If there are 30 days each month, you will run out of the 500 yuan after seven and a half days and withdraw 500 yuan from the 1500 yuan that you deposited. After another seven and a half days, you run out of this 500 yuan again. You again withdraw another 500 yuan after half a month, and so on and so forth. Therefore, your average cash reserve for this month is 250 yuan. How much interest can you earn by depositing 1500 yuan at the beginning of the month and make such withdrawals throughout the month? The total interest can be calculated as follows:

$$\begin{aligned} 1500 \times 1\% \times \frac{7.5}{30} + 1000 \times 1\% \times \frac{7.5}{30} + 500 \times 1\% \times \frac{7.5}{30} &= 3.75 + 2.5 + 1.25 \\ &= 7.5\,\overline{\pi} \\ &= 7.5 \text{ yuan.} \end{aligned}$$

Your income on interest will be 2.5 yuan more than that of only depositing 1000 yuan at the beginning of the month. With this 2.5 yuan, you can buy an ice cream. Broadly speaking, the less cash reserves that you hold at the beginning of the month, the more interest income that you can earn.

Though you can benefit in this way, could you see yourself only holding onto 66.67 yuan and depositing 1933.33 yuan in the bank only to then withdraw 66.67 yuan every morning? It is unlikely. While it may be true that you can earn more interest, it is incredibly troublesome. There will be transaction costs including the time for trips to the bank and standing in line. If you do not deposit the money but purchase bonds that can be publicly traded, you have to pay commission on those transactions. If the bond market is not that good and bond prices fall, you may unfortunately suffer capital loss.

All in all, the less the average cash reserve you hold per month, the more you can spend on depositing or buying bonds to obtain more interest. Meanwhile, the frequency by which you withdraw money or sell bonds will increase and the transaction costs will rise as well. In short, if the interest rate is higher, your willingness to hold transactional money will be weaker, and vice versa. However, with more withdrawals and transaction costs, your motive to hold transactional money will be strengthened and vice versa. Therefore, transactional money demand presents not only a positive correlation with income and transaction costs but also a negative correlation with interest rates.

14.3.2 Whalen's Precautionary Demand for Money

Keynes believes that the precautionary demand for money is only related to income. However, Edward L. Whalen and several other economists argue that factors influencing the precautionary demand for money mainly include illiquidity costs, opportunity costs to hold precautionary cash reserves, and the variance of income and spending fluctuations.

Suppose that you are a young man passionately in love. One day, you and your girlfriend go shopping together and your beautiful girlfriend comes across a fashionable set of clothes. It is fairly obvious to you that she has to have these clothes but they are really very expensive. They cost 2800 yuan! In order to please her, you decide to splurge on it. There comes the unexpected demand for money. However, you did not take enough money with you because you bought stocks and bonds. So, you are now confronted with an illiquidity problem. There are two ways to avoid disappointing your girlfriend. First, you can sell off some bonds or stocks to retrieve some money. Second, you could borrow money from your relatives and friends. In the first case, you have to pay a certain amount of commission and stamp duties. As the saying goes, lucky in love, unlucky at cards. If you really sell the bonds or stocks at the price lower than when you bought them, you shall suffer capital losses. In the second case, if you borrow money from a selfish friend who wants to make a profit by charging an interest rate of 3%, you have to pay some extra money. Although you fulfill your dream of pleasing your girlfriend, you may meanwhile feel blue about suffering from this illiquidity cost.

By drawing lessons from this experience, you are all the wiser. In order to cope with this unexpected monetary expense while shopping with your girlfriend, you start to take 6000 yuan along with you, which is more than enough to buy several sets of upscale, designer clothing. However, after three months, this 6000 yuan is still sitting untouched in your wallet. If the annual interest rate is 3%, you will lose 45 yuan of interest and run into opportunity costs. Although it is not too much, it is enough for you two to take a cab for a round trip. Opportunity costs in this case refer to giving up a certain amount of interest income for holding such cash reserves.

The total cost of holding precautionary cash reserves is constituted by the illiquidity and opportunity costs of holding this cash. If you hold more money to cope with emergencies, you reduce the expected cost of illiquidity but increase the opportunity costs of holding precautionary cash reserves. Conversely, if you hold less precautionary cash reserves, you undoubtedly reduce the opportunity cost to hold this cash but increase the illiquidity costs. Therefore, you have to find a balance between these two options. If your friends can help you with money when you are in urgent need, or if the markets for bonds and stocks are favorable and the transactional commission and stamp duty are low, your motive to hold so much cash to cope with such emergencies expenditures will be weakened. Besides, if the interest rate is high, your motive to hold precautionary money will also be weakened. Consequently, according to Whalen's analysis, the precautionary demand for money increases with rising illiquidity costs and decreases with rising opportunity costs and vice versa.

The above analysis is only an example of spending for one time. Now, let us see the case with emergency spending over and over again. There are two cases of this kind. In the first case, although your girlfriend wants to buy some indefinite things, for example, sometimes she wants to buy cosmetics, sometimes clothes, and sometimes she may want to go to a concert, but she only spends 1000 yuan each time. That is to say, there is no fluctuation in the volume of emergency expenditures. Then, in order to deal with these expenditures, you only need to hold a precautionary cash reserve of 1000 yuan. In the second case, the volume is uncertain. Sometimes, she excitedly invites you to KFC with her, which only costs you about 100 yuan. Sometimes, however, you have to pay 2800 yuan to buy designer clothes for her. Although the average expenditure for each time is also 1000 yuan, the fluctuation in the volume of expenditures is very large. Obviously, in this circumstance, if you only hold a cash reserve of 1000 yuan, you shall be caught in an embarrassment when your girlfriend wants you to buy those clothes worth 2800 yuan. It would be better for you if you took 3000 yuan in your wallet at any time. This demonstrates that, with increasing variance of emergency spending fluctuation, your demand for precautionary cash reserves will also increase and vice versa.

14.3.3 Tobin's Speculative Demand for Money

Keynes' analysis of the speculative motives behind the demand for money is imperfect. He believes that when the expected return on bonds is lower than the expected return on money, people will hold money as a store of wealth. Conversely, when the return on bonds is higher than the return on money, people will hold bonds and will not hold onto money. Only when the returns on money and bonds are the same will people hold both money and bonds. Obviously, Keynes' viewpoint concerning speculative motives of demand for money has inherently ruled out the possibility of people holding both bonds and money as a means of wealth storage, which is quite different from the fact.

To make up for the shortcomings of Keynes' speculative motives behind the demand for money, Tobin develops a new theory for the motives behind the demand for money. His basic point is that when people decide their portfolios, they will not only compare the return on assets, but also consider the risks of holding each asset. We have already discussed that the so-called risks refer to the possibility of future losses. Also, we have observed from characteristics of financial instruments the positive correlation between the returns on an investment instrument and its risks, in other words, the higher the returns, the higher its risks. For instance, suppose that you invested in a certain kind of stocks, the buying and selling of which is always at just the right time, then you could earn a considerable return on your investments in a relatively short time. However, if your luck ran dry and the price of your stocks fell at the very moment you purchased them, not only you are stuck in a rut and will not earn any money, but you will also lose your capital. For this reason, when deciding whether to hold stock or money, you will not only consider the potential returns from each option, but also take their risks into consideration.

People have three attitudes to risk, namely, risk-taking, risk-neutral, and risk-averse. Risk takers are those people who are willing to take on larger risks in hopes of earning a higher return. Gamblers are the classic risk takers. Risk-averse people are those who are only willing to take on a small risk and thereby in the hope of a relatively low return on assets. Conservatives are risk averse. People who are neutral about risk are somewhere in between the two. To them, there is no difference between risks and returns. In other words, whether it be a higher risk coupled with a higher return or a lower return with a lower risk, these people are happy either way.

Tobin believes that the majority of people is risk averse and will not take risks for "petty" gains. When compared to money, bond prices are quite volatile and as such, it has greater risk. Thus, when the return on bonds exceeds that of money, people will still prefer to hold onto money as a store of wealth, and this is because the risks of such an option are low. For this reason, based on Tobin's money demand theory of portfolio choice, the motives behind the demand for money will not only depend on interest rates, but also depend on the returns and risks of each type of financial asset. In this way, portfolio choice theory explains the phenomenon unexplained by Keynes' liquidity preference theory that people hold money, bonds, and other types of assets at the same time.

14.4 Modern Quantity Theory of Money

14.4.1 Basic Content of the Modern Quantity Theory of Money

In 1956, Milton Friedman published *The Quantity Theory of Money: A Restatement* in which he proposed the Modern Quantity Theory of Money. Friedman considers money as a type of asset, or rather, a method of wealth holding. As such, Friedman's quantity theory of money is in fact a theory of portfolio choice.

By using M_d/P to express the real demand for money, Y_p to express permanent income, ω to express the ratio of human to non-human wealth, r_m to express the expected return on money, r_b to express the expected return on bonds, r_e to express the expected return on equity and π^e to express the expected inflation rate, Friedman expresses his money demand formula as follows:

$$\frac{M_d}{P} = f(Y_p, w, r_b - r_m, r_e - r_m, \pi^e - r_m). \tag{14.9}$$

To Friedman, permanent income could also have a positive impact on the demand for money; the higher the permanent income, the higher the demand for money. Permanent income is the average of expected income over a long period of time with a very low volatility over the short-term. For instance, in an expansionary cycle, income may grow very quickly, and due to the temporal nature of this growth, changes to the average long-term income will not be very large. For this reason, during times of economic prosperity, permanent income will grow much slower than that of the particular period. Conversely, during economic downturns, income decline is also temporary in nature and the decrease of average long-term income is also smaller than that of the period. Since the volatility of permanent income is low and it is a primary determinant of the demand for money, the demand for money to a large extent does not fluctuate with the economic cycle.

Moreover, Friedman believes that individual gross wealth is a determining factor of the demand for money. Gross wealth includes income or the total proceeds from consumption and labor. Wealth can be divided into human and non-human wealth. Human wealth refers to an individual's capacity to earn money. Non-human wealth primarily refers to bonds, stocks or other physical wealth. Only when human wealth transforms into non-human wealth can it become a real value to an individual. Suppose that you have a particular skill; at this time, you only have human wealth. Only when you put this skill to good use, can you begin to earn the income that you deserve. However, since you are constrained by institutions and the labor market, the transformation of human wealth into non-human wealth is greatly restricted. Regardless of the set of skills you are born with, you can still become a "weaponless hero" when facing an incomplete market for human wealth and especially when the economy is not at its best, which makes it even harder to transform your human wealth into disposable monetary income. Conversely, there are many alternatives among the different types of non-human wealth, thus you can conveniently sell all of the stocks that you hold on the stock exchange or purchase government bonds or convert them for cash to deposit in a bank. Therefore, the higher the proportion of human wealth to gross wealth, the higher the demand for money, and vice versa.

People's willingness to hold non-human wealth depends on its relative return compared to money. The return on money is affected by two factors. The first is the interest income of money. The higher the interest earnings for holding money (cash or deposits), the higher the expected return on money, and thus the stronger motives to hold money. Next comes the convenience of banking services. If the quality of banking services is top notch, it will improve the implicit return on money and thus lower people's willingness to hold onto cash.

$r_d - r_m$ and $r_e - r_m$, respectively express the difference between return on bonds and return on money and the difference between return on stocks and return on money. The higher the value of this difference, the higher the return on bonds and stocks in comparison to that of money. We are already aware that the return on bonds arises from the interest earned and the gains/losses are a result of their price fluctuations during the period that the bonds are held; and the return on stocks includes the dividend and the capital gains/losses are due to stock price fluctuations during the period that stocks are held. As soon as either one improves, the relative expected return on money is reduced and as such, lowers people's willingness to hold onto money, and vice versa. Suppose for a moment that the return on government bonds has reached 10% while the interest rate on deposits is only 2%. Should you purchase government bonds or deposit your money in the bank, or hold cash? If you are not in a hurry to use your money, you would probably use most of your disposable money to purchase government bonds.

All in all, in Friedman's modern quantity theory of money, the primary factors that affect the demand for money are permanent income, the proportion of human wealth to individual's total wealth, and the relative return on money compared to those on bonds and stocks. The higher the permanent income, the higher the demand for money. Since the volatility of permanent income is low, the demand for money will not experience major fluctuations. The higher the proportion of human wealth to total wealth, the higher the demand for money. The lower the relative return on money with respect to stocks or bonds, the lower the demand for money.

14.4.2 The Differences Between the Modern Quantity Theory of Money and Keynes' Theory of Demand for Money

If we were to look at variables in Friedman's demand for money function, the modern quantity theory of money seems only an expansion of Keynesian portfolio choice analysis with the only difference being additional variables in the function for money demand. It seems that Friedman and Keynesian theories of money demand do not bear substantial differences. Why, though, did Friedman call his theory the "quantity theory of money"? This is primarily because there are major differences between the two theories after all.

First, in Keynes' liquidity preference-based theory, all other financial assets, apart from money, are represented by bonds. This is because he believes that the return on these assets would fluctuate together and the expected return on bonds could represent the changes in the expected returns on other financial assets; therefore, other financial assets were not necessary in his money demand function. On the contrary, in Friedman's modern quantity theory of money, bonds, and stocks, where even any physical goods could be used as a substitute for money, apart from interest rates, there are many other factors that significantly impact the demand for money.

Second, since Friedman considers money and physical goods as substitutes, the changes in the quantity of money demanded could have a direct impact on total spending. In Keynes' liquidity preference theory, only two factors, namely, income and interest rates, could affect the demand for money, and as such, changes in the demand for money could not directly impact total spending.

Third, unlike Keynes, Friedman believes that the expected return on money is not a constant. When interest rates rise, banks can earn a higher profit from loans and therefore, they would manage to attract more deposits to grant more loans and earn more profit. If there was no regulation of interest rates, banks could pay a higher interest to draw deposits, and the return on bank deposits would increase with increases in the interest rates of bonds and loans; banks would continue to offer competitive interest rate to the point where there are no more excess profits. As such, $r_b - r_m$ could maintain relative stability. If interest rate regulations exist, although banks cannot use higher interest rates to compete for deposits, they can improve the quality of services to implicitly improve the return on money, and thus maintain a relatively stable $r_b - r_m$. So, Friedman believes that interest rates have a minor impact on the demand for money. Conversely, in Keynes' preferential demand for money, interest rate is a major factor determining demand for money.

To Friedman, money demand is not sensitive to interest rates. This is not because the demand for money is insensitive to changes in the opportunity costs of other assets compared with money, but because changes in the interest rates have a small impact on opportunity costs of other assets in the money demand function.

Therefore, when the rise of interest rates causes an increase in the expected return on other assets, the expected return on money would also rise, which would offset any gains, and the opportunity costs for the different assets within the function of demand for money would remain the same. As such, changes in interest rates only have a minor impact on the demand for money.

Fourth, although Keynes and Friedman's money demand functions both have the variable of income, Friedman stresses permanent income, namely the average expected long-term income, and its fluctuations are minimal. Additionally, changes in the interest rates also have a minimal affect on the demand for money. Therefore, he believes that random fluctuations in the demand for money are small, and the demand for money function could be used to accurately predict the demand for money. Since the demand for money can be predicted and is relatively stable, the velocity of money could also be predicted and is relatively stable. In this way, changes to the money supply can affect total spending and the price level of goods, leading to the same conclusion with classical quantity theory of money. For this reason, Friedman finally decides to name his theory of demand for money as "the modern quantity theory of money: a restatement".

14.5 Demand for Money in an Open Economy: Currency Substitution and Asset Substitution

We must stress here that the above discussion on the demand for money is under the conditions of a closed economy. In reality, the demand for money under the conditions of an open economy are more much complex, because there are much more assets for people to choose from. When analyzing the demand for money in an open economy, we must clearly understand currency substitution and asset substitution.

14.5.1 What are Currency Substitution and Asset Substitution?

Currency substitution, to be brief, refers to the situation wherein domestic residents hold currencies of foreign countries or regions as a measurement of value, a medium of exchange, or a means of store of value. For example, while shopping in Shenzhen, many people use Hong Kong dollars directly. This is a kind of currency substitution as a medium of exchange. Similarly, as more and more mainland Chinese tourists visit Hong Kong, shopping in Hong Kong is becoming a "travel" must, and the majority of clerks in Hong Kong malls are also quite happy to accept Chinese yuan. When there are inconsistencies in the time of obtaining and spending foreign currency, foreign currency becomes a temporary abode of purchasing power. Then, we see currency substitution in terms of store of value. The ratio of increase in foreign currencies held by people to the increase in domestic currency in the current year is called the **currency substitution ratio**. In Table 14.1, the

Table 14.1 Currency Substitution of the Chinese Residents (Year-on-Year Growth) (Unit: 100 million yuan)

Year	1992	1994	1997	1998	1999	2000	2003	2004
Foreign Currency Deposits	138.90	390.9	344.1	1001.8	1167.8	1488.5	−318.7	−436
Domestic Currency Deposits	2693.9	6169.8	7496.0	9257.1	7280.5	6609.9	16,388	15,500.9
Currency Substitution Ratio (%)	5.16	6.32	4.59	10.82	16.04	22.5	−1.95	2.81
Year	2005	2006	2007	2008	2009	2010	2011	2012
Foreign Currency Deposits	−1254.0	−360.0	−249.0	−141.8	362.4	−76	−10.6	98.8
Domestic Currency Deposits	21,642.0	20,665.0	14,162.2	46,256.2	42,646.7	43,727.7	39,665.6	58,146
Currency Substitution Ratio (%)	−5.79	−1.74	−1.76	−0.31	0.85	−0.17	−0.03	0.17

Source: *The People's Bank of China Quarterly Statistical Bulletin* and Loan Income and Expenses from the website of the People's Bank of China

increasing amount of foreign currency deposits held by residents of China in 2000 was 148.85 billion yuan, while that of domestic currency deposits in 2000 was 660.99 billion yuan. Therefore, the currency substitution ratio in China in 2000 was 22.5%. In 2003 and 2004, due to the stronger expectation of the appreciation of yuan, residents exchanged their dollar holdings for yuan holdings, which led to a negative currency substitution ratio over these two years.

With increasingly diversified financial instruments, besides pure currency substitution, there is also **asset substitution** which means that domestic residents hold foreign currency-denominated financial assets issued overseas. For instance, if the households and enterprises of Japan hold American government bonds, it is a kind of asset substitution. If Chinese residents buy stocks issued by American companies listed on the New York Stock Exchange, it can also be called asset substitution. Asset substitution refers to the allocation and combination of global assets after comparing the risks and returns of domestic and foreign assets. Generally speaking, apart from standardized financial assets like bonds and stocks, foreign currency in cash and deposits that people hold can also be counted as a form of asset substitution. However, the main purpose that people hold them is not for asset appreciation but for "temporary abode of purchasing power" in its true sense. Therefore, when domestic residents hold cash and deposits in foreign currency, it should be considered as currency substitution. Another example is that there are qualified foreign institutional investors (QFIIs) in China which not only can purchase stocks in China but can also purchase some bonds. The corresponding qualified domestic institutional investors (QDIIs) can purchase financial assets in other foreign countries or regions (at least part of their capital account is convertible).

An implicit manifestation of asset substitution is known as capital flight. **Capital flight** is also called asset transfer or capital refuge, which refers to abnormal capital outflow in order to avoid risks or the control of authorities. According to authoritative statistics, the total amount of China's capital flight reached a staggering 87.53 billion USD in the five years from 1992 to 1996. This actually aggravated China's asset substitution. Capital flight is even more serious when there is a strong expectation on devaluation of domestic currency (especially during a sharp domestic currency devaluation or currency crisis).

14.5.2 Currency Substitution and Demand for Money

Currency substitution affects demand for domestic currency. Generally speaking, the stronger the degree of currency substitution, the less the demand for domestic currency. Conversely, the weaker the currency substitution, the higher the demand for domestic currency. When there is a fixed amount of purchasable goods in an economic system, the more the goods are traded with foreign currency as a medium of exchange, the less will domestic currency be used as a medium of exchange. Therefore, transactional demand for domestic money will be reduced. When people's aggregate saving is fixed, the more the gross deposits in foreign currency, the less the demand for domestic currency-denominated deposits. In short, there is a negative relation between currency substitution and the demand for domestic currency.

Therefore, any factors affecting currency substitution rate will influence the demand for domestic currency. In order to clearly understand the relation between currency substitution and the demand for domestic currency, it is necessary to probe deeper into currency substitution. Generally speaking, major factors influencing currency substitution include: the interest rate levels at home and abroad, the expected exchange rate fluctuation, differences in the expected returns on other assets at home and abroad, and costs of currency exchange.

As is shown in Chapter 11, when domestic and foreign interest rates differ from one to another, there will be arbitrage opportunities. People will change domestic monetary assets with lower interest rates into foreign monetary assets with higher interest rates to obtain more gains. Therefore, the more the foreign interest rate exceeds the domestic one, the more intensive people's motive to substitute currency and the higher the currency substitution ratio will be.

Exchange rate fluctuation will bring about capital gains and losses. If people predict that the exchange rate of domestic currency will depreciate substantially, they will change domestic currency assets into foreign currency assets in advance to avoid losses from domestic currency depreciation. Thus, currency substitution appears. When the exchange rate of domestic currency depreciates sufficiently, people will reconvert foreign currency assets back into domestic currency assets. Therefore, the larger the expected depreciation of domestic currency, the more motivation to conduct currency substitution. Expectation about the exchange rate can influence the currency substitution ratio, so all factors affecting exchange rate will also exert an impact on the currency substitution ratio and thus influence the demand for domestic currency.

Finally, the currency substitution ratio can also be affected by the costs of currency exchange. The higher the exchange costs, the more it costs to exchange between domestic and foreign currencies. Currency exchange costs include the convenience of exchanging currencies. For example, currencies in many countries are not fully convertible. Under such circumstances, it's very troublesome to exchange domestic currency into foreign currency. Moreover, currency exchange costs also include differences between the buying rate and selling rate. The bigger the difference, the greater the loss from currency exchanges. In brief, the more it costs to exchange currencies, the less motivation there is to conduct currency substitution.

Therefore, factors like the level of income, the fluctuation of income and spending, interest rates, relative return on other assets, the proportion of human wealth to non-human wealth, interest rate levels and return on assets in foreign countries, expected exchange rates, and currency exchange costs can all exert great influences on the demand for money.

14.6 Velocity of Money and Missing Money

14.6.1 Missing Money

The following equation can be obtained by assuming natural logarithms on both sides of the Fisher equation:

$$\ln M + \ln V = \ln P + \ln T. \tag{14.10}$$

Then by differentiating on both sides, we can obtain the following equation:

$$m' + v' = p' + t'. \tag{14.11}$$

In this equation, m' is the growth rate of demand for money, v' is the growth rate of velocity of money, p' is the growth rate of prices, t' is the economic growth rate. Because the monetary market is in equilibrium, demand for money is equal to the money supply, so m' is the growth rate of the money supply.

According to Equation (14.11), we can reach such a conclusion: when the velocity of money remains unchanged, the growth rate of money supply is equal to the growth rate of prices plus the economic growth rate.

However, from Table 14.2, we can see that China's growth rate of its money supply is far more than the sum of the growth rate of prices and the economic growth rate since the reform and opening-up. People call this excess portion of money **missing money**.

What causes missing money? The key point is that there is a strong assumption when we are deducing the above identical equation: the velocity of money is unchanged. Then, is the velocity of money a constant? Fisher deems that the velocity of money is stable over a short period. Actually, the velocity of money changes frequently, no matter in developed countries or in developing countries. For example, from Figure 14.2, we can see that apart from few years with an increasing velocity of money as compared with the previous year, China's velocity of money is basically declining, among which the declining rate of M_0 is more obvious than that of M_1. Therefore, in order to analyze missing money, we have to probe into the reasons that lead to this declining velocity of money.

14.6.2 Origin of Missing Money: Decline of the Velocity of Money

Through careful analysis, the factors that make China's velocity of money decline and then lead to missing money are as follows:

- Monetization
- Better utilization of money's function as a store of value

Table 14.2 China's Economic Growth Rate, Prices and the Growth Rate of Money Supply (Unit: %)

Year	Economic Growth Rate t'	Price Growth Rate p'	Growth Rate of the Money Supply m'	$m' - (p' + t')$
1990	11.0	3.1	34.23	20.13
1993	13.4	14.7	37.31	9.21
1994	11.8	24.1	34.53	−1.37
1997	8.8	2.8	19.58	7.98
2001	7.4	0.7	17.6	9.5
2005	10.2	1.8	17.6	5.6
2006	10.7	1.5	16.9	4.7
2007	11.4	4.8	16.7	0.5
2008	9.6	5.9	17.8	2.9
2009	9.2	−0.7	27.7	19.2
2010	10.3	3.3	19.7	9.4
2011	9.3	5.4	13.6	−1.1
2012	7.8	2.6	13.8	3.4

Source: Websites of the National Bureau of Statistics and the People's Bank of China

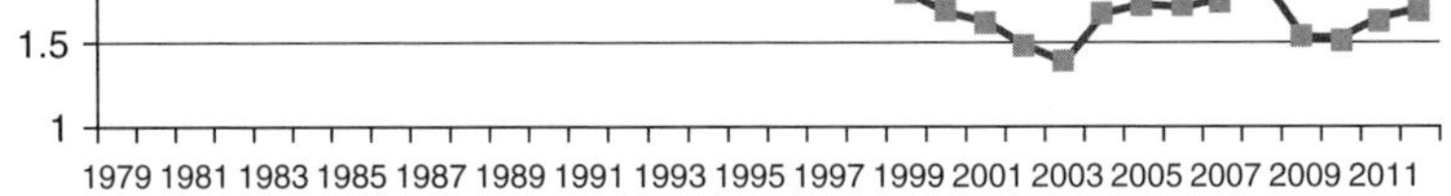

Fig. 14.2 China's Velocity of Money (times per year)
Source: Calculated with related data

- Rapid development of financial markets
- Capital flight

(a) *The First Explanation: Monetization*

After China's reform and opening-up, the principal reason for China's declining velocity of money is the deepening of monetization. According to the functions of money, there are two basic meanings that come with **monetization**. The first level is monetization of the medium of exchange, namely, increase in the proportion of transactions of goods with money as a medium in national income. For example, in the previous planned economy, housing is allocated as a kind of welfare. There is basically no transaction in commercial residential real estate markets. However, China no longer offers the welfare distribution of housing, people have to buy a house if they want one. Previously, most inputs of enterprises were allocated as planned. Now when enterprises need inputs, they have to buy them from markets. All these conditions demonstrate that China's monetization has intensified. The second level is monetization of store of value, namely, a process in which financial savings replace physical savings (see Chapter 4). The intensified monetization of medium of exchange requires the absorption of more money, and it makes the nominal velocity of money decline even though the actual velocity of money does not decline.

For example, suppose that the previous gross national income was one trillion yuan and the ratio of monetization was 0.4, that is to say, only 400 billion yuan is transacted and allocated with money as a medium and the other 600 billion yuan is distributed by administrative allocation. Let us assume that the amount of money in the economy is 200 billion yuan. Then, the actual velocity of money is 2 according to the ratio of monetization ($400 \div 200 = 2$), but the velocity based on nominal gross income reaches 5 ($1000 \div 200 = 5$). Now let us further suppose that monetization is intensified and the ratio reaches 0.8, but the actual velocity of money still remains unchanged and stays at 2, and gross nominal income is still one trillion yuan. Then, 800 billion yuan is exchanged with money as a medium. When the velocity of money is 2, monetary aggregate increases to 400 billion yuan, and the velocity of money according to the nominal gross income declines to 2.5 ($1000 \div 400 = 2.5$).

(b) *The Second Explanation: Better Utilization of Money's Function as a Store of Value*

Apart from acting as a medium of exchange, another important function of money is store of value, namely, the so-called "temporary abode of purchasing power". If the function of money as a store of value is strengthened, the velocity of money will decline. By inferring from the Cambridge equation $M_d = kPY$, we can obtain:

$$\frac{M_d}{kY} = P. \tag{14.12}$$

In this formula, M_d is the demand for money, k is the coefficient of money holding, Y is national income, and P is the price level. In equilibrium, M_d is equal to the money supply M_s. By substituting M_s into the formula (14.12) and assuming logarithm on both sides of the equation, we can obtain:

$$m' - k' - y' = p'. \tag{14.13}$$

In the above formula, m' is the growth rate of money supply, k' is the growth rate of money holding coefficient, y' is the growth rate of national income and p' is the growth rate of prices. From the above formula, we can see that the improved money holding coefficient and the increasing national income can alleviate the impact of money supply growth on the price level. Increase in the money supply does not necessarily lead to rising prices. Furthermore, whether growth in the money supply will bring about price hikes depends on whether the sum of the economic growth rate and the money holding coefficient is greater than the growth rate of money supply. When the economic growth rate is fixed, if the money holding coefficient is enhanced, the impact of increasing money supply on prices is alleviated. As shown in Chapter 4, since the reform and opening-up of China, financial deposits of Chinese residents has grown constantly, which demonstrates that monetization due to the value storage function of money is strengthened. This reduces the money as a medium of exchange in circulation and increases non-circulation money. However, only money in circulation can affect prices, so the better utilization of the function of money as a store of value will make the average velocity of money decrease.

(c) *The Third Explanation: Rapid Development of Financial Markets*

In the Fisher equation, money only acts as a medium of real goods exchanges. Many merchandise exchanges, such as purchasing a color TV, a refrigerator, or even instant noodles and a can of soda, require money as a medium of exchange. However, apart from these well-known physical goods, as current financial markets are very developed, there are a huge number of financial asset transactions. Transactions of stocks and bonds have become many people's occupation and these financial asset transactions also require money as a medium. Therefore, Keynes puts forward a modified Fisher equation:

P is used to express the price level, T is used to express total real output, V is the velocity of money, M is the monetary aggregates, A refers to gross financial assets, and P_a refers to prices. Therefore, the modified Fisher Equation is as follows:

$$M \times V = P \times T + P_a \times A. \tag{14.14}$$

Suppose that the nominal national income was one trillion yuan and the amount of money is 500 billion yuan, among which there are 250 billion yuan as a medium of exchange for financial assets. Then, the amount of money as a medium of exchange for physical goods and services is only 250 billion yuan. The actual velocity of the 250 billion yuan for physical goods and services is $4(1000 \div 250 = 4)$. The average velocity of money without eliminating money as a medium of exchange for financial assets is only $2(1000 \div 500 = 2)$. Therefore, the velocity of money calculated with the above modified Fisher Equation is probably lower than the actual velocity of money.

(d) *The Fourth Explanation: Capital Flight*

Capital flight may also slow down the average velocity of money, because domestic capital that flows to foreign lands is not involved in domestic exchanges of goods and services. Therefore, capital flight reduces money in domestic circulation and thereby, the average velocity of money. However, China's currency substitution ratio and capital flight have gradually increased for the past decade, which has reduced China's average velocity of money.

Summary

The Fisher equation demonstrates that the product of money quantity and the velocity of money is equal to that of total real output and prices. Since the velocity of money does not change over a short period of time, the increase in the amount of money supply will drive up the price level proportionally.

The Cambridge equation can be described as $M_d = K \cdot P \cdot T$, which explores the demand for money based on portfolio selection.

Keynes is the first to distinguish people's transaction motive, precautionary motive, and speculative motive to hold money, and he deems that the first two are the transaction demand for money, and the last is the speculative demand for money. The transactional demand for money only has a positive correlation with income levels, while speculative demand has a negative correlation with interest rates.

Keynesian economists furthered Keynes' theory of demand for money. Baumol holds that transactional money demand is not only related to income, but also is affected by transaction costs and interest rates. Furthermore, Whalen points out that the variance of income and spending fluctuation would influence the demand for money. Tobin further develops Keynes' speculative money demand theory, taking into consideration the influence on portfolio selection exerted by returns and risks.

Friedman believes that the major factors influencing demand for money includes permanent income, human wealth, and non-human wealth as a proportion of total wealth, and returns on bonds and stocks. Because permanent income remains relatively stable and interest rate has a minor impact on the demand for money, the velocity of money is also relatively stable. For this reason, changes to the money supply can bring about proportionate price hikes.

In an open economy, currency substitution and asset substitution will also affect the demand for money, and all the factors that influence currency substitution and asset substitution will also affect it. The expected volatility of the exchange rate, the return on assets domestically and internationally, the costs of currency exchange, and many other factors will affect currency substitution, and therefore, the demand for money is exposed to these factors as well.

Assuming that the velocity of money does not change, the growth rate of the money supply should equal the sum of economic growth and price increases. However, in many countries, the former has far exceeded the latter, and as a result, the term "missing money" appears, which refers to excess money. Main reason for the missing money is that the velocity of money is not a constant. Economic monetization, full utilization of money as a store of value, rapid development of financial markets, and capital flight — all these factors work together to decrease the velocity of money.

Key Terms

Fisher Equation; Cambridge Equation; Transactional Demand for Money; Speculative Demand for Money; Permanent Income; Currency Substitution; Asset Substitution; Missing Money; Capital Flight

Critical Thinking Questions

1. What are the Fisher equation and the Cambridge equation? How are they different?
2. What are the main ideas of Keynes' theory of demand for money?
3. What developments have Keynesian economists contributed to Keynes' theory of demand for money?
4. What are the differences between the modern quantity theory of money and Keynes' theory of demand for money?
5. What are currency and asset substitution? What are the main factors that affect currency substitution?
6. How does currency substitution affect macroeconomy? What instruments are available for the government to lower the currency substitution ratio?
7. What is missing money? What causes missing money in China?
8. Why is velocity of money unstable? Suppose that current investments are on a downturn, the unemployment rate is high, and the government plans to increase the money supply and lower interest rates to stimulate economic growth and lower the rate of unemployment. Analyze the short-term impact of these policies on the velocity of money.
9. Analyze the impact of transportation and information technology development on the demand for money.
10. Why does the modern quantity theory of money state that the velocity of money can be predicted while the Keynesian liquidity preference theory states that it cannot be?
11. If the money supply increases by 10%, and the real output is unchanged, will the average price of goods necessarily increase by 10%?
12. Suppose that you face two different situations. In the first situation, you are a freelancer with an uncertain income each month. During good times, you can earn more than 10,000 yuan; when your work slumps, you may only make a grand. In the other situation, you work for a government agency and bring in 3000 yuan each month. Given these two situations, how would your average demand for money differ in each?

Chapter 15

Interest Rate Levels and Interest Rate Structure

Learning Objectives

After studying this chapter, you will be able to:

- Understand the classical theory of interest rate determination
- Clearly understand Keynes' liquidity preference theory of interest rate determination
- Learn about the loanable fund analysis of interest rate determination
- Understand why interest rates and the rate of inflation move in the same direction
- Understand why there are interest rate differences among bonds issued by different borrowers
- Understand why the long-term interest rates are higher than short-term interest rates at the same time point

Before we begin the analyses of this chapter, let us first take a look at the following phenomena concerning interest rates. Figure 15.1 shows interbank lending rates at different times. Apart from interbank lending rates, the interest rates on government bonds, bank deposits and loans are changing as well. Second, even for the same financial instrument, if the maturity is different, the interest rate will also differ. When depositing money in a bank, you may find that the interest rate on five-year deposits is always higher than the interest rate on one-year deposits. More generally, interest rates of bonds issued by the same issuer will differ according to different maturities. The yield to maturity curve of bonds (see Chapter 9) can give a good depiction of interest rate relationships among bonds with different maturities. Normal yield to maturity curve is upward sloping, indicating that the longer the maturity, the higher the rate of return, and vice versa (see Figure 9.2). Third, as we have already seen in Chapter 10, interbank lending rates are also always higher than the repurchase rates for government bonds. Likewise, the interest rates on corporate bonds are also typically higher than the interest rates on government bonds with the same maturities.

Additionally, the interest rates on short-term financing bills announced by several companies on April 22, 2013 were significantly different, as shown in

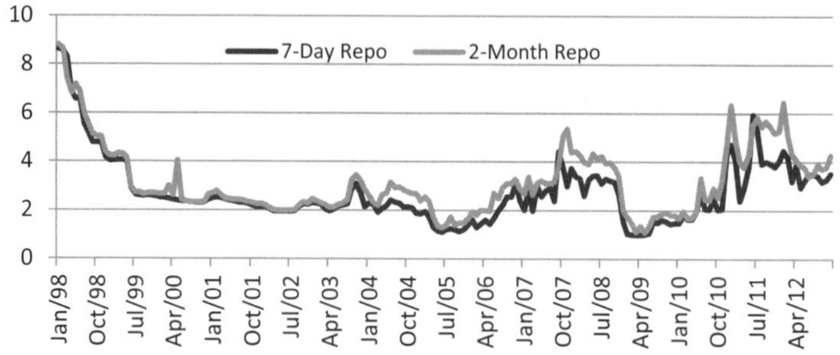

Fig. 15.1 Interbank Seven-Day and Two-Month Bond Repurchase Rates (Unit: %)
Source: Website of the People's Bank of China

Table 15.1 Selected Companies' Bond Term and their Interest Rates

Company	Xichang Steel	Huagong Tech	Jingcheng Machinery Electric	China Resources	China Southern Power Grid
Term	365	365	365	180	180
Coupon Rate (Annual)	4.83	4.43	4.1	3.65	3.60

Table 15.1. There are significant differences in interest rates for different terms, and even bonds with the same term have significantly different rates because their issuers are different.

- Why do interest rates on the same financial instrument differ for different maturities?
- Explain why differences exist in the interest rates on different bonds with the same maturities.
- Why do interest rates differ on bonds with varying maturities from the same issuer, i.e., long-term interest rates will be higher than short-term interest rates?

15.1 General Interest Rate Level Determination

15.1.1 Marxist Theory of Interest Rate Determination

Marxism believes that interest, the transformation of surplus value, is essentially a part of profits. Money itself cannot create money or added value, and can only create surplus value through production of workers after functional capitalists use money to buy the means of production and hire workers. Monetary capitalists, relying on their ownership of capital, carve up surplus value with functional capitalists. Thus, the premise of interest generation is the division of capital ownership and the right of using capital. Money, when held by the capitalists and utilized to exploit labor, turns into capital and then generates additional value, which is the ability to produce average profit. The average profits can be divided into interest and entrepreneurial income and go to different capitalists. As a result, interest is essentially the same as profit, which is a transformation of surplus value, indicating that both loaning capitalists and functional capitalists exploit the workers. Interest is a part of surplus value that loaning capitalists carve up from those who borrow money from them, while profit is the transformation of surplus value. This qualitative property of interest determines its quantitative property. The amount of interest is determined by total profit while the interest rate, which is determined by average profit rate, falls between average profit rates and zero. Interest rates are determined by both the profit rate and the distribution proportion of total profits between the lender and the borrower. The proportion is mainly determined by the relationship of supply and demand and competition. Generally speaking, the interest rate falls when supply exceeds demand, and rises when demand exceeds supply. Marx's theory on interest is instructive in explaining the determination of interest rate under the condition of socialized mass production.

15.1.2 The Classical Theory of Interest Rates

Bohm-Bawerk defines interest as value differences which result from different evaluation of goods in different periods; therefore, the theory is known as the 'Time Preference Theory' in which goods are sorted into two categories: "present goods" and "future goods". The subjective evaluation of the same goods with the same quality and quantity is different at the present time and in the future. Normally, present goods have a greater value than future goods of the same quality and quantity, and the difference between the two is the value of time. When owners postpone their consumption of goods and lend them to others, they will require the borrower to pay a discount equal to their value of time. Expressed in monetary form, discount is interest; therefore, interest is a kind of compensation for time value. Fisher argues that interest is a discount generated in the exchange between present goods and future goods and is determined by both subjective and objective factors. The subjective factor is people's time preference for present goods. The exchange of present and future goods is realized through transactions in the money market and securities market. In this process of exchange, people's time preference determines interest rates. The objective factor refers to possible investment opportunities. Entrepreneurs would consider the level of interest rates in their investment decisions. People's time preference determines money supply while entrepreneurs' choice of investment opportunities determines money demand, and the equilibrium interest rate thus is determined by the consistency of these two choices.

Marshall holds that interest rates are the compensation for waiting (savings), and are determined by capital supply and demand. Capital supply (savings) moves in the same direction as interest rates whereas capital demand (investment) is negatively correlated with interest rates. The demand and supply of capital determines interest rates. The restraints of present consumption and the wait for future rewards determine the supply of capital. Capital demand depends on investment opportunities and return. Generally speaking, interest rates rise when investments exceed savings that results in short of capital, and vice versa. The interaction between savings and investments determines the interest rate level. In fact, savings and investments themselves are affected by interest rates as well. If interest rates rise, demand for investments will fall because of the higher cost of investments. Conversely, demand for investments will rise when interest rate falls. However, savings change in the opposite direction. Higher interest rates will provoke higher savings while lower interest rates will result in fewer savings. The relationship between savings, investments and interest rates is shown in Figure 15.2.

In Figure 15.2, curve *I* represents investment demand, and it slopes from the top left to the lower right, illustrating the fact that investment demand increases as interest rates fall. For example, when the interest rate is 10%, investment demand is 10 billion yuan. When interest rates fall to 5%, investment demand increases to 20 billion yuan. The savings curve *S* slopes from the lower left to the upper right, illustrating the fact that savings increase with increases in interest rates. For example, when interest rates are 5%, savings is 11 billion yuan. When interest rates rise to 10%, savings correspondingly increase to 18 billion yuan.

However, in Figure 15.2, the equilibrium interest rate is neither 5% nor 10%. When interest rate is 5%, investment demand is 20 billion yuan. Under such conditions, investment demand will be 9 billion yuan short because savings is only

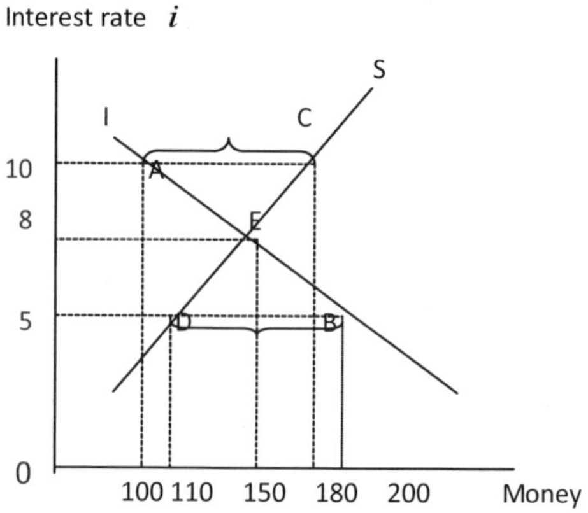

Fig. 15.2 Interest Rate Determination: Savings and Investments

11 billion yuan. Conversely, when interest rates are 10%, investment demand will decrease to 10 billion while savings will increase to 18 billion, resulting in 8 billion yuan in excess savings. When investment demand exceeds savings, interest rates will rise. Conversely, when savings exceed investment demand, interest rates will fall. Ultimately, the intersection *E* of the investment curve *I* and savings curve *S* determines the equilibrium interest rate of 8%. At this interest rate, there is neither excessive investment nor excessive savings because investment and savings are both equal to 15 billion yuan.

When the investment demand curve or savings supply curve shifts, the equilibrium interest rate will change accordingly. In Figure 15.3, when the savings supply curve remains the same and the investment demand curve shifts right from I to I_1, the equilibrium interest rate will rise from 8% to 10%. Conversely, if the investment demand curve remains the same and the savings supply curve shifts to the right from S to S_1, the equilibrium interest rate will fall from 8 to 5%. If both the investment demand curve and savings curve shift right to I_1 and S_1 respectively, the equilibrium interest rate will remain at 8%.

The main factor that causes shifts in the investment demand curve is the marginal productivity of capital. The so-called **marginal productivity of capital** refers to the additional output with an increase of every unit of capital input. When the marginal productivity of capital rises, the same amount of investment will bring a greater amount of output. Thus, at the same interest rate, investment demand will increase and the investment demand curve will shift to the right. Conversely, if the marginal productivity of capital falls, the investment demand curve will shift to the left and investment demand will decrease. As a result, the equilibrium interest rate will move in the same direction as the marginal productivity of capital.

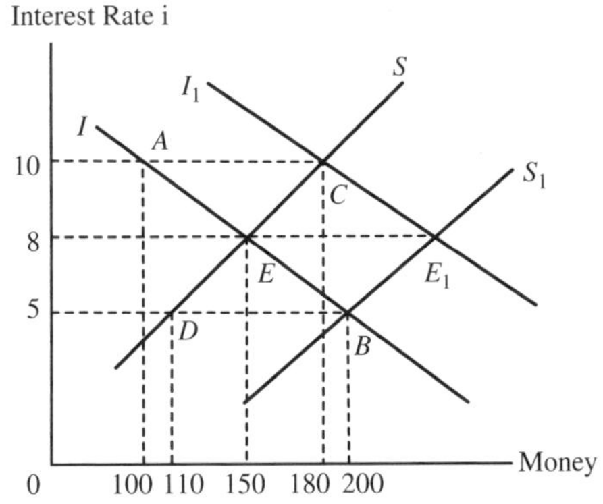

Fig. 15.3 Changes in the Equilibrium Interest Rate — Shift of the Investment Demand Curve and Savings Curve

The major reason for a shift in the savings supply curve is the marginal propensity to consume and the marginal propensity to save. If the marginal propensity to consume decreases or the marginal propensity to save increases, the savings supply curve will shift to the right. If there is no shift in the investment demand curve, the equilibrium interest rate will fall. Conversely, if the marginal propensity to consume increases or the marginal propensity to save decreases, the savings supply curve will shift to the left. If there is no shift in the investment demand curve, the equilibrium interest rate will rise.

What happens when the interest rate changes? Wicksell proposes his famous cumulative process theory. He divides the interest rate into the monetary interest rate and the natural interest rate. The monetary interest rate is the interest rate that exists in real financial markets or the interest rate that banks charge for lending. The natural interest rate is the expected profit rate obtained from using or loaning money. He holds that if the monetary interest rate is equal to the natural interest rate, then the increase or decrease of investment will have no effect on profit. Therefore, investment, production and input will not change, and the price will remain stable and at equilibrium. When the monetary interest rate is below the natural interest rate, entrepreneurs can earn a profit by increasing loans, expanding investment, and increasing production. As a result, profits and wages will rise. Conversely, when the real interest rate is higher than the natural rate, which is also called the expected profit rate, the market is unprofitable for entrepreneurs and they will reduce loans, investment, and production, resulting in a decrease in profits and wages. The decline in income will cut down on demand for the means of production and consumer goods, thus the price will fall due to a decrease in demand.

Wicksell argues that the upward or downward shift in prices caused by the changes in interest rates have an accumulative property. When the monetary interest rate is below the natural rate, and investment, production, income, and prices shift upwards, entrepreneurs will increase loans and expand investment, and thus production and prices will rise day by day. Conversely, when the monetary interest rate is below the natural rate, and investment, production, income and prices fall, entrepreneurs will reduce loans and input, and thus, production and prices will fall day by day.

Does this accumulative process last forever? Wicksell would say no, because of the "brake", the interest rate. When investment and prices increase, banks will have fewer savings. When savings cannot meet investment demand, banks will raise the interest rate in order to narrow the gap between the monetary interest rate and the natural interest rate. At this time, enterprises will not be much motivated to invest, which will slow down the rise of investments and prices. As the monetary interest rate approaches the natural interest rate, production and prices will move upwards much more slowly and come closer to a state of equilibrium. Conversely, when investment and prices fall resulting in excessive savings, banks have to reduce the monetary interest rate, which will curb the downward movement of investment and prices.

15.1.3 The Liquidity Preference Analysis

Unlike the classical theory of interest rate determination, Keynes' liquidity preference theory analyzes interest rates determinants from the perspective of money supply and demand. Keynes states that the level of interest rates is determined by the intersection of the money supply and demand curves.

(a) *Money Supply, Demand and the Equilibrium Interest Rate*

In Chapter 14, we saw that money demand is negatively correlated with interest rates. Interest rates on bonds constitute the opportunity cost of holding money, and those who hold money cannot earn the interest income that comes with holding bonds. Thus, the money demand curve slopes from the upper left to the lower right as shown in Figure 15.4. This illustrates that higher the interest rate, the less the demand for money. For example, when the interest rate is 10%, money demand is 200 units. When the interest rate falls to 6%, money demand will increase to 600 units because the opportunity cost of holding money declines.

Assuming that money supply is controlled by the central bank and is set at 400 units, then money supply will not change with interest rates. As such, the money supply curve is a vertical line. The intersection point *E* of the money supply and demand curves determines the equilibrium interest rate of 8%, and at this time, money demand is 400 units.

We also can analyze the movement of the equilibrium interest rate from Figure 15.4. Assuming that the initial interest rate is 10%, money demand would be 200 units, but the money supply is 400 units, then there is an excess supply of

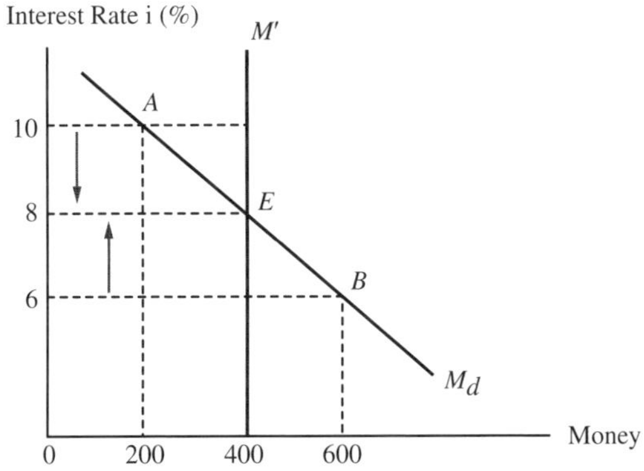

Fig. 15.4 Interest Rate Determination: Money Supply and Demand

200 units. People would use this money to purchase bonds in order to reduce their excess money. Accordingly, bond prices would rise with an increase in demand whereas the interest rate would move downwards. Conversely, if the initial interest rate is 6%, money demand is 600 units, yet the actual money supply is only 400 units, then there would be 200 units of excess money demand. At this time, people would sell a portion of their bonds to bridge this gap. Bond prices would then fall whereas interest rates would continue to rise until they reach the equilibrium point E.

(b) *Changes in the Equilibrium Interest Rate*

A shift in the money supply curve or the demand curve can lead to changes in interest rates. In Figure 15.5, if the money demand curve shifts to the top right position M' from M_d, and the money supply curve remains the same, the new equilibrium point E' is determined by the money supply curve M_s and the new money demand curve M'. At this time, the equilibrium interest rate is 10%. On the other hand, if the money demand curve shifts to the lower left position M'' from M_d while the money supply curve remains the same, the new equilibrium point is E'' and the equilibrium interest rate is 6%. At this level, the money supply and money demand are equal at 400 units.

What then are the factors that cause a shift in the money demand curve and the supply curve? In Keynes' theory of money demand, we have learned that the levels of income and prices will affect demand for real money. Assuming that the money supply is controlled by the central bank, the money supply curve will shift to the right when the central bank increases the money supply, and vice versa.

(c) *Shifts in the Money Demand Curve*

The primary factors which shift the money demand curve include changes in income and changes in prices.

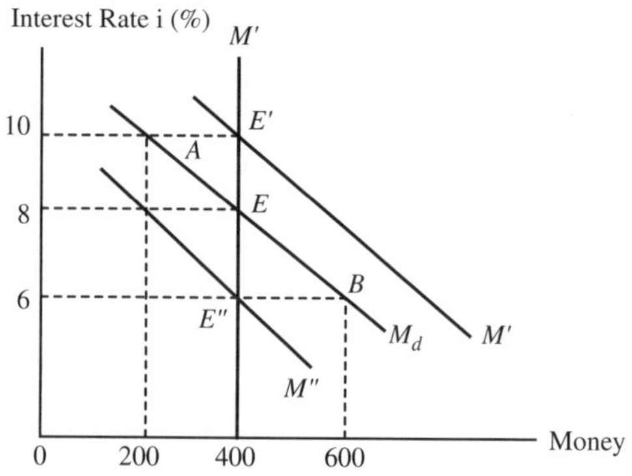

Fig. 15.5 Changes in the Equilibrium Interest Rate: Changes in Money Demand

(i) *Income*: Income influences demand for money in two ways. First, as income rises, wealth will increase accordingly, and people will prefer to hold more money as a store of value. Second, we know that the demand for money as a medium of exchange will increase when income rises, thus people will prefer holding more money. In periods of economic expansion or rapid economic growth, income rises rapidly and so too does the demand for money. At this time, if money supply growth cannot keep up with the growing demand for money, interest rates will rise. It follows that economic expansion and the rising of income will result in a shift in the money demand curve to the upper right and the interest rate will tend to rise.

(ii) *Price level*: In Chapter 14, we have also learned that people are concerned with real money balances that they hold. As price levels rise, the real value of the same amount of money will decline, and then it can buy less goods and services. In order to keep real money balances from decreasing in value, people will hold more nominal money. Therefore, the demand for nominal money will increase as price levels rise, and the money demand curve will shift to the upper right causing interest rates to rise. On the other hand, the real value of nominal money held by people will increase if price levels drop, and people can use their excess real money to purchase bonds. Thus, the money demand curve will shift to the lower left and interest rates will fall.

(d) *Shifts of the Money Supply Curve*

When the central bank implements a monetary policy, it will cause a shift in the money supply curve. For example, when the central bank expands the money supply from 400 to 600 units (as shown in Figure 15.6), the money supply curve will then shift to the right from M_S to M_s'', and the equilibrium interest rate will fall from 8% to 6%, given that the money demand curve does not shift. Conversely,

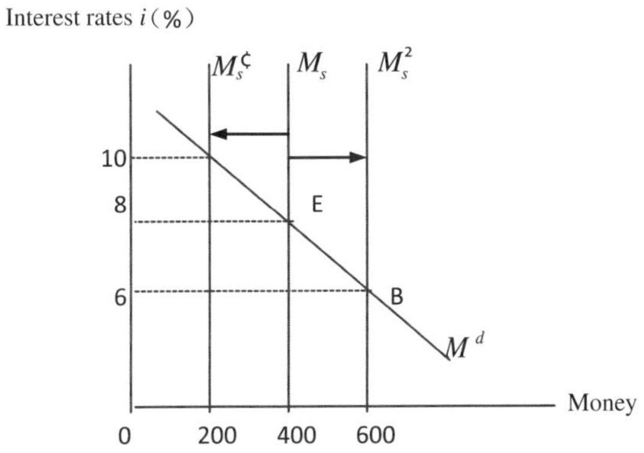

Fig. 15.6 Effect of Shifts in the Money Supply Curve on the Equilibrium Interest Rate

when the central bank reduces the money supply from 400 to 200 units, the money supply curve will shift to the left from M_s to M_s' and then the equilibrium interest rate will rise from 8% to 10%, given that the money demand curve does not shift.

Due to the liquidity effect, an increase in the money supply will result in a decline in interest rates, and vice versa. When the central bank adjusts the money supply, it will change the balances of money and liquidity held by people. For example, when the central bank increases the money supply, money held by people will increase and exceed their preferred amount, causing excessive liquidity. At this time, one option is to purchase bonds with the excessive money in hand. As a result, bond prices will increase and interest rates will decrease. Conversely, when the central bank reduces the money supply, liquidity will decrease below the preferred amount, and people will sell a portion of their bonds, which causes the price of bonds to fall and interest rates to rise. Therefore, the interest rate and the money supply are negatively correlated because of the liquidity effect. In other words, when the money supply increases, the liquidity effect will cause a decrease in interest rates. When the money supply decreases, the liquidity effect will cause interest rates to rise.

15.1.4 Loanable Funds Analysis

From the analysis of classical interest rate determination and the interest rate determination based on liquidity preference, we have realized that the classical school completely neglects monetary factors when analyzing interest rate determination. Liquidity preference analysis, on the other hand, goes to the other extreme in that it ignores the role of real factors in the determination of interest rates. The loanable funds theory combines real factors and monetary factors together to analyze the determination of interest rates.

The basic instrument of the loanable funds theory is still the money supply and demand curves. The supply of loanable funds comes from the following sources:

- Current savings. For example, part of your current income that is put into the bank will compose the supply of loanable funds.
- Inflow of foreign capital in an open economy. Nowadays, the international flow of capital has become more frequent and larger in scale. The inflow of foreign capital also increases the supply of domestic loanable funds.
- Additional money created by the banking system.
- Gains on depreciation or sales of fixed capital.
- Utilization of hoard cash.

Demand for loanable funds comes from:

- Current investment. For example, loan demands will increase when enterprises want to build a new plant or purchase new machinery to boost production.

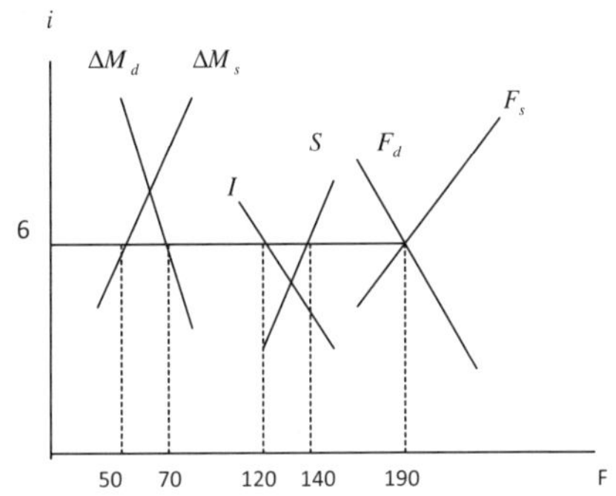

Fig. 15.7 Loanable Funds Analysis of Interest Rate Determination

- Compensation for replacement and depreciation of fixed capital. For example, the demand for money will increase when enterprises want to purchase new machinery to replace old ones.
- Newly increased demand for money.

Interest rates are determined by the intersection between the aggregate demand and aggregate supply. In Figure 15.7, ΔM_d is the newly increased money demand, I is the newly increased investment and depreciation compensation, and F_d is the loanable funds demand. Therefore, according to our definition, $F_d = \Delta M_d + I$. In the figure, if the newly increased money demand ΔM_d is seven billion yuan, and new investment and depreciation compensation is 12 billion yuan, then the demand for loanable funds F_d is 19 billion yuan. ΔM_s stands for the newly increased money supply, S stands for savings and foreign capital inflows, and F_s stands for the supply of loanable funds. Therefore, according to our definition, $F_s = \Delta M_s + S$. In the figure, newly increased money supply ΔM_s is 5 billion yuan, savings and foreign capital inflows S are 14 billion yuan, and as a result, the supply of loanable funds F_s is 19 billion yuan. At this point, the demand for loanable funds F_d is equal to the supply of loanable funds F_s, and thereby determines the equilibrium interest rate as 6%.

From further analysis of Figure 15.7, we can see that when the equilibrium interest rate is determined by the demand and supply of loanable funds, the supply and demand of newly increased money as well as savings and investments are not necessarily equal. In our example, when the equilibrium interest rate is 6%, money supply is 5 billion yuan whereas money demand is 7 billion yuan, and the excess money demand is then 2 billion yuan. On the other hand, at the same equilibrium interest rate, investment is 12 billion yuan, but savings is 14 billion yuan, thus excessive savings is 2 billion yuan. However, under all circumstances, when the supply and demand of loanable funds are equal, the gap between money demand and money supply is bound to be equal to the gap between investments and savings. In our case, the gaps are both 2 billion yuan.

15.1.5 Price Levels and Interest Rates: the Gibson Paradox

If we only look at the liquidity effect, based on the liquidity preference theory of interest rate determination, we can come up with the basic notion that an increase in the money supply will certainly cause a fall in interest rates, and vice versa. Similarly, an increase in the money supply will cause a rise in price levels, and vice versa. Based on this logic, price levels are negatively correlated to interest rates, that is, the higher the price level, the lower the interest rates. Conversely, if price levels fall, interest rates will rise.

However, this simple logical analysis is different from what we see in reality. British economist Gibson observes from the statistics of nominal interest rates and price levels over the 137 years from 1791 to 1928 that interest rates and price levels moves in the same direction; the higher the price level, the higher the interest rate, and vice versa. Figure 15.8 displays the relationship between China's loan repurchase rate and CPI. Figure 15.9 displays the relationship between America's CPI and the Federal Funds Rate. From the two figures we can clearly see that movement of the CPI and interest rates are basically in the same direction: when the inflation rate is high, the interest rate level is also high. Conversely, when the interest rates fall, the inflation rate would also fall. This positive correlation between the price level and interest rates is a far cry from the theoretical analysis. This phenomenon that the price level and nominal interest rate move in the same direction is known as the **Gibson Paradox**.

Why does the Gibson Paradox occur? It is because, apart from the liquidity effect, the changes to the money supply also have income effect, price level effect, and the expected inflation effect, all of which can raise interest rates. The income effect refers to the expansionary impact on the economy produced by an increase in the money supply, which can improve the income level and wealth of citizens. As seen in Chapter 14, an increase in the level of income and wealth will increase

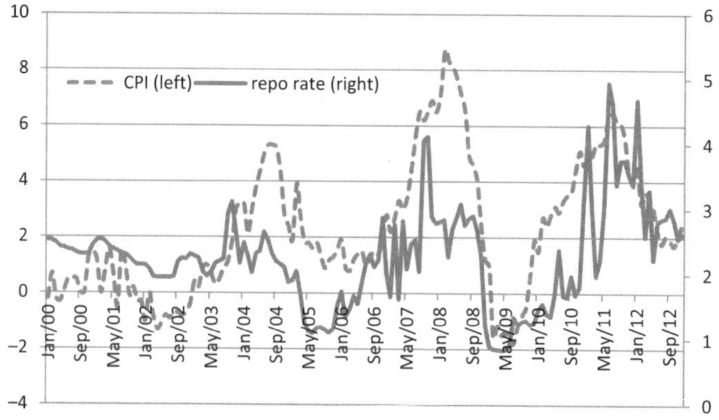

Fig. 15.8 China's CPI and Bond Repo Rate (Unit: %)
Sources: Websites of the National Bureau of Statistics and the People's Bank of China

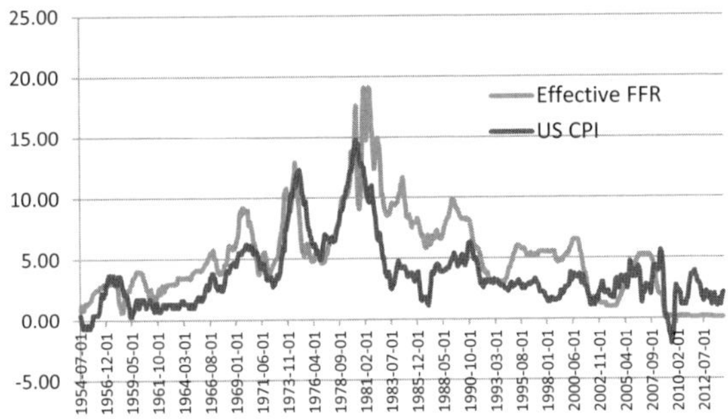

Fig. 15.9 America's Federal Funds Rate and CPI (Unit: %)
Source: Website of the St. Louis Federal Reserve

the demand for money. As such, when the central bank increases the money supply, it will automatically increase people's demand for money, which will then raise the level of interest rates.

In addition, when the central bank increases the money supply, price levels will typically increase, and an increase in price levels will raise the demand for money, which will also push interest rates higher. For this reason, the liquidity preference theory states that an increase in price levels will cause an increase in the interest rate. This is the price level effect of an increase in the money supply. Finally, an increase in the money supply may also cause people to expect an increase in future price levels, and an increase in the expected inflation rate will also raise the demand for money, which will thus raise interest rates. Therefore, the inflation effect of an increase in the money supply refers to a rise of interest rates because of an increase in the expected rate of inflation caused by an increase in the money supply. The income effect, the price level effect, and the expected inflation effect all cause interest rates to rise with an increase in the money supply. Conversely, a reduction in the money supply will cause a drop in interest rates.

As a result of these four effects, the interest rate will not necessarily fall when the central bank increases the money supply. This depends on whether or not the liquidity effect is greater than the three other effects as well as their response time to the increased money supply. Generally speaking, once the money supply has grown, the liquidity effect will immediately kick in, while the income effect and price level effect take some time to react. The response time of the expected inflation effect can either be quick or slow, which depends on the adjustment time of people to the expected inflation.

Figure 15.10 displays the three reactions of interest rates to changes in the money supply.

Figure 15.10(a) displays how interest rates will respond to changes in the money supply when the liquidity effect is greater than the effects of income, price and expected inflation. When the central bank increases the money supply at time

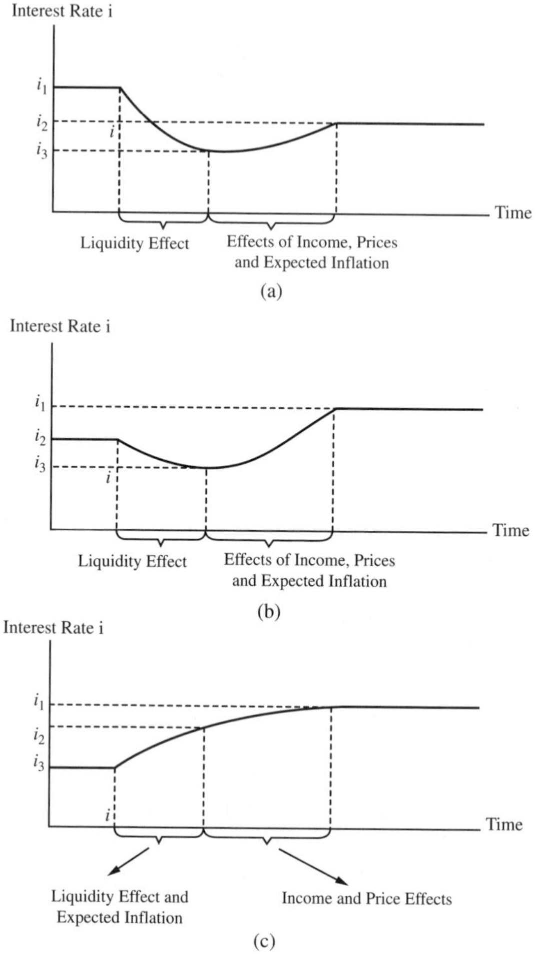

Fig. 15.10 Effect of the Money Supply Changes on Interest Rate Levels: Complete Analysis. (a) When the liquidity effect is greater than the other three effects. (b) When the liquidity effect is less than the other three effects, but adjustment for expected inflation is made slowly and (c) When the liquidity effect is less than the other three effects and adjustment for expected inflation is made quickly.

t, since the liquidity effect reacts very quickly, the interest rate will quickly fall from i_1 to i_3. After this, the three other effects will begin to come into play; as a result, the interest rate will gradually increase. Finally, though, since the liquidity effect is relatively strong, the interest rate will only increase to i_2 and cannot return to the original level of i_1.

Figure 15.10(b) displays how interest rates will respond to changes in the money supply when the liquidity effect is less than the other three effects, while expected inflation adjusts slowly. After the central bank increases the money supply, since the liquidity effect quickly comes into play, interest rates will fall from i_1 to i_3. Afterwards, since the other three effects will begin to come into play, interest rates will begin to rise. Meanwhile, since the liquidity effect is relatively weaker than the other three effects, interest rates will ultimately rise to i_2, which is higher than the initial i_1.

Figure 15.10(c) displays how interest rates will respond to changes in the money supply when the inflation expectation quickly comes into play and is stronger than the liquidity effect. In this case, once the central bank increases the money supply, interest rates will begin to rise. Afterwards, the income and price level effects will begin to come into play, and as such, the interest rates will continue to rise until they reach i_2.

15.2 Risk Structure of Interest Rates

Whenever we purchase any form of bonds, we must assume certain systematic risks and non-systematic risks. As we have learned in Chapter 5, to persuade investors to accept the risk of an investment portfolio, they must first be provided with an expected return higher than risk-free interest rate. This is a risk premium. The more that people are adverse to risk, the higher the risk premium must be. In the bond market analysis, the difference in the yields of bonds with different levels of credit is called **credit spread**. The primary risks that impact interest rate differences from one bond issuer to another are non-systematic risks, namely, default risks and liquidity risks.

15.2.1 Default Risks

Default risk, also known as credit risk, refers to the probability that the borrower cannot repay principal and interest on schedule. There are two circumstances. First, borrowers do not have enough cash flows to repay their maturing debt because of poor management. Second, borrowers have adequate cash flows, but are not willing to repay principal and interest upon maturity. Unlike most enterprises, a central government is backed by tax revenues and the right to issue banknotes. For this reason, when you purchase government bonds, there is rarely any credit risks. As such, government bonds are known as "gilt-edged bonds".

We can borrow the supply and demand graph often used in economics to analyze the effect of default risks on interest rates. Figure 15.11 is a supply and demand graph for Company A's bonds and government bonds. For convenient analysis, we suppose that Company A's bonds initially have no default risk, and for this reason, they are initially the same as government bonds and their interest rates do not have risk premiums. Also, their maturity is the same. In this way, their initial equilibrium prices and interest rates are the same, namely, $P_1^c = P_1^t, i_1^c = i_1^t$.

Now suppose that Company A suffers major losses because of poor management and thus default risks increases. In turn, the expected returns on their bonds

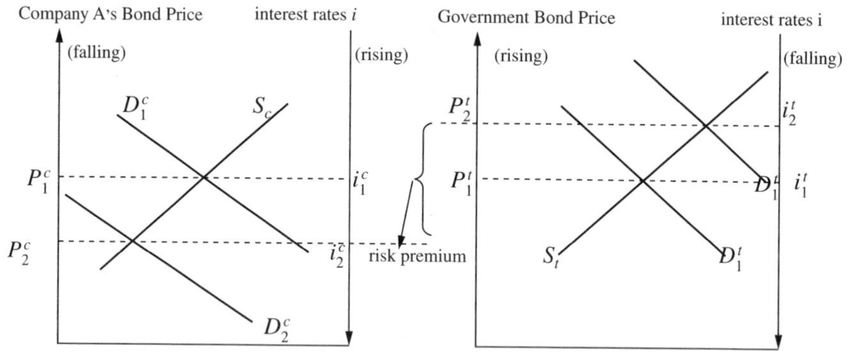

Fig. 15.11 Effect of Default Risk on Interest Rates

fall. Meanwhile, since the government bonds have no default risks, their expected return is relatively high, and as such, will be greatly preferred by investors. Since the default risks and relative return of Company A's bonds and government bonds have changed, it will also impact the investor demand for these two types of bonds. Specifically, investors will have less demand for Company A's bonds and more demand for government bonds. This change will shift the demand curve for Company A's bonds from D_1^c to D_2^c, and will shift the demand curve for government bonds from D_1^t to D_2^t. However, since the supply curves for Company A's bonds and for government bonds have not shifted, the result of a change in the demand curve will cause the price of Company A's bonds to fall from P_1^c to P_2^c, and cause the price of government bonds to rise from P_1^t to P_2^t. In this way, the interest rate on Company A's bonds will increase from i_1^c to i_2^c. Conversely, the interest rate on government bonds will fall from i_1^t to i_2^t. As a result, the interest rate of Company A's bonds is higher than government bonds by $i_2^c i_2^c$, which represents the risk premium brought by Company A's default risk. Generally speaking, bonds with default risk always have a risk premium, and the risk premium will rise with increasing risk of default. The primary reason for differences in interest rates from different bonds with the same terms is different credit risk of the issuers.

15.2.2 Liquidity Risks

In addition to credit risk, another major factor that affects bond rates is their liquidity. The higher an asset's liquidity, the less the loss when it is converted into cash. For this reason, most people will typically prefer assets with a higher liquidity. However, the higher the liquidity, the lower the rate of return. Conversely, if higher rates of return are required, a portion of liquidity must be sacrificed.

How exactly does liquidity affect interest rates? Consider this scenario: a company will issue 10-year bonds, but this type of bonds has no secondary market.

In other words, if you purchase these bonds, you must hold them for ten years before you can take back your principal with interest. Since you cannot transfer these bonds to others, these bonds are completely illiquid. In this situation, if you are in desperate need of cash five years after purchasing these bonds, you will dearly regret purchasing them in the first place instead of depositing them in the bank. After taking all of this into consideration, you would not be willing to purchase these bonds that much.

For this reason, liquidity can affect a person's demand for bonds. Let us continue our analysis of the effects created by liquidity on interest rates that we began in Figure 15.10. For a more convenient analysis, we still suppose that liquidity and terms for both Company A's bonds and government bonds are the same. As such, their initial demand curves are D_1^c and D_1^t, respectively; and their intersections with the supply curves are the initial equilibrium prices and interest rates, which are the same, namely $P_1^c = P_1^t, i_1^c = i_1^t$.

Now suppose that the liquidity of Company A's bonds changes. If you purchased them, they would be hard to get rid of, or if you were to transfer them to someone else, you would suffer a major loss. However, the liquidity of government bonds remains the same. In this way, investors would lower their demand for Company A's bonds and would increase their demand for government bonds, which would shift the demand curve for Company A's bonds from D_1^c to D_2^c and shift the demand curve for government bonds from D_1^t to D_2^t. The supply curves for Company A's bonds and government bonds, however, has not shifted, so a change in the demand curve for Company A's bonds would result in a price drop from P_1^c to P_2^c. Meanwhile, the price of government bonds would rise from P_1^t to P_2^t. In this way, the interest rate on Company A's bonds would rise from i_1^c to i_2^c. On the other hand, the interest rate on government bonds would fall from i_1^t to i_2^t. In this way, the interest rate for Company A's bonds would surpass government bonds by $i_2^c i_2^t$. The difference in interest rates caused by difference in liquidity is known as the **liquidity premium**.

Box 15.1 Why are China's Government Bond Rates Higher than Bank Deposit Rates Over the Same Period?

In 1981, China relaunched government bonds. Government bonds are known as "gilt-edged bonds", and out of all the financial instruments, government bond rates should be the lowest. However, for a relatively long period after China relaunched its government bonds, their rates were much higher than bank deposit rates for similar terms (as shown in Table 15.2), which presented the so-called interest rate "inversion". Many theorists have criticized this phenomenon.

Table 15.2 China's Government Bond Rates and Bank Deposit Rates (Unit %)

Year	Term	Government Bond Single Rate (A)	Bank Single Rate (B)	A–B	Government Bond Compound Rate (C)	Bank Compound Rate (D)	C–D
1985	5	9	8.28	0.72	7.71	7.17	0.54
1986	5	10	9.36	0.64	8.45	7.98	0.47
1987	5	10	9.36	0.64	8.45	7.98	0.47
1988	3	10	9.72	0.28	9.14	8.90	0.24
1989	3	14	13.14	0.96	12.40	11.71	0.69
1990	3	14	11.88	2.12	12.40	10.70	1.7
1991	3	10	8.28	1.72	9.14	7.68	1.46
1992	3	10.5	8.28	2.22	9.56	7.68	1.88
1993	3	13.96	12.24	1.72	12.37	10.99	1.38
1994	3	13.96	12.24	1.72	12.37	10.99	1.38
1995	3	14	12.24	1.76	12.40	10.99	1.41
1996	3	11.34	10.80	0.54	10.25	9.81	0.44
1997	3	9.18	8.28	0.3	8.45	7.68	0.77
1998	3	5.85	4.77	1.08	5.45	4.72	0.73

Having studied the risk structure theory of interest rates, you will probably have a good understanding of the interest rate "inversion" between China's government bonds and bank deposits. In fact, the presence of this kind of phenomenon is not without cause.

The inversion of China's government bond rate and bank deposit rate has a long history and institutional background. This is due to the fact that China's government bond market is gradually developing in a less developed market system. In the early stages following the relaunch of government bonds, China did not in fact have a national government bond market for circulation. Even though there were "scalpers" trading government bonds as intermediates, the government labeled them as "illegal" and as such, these so-called "scalpers" traded with a great deal of risk. Secondly, since these "scalpers" had no way of forming a national government bond exchange market, the scale of their transactions and the information as to these transactions was very limited. For this reason, government bond transactions were strongly segmented geographically, and as such, there was a wide gap in transaction prices and interest rates from place to place. In this way, the liquidity of government bonds was given a larger discount unlike gilt-edged bonds with maximum liquidity in market economies. From another perspective, China's state-owned commercial banks had always been well protected by the government, and served as a quasi-fiscal agency of the government. They raised a large amount of financing for the government, and thus, the government had to solve problems of those banks. As such, the risk of bankruptcy was slim to none. In this situation, when government bonds were issued at a higher rate than bank deposits for similar terms, there seems to be a certain degree of economic rationality.

In early 1990s, however, this situation that the interest rates on government bonds were notably higher than those of bank deposits began to change. First of all, China established a national government bond trading market, which employed modern information technology. Transaction prices were subject to ever-changing market conditions, and the volume of transactions could be very large while the transaction cost was cut down significantly. Second, after 10 years of development, state-owned commercial banks gradually began to show more and more problems, most importantly was the accumulation of non-performing loans which began to hinder their development and even endanger the fabric of the entire financial system. In other words, after 20 years of development, the liquidity structure and risk structure of government bonds and commercial bank deposits had already exhibited inverse changes: the liquidity of government bonds was higher than that of bank deposits while their risks were still slightly lower. The reason for government bond rates to be "fixed" above bank deposit rates with the same terms in the early stages of development of China's government bond exchange market no longer existed, and that is why government bond rates are lower than bank deposit rates with the same terms nowadays.

15.3 Term Structure of Interest Rates

Why do interest rates vary amongst government bonds or deposits with different terms taken by the same bank? Likewise, why are yield curves, such as those illustrated in Chapter 9, upward sloping in the right direction? These questions can be explained by the term structure of interest rates. There are several different theories used to explain the term structure: the expectation hypothesis, the theory of market segmentation, maturity choice, and liquidity premium theory.

15.3.1 Expectation Hypothesis

The expectation hypothesis states that long-term bond rates are equal to the average of short-term rate expectations prior to the long-term bond's maturity. For instance, if people expect that the average of short-term rates over the next five years will be 10%, then according to the expectation hypothesis, the interest rate for five-year bonds would also be 10%. If people feel that the average of short-term rates over the next 10 years would be 12%, then the interest rate for 10-year bonds would also be 12%.

The fundamental assumption of the expectation hypothesis is that bond buyers have no special preference for a specific maturity. Whether or not they will hold these bonds completely depends on relative return of the bonds compared to others. For this reason, when the return on some bonds is lower than that on others with a different maturity, people will stop holding this kind of bond and immediately purchase those with a relatively higher return. As such, these bonds are perfect substitutes. If these bonds can be substituted from one to another, then, because of interest rate arbitrage, the expected return on these bonds must be equivalent.

For a simplified analysis, suppose that you want to invest one yuan with a total investment term of two years. You have two options that you can choose from.

Plan A: Purchase a two-year bond and hold it until it reaches maturity. This bond calculates compound interest once a year. We shall set its annual interest rate as i_{2t}.

Plan B: Purchase a one-year bond this year with an annual rate of i_{2t}. After one year, you withdraw your principal and interest and again purchase a different bond with a one-year term. This new bond's expected annual rate is i^e_{t+1}.

In Plan A, after two years, the total amount of principal with interest would be:

$$(1 + i_{2t}) \cdot (1 + i_{2t}) = 1 + 2i_{2t} + (i_{2t})^2. \tag{15.1}$$

After deducting the principal, the actual return would be:

$$1 + 2i_{2t} + (i_{2t})^2 - 1 = 2i_{2t} + (i_{2t})^2. \tag{15.2}$$

In Plan B, after the first year of investment, the total amount of principal with interest would be: $(1 + i_t)$.

In the second year, the interest and principal of the first year are reinvested, and as the expected interest rate for the second investment of the one-year bond is $i^e_t + 1$, the total amount of principal with interest of the second investment would be:

$$(1 + i_t) \cdot (1 + i^e_{t+1}) = 1 + i_t + i^e_{t+1} + i_t \cdot i^e_{t+1}. \tag{15.3}$$

The total return in Plan B would be:

$$1 + i_t + i^e_{t+1} + i_t \cdot i^e_{t+1} - 1 = i_t + i^e_{t+1} + i_t \cdot i^e_{t+1}. \tag{15.4}$$

If these two investment plans were perfect substitutes, then their return would be completely the same. Otherwise, it would attract new arbitrage behavior which would cause the return in these two investment plans to be the same. As such:

$$2i_{2t} + (i_{2t})^2 = i_t + i^e_{t+1} + i_t \cdot i^e_{t+1}. \tag{15.5}$$

Generally speaking, interest rates are rarely above 10%, and for this reason, the value of $(i_{2t})^2$ and $i_t \cdot i^e_t + 1$ would be very small. For instance, if i_{2t} was 5%, then $(i_{2t})^2$ would only be 0.0025. As such, we can express the above equation as follows:

$$2i_{2t} = i_t + i^e_{t+1}, \tag{15.6}$$

from which we get:

$$i_{2t} = \frac{i_t + i^e_{t+1}}{2}. \tag{15.7}$$

This illustrates that the interest rate for a two-year bond should be equal to the average interest rate of two one-year bonds.

More often than not, if the term for one kind of bond is n years, its interest rate would be i_{nt}. During these n years, a series of short-term bond rates would be $i_t, i^e_{t+1}, i^e_{t+2}, \ldots, i^e_{t+n-1}$, respectively, then:

$$i_{nt} = \frac{i_t + i^e_{t+1} + i^e_{t+2} + \cdots + i^e_{t+n-1}}{n}. \tag{15.8}$$

The above equation illustrates that the long-term bond with a term of n years is equal to the average interest rate for the series of short-term bonds within this term.

For this reason, based on the Expectation Hypothesis, an increase in short-term interest rates will raise people's expectations for future short-term interest rates, and will further raise the long-term interest rates. Conversely, when short-term interest rates fall, people will expect future short-term interest rates to fall, thereby lowering long-term interest rates.

15.3.2 Market Segmentation Theory

According to the **market segmentation theory**, bond markets with different terms are completely independent and segmented; as such, the interest rate for each type of bond will only be impacted by its own supply and demand, and changes to the return on bonds with different terms will not affect its demand. For example, based on the market segmentation theory, changes to the interest rates of three-year government bonds will not affect the demand for one-year bonds. As you can see, market segmentation theory and the expectation hypothesis are polar opposites. On the other end of the extreme, the theory assumes that there are no substitutions amongst bonds with different terms.

Bonds with different maturities cannot be substituted for each other. This is because investors have a strong preference for a certain bond maturity and have no interest in other bonds whatsoever. As such, investors will typically only pay attention to the expected return for the bonds with terms that they like. This is somewhat similar to our daily lives: Perhaps Wang Xiao'er feels that Zhao Xiaosan has a few shortcomings and keeps distance from him or ignores him. Based on the theory of market segmentation, if you prefer one-year bonds, then even if there was a significant increase in the return on two-year bonds, you would still hold one-year bonds.

In accordance with the market segmentation theory, the different return on bonds with different terms is determined by the supply and demand differences of each type of bonds. Generally speaking, investors will prefer short-term bonds with lower risks, so the demand for short-term bonds would thus be higher than that of long-term bonds. Based on our analysis above of loanable fund theory, the price of short-term bonds would be higher than that of long-term bonds. As such, their interest rates would also be lower.

However, the fundamental assumption of market segmentation theory is very extreme and far from reality. In fact, there will always be a certain degree of substitution amongst bonds with different terms; a change in the return on long-term bonds will have a certain effect on the demand for short-term bonds. That is, there will always be arbitrage between the different markets. In reality, if there was a significant jump in the return on two-year bonds, you would most likely sell a portion of your original one-year bonds and purchase two-year bonds to gain the higher return. Due to investor arbitrage, the interest rates of bonds with different terms will fluctuate in unison. This is actually something that we see happening. Clearly, market segmentation theory has no way of explaining this.

15.3.3 Preferred Habit Theory and Liquidity Premium Theory

Preferred habit theory states that the interest rates on long-term bonds are equal to the average expected rates on short-term bonds before the bond becomes due, plus the maturity premium of such bond varying with supply conditions. Similar to the expectation hypothesis, preferred habit theory also supposes that bonds with different terms can be substituted. In this way, changes to the return on one type of bonds will largely affect the return on bonds with different terms. However, it is also similar to market segmentation theory in that it supposes that investors have a preference for different terms, although this assumption is not nearly as extreme as it is in the market segmentation theory. In this way, bonds with different terms are not perfect substitutes.

For example, you may like one-year bonds, but you also pay a lot of attention to changes in the return on two-year bonds. If the return on two-year bonds is incredibly high, you may also purchase a few of these bonds. However, since you prefer one-year bonds, you will only buy two-year bonds when the return is much higher. Only at that point would you be willing to purchase two-year bonds that you personally have no interest in, and the excess return is called maturity premium. If we use P_{nt} to express the maturity premium, the preferred habit theory can be

$$i_{nt} = \frac{i_t + i^e_{t+1} + i^e_{t+2} + \cdots + i^e_{t+n-1}}{n} = P_{nt}. \tag{15.9}$$

The liquidity premium theory is similar to the preferred habit theory. When we studied the characteristics of financial instruments, we learned that they have profitability, liquidity, and maturity. Generally speaking, the longer the term of a financial instrument, the lower its liquidity, and vice versa. Since the liquidity of long-term bonds is lower than that of short-term bonds, those who hold long-term bonds must take on a higher liquidity risk. As such, for investors to be willing to hold onto long-term bonds, they must be paid a liquidity premium so as to compensate for the higher risk. If we use l_{nt} to express the liquidity premium, the liquidity premium theory can be expressed as:

$$i_{nt} = \frac{i_t + i^e_{t+1} + i^e_{t+2} + \cdots + i^e_{t+n-1}}{n} + l_{nt}. \tag{15.10}$$

Since maturity premiums or liquidity premiums are typically positive, the interest rate on long-term bonds will be higher than that of short-term bonds.

Suppose that for the next five years the expected interest rates for one-year bonds will be 1.8, 2.0, 2.5, 2.7, and 3.0%, respectively. Maturity premiums (or liquidity premiums) for two- and three-year bonds would be 0.2% and 0.25% respectively. Therefore, current two- and three-year bond rates would be 2.1% [as in $(1.8\% + 2.0\%) \div 2\% + 0.2\% = 2.1\%$] and 2.35% [as in $(1.8\% + 2.0\% + 2.5\%) \div 3\% + 0.25\% = 2.35\%$], respectively.

Summary

The classical theory of interest rates states that when savings and investments are equal, the interest rate level is in equilibrium. Changes to the marginal productivity of capital, the marginal propensity to consume, and the marginal propensity to save will cause a shift in the investment demand curve and the savings supply curve, thereby changing the equilibrium interest rate.

The liquidity preference theory states that when the money supply and demand are equal, the interest rate level is in equilibrium. After the money supply curve and money demand curve have shifted, the equilibrium interest rate will also change. Changes of income and price levels can shift the money demand curve, and as such, will affect interest rates.

The loanable funds theory states that the interest rate equilibrium is determined by the supply and demand of loanable funds. The supply of loanable funds comes from current savings, foreign capital inflows, new money supply, etc. The demand for loanable funds comes from current investment, depreciation, capital outflow, etc. When the supply and demand of loanable funds are equal, the interest rate is in equilibrium, although the money supply and demand, and savings and investment are not necessarily equal. However, at this level of interest rates, the gap between the money supply and demand and the gap between savings and investment are equal.

An increase in the money supply will raise price levels and lower interest rates. For this reason, prices and interest rates are negatively correlated. In reality, however, price levels and interest rates move in the same direction, which is called the Gibson Paradox. This is explained by the impact of the liquidity effect, income effect, price level effect, and expected inflation effect on interest rates after an increase in the money supply. Give these four effects, only the liquidity effect can lower interest rates, while the other three effects will cause rates to rise.

There are differences in the interest rates for bonds issued by different borrowers, primarily because each bond has a different risk structure. Default risks (credit risks) and liquidity risks are the primary reason for varying interest rates which is the risk structure of interest rates.

As for the term structure of interest rates, the expectation hypothesis states that long-term bond rates are the average value of the expected interest rates of each short-term bond within the duration of the longer bond. Market segmentation theory states that there is no alternative between different bonds, and that investors prefer short-term bonds rather than long-term bonds. In order to encourage investors to hold long-term bonds, higher interest rates would be needed. The preferred habit theory and liquidity premium theory state that the interest rates on long-term bonds are equal to the average expected rates on short-term bonds plus maturity premium or liquidity premium.

Key Terms

Loanable Funds Theory; Liquidity Preference Theory; Risk Structure of Interest Rates; Term Structure of Interest Rates; Risk Premium; Liquidity Premium; Expectation Hypothesis; Market Segmentation Theory; Maturity Premium; Liquidity Effect; Gibson Paradox

Critical Thinking Questions

1. Describe Marx's theory of interest rates.
2. Explain the main idea behind the interest rate determination of the liquidity preference theory.
3. What is the main idea behind the loanable fund theory?
4. What is the Gibson Paradox and why does it exist?
5. Why are corporate bond rates higher than government bond rates for the same term?
6. Briefly comment on the Wicksell Cumulative Process.
7. Why do interest rates differ for similar financial instruments with the same maturity?

8. When the central bank purchases government bonds on the open market, thereby increasing the money supply, what will be the effects of this policy on the total level of interest rates?
9. Assume the relation between savings and interest rates is $S = 500+600i$ (S as savings, i as interest rates); the relation between investment and interest rates is $I = 600-400i$ (S as savings, i as interest rates); the relation between money demand and interest rates is $M_d = 300-200i$ (M_d as money demand); and the amount of money supply is 700. Calculate the interest rate level based on the classical theory of interest rate determination, the liquidity preference theory and the loanable funds theory, and compare the results.
10. Suppose that a company issues five-year interest-bearing bonds with a coupon rate of 8%. One day, the company suddenly announces that it is operating far below the expected level. How will this news impact the market rate and market prices for its bonds? If the company announces that it has developed a new product with promising prospects which has been under patent protection, how will this then affect the market price and market rate for its bonds?
11. If the market rate for one-, two-, three- and five-year government bonds are 2.5%, 2.75%, 3.0%, and 3.5%, respectively. Based on the expectation hypothesis theory, what should the rate be for a four-year government bond?
12. During the American financial crisis of 2008, the prices of bonds issued by American financial institutions and enterprises fell sharply. Liquidity nosedived, and interest rates skyrocketed. Meanwhile, the interest rates on the American government's short-term bonds fell. Prices rose even to the point that rates for short-term government bonds were negative. Briefly analyze this phenomenon based on the main ideas behind this chapter's risk structure of interest rates.

Chapter 16

Price Levels: Inflation and Deflation

Learning Objectives

After studying this chapter, you will be able to:

- Clearly understand price index and its main categories
- Understand what inflation and deflation are
- Clearly understand the social and economic impact of inflation and deflation
- Understand the causes of inflation and deflation
- Clearly understand the relationship between price levels and unemployment rate
- Clearly understand the policy measures that governments can use to stabilize prices

Regardless of whether we buy household appliances or daily necessities, we all want low costs and high quality. Prices not only have a major impact on individual purchasing decisions, but also affect each and every person's life. Price levels have a major impact on individuals, enterprises, and the entire economy. As such, when price levels are unstable, governments will typically implement policy measures to manage the prices. Price fluctuations are not only a research topic of macroeconomics, but also closely related to money and finance.

16.1 General Price Level and Its Measurement

16.1.1 Price Index

What is inflation or deflation? To understand these two terms, we must first figure out another term, that is, the general price level. The **general price level** refers to the price level that covers all goods and services in an entire society. However, in actual economic situations, a price index, instead of an absolute value, is generally used to measure changes in the general price level, and the following factors are used according to different selected statistical ranges.

- Consumer Price Index
- Producer Price Index
- GNP Deflator

The **Consumer Price Index (CPI)** is an index developed according to representative household consumption. To state a simple example, suppose that one day you go to a supermarket and purchase five bottles of Coca Cola at two yuan per bottle, four boxes of Dove Chocolate at 18 yuan per box, and three bags of Strong Jelly at 14 yuan per bag; a total of 124 yuan. However, you had to pay only 115 yuan for the same items on the same day the previous year. Therefore, the price index for these consumer goods is $\frac{124}{115} \times 100\% = 107.8\%$, which means that you pay 7.8% more now than last year. This is surely an extremely simple example, for many more kinds of goods are considered to calculate CPI in actual statistics.

CPI comprehensively reflects how price level changes influence consumption and living standards. If the CPI rises, consumers need to pay more for the same quantity of goods and services in the current year and vice versa. Therefore, CPI is most closely related to our daily lives.

The **Producer Price Index (PPI)**, as its name implies, is a price index of raw materials and other inputs, which enterprises purchase. It depicts changes to production costs. Therefore, PPI greatly influences corporate profits. If the PPI rises, enterprises need to pay more for the same quantity of inputs, which means producing the same amount goods or services will cost more, and vice versa.

The **GNP Deflator** is a ratio of GNP measured at current year's prices to that measured at a fixed price. For example, suppose that GNP in 2001 calculated based on the price of various goods is 10 trillion yuan, compared to 9 trillion yuan in 2000. Therefore, the GNP Deflator of 2001 to 2000 is $\frac{10{,}000}{90{,}000} \times 100\% = 111\%$, that is to say, compared with that of 2000, the general price level in 2001 rose by 11.1%. The reason why the GNP Deflator is superior to the CPI and PPI is that in statistics, GNP covers the price changes of consumer goods, capital goods, and raw materials, and thus can comprehensively reflect price changes of all goods and services within an entire society.

16.1.2 Two Forms of Price Index Fluctuation: Inflation and Deflation

The direction of change in the general price level can be divided into inflation and deflation. **Inflation** is a process in which the general price level continues to rise. First, it refers to a rise in the general price level rather than rise in the price of certain goods or services, that is to say, the price index is definitely above zero during inflation. Second, this increase must last for a certain period of time rather than a seasonal or temporary rise. For example, the general price rise of consumer goods around the Spring Festival cannot be viewed as inflation. Finally, the general price level must rise beyond a certain degree. If the price continues to rise moderately it is not inflation either, for instance the growth rate is less than 1% each year. However, as far as the extent of the general price level rise is

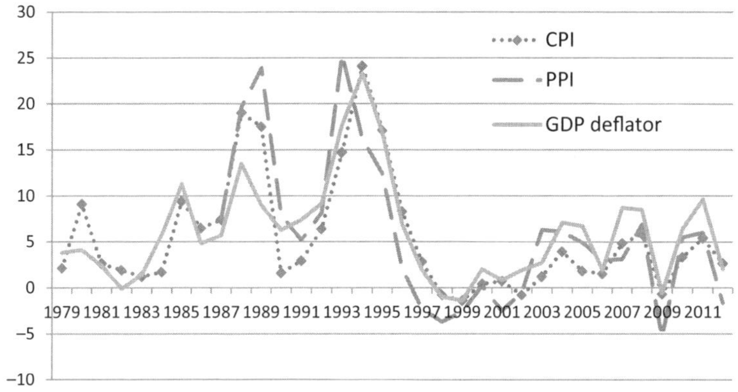

Fig. 16.1 China's GDP Deflator, CPI, and PPI (Unit: %)
Source: *China Statistical Yearbook*, China Statistics Press, and calculations of the author

concerned, there is no clear and specific limitation as to what is considered inflation. Based on the above rules, the entire world faced decades of inflation prior to the 1990s.

In contrast to inflation, **deflation** refers to a process in which prices continue to fall. Similar to inflation, deflation happens only when the general price level falls, rather than the prices of certain goods or services Furthermore, there is no deflation if the general price level falls seasonally or temporarily, for deflation is a process which lasts over a period of time (Figure 16.1).

We must distinguish changes in the general price level from changes in the price index when we judge inflation or deflation. The general price level is an absolute value, while the price index is a relative value. Inflation does not mean that the price index is rising, nor does deflation mean a fall in the price index. As the price index only reflects the direction and degree of changes in the general price level, an increase in the price index does not mean an increase in the general price level, and vice versa. For example, the CPI and PPI in China continued to fall from 1994 to 1996 but never fell below 100, which means that the general price level continued to rise but at a slower pace. Therefore, we still consider this a period of inflation. During inflation, a drop in the price index only means a decrease in the rate of inflation. Conversely, during deflation, an increase in the price index does not necessarily mean inflation, it actually means that deflation is mitigated.

16.2 Economic Effects of Price Level Fluctuations

Price fluctuations have various effects, which impact both our daily lives and the macroeconomic situation of an entire country. Generally speaking, price level fluctuations have the following effects.

16.2.1 Redistribution of Wealth

Price level fluctuations can redistribute wealth. Inflation can cause redistribution in favor of debtors and against creditors. Conversely, deflation causes redistribution in favor of creditors and against debtors. The reason why such kinds of redistribution occur lies in the fact that debtors usually calculate debt based on the nominal principal when paying off the debt.

Suppose your cousin borrows 10,000 yuan from you and guarantees that he will pay off within one year without interest. You do not charge any interest from him (you might be blamed for being unfriendly if you lend relatives money with interest). Being the good friend that you are, you would lose money from inflation. On one hand, if there is 10% inflation during this year, that is to say, the general price level is 10% higher than before, your principal is only worth 9000 yuan one year later. In this case, as a creditor and your cousin, you suffer a loss because of inflation. On the other hand, if there is 10% deflation, that is, the general price level is 10% lower, your principal will be worth 11,000 yuan one year later when your cousin repays the money.

Let us take a more specific example. Suppose that Chunlan air conditioners are priced at 2500 yuan, a Changhong TV set is priced at 3000 yuan, and a simple set of modular furniture is priced at 4500 yuan, and you can afford all of these items with exactly 10,000 yuan. If there is 10% inflation, and we simply suppose that their prices are all 10% higher, one year later you would need to pay 2750 yuan for the Chunlan air conditioner, 3300 yuan for the Changhong TV set, and 4950 yuan for the set of modular furniture, which would cost you a total of 11,000 yuan. When you purchase the above items with the 10,000 yuan your cousin pays back one year later, you will suffer a loss of 1000 yuan. Conversely, you will have a surplus of 1000 yuan if their prices are 10% lower.

Price level fluctuations can redistribute wealth, and as such, money's function of store of value is weakened during inflation. Conversely, during deflation, money's function of store of value is strengthened. During inflation, people are less willing to save as money's function of store of value is weakened. During hyperinflation, people will greatly reduce their savings and will instead rush to purchase durable goods or tangible assets as a means of storing value. To take a personal example, in 1988, I went home on summer vacation, and saw many farmers rushed to buy up salt when they got wind of price hikes, though they only had very little salt for every meal.

16.2.2 Redistribution of Income

Despite wealth redistribution, price level fluctuations can also spur income redistribution. Generally speaking, since it takes a while to adjust wages, people's income will not fluctuate simultaneously with price level fluctuations. For this reason, it exerts a great influence on our actual income when measured with physical objects.

To be more specific, if the rising rate of wages cannot catch up with that of the price level, the actual income of wage-earners will be reduced by inflation, thereby lowering their real living standards. During inflation, employers will not raise wages by the month but the price level rises day by day. As such, inflation always arouses many complaints among people. Its effect is felt more keenly by the elderly who receive fixed-amount retirement pensions and the poor who manage to get by with government support, making it even harder for them to make ends meet. As such, depression, dissatisfaction, and even crimes tend to increase during inflationary period. Conversely, if nominal wages are regulated too slowly during deflation or wages are not reduced, deflation would increase actual income and improve real living standards. Suppose that this year you earn 100 thousand yuan, just as much as last year, and the price of houses, cars, household appliances, fuel, rice, oil and salt has fallen compared with last year. If you did not purchase a house or car last year, you would be happy because your actual income has increased due to deflation.

16.2.3 Price Fluctuations and the Efficiency of Resource Allocation

Frequent price fluctuations make choices more difficult, thereby lowering the efficiency of resource allocation. In the above example, the price of Chunlan air conditioners, Changhong TV sets, and modular furniture are 10% higher or 10% lower. In fact, the prices of all kinds of goods and services do not change in accord with the general price level. Keep in mind that the general price level refers to the weighted average value of prices of goods and services of the entire society, while the price index refers to the weighted average value of changes in prices of goods and services. Actually, during inflation, the prices of some goods and services rise more, while others rise less. As such, relative prices change because of inflation. If frequent price level fluctuations distort relative prices, resource allocation will become distorted.

For instance, suppose that an enterprise intends to make an investment amounting to one billion yuan in either fridges or TV sets. A 29 inch flat screen TV set is 2500 yuan, while a fridge is 3000 yuan. With the investment of one billion yuan, the annual capacity of TV sets is 200 thousand sets, while that of fridges is 160 thousand. Hence this investment will bring the enterprise a cash flow of 500 million yuan at the unit price of 2500 yuan if investing in TV sets. If investing in fridges, the enterprise can receive a cash flow of 480 million. Holding all else equal, at the present relative price level, investment in TV sets is distinctly more cost-effective than in fridges.

Suppose again that during this investment, there is 10% inflation, but neither the price of TV sets nor that of fridges rises by 10%. Actually, TV set prices rise by 8%, while fridge prices rise by 15%, that is to say, TV set prices rise to 2700 yuan, while fridge prices rise to 3450 yuan. Suppose the annual capacity is not affected by inflation, then investment in TV sets will bring a cash flow of 540 million yuan a year and investment in fridges will bring 552 million yuan if we do not consider other costs. Obviously, investment in fridges is better than that of TV sets. Therefore, the previous favorable project has now become unfavorable because inflation has changed the relative prices between TV sets and fridges.

In addition, frequent price level fluctuations also make it more difficult for people to choose deposit methods. It will help you understand if we return to Chapter 3 which analyzes the impact of inflation on savings. In that example of saving money for a down payment on a house, at current house prices, you need to save 29,633 yuan a year given the down-payment of 100,000 yuan and the interest rate of 6%. However, if the house price rises by 8% per year during those three years, you would actually need 125,971.2 yuan for a down payment, which is 20% of the total price. Therefore, at the interest rate of 6%, you have to save 37,329 yuan per year to meet this requirement. In such a case it will not be enough if you still save 29,633 for a down payment of 100,000 yuan. You cannot move into the new house as scheduled if there are no extra funds to bridge this gap.

16.2.4 Influence on the Financial System

Large price level fluctuations also exert an influence on the financial system. As we see in Chapter 2, with an increase in the net value of debtors, the risk of moral hazard or adverse selection is reduced. During inflation, prices of various assets, especially real estate, will rise, and thus the net value of enterprises would continue to increase, lowering the possibility of moral hazard and adverse selection when banks and other lenders issue loans, which would cause an increase in loans offered by these banks. When deflation occurs, especially when the prices of assets continues to fall, the net value of debtors will decrease and the possibility of moral hazards and adverse selection will increase. In addition, since price levels fall with a corresponding fall in the price of goods and services, corporate profitability also falls. Without enough cash flows, these enterprises cannot pay off their debts acquired during inflation. Consequently, there will be a large number of non-performing loans. From 2001 to 2005, under the expectation of rising home prices and low interest rates, US banks issued a large number of subprime mortgages. From then on, however, as interest rates rose and house prices fell, many borrowers defaulted, which ultimately led to the worst financial crisis in the United States since 1933. Among the top five investment banks in Wall Street, Bear Stearns was acquired and Lehman Brothers went bankrupt.

16.2.5 Menu Cost

Finally, frequent price level fluctuations can produce menu costs. **Menu costs** are the costs incurred by changes of price tags due to price fluctuation. Menu costs cover all the costs involved in printing price tags, such as the cost of paper and

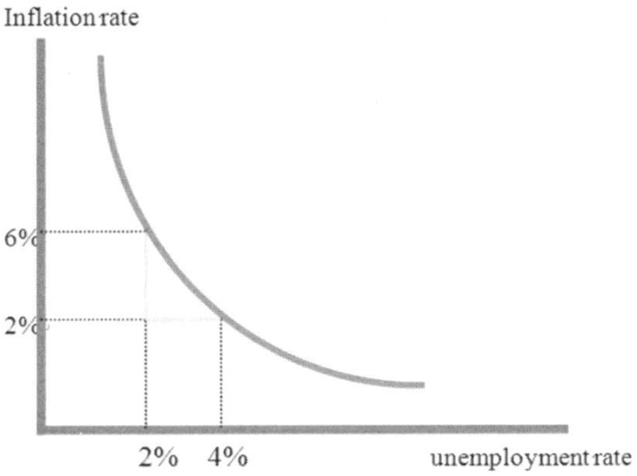

Fig. 16.2 Inverse Relationship between the Rate of Inflation and the Unemployment Rate — the Phillips Curve

printing expenses, and also include the cost of labor for refilling price tags and advertising expenses for new prices. Compared with its price, the menu cost of a single product is negligible, but the menu costs of products in an entire society amounts to a huge sum.

16.3 Price Levels and Employment: The Phillips Curve

New Zealand economist William Phillips observes from British statistical data an inverse relationship in the unemployment rate, and inflation, that is, the lower the rate of inflation, the higher the unemployment rate, and vice versa. For example, as we see in Figure 16.2, when the rate of inflation is 6%, the unemployment rate is 2%; however, when the former is 2%, the latter increases to 4%. This kind of inverse relationship between the unemployment rate and the rate of inflation is called **the Phillips Curve**. Later, some economists found that similar phenomenon exists in many other countries, thus the Phillips curve has become generalized.

Why is there an inverse relationship between the rate of inflation and the unemployment rate? The reason is that when unemployment rate falls, the supply of labor will also decrease, thus the growth rate of monetary wages will increase, which further pushes prices. Conversely, when the unemployment rate is rather high, an excessive supply of labor will lower the growth rate of monetary wages, which further decreases the rate of inflation.

The Phillips curve provides government with a menu of policy alternatives. Since it is difficult to strike a balance between stable prices and low unemployment rate, the government has to choose a tolerable inflation rate and unemployment rate. For example, suppose the government considers an inflation rate from 2% to 6% and an unemployment rate from 2% to 4%. It would then take every means to ensure that the inflation rate and unemployment rate will remain within these scopes. According to the Phillips curve, when government decreases the inflation rate, it is at the cost of rise in unemployment, which would also slow down the economic growth rate. In this way, the lost of economic growth in order to reduce 1% of inflation rate is known as the "sacrifice ratio". In other words, the sacrifice ratio is the flexibility of output decrease to inflation rate decrease.

However, only under circumstances of no expectation can the above inverse relationship between the rate of inflation and the unemployment rate exist. In fact, people are concerned with actual wages instead of nominal wages; therefore, workers would demand an increase in wages to prevent a drop in actual wages due to inflation. When inflation expectation is considered, the inverse relationship between inflation and unemployment rate would disappear. This is because a natural unemployment rate exists in economy. The **natural rate of unemployment** refers to the unemployment rate when the supply of labor is equal to market demand, or in other words, the rate of inflation is zero. Wages and prices are relatively stable when the unemployment rate is equal to the natural rate of unemployment. Inflation occurs when the unemployment rate is lower than the natural rate of employment, because under such conditions the general price level increases from a rise in wages when the demand for labor is greater than its supply. Conversely, the general price level would decrease when the unemployment rate is larger than the natural rate of employment.

Now suppose that the government considers the unemployment rate too high and intends to take measures to lower it. For convenience's sake, we assume that the present natural rate of unemployment is 4%, as seen in Figure 16.3, in which the rate of inflation is zero. However, the government tries to decrease the

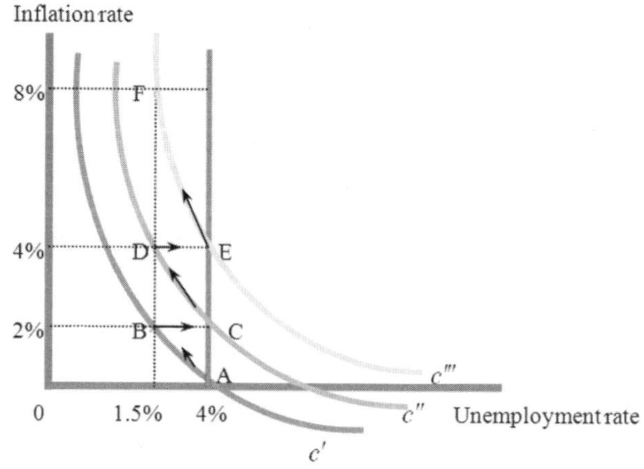

Fig. 16.3 The Phillips Curve with Expected Inflation

unemployment rate to a favorable level, for instance 2.5%, by means of regulating inflation. Suppose that the Phillips curve is c' when the original natural rate of unemployment is 4% and the rate of inflation is zero. From this curve, we can see that if the government decreases the unemployment rate from 4% to 2.5%, inflation rate will increase by 2%. Suppose that for the first time the government manages to decrease the unemployment rate to 2.5% which results in an inflation rate of 2%. In this case, people would demand that wages increase by at least 2% to prevent a drop in actual wages, which would shift the Phillips curve from c' rightward to c''. From c'', we can see that the unemployment rate corresponding to the inflation rate of 2% is still the natural rate of unemployment of 4%. Suppose that the government again intends to take measures to decrease the unemployment rate from 4% to 2.5%. The inflation rate thus would further increase to 4%, for which workers would demand a wage increase of 4%. This would again shift the Phillips curve further to the right to c'''. If the government continues to lower the unemployment rate below the natural rate of unemployment, it would only spur excessive inflation, and the unemployment rate would eventually return to the natural rate of unemployment. Therefore, when there is inflation expectation, any attempts by the government to lower the unemployment rate below the natural rate of unemployment would be in vain. For this reason, the Phillips curve is a straight, vertical line in the long run.

The vertical Phillips curve shows that the unemployment rate has nothing to do with the money supply or inflation rate. Therefore, an increase in the money supply will not decrease the unemployment rate or increase actual output; it would only lead to an increase in the general price level. This phenomenon is known as the neutrality of money.

The neutrality of money theory is based on fundamental assumptions of perfect expectations and perfect flexibility of prices and wages. Perfect expectations means that all enterprises and individuals can foresee the central bank's monetary policies and their impact on the economy, and they can adjust their own behavior based on these expectations. Since prices and wages are completely flexible, when the money supply increases, individuals will expect a rise in prices. In order to ensure that their real wages remain the same, they will demand wage growth in keeping with the price hike. In reality, however, prices and wages are not completely flexible. Prices or wages cannot change quickly in response to the external environment changes. This is what we refer to as **sticky prices** or **sticky wages**. In addition, gaining, processing, and handling information all have costs that will go into the decision-making of enterprises or individuals. Under this condition, they may not have full access to all the information available, which is known as **sticky information**. When there are sticky prices or sticky information, people cannot fully adjust to changes in monetary policy, and monetary policy may impact real economic activity. As such, there is still a degree of inverse relation between inflation (volatility) and unemployment rate (volatility).

16.4 Causes of Price Level Fluctuations: Aggregate Demand and Aggregate Supply Analysis

16.4.1 Aggregate Demand Curve and Aggregate Supply Curve

We will use the aggregate demand curve and aggregate supply curve to analyze the reasons behind price level fluctuations. The **aggregate demand curve** depicts the relationship between different general price levels and the aggregate demand. The **aggregate supply curve** depicts the relationship between different general price levels and the aggregate supply. Generally speaking, the aggregate demand curve is downward sloping from the left to the right whereas the aggregate supply curve is upward sloping from the left to the right (see Figure 16.4).

In Figure 16.4, *D* is the aggregate demand curve, and *S* is the aggregate supply curve. When the average price level is 105, aggregate demand is 600 and aggregate supply is 1100. When the average price level falls to 90, aggregate demand will increase to 1100 but aggregate supply will decrease to 500. Only when the general price level is 100 will the aggregate demand and aggregate supply be equal, in this case at 800. Only at this point will the general price level and output be in equilibrium.

Why is the aggregate demand curve downward sloping? This is because when the nominal amount of money remains the same, a drop in prices will cause an increase in real money, which will lower interest rates and lower the financing costs of capital goods, thereby spurring investment. Moreover, as interest rates fall, it will encourage current spending and a reduction in savings. For this reason, a drop in the general price level will increase consumption demand and investment demand through interest rates. Additionally, in an open economy, falling interest rates will encourage domestic capital outflows, which will lead to devaluation of local currency, increase in exports, and eventually an increase in aggregate demand.

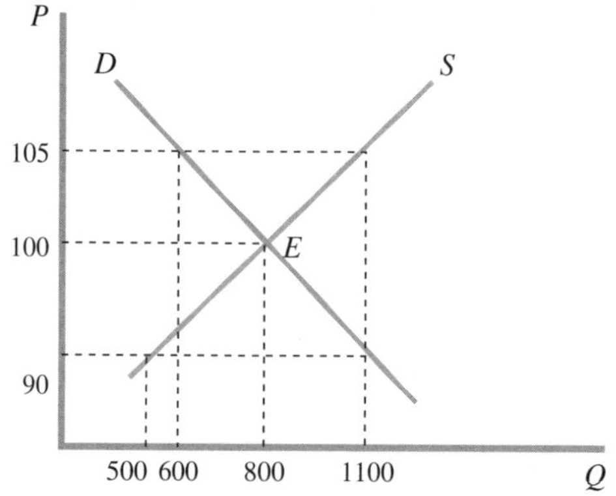

Fig. 16.4 Aggregate Demand Curve and Aggregate Supply Curve

Why then is the aggregate supply curve upward sloping? This is because the goal of enterprises is to maximize profits, and the supply of output depends on the profit earned on each and every unit. If profits increase, output will also increase, and vice versa. Since production costs are fixed in the short term, when the general price level increases, output prices will rise compared with production costs, which will cause a short-term growth in profits and thereby spur production expansion. As a result, the aggregate supply curve is upward sloping.

16.4.2 Price Level Fluctuations: Shifts in the Aggregate Demand Curve

When the aggregate demand or supply curve shifts, the general price level and total output may change. For the sake of convenience, when analyzing shifts in the aggregate demand curve, we assume that the aggregate supply curve remains the same.

In Figure 16.5, the initial aggregate demand curve and aggregate supply curve are D' and S, respectively. Their intersection determines the equilibrium price of 100. For several reasons, the aggregate demand curve shifts, whereas the aggregate supply curve remains at S. First, we suppose that the aggregate demand curve shifts right to D''. Its intersection with the aggregate supply curve determines the equilibrium price of 105. Given that the aggregate supply curve is the same, a rightward shift in the aggregate demand curve will raise the general price level. Conversely, if the aggregate demand curve shifts left, for instance, say it shifts to D''', then its intersection with the aggregate supply curve determines the equilibrium price of 95. Therefore, given the aggregate supply curve does not shift, a leftward shift in the aggregate demand curve will lower the general price level.

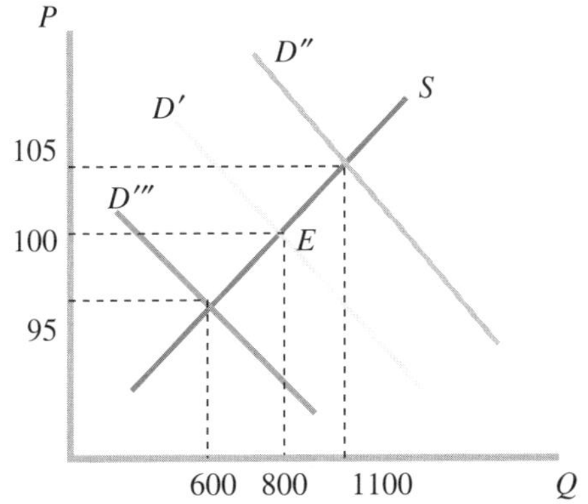

Fig. 16.5 Price Level Fluctuations: Shifts in the Aggregate Demand Curve

What causes shifts in the aggregate demand curve? The answer is whatever causes changes in aggregate demand will cause a shift in the aggregate demand curve. More specifically, money supply, government spending, net exports, propensity to consume, and the economic prospects held by enterprises will cause a shift in the aggregate demand curve. When the money supply, government spending, and net exports increase, the propensity to consume improves, and economic prospects held by enterprises are promising, the aggregate demand curve will shift to the right. Conversely, when the money supply, net exports, and government spending fall, and the prospects held by consumers and enterprises are not so promising, the aggregate demand curve will shift to the left, thereby changing the general price level.

16.4.3 Price Level Fluctuations: Shifts in the Aggregate Supply Curve

We now analyze how the aggregate supply curve impacts price levels. For the sake of convenience, when we analyze the aggregate supply curve, we suppose that the aggregate demand curve does not shift. In Figure 16.6, the initial aggregate supply curve is S, and its intersection with aggregate demand curve D determines the equilibrium price level of 100. Now suppose that the aggregate supply curve shifts left from S to S'. The intersection of S' and aggregate demand curve D determines the equilibrium price level of 105. As you can see, when the aggregate demand curve remains the same and the aggregate supply curve shifts to the left, the general price level will rise.

If the aggregate supply curve shifts right instead of left, what will happen then? If the aggregate supply curve shifts right to S'', its intersection with the aggregate demand curve D determines the equilibrium price of 90. As you can see, when the

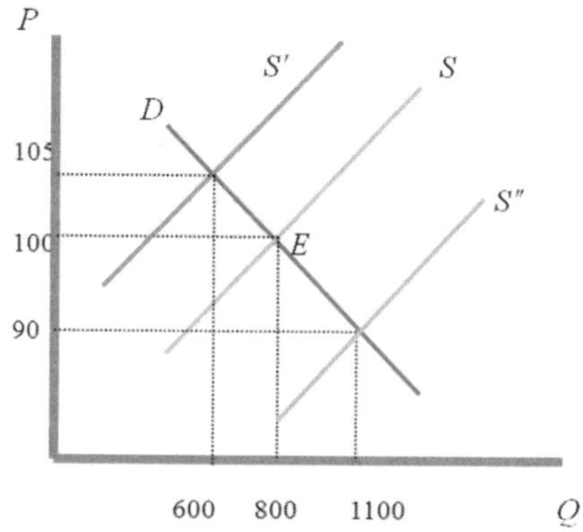

Fig. 16.6 Price Level Fluctuations: Shifts in the Aggregate Supply Curve

aggregate demand curve remains the same and the aggregate supply curve shifts to the right, the price level will fall.

What causes this shift in the aggregate supply curve? Broadly speaking, the following are the primary reasons that cause the aggregate supply curve to shift:

- Changes in Production Costs
- Expected Prices
- Technological Changes
- Institutional Changes

(a) *Changes in Production Costs*

Production costs have a major impact on corporate profitability. When production costs rise, corporate profits will fall and enterprises will cut back on investment, thereby shifting the aggregate supply curve to the left. Conversely, when production costs fall, the aggregate supply curve will shift to the right. As such, price changes of raw materials and capital goods will shift the aggregate supply curve. For instance, during the petroleum crisis, petroleum prices skyrocketed and caused an increase in the resource costs of enterprises, which shifted the aggregate supply curve to the left, thereby raising the general price level. This is exactly what happened in Western countries in the early 1970s. When costs rise and shift the aggregate supply curve to the right and then drive up inflation, we call it **cost-push inflation.**

A primary portion of production costs is wages. When the supply of labor is greater than its demand, the cost of wages will fall. Conversely, when the labor supply cannot meet demand, it will push the cost of wages up. For this reason, holding all else equal, an increase in wages will shift the aggregate supply curve to the left. Conversely, when the cost of wages falls, it will shift the aggregate supply curve to the right. In economics, when wage costs rise and shift the aggregate supply curve to the right and then drive up inflation, we call it **wage-push inflation.**

(b) *Expectations*

Expectations will also have a major impact on wages because people are concerned with their actual wages instead of the nominal wages measured by money. When nominal wages remain the same and the general price level rises, a certain amount of nominal wages will buy less goods and services. When inflation expectation exists, workers will demand higher wages to prevent actual wages from falling because of price hikes. If the enterprise gives in and raises wages, production costs will then rise, lowering the profit per unit, which will shift the aggregate supply curve to the left. The higher the expected inflation, the higher the demand for higher wages will be, which will then cause a significant leftward shift in the aggregate supply curve. In this way, the general price level will also greatly increase.

(c) *Technological Changes*

In our modern, high-tech society, a wide variety of new technologies hit the market every single day. Technological changes will improve production process and may also open up the world to new products and markets. Technological changes, which improve the production process, will enhance the productivity of enterprises, thereby enabling them to have greater output with the same raw materials and capital investment or have greater output per unit of time. For instance, Henry Ford's production line greatly improved the efficiency of automobile production. The development of information technology also improved organized production and greatly lowered management costs. Furthermore, technological changes, which develop new products or new markets, will bring a new increase in profits, thereby spurring an increase in the aggregate supply. For instance, the development of mobile communication technology and global Internet technology has greatly improved the structure of information technology. For this reason, technological changes will shift the aggregate supply curve to the right, and thereby lower prices.

(d) *Institutional Changes*

In addition to the enhanced productivity due to technological changes, effective institutional reforms will also improve the productivity, and thus shift the aggregate supply curve to the right. If an institutional reform improves the return and risk structure of economic activities or establishes a better system of performance evaluation, compensation and incentives, people will have more enthusiasm and creativity. In its transition to a market economy, China improved work incentives and constraints by market-oriented reforms and thereby largely enhanced the overall work efficiency. As such, institutional changes will shift the aggregate supply curve to the right and thus lower prices.

16.4.4 Price Level Fluctuations: The Aggregate Demand Curve and the Aggregate Supply Curve

Will a rightward shift in the aggregate demand curve always cause a rise in the price level? Will a leftward shift in the aggregate demand curve always cause a fall in the price level? It is not always a certainty. When both the aggregate demand and aggregate supply curves shift, the rise or fall of the price level depends on the relative movement of the two curves.

Figure 16.7 depicts changes to the general price level when both the aggregate demand and aggregate supply curves shift. Figure 16.7(a) depicts a rightward shift of both curves in which prices fall. In this figure, the initial aggregate demand and aggregate supply curves are D and S, respectively, and their intersection determines the equilibrium price of 100 and the equilibrium output of 800. When there is a shock to the aggregate demand and aggregate supply, both curves shift rightward to D' and S', respectively. However, the shift in the aggregate demand curve is not as

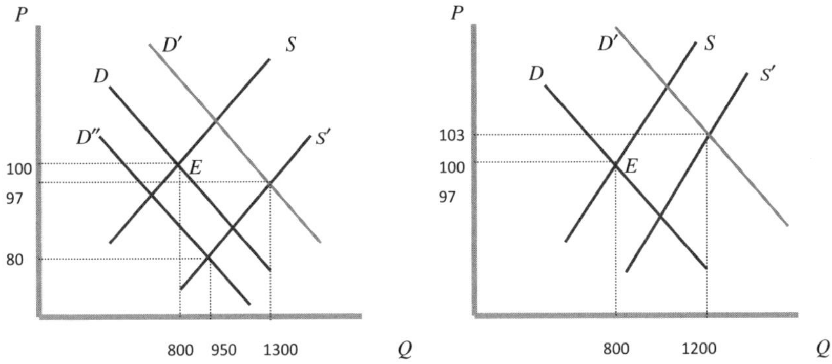

Fig. 16.7 Price Level Fluctuations: The Aggregate Demand and Aggregate Supply Curves — (a) Falling Prices and (b) Rising Prices

significant as the shift in the aggregate supply curve, so the equilibrium price falls to 97 while output rises to 1300. In Figure 16.7(a), if the aggregate supply curve shifts right while the aggregate demand curve shifts left, perhaps to D'', then at the intersection of D'' and S' the equilibrium price falls to 80 while output increases to 950.

Figure 16.7(b) depicts that when the aggregate demand and aggregate supply curves both shift right, prices will rise. In this figure, the initial aggregate demand and aggregate supply curves are D and S, respectively. Their intersection determines the equilibrium price of 100 and the equilibrium output of 800. When there is a shock to the aggregate demand and aggregate supply, both curves shift right to D' and S' respectively. However, since the aggregate demand curve shifts further right than the aggregate supply curve, the new intersection determines a higher equilibrium price level of 103 and a higher output of 1200.

With this simple tool, it is easy to analyze the deflation of recent years throughout the world and in China. In terms of aggregate demand, military spending greatly reduced after the end of the Cold War, and as such, large countries cut back on their spending. In terms of aggregate supply, the rapid development of science and technology such as information technology, various measures that governments took to break monopolies and stimulate competition as well as other factors all shifted the aggregate supply curve to the right. Due to the effects of aggregate supply changes, China maintained relatively high economic growth while prices fell continuously. From this perspective, the deflation of recent years is "good" deflation.

16.5 Policy Measures to Stabilize Prices

What economic policies can governments take to stabilize price levels? In general, governments primarily use the following stability measures: fiscal policy, monetary policy, and income and price controls.

16.5.1 Fiscal Policies

Fiscal policies can not only shift the aggregate demand curve but also shift the aggregate supply curve. Expansion of government spending will shift the aggregate demand curve to the right, thereby raising prices. Conversely, contraction of government spending will shift the aggregate demand curve to the left, thereby reducing the pressure on the price rise.

Increases in government spending may expand the fiscal deficit. Typical measures to finance for the fiscal deficit are: raising taxes, borrowing from the central bank, or issuing government bonds. Tax increases may provoke oppositions and are not very practical politically. Borrowing from the central bank is a convenient method to finance for fiscal deficit, which is often referred to as the **monetization of deficits**. If you recall for a moment the base money, you should be fairly aware that monetization of deficits will weaken the independent nature of the central bank and may shock monetary policy, and as such, countries with relatively sound macroeconomic regulations prohibit the government from borrowing or over drafting from the central bank. A better option is to issue bonds, which is known as **deficit debtization**. When people are not very willing to invest, the government can increase bond offerings, expand government spending and thereby shift the aggregate supply curve to the right, increase output, and raise prices. This is the typical macroeconomic policy to counter deflation and weak economic growth. In the several years after 1998, the Chinese government issued large-scale government bonds to stimulate economic growth. Some economists predict that such issuance greatly encourages economic growth over the years. By the end of 2008, the Chinese government launched a public spending plan worth 4 trillion yuan to prevent deflation and sustain growth. To implement the expansionary fiscal policy, the total scale of government bonds issued in 2009 reached 950 billion yuan.

Another tool of fiscal policy is to adjust tax rates. In general, governments can raise tax rates during inflationary periods and lower them during deflationary periods. However, different types of taxes have different effects on the aggregate demand. For instance, raising personal income tax rate will reduce wages, which will then shift the aggregate demand curve to the left. Conversely, if the government lowers personal income tax rates, the aggregate demand curve will shift to the right, which will push prices up. Governments can raise or lower tax rates on interest to encourage greater spending or greater savings. To contain excessive consumption demand, the government can lower tax rates on interest to raise the after-tax real interest rate on savings and encourage people to reduce current spending and increase future consumption. Conversely, if deflation occurs, the government will raise tax rates on interest to lower the after-tax real interest rate on savings, thereby encouraging people to increase current spending and reduce savings. Against the background of deflation where consumption demand hardly grew while savings rapidly grew, China started to impose a 20% tax on interest income in 1999. Beginning in 2008, China carried out structural tax cuts in response to the negative impact of the financial crisis on economic growth and prices.

Tax policies also shift the aggregate supply curve. For instance, during inflationary periods, the government will raise tax rates to prevent excessive growth of investments. In the short run, this move will reduce the investment demands of enterprises, thereby shifting the aggregate demand curve to the left. However, the reduction in corporate investment will also lower their profitability, which will undermine their enthusiasm to expand production, thereby shifting the aggregate supply curve to the left. The leftward shift of both aggregate demand curve and aggregate supply curve would lead to a higher price level at an even lower output. Therefore, we can see that the effect of tax policies on price level is quite different in the short run and in the long run.

16.5.2 Monetary Policies

Friedman once said that "inflation is always and everywhere a monetary phenomenon." That is to say, inflation is caused by excess in the money supply, and deflation then is caused by an insufficiency in the money supply. Therefore, increases or reductions in the money supply should be able to assist in stabilizing prices.

Monetary policy is a measure used by the central bank to increase or reduce the money supply or raise or lower interest rates to stabilize prices. Monetary policy adjustments will shift the aggregate demand curve. Increases in the money supply and a fall in interest rates will stimulate aggregate demand and raise prices. Conversely, a reduction in the money supply or higher interest rates will reduce aggregate demand and lower prices. During periods of inflation, then, the central bank will use contractionary monetary policy, as China's central bank used in the years prior to 1997. During periods of deflation, the government will take expansionary monetary policy and increase money supply, which was the policy of China for several years after 1997. From 2005 to the first half of 2008 and from 2010 to 2011, inflation rate rose in China and the People's Bank of China adopted contractionary monetary policy such as raising interest rates and the required reserve ratios.

16.5.3 Income and Price Controls

Income controls shift the aggregate demand curve by raising or lowering wages. Based on our previous analysis, we know that an increase in wages will shift the aggregate demand curve to the right, while an increase in the cost of labor will shift the aggregate supply curve to the left. If inflation is in fact wage-driven, restricting wage growth will lessen the rightward shift in the aggregate demand curve and may also lessen the leftward shift of the aggregate supply curve, which is conducive to price stability. Conversely, when small consumption demand results in slow economic growth and deflation, the policy will be adopted to raise people's income, the reason behind which is that when people have more money they will naturally buy more clothes or have more coffee. In several years following 1997, China raised the wages of civil servants several times to address deflation.

In addition, during periods of hyperinflation, the government can use price controls. **Price controls** are restrictions on price hikes for various goods and services. For instance, in late 1960s, the US entered a period of higher and higher inflation, and President Nixon implemented price controls for three months and achieved good results. From the middle of 1971 to the middle of 1972, prices in the US only increased by 3.2%.

However, price controls will cause shortages and thus often face severe criticism. These shortages are a form of **hidden inflation**. Because of these shortages, you will not be able to purchase certain goods even if you are satisfied with the prices. During the Nixon price-control period, the US faced this problem. Since the price of chicken was strictly controlled, the supply of chicken was clearly insufficient. During China's planned economy era, the government set prices of various goods, and shortages were common. Against this background, once price controls were loosened, the hidden inflation would reveal itself as open inflation and price hikes would continue. After Nixon loosened price controls, the rate of inflation in the US reached 11% in 1974. China's inflation during the 1980s also originated in hidden inflation.

Summary

Main indicators of general rice levels include consumer price index, producer price index, and the GNP deflator. Inflation refers to a significant and continuous increase in the general price level. Deflation is a continuous decrease in the general price level.

Price level fluctuations redistribute wealth and income, and also change relative prices, thereby distorting resource allocation. This makes it difficult for people to plan for future spending and savings, and may also add to menu costs.

There is an inverse relation between the rate of inflation and the rate of unemployment, which is represented by the Phillips curve. However, when inflation expectations exist, the inverse relation between the unemployment rate and prices disappears, and the Phillips curve will become a straight vertical line. At this time, any government policies and measures to reduce the unemployment rate will be in vain and will only increase inflation. However, when sticky prices, wages, or information exist, money is not necessarily neutral.

Shifts in the aggregate demand and aggregate supply curves cause price level fluctuations. All factors that affect the aggregate demand and supply will also affect the general price level. Changes in the amount of money supply, government spending, net exports, propensity to consume, and economic prospects held by enterprises will shift the aggregate demand curve. Labor market conditions and wage levels, expected prices, technological changes, and institutional changes will shift the aggregate supply curve.

The government can use fiscal policies, monetary policies, income policies, and price controls to stabilize prices. Fiscal policies may shift the aggregate supply curve and may also shift the aggregate demand curve. Monetary policies are primarily demand management policies. Similar to fiscal policies, income policies will shift both the aggregate supply and aggregate demand curves. Price controls may have an immediate effect to stabilize prices, but they will create further shortages and hidden inflation.

Key Terms

General Price Level; Consumer Price Index; Producer Price Index; GNP Deflator; Inflation; Deflation; Phillips Curve; Natural Rate of Unemployment; Cost-Push Inflation; Wage-Push Inflation; Price Controls; Demand-Pull Inflation; Hidden Inflation

Critical Thinking Questions

1. What is the general price level? What indicators are there to measure the general price level and what are their strengths and weaknesses?
2. What is the difference between inflation and deflation?
3. How do fluctuations in the general price level impact the economy?
4. What is the Phillips curve? Why does it exist?
5. What is the natural rate of unemployment?
6. What is the effect of inflation expectation on the Phillips curve?
7. Why does the general price level fluctuate?
8. What measures can governments take to stabilize the general price level?
9. How did the Iraq War during Bush's Presidency impact aggregate demand and general price level?
10. "Inflation is too much money chasing too small an amount of goods", or "inflation is always and everywhere a monetary phenomenon". Do these sayings make sense? Why?
11. If inflation is a monetary phenomenon, that is, inflation only occurs when prices hike continuously due to excessive increase in the money supply, then does deflation occur because of a sustained decrease in the price level due to a reduction in the money supply? Comment on China's "deflation".
12. Should we really be all that worried when prices continue to fall? Why?

Chapter 17

Exchange Rate Determination and the Exchange Rate System

Learning Objectives

After studying this chapter, you will be able to:

- Understand the economic impact of exchange rate fluctuations
- Learn how to employ purchasing power parity to analyze exchange rate determination
- Understand the theory of interest rate parity
- Understand the primary factors that impact exchange rate fluctuations
- Clearly understand the strengths and weaknesses of fixed and floating exchange rate systems
- Understand what the currency board system is
- Understand what a pegged exchange rate is
- Understand the exchange rate target zone system and its role in stabilizing exchange rates
- Understand the strengths and weaknesses of optimal currency area

When studying the foreign exchange market we have learned about the exchange rate, as well as the foreign exchange risks of the forex market and the methods to manage them. What are the main factors that determine exchange rates? Why would a speech by the Chairman of the US Federal Reserve or the Federal Reserve's adjustment of interest rate level give rise to US dollar exchange rate fluctuations in international financial markets? Before we begin the analysis of this chapter, let us first take a look at the exchange rate fluctuations of the Chinese yuan against the US dollar, and against the Japanese yen over the last 10 years.

Figure 17.1 depicts the exchange rate fluctuations of the Chinese yuan against the US dollar and against the Japanese yen beginning in 1994. We can see that from July 1994 to May 1995, the exchange rate of Chinese yuan against the US dollar had increased considerably, that is, the US dollar depreciated against the Chinese yuan. For over a year, there were small fluctuations in the Chinese yuan to US dollar

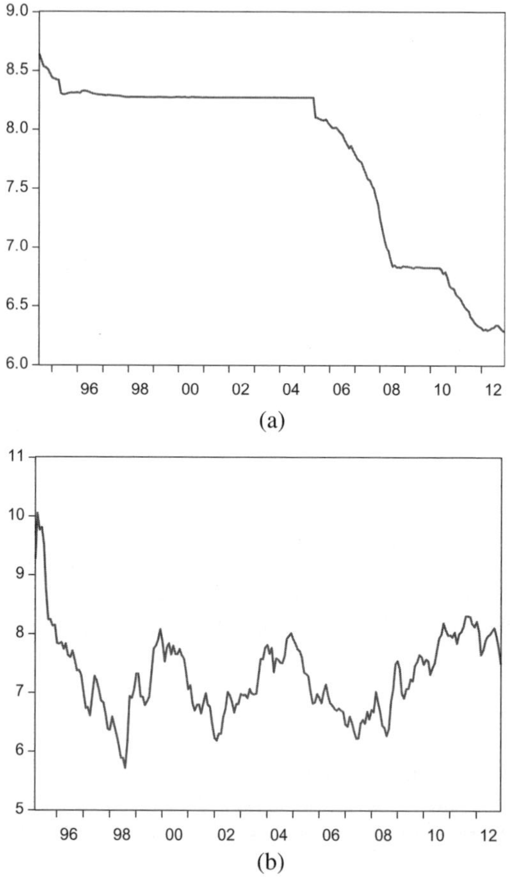

Fig. 17.1 (a) Yuan–Dollar Exchange Rate (Unit: Yuan/Dollar) and (b) Yuan–Yen Exchange Rate (Unit: Yuan/100 Yen)

exchange rate. From 1997 on, the exchange rate between the Chinese yuan and US dollar was practically a horizontal line. From July 2005, however, the exchange rate of the Chinese yuan against the US dollar had broken down, and the Chinese yuan had begun to appreciate against the US dollar until 2008. Unlike the distinct curved shape of the Chinese yuan to US dollar exchange rate, the exchange rate of the Chinese yuan against the Japanese yen has been quite volatile.

What factors led to the different shapes of the yuan–dollar exchange rate curve and the yuan–yen exchange rate curve? What kind of impact do exchange rate fluctuations have? How do we determine the exchange rate? This chapter will analyze these issues.

17.1 The Economic Impact of Exchange Rate Fluctuations

Exchange rates are an important link between domestic goods, services and financial markets, and those abroad, and therefore, exchange rate fluctuations will have a significant impact on the economy and investment activities.

17.1.1 Exchange Rates and Import and Export Activities

A decrease in the exchange rate of local currency will reduce the price of domestic goods and services sold in a foreign country, causing foreign residents to increase their demand for these goods and services. Meanwhile, demand of domestic residents for imported goods will decrease. As such, a depreciation of local currency may improve the international balance of payments. Suppose that the exchange rate of the US dollar against the Chinese yuan is 1:8, that is, 1 USD can be exchanged for 8 Chinese yuan. A T-shirt made by a domestic clothing manufacturer is worth 200 yuan. Based on the current rate of exchange, the market price of the same T-shirt in the United States should be 25 USD. Now assume that Chinese yuan has depreciated with the exchange rate dropping to 1:10. Given that the domestic price of the T-shirt does not change, the new price in the United States is now 20 dollars. In this way, the depreciated exchange rate for the Chinese yuan has made the T-shirts cheaper in the US market, which may boost sales. If the local currency instead appreciates, it will hurt exports. This is because the price of domestic goods and services in foreign markets has risen due to appreciation, which may discourage foreign demand for domestic goods.

As a result of depreciation, the domestic price of foreign goods and services will be much higher in terms of the local currency; therefore, depreciation in the local currency exchange rate may hurt imports. Suppose that the price of an IBM laptop in the United States is 2000 dollars. If we do not consider tariffs or other factors, and if the exchange rate of the US dollar against the Chinese yuan is 1:8, the price for the laptop in China would be 16,000 yuan. However, when the exchange rate depreciates to 1:10, the price will rise to 20,000 yuan. In this way, local currency devaluation may discourage the domestic demand for imports.

17.1.2 Exchange Rates and the Stability of the Financial Market

Exchange rate fluctuations may produce exchange rate risks, and as such, they may have a relatively large influence on international capital flows. Assume that you have a deposit worth 100,000 dollars. When the exchange rate of US dollars against Chinese yuan is 1:8, your deposit is worth 800,000 yuan. When the exchange rate depreciates to 1:10, which means one US dollar exchanges for 10 Chinese yuan, the US dollar deposits can be converted back to one million yuan. Conversely, when yuan appreciates, for example, the exchange rate rises to 1:6, which means one US dollar can only exchange for six yuan, the US dollar deposits can only be converted into 600,000 yuan. As such, exchange rate fluctuations are just the same as fluctuations in the stock price; they may bring you profitable gains, but they may also bring you losses on principal.

Box 17.1 Disaster of Local Currency Appreciation: Japan's Financial Losses

In September 1985, James Baker, the US Secretary of Treasury, Noboru Takeshita, the Japanese Minster of Finance, Gerhard Stoltenberg, the Minister of Finance of the former Federal Republic of Germany, Nigel Lawson, the British Minister of Finance, and Pierre Bérégovoy, the French Minister of Finance, met together with central bank governors of the five nations at the New York Plaza Hotel to address the issue of trade imbalance, and reached an agreement to lower the high US dollar exchange rate. This is the well-known Plaza Accord. After Plaza Accord, the yen–dollar exchange rate increased significantly.

At the beginning of the 1980s, due to a wide gap between the interest rates of the two countries, Japanese institutional investors had bought huge US Treasury Bonds with a high interest rate. All of these investments were settled in US dollars. As a result, the Plaza Accord brought a foreign exchange loss to net foreign assets of Japan, amounting to approximately 3.5 trillion yen. These losses damaged life insurance investors, other institutional investors, and individual investors. Moreover, the Japanese exporters had also been investing their earnings in US dollar bonds. Upon maturity of the bonds, they found that the Japanese yen appreciated and the dollar depreciated, and the amount they received had reduced by 60% compared to what they had spent to purchase those bonds.

Japanese economists were quite angry: of the three rounds of capital exports, in the British Victorian era, British pound export was denominated in sterling; after World War II, US capital export was denominated in US dollars; yet since the 1970s, Japanese capital export had not been denominated in Japanese yen. In this way, this sharp appreciation of the Japanese yen against the dollar threw Japan into dire straits!

— Motoyoshi Yoshikawa, 2000 (ed.) *Japan's Financial Losses*
Beijing: China Youth Press

From this simple example, we can see that when local currency depreciates, holding US dollars is favorable. Conversely, when local currency tends to appreciate, holding US dollar deposits is not a good choice, because exchange rate fluctuations will swallow your original principal. Because of this, when the local currency is expected to depreciate against the dollar, many people will exchange the local currency into dollars, and vice versa. Thus, when people adjust their expectations on the exchange rate of local currency and trade on the foreign exchange market in order to avoid the risks of exchange rate fluctuation or to obtain arbitrage, it may increase those fluctuations. In addition, when expecting depreciation or further depreciation of local currency, people will sell their local currency denominated assets and purchase assets in foreign currencies, which in turn will lead to remarkable price fall in national stock and bond markets, thereby further increasing the demand for foreign exchange and further depreciating local currency. In this way, the local currency exchange rate, the domestic bond market and the domestic stock market will exhibit a "three-fold decline".

17.1.3 Exchange Rates and the Domestic Economy

Exchange rate fluctuations may impact domestic economic growth, employment and price levels. Since local currency depreciation may stimulate the growth of exports, it would expand aggregate demand. If there are enough idle resources, an expansion in aggregate demand will boost economic growth and increase domestic employment. However, if the country has already reached full employment, the increase in net exports caused by the depreciation of local currency will not expand employment opportunities, and will only lead to a high rate of inflation. Conversely, when local currency appreciates, aggregate demand and employment will fall.

In addition, exchange rate fluctuations will also affect the adjustment of the industrial structure. For example, if local currency depreciates, it will stimulate foreign demand for domestic products, which in turn will raise the local currency denominated prices of exported goods. If the structure of domestic demand remains the same, local currency depreciation will raise local currency denominated prices of exported goods, generating more profits for production of exported goods. This will induce further domestic production of exported goods and increase the country's openness to the outside world. As you can see, exchange rate fluctuations have a profound impact on asset allocation.

17.2 Exchange Rate Determination

In the above analysis, we took a look at the economic impact of exchange rate fluctuations. But why do exchange rates fluctuate?

17.2.1 The Law of One Price and the Theory of Purchasing Power Parity

The differences in the price levels and the rates of inflation in two countries have a significant impact on their exchange rates. In order to analyze the role of price levels in determining the exchange rate, we must first understand the law of one price. The **law of one price** states that, under the conditions of free trade, the same goods should have the same price denominated in the same currency, regardless of where around the world they were produced. Suppose that an IBM laptop in the United States sells for 2000 dollars, while China's Lenovo Zhaoyang laptop sells for 16,500 yuan. In order to set the price for a single IBM laptop in China at 16,500 yuan, the exchange rate of US dollars against Chinese yuan should be 8.25, which means one US dollar can be exchanged for 8.25 yuan.

If the same type of product has a different price in different parts of the world in the same currency, there is room for international arbitrage that would equalize the prices of this product. Suppose that the same Lenovo Zhaoyang laptop is worth 16,500 yuan in China, but the exchange rate deviates from the law of one price parity, and the US dollar to Chinese yuan exchange rate is 1:8.500. As such, the same IBM laptop would cost 17,000 yuan in China, 500 yuan more than the Lenovo Zhaoyang laptop. On the other hand, the Lenovo Zhaoyang laptop would only cost 1941.18 dollars, which is cheaper than the IBM, which worth 2000 dollars. In this way, demand for the IBM laptop will fall, and the demand for the Zhaoyang laptop would increase, which would ultimately equalize the price in one currency of both laptops.

Therefore, in accordance with the one price law, the exchange rate between the two currencies depends on the ratio between prices of similar goods, which is the **theory of absolute purchasing power parity**.

A simple and mechanical application of purchasing power parity is the Big Mac index. The Big Mac is a type of hamburger produced by McDonald's that can be bought in nearly all corners of the world. The Big Mac index assumes that if the price of the hamburger was denominated in a single currency, it should be the same at each and every location. In other words, it establishes a purchasing power parity. If Big Macs in some countries are cheaper than those in the United States, then those currencies are undervalued relative to the dollar, and vice versa. The Big Mac purchasing power parity exchange rate between the two countries is the local price of a Big Mac in one country divided by its local price in the other country. If this rate is lower than the actual exchange rate, it indicates that the currency of the former country is undervalued. Conversely, if this rate is higher, then it indicates that the currency of the former country is overvalued.

In addition, differences in their rates of inflation will also cause fluctuations in the exchange rate. Suppose that the rate of inflation in the United States is 5%, while China's inflation is at 8%. After inflation, the IBM laptop costs 2100 dollars in the United States, while the Lenovo Zhaoyang laptop sells for 17,820 yuan in China. In the event of inflation to different degree in the two countries, and in accordance with the law of one price the US dollar to Chinese yuan exchange rates has become 1:8.4857 compared to the original 1:8.25, the yuan would have devalued by 2.85%. Generally speaking, if both countries suffer from inflation, the currency of the country with a higher rate of inflation will depreciate, while the currency of the country with a lower rate of inflation will appreciate. The notion that the fluctuations of the exchange rate between two countries depend on differences in inflation rate of the two countries is the **theory of relative purchasing power parity**.

However, the theory of purchasing power parity (PPP) does not fully explain the exchange rate between the two currencies. Consider for a moment all of the thousands of different products in each and every country, you can imagine the millions of variations in the ratio of prices in different currencies. Furthermore, the conditions for the PPP theory are similar goods with similar qualities, without the limitations of customs tariffs and trade barriers. However, is Lenovo's Zhaoyang laptop of the exact same quality of the IBM laptop? Because of restrictions such as tariffs and trade barriers, the international flow of goods is not always free, and thus the law of one price is difficult to hold. Therefore, the PPP theory is oversimplified.

17.2.2 Supply and Demand Analysis of Exchange Rate Determination

Like any product market, changes in market supply and demand are fundamental to determine price. Exchange rates are not the exception, and exchange rate of a currency is determined by its demand and supply. When the demand for foreign currency decreases, and the demand for local currency increases, local currency will appreciate. Conversely, when the demand for foreign currency increases and the demand for local currency decreases, the local currency will depreciate. Therefore, any factors that impact the supply and demand of foreign currencies will affect exchange rates and their volatility. There are mainly three types of factors affecting foreign exchange supply and demand:

- Foreign exchange supply and demand from imports and exports. The factors that affect the import and export of goods and services will affect the exchange rate. We will name these factors real factors.
- Foreign exchange supply and demand from international financing and investment. The factors that affect international capital flows will also affect exchange rates. We will call them financial factors.
- Foreign exchange supply and demand as a result of speculation in foreign exchange market. We will call the factors that affect foreign exchange speculation and exchange rates the expectation factors.

(a) *Real Factors*

The real factors that determine and affect exchange rates include:

- Relative price levels
- National income and economic growth

- Technology and productivity
- Tariffs and quotas

(i) *Relative price*: Price is the primary mechanism behind the supply and demand of goods and services. When the price of domestic goods and services increases in relation to similar foreign goods and services, the demand for domestic goods and services will decrease, and the relative demand for foreign goods will increase, thereby increasing the demand for imports and increasing the demand for foreign exchange. On the other hand, when the relative price of domestic products increases, the price competitiveness of domestic products in the international market will also fall, which will curb exports, and foreign exchange earnings and supply of foreign currency will decrease accordingly. In this way, an increase in the relative price of domestic goods and services will increase the demand for foreign exchange, reduce the supply of foreign currency, and as such, foreign currency will have a tendency to appreciate while local currency depreciates.

(ii) *Technology and Productivity*: If domestic technology is advanced and the productivity of labor is relatively high, unit inputs for goods and services produced by domestic enterprises will be relatively low. In this way, domestic enterprises can sell their goods and services at a lower price while still earning profits. Since the price of domestic goods and services fall, their competitiveness on the international market will increase with a corresponding increase in exports leading to an increase in the foreign demand for domestic currency. Due to the growth in exports, the supply of foreign currency will also increase. As a result of these effects, the price of local currency will appreciate. Conversely, if domestic technology falls behind and the productivity of labor is low, local currency will depreciate.

(iii) *Tariffs and trade barriers*: International trade is not completely free. Tariffs and trade barriers are the two major policies and measures that impede the international free trade. There are tariffs between the member states of the World Trade Organization (WTO). Why does a Ford car only sell for a little over 20,000 dollars in the United States, when the same car will cost at least 300,000 yuan in China? The main reason is that a higher tariff is imposed on Chinese automobile imports. As a result of the tariff, prices of the imported products increase, and thus demand for these products falls. Therefore, tariffs reduce the domestic demand for foreign currency, and local currency tends to appreciate. Conversely, if the government lowers tariffs, the domestic competitiveness of foreign products will be enhanced. Then, demand for imported products will increase, as will the demand for foreign currency. Therefore, foreign currency will tend to appreciate, whereas local currency will depreciate. Similarly, when the government imposes a quota, the demand for foreign currency will reduce, which will raise the relative exchange rate for local currency. If the domestic government lifts the quota, the potential demand for foreign goods will be met more easily, and as a result, foreign exchange spending will increase and local currency will tend to depreciate.

(b) *Financial Factors: Interest Rate Differences*

Apart from the current account of the international balance of payments, capital flows on the international financial market also have a major impact on the supply and demand of foreign currency. The primary factor that impacts international capital flows is the return on similar assets in two countries. We have often said that, when holding all else equal, people will invest in assets with a higher return. Portfolio choices may also be on an international scale. Unlike local currency denominated assets, when investing in foreign assets, their return depends not only on their own interest rates or asset prices, but also on the volatility of exchange rate.

For the sake of convenience, we shall consider the following situation. The interest rate of one-year US dollar deposits is 5%, and that of one-year yuan deposits is only 3%, which results in room for arbitrage. Assume that you have deposits of 800,000 yuan, and the US dollar to Chinese yuan exchange rate is 1:8. Then, you could convert this deposit into 100,000 dollars. Because there is room for arbitrage, you can convert your deposit of 800,000 yuan into 100,000 USD, and have one-year dollar deposit. Based on the 5% interest rate for deposits in US dollars, your total principal and interest after one year would be:

$$100 \times (1 + 5\%) = 105 \text{ (1000 USD)}.$$

If the US dollar to Chinese yuan exchange rate does not change over the year, your total principal with interest denominated in yuan would be:

$$105 \times 8 = 840 \text{ (1000 yuan)}.$$

If you chose yuan deposit instead of dollars, then, your total principal and interest would be:

$$800 \times (1 + 3\%) = 824 \text{ (1000 yuan)}.$$

As you can see, if you chose to deposit yuan, you would earn 16,000 yuan less in interest. Since there is an opportunity for arbitrage, as long as capital flows freely, a large amount of US dollars will flow in, and ultimately the interest rates for deposits in dollars and yuan will be equal. Of course, this difference in returns assumes that the exchange rate of US dollars against Chinese yuan does not fluctuate. As we mentioned in Chapter 11, during arbitrage, when the exchange rate of two currencies fluctuates, the possible gains from arbitrage are sometimes much higher, sometimes much lower, and these fluctuations may even bring losses.

What sort of impact does arbitrage have on exchange rates? We now make the following general assumptions: i_c is the one-year interest rate for yuan deposit, i_d is the one-year interest rate for US dollars deposit, e_0 is the current Chinese yuan to US dollar exchange rate (direct quotation), and e_1 is the exchange rate after one year. We also assume that you have one yuan.

One year after you deposit this one yuan, you will earn a total of:

$$1 \times (1 + i_c) = 1 + i_c. \tag{17.1}$$

If you deposit in dollars instead of yuan, you would go through the following steps:

Step 1: Exchange your one yuan into dollars based on the exchange rate e_0, the total amount of dollars you could exchange for would be: $\frac{1}{e_0}$ (ignoring exchange fees).

Step 2: Deposit the dollars that you received. After one year, your total principal with interest in US dollars would be:

$$\frac{1}{e_0} \times (1 + i_d)_0.$$

Step 3: After one year, you would exchange your principal and interest for yuan based on the exchange rate of e_1, totaling:

$$\frac{1}{e_0} \times (1 + i_d) \times e_1 = \frac{e_1}{e_0}(1 + i_d). \tag{17.2}$$

When capital flows freely, the interest rates for both deposits will be equal:

$$1 + i_c = \frac{e_1}{e_0}(1 + i_d). \tag{17.3}$$

Simplifying the above equation, we would get:

$$\frac{e_1}{e_0} = \frac{1 + i_c}{1 + i_d}. \tag{17.4}$$

Since we already know e_0, i_c, and i_d in advance, if there is any difference between the interest rates for yuan and dollar deposits, the exchange rate will fluctuate over the year. In which direction will it fluctuate? If the interest rate for yuan deposits is higher than that of dollar deposits, as in $i_c > i_d$, then: $\frac{e_1}{e_0} = \frac{1+i_c}{1+i_d} > 1 \Rightarrow e_1 > e_0$. This indicates that the forward exchange rate will increase after one year, and yuan will depreciate.

Conversely, if the current interest rate for yuan deposits is lower than that of dollar deposits, as in $i_c < i_d$, then: $\frac{e_1}{e_0} = \frac{1+i_c}{1+i_d} < 1 \Rightarrow e_1 < e_0$. This indicates that the forward exchange rate will decrease after one year, and yuan will appreciate.

How much would the exchange rate rise (fall) after one year when there is a difference in the interest rates between yuan and dollar deposits?

If we subtract 1 from both sides of $\frac{e_1}{e_0} = \frac{1+i_c}{1+i_d}$, we shall have:

$$\frac{e_1 - e_0}{e_0} = \frac{1 + i_c - 1 - i_d}{1 + i_d} = \frac{i_c - i_d}{1 + i_d}. \tag{17.5}$$

Suppose the increase (decrease) rate of the exchange rate is: $\frac{e_1 - e_0}{e_0} = \rho$.

Thus:

$$\rho + \rho \cdot i_d = i_c - i_d. \tag{17.6}$$

Since i_d and ρ are percentages, $\rho \cdot i_d$ is small enough that it is negligible, so that we have:

$$\rho = i_c - i_d. \tag{17.7}$$

This is the **interest rate parity** formula. This shows that when domestic interest rates are higher than foreign interest rates, forward exchange rates will be at a premium and yuan will depreciate. Conversely, when domestic interest rates are lower than foreign interest rates, forward rate will be at a discount, and yuan will appreciate. Moreover, the forward premium (discount) is equal to the difference in interest rates.

Why will the forward exchange rate be at a premium or a discount when domestic and foreign interest rates are different? This is because arbitragers tend to combine arbitrage with swaps in order to avoid the risks of exchange rate fluctuation. In this case, since capital will flow from countries with a relatively low return to those with a relatively high return, there will be an increasing demand on the spot market for currency of those countries with a higher return, and the exchange rate of that currency on the spot exchange market will rise. On the other hand, arbitragers will sell off the currency of the country with a higher return on the forward market; therefore, the exchange rate of that currency will fall while that of the currency with a lower return will appreciate on the forward market.

The shortcomings of the interest rate parity theory are obvious. When there is a large difference between yuan and dollar interest rates, will people in China be able to convert the yuan that they hold into dollars and deposit them in the United States or purchase US treasury bonds? To date, this is obviously impossible, because the Chinese yuan is not a freely convertible currency. Foreign exchange and capital controls prevent free flows of currency and capital, and thus, interest rate parities are not necessarily established. Second, even if currency is freely convertible and capital can flow freely, the interest rate parity theory does not take into account transaction costs. If you convert your yuan into dollars and remit them to the US to deposit in a bank or buy US Treasury bonds, there will be related costs, such as bank charges and remittance fees. Because of these transaction costs, the forward rate premium or discount may not be exactly equal to the difference in interest rates.

(c) *Expectations*

Exchange rate expectations also have a significant impact on the exchange rates. When people hold foreign currency as a form of asset, exchange rate fluctuations would be similar to domestic stock or bond price fluctuations, which will generate capital gain or loss for the holders. When you expect a future rise in the price of a certain stock, you may purchase a great deal of this stock. Conversely, if you expect that the price of the stock you hold will fall, you will likely sell it now in order to avoid potential losses. This is the same in the foreign exchange market. When investors expect that the exchange rate of US dollar against the Japanese yen will rise, that is, the yen will depreciate, they will sell their yen and purchase dollars prior to the depreciation. These expected changes give rise to exchange rate fluctuations.

There are many factors that affect our expectations. Our judgments of the future are based on basic economic factors, which include: national income and economic growth, economic structure, the performance of the financial sector, and so on. If the unemployment rate announced by the United States is very high, foreign exchange investors may expect that the US Federal Reserve will reduce interest rates to stimulate investment and increase employment. These interest rate cuts will change the return on US dollar assets relative to that on assets in other countries, thereby devaluing the dollar. When a country's economic structure and economic performance is not good, investors will expect that this country's currency will inevitably depreciate. As such, they will sell off its currency. This is precisely why Soros attacked Southeast Asian currencies and led to the Asian financial crisis of 1997. There is the Chinese saying goes "flies never visit an egg that has no crack"; which explains how people form their exchange rate expectations.

17.3 Exchange Rate System

Now, let us go back to the question at the beginning of the chapter: Why was the Chinese yuan to US dollar exchange rate curve a horizontal line from 1997 to July 2005? Afterwards, why was there no such relationship between the two currencies? Why does the Chinese yuan to Japanese yen exchange rate fluctuate? These questions are related to exchange rate systems.

This so-called **exchange-rate system** refers to a series of arrangements or provisions made by the monetary authorities of one country with respect to the basic mode of changes in the exchange rates of local currency against foreign currencies. Generally speaking, the exchange rate system is divided into fixed exchange rate system and floating exchange rate system in accordance with the provisions concerning the exchange rate volatility.

17.3.1 Fixed Exchange Rate System and Floating Exchange Rate System

Under a **fixed exchange rate system**, the real exchange rate can only fluctuate within a very narrow range due to the restriction of parity. For example, the authorities stipulate that the exchange rate of local currency against other currencies should not fluctuate by more than 1%. Under a **floating exchange rate system**, the prevailing exchange rates are not subject to parity but vary with the supply and demand in the foreign exchange market. Floating exchange rate system can also be divided into free floating and managed floating. **Free floating** is an exchange rate system in which the monetary authority has no intervention in the foreign exchange market but lets exchange rates float freely with changes in the market supply and demand. As sharp volatility of exchange rate will have a significant impact on the economy, many countries do not have a free floating exchange rate system and rather opt for a **managed floating exchange rate system**, under which the monetary authorities intervene in the foreign exchange market to make exchange rates float in a desirable direction.

Nowadays, fewer countries use the fixed exchange rate system, while more tend to choose the floating exchange rate system. Compared to the fixed exchange rate system, the floating exchange rate system has the following advantages:

First of all, under the floating exchange rate system, countries can automatically achieve balance of international payments without having to sacrifice domestic economy, thereby strengthening independence of national monetary policy. Under the fixed exchange rate system, authorities are obliged to maintain the exchange rates of the national currency at a fixed level. In this way, domestic economic goals are, to a large extent, subject to the international balance of payments. For instance, when there is a large surplus, the domestic currency exchange rate will tend to rise. In order to prevent this rise, authorities will increase the supply of local currency so as to reduce the pressure to appreciate. However, an increase in the domestic money supply will lead to inflation. Conversely, if domestic economy overheats and leads to hyperinflation, the central bank should tighten the money supply and raise interest rates to stabilize the domestic economy. This, however, will cause appreciation of local currency and a deficit in the international balance of payments. For this reason, under a fixed exchange rate system the central bank's monetary policy is faced with **conflict of internal and external equilibrium**. Under a floating exchange rate system, the central bank is not obliged to hold exchange rates at a fixed level. Rather, the exchange rate fluctuates with changes in supply and demand in the forex market. In this way, any imbalances on the balance of payments can be eliminated through exchange rate fluctuations. Fiscal and monetary policies can then focus on national economic goals.

Second, floating exchange rate system can avoid the international spread of inflation. Under a fixed exchange rate system, inflation spreads rapidly across countries. There are two channels by which this happens. First, because the exchange rate remains the same, inflation in foreign countries will directly result in a proportional rise in the price of domestic goods and services. For example, assume that the Chinese yuan to US dollar exchange rate is 1:8. When prices rise in the United States by 5%, the price of imported products from the United States to China, denominated in Chinese yuan, will also increase by 5%. Second, inflation in foreign countries will bring an increase in the domestic money supply through foreign exchange reserves, thereby indirectly raising the rate of domestic inflation. This is because when other countries experience inflation and there is no domestic inflation, domestic exports will increase and imports will decrease, which results in a balance of payments surplus. Under a fixed exchange rate system, such a surplus will increase the central bank's foreign exchange reserves, thereby increasing domestic supply of base currency (recall Chapter 13), and then domestic money supply will increase due to the money multiplier effects, which leads to inflation. Under a floating exchange rate system, inflation in foreign countries will not affect a country's foreign exchange reserves, and only through the relative PPP will the exchange rate of local currency rise, offsetting the impact of inflation abroad on domestic price through imports and exports.

Third, there is no need of large amount of foreign exchange reserves under the floating exchange rate system, and free trade and efficiency of resource allocation are improved. Under the floating exchange rate system, a country is not obligated to set exchange rates at a fixed level, which means that there would be no need to have a large amount of foreign exchange reserves as required under the fixed exchange rate system to intervene in the foreign exchange market. These savings from foreign exchange reserves can be used to import more capital goods and to underpin economic development and employment. At the same time, the floating exchange rate system helps to balance the international payments, and as such, the country can avoid the trade control measures that are needed under the fixed exchange rate system for the purpose of balancing international payments, thereby preventing distortions in resource allocation and enhancing economic efficiency.

Finally, because the balance of payments can be adjusted quickly and automatically under the floating exchange rate system, there will not be any cumulative, long-term deficit or surplus, which thus avoids significant international financial panic. In this sense, the floating exchange rate system ensures the stability of the foreign exchange market and the international monetary system. Under the fixed exchange rate system, the official exchange rate does not fluctuate with changes in the supply and demand on the foreign exchange market, and more importantly, official exchange rates often over-estimate local currency, thus the fixed exchange rate itself is not stable. If the currency is largely overvalued, it will depreciate sharply in response to external shocks, which may have a devastating blow to enterprises and financial institutions in the country. Fixed exchange rate systems are often very fragile for the following two reasons. First, the fixed exchange rate provides a stable value of currency, which indicates low risk in the view of foreign investors and thereby encourages capital inflows. While capital inflows will encourage economic growth for a given period, they will also cause excessive lending. Rapid increase of loans may result in huge loan losses, deterioration of banks' balance sheets, and potential financial crisis. In contrast, exchange rate fluctuations under the floating exchange rate system make private enterprises, banks and governments aware of risks in external debts. Moreover, such fluctuations can also provide policy makers with an early warning signal that policies must be adjusted to prevent potential financial crises. Second, compared with the floating exchange rate system, the fixed exchange rate system is more vulnerable to speculative shocks, which may lead to a collapse of the system. When faced with speculative shocks, governments will abandon their fixed exchange rate system, because very few central banks adhere to a target exchange rate regardless of other factors. In order to crack down on foreign exchange speculation, monetary authorities have to substantially raise the level of interest rates, which will adversely affect domestic investment, employment, government deficit, and income distribution. Although the government is committed to maintaining the stability of exchange rates regardless of domestic employment and investment, this commitment is not credible, and thus the fixed exchange rate system is very vulnerable to speculative shocks.

Of course, it has also been suggested that the above advantages of the floating exchange rate system are also its shortcomings.

First of all, the floating exchange rate system brings great uncertainty to international trade and investment. Exporters cannot determine future changes to exchange rate, and therefore tend to stick to the domestic market. In terms of trade, when prices and revenue for imports and exports are uncertain, the costs of trade will increase even with the use of forward transactions. Moreover, not all foreign exchange risks can be eliminated through foreign exchange forward transactions. For instance, it could hardly avoid the exchange rate risk arising in the period from quotation to contract execution in imports and exports or avoid the exchange rate risks of long-term external debts. Similarly, in terms of investment, changes in the exchange rate may also bring capital losses to investors that will offset their gains. In this way, floating exchange rate systems could hinder international trade and investment.

Second, it is worth noting that under the floating exchange rate system, countries will often trend towards inflation. Why? First, fixed exchange rate system imposes larger pressure on governments with fiscal surplus, and floating rate will undermine the "price discipline" of these countries. Second, under the floating exchange rate system, a decline in the exchange rate will inevitably result in higher prices of imported goods, which will directly or indirectly lead to rise in domestic price levels and may form a vicious cycle of "increase in price, decline in the exchange rate". When the exchange rate rises, domestic prices cannot be lowered because of the ratchet effect. Experience has shown that overvaluing a currency to reduce domestic inflation has often had disappointing results. For this reason, the floating exchange rate system is prone to cause inflation.

Finally, floating exchange rate has a negative effect on the allocation of domestic resources. This means that when the exchange rate drops significantly, the country's resources will flow to the export sector and import substitution sector whose international competitiveness is enhanced as a result of the exchange rate decrease. However, once the rate goes up, these resources will be in excess and will flow out again. Thus, exchange rate fluctuations will distort resource allocation.

17.3.2 Pegged Exchange Rates, Currency Boards and Exchange Rate Target Zones

On the basis of fixed exchange rates and floating exchange rates, there are three special exchange rate systems:

- Pegged exchange rate system
- Currency board system
- Exchange rate target zone system

(a) *Pegged Exchange Rate Systems*

The **pegged exchange rate system** is the exchange rate system adopted by a country whereby a fixed exchange rate is maintained between its local currency and other key currencies, while the exchange rate between its currency and non-key currencies is allowed to fluctuate relative to that between key currencies and non-key currencies. In several years following 1997, the exchange rate of the Chinese yuan against the US dollar was nearly horizontal because the yuan was in fact pegged to the US dollar. So, no matter what happened, the exchange rate of the Chinese yuan against the US dollar was essentially constant. However, if the exchange rate of the US dollar against the Japanese yen fluctuates, the exchange rate of the Chinese yuan against the Japanese yen would also fluctuate. Suppose the exchange rate of the US dollar against the Chinese yuan was pegged at 1:8.2500, and the exchange rate of the US dollar against Japanese yen was 1:82.5, that is, 1 dollar could be exchanged for 82.5 yen, then the exchange rate of Chinese yuan against Japanese yen would be 1:10, that is, 1 yuan can be exchanged for 10 yen. If, however, the yen–dollar exchange rate depreciates to 1:98.5, that is, 1 dollar exchanges for 98.5 yen, the yen–yuan exchange rate would also depreciate accordingly to 12:1, namely, 1 yuan can exchange for 12 yen. This is why we see frequent fluctuations of the yuan–yen exchange rate while almost constant exchange rate of yuan against US dollar.

We have already seen that in the pegged exchange rate system, the exchange rate of local currency against the pegged key currency is fixed, and while the exchange rate of local currency against non-key-currencies constantly fluctuates. However, why is such a system not a floating exchange rate system? Why is it considered a fixed exchange rate system? This is because, for example, although the exchange rate of the Chinese yuan against the Japanese yen fluctuates, it is not directly due to changes in the supply and demand of foreign exchange, instead, it is caused by dollar–yen exchange rate fluctuations. Under a pegged exchange rate system, even if the demand and supply relationship between yuan and the yen has changed, which requires an adjustment to the exchange rate, the yuan–yen exchange rate will not change unless changes occur to the exchange rate of the US dollar against the Japanese yen.

(b) *Currency Board System*

The **currency board system** is an exchange rate system in which the law explicitly stipulates that local currency maintains a fixed exchange rate with the convertible currency of another country, and specially restrains the issue of banknotes to guarantee the performance of such a legal obligation. This system usually requires that the currency issue must be backed by a certain amount of foreign currency as a reserve, and this reserve should be maintained in the currency circulation. For example, Hong Kong implements the currency board system, and it requires note-issuing banks (HSBC, Standard Chartered Bank, and Bank of China) to place equivalent US dollars with the Exchange Fund at the fixed exchange rate of 1 US dollar to 7.8 HK dollar each time when they issue banknotes, which will then be converted to debt obligations in HK dollar and will serve as the required reserve for issuing banknotes.

The currency board system is a special kind of fixed exchange rate system. It differs from an ordinary fixed exchange rate system in that: First of all, the exchange rate is subject to stringent legal provisions. These legal provisions are open to the public, and as such, it is extremely difficult for the government to change the exchange rate. If the government changes the rate, it will inevitably harm its credibility. Second, there are legal restrictions as to the source of reserve currency. The currency board can issue banknotes only when it holds foreign currency as reserves, which is the "backing rule". Because of this rule, the currency board is strictly limited in terms of budget deficit financing. According to legal provisions, banks that issue banknotes must have a proportionate amount of foreign currency. If these banks do not have sufficient foreign exchange reserves, it will be extremely difficult for the government to borrow money from these issuing banks to deal with fiscal deficits.

The primary benefit of a currency board system is that it gives high credibility to monetary policy. The effects of various policies developed by the government to a large extent depend on its long-term reputation in people's mind. When the government adopts the currency board system and provides effective support, monetary authorities and government deficit financing are subject to stringent restrictions, so the public is given a clear idea of the government's intentions, allowing them to adjust their expectations and making the government policies function. In countries with high inflation where the government policies could hardly work, the currency board system will have a profound effect and may rebuild the government's good reputation. However, the currency board system can also lead to rigid nominal exchange rate and fragile financial systems, which will sacrifice some of the functions of the central bank. For example, under the system, the currency issue is no longer subject to the desires of the monetary authority or the actual economic situation, but instead depends on the amount of available foreign exchange reserves. Therefore, the monetary authorities have lost their independence of currency issues and the role of lender of last resort.

(c) *Exchange Rate Target Zone System*

An **exchange rate target zone system** is an exchange rate system of restraining exchange rate fluctuation within a specified range. Under the system, the authorities, first of all, determine the central exchange rate and then determine the range of rate fluctuations. For example, exchange rate can only fluctuate up or down 5% of the central rate.

Exchange rate target zone system is unlike other exchange rate systems. Compared with the managed floating exchange rate system, there are two differences. First, the authorities set a specific range of rate fluctuations in advance. Under a managed floating exchange rate system, the government does not identify the interval of exchange rate fluctuations in advance, but if the exchange rate volatility exceeds the acceptable range, the government will intervene. Second, in a target zone system, the monetary authority is more concerned with changes in the exchange rate, and if necessary, will restrict those changes in the exchange rate as much as possible in the target zone. Compared with a pegged exchange rate system, under the exchange rate target zone system, the government will not commit to intervening in the foreign exchange market under any circumstances so as to maintain the exchange rate at the pre-determined fixed central exchange rate. Therefore, exchange rate changes will be of a greater magnitude.

To a certain extent, the exchange rate target zone system has the function of an automatic stabilizer. We assume that the government-mandated target zone can be fully trusted, and that the exchange rate will always fluctuate in the target zone. In other words, the government will only intervene when the exchange rate reaches the upper or lower limits. In this case, when the exchange rate fluctuates near the limit of the target zone, foreign exchange traders will expect the government to intervene and quickly make necessary adjustments to force the exchange rate back towards the center. If this is the case, these traders would act before the government intervenes and the exchange rate moves back to the center. Due to this sort of trader behavior, the exchange rate will not surpass the boundaries of the target zone and automatically adjust towards the center even if the government does not intervene. Therefore, the exchange rate target zone system automatically stabilizes exchange rate fluctuations. In other words, under the exchange rate target zone system, the exchange rate fluctuates up or down around the center. Once the rate strays from

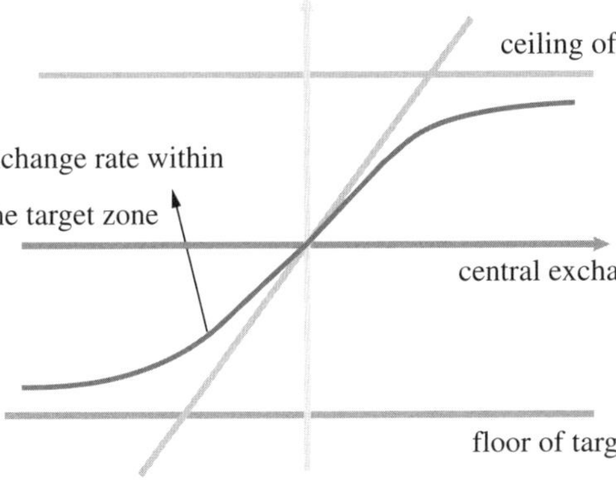

Fig. 17.2 Honeymoon Effect of the Exchange Rate Target Zone

the central exchange rate to a certain extent, it will spontaneously adjust and return to the central rate. This is as if two lovers have decided to take some time apart, but of course, after some time, they yearn anew for each other. As such, we call this the "honeymoon effect" of the exchange rate target zone (Figure 17.2).

However, the "honeymoon effect" of the exchange rate target zone can be established only if the government has credibility and the economic and monetary situation is sound. If the economic and financial fundamentals experience a large shift in a certain direction, people will anticipate that the central exchange rate of the exchange rate target zone will also undergo a large adjustment. When this happens, the exchange rate target zone loses its credibility. For example, the central exchange rate that the government determines when things are going well will be seriously overestimated if the economy suffers a shock, and thus the target zone will not have credibility or sustainability. When this happens, the market exchange rate changes will no longer be automatically inclined towards the government's pre-determined central exchange rate. Conversely, at this time, changes in the exchange rate will be very severe and often exceed typical changes seen under a floating exchange rate system. Compared to the "honeymoon effect", this change in the exchange rate is as if a husband and wife realize that the romance of love had gone out over time and decide that their personality clash makes it no longer possible to hold their marriage. They get a divorce and part ways. As such, this is known as the "divorce effect" of the exchange rate target zone.

17.3.3 RMB Exchange Rate System

After the founding of new China, the exchange rate system of the Chinese yuan underwent several evolutions. In 1994, China reformed its system of foreign exchange control and also implemented the managed floating exchange rate system.

However, because of the impact of the Asian financial crisis in 1997 and in order to stabilize the Chinese yuan exchange rate and avoid competitive depreciation as other Southeast Asian currencies, China resolutely decided that the fluctuations of yuan–US dollar exchange rate should not exceed 1%. Since then, China has actually implemented a pegged exchange rate to the dollar. In this exchange rate system, the exchange rate of yuan against USD is basically fixed; and as depicted in Figure 17.1(a), the rate curve is horizontal. However, because the exchange rate of US dollar against other currencies (such as the Japanese yen) is floating, the yuan–yen exchange rate changes whenever the US dollar–yen exchange rate changes.

On July 22, 2005, the People's Bank of China announced the introduction of a new exchange rate system. On the day after the announcement, Chinese yuan would no longer be pegged just to the US dollar. and China started to adopt a managed floating exchange rate regime based on market supply and demand with reference to a basket of currencies, in a view to maintaining the stability of Chinese yuan exchange rate at a reasonable level. Meanwhile, during this reform, the yuan appreciated by 2% against the USD, that is, 1 USD could be exchanged for 8.11 yuan instead of original 8.27 Chinese yuan.

Also, the People's Bank of China expanded the volatility range of exchange rate of the Chinese yuan against non-dollar currencies on the interbank foreign exchange spot market. Specifically, the range was extended from 1.5% to 3%. People's Bank of China also adjusted the management of bank customer's quoted rates in dollars, and implemented management of the spread range. In particular, the spread of selling price and bid price for US dollars should not exceed 1% from the central parity, and the cash offer price and bid price should not exceed 4% of the central parity. In April 2012, the People's Bank of China expanded the floating range of yuan–US dollar exchange rate from 0.5% to 1%, further enhancing the flexibility of exchange rate and also making it more sensitive to the external economy. All in all, after the reforms on the exchange rate system in 2005, the Chinese yuan experienced an overall trend of appreciation with bi-directional fluctuations, indicating the enhanced flexibility of the yuan.

17.4 Optimal Currency Areas

The theory of optimal currency areas was developed in the 1960s. At that time, western economic circles fiercely argued over the pros and cons of fixed exchange rate system and floating exchange rate system. In this debate, American economist Robert Mendelssohn put forth the optimal currency area theory. He believes that a shift in demand is the main cause of imbalances in the international balance of payments. For example, when the demand for US goods shifts towards a demand for Japanese goods, it will cause an imbalance in the balance of payments between the United States and Japan. Meanwhile it will also cause unemployment in America and inflation in Japan. If the two countries adopted a fixed exchange rate and wanted to eliminate imbalances of international payments, then it would lead to a rise in Japanese prices or fewer jobs and wage cuts in America. It would be impossible to eliminate both inflation in Japan and unemployment in America.

Mendelssohn believes that the establishment of an optimal currency area would solve these problems. An **optimal currency area** is an independent currency area composed of the regions where economy is open, flow of goods, labor, and capital are free, industrial structures are different but economic growth and inflation rates are close, and economic and monetary policies are comparatively coordinated. The primary features of optimal currency area are that within the currency area, factors can flow freely, exchanges rates are unified, and member states coordinate their monetary and fiscal policies. In the area, member states adopt a fixed exchange rate system to ensure the full convertibility of various currencies within the area. "Optimal" appears in the following ways: the currency area can achieve full employment, price stability, and external balance of payments through coordinated monetary and fiscal policies and flexible exchange rate policies.

The optimal currency area comes with both advantages and disadvantages. The benefits are as follows. First, the unified currency increases the openness of the economies within the area, and is conducive to free flows of goods and capital and efficient allocation of resources throughout the area. Second, when international balance of payments becomes imbalanced, the country can manage to achieve balance either through imports and exports on the goods market or through capital flows on the financial market. Third, the currency area eliminates exchange rate uncertainty and speculation, thereby reducing disturbance of balance of payments and reducing the demand of member states for international reserves. Fourth, it promotes coordinated monetary and fiscal policy among member states.

Of course, the establishment of a currency area is not without cost, and participating countries have to pay price. First, in order to stabilize the exchange rate or use a common currency, member states must maintain the same rate of inflation. Second, member states must make every effort to maintain the balance of international payments. Third, because the currency area will require concerted policy measures in order to maintain a common exchange rate system within the currency area, member states must give up policy independence to some extent. Upon the establishment of the euro zone, the euro zone member states no longer had any control over monetary policies to adjust unemployment rates or economic growth. Instead, monetary policy within the euro area is developed and implemented by the European Central Bank and is not subject to governments of euro zone member states. Also, the smooth operation of the currency area relies on people's absolute confidence in long-term fixed rates and the full convertibility of currency amongst member states. This requires that monetary authorities work in close coordination and may even call for the establishment of a supranational central bank. In this way, macro-control of the currency area will require member states to automatically give up monetary policy and, at the same time, fiscal policy of those countries will be subject to constraints.

Summary

Exchange rate fluctuations affect imports and exports and also affect the stability of the financial market. These fluctuations have a profound impact on domestic economic growth, employment, price levels, as well as the adjustment of the industrial structure.

The principal factors that determine exchange rates including real factors, financial factors, and expectations. Real factors include technology and productivity, economic development, the relative level of prices, tariffs, quotas, and so on. The financial factors that affect the exchange rate are primarily differences in the rates of return. Expectations also affect the supply and demand of foreign currency, and further affect the fluctuation of the exchange rate. Both real and financial factors affect expectations.

Absolute purchasing power parity theory suggests that the proportional price levels of the two countries determine the exchange rate between two currencies. Relative purchasing power parity theory suggests that the exchange rate fluctuations are determined by the rates of inflation in the two countries. The Big Mac index is a simple application of the purchasing power parity theory.

Differences in interest rates also have a significant impact on exchange rate fluctuations. Interest rate parity theory suggests that the exchange rate of countries with higher interest rates tends to appreciate on the spot market while the exchange rate of countries with lower interest rates tends to depreciate on the spot market. Conversely, because of hedging, the currency of the country with a higher interest rate will be at a discount on the forward market, while the currency of country with lower interest rates will be at a premium on the forward market.

The exchange rate system is a series of arrangements or provisions made by the monetary authority of one country with respect to the basic mode of changes in the exchange rates of local currency against foreign currencies. On the basis of fixed exchange rate systems and floating exchange rate systems, a variety of more flexible systems have evolved, such as the pegged exchange rate system, the currency board system, and the exchange rate target zone system.

Compared to fixed exchange rate systems, floating exchange rate systems have the following benefits: the balance of payments can be realized automatically, the central bank's monetary policy is independent, a great amount of foreign exchange reserves are not needed, and resources allocation is enhanced.

In order to mitigate the impact of exchange rate fluctuations, countries with similar levels of economic development can establish optimal currency areas. An optimal currency area can coordinate the fiscal and monetary policies of member states and promote the rational flow of factors, but member states have to give up some autonomy in terms of economic policy.

Key Terms

Law of One Price; Purchasing Power Parity; Interest Rate Parity; Exchange Rate System; Fixed Exchange Rate System; Floating Exchange Rate System; Free Floating; Managed Floating; Pegged Exchange Rate System; Currency Board System; Exchange Rate Target Zone System; Honeymoon Effect; Divorce Effect; Optimal Currency Area

Critical Thinking Questions

1. What is the economic impact of exchange rate fluctuations?
2. What is the law of one price? What factors affect it?
3. What is the main idea behind the purchasing power parity theory? How would you comment on it?
4. Describe the main content of the interest rate parity theory.
5. What are the advantages and disadvantages of a fixed exchange rate system and a floating exchange rate system?
6. What is a pegged exchange rate? Why is the pegged exchange rate considered as a fixed rate and not as a floating exchange rate system? What are the advantages and disadvantages of a pegged exchange rate system?
7. What is a currency board system?
8. What is an exchange rate target zone system? What kind of impact does it have on exchange rate fluctuations?
9. What is an optimal currency area? What are the advantages and disadvantages of an optimal currency area?
10. Alan Greenspan, Board Chairman of the US Federal Reserve, announced lower interest rates in the United States, while the interest rates of other countries remained the same. What kind of response will this create in the foreign exchange market?
11. In 1994 and 1995, the rate of inflation was 21.7% and 14.8% respectively in China. However, from Figure 17.1 of this chapter, we can see that during those two years, the Chinese yuan continued to appreciate against the US dollar. This has created a confusing paradox: the value of yuan was in a constant state of depreciation in China, yet its value was constantly increasing abroad. How do you explain this paradox?
12. After the Southeast Asian financial crisis, a few countries including Thailand, Malaysia and Indonesia abandoned their original fixed exchange rate systems and shifted to a floating exchange rate system. Why did they switch?
13. In the China Monetary Policy Report Q3 2007, the People's Bank of China says that the role of interest rates and exchange rates in currency adjustment would be strengthened. Then, the Chinese yuan began to appreciate against the US dollar till July 2008 (Figure 17.1). Analyze the possible economic impacts of this accelerated appreciation of the Chinese yuan.

14. From 2009 to 2013, the US adopted the monetary policy of quantitative easing after the Federal Funds Rate was cut down to 0–0.25% in response to the financial crisis (see Chapter 20). After Prime Minister Abe took office in 2012, Japan implemented more loose monetary policies after the interest rate stayed at zero percent for a long time. Analyze the impact of the monetary policy of the United States and Japan on the exchange rates of US dollars and Japanese yen respectively. What impact would this have on the Chinese yuan?

Chapter 18

Balance of Payments

Learning Objectives

After studying this chapter, you will be able to:

- Understand the balance of payments
- Clearly understand the balance of payments statement and its items
- Understand the factors that affect the balance of payments
- Understand the Marshall–Lerner condition
- Understanding the J-curve effect of exchange rate depreciation
- Understand international reserves
- Understand the conflict between internal and external equilibrium in an open economy
- Clearly understand principles of policy mix in an open economy

Modern society is an open society. As a result of increasing economic globalization, economic exchanges between countries are becoming more frequent and on an ever increasing scale. When cut off from the world, no country can possibly achieve a sound development. The balance of payments reflects the position of a country in the global economic system. The balance of payments aggregates and its structural changes will have a major impact on a country's domestic economy. This chapter describes the basic concepts behind the balance of payments.

18.1 Balance of Payments and the Balance of Payments Statement

18.1.1 What is the Balance of Payments?

The **balance of payments** is a systematic record of the economic transactions between residents of one country with those of foreign countries within a certain period of time. These economic transactions refer to the transfer of economic value from one economic entity to another; for example, Konka's color TV exports to the European Union. There are five different categories of economic transactions based on the content and direction of such transfer as recorded in the balance of payments:

- Exchange between financial assets and goods and services, namely the trade of goods and services, such as using foreign exchange to purchase foreign home appliances, import raw materials or equipment, and other capital goods.
- Direct exchange of goods and services without the use of foreign currency as a medium of exchange.
- Exchange between financial assets, such as when domestic residents purchase shares issued by foreign companies or foreign government bonds. Similarly, foreign residents can also purchase the shares or bonds issued by domestic enterprises.
- Uncompensated one-way transfers of goods and services, such as animals provided by China free of charge to Afghanistan zoo, or China's assistance to some African countries to build railways and ports.
- Uncompensated one-way transfers of financial assets, such as the 100 million dollars of financial assistance China provided in support of Afghan reconstruction.

Economic transactions as recorded in the balance of payments must be between residents and non-residents. Only economic transactions between residents and non-residents are considered as international economic transactions. Remember, said residents in the context of balance of payments are not only typical residents such as your neighbors. They include all entities engaged in economic activities, such as individuals, governments, non-profit groups, and enterprises. Even foreign citizens, so long as they have been engaged in long-term productive or consumptive activities domestically, are also considered as domestic residents (even though they are not citizens of your country, and enjoy no right of participating in the country's political affairs). For example, Frenchman David is studying in China, and as such, he has been added to China's resident statistics. However, official diplomats or foreign military personnel stationed abroad do not fall under the domestic residents. For example, the Russian Ambassador to China also shops and makes purchases in China, but does not belong to Chinese residents. Businesses are also included as residents that engage in economic activities. For example, the Chinese branch of IBM is considered a Chinese resident instead of a United States resident. International institutions, such as the United Nations, the International Monetary Fund, and the World Bank are deemed non-residents of any nation.

18.1.2 Balance of Payments Statement

In order to fully reflect economic transactions between domestic residents and foreign residents, a balance of payments statement must be prepared. The **balance**

of payments statement is a statement reflecting the economic transactions between residents of one country and those of other countries within a certain period. The balance of payments statement adopts the principle of double-entry bookkeeping, and is divided into debit and credit. The credit items are: exports of goods and services, income revenue, the acceptance of goods and capital as aid, increases in financial liabilities, and reductions in financial assets. Debit items are: imports of goods and services, income payments, goods and financial aid sent abroad, increases in financial assets, and reductions in financial liabilities. The balance of payments statement mainly contains four accounts, namely current account, capital and financial account, reserves, errors, and omissions.

(a) *Current Account*

The **current account** reflects the transfer of physical resources between one country and other countries. Current accounts usually have four components: goods, services, income, and current transfers.

Goods are the most important item of the current account and even of the balance of payments statement as a whole, and it records a country's import and export situation of goods such as color TVs, refrigerators, machines, etc. Exports are accounted for on the credit side, while imports are accounted for on the debit side. The difference between imports and exports is called the **trade balance**. If the values of imported goods are greater than exported goods, the country is experiencing a **trade deficit**. Conversely, if the values of imported goods are less than exported goods, the country is experiencing a **trade surplus**. For example, China's imports amounted to 2.0569 trillion dollars in 2012, while exports amounted to 1.7353 trillion dollars. That is to say, China had a trade surplus of 321.6 billion dollars.

Services record service export and import. Service export refers to domestic services supplied abroad. Service import refers to foreign services supplied domestically. Transactions of this item are relatively complex, often including shipping, tourism, communications, insurance, banking, services, construction, computer and information services, patent transfers, and so on. In the balance of payments statement, credit side registers service revenues, namely domestic services exported abroad, while the debit side registers service payments, namely the import of foreign services. In 2012, service revenue in China's balance of payments statement was 191.4 billion dollars, while service expenditure was 281.2 billion dollars. Therefore, the service trade deficit was 89.7 billion dollars.

Income is a record of the factor income payments arising from international flows of factors of production. Such international flows include import and export of labor as well as capital. Thus, this item has two sub-items, i.e., compensation of employees and investment income. Compensation of employees reflects remitted income of Chinese individuals who work abroad (less than one year), as well as wages and benefits paid to foreign employees who work in China (less than

Table 18.1 China's Balance of Payments Statement for 2012 (Unit: 100 million USD)

Item	Balance	Credit	Debit
I. Current Account	1931	24,599	22,668
A. Goods and Services	2318	22,483	20,165
1. Goods	3216	20,569	17,353
2. Services	−897	1914	2812
B. Income	−421	1604	2026
1. Compensation of Employees	153	171	18
2. Investment Income	−574	1434	2008
C. Current Transfers	34	512	477
II. Capital and Financial Account	−168	13,783	13,951
A. Capital Account	43	45	3
B. Financial Account	−211	13,738	13,949
1. Direct Investment	1911	3079	1168
1.1. Abroad	−624	234	857
1.2. In China	2535	2845	311
2. Portfolio Investment	478	829	352
2.1. Assets	−64	237	301
2.1.1. Equity Securities	20	120	100
2.1.2. Debt Securities	−84	117	201
2.2. Liabilities	542	593	51
2.2.1. Equity Securities	299	348	49
2.2.2. Debt Securities	243	244	2
3. Other Investments	−2600	9829	12,429
3.1. Assets	−2316	1402	3718
3.1.1. Trade Credits	−618	4	622
3.1.2. Loans	−653	244	897
3.1.3. Currency and Deposits	−1047	1027	2,074
3.1.4. Other Assets	3	127	125
3.2. Liabilities	−284	8428	8712
3.2.1. Trade Credits	423	503	80
3.2.2. Loans	−168	6480	6648
3.2.3. Currency and Deposits	−594	1339	1933
3.2.4. Other Liabilities	54	106	51
III. Reserve Assets	−966	136	1101
3.1. Monetary Gold	0	0	0
3.2. Special Drawing Rights	5	7	2
3.3. Reserve Position in the Fund	16	16	0
3.4. Foreign Exchange	−987	112	1099
IV. Net Errors and Omissions	−798	0	798

Source: China's State Administration of Foreign Exchange Website

one year). Investment income includes profit and interest payments and reinvested earnings under direct investment, portfolio investment income (dividends, interest, etc.), and other investment income (interest). In China's balance of payments for 2012, investment income on the credit side was 160.4 billion dollars and 202.6 billion dollars on the debit side, suggesting that China had higher earnings from its investment abroad than foreign investors earned in China during that year.

Current transfers, also known as free transfers or one-way transfers, include general government and private transfers. The general government transfers primarily include debt forgiveness, intergovernmental economic and military assistance, war reparations, and donations. Private uncompensated transfer mainly includes expatriate remittances, annuities, grants, and so on. The credit side records uncompensated foreign transfers to China, while the debit side records uncompensated transfer from China to foreign countries. In 2012, China's uncompensated transfers on the credit side amounted to 51.2 billion dollars, and on the debit side, these transfers amounted to 47.7 billion dollars. This shows that China's acceptance of foreign aid is greater than China's assistance towards other countries.

(b) *Capital and Financial Accounts*

Capital accounts include capital transfers such as debt relief, migrant transfers, and so on. Financial accounts include all transactions involving changes in the ownership of China's foreign assets and liabilities. Financial accounts are further divided into direct investments, portfolio investments, and other investments based on the different methods of investment, and are also divided into assets and liabilities based on the direction of capital flows. Direct investment is divided into foreign direct investment in China (considered as liabilities) and China's direct investment abroad (considered as assets).

Direct investment refers to situations in which residents of one country directly establish branches abroad, or purchase enough shares in a foreign enterprise to acquire a certain control right in the enterprise. In the balance of payments statement, direct investment includes foreign direct investment in China and China's foreign direct investment abroad. The debit side of "Abroad" refers to the outflow of capital invested abroad and the outflow of funds in the transactions between parent companies and subsidiaries. On the credit side, this is expressed as divestment and liquidation by China as well as the inflow of external funds in the transactions between parent companies and subsidiaries. The credit side of foreign direct investment "In China" refers to direct investment made by foreign investors in setting up an enterprise in China, including equity capital, reinvested earnings and other capital. On the debit side, this refers to the divestment and liquidation of foreign enterprises and the remittance of funds out of China. In terms of direct investment for 2012, China reported 307.9 billion dollars on the credit side, and

116.8 billion dollars on the debit side. As such, foreign net investment in China amounted to 191.1 billion dollars.

Portfolio investments refer to domestic residents' purchases and sales of foreign bonds and stocks that are not included in direct investment, such as US Treasury bonds purchased by the Chinese government or IBM stock purchased by Chinese residents. Alternatively, this also includes situations in which foreign residents trade domestic bonds and stocks (including capital repayments). Unlike direct investors, portfolio investors are primarily concerned with capital safety and expected capital gains rather than long-term prospects of the invested enterprise. These portfolio investors tend to transfer capital when they expect changes in business prospects. In the balance of payments statement, portfolio investments are divided into assets and liabilities. "Assets" on the debit side expresses an increase in Chinese holdings of non-resident securities assets, while "Assets" on the credit side denotes a reduction in such assets. "Liabilities" on the credit side expresses the amount financed through China's stock and bond issues for the current period. "Liabilities" on the debit side expresses current stock recovery and bond repayments. For example, in 2012, 12 billion dollars were credited under "Portfolio Investment Liabilities–Equity Securities", which reflects the amount of equity financing abroad for that year.

Other investments are all other financial transactions aside from direct investment and portfolio investment. These investments can be divided into trade credits, loans, currency and deposits, and other assets and liabilities. They are also divided into assets and liabilities. "Assets" on the debit side refers to an increase in assets. On the credit side, this refers to a reduction in assets. "Liabilities" on the credit side refers to an increase in liabilities. On the debit side, this refers to a reduction in liabilities.

(c) *Reserves*

Reserves are a very important item in the balance of payments statement. **International reserves** refer to the reserves held by monetary authorities (primarily the central bank) which can be used to satisfy foreign assets requirements of the balance of payments, which includes monetary gold, special drawing rights, reserve positions in the International Monetary Fund (IMF), and claims on non-residents (foreign exchange assets).

Monetary gold is a financial asset held by a country's monetary authority. Non-monetary use of gold is not included. For example, gold necklaces and jewelry sold at the mall are not included in a country's reserve assets. **Foreign exchange reserves** are external liquid assets held by monetary authorities, mainly bank deposits and Treasury bills. When the Chinese government holds US Treasury bonds or US dollar deposits, they are included in China's foreign exchange reserves. The world's major reserve currencies are the US dollar, the Euro, the yen, and the pound.

The reserve position in IMF refers to the assets member countries of the IMF can freely draw upon, including the foreign exchange as a portion of the members' quota payment to the IMF and the portion of domestic currency holdings that has been used by the IMF. The IMF was established to provide short-term funds to members who suffer balance of payments difficulties. The loan ceiling for a member is 125% of its quota. For a member, 25% of the quota is subscribed with gold, US dollars or special drawing rights. The remaining 75% is payable in their domestic currencies. The former (25%) is known as "reserve tranche" loans, which may be used without the approval of the IMF, and which is a type of reserve asset as members may, at any time, purchase using their domestic currency (as long as they buy back their own currency within a specified time). Another part of the reserve position is the domestic currency that IMF uses to meet the funding needs of other members. This portion is IMF debt, and the IMF can reimburse members at any time. In other words, it may be unconditionally used by members to fund a deficit in the balance of payments. When the IMF provides the domestic currency to other members, its holding of this currency is lowered below 75% of the quota.

A **special drawing right** is a kind of paper asset that the IMF allocates to members in accordance with their quotas and can be used to repay IMF loans and deficits in a member's balance of payments. Special drawing rights (SDRs) that have been allocated by the IMF and yet remain unused are parts of the international reserve. SDRs are the rights to use funds. Compared with other assets, there is a distinct difference: First of all, SDRs do not have a built-in value; they are paper asset artificially created by the IMF. Second, they are not like gold and foreign currency, which is obtained through trade or non-trade means, nor are they like reserve positions that are paid quota funds, but rather are given for free by the IMF on a pro rata basis to members. Finally, they only play a role between the IMF and governments and cannot be used by private enterprises. SDRs cannot be directly used as a means of payment in trade or non-trade activities and have strictly limited purposes.

(d) *Errors and Omissions*

The last item in the balance of payments statement is the "Errors and Omissions". Based on accounting needs, this item is created to offset statistical deviations and ensures that the positive and negative entries reach a net total of zero, therefore serving the purpose of "balance".

18.2 Balance of Payment Imbalances

18.2.1 Reasons for Balance of Payment Imbalances

Generally speaking, imbalances are the norm for a country's balance of payments. There are two forms of imbalances: surpluses and deficits. A **balance of payments surplus** refers to when income from the current accounts and capital accounts of a country in international economic transactions are greater than expenditures from these accounts. If expenditures were greater, this would be a **balance of payments deficit**. Generally speaking, there are two levels of a balance of payments surplus or deficit: current account surplus (deficit) and capital and financial account surplus (deficit). Therefore, a balance of payments surplus (deficit) includes a trade surplus (deficit), current account surplus (deficit), and capital and financial account surplus (deficit). If there is a current account surplus and a capital and financial account surplus, we call it a twin surplus.

There are many reasons for these imbalances, each of which can be analyzed from a different perspective.

(a) *Savings — Investment Gap and Balance of Payment Imbalances*

From the perspective of aggregate demand, national income Y can be divided into four categories, namely private consumption C, investment I, government consumption G, and exports E, that is:

$$Y_{\mathrm{d}} = C + I + G + E. \tag{18.1}$$

From the aggregate supply perspective, the national income can also be divided into four categories, namely private consumption C, private savings S_P, government revenue T, and imports M, that is:

$$Y_{\mathrm{S}} = C + S_p + T + M. \tag{18.2}$$

When national income is balanced: $Y_{\mathrm{d}} = Y_{\mathrm{S}}$

$$C + I + G + E = C + S_p + T + M, \tag{18.3}$$

from which we get:

$$S_p + (T - G) - I = E - M. \tag{18.4}$$

The difference between government taxation and government consumption is government savings. The sum of government savings and private savings is gross national savings S. If NX represents net exports, namely the difference between exports and imports:

$$S - I = NX. \tag{18.5}$$

Equation (18.5) shows that the difference between savings S and investment I is equal to net exports NX. If national savings S is less than investment I, net exports NX will always be negative. In other words, if savings are less than investment, there will be a trade deficit. Conversely, if national savings are greater than investment, there will be a corresponding trade surplus.

Nowadays, the United States as a representative of many developed countries, has had a long period in which domestic savings have been less than investment, thus resulting in a large trade deficit. China, as a representative of some emerging market economies, has exhibited domestic savings greater than investment, and thus has a significant trade surplus. This is called the global economic imbalance.

Based on this relation of equality between savings–investment gap and net exports, the root causes and solutions of trade surpluses or deficits can be analyzed. For instance, some suggested that at one end of global economic imbalance, the enormous US trade deficit was caused by insufficient US savings. In 2005, the US national savings rate was only 1.29%. Therefore, in order to reduce the US trade deficit, we should improve the US savings rate. On the other hand, Ben Bernanke, who began to lead the Federal Reserve on January 31, 2006, suggested that America's trade deficit and the surpluses of other countries were due to too little consumption and too much savings on the part of other countries. Therefore, in order to alleviate the US trade deficit, other countries should reduce their savings rates and increase domestic consumption.

(b) *Fiscal Deficit and Trade Deficit*

Sometimes governments will be faced with both a trade deficit and a fiscal deficit. This phenomenon is known as a **twin deficit**. A twin deficit has existed in the United States since the 1970s. Similar to the fact that there will always be a trade deficit when national savings are less than investment, there is also a natural link between a government's fiscal deficit and a trade deficit. If government spending is greater than government revenue, it would mean a fiscal deficit which is equivalent to negative government savings. A fiscal deficit would then reduce overall national savings, thereby broadening the gap between national savings and investment, and according to Equation (18.5), widening the trade deficit.

Of course, the derivation of the relationship between a fiscal deficit and a trade deficit is more complex than the equation above. In accordance with the analysis in Chapter 19, an expansion in the fiscal deficit would cause a rise in domestic interest rates, which, in turn, will lead to an increase in the rate of return for investment in domestic financial assets and a corresponding decrease in the rate of return on foreign investments. This would also increase the demand for domestic currency assets and cause a relative decrease in the demand for foreign assets, as well as an increase in the demand for domestic currency as opposed to a decrease in the demand for foreign currencies. As a result, domestic currency will appreciate while foreign currencies will depreciate. This would make domestic exports to foreign markets more expensive and lower the relative cost of foreign goods in domestic markets, whereby imports would ultimately be greater than exports. Therefore, a fiscal deficit will result in rising interest rates, which will lead to appreciation of domestic currency and depreciation of foreign currencies, thereby shifting the trade balance into a deficit.

(c) *International Division of Labor and Structural Disequilibrium in the Balance of Payments*

Imbalance in the balance of payments caused by an economy's structural disequilibrium is known as **structural disequilibrium**. If the supply and demand structure for a domestic product cannot keep up with changes in the international market supply and demand, the country's balance of payments will remain in a long-term structural disequilibrium. If the international market has a declining demand for a country's export where it has a comparative advantage, or if the reduced supply in the international market causes a rising price of the country's import when the country is not in a position to change its export structure, the country will run a deficit in the balance of payments. Suppose that China has a comparative advantage over the United States for toys, textiles, and other products while the United States has a comparative advantage for automobiles and IT products. As such, China will export more textiles and toys to the United States, while the United States will export more automobiles and IT products to China. If the demand for textiles and toys falls in the United States, and China, meanwhile, has an increasing demand for automobiles and IT products because of its high-speed economic growth, there will be a reduction in the textiles and toys exported by China and an increased import demand for automobiles and IT goods. This will lead to China's international trade deficit.

The deepening of economic globalization, the new international divisions of labor, and new production networks have the potential to create long-term imbalances in the balance of payments. Since the 1970s, Japan has had a constant trade surplus, while the United States has maintained a constant trade deficit, both of which have grown continuously. China, as a new and emerging market economy, has exhibited a sharp increase in its trade surplus over the last few years. In fact, the trade surplus had reached 360.68 billion US dollars in 2008. China's trade surplus over recent years is due to a large amount of foreign manufacturing that has shifted to China, as well as the use of cheap labor in China. Meanwhile, nearly one-third of the US trade deficit is due to oil imports.

(d) *Monetary Factors*

These factors result in an imbalance in the balance of payments through changes in price levels, costs, exchange rates, interest rates, or other changes caused by changes in a country's money supply. If a country issues too much currency, prices will rise, and if the exchange rate is unchanged, it will inevitably lead to fewer exports and more imports. Additionally, an increase in the money supply will lower domestic interest rates, causing an increase in capital outflows, a reduction in capital inflows and thereby a deficit in the balance of payments. Thus, it can be seen that monetary factors will not only affect the current accounts balance but will also affect the balance of capital and financial accounts.

(e) *Foreign Exchange Speculations and the Instability of International Capital Flows*

These factors result in an imbalance due to changes in exchange rate risk under a floating exchange rate system. A large amount of hot money exists in the international financial market, and these funds will flow frequently between countries in pursuit of speculative profits. Changes in short-term capital flows often result in unstable balance of payments. If, for example, speculators expect a devaluation of the domestic currency, they will sell the domestic currency and purchase foreign currencies they expect to appreciate, thereby furthering capital outflows and cause a deficit in the capital and financial accounts. From 2003 to 2012, China had a capital and financial account surplus because the Chinese yuan was expected to appreciate, resulting in a large amount of capital inflows into China.

(f) *Cyclical Factors and Emergencies*

Cyclical changes in the economy will also cause imbalances. Economic cycles are not exactly the same from one country to another; while one country is in an economic boom, another may be in recession. If the local economy is expanding, and if trade partners are handling a recession, the country will have a greater demand for imports than other countries, which will cause a trade deficit; or if the opposite is true, a trade surplus may occur. Similarly, if capital flows freely, and if a nation's economy is in prosperity, while another country is in recession, domestic investment will have a higher rate of return, thereby encouraging capital inflow into the country. This coupled with a reduction in the capital outflow will cause a capital and financial account surplus. Now, of course, economic globalization is spreading farther and wider, which means that economic cycles are becoming more consistent across countries, and therefore, the imbalances caused by differences in two countries' economic cycles are becoming less and less obvious. One-time emergencies at home and abroad will often cause a decrease in export revenue or an increase in import expenses or even cause large-scale capital flight. For example, a decline in domestic production caused by climate change or natural disasters will reduce export supply and increase import demand. Similarly, if these events occur in the nation's trading partners, they may also lower their supply of imports and their demand for the nation's exports. These factors will deteriorate the terms of trade, reduce exports, or increase imports, resulting in a balance of payments deficit. Sudden political events or crises will cause massive capital flight, which will bring a major deficit to capital and financial accounts in the balance of payments statement. An example is that of the assassination of Mexican political leaders in 1994, which greatly shook the confidence of Mexican peso holders, thereby leading to a mass exodus of Mexican capital. Such political shocks will cause a sharp rise in domestic interest rates and will devalue the domestic currency, but these factors will not sufficiently affect imports to compensate for capital flight. The Southeast Asian financial crisis of 1997 that began in Thailand not only caused a capital exodus from Thailand, but also led to capital flight in China. Although these unexpected events have a significant impact on the balance of payments, this impact is relatively short, and once these unexpected factors are eliminated, the balance of payments will restore its balance.

18.2.2 Impact of Imbalances in the Balance of Payments

With increasing economic connections and interactions between countries, instability in the balance of payments will affect the domestic economy. Whether it be a surplus or deficit, a persistent and remarkable imbalance in the balance of payments will produce a large or small negative impact on the domestic economy through a variety of mechanisms. A long-term balance of payments deficit will devalue the domestic currency. If a government wants to avoid the devaluation of its own currency, it must sell foreign exchange for domestic currency, which will not only significantly reduce its holdings of foreign exchange reserves, but also reduce the domestic money supply (recall Chapter 13), so that domestic interest rates will rise and affect domestic investment, production, and employment. In addition, a reduction in the international reserves will also affect a country's external financial strength, and its credit will decline.

Given the negative effects on a country's economy caused by a long-term balance of payments deficit, would this mean that a long-term balance of payments surplus is beneficial? Not quite. The fact is, when a country has a prolonged balance of payments surplus, it will also have a negative impact on the domestic economy, since accumulation of international reserves will cause growth in domestic money supply and pressure for a rise in prices. Since 2003, the substantial increase in China's trade surplus has caused a dramatic increase in the central bank's funds outstanding for foreign exchange. In order to stabilize the money supply, the central bank must use hedging operations, and the independence of monetary policy in managing aggregate demand is lessened. At the same time, a country's surplus also means that another country faces a deficit. A large deficit of one country is due to a large amount of imports of foreign products, which will impact domestic employment. As such, a long-term surplus will cause economic conflicts between countries and is not conducive to stable international economic relations. For instance, the Sino-US trade war, trade disputes between the United States and Japan and between the United States and the EU, to a great extent, was due to America's enormous trade deficit. An obvious example is the dispute that arose from the large US trade deficit with China. Congressmen Schumer and Graham argued for an appreciation of the Chinese yuan to correct the Sino-US trade imbalance. Otherwise, the United States would impose a punitive tariff of 27.5% on Chinese exports. Ultimately, if a balance of payments surplus is due to excessive exports, the domestic resources available for production will be reduced, and in the long run, this will certainly affect the rate of economic growth.

Now that we realize the various effects of these imbalances, how should they be addressed? When facing an imbalance, the economic system has a mechanism of automatic adjustments that will gradually restore balance. The government can also alter economic policies to help restore balance.

18.3 Adjustments of Balance of Payment Imbalances

When facing an imbalance, there are two means by which the payments can return to equilibrium: automatic adjustments and policy adjustments.

18.3.1 Automatic Adjustment of Imbalances

The automatic adjustment mechanism kicks in when there is an imbalance in the balance of payments. With the help of the intrinsic strength of the economy, the balance will self-adjust. There are different automatic adjustments for different exchange rate systems.

(a) *Automatic Adjustments under Fixed Exchange Rate System*

When a country faces a balance of payments deficit, in order to maintain a fixed exchange rate, the country's monetary authorities must reduce the foreign exchange reserves, leading to corresponding reduction in the domestic money supply. Initially, this will cause monetary tightening and rising interest rates. Rising interest rates will also lead to lower capital outflow and greater foreign capital inflows, resulting in an improved capital account. On the other hand, given a balance of payments surplus, monetary authorities can lower interest rates to increase the outflow of domestic capital and reduce the inflow of foreign capital, thereby reducing or eliminating the surplus. This is the interest rate effect of an imbalance in the balance of payments.

A balance of payments deficit will lower the domestic money supply, and cause the public to reduce the real money balances to a level they are willing to hold. In order to achieve this level of cash balances, people will directly reduce domestic spending. Also, a decrease in the money supply will lead to a rise in interest rates, which will further reduce current spending by domestic residents. A portion of domestic spending goes towards imported goods, and in this way, when domestic spending falls, demand for imports will also decline, thereby improving the balance of payments. This is the cash balance effect. Similarly, a balance of payments surplus can be addressed through domestic spending increases that will increase demand for imports, thereby automatically eliminating or reducing the surplus.

Price changes will also automatically adjust the balance of payments. When a country faces a balance of payments deficit, a reduction in the money supply will also lead to a drop in domestic prices. If the exchange rate is fixed, the price for the country's exports (as expressed in foreign currency) will fall while the relative price of foreign goods (as expressed in domestic currency) will rise, thereby increasing exports and reducing imports. This will consequently eliminate the balance of payments deficit. Conversely, when there is a large balance of payments surplus, the adjustment mechanism will work in the opposite way: with a rise in the relative prices of domestic products, exports will reduce while imports will rise, thus automatically shrinking the balance of payments surplus.

Under a fixed exchange rate system, automatic adjustments of imbalances in the balance of payments are summarized as follows:

Balance of Payments Deficit → Reduction in the Money Supply → Interest Rates Rise → Capital Inflows Increase, Outflows Decrease; Expenses Decrease, Imports Decrease → Improvement in the Balance of Payments

(b) *Automatic Adjustments under Floating Exchange Rate System*

Under a floating exchange rate system, monetary authorities do not assume the responsibility to fix the exchange rate, so the exchange rate will fluctuate with market demand and supply, and central banks cannot alter foreign exchange reserves to deal with a balance of payments deficit or surplus. However, if a country's balance of payments exhibits a deficit, the domestic demand for foreign currency will be greater than the supply of foreign currency, thereby appreciating the value of foreign currency and devaluing domestic currency Conversely, if a country's balance of payments exhibits a surplus, the demand for foreign currency will be less than supply of foreign currency, thereby appreciating the domestic currency and devaluing foreign currencies. Fluctuations in the exchange rate will automatically change the relative prices of exports and imports, and thus, the deficit in the balance of payments will be automatically eliminated due to exchange rate fluctuations.

We can describe the automatic adjustments to the imbalance in the balance of payments under a floating exchange rate system as follows:

Balance of Payments Deficit → Demand for Foreign Exchange Increases → Foreign Currency Exchange Rate Appreciates; Domestic Currency Depreciates → Exports Increase; Imports Decrease → Balance of Payments Restored to Equilibrium

Balance of Payments Surplus → Foreign Exchange Supply Increases → Foreign Exchange Rate Depreciates; Domestic Currency Appreciates → Exports Decrease; Imports Increase → Balance of Payments Restored to Equilibrium

When comparing automatic adjustments to an imbalance in the balance of payments under a fixed exchange rate system and a floating exchange rate system, you will realize that under a fixed exchange rate system, imbalances are restored through changes in domestic macroeconomic variables, which means that an external balance is achieved at the cost of damaging the domestic economic balance. Under a floating exchange rate system, the exchange rate changes to automatically adjust the imbalance and will not affect domestic money supply and price levels.

Therefore, these policies help protect the domestic economy from disturbances caused by foreign economies via the balance of payments channel.

18.3.2 Policies to Adjust Balance of Payments

When the balance of payments is imbalanced, the economy has automatic adjustment mechanisms to restore equilibrium, but these automatic adjustment mechanisms require a long period of time, and in the process, new factors may impede the restoration of the balance of payments equilibrium. Therefore, when there is an imbalance, governments will often take initiative to adopt appropriate corrective policies. Policy adjustments to improve the balance of payments can be divided into two categories: expenditure changing policies and expenditure switching policies. **Expenditure changing policies** are macroeconomic policies, including fiscal and monetary policies, which change the aggregate domestic expenditures to adjust the balance of payments. **Expenditure switching policies** are policies, primarily exchange rate policies and direct controls, which change the relative prices of imports and exports, thereby changing the demand for them. In addition, governments can also adopt exchange buffer policies to temporarily restore balance in the balance of payments. Put together, the following measures can be used by governments to adjust the balance of payments:

- Fiscal and monetary policies
- Exchange rate policies
- Direct controls
- Foreign exchange buffer policies

(a) *Fiscal and Monetary Policies*

When a country has imbalance in the balance of payments, authorities can adjust the imbalance through fiscal and monetary policies. The fiscal deficit is closely linked to the trade deficit, and therefore, when there is a substantial trade deficit, monetary authorities can improve the balance of international payments by reducing government spending to reduce the fiscal deficit or achieve a balanced budget. In accordance with Equation (18.5), the gap between national savings and investment is equivalent to the trade balance, and thus, any policies and measures that impact national savings and investment will ultimately affect the balance of payments. When facing a balance of payment deficit, the governments can change fiscal policy by reducing government spending and lowering the income tax on interest. As for monetary policy, governments can increase the interest rates, increase domestic savings, and reduce domestic investment. As long as these effects are greater than the increase in interest rates, the domestic currency will appreciate, thereby adversely affecting imports. As such, the balance of payments deficit would improve accordingly. Conversely, if the country faces a long-term balance of payments surplus, monetary authorities can increase government spending or lower interest rates and other policies that will improve final consumer demand, such as expanding consumer credit and unemployment insurance and improving pension insurance (recall the impact of savings in Chapter 4). It is precisely on the basis of this theory, and in the face of China's growing trade surplus, that China has now increasingly emphasized a reduction in the domestic savings rate to address the imbalance in the balance of payments.

However, the limitation of such a policy is that improving the balance of payments will be at the expense of the domestic economy, often conflicting with domestic economic goals. Contractionary policies reduce import costs but also suppress the domestic demand for domestic goods, which can result in an increase in unemployment. In addition, contractionary fiscal and monetary policies — whether it be to raise taxes or lower the money supply and raise interest rates — will dampen domestic investment, which will have an impact on long-term economic growth. For this reason, when the domestic economy falls into a recession and unemployment has already been a serious problem, a balance of payments deficit puts macroeconomic policymakers in a difficult position.

(b) *Exchange Rate Policies*

Exchange rate policies refer to the government's use of exchange rate changes to eliminate imbalances in the balance of payments. In general, currency devaluation of a country will suppress its imports and increase its exports. From 1970s to the mid-1980s, Japan's trade surplus with the United States continued to increase. In this context, the United States joined together with several other countries to force Japan into signing the Plaza Accords. From then on up to the end of 1995, the yen–dollar exchange rate appreciated from 1 US dollar to 254 Japanese yen to 94, and as a result, the US trade deficit with Japan was reduced from 9369 billion yen to 425.7 billion yen in 1995. Since 2000, China has witnessed successive trade surpluses, which developed countries such as US believe were caused by undervalued yuan. They thus placed political pressure on China, urging it to appreciate its currency in the hope of reducing its trade surplus. As a response to domestic monetary expansion caused by continuous trade surpluses, the People's Bank of China (PBOC) indeed adopted a currency appreciation policy.

However, when a country uses exchange rate depreciation to improve the balance of payments, the results depend on the following factors: (1) Whether or not the elasticity of demand for imports and exports meets the Marshall–Lerner condition (discussed later in this chapter); (2) Whether or not the country's existing production capacity has been fully utilized, because the shift in demand following the devaluation requires the country to increase supply of its own trade sectors. If production resources were already fully utilized prior to devaluation, even a significant devaluation would hardly improve the balance of payments as there were no more resources available for producing exports; (3) Whether or not the devaluation-caused high price differentials between domestic tradables and non-tradables can remain over a long period of time. If it can only sustain for a short time, it will be difficult to achieve the goal of improving the balance of payments; and (4) In general, a devaluation in the domestic currency will raise domestic prices, but the country must consider whether or not it can sustain the pressure of price increases. This is an important factor that must be considered with such an exchange rate depreciation policy.

(c) *Direct Controls*

To implement depreciation policies and contractionary fiscal and monetary policies to address long-term imbalances, the country must rely on market mechanisms to be successful, but this also requires a longer period of time. As for an imbalance in the balance of payments caused by structural changes, it is difficult to achieve the desired effects of the aforementioned policies. For this reason, and in particular, given structural deficits in the balance of payments, many developing countries directly intervene in international economic transactions by introducing direct controls.

Direct controls include foreign exchange controls and trade policies. As for the nature of control, they include quantity controls and price controls. The former is mainly implemented for imports, including all kinds of non-tariff barriers to imports such as import quotas, import licensing, and foreign exchange controls. The latter can be used to reduce import expenses, such as import tariffs, and can also be used to increase export earnings, such as export subsidies, export tax rebates, foreign exchange retention, and export credit preferences. Even if many countries respect free trade, when there is a large trade deficit, they will often implement trade protection policies. China's textile and footwear products are exported to the European Union, and in 2006, the EU imposed a punitive tariff of 16% on these Chinese products. Based on the results of implementation, quantity control measures can reduce import expenditures promptly in the short run, and price control measures produce essentially the same effects as exchange rate policies.

Direct control and exchange rate depreciation belong to the same expenditure switching policies, but the former is a selective control instrument, while the latter is an overall control instrument to improve the balance of payments that usually takes effect on a broader basis. Direct control measures are characterized as being more flexible and can be tailored to different import and export projects and capital flows. A country may impose no restrictions on imports of intermediate goods and consumer goods, for they are necessary for maintaining production and living standards, or imports of capital goods required to expand production capacity, but it may tightly control luxury imports. Meanwhile, on the export side, authorities can focus on offering incentives to important or non-traditional production and exports. Therefore, an appropriate use of direct control measures to correct the balance of payments deficit will not affect the overall economy. While politicians like Schumer and Graham tend to prefer protective policies, economic analysis differs greatly from political intuition: protectionism does not affect the trade balance. In the short term, raising tariffs or introducing import quotas will initially reduce imports, thereby reducing the trade deficit. However, a reduction in the trade deficit would reduce the supply of domestic currency in the foreign exchange market. On the other hand, foreign demand will require even more domestic currency for imports, which will cause a corresponding increase in the demand for domestic currency assets. These two factors together will ultimately lead to currency appreciation. Domestic currency appreciation will eventually lead to a reduction in the country's exports and increase imports to the point where net exports will return to at least the original level. It is precisely because of this that many economists strongly disapprove such proposals like Schumer and Graham's to impose trade protection policies on Chinese products.

(d) *Exchange Buffer Policies*

Exchange buffer policy refers to the use of changes in the official reserves or temporary foreign financing to offset excess demand for foreign exchange or supply. Assuming that China has a balance of payments deficit and there is an excess demand for foreign currency, the government can sell official foreign exchange reserves to meet this excess demand. Through exchange buffer policy, monetary authorities can accommodate for a temporary balance of payments deficit, and this is a simple and useful approach to avoid unnecessary exchange rate fluctuations of the domestic currency. However, the size of the official reserves is limited, and thus, authorities cannot entirely rely on this approach to cover a massive, long-term balance of payments deficit as this will cause a depletion of foreign exchange reserves or a considerable increase in external debt, but will not help solve the deficit problem.

18.4 The Role of Exchange Rates in Adjusting the Balance of Payments

18.4.1 Impact of Domestic Currency Devaluation on the Balance of Payments: Elasticity Analysis

We have already pointed out that when a country faces a balance of payments imbalance, authorities can use the exchange rate to adjust. However, the use of the exchange rate in the adjustment of the balance of payments must meet certain conditions. If these conditions are not met, devaluation of the domestic currency may not improve the balance of payments at all. We will use the elasticity approach to analyze this situation. The basic principle of the elastic approach is that changes in the exchange rate, which leads to changes in the relative prices between goods at home and abroad and between domestically produced tradable and non-tradable goods, will affect the supply and demand of exports and imports, and ultimately have an impact on the balance of payments.

In direct quotation, a rise in the exchange rate reflects the depreciation of the domestic currency and an appreciation of foreign currency. The exchange rate first determines the relative price between domestic and foreign products. If p_x expresses the price of exports in the domestic currency, p_m expresses the price of imports in a foreign currency, and e expresses the amount of domestic currency that can be exchanged for one unit of foreign currency, then the relative price (π) can be expressed as:

$$\pi = \frac{p_x}{e p_m}. \tag{18.6}$$

The relative price π is actually the **terms of trade**, and it represents the fact that one unit of exports can be exchanged for a certain quantity of imports. An increase in π means that each unit of exports can be exchanged for more imports, which is an improvement of terms of trade. Conversely, if π should fall, more imports would be needed for each unit of imports, which is a deterioration of terms of trade.

If domestic and international prices p_x and p_m remain unchanged, domestic currency depreciation will deteriorate terms of trade, and domestic products will become relatively cheap in foreign markets, while foreign products in the domestic market will become relatively expensive. This will give domestic residents an incentive to reduce import demand, and at the same time, it will also stimulate foreign residents to reduce their own domestic demand and increase their demand for the country's products.

However, will domestic currency devaluation always improve the balance of payments? This depends on the price elasticity of import and export demand. Price elasticity of import demand refers to a percentage change in import demand for every 1% change in the price of foreign products. If the price of imports drops by 1% and demand for imports thereby increases by 1.5%, then the price elasticity of import demand is -1.5. Similarly, price elasticity of export demand refers to a percentage change in export demand for every 1% change in the price of domestic exports. If export prices drop by 1% and exports increase by 2%, then the price elasticity of export demand is -2.

If B is used to express the difference between international receipts and payments prior to devaluation, X is export volume prior to devaluation and M is import volume prior to devaluation, then:

$$B = p_x \cdot X - e \cdot p_m \cdot M. \tag{18.7}$$

If η_m expresses the price elasticity of import demand, ΔM expresses the increase in import demand, and if the price of imports drops by 1%, according to the definition:

$$\eta_m = \frac{\frac{\Delta M}{M}}{1\%} \Rightarrow \Delta M = \frac{\eta_m \cdot M}{100}. \tag{18.8}$$

Similarly, if η_x expresses export price elasticity, ΔX expresses the increase in exports, and if export prices drop by 1%, according to the definition of export price elasticity:

$$\eta_x = \frac{\frac{\Delta X}{X}}{1\%} \Rightarrow \Delta X = \frac{\eta_x \cdot X}{100}. \tag{18.9}$$

Thus, domestic currency depreciation will increase export earnings of $p_x \cdot \Delta X = \frac{\eta_x \cdot p_x X}{100}$. Currency devaluation will increase the domestic currency price of imports, and therefore, following devaluation, the demand for imports will be reduced by $\frac{\eta_m \cdot M}{100}$, and the cost of imports in the domestic currency will be reduced accordingly by $\frac{\eta_m \cdot e \cdot p_m M}{100}$. At the same time, after a currency depreciation of 1%, the domestic currency price of imports will increase by 1% and, therefore, the domestic currency cost of imports will increase accordingly by $1\% \times e \cdot p_m \cdot M$. In this way, the cost of imports will increase by $(1 - \eta_m) \cdot e \cdot p_m \cdot M$ and the changes in the balance of international receipts and payments after domestic currency depreciation will be:

$$\Delta B = \frac{\eta_x \cdot p_x X}{100} - \frac{(1 - \eta_m) \cdot e \cdot p_m M}{100}. \tag{18.10}$$

It is clear that, as long as $\eta_x \cdot p_x X > (1 - \eta_m) \cdot e \cdot p_m M$, currency depreciation will improve the balance of payments. If the balance of payments is balanced before depreciation, then $p_x X = e \cdot p_m \cdot M$. Therefore, the above-mentioned conditions will change to: as long as $\eta_x > 1 - \eta_m$, or $\eta_x + \eta_m > 1$, currency depreciation will improve the balance of payments. This condition is known as the **Marshall–Lerner condition**, and it states that only when the sum of the price elasticity of import demand and price elasticity of export demand is greater than 1, will domestic currency depreciation improve the balance of payments.

Elasticity analysis warns people that when a country faces an imbalance in the balance of payments, one should not wishfully assume that depreciation would stimulate exports and curb imports. However, it is clear that the elasticity approach only analyzes the effects of depreciation on current accounts and does not take into account the effect of currency depreciation on capital flows and currency substitution. The government may announce a one-time depreciation of the domestic currency, and if people expect that the currency will further depreciate, then, in order to preserve the value of their assets, they would sell their domestic currency assets and turn to hold foreign currency assets. For currency substitution and asset substitution in countries that allow free convertibility of currency, it is expected that currency devaluation will trigger capital outflows. In countries with a strict control of currency exchange, this can cause a large-scale capital flight. Capital flight may offset the improvement of the current account due to currency devaluation.

18.4.2 Impact of Domestic Currency Devaluation on the Balance of Payments over Time: J-curve Effect

Even if it meets the Marshall–Lerner condition, domestic currency devaluation will still not immediately improve the balance of payments. There is a period of time between the implementation of domestic currency depreciation and an improvement in the balance of payments. During this period, depreciation will not improve the balance of payments. On the contrary, it may result in its deterioration. Figure 18.1 shows that at time t_0, the country's balance of payments is in a deficit; in order to adjust, the government must first implement currency devaluation policies, which may not only have a minimal impact on the balance of payments deficit but may expand it further. At t_1, the balance of payments deficit has reached its maximum, and thereafter, the deficit will gradually decrease. Only after t_2 will an improvement in the balance of payments be shown. Later, scholars called this the **J-curve effect**.

Why is there a J-curve effect? Economist Stephen Magee divided the period of time after depreciation into three phases, namely the contract phase, the conductive phase and the quantity adjustment phase. In the contract phase, import and export contracts are signed prior to the implementation of the currency devaluation policies, and export and import prices and quantities do not change just because of currency depreciation. In this way, the trade balance as expressed in the domestic currency will depend on the denomination currency specified in the contracts. If foreign currencies are used to settle imports and exports, the domestic currency price of the specified exports and imports will rise by the same extent as the currency depreciation. So, if the import costs are higher than export earnings

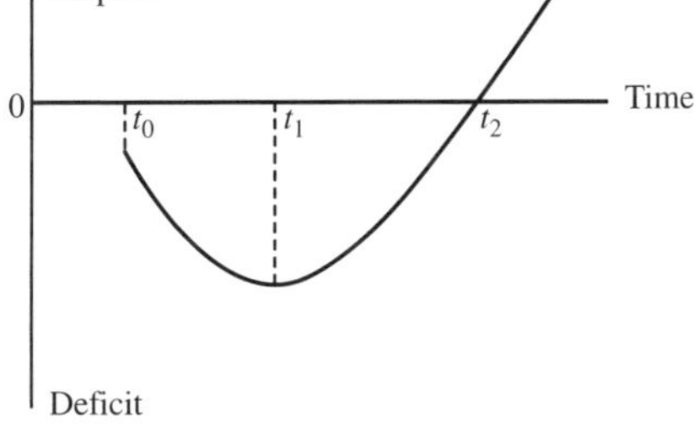

Fig. 18.1 J-Curve Effect of Currency Devaluation on the Balance of Payments

prior to depreciation, the trade deficit will further expand. In the conductive phase, import and export prices can be changed at the time of contract signing. Quantities, however, will not change because of supply and demand stickiness. Since an increase in the domestic currency price of imports will not lower the quantity, the cost of imports in the domestic currency will increase. Meanwhile, due to supply stickiness, export prices in foreign currencies will fall by the same margin as domestic currency depreciation, and as such, in terms of the domestic currency, export earnings will not increase, and thus, the deficit still will not decrease. By the quantity adjustment phase, total import and export quantities can change, and the expected effects of depreciation on the balance of payments will begin to be felt, thereby gradually shifting the deficit towards a surplus.

18.5 Conflicts between Internal and External Equilibrium and the Policy Mix

18.5.1 Conflicts between Internal and External Equilibrium

In Chapter 20, we will see that the Chinese government's monetary policy goals are economic growth, price stability, full employment, and balanced international payments. The first three goals are collectively known as the internal equilibrium, while the balance of payments is referred to as external equilibrium.

Suppose that you are both a rifle shooter and a pole-vaulter. Because you participate in two different sports, you must have two different types of sporting equipment — air rifles and poles — to be successful in both sports. If you use a rifle as a pole to jump, you will undoubtedly lose the game. Similarly, as for the government's economic policies, if the Government has a certain number of economic policy goals, then it will also need the same number of mutually independent and effective policy instruments, and only in this way can these goals be achieved. This is known as the **Tinbergen Norm**.

According to this principle, if a government uses flexible exchange rate policies, there will not be any difficulty in achieving both internal and external equilibrium. However, under a fixed exchange rate system, it will be difficult for the government to employ exchange rate as a policy tool to restore equilibrium in the balance of payments. In this case, the government can only use expenditure changing policies. As a result, there may be a conflict between internal and external equilibrium goal. This condition is called the **Meade conflict**. Clearly, one policy instrument cannot be used to achieve two goals at once. When external equilibrium requires contractionary policies, the internal equilibrium may require expansionary policies; and when external equilibrium requires expansionary policies, internal equilibrium may require contractionary policies. Specifically, when a country faces a balance of payments deficit and unemployment, or a balance of payments surplus and inflation, expenditure changing policies will be caught in a dilemma. Equilibrium in either the internal or external balance can only be achieved at the cost of the other.

18.5.2 Policy Mix in an Open Economy

However, Mundell points out that as long as fiscal policy and monetary policy is appropriate, we could achieve simultaneous internal and external equilibrium, thereby resolving this conflict. In Mundell's view, fiscal policy and monetary policy have relatively different effects on the balance of payments and nominal revenues. Because of this, countries with a fixed exchange rate system can achieve economic goals through these two independent policy instruments.

Fiscal policy and monetary policy have the same effect on national income and current accounts, and their different roles are primarily in the management of interest rates and capital accounts. Contractionary fiscal policy tends to lower interest rates, whereas contractionary monetary policy will increase the interest rates. Holding all else equal, higher domestic interest rates will improve the capital account balance, and lower domestic interest rates will damage capital account income. In this way, the two policies have different significances with regard to the balance of payments. If used appropriately, they can achieve both internal and external balances. Mundell is of the view that fiscal policy should address the internal equilibrium goals and monetary policy should address external equilibrium goals to achieve an overall economic balance. This principle is also known as the "policy mix theory".

Summary

The balance of payments is a systematic record of the economic transactions between residents of one country with those of foreign countries within a certain period of time. The balance of payments statement is a reflection of these economic activities. The balance of payments statement primarily contains current accounts, capital and financial accounts, reserves, and errors and omissions.

Emergencies, cyclical factors, structural factors, and monetary factors will result in an imbalance in the balance of payments. A massive and persistent imbalance — whether a deficit or a surplus — will bring about many adverse effects. Imbalances in the balance of payments can return to equilibrium through automatic adjustments or with the help of economic policy. Macroeconomic policies that promote equilibrium in the balance of payments primarily include exchange buffer policies, fiscal and monetary policies, foreign exchange policies and foreign exchange controls.

It is generally believed that domestic currency devaluation will improve the balance of payments and reduce balance of payments deficits. However, only if the domestic currency satisfies the Marshall–Lerner condition will devaluation improve the balance of payments. In addition, the role of the domestic currency devaluation in improving the balance of payments over time is known as the J-curve effect.

In an open economy, there will be a conflict between internal and external equilibrium. This is due to the fact that there are multiple objectives in an open economy. In accordance with the Tinbergen norm, various economic policy objectives should be accompanied with the same number of policy instruments. In order to achieve the goal of internal and external equilibrium, countries can adopt the principles of a policy mix with different economic policy instruments for different objectives. This is Mundell's policy assignment rule.

Key Terms

Tinbergen Norm; Balance of Payments; Balance of Payments Statement; International Reserves; Marshall–Lerner Condition; J-Curve effect; Terms of Trade; Conflicts between Internal and External Equilibrium; Foreign Exchange Buffer Policy; Policy Assignment Rule; Expenditure Changing Policy; Expenditure Switching Policy; Meade Conflict

Critical Thinking Questions

1. How can we properly understand the balance of payments?
2. What is the balance of payments statement? How are balance of payments accounts categorized?
3. What causes an imbalance in the balance of payments?
4. How can a large, persistent balance of payments imbalance adversely affect the domestic economy?
5. What mechanisms are available to address the balance of payments imbalance?
6. What is the role of exchange rate in adjustment of the balance of payments?
7. What are the Meade Conflict and the Tinbergen Norm?
8. How can a country achieve internal and external equilibrium simultaneously in an open economy?
9. After 1994, China has sustained a balance of payments surplus, which substantially increased the foreign exchange reserves held by the central bank. In terms of China's economic development, is this a good thing or a bad thing? Why?
10. At the end of 1997, countries affected by the Asian financial crisis such as South Korea, Thailand, Indonesia, and Malaysia all suffered substantial currency devaluation, presenting a serious challenge to China's export situation. In 1998, China experienced a rare catastrophic flood. Moreover, after 20 years of reform and development, China has changed from a shortage economy to a country with a surplus of production and insufficient domestic demand. Under these conditions, many people believed that the Chinese yuan should be devalued significantly in order to expand international demand

to compensate for the lack of domestic demand, thereby promoting economic growth. How do you view this policy proposal?

11. Since 2003, China's trade surplus has continued to increase. Due to China's compulsory foreign exchange settlement and sales system, the increase in the trade surplus caused increases of the central bank's fund outstanding for foreign exchange. Based on what we have learnt in Chapter 13, can you analyze the impact of this trade surplus on China's base money? Given this situation, some people believed that the Chinese yuan should appreciate sharply to reduce the trade surplus. Do you agree?
12. Over the past few years, the People's Bank of China has stressed that monetary policy should promote the balance of balance of payments. Do you think this goal is achievable? If yes, what measures can be taken to achieve this goal?

Chapter 19

National Income and Output Determination: The *IS–LM* Model

Learning Objectives

After studying this chapter, you will be able to:

- Clearly understand what determines national income
- Understand what multipliers are
- Understand the relationship between interest rates and national income when product market is in equilibrium
- Understand the factors that determine the slope of the *IS* curve
- Understand the factors that shift the *IS* curve
- Understand the relationship between interest rates and national income when the money market is in equilibrium
- Understand the factors that determine the slope of the *LM* curve
- Understand the factors that shift the *LM* curve
- Understand the automatic adjustment mechanisms of economic imbalances in the *IS–LM* model
- Use the *IS–LM* model to analyze the role of fiscal and monetary policies and their effects

A person's individual spending has a minimal impact on the economic growth of an entire country, but the consumption of all individuals does have a major impact on economic growth. This is not only because consumption itself constitutes a major segment of aggregate demand, but also because changes in the marginal propensity to consume have a multiplier effect, which will multiply the impact of investment, government spending, and net exports on economic growth. In this chapter, we will analyze the determinants of national income and output, the impact of product market and money market on the national income equilibrium, and the role of fiscal and monetary policies in adjusting national economic imbalance. The contents of this chapter will provide the theoretical framework for the next chapter.

19.1 Determination of Output

Within our economy, aggregate demand can be divided into four categories: (1) consumer demand or consumer spending, such as attending concerts, going to the movies, or going out to eat at a nice restaurant — all of these are considered as consumption; (2) investment spending, such as the construction of new plants and purchase of new equipment; (3) government spending, including administrative expenses, financial subsidies, etc.; and (4) net exports, namely a country's exports minus their imports.

If we set C as consumption, I as investment (demand), G as government spending and NX as net exports, then aggregate expenditure Y_{ad} is:

$$Y_{ad} = C + I + G + NX. \tag{19.1}$$

As our analysis in Chapter 4 indicates, consumption is a function of disposable income, and disposable income is total income minus taxes. If we set total income as Y, taxes as T and disposable income as Yd, then:

$$Y_d = Y - T. \tag{19.2}$$

If we then set the tax rate as t, then tax revenue is $T = t \cdot Y$, and disposable income is $Yd = (1 - t)Y$.

If a represents autonomous consumption, that is, the consumption that cannot be reduced even if income is zero, and c represents the propensity to consume, then:

$$C = a + c \cdot (1 - t)Y. \tag{19.3}$$

Thus:

$$Y_{ad} = a + c \cdot (1 - t) \cdot Y + I + G + NX. \tag{19.4}$$

When aggregate expenditure is equal to the current output, the economy reaches equilibrium, that is:

$$Y_{ad} = Y, \tag{19.5}$$

$$\text{So: } Y = a + c \cdot (1 - t) \cdot Y + I + G + NX. \tag{19.6}$$

Rearranging the equation, we have:

$$Y = \frac{a + I + G + NX}{1 - c \cdot (1 - t)}. \tag{19.7}$$

As the above equation indicates, autonomous consumption, investment spending, government spending, net exports, the propensity to consume, and the tax rate will all impact the level of national income. For instance, when autonomous consumption a is 500, investment spending I is 3000, government spending G is 1000, net exports NX is 500, the propensity to consume c is 0.8 (for every 1 yuan of disposable income, 0.8 yuan will be spent), and the tax rate t is 0.25, the equilibrium national income should be:

$$Y = \frac{500 + 3000 + 1000 + 500}{1 - 0.8 \times (1 - 0.25)} = 12{,}500. \tag{19.8}$$

So, how will a change in autonomous consumption, investment, government spending, or net exports change the national income? For instance, if all else is held equal, and investment spending increases by one yuan, how much will national income increase by? In general, this will cause an increase in national income of $\frac{1}{1-c\cdot(1-t)}$. This is a multiplier. For instance, if the propensity to consume is 0.8, and the tax rate is 0.25, then the multiplier is 2.5, that is, if investment increases by one yuan, the national income will increase by 2.5 yuan.

Suppose that in the example above, none of autonomous consumption, government spending, net exports, the propensity to consume and the tax rate changes; however, investment spending increases from 3000 to 4000. Then, the level of national income should be:

$$Y = \frac{500 + 4000 + 1000 + 500}{1 - 0.8 \times (1 - 0.25)} = 15{,}000. \tag{19.9}$$

In other words, national income increases by 2500, which is 2.5 times the increase in investment.

Conversely, if investment decreases by 1000, then national income will fall by a multiple of 2.5.

Similarly, changes in government spending or net exports will also cause a multiple increase or decrease in the national income.

Figure 19.1 demonstrates the determination of equilibrium national income. In the figure, the 45° line is the line of equilibrium levels of national income. Along this line, aggregate demand is equal to the aggregate supply. Above this line, aggregate demand is greater than aggregate supply; below this line, aggregate supply is greater than aggregate demand. In the figure, the two lines Y_{ad}^1 and Y_{ad}^2 denote two levels of aggregate demand. When aggregate demand is Y_{ad}^1, the equilibrium of national income is 1000, and when aggregate demand increases to Y_{ad}^2, the equilibrium of national income is 2000.

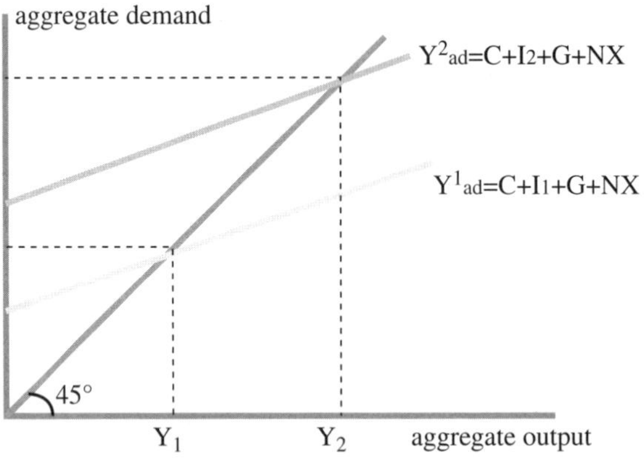

Fig. 19.1 Determination of Aggregate Demand, Aggregate Supply and National Income

19.2 Product Market Equilibrium: The *IS* Curve

19.2.1 Deriving the *IS* Curve

The *IS* curve depicts the relationship between interest rates and national income when product market is in equilibrium. To understand the nature of their relationship, we must first clearly understand the relationship between interest rates and aggregate demand.

Of the four segments of aggregate demand, three are affected by interest rates. First of all, if interest rates increase, people will typically cut back on current consumption and increase savings. As such, an increase in interest rates will typically cause a reduction in consumer demand. Conversely, a drop in interest rates will cause an increase in consumer demand and a drop in savings.

Second, in general terms, investment and interest rates are strongly correlated, that is, the higher the interest rates, the lower the investment demand, since enterprises will require a higher return on physical capital in order to compensate for financing costs. Conversely, the lower the interest rates, the lower the rate of return on physical capital that enterprises will require, and for this reason, investment demand will increase.

Finally, interest rates also affect net exports. Looking back on what we have learned in the previous chapter, the interest rate parity theory suggests that an increase in domestic interest rates will cause an appreciation in the spot rate of local currency. Conversely, a decrease in domestic interest rates will cause depreciation in the spot rate of local currency. An increase in the exchange rate of local currency will hurt domestic exports, while depreciation would cause an increase in exports. In this way, through the channel of exchange rate, an increase in domestic interest

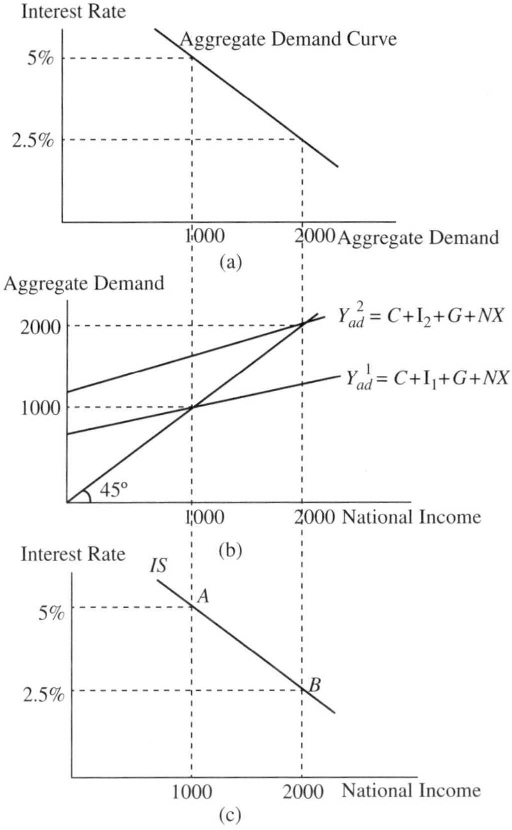

Fig. 19.2 National Income Determination When Product Market is in Equilibrium

rates will reduce net exports, while a drop in domestic interest rates will increase net exports.

By combining the above three factors, we can see that aggregate demand and interest rates are inversely related, that is, the higher the interest rates, the lower the aggregate demand, and vice versa. This relationship is depicted in Figure 19.2(a): when the interest rate is 5%, aggregate demand is 1000; when the interest rate is 2.5%, aggregate demand is 2000.

If we combine the figure of the relationship between interest rates and aggregate demand and the figure of the equilibrium level of national income when aggregate demand and aggregate supply are in equilibrium, we can draw a diagram of the relationship between interest rates and the level of national income. This is the *IS* curve. When the interest rate is 5%, aggregate demand is 1000, and when aggregate demand is 1000, the equilibrium level of national income should be 1000. As such, when the interest rate is 5%, the equilibrium level of national income is 1000, and in this way we can mark the point in which the interest rate and the equilibrium level of national income meet, which is point *A* in Figure 19.2(c). Similarly, we can also find the second point in which the equilibrium level of national income and the interest rate meet, which is point *B*. This point corresponds to an interest rate of 2.5% and a national income of 2000. If we connect point A and point B, we will get the *IS* curve.

The ***IS* curve** represents the relationship between the interest rate and the equilibrium national income when total output is equal to aggregate demand. The *IS* curve slopes downward from the upper left to the bottom right, indicating that higher interest rates will lower aggregate demand, and therefore lower the equilibrium level of national income.

19.2.2 Factors that Affect the Slope of the *IS* Curve

The slope of the *IS* curve is affected by the interest rate elasticity of aggregate demand. Interest rate elasticity of aggregate demand refers to the percentage change in aggregate demand when the interest rate changes by 1%. If the interest rate increases by 1% and aggregate demand decreases by 2%, the interest rate elasticity of aggregate demand is −2; if the interest rate decreases by 1% and aggregate demand increases by 1%, the interest rate elasticity of aggregate demand is 1.

The interest rate elasticity of aggregate demand will affect the slope of aggregate demand curve. In Figure 19.3(a), there are two aggregate demand curves: *AD* and *AD′*. When the aggregate demand curve is *AD*, if the interest rate falls from 5% to 4%, aggregate demand will increase from 1000 to 1400. When the aggregate demand curve is *AD′*, if the interest rate falls from 5% to 4%, aggregate demand will increase from 1000 to 2000. As we can see, the interest rate elasticity of aggregate demand *AD′* is larger than the interest rate elasticity of *AD*, so *AD′* is not as steep as *AD*.

The respective *IS* curves for the aggregate demand curves *AD* and *AD′* are IS_1 and *IS′*, and the latter is not as steep as the former. From this it can be seen that the larger the interest rate elasticity of aggregate demand, the flatter the aggregate demand curve and the *IS* curve, and the smaller the slope. Conversely, the lower the interest rate elasticity of aggregate demand, the steeper the aggregate demand curve and the *IS* curve, and the larger the slope.

Because of the effect of interest rates on consumer demand, investment demand, and net exports, the interest rate elasticity of consumption, investment demand, and net exports will also impact the slope of the *IS* curve. Corresponding to the interest rate elasticity of aggregate demand, the interest rate elasticity of consumption refers to percentage change in consumption when the interest rate changes by 1%. Similarly, the interest rate elasticity of investment demand refers to percentage change in investment demand when the interest rate changes by

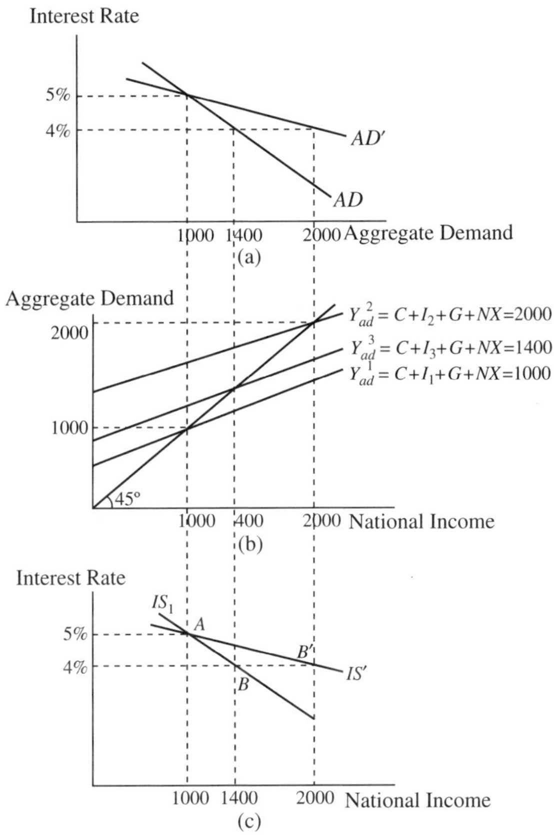

Fig. 19.3 Factors that Affect the *IS* Curve

1%, and the interest rate elasticity of net exports refers to percentage change in net exports when the interest rate changes by 1%. Here, we will primarily focus on the main factors that impact the interest rate elasticity of consumption and investment.

As mentioned in Chapter 4, changes in the interest rate affects consumption through two channels: first, a decline in interest rates will encourage people to borrow more for consumption, thereby increasing the spending; and second, a decline in interest rates will encourage people to reduce their savings and increase their current spending. For this reason, the interest rate elasticity of consumption is first subject to the effects of consumer credit. If consumer credit is far from perfect, regardless of any changes in interest rates, consumers will be unable to obtain consumer credit from banks. Thus, the interest rate elasticity of consumption would be very low, and vice versa. Lastly, any factors that affect savings may also have an effect on the interest rate elasticity of consumption. The greater the uncertainty about the future, the lower the interest rate elasticity of savings.

The interest rate elasticity of investment demand is first subject to the entrepreneurial prospects. If entrepreneurs are optimistic as to their prospects, even if interest rates rise, it will not have a major impact on investment spending. When economic prospects are better than usual, the interest rate elasticity of investment demand will be low. Conversely, when enterprises are rather pessimistic, even a small increase in interest rates will have a major impact on investment, and in this case, the interest rate elasticity of demand would be higher. Second, the interest rate elasticity of investment demand is also subject to corporate structures. If investment costs are not binding to the enterprise, higher interest rates will not inhibit the willingness to invest. When corporate structures are imperfect, the binding effect of interest rates on investment will be smaller, the interest rate elasticity of investment demand would be lower, and the aggregate demand curve would be steeper, as would the slope of the *IS* curve. This is what happens in the early stages of a transition era from planned economy to market economy.

19.2.3 Factors that Shift the *IS* Curve

The following factors may shift the *IS* curve: changes in autonomous consumption, investment spending unrelated to interest rates, government spending and tax revenue, and net exports unrelated to interest rates.

When the interest rate is fixed, an increase in autonomous consumption, investment, government spending, and net exports will shift the aggregate demand curve to the right. For instance, in Figure 19.4(a), AD shifts to the right to AD'. Along the aggregate demand curve AD', when the interest rate is 5%, aggregate demand is 1400; when the interest rate is 2.5%, aggregate demand is 2100. When aggregate expenditures are 1400 and 2100, the corresponding equilibrium level of national income would be 1400 and 2100, respectively. The new equilibrium point in which national income is 1400 and the interest rate is 5% is A', and the new equilibrium point in which national income is 2100 and the interest rate is 2.5% is B'. By connecting A' and B', we can get the new IS curve, that is IS'.

Since a change in taxes will affect disposable income, a decrease in tax rate will increase disposable income. This will increase consumption, and thereby shift the aggregate expenditure curve and the aggregate demand curve upward. An upward shift in the aggregate expenditure curve will shift the *IS* curve to the right.

Conversely, when autonomous consumption, investment unrelated to interest rates, government spending, and net exports unrelated to interest rates decrease, the *IS* curve will shift to the left. Since an increase in the tax rate will reduce consumption, higher tax rates will shift the *IS* curve downwards to the left.

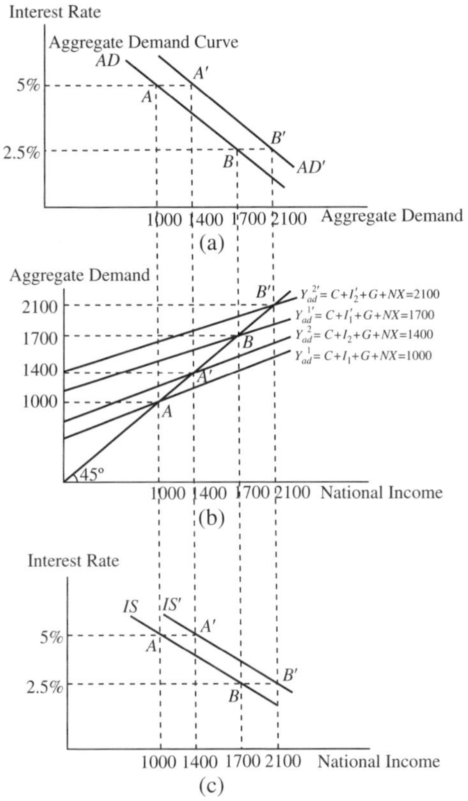

Fig. 19.4 Factors that Shift the *IS* Curve

19.3 Money Market Equilibrium: The *LM* Curve

19.3.1 Deriving the *LM* Curve

The ***LM* curve** depicts the relationship between interest rates and the national income when the money market is in equilibrium. As we have learned in Chapter 14, Keynes' theory holds that the demand for money can be divided into transactional demand and speculative demand. Transactional demand for money depends on the level of income. The higher the level of income, the higher the transactional demand. Conversely, the lower the level of income, the lower the transactional demand. Figure 19.5(c) depicts this relationship between the transactional demand for money and income. In this figure, when the level of national income is 900, the transactional demand for money is 600; when the level of national of income increases to 2100, the transactional demand for money increases to 1200.

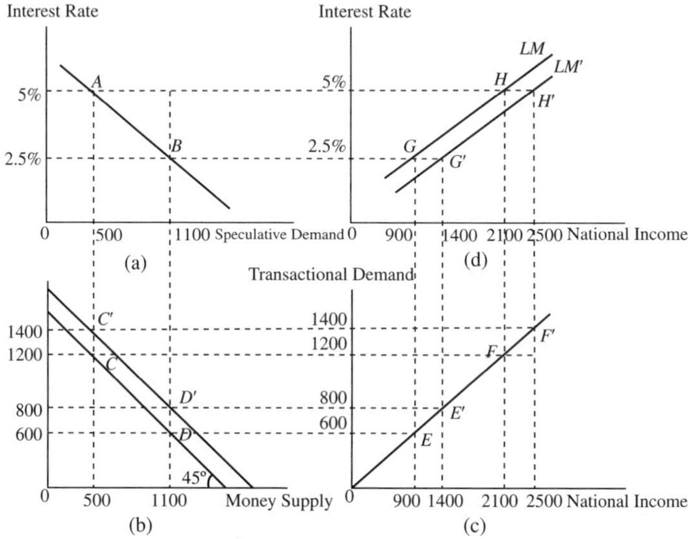

Fig. 19.5 *LM* Curve Derivation

Speculative demand is related to interest rates. The higher the interest rates, the lower the speculative demand for money. Conversely, when interest rates decline, the speculative demand for money will increase. Figure 19.5(a) depicts this relationship between the speculative demand for money and interest rates. In this figure, when the interest rate is 5%, the speculative demand for money is 500; when the interest rate is 2.5%, the speculative demand for money is 1100. In this figure, the speculative demand for money curve is downward-sloping from left to right, displaying the relationship between the speculative demand for money and interest rates.

Curve *CD* in Figure 19.5(b) is the money supply curve which has a slope of 45°. By adding the speculative demand for money in Figure 19.5(a) and the transactional demand for money in Figure 19.5(c), we can obtain the aggregate demand for money which displays the aggregate demand for money at a certain interest rate and a certain level of national income. Since an equilibrium in the money market requires that the demand for money is equal to supply of money, as such, points *C* and *D* in Figure 19.5(b), respectively indicate the two points in which the money market is in equilibrium. Point *C* corresponds to a speculative demand for money and a transactional demand for money of $500 + 1200 = 1700$ when the interest rate is 5% and national income is 2100. Point *D* corresponds to a speculative demand for money and a transactional demand for money of $1100 + 600 = 1700$ when the interest rate is 2.5% and national income is 900. By marking the point in which the interest rate is 2.5% and the national income is 900, we can obtain point G in Figure 19.5(d). Similarly, by marking the point in which the interest rate is 5% and the national income is 2100, we can obtain point H in Figure 19.5(d). By connecting points G and H, we can get the *LM* curve. Any point along this line represents a combination of an interest and the national income when the money market is in equilibrium.

19.3.2 Factors that Shift the *LM* Curve

The following factors will shift the *LM* curve:

- Changes in the money supply
- Changes in the demand for money

(a) *Changes in the Money Supply*

If all else is held equal, a change in the money supply will shift the *LM* curve. Suppose that the money supply increases from 1700 to 1900, curve CD in Figure 19.5(b) would shift to $C'D'$. However, since the money demand function does not change, when the interest rate is 5%, the speculative demand for money will still be 500. As the money supply increases to 1900, the transactional demand for money must be 1400 so that the money market is in equilibrium. As we can see in Figure 19.5(c), for the transactional demand for money to be 1400, national income must be 2500. Thus, when the money supply increases to 1900, the point where the interest rate of 5% and the national income of 2500 meet is the equilibrium point H', and in this case, the money market is in equilibrium. Similarly, only when the interest rate is 2.5%, the money supply is 1900 and the level of national income reaches 1400 will the money market achieve equilibrium. At this time, the transactional demand for money is 800, while the speculative demand for money is 1100. Thus, when the money supply is 1900, the point where the interest rate of 2.5% and the national income of 1400 meet is the equilibrium point G', and at this point, the money market is in equilibrium. By connecting points G' and H', we can get the new LM'. From this it can be seen that an increase in the money supply will shift the *LM* curve to the right. In the same way, we can deduce that when the money supply decreases, the *LM* curve will shift to the left.

(b) *Autonomous changes in the demand for money*

A shift in the speculative demand for money curve will also shift the *LM* curve. In Figure 19.6(a), the original speculative demand for money curve is AB, and when the aggregate supply of money is 1700, its corresponding *LM* curve is LM_1.

Now suppose that all else is held equal, the speculative demand for money curve shifts outward to $A'B'$. This outward shift indicates that under the same interest rates, the speculative demand for money increases. For example, in the new speculative demand for money curve, the speculative demands that correspond to the interest rates of 5% and 2.5% increase from 500 and 1100 to 700 and 1500,

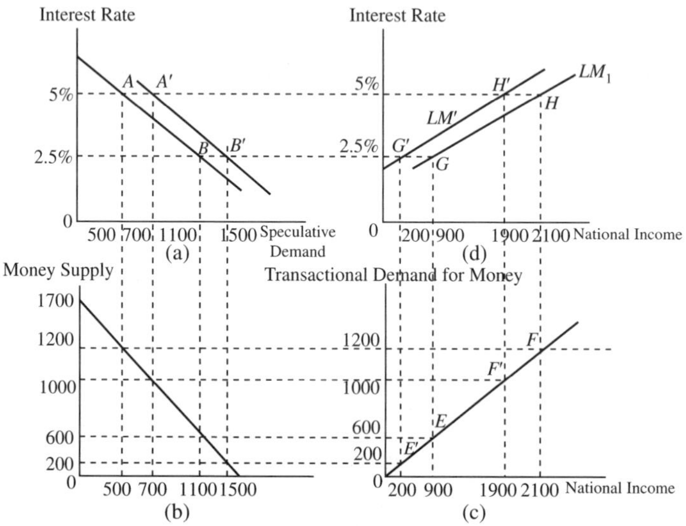

Fig. 19.6 Shifts in the *LM* Curve

respectively. Since no changes occur in the aggregate supply of money, which is still at 1700, the transactional demand for money must decrease from 1200 and 600 to 1000 and 200, respectively for the money market to return to equilibrium. At this time, the corresponding points in Figure 19.6(c) are F' and E'. The respective equilibrium points that correspond to this interest rate and national income are H' and G'. By connecting points H' and G', we can get the new *LM* curve of LM'. Relative to LM_1, the curve shifts to the left. As we can see, if the speculative demand for money curve shifts outwards and all else is held equal, the *LM* curve will shift upward and to the left. Given the same interest rates, the corresponding equilibrium level of national income will decrease. Conversely, if the speculative demand for money curve shifts down and to the left, the *LM* curve will shift down and to the right. At this time, given the same interest rates, the equilibrium level of national income will increase.

19.3.3 Factors that Affect the Slope of the *LM* Curve

In addition to the difference in position of the *LM* curves, the slope may also differ. Why would the slopes of the *LM* curves differ?

In general, the difference in the slopes is caused by the following two aspects

- The elasticity of speculative demand to interest rates.
- The proportional relationship between the transactional demand for money and the national income.

(a) *The Elasticity of Speculative Demand to Interest Rates*

The elasticity of speculative demand to interest rates is the percentage change in the speculative demand of money for each 1% change in interest rates. If M_s^d represents the speculative demand for money, ΔM_s^d represents the change in the speculative demand for money, r represents interest rates and Δr represents the change in interest rates, then:

The elasticity of the speculative demand for money to interest rate = $\frac{\Delta M_s^d / M_s^d}{\Delta r / r} = \frac{\Delta M_s^d}{\Delta r} \cdot \frac{r}{M_s^d}$.

For instance, in Figure 19.7(a), the speculative demand for money curve is AB, when the interest rate is 5%, the speculative demand for money is 500; when the interest rate falls to 2.5%, the speculative demand for money rises to 1100. In this case, the elasticity of the speculative demand for money to interest rate would be:

$$\frac{1100 - 500}{2.5\% - 5\%} \times \frac{5\%}{500} = -2.4.$$

In other words, given that speculative demand for money curve is AB, when interest rates change by 1%, the speculative demand for money will change adversely by 2.4%.

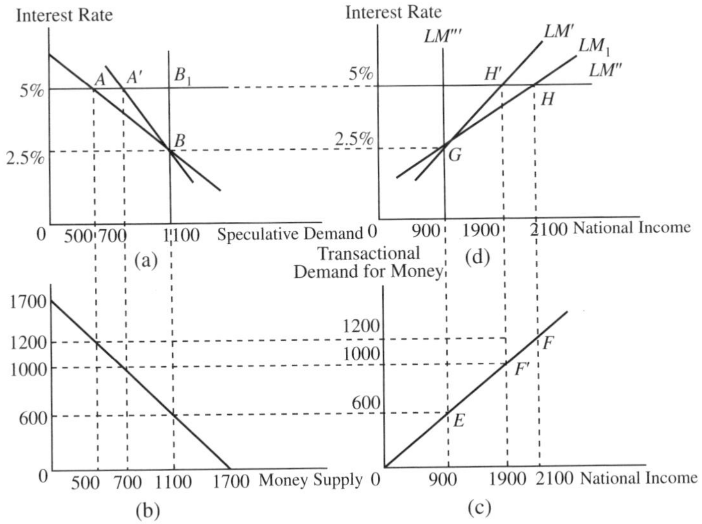

Fig. 19.7 Changes in the Slope of the *LM* Curve — Elasticity of Speculative Demand for Money

If the speculative demand for money curve is $A'B$, when the interest rate is 5%, the speculative demand for money is 700; when the interest rate is 2.5%, the speculative demand for money is 1100. In this case, the elasticity of the speculative demand for money to interest rate would be -1.14. In other words, for every 1% change in interest rates, the speculative demand for money will move in the opposite direction by 1.14%.

As we can see, the flatter the speculative demand for money curve, the higher the elasticity of the speculative demand for money to interest rate. In the extreme case where the speculative demand for money curve is horizontal, such as AA', the elasticity of the speculative demand for money to interest rate approaches infinity. On the other hand, the steeper the speculative demand for money curve, the lower the elasticity of the speculative demand for money. In the other extreme case where the speculative demand for money curve is vertical, such as BB_1, no matter how interest rates may change, the speculative demand for money will not change.

Based on the method above, we can draw out the *LM* curves of *LM1*, LM', LM'', and LM''' that respectively correspond to the speculative demand for money curves AB, $A'B$, AA', and BB_1. Thus, it can be seen that the higher the elasticity of the speculative demand for money to interest rate, the flatter the *LM* curve. In the extreme case where the elasticity of the speculative demand for money to interest rate approaches infinity, the *LM* curve forms a horizontal line. On the other hand, the lower the elasticity of the speculative demand for money, the steeper the *LM* curve. In the extreme case where the elasticity of the speculative demand for money is zero, the *LM* curve will become a vertical line.

(b) *The Proportional Relationship between Transaction Demands for Money and the National Income*

When the proportional relationship between the transactional demand for money and the national income changes, the slope of the *LM* curve will also be affected.

In Figure 19.8, suppose that the speculative demand for money curve is still *AB*, but a change occurs in the proportional relationship between the transactional demand for money and the national income. When the national income is 750, the transactional demand for money is 600, and when the national income is 1500, the transactional demand for money is 1200. In other words, the proportional relationship between the two is 0.8 instead of the original 0.67. In accordance with the method above, we can draw out the new *LM* curve, that is, LM'.

As we can see, given a certain relationship among the money supply, the speculative demand for money and interest rates and given a certain level of national income, the higher the transactional demand for money, the steeper the *LM* curve. Conversely, when the national income is fixed, the lower the transactional demand for money, the flatter the *LM* curve.

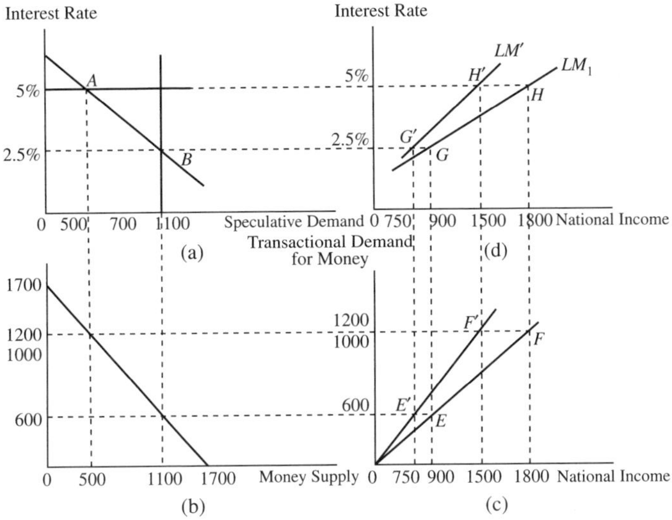

Fig. 19.8 Effect of the Transactional Demand for Money on the Slope of the *LM* Curve

19.4 The Equilibrium Level of National Income and Automatic Adjustment Mechanisms

19.4.1 Determining the Equilibrium Level of National Income in the *IS–LM* Analysis

When the product market and the money market both achieve equilibrium, the level of national income is determined as the equilibrium national income and the corresponding interest rates as the equilibrium interest rate. In other words, when the *IS–LM* curves intersect, both the product market and the money market achieve equilibrium. For instance, when the *IS–LM* curves are *IS* and *LM* in Figure 19.9, the equilibrium level of interest rates and national income are 5% and 2000, respectively.

In the figure below, there are four different regions. In Region I, the product market and the money market are both above the *IS–LM* curve, that is, the aggregate supply in the product market is greater than the aggregate demand, and the aggregate supply of money in the money market is also greater than the aggregate demand. In other words, both markets have an excess supply. In Region II, the economy is located above the *IS* curve and below the *LM* curve. Specifically, the aggregate supply in the product market is greater than the aggregate demand; however, the money market has excess demand. In Region III, the economy is located below the *IS* and *LM* curves. Specifically, the aggregate demand in the product market exceeds aggregate supply, and the aggregate demand for money exceeds its supply

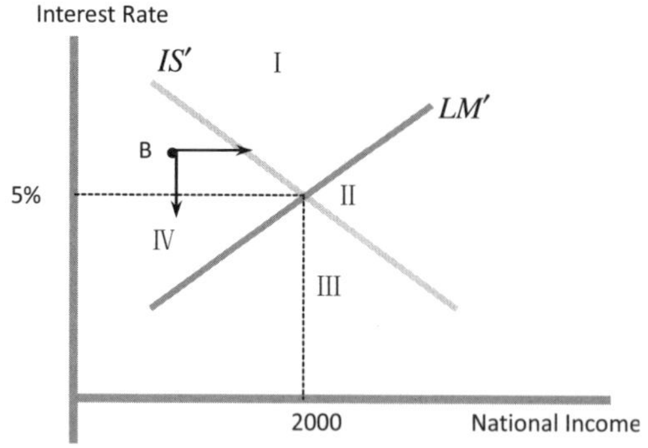

Fig. 19.9 National Income when Both the Product Market and the Money Market are in Equilibrium

in the money market. In Region IV, the economy is located below the *IS* curve and above the *LM* curve. That is, aggregate demand in the product market is greater than the aggregate supply, but the aggregate supply of money in the money market is instead greater than the aggregate demand. In each of the above regions, the economy is not in equilibrium.

19.4.2 Automatic Adjustment Mechanisms that Restore Equilibrium National Income

When the economy is not in equilibrium, it has an automatic mechanism that facilitates its recovery. Suppose that the economy is initially in the Region IV where the aggregate demand in the product market is greater than the aggregate supply, while the supply of money in the money market is greater than the demand for money. Since the supply cannot meet the demand in the product market, enterprises will increase production and the economy will move in the rightward direction. Meanwhile, since the supply of money in the money market is greater than the demand for money, money holders will purchase bonds that will push the price of bonds upwards and decrease interest rates. In this way, the economy will shift in the downward direction. Where these two meet is the point in which the economy returns to equilibrium. Similarly, regardless of which of the three other regions that the economy lies in, adjustment to output and interest rates will drive the economy to return to the equilibrium point.

19.5 Fiscal and Monetary Policies in the *IS–LM* Model

Since changes in government spending and tax revenue will shift the *IS* curve and changes in the money supply will shift the *LM* curve, the government can implement fiscal and monetary policies to lead the economy to equilibrium.

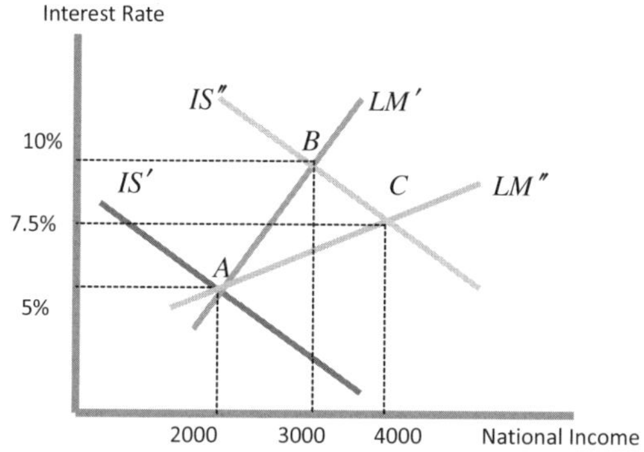

Fig. 19.10 Fiscal Policies Under the *IS–LM* Framework

19.5.1 Fiscal Policies

Fiscal policies include changes in government spending and tax policies. Through an increase in government spending or tax cuts, the government can implement expansionary fiscal policies to increase private consumption and investment spending. An increase in government spending or a decrease in tax rates will shift the *IS* curve upward, while a decrease in government spending or an increase in tax rates will shift the *IS* curve downward. The effect of fiscal policies depends on the strength of policy implementation and the slope of the *LM* curve.

Suppose that the economy is initially at the equilibrium point *A* in which the equilibrium national income and equilibrium interest rate are 2000 and 5%, respectively. However, the government is of the view that the level of national income is too low and decides to use expansionary fiscal policy to raise the equilibrium level of national income. Given different *LM* curve slopes, the effect of such fiscal policy will differ. Suppose that there are two *LM* curves: LM' and LM'', and the slope of LM' is greater than that of LM''. After the government increases spending and lowers tax rates, the *IS* curve will shift from the original IS' upward to IS''. The intersection of IS'' and LM' and that of IS'' and LM'' are point *B* and point *C*, respectively. The respective equilibrium levels of national income are 3000 and 4000, and the corresponding equilibrium level of interest rates are 7.5% and 10%, respectively. Clearly, the smaller the slope of the *LM* curve, the more efficient that expansionary fiscal policies will be in raising the income levels, and the smaller the fluctuations in the interest rates. Conversely, the larger the slope of the *LM* curve, the less effective that expansionary fiscal policies will be in raising the equilibrium level of national income, and the greater the impact it will have on interest rates.

There are two extreme cases: When the *LM* curve is horizontal and when it is vertical. For instance, in Figure 19.11, LM' is a vertical line, while LM'' is a

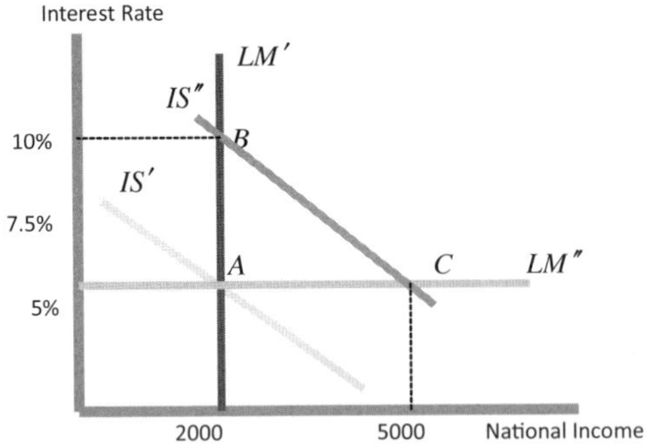

Fig. 19.11 Impact of the Slope of the *LM* Curve on the Effects of Fiscal Policies — Two Extremes

horizontal line. Assume that the economy is initially at the equilibrium point *A*, in which the equilibrium level of national income and interest rate are 2000 and 5%, respectively. If the government is of the view that the national income is too low and decides to use fiscal policies to raise it, it will shift the *IS* curve from *IS*′ upward to *IS*″. The intersection of *IS*″ and *LM*′ and that of *IS*″ and *LM*″ are *B* and *C*, respectively. Point *B* corresponds to the equilibrium level of national income of 2000 and the interest rate of 10%; point *C* corresponds to the equilibrium level of national income of 5000 and the interest rate of 5%. From this it can be seen that when the *LM* curve is vertical, expansionary fiscal policies can only raise interest rates but cannot raise the equilibrium level of national income. Conversely, when the *LM* curve is horizontal, expansionary fiscal policies will raise the equilibrium level of national income and will have no effect whatsoever on interest rates.

19.5.2 Monetary Policies

The government can also adjust the money supply to affect the equilibrium level of national income and interest rates. As we have learned before, when the government increases the money supply, the *LM* curve will shift to the right, and when the government reduces the money supply, the *LM* curve shifts to the left. After the government adjusts the money supply, the intersection between the new *LM* curve and the *IS* curve will determine the equilibrium level of national income and interest rates.

In Figure 19.12, suppose that the economy is initially at the equilibrium point *A* in which the equilibrium of national income is 2000 and the interest rate is 5%. The government is of the view that the level of national income is too low and decides to use expansionary policies to raise it. However, at this time, the government decides to use expansionary monetary polices. Suppose that after the government increases the money supply, the *LM* curve shifts from *LM*′ rightward

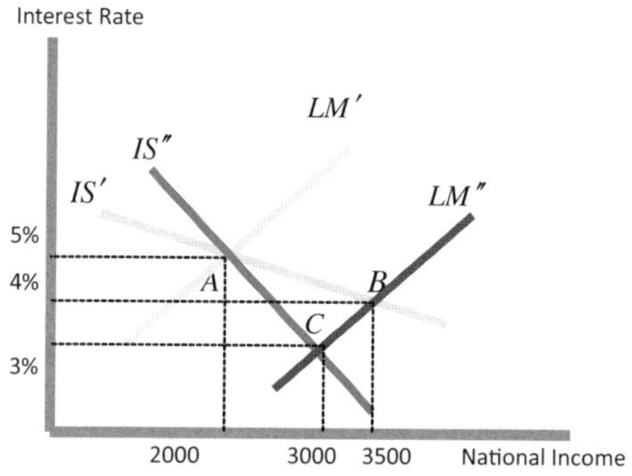

Fig. 19.12 Monetary Policies Under the *IS–LM* Framework

to LM''. The intersection of LM'' and IS' and that of LM'' and IS'' are B and C, respectively. Point B corresponds to the equilibrium level of national income of 3500 and the interest rate of 4%; point C corresponds to the equilibrium level of national income of 3000 and the interest rate of 3%. From this it can be seen that the slope of the *IS* curve has a significant impact on monetary policies: the smaller the slope of the *IS* curve, the more effective that expansionary monetary policies will be in raising the level of national income, and the smaller their effect on interest rates. Conversely, the larger the slope of the *IS* curve, the less effective that expansionary monetary policies will be in raising the level of national income, and the larger their effect on interest rates.

In the extreme case in which the *IS* curve is vertical or horizontal, expansionary monetary policies will only affect interest rates and will have no effect whatsoever on the equilibrium level of national income, or it will only affect the equilibrium level of the national income and have no effect whatsoever on interest rates.

In Figure 19.13, the economy is initially at the equilibrium point A, and at this time, the corresponding equilibrium level of national income is 2000 and the interest rate is 5%. Suppose the government uses expansionary monetary policies, and the *LM* curve shifts from LM' rightward to LM''. If the *LS* curve is the vertical line IS', the intersection of LM'' and IS' at point B determines the equilibrium level of national income of 2000 and the equilibrium interest rate of 2%. Conversely when the *IS* curve is the horizontal line IS'', the intersection of LM'' and IS'' at point C determines the equilibrium level of national income of 4000 and the equilibrium interest rate of 5%. From this it can be seen that when the *IS* curve is vertical, expansionary monetary policies will only lower interest rates but will not have any effect whatsoever on the equilibrium level of national income. Conversely, when the *IS* curve is horizontal, expansionary monetary policies will only raise the level of national income but will not have any effect whatsoever on interest rates.

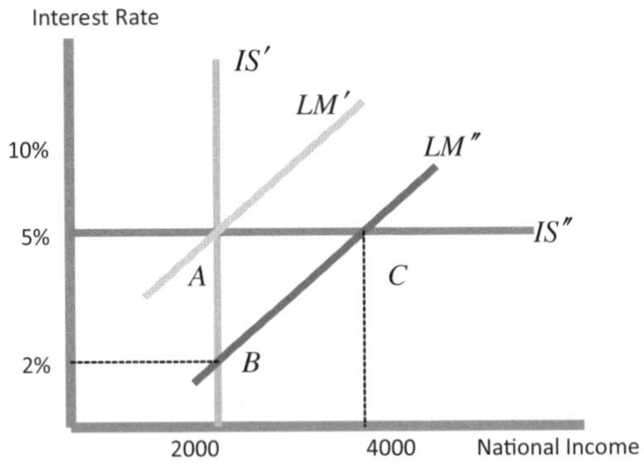

Fig. 19.13 Impact of the Slope of the *IS* Curve on the Effects of Monetary Policies — Two Extremes

Summary

Aggregate demand is comprised of consumer demand, investment demand, government spending, and net exports. When aggregate demand is equal to the current aggregate output, the economy reaches equilibrium. Autonomous consumption, investment spending, government spending, net exports, the propensity to consume, and the tax rate will all impact the level of national income. Changes in investment, tax revenue, net exports, and government spending will all have a multiple impact on national income through a multiplier effect.

The *IS* curve depicts the relationship between interest rates and the national income when product market is in equilibrium. The interest rate elasticity of consumption, investment and net export are the primary factors that affect the slope of *IS* curve, and thus anything that affects consumption, investment, and net exports will also affect the slope of the *IS* curve. Changes in government spending, tax revenue, and investment spending will all shift the *IS* curve.

The *LM* curve depicts the relationship between interest rates and the national income when the money market is in equilibrium. The interest rate elasticity of speculative demand for money and the proportion of transaction demand for money to the national income will all affect the slope of the *LM* curve. Changes in the money supply will shift the *LM* curve.

Changes in fiscal policy will shift the *IS* curve, thus affecting the level of national income and interest rates. The degree by which this will have an impact depends on the slope of the *LM* curve. Changes in the money supply will shift the *LM* curve, thus affecting the national income and interest rates. The degree by which this will have an impact depends on the slope of the *IS* curve.

Key Terms

Aggregate Demand; *IS* curve; *LM* curve

Critical Thinking Questions

1. What constitutes the aggregate demand?
2. What is a multiplier?
3. What is the *IS* curve?
4. What are the main factors that affect the slope of the *IS* curve?
5. What are the main factors that shift the *IS* curve?
6. What is the *LM* curve?
7. What are the main factors that affect the slope of the *LM* curve?
8. What are the main factors that shift the *LM* curve?
9. In the *IS–LM* model, what is the mechanism that automatically adjusts for economic imbalances?
10. As we have analyzed in Chapter 4, an improvement in consumer credit may lower the rate of savings. With this conclusion, analyze the impact an improvement in consumer credit would have on the slope of the *IS* curve.
11. Under a planned economy, enterprises have "soft budget constraints". Under these soft budget constraints, enterprises are not concerned with the cost of investment. After transitioning to a market economy, their budget constraints are enhanced significantly, as such, investment costs and risks will have a major impact on their investment decision-making. When enterprises face these different budget constraints, what kind of difference would there be in the slope of the *IS* curve?
12. Summarizing the contents of Chapter 14, analyze the impact of the rapid development of China's financial markets on the slope of the *LM* curve.

Chapter 20

Monetary Policy Operations of the Central Bank

Learning Objectives

After studying this chapter, you will be able to:

- Understand the ultimate objectives of monetary policies and how they are related
- Clearly understand the monetary policies of adjustments to the required reserve ratio, rediscounting and open market operations
- Clearly understand the roles and types of selective monetary policy instruments
- Understand the intermediate targets of monetary policy and the criteria for selecting intermediate targets
- Better understand the monetary policy of quantitative easing
- Understand the transmission mechanism of monetary policy
- Understand the effects of monetary policy
- Understand the impact of central bank independence on monetary policy
- Understand the discretionary and rule-based monetary policy paradigms
- Understand monetary policy transparency and credibility as well as accountability of the central bank

In order to iron out cyclical fluctuations in the economy, the central bank will often take monetary policy measures. Monetary policy refers to the various policy instruments that the central bank will use to increase or decrease the money supply to adjust interest rates, thereby guiding investment and consumption. Why does the central bank formulate and implement monetary policies? In order to achieve their objectives, what measures will the central bank take? After these measures have been implemented, what sort of effect will they have? The contents of this chapter will analyze these topics.

20.1 The Ultimate Objectives of Monetary Policy

20.1.1 Economic Growth

Since 1999, the global economy has been in a deflationary period, all the more so since the global recession in 2001. Since then, global economic growth has sharply declined. In 2001, the growth of the US economy declined by 2.1%. In order to stimulate growth and enable economic recovery, the US central bank — the Federal Reserve (Fed) — significantly reduced the federal funds rate 11 times over a single year. After the US financial crisis in 2008, in order to stimulate economic growth, the Fed dropped federal funds rates to the 0–0.25% range. Once interest rate could not be lowered further, the Fed used the monetary policy of quantitative easing by which they purchased a large volume of various types of assets to increase the money supply. Japan's central bank went one step further. Since the 1990s, Japan's economy has been stuck in a severe recession, and in order to promote economic recovery, Japan implemented a zero interest rate policy. Nevertheless, Japan's economy lost two decades, experiencing only weak growth. To spur economic growth, the Japanese central bank was the first in the world to use the monetary policy of quantitative easing, not only purchasing Treasury bills but also purchasing stock. After 1997, in order to stimulate economic growth, China also expanded money supply and on multiple occasions lowered deposit and loan rates. In October 1997, the interest rate on one-year deposits fell to 5.67%. By February 23, 2002, the rate had fallen to 1.98%. Given the economic shock of the global financial crisis in 2008 and the European sovereign debt crisis in 2011, in order to "maintain growth", China again used expansionary monetary policy. The majority of central banks throughout the world will implement monetary policies to maintain a certain level of economic growth. Of course, this does not mean that monetary policy should focus on pushing the growth rate as high as possible. Rather, it is best to keep real economic growth in line with the potential growth as determined by technology, environment and resources, etc. When the real growth rate of the economy is far higher than the potential growth rate, it causes inflation. Conversely, when the monetary policy is too much stringent and when the real growth rate is far lower than the potential growth rate, the unemployment rate may become too high.

Maintaining a certain rate of economic growth is one of the important objectives of monetary policy, as a decline in the rate of economic growth will not only reduce the cash in people's hands, but also consumption and welfare. Also, a decline in the economic growth rate or a serious economic recession can cause a serious social and psychological burden. In our modern society, people will consciously or unconsciously measure their personal success based on how much they make, and a decline in the economic growth rate will also cause a decline in personal income that will distort people's evaluation of their self-worth and abilities and thus do a great deal of harm to society.

20.1.2 Price Stability

Price stability is the most important monetary policy objective that the central bank will pursue. Whether prices continue to rise under inflation or continue to fall under deflation, both will have a major impact on the economy. As for the economic impact of price fluctuations, we have already analyzed this in detail in Chapter 16.

Since price fluctuations from both inflation and deflation have adverse effects on the economy, the central bank of each country will invariably set price stability as the primary objective of monetary policy. Nowadays, more and more central banks have selected price stability as the only ultimate objective of monetary policy. As stipulated by the *Law of the People's Bank of China*, the monetary policy of the People's Bank of China is formulated to maintain price stability and promote economic growth. With the rapid growth rate of China's investment in 2004, price indices also rose for several months. In order to prevent a bigger rise in the price index, central banks raised the required reserve. Since the CPI rose by over 5% for three consecutive months in the third quarter, the central bank raised benchmark interest rates on deposits and loans on October 28. Similarly, in order to stabilize prices and public expectations for inflation, after June 2004, the Federal Reserve raised the target value of federal funds rate 17 times in a row. Conversely, when prices continue to fall, deflation will occur, and the central bank will typically use stimulative monetary policy.

Of course, price stability does not necessarily mean that the central bank will fix prices. In fact, the central bank is not so resourceful and fixed prices will also impair economic efficiency. Today, the monetary policy objective of price stability for many central banks is typically to allow inflation to fluctuate in a small range around 2%. When the inflation rate is significantly higher than 2%, the central bank may use contractionary monetary policies, and vice versa.

20.1.3 Full Employment

Unemployment is not only an economic issue but will also cause a great deal of social issues, such as psychological stress or crimes and unhappiness of families. When an unfortunate husband and wife are both unemployed, there is either no guarantee to their livelihoods or only a little unemployment benefits for them to draw on. In this way, their lives will not only be stretched thin, but also be hard pressed when they try to put their kids in college. In addition, high unemployment is also a direct source of social unrest. Thus, full employment was once a monetary policy objective pursued by various countries.

However, full employment does not mean that no one is unemployed. Within our society there will always be a degree of unemployment, including frictional unemployment, seasonal unemployment, and voluntary unemployment. If you are unsatisfied with your current job and decide to resign to find a better-paid or otherwise more desirable job, there will be a period of time before you find this new job. During this period of time, you are **frictionally unemployed**. **Seasonal unemployment** is due to seasonal changes that will cause unemployment, and this type of unemployment is most prevalent in sectors related to agricultural production. In addition, there are also those who are **voluntarily unemployed**, and no matter how great a work environment or what sort of benefits that you provide them with, they will still reject the jobs. As such, monetary policy cannot eliminate voluntary unemployment.

Thus, full employment does not mean zero unemployment. A certain level of unemployment is also beneficial to economic development and structural adjustments. If there is no frictional unemployment, it becomes more difficult for new enterprises to find suitable workers and innovate. This is just like when there is no vacant place for rent. If you have to work at a new place, separate, satisfactory, and inexpensive accommodation would be difficult to come by. However, when there are vacant houses available for rent, everything will be easier. For this reason, monetary policy also allows for a certain unemployment rate, and given this unemployment rate, the supply and demand in the labor market will be equal and the labor market will be in equilibrium. At this time, the unemployment rate is called the **natural rate of unemployment**.

20.1.4 Balance of the Balance of Payments

As we have learned in Chapter 18, a serious imbalance in the balance of payments, whether it be a long-term surplus or deficit, will have a number of adverse effects on the economy. For this reason, the balance of the balance of payments is also an important objective of monetary policy. However, the balance of the balance of payments is not absolute. In the short term, a surplus or deficit in the balance of payments is not a cause for concern. Also, in the long term, one year of surplus or deficit may compensate for a different year's deficit or surplus. If this can be achieved, the balance of payments can be considered balanced. Additionally, not every country will regard the balance of the balance of payments as a monetary policy objective. Since the 1970s, countries with a trade deficit have always had a trade deficit, and those with a trade surplus have always had a trade surplus, with these deficits/surpluses continuing to widen. The United States is one of the former countries, while Japan is one of the latter. However, the Federal Reserve and the Japanese central bank did not take steps to rectify their imbalance.

20.1.5 Financial Market Stability

Nowadays, financial markets have an even greater impact on the real economy, which is why financial market stability has also become an important objective and concern of monetary policy. When banks face liquidity difficulties, central banks must give full play to their function as the lender of last resort to prevent further deterioration of banking system liquidity difficulties that may lead to financial panic. Additionally, exchange rate volatility will also have an adverse effect on imports and exports. Therefore, when exchange rates on the exchange market fluctuate in a way which the central bank had not expected, the central bank will use various monetary policy measures to intervene and stabilize the exchange rate. Finally, stock market and other capital market instability will send a shock to investment, consumption, and the economy as a whole. Nowadays, when central banks formulate and implement monetary policy, they will also take into account capital market conditions. It is precisely because of the above reasons that central banks will play an important role in financial market stability. The People's Bank of China will offer refinancing to troubled financial institutions. In order to stabilize the Chinese stock market in 2005, the People's Bank of China provided tens of billion yuan in refinancing to several securities companies. As the US subprime mortgage crisis of 2008 continued to deteriorate, the US central bank — the Fed — used various channels to provide a number of financial institutions and markets with credit and liquidity support. When the price of financial assets falls sharply, and financial institutions face liquidity difficulties, the large-scale liquidity assistance that the central bank provides makes it the "firefighter" in the financial system.

20.1.6 Conflicting Objectives

When conflicts exist between some of the monetary policy objectives, the pursuit of some objectives may make it impossible for central banks to attend to others.

First of all, a conflict exists between price stability and full employment. As indicated by the Phillips curve, an inverse relationship exists between prices and the unemployment rate. The higher the rate of inflation, the lower the rate of unemployment, and vice versa. When the unemployment rate is high, in order to add jobs, the central bank would need to adopt a loose monetary policy by expanding money supply and lowering interest rates to stimulate corporate investment and increase the demand for labor. However, a rapid expansion of the money supply would also cause inflation. On the other hand, in order to stabilize prices, the central bank must tighten monetary policies to reduce the money supply and raise interest rates, which will harm corporate investment and increase unemployment. Therefore, a country cannot pursue price stability and full employment at the same time. A classic example of this conflict occurred in the early 1980s when Paul Volker, Chairman of the Federal Reserve, significantly raised federal funds rates to control the high rate of inflation. As a result, over 1 million people became unemployed. One American architect, Howard, expressed the impact on employment of the Federal Reserve's price stability measures, saying "We used to pass people by and say 'How's it going?', but nowadays, we just say 'How much longer can you hold out? Will you make it to the end of the year?'".

Another conflict exists between price stability and the balance of the balance of payments. When prices rise, domestic currencies will depreciate, and when exchange rates do not adjust accordingly, the price of imported goods will be relatively low, which will have an adverse effect on domestic exports and thus exacerbate the balance of payments. On the other hand, if the domestic prices continue to fall, and the exchange rate does not adjust, the price of domestic products will be relatively low on the international market, which would stimulate an increase in exports and a corresponding decrease in imports and create a surplus-type imbalance.

A conflict also exists between economic growth and balance of the balance of payments. When an economy grows too fast, demand for imports will increase, and a substantial increase in imports will cause a deficit. In the event of imbalance of the balance of payments, though decreasing the domestic demand may help put it right, economic growth will be adversely affected as well. Since 2003, China's trade surplus has continued to increase, and even though the government is of the view that an imbalance is a "serious" issue, it is also worried that a decline in exports would undermine the growth of the economy. As such, China seems to be caught in between a rock and a hard place.

Finally, a conflict also exists between price stability and financial market stability. When inflation becomes serious, in order to suppress an excessive price hike, the central bank will tighten monetary policies by reducing the money supply and raising interest rates. An increase in interest rates would cause a fall in bond prices. Meanwhile, when interest rates rise, it would be more favorable to hold onto deposits, and investors may reduce their investment in bonds or stocks which would then cause a reduction in the supply of funds on the financial market. Additionally, after interest rates have risen, corporate financing costs will also rise, which means that the profitability of listed companies will fall accordingly, thereby disrupting the stock market. Along the same lines, we can also see that a significant conflict exists between economic growth and financial market stability. In order to stimulate economic growth, the central bank will increase the money supply and lower interest rates, which will significantly change investor expectations and further overheat financial markets. This makes reverse adjustment necessary, may cause the economy to fall into long-term recessions.

Since these conflicts exist amongst the varied monetary policy objectives, nowadays, more and more central banks are shifting towards a single objective monetary policy framework: price stability has virtually become the only ultimate objective of monetary policy. These central banks define price stability as a state when changes in the general price level do not have a significant influence on the public investment and consumer decisions and expectations. In this state, a desirable rate of economic growth and rate of employment are achieved, though balancing the balance of payments does not appear to be within the scope of consideration.

20.2 Instruments of Monetary Policy Operations

In order to achieve monetary policy objectives, central banks must have corresponding policy instruments. Based on the different effect of monetary policies of the central bank on commercial banks and interest rates, monetary policy instruments can be divided into direct controls and indirect controls.

Direct control monetary policies are primarily the central bank's direct credit controls used to regulate money supply or interest rates to achieve the objectives of monetary policies. Direct credit controls are most common in planned economies, which includes **credit rationing** and interest rate controls. Credit rationing is the central bank's limitations on the scale and purpose of commercial bank credit based on the needs of the economy and as a means of avoiding excess credit expansion. For example, as stipulated by the central bank, a certain commercial bank can only issue a maximum of 50 billion yuan in loans over a given year. Interest rate controls by the central bank are the act of stipulating the interest rates of deposits and loans to prevent commercial banks from raising or lowering interest rates to fight for deposits or loans, as such vicious competition would threaten the stability of the banking system. However, the effect of direct credit controls is generally very poor and may also distort the efficiency of resource allocation, and for this reason, most central banks will typically use indirect monetary policy instruments.

Indirect control monetary policies are monetary policies that are implemented through the market as a means of influencing the reserves of commercial banks as well as adjusting money supply and market rates. Based on their different influence on the economy, indirect monetary policy instruments can be divided into:

- General Monetary Policy Instruments
- Selective Monetary Policy Instruments

20.2.1 General Monetary Policy Instruments

General monetary policy instruments refer to policy instruments that impact the monetary and economic system as a whole; selective monetary policy instruments only impact a portion of the system rather than the whole. There are three types of general monetary policy instruments:

- Adjusting the required deposit reserve ratio
- Rediscount mechanisms
- Open market operations

(a) *Adjusting the Required Deposit Reserve Ratio*

The required deposit reserve ratio is the basis of the required deposit reserve system. Additionally, the system also provides for the liabilities of financial institutions that need required reserve, the assets that can serve as a reserve, and the calculation of reserve periods (e.g., whether the reserve is calculated biweekly or on a monthly basis; whether the reserve is calculated on the basis of the balance of the period or the average liabilities over the period), and whether or not the central bank will make interest payments on the reserve. Both in China and in Western countries, central banks traditionally do not make interest payments on reserves, and for this reason, the higher the required deposit reserve ratio, the less fund that commercial banks can freely utilize and the greater the cost of opportunity. Therefore, the required deposit reserve ratio is also known as "reserve tax".

In terms of monetary controls, adjusting the required deposit reserve ratio has two effects on the amount of money. First, an adjustment in the ratio will change the reserve structure of the banking system. By increasing the ratio, the banking system will have to transfer a portion of excess reserve to the required reserve, which lowers the basis on which the banking system can create deposits. Conversely, when the central bank lowers the required reserve ratio, a portion of the banking system's required reserve will become excess reserve, and commercial banks can utilize this portion of excess reserve to create deposit currency. Second, the required reserve ratio is an important factor that affects the monetary multiplier. Raising the required reserve ratio will lower the monetary multiplier. On the contrary, lowering the ratio will raise the monetary multiplier, thereby improving the capacity of the banking system to expand the money supply.

Box 20.1 The Global Trend for Lowering Required Deposit Reserve Ratios

In recent years, many central banks throughout the world have lowered required reserve ratios or have simply abolished the required deposit reserve system. From December 1990 to April 1992, the US Federal Reserve eliminated the required reserve for time deposits and lowered the required reserve for checkable deposits from 12% to 10%. After October 2008, the US began to make certain interest payments on required reserves of commercial banks. In April 1992, Canada eliminated all required reserves for time deposits of greater than two years. The central banks of Switzerland, New Zealand, and Australia have all completely eliminated required reserves. In short, there are more and more indications of a trend that central banks are lowering required reserve ratios or are even eliminating their required reserve systems.

The countries that have lowered the required deposit reserves have done so for several reasons. First of all, in addition to the required deposit reserve ratio, the cash leakage rate and the excess reserve ratio also are important factors that determine the monetary multiplier, and for this reason, lowering

(*Continued*)

Box 20.1 (*Continued*)

the required reserve ratio will not make the central bank lose controls over the monetary multiplier. Second, in Western countries, central banks do not make interest payments to commercial banks on required reserves, and required reserves reduce the funds that commercial banks can use to profit from investment. Required reserve ratios actually increase the capital costs of commercial banks and lower their competitiveness, and lowering the required reserve ratio can improve commercial bank competitiveness to a certain degree. Third, the capital adequacy management as stipulated in the Basel Accords has partially replaced the function of the required reserve ratio to constrain the credit expansion of commercial banks. Finally, many countries have set certain market interest rates as intermediate targets of monetary policy and have focused on their smooth operation. Adjusting the required deposit reserve ratio can have a relatively huge impact on the liquidity of the financial system and thus cause a considerable change in market rates, which is in conflict with the smooth operation of interest rates.

It is generally believed that one of the primary advantages of adjusting the required reserve ratio to control the money supply lies in the equal effect that it has on banks. However, adjusting the ratio also has two weaknesses. First, it is the "giant axe" among monetary policy instruments, which has such a huge impact on the money supply that it makes fine-tuning impossible. Therefore, the volatility of market rates before and after the central bank adjusts the required deposit reserve ratio will be relatively high. Second, when the central bank raises the required reserve ratio, those banks with a very low amount of excess reserves will face liquidity problems. Frequent adjustments of the required reserve ratio will make liquidity management difficult for banks and will increase the difficulty for its rational use of funds. For this reason, central banks rarely use required reserve ratio adjustments to control the money supply.

(b) *Rediscount Mechanisms*

Rediscounts are the act whereby commercial banks have their commercial paper discounted by the central bank. Of the various monetary policy operations, rediscount mechanisms simply means that central bank changes the **rediscount rate** and influences the willingness of commercial banks to apply for loan discounts, thereby influencing their reserves and base money. The rediscount rate is the interest rate charged by the central bank when providing commercial banks with discounting, which in fact, is a necessary cost that must be paid by commercial banks for loans discounted by the central bank. When the central bank increases the discount rate, it raises the cost on commercial banks for rediscount loans from the central bank, and thus lowers the amount of rediscounts that commercial banks will request from the central bank, thereby lowering their base money. Conversely, when the central bank lowers the rediscount rate, rediscounting becomes much more attractive to commercial banks, and rediscounts will increase, thereby increasing the base money and money supply.

In addition to adjusting the rediscount rate, the central bank can also implement limitations on the amount of rediscounts and specify standards on rediscounted bills. For example, the central bank may stipulate that only the commercial paper of enterprises with a AAA credit rating can be rediscounted, thus greatly limiting the scope of bills that can be rediscounted. As stipulated by the central bank, the maximum amount of a commercial bank's loans that can be rediscounted by the central bank is limited to 50 million yuan. At this time, even if the commercial bank is willing to accept the central bank's rediscount rate, their rediscount demands cannot be fully met, and the commercial bank may also experience "rationing".

The central bank's rediscounting to commercial banks can be divided into three categories, namely adjustment rediscounts, seasonal rediscounts, and extended rediscounts. Adjustment rediscounts are used to assist commercial banks in addressing the issues of temporary insufficient liquidity and short positions, the term of which is very short. Seasonal rediscounts are used to resolve liquidity pressures on banks due to seasonal changes. For example, during the agricultural harvest season, farmers will sell a large amount of agricultural goods, increasing the demand for funds within the transaction of these goods. In order to meet this seasonal demand for money, banks can use seasonal rediscounting. When a commercial bank's deposits drastically decrease or when faced with a severe liquidity crunch, the bank can request an extended rediscount from the central bank, the term of which is generally longer.

In fact, rediscount mechanisms to a large extent allow the Central Bank to play its role as the lender of last resort to resolve the insufficient required reserve and liquidity problems of commercial banks. Additionally, as a policy instrument, rediscounting also has an "**announcement effect**" that signals the future monetary policy intentions of the central bank, thereby affecting the expectations of commercial banks or the general public. When the central bank raises the rediscount rate, people may believe that the central bank will tighten the money supply and that the inflation rate will fall. If this is the case, during times of high inflation, it will reduce panic buying caused by price increases. Conversely, if the central bank lowers the rediscount rate, the public may believe that it is a signal of expansionary monetary policies that will raise prices and increase the willingness to spend. However, the "announcement effect" may have the exact opposite effect that will confuse public expectations. For example, when the central bank lowers the rediscount rate, the public may believe that this is the central bank's natural reaction to an economic recession, and if the public believes that the central bank's monetary policies cannot stimulate the economy to the point of a recovery, they may expect that their income will fall, which will further their spending cuts. In this case, it will have a tightening effect on the money supply.

When the central bank adjusts the rediscount rate, despite the change in borrowing costs for commercial banks, whether or not the central bank can achieve its expected results still depends on the response elasticity of commercial banks to the change in the rediscount rate. If commercial banks are not sensitive to changes in the rediscount rate, it will be difficult for the central bank to control the money supply through rediscount mechanisms. Furthermore, the number of instruments commercial banks are willing to rediscount is based completely on their own objectives, and as such the central bank is in a passive position. There is a saying that sums this up, that "you can lead a horse to water, but you can't make him drink".

(c) *Open Market Operations*

Open market operations is the central bank's purchases or sales of marketable securities on the securities market so as to affect the reserves of the banking system and further affect the money supply. When the central bank purchases government bonds in the open market, the reserves of the banking system will increase and will thereby lay a foundation for the banking system's creation of money. Conversely, when the central bank sells government bonds on the open market, it will reduce the reserves of the banking system, thereby contracting the money supply.

In general, the ideal instrument for the central bank's open market operations is short-term government bond. This is because when a central bank conducts open market operations in the bond market, a portion of bond holders will become the beneficiaries of the monetary policy, while other bond holders will become the victims. In order to avoid a significant fluctuation in bond prices due to open market operations, the central bank must select a bond market with a relatively large capacity and low potential risks. As for long-term government bonds, even with their reliable credit guarantee, their market capacity is also relatively small and their liquidity low. Additionally, central bank monetary policies can only have an effect on short-term rates, whereas the rates on these government bonds are long term, and thus cannot meet the demands of the central bank's open market operations. As for corporate bonds and stocks, their markets are too small to withstand the central bank's open market activities, and the potential risks are also enormous. Since corporate stock prices are the "barometer" for a company's performance, a change in corporate stock prices will reflect the confidence of shareholders and the market valuation of the company's assets, but the central bank's open market operations are not for profit. Therefore, if corporate stock were used as an instrument of open market operations, the changes induced by central bank activities in the price of corporate stock would not reflect the objective evaluation of the public market towards the company's assets, and the movement of this stock price may lead to a distorted resource allocation. The crux of this problem lies in the fact that if these two securities with low market capacities were to be used for the central bank's open market operations, it would lead to price volatility, which would not only be unfair but would also lead to extremely high social costs. The open market operations would be doomed to fail and would not achieve the policy's expected results. Since the amount of securities held by those financial institutions that engage in securities vastly exceeds their own capital, if they suffered a serious blow due to the open market activities, they may abandon the role of market maker and retreat to only serving as a broker between the buyer and seller, which will doubtlessly reduce the efficiency of the capital market. Clearly, only government bonds, specifically short-term government bonds, can meet the two requirements of the central bank's open market operations. Whether in terms of quality or quantity, other bonds are not comparable to short-term government bonds, which are the ideal and most effective financial instrument for open market operations. It is precisely because of this that in countries with mature open market operations, governments will frequently issue a large volume of short-term government bonds in order for the central bank to implement monetary controls.

Nevertheless, open market operation instruments are not restricted to short-term government bonds alone. If the central bank holds a low balance of government bonds and yet it needs to curb inflation by recovering the base money, controlling money supply growth and raising interest rates, it can issue its own bonds (i.e., central bank bills). The People's Bank of China issues large volumes of central bank bills to hedge the funds outstanding for foreign exchange (see Chapter 13). When the financial market is in turmoil and liquidity is insufficient, the central bank can also directly purchase certain financial instruments, thereby directly improving the liquidity of the financial market. For example, after the US subprime mortgage crisis, the Federal Reserve purchased commercial papers and asset-backed securities. When the central bank of Japan implemented quantitative easing, they even purchased stocks as a means of open market operations.

Open market operations can either be proactive or reactive. Proactive open market operations are designed to change the reserves and base money within the banking system. Reactive open market operations thus are designed to offset the impact to the monetary base caused by changes in other factors, thereby causing the base money to remain relatively stable. If there are macroeconomic signs of a recession, reduced investment and stagnant consumption, the central bank will use proactive open market operations and purchase a large volume of government bonds in order to expand the money supply and increase reserves in the banking system. Another example is that an increase in government deposits will reduce the base money. If the central bank does not want this to happen, it can also use open market operations to purchase government securities to offset the reduction in the base money. This is a type of reactive open market operation.

Of course, the purchase and sale of government bonds in open market operations is different from you buying a can of soda, in which you hand over the money with one hand and grab the soda with the other, nor is it like your purchase and sale of stocks in which you will purchase a certain type of stock, and sell it when having earned a certain amount of capital gains. If you do not have high expectations for this stock, you probably would not purchase it again. Open market operations are often through repos and reverse repos. Of course, sometimes the central bank will also purchase and sell through spot trading as a means of implementing open market operations. Repo refers to an agreement signed between the Central bank and a financial institution that the Treasury bills held by the central bank will be temporarily transferred to the latter at an agreed price; meanwhile, the central bank has also agreed to buy back these bonds at a certain date in the future based on a negotiated price. During a repo, the central bank's transfer of their Treasury bills to a commercial bank is reflected on the central bank's balance sheet as a reduction in government bonds and an equivalent reduction in financial institution reserves on the liabilities side. Thus, the central bank's repo operations are a means of recovering the base money.

Conversely, if the central bank wants to inject base money, it can use the open market operation of reverse repos. Open market reverse repos refer to when the central bank and a commercial bank or other financial institution sign an agreement in which the latter will transfer their Treasury bills to the central bank at an agreed price, and meanwhile, the central bank has also agreed to sell back these bonds to the original financial institution on a certain date in the future based on a negotiated price. During a reverse repo, the asset side of the central bank's balance sheet shows an increase in government bonds, while the liabilities side shows an increase in commercial bank reserves.

Compared to the required reserve ratio and rediscounting policies, open market operations have the following advantages:

(1) The central bank can take the initiative when using open market operations, such as when to purchase and when to sell securities to change the banking system reserves; such timing can be controlled by the central bank. (2) Open market operations are uniquely flexible in terms of the amount of securities sold, which is completely determined by the needs of the central bank, and for this reason, open market operations have also been called "fine-tuned" monetary policy instruments. (3) It is easy to carry out a reverse correction. If the central bank suddenly realizes that the money supply has expanded excessively due to open market operations, it can immediately offer securities on the open market to recover the excess base money, and vice versa. (4) Open market operations are easy and quick. The securities exchange system has become very advanced these days, and as long as trade orders are issued, the transaction will usually be completed in a very short period of time. (5) The central bank's open market operations can also affect the interest rate structure. For example, if the central bank uses open market operations to purchase

10 million yuan worth of short-term Treasury bills and also sells 10 million yuan worth of long-term government bonds, it may raise the price of short-term Treasury bills and lower the price of long-term Treasury bonds, and for this reason, even if the total amount of the base money is not effected, a higher price for short-term Treasury bills will lower interest rates and the lower price of long-term government bonds will raise interest rates.

20.2.2 China's Practice of General Indirect Monetary Controls

In 1998, China abandoned traditional credit scale controls as a means of direct financial control, and instead adopted the indirect monetary controls of open market operations and the adjustment of the required deposit reserve ratio. Indirect monetary policy has begun to play an increasingly important role in China's macroeconomic controls.

(a) *The Use of Required Deposit Reserve Ratio in China*

For a long period of time after market reforms, China implemented a very high required deposit reserve ratio. The high reserve requirement at that time was meant to tie in with the People's Bank of China's direct credit scale control measures with the typical characteristics of financial repression (see Chapter 22). In order to promote financial deepening, improve the autonomy of commercial banks and reform China's monetary control instruments, China introduced the deposit reserve reform in the 1990s. Also, when the macroeconomic situation was favorable, the central bank lowered the deposit reserve ratio. When China reformed the monetary control mechanisms in 1998, the world had not yet recovered from the aftermath of the Southeast Asian financial crisis. Meanwhile, China had experienced deflation due to a structural lack of demand at the end of 1997, and prices, economic growth, and the money supply all continued to decline. In this situation, the Chinese lowered the reserve requirement from 13% to 8% in 1998. However, after this drop in the required deposit reserve ratio, private investment did not pick up and the demand for bank credits remained sluggish. Thus, in 1999, the People's Bank of China again decided to lower the required deposit reserve ratio from 8% to 6%.

In the following three years, adjusting the required reserve ratio, as a policy instrument, had been shelved. However, after mid-2002, since investment demand was rapidly increasing, especially with the continuous increase of the Chinese trade surplus and the strong appreciation expectation of the Chinese yuan, large-scale foreign capital inflows began and led to a substantial increase in the People's Bank of China's holding of foreign assets. Meanwhile, the domestic money supply also continued to rise, which increased the pressure of inflation. Thus, in September 2003, the reserve requirement for commercial banks was raised from 6% to 7%. Since then, China has entered a monetary policy cycle of continued increases in the required reserve ratio. From September 2003 to the end of 2012, the People's Bank of China has increased the required reserve ratio over 30 times. As shown

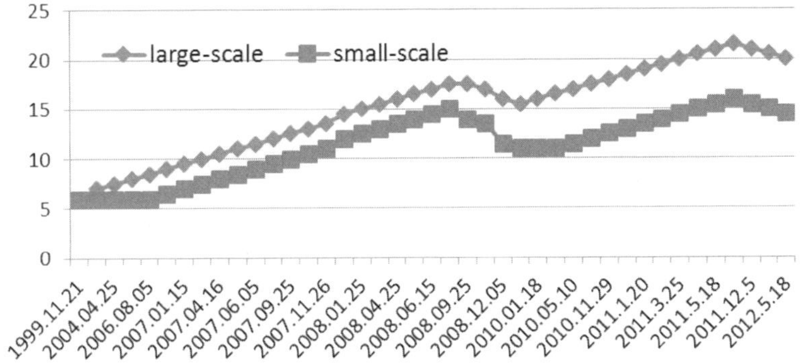

Fig. 20.1 China's Required Reserve Ratio for Large-Scale and Small-Scale Financial Institutions (Unit: %)

Source: Website of the People's Bank of China

in the figure, the ratio had gone up to as much as 21.5%. Of course, during this period of time, from the fourth quarter of 2008 to 2012, the central bank also lowered the ratio and increased the supply of liquidity to "maintain economic growth". Over the last decade since 2003, the world's major developed countries have lowered their required deposit reserve ratios or have abandoned them all together, but the Chinese central bank had to do the opposite with the primary direct purpose of counterbalancing the expanding liquidity pressure due to a growth in foreign exchange reserves. Adjusting reserve requirements has become China's liquidity management tool to deal with the balance of payments imbalance or respond to deterioration in the economic environment. China's central bank is of the view that: "deposit reserves have the function of 'deep-freezing' liquidity, and may be used as a hedging instrument in the event that the central bank reactively discharges base money. By increasing the required deposit reserve ratio, a portion of excess liquidity can be deep-frozen, which can lessen the pressure on the central bank to issue securities and enhance the role of open market operations in adjusting interest rates and credit".[1]

In addition to the high reserve requirement, China's application of the required deposit reserve ratio has two other notable features, namely the dynamic adjustments of the reserves and the differentiated required deposit reserve system. This so-called dynamic adjustment refers to the dynamic changes the central bank has made on the scope of ordinary deposits subject to reserve requirement, based on the state of financial development and the needs of monetary policy controls. In recent years, on-balance-sheet financial products, time deposits of Treasury cash, ordinary deposits of controlling financial companies, and securities margin deposits

[1]The People's Bank of China: *Monetary Policy Report, Quarter 2, 2006*, Website of the People's Bank of China.

are all included in the category of ordinary deposits subject to reserve requirements. A differentiated required reserve system was first implemented in March 2004, allowing the applicable reserve ratios for financial institutions to be linked with their capital adequacy ratios and other indicators of asset quality. If the capital adequacy ratio declines and the ratio of non-performing loans increases, a higher ratio of required deposit reserves would apply, and vice versa. In 2011, the People's Bank of China, according to the requirements of macro-prudential management and liquidity management, introduced the dynamic differentiated reserve adjustment mechanism that imposes differentiated reserve requirements on financial institutions with low capital adequacy, rapid credit growth and increasing potential pro-cyclical risks. The dynamic differentiated reserve requirements combine the requirements of credit growth and counter-cyclical capital in order to establish an incentive mechanism for commercial banks and guide the size of financial institution lending.

(b) *Rediscounting*

After China's reforms to monetary control mechanisms in 1998, rediscount began to occupy a position in China's monetary controls. The People's Bank of China set up a rediscounting counter at its head office to accept, examine and process rediscount applications from the head offices of commercial banks. Meanwhile, authorized rediscount counters were also set up at its first-tier branches and in cities with independent planning to accept, review and process bank rediscount applications within their jurisdiction and within the rediscount limit approved by the head office. The People's Bank of China, in accordance with the macro-financial control and the need for structural adjustments, will publish from time to time a list of industries, companies and products that will receive priority support for rediscounting. The authorized counters will select bills for rediscounting accordingly and will arrange for the investment of the rediscounted funds. Priorities are given to the financial institutions with experience in commercial bills and a good record of business practice as well as to the cross-region and cross-system discounted bills. The People's Bank of China controls the total amount of rediscounting at each authorized counter, and the rediscounting limit of each authorized counter is subject to the need for timely financial adjustments. The rediscount quotas of each authorized counter is centrally managed and coordinated, and rediscount quotas cannot be sequentially assigned.

The People's Bank of China also implements a quantitative assessment of the performance of the rediscounting operations of each authorized counter to implement ratio controls over the total amount, terms and investments. (1) Total amount ratio: in terms of the amount accrued, the ratio of rediscounts, discounts, and commercial bills cannot be higher than 1:2:4; (2) term ratio: the cumulative amount of rediscounts with terms of less than three months (including three months) cannot be lower than 70% of the total amount of rediscounting; (3) investment ratio:

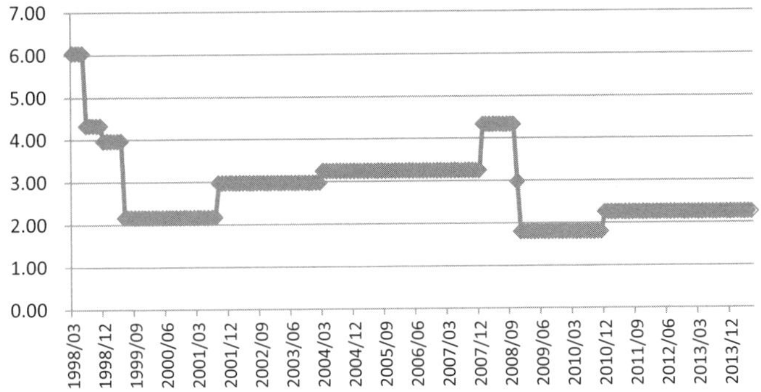

Fig. 20.2 China's Adjustments of Rediscount Rate (Unit: %)
Source: Website of the People's Bank of China

the rediscounts towards national key industries, sectors and products cannot be less than 70% of the total amount of rediscounting, and the rediscounts towards wholly state-owned commercial banks cannot be less than 80% of the total. As you can see, rediscounting policies not only can control the total amount of rediscounted bills but can also be used for structural adjustments.

In addition to the above control of the total amount and structural adjustments, the rediscount rate also plays another important role within China's rediscount mechanism. After the reforms to the formation mechanism of China's rediscount rates in March 1998, the rediscount rate fell 4 consecutive times. In particular, by taking advantage of the opportunity to adjust the deposit and loan rates of financial institutions, the rediscount rate was reduced from 3.96% to 2.16% on June 10, 1999, the purpose of which was to improve the initiative of commercial banks to discount bills and thus develop the bill market. The bill market developed rapidly in 2000. In that year, the amount of commercial bank acceptances and the cumulative amount of discounts were more than 670 billion yuan and 630 billion yuan, respectively. Rediscounting by the People's Bank of China reached 125.8 billion yuan, an increase of 75.8 billion yuan from 1999. Rediscounting became one of the important channels of the central bank for injecting base money, which not only expands the financing channels of financial institutions, particularly those small and medium-sized, but also effectively resolves the issue of defaults between enterprises.

In September 2001, the central bank raised the rediscount rate from 2.16% to 2.97%. In February 2002, China once again reduced the deposit and lending rates of financial institutions, but the People's Bank of China did not lower the rediscount rate at that time. The decline in the deposit and lending rates of financial institutions led to a decrease in bill discount rates, though the rediscount rate remained at the level of 2.97%. Compared to deposit and lending rates, a relatively high rediscount rate will raise the cost of central bank financing imposed on commercial banks,

Table 20.1 Amount of Rediscounting Provided by the People's Bank of China and Year-end Balance (Unit: 100 million yuan)

	Amount of Rediscounting Provided by the Central Bank	Year-End Balance of Rediscounting
2003	405	65
2004	223.7	33
2005	25	2.39
2006	39.9	18.2
2007	138.22	57.43
2008	109.7	Unknown
2009	248.8	181.2

Source: The People's Bank of China, *Monetary Policy Report*

which will lead to a significant reduction in the amount of rediscounted bills. This was a beneficial attempt by the Chinese central bank to further explore rediscount mechanisms as a means of regulating and controlling the base money.

In 2003 and early 2004, in order to curb the rapid growth of investment and the money supply, the central bank not only scaled up open market operations and raised required deposit reserve ratio, but also used the rediscount mechanism. The central bank added 0.27 percentage points to the benchmark rediscount rate of 2.97%, bringing the rediscount rate to 3.24%. In November and December of 2008, the central bank lowered the rediscount rate again in order to provide liquidity support to commercial banks. However, since 2003, the rediscount mechanism has not in fact played any significant role in China's monetary policy operations. As indicated in Table 20.1, compared to trillions of yuan in base money, the amount of rediscounting and year-end balances are almost negligible.

(c) *Open Market Operations*

China's exploration of indirect monetary control mechanisms started with the central bank's open market operations. On April 9, 1996, the People's Bank of China began to put into practice open market operations, mainly in the form of Treasury bill repos. Every Tuesday, it would issue a repo tender to 14 commercial banks that as primary dealers would bid on the repo rate and quantity. The central bank will then determine the interest rate and quantity based on the actual successful tender. In 1996 there were a total of 51 effective tenders and repos, by which the central bank injected more than 2 billion yuan in base money into the economy. Despite the fact that this injection was still quite small considering the hundreds of billion yuan of base money, it marked a fundamental change in China's monetary regulation and control mechanisms.

However, by 1997, open market operations were formally suspended because commercial banks were inadequately involved in bidding, both in terms of number and frequency. Only when China abandoned credit scale controls in 1998 did open market operations begin to recover. Assuming an increasingly prominent role within the central bank's monetary policy instruments, they have become China's routine operational method of fine-tuning its currency. In 1998 and 1999, due to sluggish money supply and bank credit growth, the central bank injected a great amount of base money through open market operations. Since 2000, given the appreciation expectation of the Chinese yuan and the widening difference between Chinese and foreign interest rates, foreign hot money began to flow into China, which led to an increase in the funds outstanding for foreign exchange. This forced the central bank to use open market operations to withdraw base money from circulation. In 2002, the central bank withdrew over 100 billion yuan in base money through open market operations. In 2003, this role of open market operations was even more evident. In that year, the central bank withdrew about 270 billion yuan worth of base money through open market operations.

Initially, China's open market operations were primarily through government bond repos and reverse repos. In 1998 and 1999, the central bank's open market operations were primarily through injecting base money into the financial system, and for this reason, open market operations were through the acquisition of bonds from primary dealers on the open market. In 2000 and 2001, even though the overall central bank open market operations were to withdraw base money, the withdrawal was not too large and the amount of government bonds held by the central bank was basically enough to meet the needs of open market operations.

However, when the central bank faces an external shock that causes a surge in the base money and loans, the central bank would become strained if the amount of securities held were limited when it tries to offset the shock with open market operations and curb excessive growth of lending and money supply. In 2002 and 2003, a surge in funds outstanding for foreign exchange required the central bank to sell a large amount of bonds or recover base money through repos, but the amount of bonds held by the central bank could not meet this demand. Thus, the People's Bank of China had no choice but to issue its own bank bills on June 25, 2003 to withdraw the base money, and through issuing these bills, it recovered 193.75 billion yuan of base money in that year. After 2003, the issue of central bank bills practically replaced Treasury bill repos as the only method of open market operations, and both the quantity and balance of central bank bills increased. With the increase in the quantity of central bank bills and in market rates, if central bank bills were to be used continuously to offset monetary expansion brought about by the huge amount of foreign assets, the People's Bank of China would not only have to pay a higher amount of interest, but also need to issue more and more central bank bills. Therefore, required deposit reserves gradually replaced central bank bills as the primary instrument for offsetting foreign assets. Since 2010, the position of central bank bill issuances within the various open market operations rapidly declined (see Figure 13.4).

The central bank issues central bank bills through rate tenders and quantity tenders. In a rate tender, the size of issue is predetermined and dealers bid for the interest rate (price) of issuance. The rate tender is also called "discount-based issue by price tender". Issuing central bank bills in this way is conducive to the formulation of a more reasonable interest rate and can help better implement the central bank bill issuance plan, thus the central bank can have more effective control over the supply of base money. The weak point, however, is that when market rates rise and a discount-based issue by price tender is used, the interest rate for the issuance of central bank bills will also significantly rise, which will raise the cost of central bank bills, accordingly.

In a quantity tender, the central bank bill rate is pre-determined by the central bank, while primary dealers bid for the issue size based on the given interest rate. When money market rates fluctuate considerably, and when the central bank hopes to use the central bank bill rate as a means of guiding the movement of market rates or as a means of controlling the cost of central bank bills, they will often issue the bills through a quantity tender. However, when the central bank determines the bill rate on its own, it will often differ greatly from the expectations of primary dealers. When primary dealers refuse to accept the rate determined by the central bank, the issuance of central bank bills will experience an abortive tender, and it will be difficult for the bank to reach the planned issuance. For instance, in 2003, both the 55th and 56th issue of central bank bills adopted the quantity-tender method. For the 55th issue, 3.82 billion yuan worth of three-month bills were subscribed, just 25.5% of the total tender amount of 15 billion yuan. The 56th issue, with a six-month term, had only 6.25 billion yuan subscribed, just 41.7% of the total of 15 billion yuan.

Regardless of whether they are bond repos, reverse repos, or central bank bills issuances, all open market operations are completed between the central bank and primary dealers. In other words, the People's Bank of China will not undertake bond transactions or repo transactions directly with all commercial banks. The primary dealers of open market operations are only those qualified financial institutions such as commercial banks, securities companies, insurance companies, and investment trusts that have been approved to directly engage in bond transactions with the People's Bank of China. These financial institutions can spread the monetary policy operations of the central bank throughout the entire financial system by trading with other financial institutions in the money or bond markets, which will correspondingly increase the efficiency of the central bank's open market operations.

In terms of form, there is a large difference between bond repos and central bank bills issuance. Bond repos are through the pledging of bonds held by the central bank itself to commercial banks so as to recover excess liquidity from these commercial banks. The issuance of central bank bills recovers commercial bank liquidity by increasing the liabilities of the central bank. Both repos and central bank bills are liabilities of the central bank, and they play the same role of recovering liquidity. The issuance of central bank bills reduces the demand for the People's Bank of China to pledge bonds for repos, which will correspondingly increase the instruments of the central bank's open market operations. As for the primary dealers, central bank bills can circulate, which will correspondingly increase the liquidity of held financial instruments and is conducive to the liquidity management of these financial institutions. Therefore, in the short term, the issuance of central bank bills plays an important role in controlling and regulating monetary policy objectives and stabilizing the supply of the base money.

20.2.3 Selective Monetary Policy Instruments

(a) *Consumer Credit Controls*

Nowadays, a great deal of our consumption can be done through credit, such as auto loans and the consumption of durable goods. However, when consumer demand grows too quickly, it may cause or exacerbate inflation. Conversely, if consumer demand is in serious shortage, it may lead to an increase in inventories, which will hinder the investment willingness of enterprises and mire the economy in a recession. In order to reduce the consumer demand fluctuations and the cyclical economic fluctuations that they bring about, the central bank can use consumer credit controls. When the economy overheats and the inflation rate is relatively high, the central bank can tighten consumer credit. Conversely, when economic growth is weak and consumer demand is sluggish, it can take measures to increase consumer credit.

A primary component of consumer credit is housing credit. Most of us apply for home mortgage loans from commercial banks. As we have already analyzed, in order to control the moral hazards and adverse selection of home mortgage loans brought about by asymmetric information, commercial banks will typically require borrowers to pay a certain percentage in a down payment. In fact, down payments have become an instrument of credit control. For instance, excessive demand for housing has led to a rapid rise in housing prices, and in order to prevent a real estate bubble, the central bank may require commercial banks to raise the down-payment percentage when issuing home mortgage loans, say, from 20% to 40%. In this way, the central bank can suppress the current effective demand for housing, and vice versa.

(b) *Securities Margin Ratio Controls*

Securities margin ratios refer to the portion of cash that the buyers must pay when purchasing securities. If the securities margin ratio is stipulated at 40%, if you purchase 1 million yuan worth of securities, you must pay 400,000 yuan in cash, while the remaining 600,000 yuan can be paid with a loan. If the securities margin ratio is low, people will not be constrained by their own funds, which may lead to serious moral hazards. If the securities margin ratio is high, say in the extreme case of 100%, the ability to purchase securities would be completely limited to a person's own funds, and for this reason, it can effectively curb speculation on the securities market. With the rise of China's margin trading and short selling, margin-based trading of securities has begun to play an ever-bigger role. In the near future, securities margin ratio controls may become an important selective monetary instrument directed towards the financial market.

(c) *Moral Persuasion*

Moral persuasion is also called window guidance. It is, in essence, the central bank's indication of its position towards various banks and the use of the central bank's influence to implement monetary policy objectives. When there are serious real estate and stock market bubbles, the central bank may advise commercial banks to take note of the risks of these loans and induce them to gradually reduce the amount of loans to these areas. Since the long term interests of the central bank is the same as those of commercial banks, in some cases, moral persuasion is incredibly effective. However, unlike other policy instruments, the effectiveness of moral persuasion primarily depends on the reputation of the central bank and the cooperation between it and commercial banks, and the central bank is thus in a relatively passive position. For this reason, moral persuasion can only be a complementary monetary policy instrument.

(d) *Advantages of Selective Monetary Policies*

Unlike the three-pronged general monetary policy instruments, selective monetary policy instruments only affect certain sectors of the economy and not the whole, which allows the central bank to target specific sectors for credit control. If prices are soaring in the stock and real estate markets and a serious bubble emerges, the central bank's open market operations or a rise in rediscount rates can tighten the money supply, but can hardly contain stock and real estate bubbles. Since the money supply is tightened, it will be difficult to meet the demand for loans from other areas such as technological development and may lead to a rise in interest rates, which will seriously hinder the willingness of enterprises to invest and may result in increased unemployment. Obviously, given these conditions, "piecemeal" is the best approach.

20.3 Instrumental Variables and Intermediate Targets of Monetary Policy

20.3.1 What are Instrumental Variables and Intermediate Targets?

After the central bank has used monetary policy instruments, they cannot simply reach the ultimate objectives immediately and can only change commercial bank reserves, the amount of cash in circulation or short-term interest rates. After

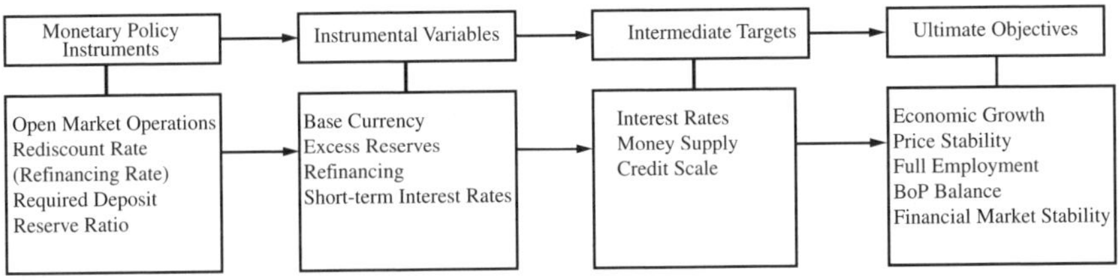

Fig. 20.3 Relationship Between Monetary Policy Instruments, Instrumental Variables, Intermediate Targets and Ultimate Objectives (Base Money)

the central bank has changed these **instrumental variables**, there is still quite some time before the ultimate objectives of monetary policies can be achieved. Therefore, the central bank must set **intermediate targets** between the monetary policy instrument and the ultimate objective. The relationship between monetary policy instruments, ultimate objectives, instrumental variables, and intermediate targets can be represented graphically as seen in Figure 20.3.

20.3.2 Selection Criteria for Instrumental Variables and Intermediate Targets

The instrumental variables and intermediate targets of monetary policies are not arbitrarily determined, and if an indicator is to become the instrumental variable or intermediate target of monetary policy, it must first satisfy three criteria, namely measurability, controllability, and relevance.

(a) *Measurability*

Measurability can be understood in two ways. First, these variables can be quantified. Second, the central bank can promptly access accurate data on these variables. Without these two criteria, the variable is not measurable. Psychological factors and emotions may influence buying behavior and attitudes towards work, and as such, will have a certain influence on economic growth and employment, but they cannot be quantified. Our individual consumption expenditures can be quantified, though if the central bank were to obtain this data, there would be a certain period of time lag, and this information cannot be obtained in a timely manner.

(b) *Controllability*

Controllability means that the variable can, in general, be directly controlled by the central bank. Otherwise, this indicator of monetary policy would not have much use. Emotions and psychological factors of the public cannot be controlled by the central bank, nor can individual consumption expenditures be directly controlled by the central bank through monetary policies. If an indicator cannot be controlled by the central bank, its usefulness would be much lower.

(c) *Relevance*

Relevance means that the intermediate variables of monetary policy must have a high degree of relevance with the ultimate objectives of monetary policy, and changes in the intermediate targets of monetary policy may immediately give rise to a certain degree of change in the ultimate objectives. Only when there is a high degree of relevance, can the central bank determine the conditions of the ultimate objective in accordance with these intermediate variables.

20.3.3 Instrumental Variables of Monetary Policy

Instrumental variable indicators are typically short-term interest rates, the base money, excess reserves, and refinancing.

(a) *Short-Term Interest Rates*

The central bank can easily obtain relevant data on short-term interest rates, which means short-term interest rates meet the requirement of measurability. As for controllability, the central bank can independently adjust rediscount rates. However, different financial instruments have different rates, and short-term rates include interbank lending rates, repo rates, and so on. These short-term rates are formed in the money market and cannot be controlled by the central bank. As for relevance, long-term interest rates play an important role in terms of investment, consumption and the national income, and for this reason, since long-term interest rates have a much more direct influence on capital costs, whereas changes in short-term interest rates (money market rates) are primarily concentrated on the liquidity of financial institutions and are only one of the factors that affect long-term interest rates.

(b) *Base Money*

In accordance with the base money equation of Chapter 13, the base money is equivalent to difference between the central bank's assets and its liabilities of government deposits, central bank bonds, capital, etc. The central bank can obtain accurate data on the base money from its balance sheet. Even though the central bank cannot control government deposits as well as other items on the liabilities side, it can offset the impact of their changes on the base money through asset activities. For instance, given no change in commercial bank reserves, a certain factor leads to a change in the amount of cash in circulation, thereby reducing the initial base money by 1 billion yuan. In this case, the central bank can quickly purchase 1 billion yuan in government bonds in the open market to offset the 1 billion yuan reduction in the base money, thereby maintaining the base money's original level. As for relevance, if the change in the base money is due to a change in the amount of cash in circulation, this may directly impact prices. If the change in the base money is due to a change in the amount of commercial bank excess reserves, it will change the ability of commercial banks to create credit, which will also directly impact investment. Thus, no matter how you look at it, base money is a relatively ideal instrumental variable.

(c) *Excess Reserves*

Excess reserves consist of two parts: the excess reserves commercial banks have deposited with the central bank and vault cash. The central bank can directly obtain the data of excess reserves deposits by subtracting the required deposit reserve from the reserve account of commercial banks. However, the vault cash of commercial banks is not clearly reflected in central bank balance sheet, and excess reserves are thus not as measurable as the base money. Additionally, even though the central bank can use open market operations to influence the excess reserves of commercial banks, the ultimate amount of excess reserves held by commercial banks are determined by the maximization of their own interests, risk preferences, and other such factors. Therefore, the commercial bank excess reserve ratio is not a readily controllable indicator for the central bank. Finally, excess reserves are quite relevant, and are at least strongly correlated to the total amount of credit and deposit fluctuations. When the economy booms, the demand for loans increases and commercial banks will reduce their excess reserve and increase lending so as to meet the demand for investment and promote economic growth. For this reason, the central bank can influence the excess reserves of commercial banks to a certain degree, and thereby achieve the purpose of influencing economic activity.

(d) *Refinancing*

Refinancing refers to the central bank's provision of loans to commercial banks and is one of the main channels through which the Chinese central bank injects base money into circulation. It is directly reflected on the asset side of the central bank balance sheet. The central bank can directly obtain authentic data on refinancing from its balance sheet. Through adjusting the scale of refinancing, the central bank can influence commercial bank excess reserves, and thus, refinancing has a strong correlation with the credit scales of commercial banks. In general, only when enterprises substantially increase their credit demands on commercial banks will commercial banks apply to the central bank for refinancing, and for this reason, refinancing is pro-cyclical. In terms of controllability, refinancing is an asset activity of the central bank, and, the central bank in theory can control the scale of refinancing in accordance with its own objectives. However, an inverse mechanism has always existed in China's money supply (credit supply), causing the refinancing scales set by the central bank to be repeatedly exceeded, and at those times, the central bank had its hands tied when it comes to controlling refinancing. Since 1997, however, due to the capital surplus in which savings has been greater than investment, the central bank has had a better control over refinancing.

20.3.4 Potential Intermediate Target Variables

(a) *Interest Rates*

Interest rates are one of the intermediate targets that Keynesians have always insisted on. The grounds for this lie in the following: (1) As for measurability, interest rates can be quantified and the central bank can promptly obtain relevant data on changes in interest rates. By simply looking at the daily financial newspaper, one can basically find relevant data on interest rates. However, in economic theory, the term "interest rate" refers to the weighted average interest rate of all borrowing, and the published data only refers to stated interest rate on borrowings from the open market or banks, which do not include the implicit internal rates of companies, nor do they include the other costs related to bank or open market borrowings. For this reason, the measurability of interest rates is not the most ideal. (2) There is a high degree of relevance between interest rates, investment and consumption. Rising interest rates may lower both investment and consumption, and vice versa. Second, interest rates are pro-cyclical in that if the economy is prosperous, and investment and consumer demand both increase, interest rates will rise. Conversely, when the economy is in a recession and investment and consumer demand decline, interest rates will fall. However, this is only a theoretical analysis. In reality, what exactly is the relevance between interest rates and economic activities? This is not easy to determine, because economic behavior is also influenced by factors other than interest rates. As we noted in Chapter 4, the ultimate impact of changes in interest rates on consumption and savings is uncertain. Moreover, because of asymmetric information, lenders cannot clearly distinguish loan risks. At a given level of interest rates, lenders will use credit rationing, and some enterprises will simply not obtain loans or will only receive a portion of what they need, and as such, interest rates are of no help to them. As for the published data on interest rates, it is impossible to eliminate these factors. (3) As soon as you think about the controllability of interest rates, you might immediately think of the deposit and loan rates determined by the People's Bank of China, and controllability does not seem to be an issue. However, this is a special case of regulated interest rates. In a fully market-oriented country, even deposit and lending rates are not the decision of the central bank. The only rate that the central bank can control is the rediscount rate. Additionally, there are also Treasury bill rates, interbank lending rates, capital market bond rates, etc. Even if the central bank could initially influence these rates, it would only be temporary. If the central bank lowers interest rates and promotes an increase in investment and consumption, thereby causing an increase in the national income, these changes would also form an upward pressure on interest rates. In an open economy, the central bank's interest rate adjustments are also subject to exchange rate fluctuations. Finally, investment and consumption is primarily influenced by long-term interest rates and not short-term interest rates, and the central bank can only control short-term rates, which is a primary reason for the central bank's poor controllability over interest rates.

(b) *Money Supply*

As for the measurability of money, the central bank can easily look at various monetary aggregates data. What we need to discuss here are relevance and measurability. As for relevance, changes in the money supply have a certain effect on investment, consumption, and net exports and also have a certain degree of relevance with ultimate objectives. However, since there are different levels of monetary aggregates, an aggregate may be strongly related to one component of the ultimate objectives, yet loosely related to the others. For example, M_0 and M_1 have the highest liquidity, and changes in monetary liquidity are most closely related to prices. Specifically, the growth of M_0 and M_1 relative to M_2 will come with price increases, and vice versa. However, they are poorly related to investment, employment, and economic growth. In terms of controllability, the cash in circulation is reflected on the liabilities side of the central bank's balance sheet, and the central bank can use various measures to completely control the cash in circulation M_0. However, M_1 and M_2 are different. In addition to the base money, any variables within the monetary multipliers will impact the value of the multiplier, and these factors cannot be controlled by the central bank. As such, as an intermediate variable, apart from M_0, the controllability of M_1 and M_2 is poor. Table 20.2 shows that since 1998, the actual growth rate of broad money has significantly differed from the target growth rate, which indicates that money supply is not completely controllable.

Table 20.2 The Target Value and Actual Value of the Growth of China's Money Supply (Unit: %)

	M_2		M_1	
Year	Target Growth Rate	Actual Growth Rate	Target Growth Rate	Actual Growth Rate
1998	17	11.9	16–18	15.3
2000	15–17	16.0	15–16	12.3
2002	13	16.82	13	16.78
2004	17	13.6	17	14.6
2005	15	11.8	15	17.57
2006	14	17.5	16	16.9
2007	16	16.7	—	21
2008	14	17.8	—	9.1
2009	17	29.74	—	34.63

Source: Website of the People's Bank of China

(c) *A Further Comparison of Interest Rates and the Money Supply*

Whether interest rates or the money supply is a better intermediate target depends on whether the economic shock comes from the real sector or the monetary sector. If the economic shock is from the monetary sector, the intermediate target should be interest rates. If the economic shock is from the real sector, the intermediate target should be the money supply. We can use the *IS–LM* curve that we learned previously to form a clearer conclusion.

First, we shall assume that the economy is initially in equilibrium and that the *IS–LM* curves are respectively located at LM_1 and IS_1. Now, suppose that an unexpected shock jolts the economy. This shock can occur in two cases. The first is that the economic shock arises in the real sector and not the monetary sector. The second case, then, is that economic shock arises in the monetary sector and not the real sector. In the first case, we can use the *IS–LM* framework of Figure 20.4, where the *LM* curve is still located at LM_1, but the *IS* curve has shifted, say, from IS_1 to IS_2 because of the shock to the real economy. The intersection of LM_1 and IS_1 is the point E_1, which determines the initial equilibrium of national income of Y_1. If this is the case, and if the central bank were to set the money supply as the intermediate target, that money supply would be determined at LM_1, and at this time, with the shift of the *IS* curve, the equilibrium national income determined by the intersection of LM_1 and IS_2 at E_2 would shift from Y_1 to Y_2. However, if the central bank were to select interest rates instead of the money supply as an intermediate target, what would happen? Since interest rates have become the intermediate target of monetary policy, the *LM* curve would become a horizontal line (think about it), or LM_2, and the equilibrium national income, determined by the intersections of LM_2 and IS_1 and IS_2 at the points E_1' and E_2', would be Y_1' and Y_2', respectively, and the volatility of the national income would be greater

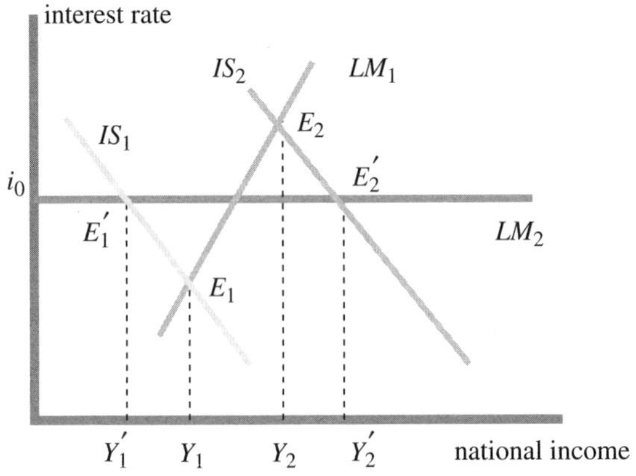

Fig. 20.4 Intermediate Targets of Monetary Policy During a Shock to the Real Sector

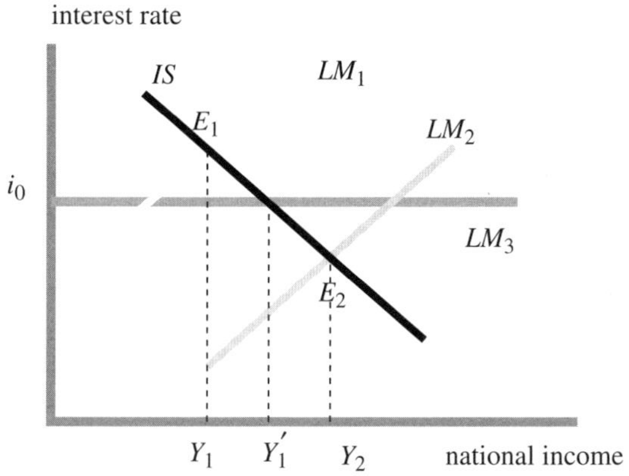

Fig. 20.5 Intermediate Targets of Monetary Policy During a Shock to the Monetary Sector

than when the money supply is set as the intermediate target. Thus, we can make the first conclusion that if the economic shock arises from the real sector and not the monetary sector, compared to interest rates, money supply as an intermediate target would cause less fluctuation in the national income, that is, it does a better job of stabilizing the economy.

In the second case, the economic shock arises from the monetary sector instead of the real sector. Thus, as in Figure 20.5, the *IS* curve does not shift, but the monetary shock will cause a shift in the *LM* curve, say, a shift from LM_1 to LM_2. In this case, if the central bank still decides to select the money supply as its intermediate target, there is a level of uncertainty as to the actual national income, which would be somewhere between Y_1 and Y_2. If interest rates are the intermediate target, then the shift in the *LM* curve will be to LM_3, and the equilibrium national income determined by its intersection with the *IS* curve would be Y_1'. Clearly, in this case, the economy is more stable when the intermediate target is interest rates. In this way, we can come to our second conclusion that when the economic shock primarily comes from the monetary sector instead of the real sector, interest rates as an intermediate target, do a much better job of stabilizing the national income.

(d) *Credit Scale*

In the 1980s, Milton Friedman of Harvard University proposed outstanding loans or debt as an intermediate target of monetary policy. Credit is the primary source of financing for business capital investment and capital flows, and it is pro-cyclical in that when the credit scale increases, investment and consumption will also increase, thereby promoting economic growth. The reverse is also true. However, with the development of direct investment and adjustment of financial restructuring, the degree of correlation between credit scale and economic growth may have been weakened. At the same time, because of the existence of credit, there may also be a degree of false prosperity, which may exacerbate fluctuations in the economic cycle. As for controllability, the credit scale controls of the central bank can set a ceiling on the credit scales of commercial banks through administrative provisions, and as such, the central bank's control of the scale of credit seems to be quite strong. However, as with refinancing, an inverse mechanism exists, and credit scale is often beyond what the central bank has determined. Also, credit scale controls are contrary to market-oriented reforms. From 1998 onwards, China has abandoned credit scale controls and has instead implemented asset and liability ratio management so that the amount of credit issued by commercial banks is entirely dependent on the scale of their liabilities, profit objectives, and risk controls, furthering the decline in the central bank's control of credit scale.

20.3.5 Zero Interest Rate and Quantitative Easing

As mentioned above, both interest rates and the money supply are potential candidates for intermediate targets of monetary policy. If a country's central bank sets interest rates as an intermediate target, when the interest rate is at or close to zero and yet economic growth remains weak with high unemployment, what should be the operating objective of monetary policy? This is not a hypothetical question, and has become a reality for the central banks of Japan, the United States, Britain, and Europe. For example, in 2010, the US Federal Reserve lowered the target federal funds rate to 0–0.25%, but the US unemployment rate remained high at about 10%. In this case, if monetary policy were to pull the economy out of stagnation or out of its quagmire of low growth, a new path would be necessary. This new path is **quantitative easing**, which media tends to refer to as QE. QE is introduced when the benchmark interest rates for monetary policy are at or near zero. The central bank announces that it will purchase Treasury bills or other assets at a given frequency and at a given quantity or through other such measures so as to increase the money supply or market liquidity and change the interest rate term structure and stimulate economic activity. The monetary policy of QE is implemented in different ways in different countries and at different periods of time. Based on the different asset categories and quantities purchased by the same central bank, QE monetary policies are often distinguished as QE1, QE2, ...

At this point, we will take the operations of the US Federal Reserve as an example. After the US subprime mortgage crisis, the US economy suffered a heavy blow; the economic growth rate declined rapidly and the financial market fell into a liquidity crunch. In order to inject liquidity into the financial system, the Federal Reserve announced in November 2008 that it would purchase 100 billion dollars worth of bonds issued by Fannie Mae, Freddie Mac, and the Federal Home Loan Bank and 500 billion dollars worth of asset-backed securities guaranteed by them. This is the asset purchase plan which people now call QE1. In fact, by March 2010, it had purchased a total of 1.25 trillion dollars of mortgage-backed securities, 300 billion dollars worth of Treasury bills and 175 billion dollars worth of institutional securities. However, the US economy did not rapidly recover from its difficulties because of the Federal Reserve's asset purchase plan, and therefore, in November 2010, the Fed launched a second phase of quantitative easing (QE2) in which the Fed purchased 75 billion dollars worth of long-term Treasury bonds each month (for a total of 600 billion dollars). In September 2011, the US Federal Reserve had implemented **Operation Twist** worth 400 billion dollars, in which the Fed purchased Treasury bills with a remaining maturity between 6 and 30 years and sold or redeemed the Treasury bills with the same nominal value and a remaining maturity of less than three years, lowering long-term interest rates and loan costs, thereby stimulating mortgages and economic growth. In September 2012, the Federal Reserve introduced a third phase of quantitative easing (QE3), in which the Fed would purchase 40 billion dollars worth of mortgage-backed securities each month, and would continue the original Operation Twist. With the addition of long-term US Treasury bill purchases under Operation Twist, in the last four months of 2012, the Federal Reserve had purchased assets at a pace of 85 billion dollars per month. After implementing the monetary policy of quantitative easing, the US unemployment rate gradually declined, the economic growth was better positioned to withstand the adverse impact of the European debt crisis, and the Dow Jones stock index had broken through its previous high point in early 2013, setting a new record high.

20.4 Transmission Mechanisms of Monetary Policy

The **transmission mechanisms of monetary policy** refer to the processes through which the central bank leverages monetary policy instruments to operate on instrumental variables and thereby attain the ultimate objectives of monetary policy. More generally, it refers to the channels used to achieve the ultimate objectives of monetary policy after the monetary policy has been implemented. Surrounding the transmission mechanism of monetary policy, different schools have different ideas, such as the "monetary perspective" and "credit perspective". Additionally, monetary policies are in fact a policy of aggregate demand management, and apart from government spending which is not affected by the central bank's monetary policies, investment, consumption, and net exports are all affected by monetary policy. Thus, the transmission mechanism of monetary policy should be analyzed from the three aspects of investment, consumption, and international trade.

20.4.1 The "Money View" and the "Credit View"

How do monetary policies affect aggregate demand? The traditional view is that changes in the money supply impact aggregate demand. According to this view, if the central bank were to lower the speed of growth in the aggregate demand or control the rate of inflation, it would sell bonds through open market operations, contract reserves from the banking system and reduce the money supply. This drop in the money supply may lead to a rise in short-term interest rates, as well as a rise in long-term interest rates. A rise in interest rates may then influence the cost of capital (including housing and consumer durables), which will suppress aggregate demand and control prices. Higher interest rates will raise the exchange rate for local currency and will suppress export demand. This standard view of the monetary policy transmission mechanism has also been called a "**money view**".

The monetary perspective is based on several very strong assumptions, namely all non-monetary assets are perfect substitutes, which means there is no difference between government bonds, commercial paper, corporate bonds, stock, bank loans, and consumer credit. It also assumes that enterprises are not concerned with liability structures and that there is no difference between external and internal financing. However, since asymmetric information in the financial markets can result in credit market friction, the "**credit view**" of the monetary policy transmission was formulated, which stresses the unique role of credit market friction within the monetary policy transmission. Mechanisms under the credit perspective are often divided into the lending channels and the broad financial accelerator mechanism.

The **bank-lending channel** emphasizes the nature of bank credit as well as the unique role of banks within the financial structure. If monetary policies affect the reserve position of banks, it will lead to changes in interest rates and prompt banks to restructure their assets and liabilities. The ultimate impact of monetary policy on bank deposits and the money supply will be reflected in an adjustment of banking sector liabilities. However, any factors affecting the banking sector reserves and interest rate factors will also impact the credit supply of banks as well as the asset side of bank balance sheets. If banks cannot adjust their holdings of securities or issue liabilities not backed by reserves to raise funds to offset the impact of declining reserves, these banks will tighten their loans. If borrowers have no other channels by which they can raise funds, changes in the availability of bank loans will also impact total expenditures. For this reason, the key of the bank-lending channel lies in the fact that in the liabilities side of bank balance sheets, deposits have no good alternatives. Also, for some borrowers, there are no other alternatives to bank loans.

The **broad credit channel** is also known as the borrower balance sheet channel. As indicated in Chapter 2, incomplete information in financial markets will affect financial contracts, and may lead to credit rationing, or cause a difference in the internal and external costs of financing, which is called by Bernanke the "external financing premium". The difference between the internal and external costs of financing results from asymmetric information because the lender cannot supervise the borrower without costs, which results in agency costs. As indicated in Chapter 2, good collateral and net worth of the borrowers will lessen the asymmetric information problem of the borrowers and lenders; therefore the availability of funding and its cost and investment expenditures are influenced by corporate cash flows and net worth. When internal financing decreases and leads to a relative rise in the cost of external financing, enterprises cannot help but rely on the more expensive external financing. Under such circumstances, how will the economy be influenced by monetary policy? Take contractionary monetary policy as an example. It will make it hard to obtain external financing, aggregate demand will be affected, the economic growth will slow down, and cash flows and the profit of enterprises will decrease. A decrease in cash flows and profit of enterprises will worsen the asymmetric information problem, increase agency costs and the premium on external financing, thus bringing about a greater contractionary effect on expenditures. Therefore, friction in credit markets will spread, amplifying the influence of the initial monetary tightening on aggregate expenditures and furthermore, on the growth rate of the economy. This is called the **financial accelerator**.

20.4.2 Investment Channel

(a) *Keynes' Interest Rate Channel*

Keynesians believe that once the money supply increases, it will cause a decrease in interest rates, and this decrease will also lower the cost of investment, thus contributing to an increase in investment spending, and increased investment will lead to an increase in the national income. Conversely, when the money supply decreases, it will cause an increase in interest rates, and this increase will cause a reduction in investment spending, thereby causing a reduction in the national income. For this reason, Keynes' interest rate channel can be described as follows:

$$M \uparrow \rightarrow i \downarrow \rightarrow I \uparrow \rightarrow Y \uparrow, \quad \text{or vice versa,} \quad M \downarrow \rightarrow i \uparrow \rightarrow I \downarrow \rightarrow Y \downarrow .$$

(b) *Tobin's q Theory*

Tobin developed the q theory of the relationship between stock prices and investment spending. The **Tobin's q** is the ratio between an enterprise's market value and the replacement cost of capital. If the value of q is greater than 1, it indicates that the market value is higher than the replacement cost of capital, and the costs of the construction of a new plant and the purchase of new equipment will be lower than the cost of acquisition by an enterprise with a comparable size. If, for example, the market value of enterprise A is 200 million yuan and the replacement cost of capital is only 160 million yuan, the value of Tobin's q would be 1.25. In this case, if enterprise B were to enter enterprise A's industry, it has two available choices. One is to acquire enterprise A, the other is to construct their own plant and purchase new equipment. For comparison, the cost to acquire enterprise A is 200 million yuan, while the cost of constructing a plant of similar size and purchase all of the necessary equipment would only be 160 million yuan. Clearly, the best choice for enterprise B is to construct a new plant and purchase new equipment. At this time, it would expand investment spending.

Conversely, if q is less than 1, it indicates that the market value is less than the replacement cost of capital, and that the cost to construct a new plant and purchase new equipment would be higher than the cost of acquiring another enterprise with a comparable size. If, in the above example, enterprise A's market value was 160 million yuan, while their replacement cost of capital was 200 million yuan, the value of Tobin's q would be 0.8. At this time, enterprise B's acquisition of enterprise A would cost them 40 million yuan less than it would cost to construct a new plant and purchase new equipment. Therefore, in this case, the total investment expenditure will not increase.

How, then, does monetary policy impact the value of Tobin's q? After increasing the money supply, people will realize that the actual value of the money in their hands is greater than what they really need, and thus, there will be an excess amount of cash for investment. One option of investment may be the purchase of stock, and because of this increased demand for stock, stock prices will rise, thereby improving the market value of enterprises and the value of Tobin's q. Thus, if P_s represents the price of stock, the monetary policy transmission mechanism through Tobin's q would be:

$$M \uparrow \rightarrow P_s \uparrow \rightarrow q \uparrow \rightarrow I \uparrow \rightarrow Y \uparrow,$$ and if the money supply is reduced, then:

$$M \downarrow \rightarrow P_s \downarrow \rightarrow q \downarrow \rightarrow I \downarrow \rightarrow Y \downarrow .$$

(c) *Loanable Funds Channel*

Another channel through which monetary policies affect investment spending is the channel of loanable funds. When the central bank uses easing policies such as purchasing a large volume of government bonds in the open market or reducing rediscount rates, the excess reserves of the commercial banking system will increase, which can be used to increase the amount of funds available for loans. At this time, it will be easier for enterprises to meet their demand for loans, which will increase investment spending, and investment spending will then lead to the further growth of the national income. If we set L_a as the amount of loans, then one of the transmission channels of loanable funds would be:

$$M \uparrow \rightarrow L_a \uparrow \rightarrow I \uparrow \rightarrow Y \uparrow.$$

Conversely, if the central bank reduces the money supply, it would have the opposite effect. That is:

$$M \downarrow \rightarrow L_a \downarrow \rightarrow I \downarrow \rightarrow Y \downarrow.$$

Even if the central bank does not use open market operations or adjust the rediscount rate to change the amount of loanable funds of commercial banks, for the selective monetary policy instruments, the credit channel would also play an important role. When the central bank raises the securities margin ratio, the amount of loans used for stock investment will decrease, as will the price of stock, thereby lowering the value of Tobin's q, and in this way, there would be an increase in the amount of acquisition activity on the capital market and a corresponding reduction in the aggregate expenditures of the entire society on physical capital. Conversely, if the central bank lowers the securities margin ratio, the amount of loans used for purchasing stock would increase, which would raise the price of stock and the value of Tobin's q, thereby increasing investment spending. Thus, another transmission channel of loanable funds is as follows:

$$\text{Securities margin ratio} \downarrow \rightarrow \text{Loans used for stock investment} \uparrow$$
$$\rightarrow Ps \uparrow \rightarrow q \uparrow \rightarrow I \uparrow \rightarrow Y \uparrow .$$

(d) *Channel of Asymmetric Information*

A transmission mechanism closely related to loanable funds is the effect of asymmetric information. Asymmetric information generates moral hazards and adverse selection, the solution of which is the net worth. A higher net worth means that the borrower of the loan actually has more collateral, and thus, when exposed to risks, the borrower will also assume a greater share of the losses. Thus, the higher the net worth, the lower the likelihood that the borrower will engage in high-risk, opportunistic behavior.

How then can monetary policies be transmitted through net worth? In the analysis above, changes in the money supply or an adjustment in the securities margin ratio will have a large impact on stock prices, and changes in stock prices will impact corporate net worth and corporate moral hazards and adverse selection. Thus, the transmission of monetary policies through asymmetric information can be expressed as follows:

$$M \uparrow \rightarrow Ps \uparrow \rightarrow \text{Corporate net worth} \uparrow \rightarrow \text{Adverse selection} \downarrow \text{ Moral hazards} \downarrow$$
$$\rightarrow \text{Loans} \uparrow \rightarrow I \uparrow \rightarrow Y \uparrow .$$

20.4.3 Consumer Spending Channel

(a) *Interest Rate and Income Channel*

An increase in the money supply will lead to lower interest rates, an increase in consumer spending and a reduced willingness to save. Meanwhile, the increase in the money supply will lead to a temporary increase in people's income, and based on the permanent income theory, an increase in temporary income will lead to an increase in consumer spending. Conversely, if the central bank uses monetary policies to lower the money supply, it will have the opposite effect and reduce consume spending. If C is used to represent consumer spending, and if Y_t is used to represent temporary income, the transmission mechanism of interest rate and income can be expressed as follows:

$$M \uparrow \rightarrow i \downarrow$$

$$Y_t \uparrow \rightarrow C \uparrow \rightarrow Y \uparrow .$$

(b) *Wealth Effect*

As we saw in Chapter 4, the life-cycle hypothesis of savings suggests that consumers even out their consumption across their entire life, and consumer spending is determined by the lifetime wealth of consumers rather than by their current level of income alone. A consumer's lifetime wealth includes all financial assets, such as stocks or bonds. When the prices of stocks or bonds rise, a consumer's lifetime wealth will increase, and in this way, their spending will expand. For this reason, the wealth effect as a channel for influencing consumer spending would be:

$$M \uparrow \rightarrow Ps \uparrow \rightarrow \text{Lifetime Wealth} \uparrow \rightarrow C \uparrow \rightarrow Y \uparrow .$$

(c) *Liquidity Effect*

The liquidity effect is the impact on the financial position of consumers when the liquidity of the asset they hold changes, thereby influencing consumer spending. When consumers face a greater likelihood of liquidity difficulties, consumer spending may decrease accordingly. If the likelihood of liquidity difficulties decreases, consumer spending may increase. If the prices of stocks, bonds or other financial assets increase, the financial assets held by consumers will not only be easy to sell in the open market, but the possibility that they will suffer losses will also become smaller. Therefore, the likelihood that consumers will face liquidity difficulties will decrease, and vice versa. Thus, a transmission channel of the liquidity effect would be:

$$M \uparrow \rightarrow Ps \uparrow \rightarrow \text{Value of financial assets} \uparrow$$

$$\rightarrow \text{Likelihood of liquidity difficulties} \downarrow \rightarrow C \uparrow \rightarrow Y \uparrow .$$

The liquidity effect also exists in the selective monetary policy instrument of consumer credit ratio controls. If consumer credit ratios fall, it will be more difficult for consumers to overcome liquidity difficulties by obtaining credit from banks and other financial institutions, and in this way, they will reduce their consumer spending. Conversely, if consumer credit ratios rise, consumers can be granted a greater amount of credit for consumption, and consumer demand will thereby increase. One exception to the consumer credit ratio is the down-payment rate for home mortgages. If the down-payment rate rises, home-buyers must accumulate more money to pay the down payment, and as such, the effective demand for homes will decrease, and vice versa. Thus, the second transmission mechanism of the liquidity effect would be:

$$\text{Consumer credit ratio} \uparrow \rightarrow \text{Availability of consumer credit} \uparrow$$
$$\rightarrow \text{Likelihood of Liquidity Difficulties} \downarrow$$
$$\rightarrow C \uparrow \rightarrow Y \uparrow .$$

20.4.4 International Trade Channel

In an open economy, net export is an important component of a country's aggregate demand. However, next exports are also greatly influenced by changes in the exchange rate. When foreign currency exchange rates rise and the domestic currency exchange rate falls, the domestic commodity prices will be reduced accordingly on the international market, and for this reason, exports may increase and imports may decrease accordingly. Conversely, when the domestic currency exchange rate rises and foreign currency exchange rates fall, the competitiveness of domestic commodities on the international market will diminish accordingly and net exports may decline.

How can monetary policies impact exchange rates? An expansion in the money supply will lower interest rates. If foreign interest rates do not decrease accordingly, the spread between the domestic and foreign interest rates will widen. According to the interest rate parity theory, at this time, the domestic currency exchange rate will fall and foreign currency exchange rates will rise. Conversely, if the money supply is tightened, through the role of the interest rate parity, the domestic currency exchange rate will rise and foreign currency exchange rates will fall. If we set e as the exchange rate (direct quotation) and NX for net exports, the transmission mechanism through international trade can be expressed as follows:

$$M \uparrow \rightarrow i \downarrow \rightarrow e \uparrow \rightarrow NX \uparrow \rightarrow Y \uparrow .$$

20.5 Effects of Monetary Policy

The **effects of monetary policy** are the degree by which the ultimate objectives of the monetary policy can be achieved after the central bank has put the monetary policy into play. If the central bank has implemented a monetary policy and it can quickly lead to the determined targets of the monetary policy's ultimate objectives, the monetary policy is relatively effective. However, if it takes quite some time to achieve the determined targets of the monetary policy, the monetary policy is not very effective.

20.5.1 Time Lag of Monetary Policy

The **time lag of monetary policy** is the period of time between the point where economic changes necessitate monetary policy implementation and the point where the variable of the ultimate objective changes. If we closely look at the traffic after the red light changes at an intersection, it is fairly easy to understand time lag. It is not that the cars will immediately cross the intersection when the red light turns green; instead, the cars at the back will wait for a longer period of time. This is the analogy of lagging behind.

The time lag of monetary policy can be divided into recognition lag, decision lag, and response lag. If the central bank cannot immediately obtain information on changes in the economy, since there is a period of time required to obtain statistical data, and the period of time between the change in the economy to the point in which the central bank recognizes which monetary policy should be used to regulate the economy is the **recognition lag**. Meanwhile, the central bank cannot immediately implement such a monetary policy once they recognize which policy is needed, because the central bank will often need to discuss such issues as the direction and strength of operation of the monetary policy and formulate a detailed action plan for the monetary policy. The result is a **decision lag**. If there is any controversy with regards to the judgment of the economic situation or the specific implementation amongst the monetary policy decision-makers, the decision lag may be very long. After central bank has implemented a monetary policy, initially, it may only change the base money, the excess reserves of the banking system and the short-term interest rates, but only changes in the money supply and long-term interest rates will influence investment, consumption, and net exports and will finally have an impact on the ultimate objective of the monetary policy. The time from when the central bank operates the monetary policy instrument to the point in which a change occurs in the variable of the ultimate monetary policy objective is the **response lag**.

Due to time lags in monetary policy, the policies initially intended on stabilizing the economy may instead lead to economic instability. For instance, after the central bank has operated a monetary policy and as they wait for it to begin to function, the economic situation might have already reversed. For example, the central bank's expansionary policy that has been developed to address a recession may only begin to function when economy is already prospering; this may lead to constant price hikes and may even lead to serious inflation. Conversely, if the central bank implemented contractionary monetary policies in the previous year when the economy was prosperous but the economy has shifted from prosperity into a recession before the policy begins to function, it will only further deteriorate the economic situation. Since time lags exist, the central bank may not reach the ultimate objectives of monetary policy upon their implementation.

20.5.2 Efficiency of Monetary Policy Transmission Mechanisms and the Effect of Monetary Policy

After the central bank implements a monetary policy, it must go through various transmission mechanisms to alter the variables of the ultimate objective, and as such, the effectiveness of monetary policy transmission mechanisms will have a significant impact on the effectiveness of monetary policies in achieving their ultimate objectives. If a transmission mechanism does not work well, the central bank will find it difficult to achieve monetary policy objectives. Sometimes economic variables impact the efficiency of monetary policy transmission mechanisms, while at other times, institutional variables will affect their efficiency.

As we analyzed in Chapter 19, the slope of the *IS–LM* curve will have an impact on monetary policies. The flatter the *IS* curve, the more effective that monetary policies will be in adjusting the national income and the smaller their impact on interest rates. Conversely, the flatter the *LM* curve and the steeper the *IS* curve, the smaller the impact that increases or decreases in the money supply will have on the national income and the larger their impact on interest rates. This analysis shows that all factors that affect the slopes of the *IS* and *LM* curves will also have an impact on the efficiency of monetary policies. One of the most important factors is the interest rate elasticity of the demand for money and the interest rate elasticity of investment demand. This point has already been analyzed in the previous chapter.

20.5.3 Central Bank Independence and the Effect of Monetary Policy

Central bank independence refers to the extent to which other domestic interest groups can influence the functions of the central bank, and this independence primarily includes two aspects, that is, policy independence and credit independence. **Policy independence** is the degree of autonomy that the central bank has in the formulation and implementation of monetary policies. If the bank can implement and formulate monetary policies based on policy objectives and without external interference, this central bank has a high degree of policy independence. Policy independence is subject to the influence of a country's political power structure and interest groups, and in a country that tends towards centralized power, the central bank has relatively weak policy independence. **Credit independence** refers to the degree by which the fiscal deficit relies on the central bank, and if the government primarily relies on borrowing or over drafting from the central bank to compensate for fiscal deficits, the credit independence of this central bank is relatively weak.

Clearly, credit independence is subject to the degree of development of a country's financial markets. Countries with relatively broad financial markets tend to grant their central banks a high degree of independence. The reason for this is that the more massive the financial system, the more serious the adverse consequence that may be caused by inflation and its uncertainty in the process of savings and investment management. Second, more developed financial markets allow governments to finance relatively large budget deficits through the financial markets themselves. In addition to the fiscal deficit, different foreign exchange management systems will also have an effect on the credit independence of central banks. Under China's foreign exchange settlement and sales system, the supply of base money will fluctuate with changes in the balance of payments, and for this reason, the settlement and sales system also greatly weakens the credit independence of the People's Bank of China.

The independence of a central bank will have a large impact on monetary policies. First of all, the greater the policy independence of the central bank, the shorter the time lag of monetary policy actions. Because the central bank has a relatively great degree of independence, when it comes to recognizing changes in the economy, it can promptly take appropriate actions and does not have to wait for the delayed "approval" of higher authorities. Meanwhile, the greater the policy independence, the shorter the amount of time for bargaining in the formulation and implementation of monetary policies. Additionally, in countries in which the central bank is more independent of politics, it is more likely to be committed to price stability. Conversely, those central banks that have a smaller degree of independence are more likely to accept higher inflation in exchange for a lower unemployment. Second, the greater a central bank's credit independence, the smaller the influence that the fiscal deficit will have on the supply of base money. Therefore, on an average, the lower the independence of a central bank, the higher the inflation. For example, the central bank of Germany is the most independent of politics, and Germany also has the lowest rate of inflation. Conversely, the central bank of New Zealand has a relatively low degree of independence, and as such, New Zealand has a relatively high inflation rate. Experience has also shown that in countries where the central bank has a higher degree of independence, the average annual economic growth rate is also higher than that of countries with a less independent central bank.

20.6 The Principles of Monetary Policy

20.6.1 Discretionary or Rule-Based Monetary Policies

(a) *What are Discretionary and Rule-Based Monetary Policies?*

The discretionary monetary policy refers to the flexibility of the monetary authority or central bank to use different monetary policies at different times and based on different economic situations to achieve the most necessary policy objectives at the current time. In particular, contractionary policies should be implemented to curb inflation during times of inflation, and expansionary policies should be used to stimulate the economy and promote a recovery from recessions. Discretionary monetary policies enhance the flexibility of central banks in the formulation and implementation of monetary policies. Because the economy is always changing and developing, and the central bank will act in accordance with the changes in the economy, it seems that they would be better able to achieve macroeconomic stability. Just as "a general in the field is not bound by the orders from his sovereign", a general can only ensure a brilliant victory by becoming flexible to environmental and conditional changes. For several decades after the development of Keynesian theory of state intervention, discretionary monetary policies have been widely adopted by central banks.

However, nowadays, more and more central banks implement rule-based monetary policies. **Rule-based monetary policies** refer to the guidelines of a monetary policy framework that are developed for the central bank prior to the formulation and operation of monetary policies. One of the first people to propose rule-based monetary policies was the monetarist guru, Milton Friedman. According to his modern quantity theory of money, there exists a stable relationship between the quantity of money and prices, and the central bank should maintain a certain growth rate of money supply. In the 1970s, modern monetarism flourished, and the US central bank — the Fed — used Friedman's quantity of money rules, announcing the growth rate of the money supply at the start of each year. Afterwards, the Federal Reserve took appropriate monetary policy measures to ensure that the growth rate of the money supply remained within its declared objective. However, as we saw in Chapter 13, the factors that affect the money supply are quite complex, and in addition to the central bank's formulation and implementation of monetary policies, individuals, enterprises, and banks all will have a considerable impact on the money supply. Thus, at that time, the Federal Reserve's control over the money supply did not work very well, which has in a way similar to the People's Bank of China, who was unable to maintain the declared goal of money supply growth at the start of each year. As a result, by the early 1990s, the US had already abandoned the monetary policy regulations of a fixed money supply growth rate.

Instead, the Federal Reserve replaced it with a different policy rule, namely the Taylor rule, which was named after its inventor, the American economist John Taylor. Through his study of the real performance of the monetary policies of countries such as the United States, the United Kingdom, and Canada, he realized that of the factors that affect prices and economic growth rates, real interest rate is the only variable that maintains a stable and long-term relationship with the two objectives. In view of this, he believed that adjusting the real interest rate should be the primary mode of operation for monetary authorities. We can start to describe the

Taylor rule with an idealistic state. Assuming that there exists a "real" equilibrium federal funds rate within the economy. At this rate, the employment rate and prices are maintained at a reasonable level by natural laws. This equilibrium interest rate refers to the nominal interest rate minus the expected rate of inflation. According to Taylor's research, the real equilibrium interest rate in the United States was approximately 2%. If the aforementioned relationship between the real interest rate, economic growth rate, and the level of inflation (as defined by Taylor) were to fall apart, monetary authorities should take measures to rectify the situation. First of all, the nominal interest rate of the federal funds should respond to changes in the rate of inflation and adjust accordingly, and thus, the real equilibrium rate can be achieved. Second, if the growth rate of output exceeds its potential level, the real interest rate must increase. If the inflation rate exceeds the target level, the real interest rate will also need to increase accordingly. If the Federal Reserve were to follow such a rule, it would maintain a steady and sustainable rate of economic growth in such an ideal state. Shortly after the Taylor rule was introduced to the world, Former Federal Reserve Chairman Alan Greenspan, the "Economic Czar" put the rule to practice. The Federal Reserve abandoned the fixed rate of money supply growth and instead announced adjustment in the target value of the federal funds rate in accordance with changes in the expected rate of inflation and the rate of economic growth. It would then adjust rediscount rate and launch open market operations to ensure the actual federal funds rate was about the same as the target interest rate of the Federal Reserve. As a result, the Greenspan Era of US monetary policy achieved considerable success, and contributed to the longest postwar period of US economic prosperity.

To a certain extent and for a certain period of time (1994 to September 2001) the US Federal Reserve was the only central bank to use the Taylor Rule as the basis for formulating and implementing monetary policies (it had apparently not been explicitly declared). In the early 1990s, another monetary policy rule appeared at nearly the same time as the Taylor Rule — inflation targeting. After the Bank of New Zealand took the lead and adopted the monetary policy framework, more than 20 other countries, such as the United Kingdom, Canada, Australia, and Brazil, adopted the framework. To put it simply, **inflation targeting** is when a central bank first explicitly declares a specific rate of inflation and the monetary policies of the central bank will then attempt to ensure that the rises in the price level will remain within the declared range. For instance, the British central bank — the Bank of England — announced the target inflation rate of 2%, and the central bank of Australia set the target inflation rate at 2–3%, etc. In 2006, the British inflation rate had reached 2.5%, and owing to higher oil and banana prices, the Australian inflation rate reached 4.0%, both exceeding the target inflation rates. The Bank of England and the Australian central bank thus decided to increase the interest rates of lending to banks in order to bring prices back to their target rates. As practice has shown, in countries where inflation targeting has already been implemented, prices have always been stable, while prior to the implementation of inflation targeting, these countries had experienced relatively serious inflation.

The countries who adopted inflation targeting have given their central banks clear and specific target rates of inflation, and thus the central banks must have a high degree of independence, which includes both credit and policy independence. Credit independence means that the fiscal deficits of those countries that have opted for inflation targeting cannot be financed by the central bank, and requires the deepening of domestic financial markets that can sufficiently absorb the Treasury bonds issued. In addition, a decrease in the rate of economic growth or an increase in the unemployment rate cannot interfere with the central bank's operation of monetary policies, and the stabilization of prices by the central bank cannot come under the political pressures, and in this way, the central bank can try to achieve the target inflation rate without distractions.

(b) *The Debate Between Discretionary and Rule-Based Policies*

Under the discretionary monetary policy framework, central banks do not need to make public, clear, and specific commitments to ultimate monetary policy objectives. They have the discretionary power to adjust monetary policies based on current changes in the economy and to flexibly respond to new information and unexpected situations. This is the biggest advantage of discretionary monetary policies.

However, there are two issues with regards to discretionary monetary policies. First of all, it does not limit incompetence or the central bank's abuse of power. For instance, in Western countries where central banks have too much discretionary power over monetary policy, monetary policies may be manipulated to influence election results. If the current president's votes depend on the economic situations during his term, and the central bank is on good terms with the incumbent president, it may adopt overly expansionary monetary policies to stimulate production and employment, the inflation caused by which will not be seen in the near future. In this way, discretionary monetary policy may aggravate the political–economic cycle of the economy.

Second, under a discretionary monetary policy framework, the real inflation rate may be higher than the desirable rate of inflation. If the governor of the central bank knows that there is no long-term alternative between inflation and unemployment, the central bank will often announce the objective of stabilizing price levels. However, since the public has already formed expectations on the steady inflation prior to the announcement, the central bank will face a short-term problem of alternating between inflation and unemployment, and they may give up the objective of price stability so as to reduce unemployment. That a central bank says one thing and does another in terms of its monetary policy is referred to as the time inconsistency of the monetary policies. When the actions of the central bank fail to match up with their words, the public will "live and learn" and will no longer trust the central bank's commitment to stable prices, which will raise public expectations on the real rate of inflation over the announced level of the central bank.

One method of avoiding these issues of discretionary monetary policy is to implement rule-based monetary policies. The supporters of such rules believe that monetary policy rules can increase the constraints on monetary authorities and enhance the credibility of policies and the confidence of the public that the central bank does not perform inflationary policies or abuse their power. For instance, in countries that have adopted inflation targeting, if the general price level exceeds the determined target value, the central bank must act decisively to lower the rate of inflation back to the target area. This is the central bank's duty to the public as well as their commitment as to price stability objectives. Since the central bank must fulfill their commitments, the time inconsistency and political cycle problems under discretionary policies can be avoided. In addition, since the rate of price increases is determined in advance and known to the public, if the central bank truly honors this commitment to stable prices, the public can adjust their own investment and consumption strategies based on the rate of price increases, and the central bank may expend less effort in monetary policy adjustments.

20.6.2 Transparency, Communication, and Accountability of Monetary Policy

For quite a long time, the decision-making, operation, and specific objectives of monetary policy were always obscure to the public to the point where a great deal of macroeconomic information, such as the money supply, monetary policy meetings, and so on were confidential and only after monetary policies had been implemented for a long period of time could they become "decrypted". However, with the development of rational expectations theory and the game theory of information economics, after central bank independence was increased, monetary policy transparency was also becoming an international trend for central banks. Monetary policy transparency refers to the disclosure of information relevant to the formulation and implementation of monetary policies, and it also refers to an environment, in that policy objectives and laws, institutional and economic frameworks, policy-making and its principles, as well as data and information related to monetary and financial policies and institutional accountability is made available to the public on an easy to understand and easy to access basis and in a timely manner. It is generally believed that improving monetary policy transparency is conducive to enhancing the credibility of monetary policies and helps guide the public to form rational expectations, thereby improving the potential efficiency of the market.

Monetary policy transparency covers multiple levels. At the political level, it refers to the openness of monetary policy objectives; for instance, the central bank will announce that the target inflation rate is 2%. At the economic level, transparency refers to whether or not economic information used for monetary policies is available to the public, such as data on economic performance, models that predict or assess the effect of policy-making as well as the central bank's internal forecast on economic performance. For instance, the central bank will promptly disclose information on the monetary and financial aspects of statistical data and price changes. Concerning procedures of monetary policy, transparency refers to whether or not the policy-making process is made known and understood by the public, including clear monetary policy rules or strategies, as well as a true record of the decision making process, meetings, and voting records. Nowadays, most central banks will immediately release a corresponding statement after the closing of their monetary policy meeting. This statement will disclose the results of the discussions (such as whether or not interest rates will be adjusted), how members voted, the judgment of the current and future macro-economic situation, as well as appropriate monetary policy actions. At the operational level, transparency refers to whether or not the implementation process and results of monetary policies are available to the public in a timely manner, such as error controls, the macroeconomic fluctuations and shocks that may affect policy transmission. For instance, the central bank will promptly announce the conduction of open market operations in order to adjust market interest rates.

The transparency of monetary policy is closely linked to the communication between the central bank and the public. Nowadays, many central banks stress the importance of communication and exchanges with the public. The communication and exchanges of information not only include the interpretation of current policies, but also the direction of future policies, and there should also be a variety of ways to communicate, such as holding a press conference after a monetary policy meeting and answering questions from reporters and the public. The central bank can also use questionnaires to understand the degree of public satisfaction in terms of current prices as well as the public expectations for the future. Through communication, the central bank is able to allow the public to better understand and grasp monetary policies, and the central bank can also get a better understanding of the public expectations for the future, which in turn will facilitate monetary policy adjustments. Effective communication is not only capable of improving the central bank's credibility, it can also help avoid the development of monetary policy that far exceeds expectations, which would cause unnecessary economic fluctuations. It also helps the central bank in the accurate understanding of relevant micro information to ensure a better-informed policy making process. Many people believe that it is precisely because the US Federal Reserve has become more open to the public that the release of information after a policy committee meeting has become a more powerful instrument that affects policies than interest rate policies themselves. As practice has proven, in countries like the United States and the United Kingdom, communication can greatly improve the efficiency of monetary policies.

Apart from transparency and communication, nowadays there is an increasing emphasis on the accountability of central banks. Accountability refers to the various obligations that a central bank must bear in order to complete pre-determined monetary policy objectives. Accountability is linked to the credibility of monetary policy objectives. If a central bank's ultimate objectives and its monetary policy behaviors are unmindful of their consequences, the clear and specific quantitative objectives of the pre-determined monetary policy may not be credible. Each country has a different means by which they improve the credibility and accountability of central bank monetary policies. For example, the US Federal Reserve will regularly submit monetary policy and economic outlook report to Congress, accept Congressional inquiries on monetary policy and provide testimony. The European Central Bank will not only submit a report at the end of the year and at each quarter but will also submit the Monthly Bulletin, which provides a comprehensive assessment of economic conditions under monetary policy decisions. In addition, the European Central Bank will also regularly meet each quarter with the Economic and Monetary Affairs Committee of the European Parliament to report on the European central bank's monetary policies and answer any relevant questions. The Reserve Bank of New Zealand has an even more stringent approach in that if the quarterly inflation targets were not met, the government will dismiss the Chairman. By increasing the accountability of the central bank's monetary policies, it will also raise their credibility accordingly so as to stabilize corporate expectations on monetary policies. As the saying goes, "a man is nothing if he is not trusted"; effective monetary policy is probably the same.

Summary

Monetary policy refers to the various policy instruments that the central bank will use to increase or decrease the money supply to adjust interest rates, thereby guiding investment and consumption. The traditional ultimate objectives of monetary policy were primarily economic growth, full employment, price stability, balance of the balance of payments, and stable financial markets. Conflicts exist amongst these ultimate objectives. Nowadays, price stability has practically become the only ultimate objective.

In order to achieve the ultimate objectives of monetary policy, central banks must have corresponding policy instruments. Monetary policy control instruments can be direct or indirect, with indirect monetary controls being used more often today. Indirect controls can also be divided into general and selective monetary policy instruments. The former includes required reserve ratios, open market operations and rediscounting. The latter primarily includes consumer credit controls, securities trading margin ratio controls and moral persuasion.

When the central bank implements monetary policies, they must also select instrumental variables and intermediate variables. Interest rates, the supply of base money and refinancing can be used as instrumental variables. Interest rates and the money supply can be used as intermediate target variables. This depends on whether the economic shock is from the real sector or the financial sector. If the economic shock occurs in the real sector, adjusting the money supply would be more appropriate; if the shock occurs in the financial sector, it would be better to adjust interest rates.

Monetary policy instruments influence the ultimate objectives of monetary policy through the following channels: the investment channel, the consumption channel, the capital market channel and the international trade channel.

There is a time lag between the formulation and implementation of monetary policy by the central bank and the realization of its ultimate objectives. The interest rate elasticity of the demand for money and the response elasticity of investment to interest rates will influence the results of monetary policy. Central bank independence also has an important influence on monetary policies. Central bank independence includes policy independence and credit independence. The greater the independence of the central bank, the lower the rate of inflation and the higher the rate of economic growth.

Monetary policies can be divided into discretionary and rule-based policies. Nowadays, more and more countries will implement a framework of rule-based monetary policies. Central banks are also increasingly emphasizing the transparency, credibility and accountability of monetary policies.

Key Terms

Monetary Policy; Objectives of Monetary Policy; Full Employment; Frictional Unemployment; Seasonal Unemployment; Monetary Policy Instruments; Open Market Operations; Transmission Mechanisms of Monetary Policy; Intermediate Targets of Monetary Policy; Quantitative Easing; Operation Twist; Financial Accelerator; Money veiw; Credit view; Time Lag of Monetary Policy; Central Bank Independence; Policy Independence; Credit Independence; General Monetary Policy Instruments; Selective Monetary Policy Instruments; Inflation Targeting; Recognition Lag; Response Lag; Decision lag; Taylor Rule; Monetary Policy Transparency

Critical Thinking Questions

1. What are the ultimate objectives of monetary policy? How are they related? How would you define “currency stability”?
2. What are monetary policy instruments? What kinds of instruments are available?
3. What are the advantages and disadvantages of adjusting the required deposit reserve ratio, open market operations and rediscounting?

4. When the central banks implement open market operations, why will they use government bonds as an operating instrument?
5. What are selective monetary policy instruments? What are the benefits of using selective monetary policy instruments?
6. What are the instrumental variables and intermediary variables of monetary policy? What is quantitative easing?
7. Which is more appropriate as an intermediary target: interest rates, money supply, or credit scale?
8. After the central bank has operated monetary policy instruments, what channels can they use to reach their ultimate objectives?
9. What is the credit perspective of monetary policy transmission?
10. What is the time lag of monetary policy? What sort of impact does it have on monetary policy?
11. What sort of impact does central bank independence have on monetary policies?
12. What sort of effect will the central bank's repurchase of 10 billion yuan worth of government bonds on the open market have on the base money?
13. After 1994, the Chinese government could not borrow or overdraft from the central bank and could only issue bonds as a means of making up the deficit. How did this affect the independence of China's central bank?
14. Based on everything we learned about the foreign exchange settlement and sales system, analyze the effect that changes in the balance of payments will have on the monetary policies of the People's Bank of China. Has the exchange settlement and sales system lowered the credit independence of the People's Bank of China?
15. Since the market-oriented reforms, China's private sector has continued to account for an ever larger segment of the economy, while the proportion of state-owned enterprises has continued to decline. These two different types of enterprises respond in different ways to changes in interest rates in that the former tends to be more sensitive. Analyze the effect that this change to China's economic structure will have on the effectiveness of indirect monetary policy controls.
16. Based on what we learned in Chapter 4 and Chapter 19, analyze the effect that the growth of Chinese consumer loans as a proportion of commercial bank loans has had on the effectiveness of monetary policy.
17. In 2012, the People's Bank of China twice lowered the commercial bank required deposit reserve ratio. Analyze the impact of these policy changes on the economy.
18. Near the end of the year and on the eve of the Spring Festival, the People's Bank of China will typically implement reverse repo open market operations. Why?
19. In November 2008, the State Council issued *Several Opinions of the General Office of the State Council on Providing Financial Support for Economic Development* and indicated that they would lower the frequency and scale of central bank bill issuances. Attempt to read into the intentions of this policy and illuminate the orientation of such a monetary policy.
20. Analyze the macroeconomic impact of the US quantitative easing policy.
21. Use the financial accelerator theory to briefly analyze the macroeconomic impact of a fall in the price of assets.

Part IV

Financial Development and Stability

Govern a great nation as you would cook a small fish.

— Lao Tzu

That government is best which governs least.

— Thomas Paine

I permit myself to note in this connection the words said to me by a very high personage of the Republic: "I know my country well. It is capable of supporting anything with calm except a financial crisis."

— Raymond Philippe

Chapter 21

Financial Development and Financial Structure

Learning Objectives

After studying this chapter, you will be able to:

- Understand financial development
- Clearly understand the motivations behind financial development
- Understand the financial interrelations ratio
- Understand demand-following and supply-leading financial development
- Learn about the basic components of the theory of endogenous financial development
- Clearly understand the basic characteristics of the modern financial structure
- Understand the primary factors which impact the modern financial structure
- Learn about the financial globalization in financial development

Financial development is one of the basic phenomena that has accompanied the progress of the human race since the emergence of currency. What is financial development? What are the basic trends and patterns of financial development? What are the main factors influencing financial constraints? What is the direction of future financial development? This chapter will primarily focus on these aspects.

21.1 Financial Development

21.1.1 What is Financial Development?

We often come in contact with the word "development", such as economic development, corporate development, career development, and so on. We also often see the word financial development in newspapers and magazines. Then what is financial development?

Financial development is the process of constantly improving and expanding financial functions and thereby boosting financial efficiency and economic growth. It manifests as follows: currency as a common means of exchange, the diversification of financial instruments, currency and financial assets as the best means for individuals to save for future spending, and the price of financial instruments playing an important role in the allocation of financial resources. Financial development accompanies changes in the financial structure and the ever-increasing efficiency of finance.

Financial development is also driven by financial innovation. **Financial innovation** covers activities to create new financial instruments, organizations, and systems to allocate financial resources more reasonably, so as to increase income or mitigate risks. It can be said that financial innovation is an important path for achieving financial development, just as the technological innovation for the development of a nation. With constant financial innovation, the functions of financial services offered by financial organizations are very similar to those offered by traditional banking institutions. After the US financial crisis in 2008, this kind of financial activity which transforms terms and liquidity while also acting as a medium of credit and a means of credit creation, but which is not governed by regulatory rules of the banking industry is collectively referred to as the **shadow banking system**. The shadow banking system as a medium of credit can provide financing and liquidity to both enterprises and other participants.

The development of finance results in refined functions of finance, which significantly contributes to economic development and social change. In the history of mankind, economic development has always been accompanied by financial development. From the days of barter exchange to the emergence of physical currency, and again with the emergence of the modern era of electronic money, over this lengthy process, new financial instruments, and financial systems have always emerged. Nowadays, the large array of purchase and sale order on the busy trading floor of a securities company are exactly the result of financial development. For an ancient Chinese emperor to obtain information from remote regions, he would need to wait for 10 or 15 days even if he used the most efficient courier system. Nowadays, ordinary people can instantly obtain emails from their friends halfway across the world. The Shanding cave people in Beijing in ancient times did not know what trading or currency was, but nearly each and every person in a modern metropolis knows how to organize their lives with finances. In short, financial development has greatly improved the well-being of mankind.

21.1.2 Motivations for Financial Development and Innovation

What factors contribute to financial development and financial innovation? When we look at the history of financial development, it is not difficult to realize that the following factors stimulate financial development and financial innovation:

- Lowered Transaction Costs
- The Circumvention of Risks

- The Circumvention of Regulations
- The Development of Information Technology

(a) *Lower Transaction Costs*

As we saw in Chapter 1, the emergence of currency overcame the issue of the double coincidence of wants, and the depth and breadth of the expansion of trading promoted the division of labor and the further development of exchange. Financial institutions, such as commercial banks, also greatly lowered the information search costs of those with surplus funds who want to invest. The specialization of information gathering and analysis has also reduced the cost of transactions.

The latest example of financial development that leads to reduction in transactions costs is the birth and use of the euro. From January 2002 onwards, the euro, a new currency, officially began to circulate amongst EU member states, and the original currencies of the 15 member states were gradually withdrawn from circulation. By March 2002, the euro was the only currency in circulation amongst these 15 states. The birth of the euro was a great currency initiative in the history of mankind, and because of the formation of the European Monetary Union, the transaction costs amongst EU member states was greatly reduced, which promoted the free movement of commodities, labor, and capital and the cross-border resources allocation that is free from the sovereign state interference. This also results in an improvement of social welfare within the EU. Prior to the official circulation of the euro, if you were to travel to any of the 15 member states, you have to carry currency issued by the member state, and would lose a lot of money in the exchange from one currency to another, as well as waste a great deal of time in the process. Nowadays, all you need is a single currency, the euro, and you can take trip throughout all countries within the EU.

(b) *Circumvent or Transfer Risks*

Another strategy which promotes financial development is to circumvent or transfer risks. With the separation of savings and investment, finance obtained a relatively independent form of existence which has led to a degree of uncertainty which people must face when investing. Coupled with several other unexpected events, people's daily production and lives were suddenly faced with the risk of suffering economic losses. In order to avoid a variety of financial risks, new financial organizations and financial instruments were invented. For instance, the emergence of various types of insurance companies has allowed people to salvage their losses at a relatively small price. Similar to commercial banks, the arrival of such financial institutions has lowered the liquidity risks which human society faced in the transfer of savings into investment (Chapter 2).

Various secondary financial securities markets emerged in order to find a mechanism to determine the capital market price and lower the liquidity risks of holding these securities. Securities investment funds also lower the risk of securities investment through financial experts and by expanding the scope of investment portfolios (Chapter 9). The emergence and development of various derivative financial instruments, such as forward transactions, options, swaps and futures all initially emerged in order to give people and companies an effective means to prevent financial risks. Financial institutions have also transferred risk through innovative financial instruments. A typical example of this is the securitization of credit assets in which certain non-standardized loan contracts which commercial banks could not originally trade are sold to special purpose companies, and are then broken down into standardized bonds with the same nominal value, duration and interest rate and are circulated on the secondary market. This is a typical arrangement for transferring risks, because once the original borrower defaults, the ultimate losses occur to those who hold the securitized assets.

Another financial innovation with a growing reputation for mitigating and transferring risk after the financial crisis in 2008 is **credit default swaps** (CDS). CDS are a risk-transferring financial arrangement: after default swap buyers pay a regular fee to the default swap sellers (known as credit default spreads), and once a default arises, such as that of bonds, buyers have the right to sell the bonds to the default swap seller at their nominal value, thereby effectively mitigating and transferring the credit risk. Since the 1990s, these financial products rapidly developed in the financial markets of developed countries.

Of note is the fact that these financial innovations were originally carried out in order to circumvent regulations, and when prices become volatile, they produce a higher risk. For instance, the futures transactions in Chapter 12 play the role of a leverage in that as soon as the futures price changes in a different direction from expectations, traders will suffer huge losses. Although several innovative financial instruments can successfully mitigate and transfer risks to the entire financial system, risks are still an objective reality, and these instruments simply transfer the risks which were originally run by individual financial institutions to a wide range of institutions and investors. As soon as there is a credit risk default, it will lead to a wider dissemination of risk within the financial system.

(c) *Circumvent Controls or Regulations*

Finance is one of the areas subject to a relatively high degree of government regulation. The most prominent means by which the government regulates finance includes required reserve regulations and interest rate controls. The government may compulsorily require commercial banks to pay a certain reserve at the Central Bank. As there is no interest on reserves in Western countries, the more reserve fund commercial banks have deposited with central banks, the less fund they can use for lending, and thus the lower the return on funds. For this reason, the reserve is also known as a "reserve tax".

In addition to reserves, many countries also impose strict controls on interest rates. For instance, the original American Regulation Q stipulated the maximum limit of interest rate payments on time deposits. However, if market rates rose above the limit stipulated by Regulation Q, depositors can withdraw bank deposits for other investments thereby lowering the scale of bank lending. This phenomenon is known as **disintermediation**. When disintermediation occurs, it weakens the profitability of banks.

We often say that "while the priest climbs a post, the devil climbs ten", and wherever there is regulation, there will always be a fight against it. In order to avoid the reserve regulations and interest rate controls of authorities, commercial banks have developed several new financial instruments, such as eurocurrency. **Eurocurrencies** are currencies circulated outside the currency issuing countries. In this case, Europe is not Europe in its geographical sense. If, for example, someone deposits US dollars in Japan, this deposit is a eurodollar deposit. If Japanese yen are deposited in a British bank, this deposit is a euroyen deposit. Often, national authorities do not require that foreign commercial banks pay a required deposit reserve, and for this reason, by drawing eurocurrency, commercial banks do not have to pay a required reserve, thereby expanding the amount which can be used for lending or other earning assets.

In the United States, the greatest cost of Regulation Q occurred in the savings and loan associations, and since the market rate exceeded the maximum limit of payments on savings and loans, these banks lost a lot of money. In this case, they would need to open up new sources of funding to maintain profitable loans. The financial innovations undertaken by savings and insurance institutions in order to avoid interest rate regulations are primarily negotiable order of withdrawals and automatic transfer service accounts. Negotiable orders of withdrawals are not legally treated as checks, are not subject to relevant checking account restrictions, and can earn interest. Later on, other financial institutions, including commercial banks, also developed negotiable orders of withdrawals to compete for deposits. In 1980, the United States was finally forced to admit the legitimacy of negotiable order of withdrawals.

Automatic transfer service accounts are a type of checking account in which checking account balances above a certain amount are automatically transferred into an interest-bearing savings account. When checks are issued from the automatic transfer service account, the necessary funds for the check are automatically transferred from the savings account to the checking account. In this way, the balance in the interest-bearing savings account has become a portion of the depositor's checking account, and as such, they are available for the issuance of checks. However, legally speaking, this is a savings account and is not a checking account which makes interest payments to depositors.

China's deposit rate regulations also drive financial innovation. The benchmark interest rate determined by the People's Bank of China is relatively low, sometimes even lower than that of the rate of inflation. In order to avoid the regulations on deposit rates, a large number of bank wealth management products arose. Bank wealth management products are not considered as deposits, and their expected rates of return naturally are not subject to the limitations of central bank interest rate policies, thus, winning the favor of more and more investors. Similarly, there are also a variety of trust products. Of course, Chinese financial innovations such as these which avoid interest rate regulations have also changed the risks which investors must bear.

As for countries such as China, in addition to reserve regulations and interest rate controls, prior to 1998, the government had always implemented a degree of control on commercial bank loans. At the start of each year, the central planning authorities developed a credit scheme for the given year. Because the credit scale was controlled, commercial banks, in principle, could only issue loans within the scheme, and enterprises could only obtain a credit scale within that scheme. However, it was often difficult for enterprises to meet their needs under the central bank credit scale. More importantly, in the credit scheme of the state-owned banking system, private enterprises and other non-state-owned enterprises had a great deal of trouble in obtaining formal credit support from banks. Non-state-owned Chinese enterprises which arose in the 1980s could only look for required funds for production development outside of the national credit scheme, as did state-owned enterprises whose funding needs were not fully satisfied by state-owned bank credit schemes. The Chinese interbank funding market, the Treasury bond repo market and the stock market all began in this way. These financial activities which were in accord with the demands of developing a market economy brought a major shock to the planned economy, and the government also recognized that the existence and operation of these markets could indeed improve financial efficiency. As such, the rules of the existing system were modified, and these informal financial activities which were originally outside of the system were then incorporated into the nation's licensed financial system, which greatly contributed to the development of China's financial system and financial instruments.

(d) *The Development of Information Technology*

Scientific and technological development provides financial development with technical support. In particular, the development of modern information technology has led to a proliferation of innovations in the field of finance. Electronic money, bank-securities accounts, and online transactions have become new vocabulary popularly used in the field of finance. As long as you hold a bank's debit card or credit card, and as long as you make a purchase or acquire other services at one of the issuer's authorized merchants, you do not have to carry cash. This is an **electronic payment system (EPS)**. If you want to purchase stock, even if you are as far away as in Urumqi, you can also look at changes in the stock trading on the Shanghai Stock Exchange through a satellite transmission of information, thereby facilitating your investment decisions. The development of information technology has also greatly changed the services of financial institutions, and the classic examples are those of self-service banks and financial supermarkets. Usually via automated teller machines (ATMs), self-service banking allows customers to make small deposits or withdrawals 24 hours a day without the need to stand in line at the bank counter during working hours. The development of modern information technology also led to the development of UnionPay. Prior to UnionPay, if you held a China Merchants Bank card, you would not be able to access your account at a Bank of Communications ATM. Similarly, if you have a Pacific card from the Bank of Communications, you cannot use it at the China Merchants Bank ATM to withdraw funds. With UnionPay, however, all card-issuing banks created a network, and through this network, customers of the various banks could use the shared ATM transaction platform, and as long as your bank card has a UnionPay label, you can make a withdrawal from any of these ATMs.

In other countries, improved market access to securities information due to the development of information technology has led to the emergence and development of so-called junk bonds. Prior to computers and modern communication technology, it would be incredibly difficult for you to learn about the financial information of listed enterprises, just as difficult as it would be to distinguish their credit situation. In this way, bonds could only be issued by large, well-organized enterprises. However, with the development of information technology, the ability of investors to distinguish risks was greatly improved, and many investors were more willing to purchase the junk bonds with a relatively high risk but an even higher expected return of those lesser known enterprises. In America, the junk bond market has experienced a rapid development.

21.2 The Financial Interrelations Ratio of Financial Development

One of the most important indicators for measuring a country's financial development is the financial interrelations ratio. The **financial interrelations ratio** is a ratio of broad money balances and a country's GDP, namely:

$$\text{Financial Interrelations Ratio} = \text{M}_2 \div \text{GDP}.$$

The earliest mention of the financial interrelations ratio was Goldsmith's *Financial Structure and Development*. After analyzing decades of data from 35 different countries, he realized that the financial interrelations ratio would continue to rise with GDP growth. Nowadays, people typically use the financial interrelations ratio to measure a country's financial development. Even though the financial interrelations ratio will grow with national income, its growth is not without end. Actual observation and theoretical research has shown that once a country reaches a certain stage of development, specifically when the relevant financial interrelations ratio reaches 100% to 150%, the ratio will tend to stabilize.

Why does the financial interrelations ratio reflect financial development? This is because an increase in the financial interrelations ratio is in fact a process of economic monetization, that is, when the financial interrelation ratios are high, the degree of economic monetization will also be high. Based on the three functions of money as a means of exchange, a means of payment, and a store of value, economic monetization should also include three levels of meaning: First, an increase in the volume of commodity transactions through the medium of money as a proportion of gross national product. Secondly, an increase in the proportion of monetary income in the proportion of income distribution and a decrease in the physical distribution. Third, a constant increase in the ratio of household financial assets to GNP. As such, an increase in the financial interrelations ratio reflects the widespread use of money as a medium for the exchange of goods or services. It also reflects an increase in money as a proportion of income distribution, which gives people a more autonomous choice when it comes to the consumption of physical products or services. Furthermore, it reflects an enhanced function of money as a store of value, which mobilizes savings and accelerates capital formation. Thus, the level of the financial interrelations ratio and its changes reflect the extent by which enterprises, households, or governments need to resort to external financing in the form of borrowing or issue securities, and also reflects the extent by which their internal savings can meet their capital requirements.

However, simply determining a country's degree of financial development based on the financial interrelations ratio will also bring about a lot of problems. In fact, the interrelations ratio of a large number of developing countries who have experienced many years of development is already high, to the point where the ratios have exceeded that of developed countries. In 2001, China's financial interrelations ratio was beyond 140% (Figure 21.1), which was higher than that of America in the same year. In 2005, the US financial interrelations ratio was 53%. In fact, over the last 20 years, China has always had a higher ratio than that of the US. Does this mean that China's financial development is at a higher degree than America? The

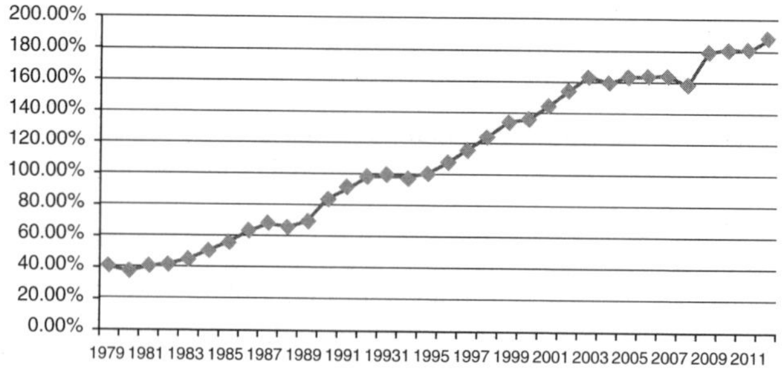

Fig. 21.1 China's Financial Interrelations Ratio
Source: National Bureau of Statistics, the People's Bank of China

answer is anything but yes. This is because the financial interrelations ratio only measures the growth of a country's finance, and does not reflect the efficiency of allocating financial resources. In fact, some measures do not promote financial development but will still promote growth in the overall volume of financing. For instance, prior to 1998, consumer credit did not occupy its rightful place in China's banking system, and incomplete consumer credit raised the savings rate of unwilling households, which thereby promoted a rise in the savings rate of Chinese households and growth in aggregate savings. Clearly, when the lack of consumer credit led to an increase in the rate of savings, the resultant increase in the financial interrelations ratio could not be counted as a case of financial development.

21.3 The Path of Financial Development

21.3.1 Demand-Following and Supply-Leading Financial Development

There are two types of financial development: demand-following financial development and supply-leading financial development.

Demand-following financial development is financial development that is driven by the development of the real economy. Due to sustainable market expansion, product diversification and the needs of spreading risk and controlling transaction costs, there is a demand for financial products and services. This type of financial development is essentially a reaction to demand for financial services in the real economy. It is like the production of electric fans or air conditioning which came out of a demand for cooling off in the summer, and only when people have a certain demand will there be a development to provide such a product to meet this demand. The emergence of currency is a demand-following financial development in response to the division of labor and the deepening of transactions. The stock market is also a case in point as it emerges as a response to enormous demand for capital that comes from socialized production.

Supply-leading financial development precedes the demand for financial services in the real economy, and it automatically plays an active role in economic growth. As different financial organizations emerged, they began to compete with each other. In order to earn more profits and attract more customers, these financial organizations may take the initiative to develop new financial instruments, which also further reduces risks and transactions costs. For instance, the American financial institutions, which we mentioned previously, developed negotiable order of withdrawals and automatic transfer service accounts in order to circumvent the interest rate ceiling of Regulation Q, and this sort of development is considered as supply-leading financial development. Supply-leading financial development is very similar to when an enterprise launches a new product, and then stimulates consumer's desire to buy through a large amount of advertising which labels the consumption of this product as a trend. In fact, without this kind of conspicuous consumption people would still be very comfortable. For example, urban fitness centers, over the years, have become a supply-leading type of development. Even if these fitness centers did not exist, people would still find ways to naturally exercise and become fit. However, because these fitness centers pump out a lot of advertising, they provoke consumers into having a desire to exercise in such a trendy way. In supply-leading financial development, the financial sector actively mobilizes resources which are stuck in traditional sectors and transfers them to the modern sectors which can promote economic growth, thereby promoting efficient resource allocation. For example, with the rise of these fitness centers, some young people no longer go jogging, and as such, this trendy kind of fitness has replaced traditional training methods.

21.3.2 Endogenous Financial Development Theory

(a) *Income Constraints and Financial Development*

As the analysis above has pointed out, statistics have shown that with GDP growth, the financial interrelations ratio will also increase as a result. The endogenous financial development theory seeks to clarify how financial organizations and financial markets will evolve with changes in per capita income. The theory is that when an economy is in the early stages of development, the per capita income and per capita wealth will be very low, and people will be unable to pay fixed entry costs, or rather, only a few people can pay for transactions, and thus the unit cost of transactions would be too high. Therefore, there would be too few people who would take advantage of financial intermediaries and financial markets. A shortage in the demand for financial services would mean no supply of financial services, and as such, there would be no basis for the existence of financial intermediaries and financial markets. This is the same as the decreased demand for trendy fitness when the income level is generally low. When market demand is insufficient and is constrained by income levels, vendors will suffer a loss if they develop high-end fitness products. In this sense, the demand for financial services is still a luxury.

When economic development reaches a certain stage, some people will get rich first because their income and wealth have reached a critical value, and they will then have an incentive to take advantage of financial intermediaries and financial markets after paying a fixed entry fee. In this way, financial intermediaries and financial markets can be established. With the further development of the economy, the number of people with income and wealth that has reached a certain value will grow, and more and more people will take advantage of financial intermediaries and financial markets, thereby promoting the continuous development of financial intermediaries and financial markets. This is similar to the development of trendy fitness products, and only when the level of income is generally high, will there be a sound market basis for trendy fitness products.

From the point of view of endogenous financial development, the more complex that financial services become, the higher the entry costs and transaction costs. But whatever the case, as the level of per capita income and wealth increases, the financial system also becomes more complex, so as to investigate into and supervise the projects and investors, mobilize the resources and thus take full advantage of favorable opportunities for production. If per capita income is high, people will purchase financial services to take full advantage of investment opportunities. Conversely, if the level of per capita income is low, people will realize that the additional revenue from these financial services cannot cover their costs, and thus, these people will not purchase these financial services and be satisfied with only the existing, simple financial intermediary services. From this it can be seen that the demand for financial intermediary services will grow with income levels, and in this sense, the demand for financial services and the development of financial intermediaries are both a result of economic growth and development.

Box 21.1 Why China's Securities Exchange Was Only Formally Created in the Early 1990s

In the beginning of China's shift to a market economy, there was an inherent requirement for financial liberalization and enterprise reform to be led by the capital markets. However, throughout the 1980s, China never established a formal securities exchange system like what it had done in the stock market. People have attributed this to constraints in terms of ideology and understanding. In fact, even if there were no non-economic restraints, it would still be infeasible then to establish a formal securities exchange system and introduce a comprehensive joint-stock reform for state-owned enterprises.

This is because the endogenous constraints to economic development played a very important role. In the early years of the reform, China's level of economic development was low and the per capita income, the household financial savings rate, and total amount of savings was very limited. For example, in the early stages of the reform in 1978, China's per capita financial assets amounted to only about 120 yuan. After 10 years of reform, the financial assets of Chinese households in 1991 was nearly 2000 yuan. Thus, prior to 1991, China's demand for financial assets was more limited to the "essentials". So, in spite of the fact that market reforms then had an endogenous demand for the development of stock, bonds and other financial markets, however, because of the low level of per capita wealth, their development, objectively speaking, was constrained by the demand for financial assets. With China's economic growth, the level of per capita

(*Continued*)

Box 21.1 (*Continued*)

income and the balance of per capita financial assets increased, and the capacity for people to take on risks was also enhanced, and thus, the demand for "luxury" financial assets was also increased. From this perspective, we can easily understand why the Shanghai Securities Exchange was only established at the end of 1991. Similarly, this also indicates that, without a doubt, China's gradual pursuit of financial liberalization was on a strong theoretical basis (Figure 21.B1).

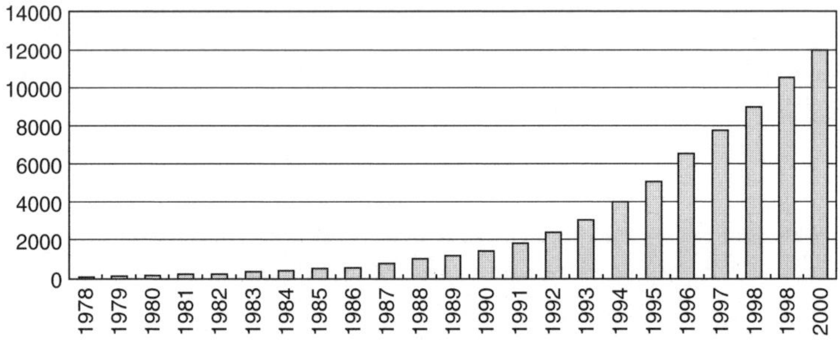

Fig. 21.B1 Changes in the Structure of China's Per Capita Financial Assets (Unit: Yuan)
Source: The People's Bank of China Annual Reports

(b) *Alternatives and Complementarities: The Relationship Between Financial Markets and Financial Intermediaries in the Different Stages*

The endogenous financial theory also indicates that in different stages of economic development, the relationship between financial markets and financial intermediaries will be different. In the early stages of economic development, financial markets and financial intermediaries are complementary and mutually reinforcing, in that the full development of financial intermediaries will promote the development of financial markets. In the early stages of economic development, there is a potential source of savings within society and the economy, and the development of financial markets is largely dependent on the mining of this source of savings. Rather than reducing the sources of funding to financial intermediaries, financial market competition enables the intermediaries to benefit from market development. In other words, financial markets and financial intermediaries may have a complementary and mutually reinforcing relationship. In addition, in the early stages, financial intermediaries may be more efficient than the financial market, and as such, if there is no outside interference, bank-led financial systems are relatively efficient, and banking and the activities of other such financial intermediaries will dominate the financial activities of the society. As an economy develops, and after the financial markets reach a certain degree of development, the potential source of savings throughout the entire society will be used to their fullest, and at that time, the financial market will further develop and will transfer savings from financial intermediaries to the financial market. In this way, financial intermediaries and financial markets will become alternatives.

21.4 The Modern Financial Structure

21.4.1 The Basic Characteristics of the World's Modern Financial Structure

Financial development will always accompany changes in the financial structure. The financial structure is the proportional breakdown of various financial institutions and financial instruments throughout the financial system. Now, the world financial structure has the following basic characteristics:

First of all, once China made clear its commitment to establishing a socialist market economy, there was a general consensus that the stock market should be vigorously developed. Because of this, many people believe that the issuance of shares should become an enterprise's most important source of financing. The truth is, though, that even in highly-developed market economies like that of the United States, the issuance of stock is not an important channel for corporate financing. For instance, from 1970 to 1985, of the various sources of corporate financing in the United States, equity financing as a proportion of total financing is only 2.1%. However, the use of equity financing gradually increased as a proportion of Chinese financing (Figure 21.2). In the early 1980s, funds raised from the issuance of shares by Chinese enterprises was nearly zero, but in 2000, 4.68% of Chinese fixed asset investments were from the funds raised by stock issuances. Over the years, this proportion has been on the rise. However, in 2007, this trend appeared to be on the reverse.

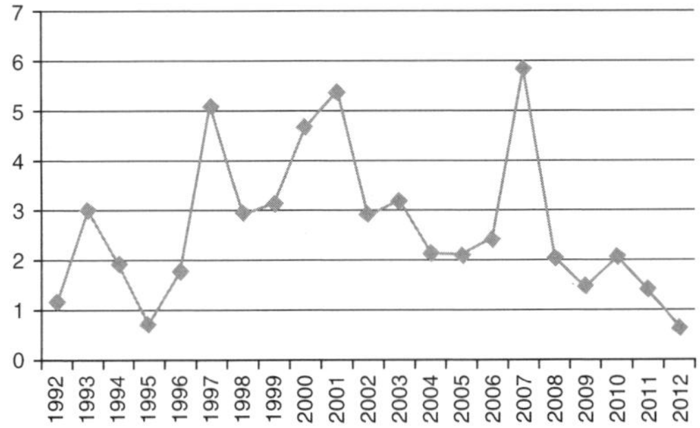

Fig. 21.2 Equity Financing as a Proportion of Chinese Fixed Assets Investment (Unit: %)

Source: National Bureau of Statistics, website of the China Securities Regulatory Commission

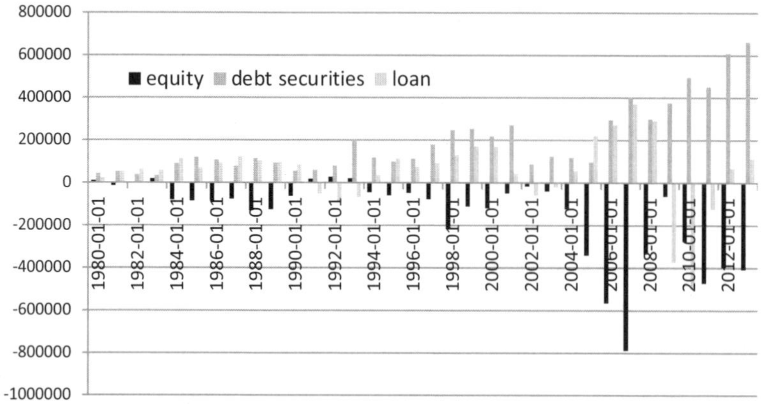

Fig. 21.3 The Financing Structure of Non-Financial Corporate Business (Unit: Million US Dollar)
Source: The Funds Flow Statement of the US Federal Reserve

Secondly, the majority of the external financing of the industrial and commercial enterprises around the world came from bank loans. In the United States, the amount of funds raised through bank loans on an average year were 25 times that of funds raised through stock (Figure 21.3). That is to say that, simply in terms of financing, even in highly developed, modern capital markets like that of the United States, banking is much more important than the stock market.

Third, corporate bonds are an important channel of external financing for many companies, but only large-scale and well-organized companies are allowed access to stock market financing. As such, it is almost impossible for individuals and small enterprises to finance through issuance of negotiable securities in organized capital markets like New York, Shanghai, and Shenzhen securities exchanges. For instance, home buyers cannot issue bonds or stock, and sole proprietors cannot issue a public offering in order to open up a cozy, romantic café. Unlike other countries, China's stock market was much more important than the corporate bond market for a long period of time. In 2000, China's corporate bond financing was only 4.04% of equity financing (Figure 21.4). However, after 2005, more and more Chinese enterprises relied on the issue of bonds for financing.

Fourth, when borrowers apply for loans, they are required to provide collateral or third party guarantees. When we apply for loans to purchase real estate, the banks which provide loans require the purchased house as collateral. Such requirements for collateral or third party guarantees are common when banks issue loans. Unsecured loans, which are loans with no collateral or third party guarantees, practically do not exist.

Fifth, from the perspective of the fund surplus sector, the proportion of secure assets, such as government bonds and demand deposits, is declining. Risky assets

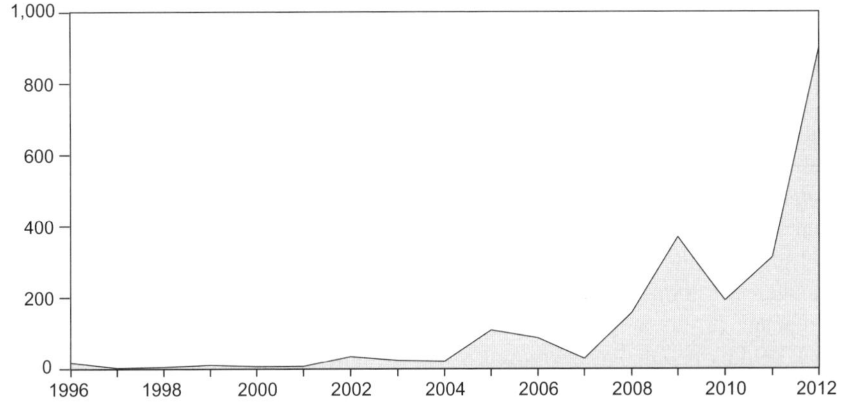

Fig. 21.4 A Comparison of China's Corporate Bond Financing and Equity Financing
Source: *China Statistical Yearbook* and the Website of the People's Bank of China

such as stock, are thus rising. However, nowadays, many people will not directly purchase listed stock, but will instead purchase into securities investment funds to indirectly hold stock. By the end of 1998, there were only five securities investment funds in China, but by the end of 2012, there were over 1100 securities investment funds, with total assets of more than 2.8 trillion yuan.

Finally, the proportion of life insurance and pension funds is also on the rise.

21.4.2 Why the Modern Financial Structure Presents Such Characteristics

What has led to such characteristics in the modern financial structure? The structure is primarily, for the following reasons:

- Transaction Costs and Risk Diversification
- Asymmetric Information
- Government Behavior and Institutional Changes
- The Coming of an Aging Society

(a) *Economies of Scale and Transaction Costs*

An important function of the financial system is to lower costs, and this is because the use of financial intermediaries has the advantage of economies of scale, and as such, the unit cost of each investment is effectively reduced. In addition, due to economies of scale, a great deal of funds are pooled together, which is conducive to dispersed investment and which can lower the investment risks of individuals. As such, in many countries, there has been a rapid growth of capital market intermediaries such as mutual funds. By the end of 2005, China had a total of

186 fund management companies. The 373 funds under these companies managed 930 billion yuan worth of assets. By the end of 2012, the total scale of China's fund assets had reached more than 2.8 trillion yuan.

Another important reason why intermediary institutions can lower transaction costs is because they do a better job of developing specialized expertise. Mutual funds, banks, and other financial intermediary institutions developed specialized computer expertise, which enabled them to offer more convenient services at an extremely low cost. Institutional investors, like securities investment funds, pool together the scattered surplus funds and engage in so-called expert wealth management, joint investment, and risk-sharing to utilize the advantages of scale to manage profits and risks. Thus, in developed countries, the amount of listed stock held by people has decreased, while the amount of common fund shares has increased.

(b) *Asymmetric Information*

Asymmetric information has a major influence on the modern financial structure.

(i) *Asymmetric information and financial intermediaries*: Financial intermediaries have become experts in producing information to distinguish the level of credit risk. They have the capacity of obtaining funds from depositors, only to then evaluate and select the potential borrowers and lend money to those they consider as good companies, and in this way, they can obtain higher expected returns from these loans than the interest they pay depositors. The main reason why banks have the ability to make a profit on producing information is that they primarily issue private loans instead of purchasing securities through open market transactions. As such, they avoid the free-rider problem of information production. Since private loans are not traded on the open market, other investors cannot see what banks are doing, and as such, it would be difficult for them to bring the price of loans to a high level that can hardly cover the bank's high cost of information production. As intermediaries, banks hold a large volume of loans which are not publicly traded on the market. This is the key by which they overcome the problem of asymmetric information on the financial market and this is also the main reason why bank loans have become one of the most important sources of corporate external financing.

(ii) *How asymmetric information affects corporate external financing*: The better a company's reputation, the easier it is to obtain information about this company on the market. For investors to determine the quality of these companies, it is easier to determine their strengths and weaknesses. Since investors do not care about the adverse selection of reputable companies, they are willing to directly invest in securities. This is the reason why big companies are the only ones who issue negotiable securities.

(iii) *How asymmetric information affects debt and equity contracts*: After the separation of savings and investment, the problem of asymmetric information arises between capital providers and users. In order to avoid the adverse selection and moral hazards of asymmetric information, there must be appropriate contractual agreements within financing activities. Any financing activity may be regarded as a contractual agreement. If moral hazards of a contract only exist under certain conditions, it will greatly reduce the supervision required by managers and will greatly cut down the cost. As such, this kind of contract is very attractive. Compared to equity contracts, debt contracts happen to have these characteristics, because they are a contractual agreement in which borrowers must pay a fixed amount in regular intervals to the lender (bond investor). When a company's profits are relatively high, lenders will receive contractual payments without having to ascertain the profits of the company. If corporate management personnel conceal profits, or act in a way which benefits themselves but does not add to the profits of the enterprise, as long as it will not have any impact on the company's ability to meet its obligations on time, lenders need not mind. Just like Zhao Xiaosan's lending of money to Wang Xiao'er in Chapter 6, he need not be too concerned about whether or not Wang Xiao'er withholds some of his operating revenue. Only when a company is unable to meet its obligations will lenders need to audit the company's dividends, and only in this case will lenders act like shareholders of the company: in order to get a fair share, they will need to know about the company's revenue. Such companies do not require a lot of monitoring, and as such, audit costs are low, and investors will thereby prefer this type of debt contract as opposed to equity contracts.

(iv) *How asymmetric information affects the structure of debt contracts*: Of course, if debt contracts are used in place of equity contracts, it will not completely resolve the issue of adverse selection and moral hazards. How does asymmetric information, which also exists in this type of contract, affect debt contracts?

In a debt contract, restrictive clauses will typically be imposed as a way of excluding those borrowers who are engaged in undesirable activities. Restrictive clauses primarily have the following four aspects: first, the borrower must specifically state the purpose of the loan. For instance, the home mortgage that you apply for at the bank cannot be used for stock speculation. Second, restrictive clauses can urge borrowers to engage in those activities which will better facilitate loan repayment. For enterprises, the main point lies in encouraging borrowers to maintain a high level of net worth, thereby reducing the risk of moral hazards. Third, borrowers are required to provide collateral or third party guarantees. If we want to borrow money to buy a house, banks will require the house we purchase as collateral, and in the event that the borrower defaults and cannot repay their principal and interest upon maturity, then the bank will require that the borrower sells the real estate purchased so as to pay off the outstanding loan. Fourth, they may require that borrowers provide financial statements on time so that the lenders can monitor the borrower's activities at any time as well as the status of their operations.

(c) *Impact of Government Behavior on the Financial Structure*

Government behavior affects the financial structure in two ways, namely, through taxation and institutional rules.

(i) *Impact of taxation on the financial structure*: Taxes have a significant impact on the financial structure. Taxation lowers the overall cost of bond financing below that of equity financing. In debt financing, the calculated interest is included in the cost of debt and can reduce the tax base. In equity financing, there is a "double taxation" on both the corporate legal person and the shareholders. Companies partially financed by debt will have a greater value than those fully financed by equity (see Chapter 6).

(ii) *The government's institutional supply and financial structure*: One important reason for the large differences from one country's financial structure to another is that the institutional arrangements in these countries are not entirely the same. The institutional arrangements set down the rules for people's behaviors. Within the permitted scope of these arrangements, financial activities account for a large proportion. Financial activities which are outside of the scope are severely punished, and in this context, very few of the financial activities are disclosed. In direct financing, China's structure displays very different characteristics from other countries. Prior to the 1980s, China's financial structure included no financial assets like stock or corporate bonds, nor were there any securities investment funds, and this was because under a planned economic system, corporate financing was primarily through fiscal appropriation. At that time, it was illegal for enterprises to issue stock, and as such, the amount of equity financing was practically zero. However, when equity financing was permitted by the government and a corresponding formal system was established, it developed rapidly, and China's stock market boomed over the last decade.

Relative to equity financing, the development of China's corporate bond market was very slow in a long period. This is mainly because it was not involved in the reforms to the system of enterprises, and the issuance of corporate bond did not bring about any corresponding changes to this system. During China's economic reforms, especially when enterprise system reforms became the focus of the entire economic reforms, the government naturally included the stock market into a formal financial arrangement. Conversely, corporate bonds could not play a role as the government had desired in facilitating the reform of enterprises, thus receiving less attention from the government in quite a long period of time. Secondly, since corporate bonds are a type of debt financing activity, the issuer should have a relatively strong ability to repay debt. Enterprises' ability to repay debt depends not only on their future cash flows, but also on their related property ownership. When an enterprise's property rights do not constitute a powerful constraint on its debt, there is a serious risk of moral hazards, or there may be adverse selection within debt financing. From this perspective, the development of the stock market is the basis for the development of corporate bonds.

(d) *The Coming of an Aging Society*

Population aging has had a phenomenal impact on financial structures. In major industrialized countries, there has been a long-term decline in fertility, and with a recent decline in mortality rates in the older population, a resulting trend has emerged in the form of an aging population. Since the 1950s, the population of people 65 years of age or older in the United Kingdom and Canada has increased by a third or more. In the United States and Germany, this population has increased by half, while in Japan, this population has doubled. Over the next decade, this aging phenomenon is expected to continue. According to UN projections, the population over age 65 in the main countries (except for the United Kingdom) within the Organization for Economic Cooperation and Development (OECD) is expected to double by 2025. By that time, the elderly population will account for one-fifth to one-fourth of the entire population. Because the population is aging, retirement and pension funds are given more weight within the financial structure. China's aging society is also on its way, and with this demographic change, it can be predicted that life insurance and pension insurance will occupy an increasingly important position in the Chinese financial structure. Also, an aging population will also increase the demand for safer assets with relatively stable earnings, and as such, there may be greater development in markets for fixed-yield securities, such as bonds.

21.5 The Financial Globalization in Financial Development

21.5.1 Economic Globalization and Financial Globalization

Today, one striking aspect of financial development is financial globalization. Financial globalization has four characteristics:

First and foremost, with the emergence of cross-border financial activities as well as financial assets and liabilities, there is now a global movement of financial resources. In accordance with the principle of comparative advantage, the world's scarce resources can be more reasonably allocated in a broader geographic area. When enterprises issue stock to raise funds, they are also transcending the limitations of national frontiers, and many more companies are listed overseas. For example, China's Tsingtao Beer, Sohu, and other companies are listed in America. Similarly, Lenovo Group, China Unicom, China Construction Bank, the Industrial and Commercial Bank of China, and the Bank of China are all listed on the Hong Kong Joint Stock Exchange. China has also gradually lifted restrictions on capital markets, allowing qualified foreign institutional investors (QFIIs) to invest in Chinese securities. In the early stages of China's market reforms, the economy attracted a large amount of foreign direct investment. Foreign companies set up factories in China, allowing China to take advantage of their technology and capital, while China provided a large amount of cheap labor. The global allocation of capital has been an important driving force behind global economic growth over the last decade.

Second, financial activities and financial markets operate under harmonized rules. An increasing number of international financial organizations have developed harmonized rules and standards for global financial activities, such as the regulatory standards of the Basel Accord for global banking which requires that the capital adequacy ratio of commercial banks shall not be less than 8% (see Chapter 24), and this harmonization is constantly improving. The International Organization of Securities Commissions and the International Association of Insurance Supervisors also respectively developed the harmonized standards of sound operations and supervision in international securities and insurance. The World Trade Organization, the World Bank, the International Monetary Fund, and the Bank for International Settlements also play an important role in resolving trade disputes, promoting international direct investment, coordinating international currencies, stabilizing exchange rates, and providing loans or emergency assistance to member countries.

Third, the homogeneous financial assets tend to have nearly the same price on the international market, which indicates that arbitrage opportunities that had arisen from a variety of barriers have been greatly reduced because of financial globalization. For example, the price of gold calculated in the same currency is almost equal, anywhere in the world.

Finally, the globalization of financial activities has allowed the financial risks of individual countries to affect neighboring countries and regions. Like viral flu, hepatitis B, and atypical pneumonia which are all contagious, the contagious effects of financial risks are also global, to a certain extent. For instance, the financial crisis which first occurred in Thailand in 1997 quickly spread to other Southeast Asian countries, and even the Republic of Korea and Japan were not spared. In 2008, what was initially only a US sub-prime mortgage crisis evolved into the global financial crisis. Global stock markets suffered heavy losses, and China was no exception. This was all the more so in Iceland, where not only the currency significantly depreciated and the stock market crashed, but the country itself went bankrupt, and thus, against the background of globalization, the destructive power of contagious risks became all the more evident. The European sovereign debt crisis which began in 2010 was, to a considerable extent, a continuation or a result of the US sub-prime mortgage crisis. In the context of globalization, as soon as one country experiences systematic financial risks (especially major powers), it will be difficult for other countries to be spared, as the saying goes: "To be hit by a stray bullet without being in a war."

21.5.2 The Basic Factors Which Drive Financial Globalization

Financial globalization is not groundless, but is instead built upon a profound economic, technological, and institutional infrastructure. In short, the following four factors have contributed to the development of financial globalization.

(a) *The Globalization of Trade*

Now, the global economy is increasingly becoming a whole. Chinese consumers can use American IBM computers, Ford automobiles, and Boeing aircrafts, just like they can use Japanese Matsushita electronics and Toyota automobiles. Meanwhile, Americans and Europeans can also buy China's textiles and household appliances. If you walk into an American, European, or other developed economy's shopping mall, you may find out that a lot of the goods are labeled "Made in China". On the back of Apple products, such as the iPhone or the iPad, is written "Designed by Apple in California. Assembled in China". Through international trade, the global economy has been forged into an integral whole.

Since the 1990s, the annual growth rate of the global trade of goods and services has been 6.5%, which is much higher than the annual growth of global GDP at 3.36%. In 2000, the world's total output, based on the official exchange rate, was approximately 31.8 trillion dollars, or 43.8 trillion dollars based on purchasing power parity; the gross imports and exports of global commodities was 12.8 trillion dollars, and the total output's degree of dependence on foreign trade was 40.4%. By 2012, the gross amount of global exports of goods and services had reached 22.75 trillion dollars, which accounted for more than 30% of the world's GDP. With the development of the international division of labor, the formation of new international production networks, and the reorganization of international supply chains, the global trade of goods and services is growing constantly. The global trade of goods and services requires the support of appropriate financial services and transactions. For instance, the development of global trade demands transnational capital settlements, and in order to avoid exchange rate risks, it requires the use of the global foreign exchange market for hedging transactions. The globalization of trade is the initial motivation for financial globalization.

(b) *International Capital as a Driving Force*

From 1991 to 2000, the annual average growth of global net private direct investment greatly exceeded that of the world's GDP and international trade. According to statistics released by the United Nations Conference on Trade and Development, the total amount of global transnational investment had reached 1.1 trillion dollars in 2000, a 14% growth since 1999. The statistics also showed 80% of foreign direct investment flowed to developed countries, and the regions which attracted most transnational direct investment were Western Europe, with an annual investment of 597 billion dollars. The United States attracted the most transnational direct investment, at a total of 260 billion dollars in investments. About 190 billion dollars of transnational direct investment flowed to developing countries. In 2011, the total amount of global transnational investment was more than 1.5 trillion dollars (transaction amount for the year), of which, developing economies attracted approximately 680 billion dollars in foreign direct investment, while developed economies attracted 750 billion dollars in direct investment. In addition, capital flows occur on a much greater scale in the form of so-called hot money. Hot money is short-term international capital used for exchange rate spreads, interest rate spreads, or other such earnings. In particular, when interest rates in developed economies are very low, and when interest rates in emerging economies are relatively high, there will be a greater scale of hot money. This is why the scale of China's foreign exchange reserves has increased significantly since 2001, and one of the main reasons behind the sharp rise in real estate prices.

(c) *The Development of Multinational Corporations and Multinational Financial Institutions*

According to statistics, by the end of 1999, global transnational corporations increased to 63,000 companies, with more than 700,000 overseas subsidiaries which accounted for 60% of all global trading, and a 70% stake in the global high-tech industry, 40% of the world's GDP, and more than 90% of all international direct investment. Transnational corporations are active in various parts of the world, and have caused a general breakdown in national boundaries as well as a shift in international division of labor which is now on the basis of modern technology and industrial processes, rather than natural resources, and which is within industries and along the boundaries of the factors of production, rather than between and along the boundaries of industries. This has also led to developments in the free global flow of the factors of production. It can be said that the development of transnational corporations is one of the main driving forces which promote financial globalization.

In the global development of transnational corporations, the development of transnational financial institutions is particularly noteworthy. This is because, compared to the typical industrial and commercial enterprises, financial institutions are much more penetrating and are an important force for promoting financial globalization, as are they an important part of this financial globalization. Currently, transnational banks operate trillions of dollars worth of international loan capital on a global scale. As for transnational banks, Citibank, HSBC, and Standard Chartered Bank all have branches in China. Bank of China, China Merchants Bank and China Construction Bank all have branches in Europe and America in order to conduct business overseas. In the global direct capital markets, transnational investment banks are engaged in mergers and acquisitions, underwriting corporate stocks, and other such financial activities; they are truly global in terms of their business perspective and scope of operations. For instance, the stocks of China Merchants Bank and Sinopec are underwritten by China International Capital Corporation, a joint venture of China Construction Bank and Morgan Stanley. Well-known investment banks such as Goldman Sachs also conduct business in China, and in fact, Goldman Sachs has more than 1000 employees working in China, and they assumed the underwriting of China Mobile, which is listed in Hong Kong.

(d) *The Development of Modern Information Technology*

The development of information technology has made the world much smaller, and even though great oceans separate Beijing from New York and New York from Paris, the development of information technology has connected the "global village" so that they can easily obtain information within the other "neighborhoods". After the September 11 attacks, this shocking news quickly spread throughout the "global village". In August 2008, billions of people around the world simultaneously watched the opening ceremony of the Beijing Olympics. In the financial markets, Chinese investors can instantly access US stock market prices, and the prices of US gold and crude oil futures.

The development of information technology has closely linked together financial markets and financial institutions scattered all across the world. First and foremost, the development of information technology has allowed for the simultaneous dissemination of information about financial products and thus greatly reduced the global arbitrage opportunities for the same type of products, because as soon as there is a price difference, traders who focus on global finances will quickly take the opportunity to make a profit. Second, the development of information technology has allowed global capital allocation to be completed in an instant, and simply by typing on the keyboard, huge sums of money can flow across national borders. Third, the development of modern information technology has made financial globalization technologically feasible. It has greatly reduced transaction costs, allowing traders to carry out transactions 24 hours a day in international financial markets, especially in the foreign exchange market.

(e) *A Financial System Based on Financial Globalization: The Wave of Financial Liberalization*

Prior to the 1970s, the financial sector was subject to some of the most severe government regulations, with strict restrictions imposed on interest rates, exchange rates, currency convertibility, commercial banks, etc. The government regulations on finance were not only limited to the developing countries adopting financial repression, but even developed countries implemented stringent financial controls. For instance, the American Regulation Q stipulated that the interest rate payments by commercial banks could not exceed a certain limit nor could interest be paid on demand deposits. A great majority of countries throughout the world required commercial banks to pay a required deposit reserve, although central banks did not pay interest on these required reserves. In this way, the higher the required reserve to be paid, the less fund that was available to commercial banks to make a profit. Thus, people also refer to required reserves as a reserve tax.

Most financial regulations limit the scope of business of financial institutions, and under these strict controls, financial globalization, in its real sense, could never occur. Since the 1970s, however, developed and developing countries alike have all been swept up by the wave of global financial liberalization, and most countries have adopted various measures to promote financial liberalization, deregulated interest rate, and currency convertibility, and eased the controls over commercial banks and capital flow. This global wave of financial liberalization has allowed investors and fund-raisers to invest and engage in financing activities at lower costs, more freely, and on a global scale. The financial liberalization regime provides a solid basis for financial globalization.

21.5.3 The Future Development of Financial Globalization

With the further development of information technology, the closer ties between countries in trade and investment, as well as the accelerated financial deregulation and liberalization processes around the world, financial globalization will also gain momentum in the coming years. For countries around the world, whether they be deep in the heart of Africa or developed countries in North America, whether they be European or East Asian, the financial industries of these various countries will come closer together, merging into a whole. The financial development of one country will have a significant impact on others, as will that country be affected by the development of other countries.

Summary

Financial development is the dynamic process of constantly improving and expanding the functions of finance and thereby promoting financial efficiency and economic growth. Financial development accompanies changes in the financial structure and the ever-increasing efficiency of finance. The financial development is primarily driven by the following motivations: the lowering of transaction costs, the circumvention of risks and regulations, and the development of information technology.

The financial interrelations ratio is the ratio between the balance of broad money and a country's GDP. The financial interrelations ratio will constantly rise with GDP growth.

The two paths of financial development are demand-following and supply-leading. If financial development is only a passive response to the demand for financial services in the real economic sector, it is demand-following. In supply-leading financial development, the financial sector actively mobilizes resources which are stuck in traditional sectors and transfers them to the modern sectors which can promote economic growth, thereby promoting efficient resource allocation.

According to the endogenous financial development theory, only when an economy develops to a certain degree and when the per capita income exceeds a certain critical value, people will then take advantage of financial intermediaries and financial markets on a large scale. However, in different stages of economic development, there is a different relationship between financial intermediaries and financial markets, and in the early stages, they are complementary, but in the later stage of development, they are alternatives.

Modern financial structures have several important characteristics: stock is not the most important source of financing, and bank loans and corporate bonds are far more important. Only large enterprises will raise fund on the stock market, and life insurance and pension funds are gaining an increasingly important position in the financial structure. The reasons are as follows: transaction costs and risk diversification, asymmetric information, government behavior and institutional changes, and finally, the arrival of an aging society.

A striking aspect of financial development is financial globalization. The process of financial globalization is driven by the globalization of trade, international capital flows, the development of transnational corporations and transnational financial institutions, and modern information technology.

Key Terms

Financial Development; Financial Structure; Financial Interrelations Ratio; Economic Monetization; Junk Bond; Demand-Following Financial Development; Supply-Leading Financial Development; Financial Globalization; Financial Innovation; Disintermediation; Eurocurrency; Shadow Banking; Credit Default Swaps

Critical Thinking Questions

1. What is financial development?
2. What are the motivations behind financial development?
3. What is demand-following and supply-leading financial development?
4. What is the endogenous financial development theory about?
5. What are the intrinsic motivations for changes in an enterprise's financing structure?
6. What are the basic characteristics of the world's modern financial structure?
7. What are the underlying factors which contribute to the world's modern financial structure?
8. Do you believe that China's financial structure should be the same as America's? Why?
9. Analyze the changes that will happen to China's financial structure.
10. Some people say that China's financial sector should develop beyond its normal limits. Please use the endogenous financial development theory to briefly comment on this.

Chapter 22

Financial Deepening and Financial Liberalization

Learning Objectives

After studying this chapter, you will be able to:

- Learn about the basic features of the financial systems of developing countries
- Understand financial repression, its means and its impact
- Understand why the capital and money of a developing country are complementary
- Understand why a virtuous cycle may exist between savings and growth
- Clearly understand the primary policy measures for increasing the savings rate of developing countries
- Understand financial liberalization and its objectives
- Understand the liberalization of the banking sector
- Understand capital market liberalization
- Understand interest rate liberalization
- Understand the liberalization of the foreign exchange market and currency convertibility

Since the 1970s, the world has been swept up in a wave of economic liberalization. The financial sector is no exception, particularly the economic liberalization of several developing countries, the scope, extent and speed of which constitutes some of the most dazzling of international economic policy changes. In the financial sector, financial liberalization is primarily based on the theory of financial deepening. In this chapter, we will introduce the theory of financial deepening and the basic content of financial liberalization.

22.1 Characteristics of Financial Systems and Financial Repression of Developing Countries

22.1.1 Characteristics of Financial Systems in Developing Countries

In 1973, American economists Ronald McKinnon and Edward Shaw respectively published *Money and Capital in Economic Development* and *Financial Deepening in Economic Development*, which were the first systematic analyses of the characteristics of financial systems in developing countries. Based on their findings, the financial systems of developing countries share the following four characteristics:

(1) The majority of developing countries, especially undeveloped and poor countries, will have a relatively lower degree of monetization than advanced industrialized countries. This demonstrates the predominance of natural economies and a barter system in developing countries.

(2) The financial systems of the majority of developing countries have a dual nature in that there exist the "modern" financial sector and financial markets — which have been mainly introduced from Western industrialized countries and which features modern operations management — and alongside with it the local "traditional sector" which is constituted by scattered and small-scale private financial institutions such as exchange shops, revolving savings and credit associations and pawnshops. The "modern sector" is largely concentrated in major cities, while the "traditional sector" is commonly found in small towns and countryside.

(3) Financial markets, especially capital markets, are generally undeveloped. In some developing countries, there is no capital market whatsoever, and even if there is, it is still in its incubation period or in the very early stages of development. Furthermore, commercial banks, especially state-owned commercial banks, will typically hold a definite position of dominance. Non-banking financial institutions and private financial institutions, even those with very modern operational management, will only hold a subordinate position. In this way, underdeveloped or unevenly developed financial organizations, systems and financial markets will be unable to carry out the large-scale mobilization of savings to support investments.

(4) The government authorities of most developing countries will implement strict financial controls. Bank deposit and lending rates are typically established by the government and cannot properly reflect a capital surplus or deficiency. Exchange rates are also established by the authorities and do not accurately reflect the supply and demand of foreign currency. State-owned banks are massive and enjoy many "privileges", which may easily lead to a lack of competition in the financial sector, inefficiency, and correspondingly, they will often serve as an instrument for offsetting the government's fiscal deficit.

22.1.2 The Financial Repression of Developing Countries and the Means of Financial Repression

In correspondence with the four characteristics, **financial repression** prevails in developing countries. Financial repression refers to compulsory administrative intervention in the financial system conducted by governments of developing countries for specific purposes, making it impossible for the financial system to give play to its role in guiding reasonable resource allocations by market mechanisms.

The primary means of financial repression include:

- Special Credit Institutions
- High Reserve
- Interest Rate Controls
- Foreign Exchange Controls

(a) *Special Credit Institutions*

To implement their development plans, the government of a developing country will establish special credit institutions, such as policy banks, in order to provide cheap credit to sectors and industries which the government favors. **Cheap credit** is a low-interest loan that can neither reflect market supply and demand nor the risk profile of fund users. Preferential interest rate loans are the classic example of cheap credit. Special credit institutions are financed primarily through central bank loans, the funds of which, having been borrowed from the central bank, can be used at unbalanced low rates to promote imports and exports, provide credit to rural households, subsidize government-designated industrial projects, etc.

The financial systems of developing countries are subject to strict financial control by the government authorities when special credit institutions are established. When "organized" financing is arranged in such a harsh manner, there are not many remaining competitive factors which can affect deposit rates and the cost per unit, and thus there is no impetus for reducing the gap between deposits and lending rates or lowering management costs. Under such financial repression, even after deducting the factor of economies of scale, the operating cost per unit of the various intermediary institutions is still very high. The greater the gap between deposit and lending rates, the less pressure on commercial banks to cut costs.

In those developing countries which have not established special credit institutions, commercial banks will often be subject to too much government intervention, and governments may force commercial banks to grant a large amount of "policy" loans, hence becoming the government's quasi-fiscal institutions. These institutions will then provide substantial financial subsidies to enterprises in those sectors and industries which the government favors. Because of government intervention in the process of commercial bank credit allocation, and because of the multi-faceted purpose of the government behavior, naturally, cost-effective resource allocation does not come first in credit allocation. Over time, the policy-related losses of commercial banks will become an increasingly heavy burden and may become one of the most difficult hurdles of future financial reforms. This is well illustrated by the situation in China. Prior to the establishment of the three large policy banks in 1994, four large state-owned commercial banks assumed a large amount of the financing obligations as required by the government, which, under the influence of unreasonable enterprise property rights, led to massive non-performing loans.

(b) *High Reserve Requirements*

In order to strengthen the centralized control of financial resources, the governments of developing countries will typically implement high required reserve ratios, and as such, the deposits drawn by commercial banks will be directly transferred to central bank accounts which is conducive to the central bank's credit controls on commercial banks. Because of the high reserve requirement, commercial banks will have less discretionary funds. High reserve ratios are typically accompanied by directed credit allocation, in that commercial banks will typically be subject to mandatory administrative interventions from various levels of the government when they allocate their credit resources, and as such, they are not very autonomous. For instance, after the four state-owned specialized banks were established in China in 1984, the initial required deposit reserve that they deposited in the central bank was as high as 40%. As such, these banks had little or no discretionary funds for issuing loans, and the amount of loans issued by commercial banks was completely dependent on the central bank's credit scheme.

High reserve ratios are closely linked to a government's controls in the form of direct credit schemes. Because of the implementation of the government scheme, deposit reserve ratios have almost no effect on monetary multipliers. However, to commercial banks, high required deposit reserve ratios will lower their amount of discretionary funds and thereby lower the funds which can be used for profitable project financing. In this way, they are a disguised high deposit reserve tax imposed on commercial banks to support the central bank's credit scheme. To compensate commercial banks for the losses, the government has established corresponding mechanisms which artificially expand the rate differential between savings and loans (as shown in Table 22.1) and pay a relatively high amount of

Table 22.1 China's One-Year Deposit and Lending Benchmark Interest Rate (at the End of the Year)

	1990	1995	1998	2000	2002	2004	2006	2008	2010	2012
Deposit	8.64	10.98	3.78	2.25	1.98	2.25	2.52	2.25	2.75	3.00
Lending	9.36	12.06	6.39	5.85	5.31	5.58	6.12	5.31	5.81	6.00
Spreads	0.72	1.08	2.61	3.6	3.33	3.33	3.6	3.06	3.06	3.00

interest on required reserves. As China's current market rates continue to decline, the central bank still pays interest on commercial bank reserves at a rate of 1.89%. In this situation, especially when market rates continue to decline, commercial banks will not actively issue commercial loans beyond what is regulated by the government.

(c) *Interest Rate Controls*

Another means of financial repression is setting an interest rate ceiling. As the real interest rates are often negative due to inflation, financial assets holders may need to "pay back" interest. Under such financial repression, deposit rates cannot reflect the time preference of depositors' consumption and excessively low rates repress the willingness to save, which results in an insufficient supply of capital. On the other hand, due to lending rate restrictions, borrowers can obtain loans based on an interest rate that is low or in effect negative. Negative real deposit rates will inhibit the voluntary demand for actual claims on financial intermediaries, lowering the ability of such financial institutions to allocate savings for investment.

Since the real lending rates are low or even negative, the only way to resolve the excessive demand for loans on intermediary institutions is through a reliance on rationing. Rationing comes at quite a cost, as it breeds corruption and also allows borrowers and officials at intermediary institutions to earn a monopoly income from the difference between the low, regulated lending rates and the real market break-even interest rates. Also, the rationing order will often be disrupted if borrowers do not repay their loans or if they unreasonably retain possession of the rationed funds by extending their loan period. Additionally, low real interest rate ceilings will increase the likelihood of intermediary institutions to avoid risk and maintain a preference for liquidity. Because the government-regulated interest rates are unified, when commercial banks issue loans to borrowers with different credit risks, they cannot earn a corresponding risk premium, which stifles the willingness of commercial banks to lend to relatively high-risk enterprises, and encourages banks and other intermediary institutions to provide special offers to the creditworthy customers, especially those companies with a history of long-term stable operations. As such, there is little incentive to develop new lending opportunities, and these institutions are satisfied with transferring a large amount of funds in the form of excess reserves to the monetary authority or transferring such funds to the Ministry of Finance when they hold onto government securities. As soon as the opportunity arises, monetary or fiscal authorities will transfer these funds to development banks for their use.

(d) *Foreign Exchange Controls*

Foreign exchange controls refer to the restrictive measures adopted by a government in regards to the receipts and disbursements, settlements, transactions and use of foreign exchange. Exchange controls come in the form of direct and indirect controls. The former refers to a variety of compulsory management and control measures directly imposed by regulators on various foreign exchange services. The latter refers to the act of implementing a licensing system, import quotas and other such arrangements so as to produce indirect effects on foreign exchange services and achieve the purpose of exchange controls.

The content of exchange controls will differ from country to country and from time to time. The general framework of exchange controls will include the following aspects: exchange controls on trade transactions, which can be divided into exchange controls on import and exchange controls on export; the former may include an import licensing system and import quotas, while the latter, in addition to restrictive arrangements such as export licenses, also includes export-promotion measures; non-trade exchange controls, i.e., controls on foreign exchange receipts and disbursements not under trade and capital accounts; controls on the import and export of capital; controls over the import and export of domestic currency, foreign currency and gold as well as controls on foreign exchange purchases and sales. Originally, China was a country with strict foreign exchange controls, but with the deepening of market and economic reforms, China's exchange controls are becoming more relaxed.

22.2 The Complementarity of Money and Capital and the Virtuous Cycle of Savings and Growth

22.2.1 The Complementarity of Money and Capital

Unlike developed countries, the economy of a developing country is segmented and the economic units are primarily internally financed, with little external financing. In this case, savers are investors. Because of the inseparability of investment, there must be a large amount of accumulated savings before investments can be made. For instance, even after China's economy had already reached a considerable degree of development, many underdeveloped rural areas still belonged to this category. After the fall harvest, farmers will withhold a portion of their seeds for the coming year, and this kind of physical savings is also an investment. Alternatively, a farmer will purchase cattle with the income earned after selling off some of their grain. This is the typical way in which rural savings is transferred to investment. Because external financing is subject to a lot of restrictions, a single producer will find it difficult to invest through modern financial arrangements in order to take advantage of optimal production technology. If there is no external financing, it will be difficult to achieve agricultural mechanization, and farmers will find it difficult to improve their agricultural infrastructure.

Because external financing is subject to limitations, people in developing countries with underdeveloped financial systems must first have a sufficient amount of monetary savings to increase internal financing before they enter into a desirable investment. In this way, the greater the willingness to invest, the larger the scale of monetary savings, and as such, the monetary balance will display a very strong complementarity with that of capital. In other words, the higher the demand for capital, the higher the demand for money. Thus, in developing countries and given a certain level of income, if one wants to raise accumulation rate of desired capital (the savings rate), the average ratio between real money balances and the income will increase.

Investment willingness will be influenced by the rate of return on capital. When the rate of return increases, investment willingness will increase. Conversely, if the rate of return decreases, the propensity to invest will also decline. Since the demand for real money balances changes in the same direction as that of investment spending, capital investment yields rise with an increase in the demand for real money balances.

Given a certain rate of return on capital, a higher yield on monetary holdings will cause an increase in internal accumulation rates. Conversely, if the effective yield on monetary holdings decreases, it will hurt monetary savings. Thus, an increase in the effective yield on money will encourage more savings, less consumption, and an increase in internal financing. In this way, it will reduce capital constraints and also increase physical capital investments. This is the **tube effect**. As in Figure 22.1, r represents the nominal rate of deposits, $\dot{p}$ represents the rate of inflation, and as such, $r - \dot{p}$ represents the effective yield on money. When real interest rates are 0.8%, because the return on monetary holdings decreases, people will not be willing to make monetary savings, and the investment to income ratio will only be 10%. With an increase in the effective yield on money, the willingness to save will also increase, as will internal financing, and thus, the investment scale of physical capital will also expand accordingly. When the effective yield on money is 3%, the investment to income ratio will increase to 30%.

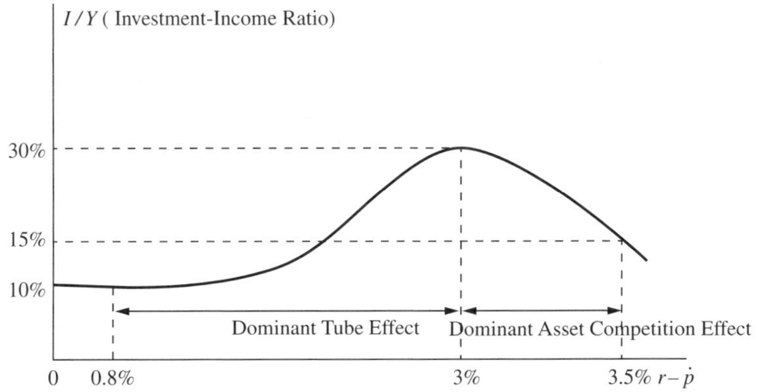

Fig. 22.1 Endogenous Investment and Financing as Influenced by Effective Yield on Money

However, as soon as real interest rates reach a level that ensures the optimal marginal revenue and internal revenue of internal financing, **asset competition effect** will dominate and reduce total investment flows. In other words, when the real return on monetary holdings is already very high, a further increase in this type of earnings will often lead to cash balances in place of physical capital, and this is because holding cash balances has become much more attractive. If the rate of return on physical capital investment is 3%, when the real interest rate on money exceeds 3%, the asset competition effect will dominate. For example, when the real interest rate reaches 3.5%, the effective yield on monetary holdings will be far greater than the rate of return on physical capital investment. When this happens, people would rather hold onto money and would not be willing to transfer their monetary savings to investment in physical capital. When the real interest rate is 3.5%, the physical capital investments to income ratio will fall to 15%.

22.2.2 The Virtuous Cycle of Savings and Growth

How then can a developing country raise the rate of savings and capital accumulation? In order to achieve such an objective, developing countries should promote financial liberalization reforms, promote financial deepening, improve the nominal rate of return on money and lower the rate of inflation. Through financial reforms, financially repressed developing countries can achieve a virtuous cycle of savings and growth.

McKinnon used the simple Harrod–Domar economic growth model to illustrate the virtuous cycle of financial reforms, growth and savings. If we set the rate of savings as s, Y as national income, and S as the amount of savings, then:

$$S = s \cdot Y. \tag{22.1}$$

If the output–capital ratio is σ, and K is capital, then:

$$\sigma = \frac{Y}{K}. \tag{22.2}$$

If we set ΔK as the increase in capital and ΔY as the increase in output or national income, then:

$$\Delta Y = \sigma \cdot \Delta K. \tag{22.3}$$

The increase in capital is attributed to investment, and if we set investment as I, then:

$$\Delta Y = \sigma \cdot I. \tag{22.4}$$

If the growth rate is y, then:

$$y = \frac{\Delta Y}{Y} = \frac{\sigma \cdot I}{Y}. \tag{22.5}$$

The equilibrium of the national income requires savings S to equal investment I, namely:

$$I = S = s \cdot Y. \qquad (22.6)$$

Plugging Equations (22.6) into (22.5), we would obtain the following formula:

$$y = s \cdot \sigma. \qquad (22.7)$$

This is the famous Harrod–Domar economic growth model which indicates that the rate of economic growth is equal to the product of the output-capital ratio and the rate of savings.

McKinnon believed that the growth rate of income would have an influence on the rate of savings, so the rate of savings is an increasing function of the growth rate of income:

$$s = s(y, \rho), \qquad (22.8)$$

of which ρ represents financial deepening variables other than economic growth rate which have an influence on the rate of savings after financial liberalization. Also, $0 < S < 1$. Thus:

$$y = \sigma \cdot s(y, \rho). \qquad (22.9)$$

Equation (22.9) indicates the interactions between economic growth, savings and financial deepening. Next, we have used a graph to illustrate the virtuous cycle of financial reform, savings, and growth. In Figure 22.2, the horizontal axis indicates the rate of economic growth, while the vertical axis is equal to the product of the rate of savings and the capital-output ratio. The 45° dotted line represents a

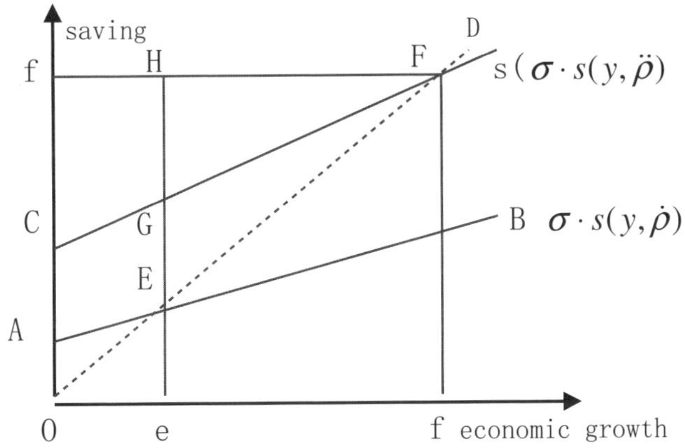

Fig. 22.2 Financial Reform — The Virtuous Cycle of Savings and Growth

path of balanced growth, namely the economic growth rate is equal to the product of the rate of savings and the capital–output ratio. Suppose that line AB is the savings rate function $s(y, \rho)$ under financial repression, with ρ representing financial repression, and in this case, the effective yield on monetary holdings is low and the money to income ratio is also very small. Correspondingly, the rate of savings curve AB is also located in a lower position, and point E in which AB intersects the 45° dotted line is the equilibrium point of economic growth. Now, suppose that the government implemented financial reforms, in that ρ will become $\ddot{\rho}$. There are two effects which financial reforms will have on savings, namely: the rate of savings curve AB will shift upwards to CD, and the slope of line CD will be greater than that of line AB which reflects the increased willingness to hold onto monetary assets after financial reforms. With the shift of the rate of savings curve from AB to CD, the equilibrium economic growth rate will also drastically increase from point e to point f. Prior to an actual increase in y, the expansionary effect of financial reforms will be limited to the fluctuations from E to G. Once y has increased to the new level of equilibrium, GH is a further increase in savings.

22.3 Financial Liberalization

To developing countries, one of the most important measures for increasing the rate of savings is to promote financial liberalization reforms and promote financial deepening. **Financial liberalization** is when a government abandons administrative interventions in the financial system and allows the financial market to give play to its fundamental role in the allocation of financial resources. **Financial deepening** is the process of optimization of a financial structure and the constant expansion and improvement of financial functions. To financially repressed developing countries, financial liberalization is a necessary means of financial deepening.

22.3.1 Benefits of Financial Liberalization

McKinnon and Shaw believed that financial liberalization would increase remunerations to domestic private sector savings and would also provide more opportunities to disperse the holdings of domestic financial assets. Furthermore, in the context of liberalization, financial institutions, in order to strive for more profits and increase their market share, would actively create new financial services and financial products. China is the most obvious example. In the early stages of reform, deposits, cash and loans were the only financial products available in China, whereas today, despite the fact that China's financial sector is still strictly regulated, stock, bonds, funds, futures, and foreign exchange have become an important component of ordinary lives, and residents now have a much broader range of assets to select from. Thus, financial liberalization will open the eyes of savers and change their expectations in terms of earnings, so that future consumption becomes more attractive, which would thereby increase the savings rate of the domestic private sector. An increase in the rate of savings will expand the scale of financial institutions and provide more sources of funding for increasing physical capital investments, which would thereby alleviate the capital shortages of developing countries.

Secondly, financial liberalization will cause fiscal activities to be replaced by financing activities that mobilize and allocate savings. It will lower the inflation rate and the dependence on foreign aid, and through an expansion and diversification of financial markets, open up new channels for the optimal allocation of savings. For instance, prior to China's reforms, corporate investment primarily relied on allocations within the fiscal budget. After the economic reforms which began in 1978, and having replaced allocation with lending and pushed through reforms to the indirect financing of bank credit and direct financing of capital markets, China's financial liberalization diversified China's mechanisms for allocating savings. Additionally, in a strictly regulated financial environment, the allocation of savings lacked effective competition, and as a result, there will always be a lot of rent-seeking behavior when it comes to the allocation of savings resources. What people usually refer to as "having connections" or "going through the back door" are classic examples of rent-seeking behavior. Rent-seeking results in a lack of screening mechanisms that comply with the principles of efficiency in the allocation of savings, because whoever has better "connections" or more "back doors" will be the person who can earn a greater amount of savings resources, and in this way, the allocation of savings is not very efficient as it could be. Conversely, in a free and integrated capital market, the open competition over savings between varieties of investment projects will lead to the allocation of savings to more efficient sectors. Financial liberalization is an important prerequisite for the competitive and innovative distribution of the flow of savings.

Third, if labor is a highly elastic substitution for capital, an increase in real interest rates after financial liberalization will increase capital costs. This will encourage enterprises to conserve scarce capital and employ a larger labor force. On the one hand, this will generate employment, but on the other hand, it will also increase wages within the share of national income, and as such, financial liberalization is conducive to the promotion of equality in income distribution.

Finally, the liberalization of foreign exchange markets will lead to free fluctuations in short-term exchange rates and exchange rates will better reflect supply and demand in the foreign exchange market as well as the relative position of the country within the international economic system. We know that one of the important factors which decide a country's currency exchange rate is the relative strength of the country's economy within the international economic system. If the economy is strong, the country's currency will become a strong currency. Conversely, if the economy is weak, so is the country's currency. If the free exchange rate properly reflects a country's economic situations, it will provide a useful signal for the authorities to adopt appropriate macroeconomic policies. Additionally, the free fluctuations of the exchange rate will also automatically stabilize the international balance of payments, enhance the independence of the central bank in its formulation and implementation of monetary policies, and reduce the conflicts between internal and external equilibrium.

The liberalization of the foreign exchange market requires a freely convertible currency, in that the residents of a country can freely convert the domestic currency for foreign currency, such as converting Chinese yuan for US dollars, euros, or pounds. As far as the residents are concerned, currency convertibility expands the range of asset choices, because foreign currencies can be treated as a type of investment for profit-making purpose. Currency convertibility reduces the liquidity risks of savings, can be used as a particularly powerful policy instrument, and can raise the real interest rate of savers to the scarcity price level of savings. Furthermore, to undeveloped economies, the only way to draw foreign savings is through foreign exchange liberalization, which lowers the demand price for foreign savings. Foreign exchange liberalization reduces smuggling, and thus, foreign exchange liberalization and floating exchange rate systems are conducive to improving the fiscal situation of governments.

In short, from the point of view of Ronald McKinnon, Edward Shaw, and other such liberals, financial liberalization is quite a rosy picture!

22.3.2 Content of Financial Liberalization

Financial liberalization will primarily include the following aspects:

- Capital Market Liberalization
- Liberalization of the Banking Sector
- Interest Rate Liberalization
- Liberalization of the Foreign Exchange Market and Currency Convertibility

(a) *Capital Market Liberalization*

Capital markets are an important channel and mechanism for transferring savings into investment. However, in developing countries, the direct financing of capital markets is typically undeveloped, even to the point where there is no formal organized capital market, and as such, the financial structure of developing countries will also be very incomplete. In order to promote the restructuring of the economy and financial liberalization, and under the influence of the theories of financial deepening and liberalist ideology, developing countries have adopted various measures to promote the development of capital markets. In particular, for those socialist developing countries like China, developing capital markets is an important means for the government to withdraw from competitive economic sectors and to support the reform of state-owned enterprises. Given the particularity of this mission and the transition period China has been in, the Chinese capital market had been, in the very beginning, led down a very different path of development than the naturally evolving capital markets of developed countries, and it is still tightly controlled by the government.

Fundamentally speaking, the liberalization of capital markets is the cultivation of a spirit and system of free capital. As such, the real significance of capital market liberalization is not simply that the price of capital is determined by market supply and demand, but it also covers the free movement of surplus funds to those sectors which face shortages, and the use of automatic screening mechanism of capital markets to allocate capital, distribute proceeds, and share risks, rather than the government's distribution of capital to particular enterprises or sectors.

In a broad sense, capital markets include stock markets and bond markets, which are functionally different in terms of the distribution of proceeds, the assumption of risks, corporate governance, and asymmetric information. Thus, even though they both promote the transfer of savings to investment, they are not functional alternatives in other aspects. What this means is that the liberalization of capital markets, in its true sense, is that those with surplus funds and those with a shortage of funds can select stock or bonds based on their own risk preferences, their own pursuit of profit and capital cost burdens and thus promote a coordinated development between the stock and bond markets.

(b) *Liberalization of the Banking Sector*

The second aspect of financial liberalization is the removal of the government's controls over the banking sector and thus the implementation of a free banking system. A free banking system will typically imply the following:

- Lifting restrictions on the banking market access and the permission for the private sector to freely engage in banking.
- The liberalization of banking services. The asset and liability business of commercial banks are no longer constrained by direct government controls, and banks are engaged in legitimate business activities under the government's regulatory system.

However, in theory, there is a degree of controversy as to whether or not a free banking system should be adopted. Advocates of free banking systems are of the view that because the free trade of goods is beneficial, a free banking system should also be efficient. Similar to the wide range of choices available to us when we go shopping at the supermarket, in a free banking system, the range of financial services which we can select from will also greatly expand. Additionally, deregulated banking systems also have an intrinsic stability. This is because bank managers understand that their long-term survival depends on the confidence of their depositors, and to that end, banks will be very cautious in their lending to retain enough capital to cushion losses and accept external oversight and public audits. In addition, just as people get hepatitis B vaccine to prevent the infection, or rather people will stay away from the infected persons to avoid coming down with atypical pneumonia, when good banks catch wind of the threat of "infection", they will strengthen themselves against it to ensure that they will not be affected by the insolvency of other banks, and thus, under a free banking system, one bank's insolvency will not lead to a bank run and will not threaten the security of the entire financial system.

Liberalists still believe that government regulations will typically limit inter-bank competition, lower the efficiency of banks, and thus lead to a greater risk of moral hazards in terms of banking operations. For instance, they believe that as soon as deposit insurance is introduced, depositors will have no incentive to monitor the bank conduct and bank managers will no longer worry about public confidence. In this case, the rational response of banks will be to reduce capital, and to compete for market shares, good banks will imitate bad banks and be encouraged to take on excessive risks. If successful, they will earn a considerable amount of additional revenue, but as soon as they fail, their losses will be passed on to the deposit insurance company. In addition, the mechanism for the central bank to act as the lender of last resort may also create serious moral hazards within the commercial banking system. Bank managers believe that as soon as a bank faces serious difficulties, the government will, out of consideration for stability, come to its help rather than sitting idly by, and thus, under government regulations, commercial banks may engage in high-risk investments. In light of this, a financial system which is subject to controls is not as stable as a *laissez-faire* financial system.

However, banks, after all, are different from the typical product market. The following examples will vividly illustrate the differences between the bank credit market and general product markets.

In the slaughter market, consumers can not only learn the price of pork, but they can also determine its quality. In some countries, the government has established a quality supervision agency. If there are rumors that toxins exist in some of the meat, people will lose their trust in the butchers or the government's quality supervision authorities, and people will stop buying meat products, which may lead to bankruptcy in the slaughter market. However, a butcher's bankruptcy would not produce strong externalities. Also, very few butchers would refuse to accept cash for the meat they sell. Bankers, on the other hand, certainly would not provide loans to all those people who would be willing to apply for loans at the interest rates required by the bank. The former is a simple spot transaction of cash for goods, while the latter is a commitment to future payments, and the bank is not entirely clear as to the borrower's honesty and reliability. In the determination of a borrower's credit, it is important for banks to include overhead, while butchers do not have to worry about the credibility of a customer's cash purchase.

As you can see, the largest difference between the bank credit market and product markets is asymmetric information and externalities. Most economists will analyze the rationality of the government's controls on banking from these two perspectives. Some economists worry that completely *laissez-faire* competition among banks would be very destructive, and they believe that bankers with an appetite for risk will engage in high-risk, high-yield loans, and other bankers who were originally cautious would also engage in high-yield, high-risk loans to avoid losing their business and market share. In this way, there would be an excessive expansion of bank assets, and ultimately, banks and the economy as a whole, would collapse. Additionally, there are strong externalities within bank operations, which include positive externalities and negative externalities. Positive externalities include the creation of a generally acceptable medium of exchange and a store of value. Negative externalities include the collapse of confidence within the entire banking system caused by a single bank's insolvency, which would lead to comprehensive bank failures. In the event of a crisis within a free banking system, positive bank externalities would quickly disappear and negative externalities would rapidly spread and expand.

The theory of financial constraints also believes that bank regulations are effective. According to this theory, governments limit the free access of banks to provide rental opportunities to existing banks. This rent would disappear under the perfect competition of a free banking system, and as such, government regulations provide a "privileged value" to existing banks. Because the "privileged value" of rental opportunities improves the expected bank earnings, banks may become more cautious over the course of operations, which will lower the chances of moral hazards and adverse selection, thereby contributing to the stability of the banking system. Conversely, if full liberalization were implemented, this would reinforce the competition between banks, but competition would erode their profits, and lower earnings would mean that the privileged value of banks would decrease, as would their expected future earnings. This reduction in expected future earnings would lower the incentive for cautious lending, and thus would increase the risk of moral hazards. More importantly, liberalization would loosen the restrictions on banks, opening the door to activities which had been prohibited, such as derivatives and other such high-risk business; this is equivalent to creating opportunities for gambling and speculation. Once gambling becomes successful, it will generate a considerable amount of revenue for bank managers, but as it fails, bank shareholders or depositors will have to bear the losses. So, a free banking system can reduce bank stability.

(c) *Interest Rate Liberalization*

The third aspect of financial liberalization is interest rate liberalization. Interest rate liberalization is when a government abandons administrative interventions and removes the stipulation for interest rate ceilings or floors and interest rates are thus determined by the changes in the market supply and demand of funds.

Whether in developed or developing countries, governments have, or are still controlling the level of interest rates. For instance, the United States imposed Regulation Q to set a limit on the interest rate payments which banks could make to borrowers. Chinese deposit and lending rates are also controlled by the People's Bank of China, which in accordance with macroeconomic changes and the needs of monetary policy, will make adjustments to the benchmark deposit and lending rates from time to time. Unlike the evening-out trend for interests rates in the more marketized money markets, there are discontinuities when central banks adjust deposit and lending rates, with these adjustments occurring every few months, or in some cases, every few years. In this way, deposit and lending rates cannot reflect the supply and demand for funds. More importantly, the deposit and lending rates which are uniformly stipulated by the central bank cannot embody the risk profiles of different borrowers. High-risk borrowers will not have to pay a risk discount when they borrow, and when banks issue loans to these high-risk borrowers, they cannot be compensated for the added risk. As a result, interest rate mechanisms will play a distorted role in the allocation of savings resources.

Within the financial system, there is a wide variety of financial instruments, and they will have different interest rates just as different products will have different prices. As such, interest rate liberalization is in fact the liberalization of the interest rate system. At present, the degree of marketization in China's money market rates and Treasury bond rates is already high, and movements in the money market rates reflect the supply and demand of Chinese funds.[1] Now, the core of China's interest rate liberalization is the liberalization of bank deposit and lending rates so that commercial banks will offer different interest rates based on the risk profiles of different borrowers.

For interest rate liberalization to be able to improve the efficiency of resource allocation, first of all, changes in interest rates will be a rather important constraint on the financing costs of borrowers, because enterprises will have a highly elastic response to interest rates, which requires a relatively sound corporate governance structure. Second, the commercial banking system should also be relatively sound, and changes in market rates should lead to changes in commercial bank revenue and costs, and as such, commercial banks should be sufficiently sensitive. Finally, following interest rate liberalization, market rates will continue to fluctuate, which adds to the interest rate risks of borrowers and commercial banks. In

[1]After China established a unified national interbank lending market in January 1996, a nationally unified interbank lending rate was formed, though the authorities later removed the restrictions on such interest rates. When the nationally unified interbank bond market was established in 1998, interest rate controls on this market were also removed.

order to let borrowers and commercial banks effectively avoid the risk of interest rate fluctuations, financial instruments which can easily manage interest rate risks should be developed.

(d) *The Liberalization of the Foreign Exchange Market and Currency Convertibility*

In repressed economies, governments should also remove controls on foreign exchange and exchange rates, and implement free-floating exchange rate systems, which will cause a fluctuation in exchange rates in accordance with relevant changes in the foreign exchange market supply and demand.

In addition to the marketization of the exchange rate system, governments should also remove restrictions on currency convertibility. **Currency convertibility** refers to when holders of a currency can freely convert one currency into another major international reserve currency according to the market exchange rate. It includes current account convertibility and capital and financial account convertibility. For instance, when you go to visit Switzerland, if you can freely convert Chinese yuan for the US dollars or Swiss francs without any restrictions, then the Chinese yuan would be convertible under current accounts. If you can convert Chinese yuan for US dollars without any restrictions when you want to purchase government bonds issued by the US government or purchase stock issued by an American company listed on the New York Stock Exchange, then the Chinese yuan would be freely convertible under capital accounts.

Current account convertibility of a currency is a fundamental obligation for member states of the International Monetary Fund. As requested by the IMF, without the approval of the organization, the member states are not allowed to impose exchange restrictions on the current international transaction payments and fund transfers. This so-called "current transaction payments", is presented in a simplified manner, under the current accounts which we have introduced when we discussed the international balance of payments. Discriminatory currency arrangements and multiple exchange rate practices are prohibited. The multiple exchange rate practices mainly include: different exchange rates for different transactions with an exchange rate spread greater than 2%, dual or multiple exchange markets, and retention quotas, exchange taxes and exchange guarantees. Discriminatory currency arrangements primarily refer to bilateral payment arrangements, which may lead to transfer restrictions on non-residents and multiple currency practices.

Capital and financial account convertibility refers to the free convertibility of capital inflows and outflows. Capital and financial account convertibility can provide the residents of a country with a broader range of financial asset choices, which will place the central bank under competitive pressure as to monetary stability. If the central bank disregards the needs of economic development and issues an excessive amount of currency which triggers a relatively high rate of inflation and devalues the domestic currency, in order to preserve the value of assets and when the currency is convertible under capital accounts, domestic residents can conveniently sell their assets to purchase foreign currency assets, or, if they lose confidence in the domestic currency, can hold foreign currencies instead. Large currency substitutions and asset substitutions will cause increasing pressure on the central bank as to currency issue and monetary stability, which will, in the end, be conducive to a stable domestic currency. Second, currency convertibility under capital accounts can provide many more profitable opportunities as capital is now allocated on a global scale and truly based on the principle of comparative advantages. This improves the efficiency of capital allocation and greatly promotes the process of financial globalization.

However, currency convertibility typically requires a number of prerequisites, so not all countries can begin to implement freely convertible currency. These prerequisites include: first of all, there must be an appropriate exchange rate. This is because an appropriate exchange rate is consistent with an external balance, and under the conditions of a continued decline in international reserves or a continued depreciation of the currency, an appropriate exchange rate is absolutely necessary in order to continue to maintain currency convertibility. Second, a country must have sufficient international liquidity and foreign exchange reserves. This is conducive to resisting temporary shocks of balance of payments imbalances and avoiding exchange rate fluctuations. Third, a country must have sound macroeconomic policies and a stable macroeconomic environment. If a country's rate of inflation is much higher than that of its trading partners, it will not be able to maintain its balance of balance of payments without a currency devaluation or strict controls on payments. Finally, a country must have a proper environment in which an economic entity is motivated and able to respond to market prices and in which price distortion is almost eradicated. The former three conditions are to ensure that the implementation of currency convertibility will not lead to macroeconomic instability, and the fourth condition is to guarantee that currency convertibility will bring about the expected economic benefits.

22.4 China's Financial Liberalization and Market Reforms

22.4.1 Capital Market Liberalization

Beginning in the early 1980s, new private enterprises emerged outside of China's state-owned institutions, but at that time, they were unable to obtain the necessary financial support from the national banking system, and as such, they had no choice but to stray into the gray areas outside of the government-approved financial system, and the spontaneous stock offerings became one of the means through which they could obtain financing. After the market reforms, China's capital market began to develop, which arose out of the government's need to reform SOEs, and having experienced such enterprise reforms as replacing allocation with lending and the contract system, the government finally realized that without fundamental reforms to the property rights system of enterprises, the Chinese corporate governance would be very inefficient. Reforms to the SOE shares system became the ultimate path for China's SOE reforms. Thus, it is not surprising that, prior to 2005, China's stock market primarily consisted of listed companies which had been restructured from state-owned enterprises. However, after 2005, more and more private Chinese enterprises were listed, and the issue of new shares was predominantly from private enterprises. As a result of the establishment and development of China's multi-level stock market, venture capital, and private equity capital markets have also become increasingly popular.

When China implemented reforms to the SOE shares system, the shares were purposefully divided into three categories, i.e., state-owned, corporate, and public shares, in order to gain ideological support for the reforms. In order to ensure a controlling stake in state enterprises, state-owned shares and corporate shares could not be circulated at that time, and only public shares could be traded on the Shanghai and Shenzhen stock exchanges. This resulted in a typical phenomenon for Chinese stock companies, namely "split shares" and "the same shares with different rights". China began split share reforms in 2005, and because the premium rate on the public subscription for shares was relatively high, the subscription for state-owned shares and corporate shares was often at par value (usually 1 yuan). Having provided an appropriate financial compensation to holders of public shares, state-owned shares or corporate shares could be freely circulated on the market.

The medium and long-term bond market is also an important part of capital markets. On the one hand, this is because China lacked a culture of corporate credit in the early stages of the market reforms, business efficiency was relatively low, and the government was worried that a large-scale issuance of corporate bonds would lead to widespread default risks. On the other hand, corporate bonds are different from stock, and they cannot change the structure of corporate ownership. For this reason, when China's stock market underwent considerable development, corporate (company) bonds were suppressed for a long period of time, and government controls were quite severe. This continued until 2005. After the People's Bank of China permitted the issuance of short-term corporate bonds of less than a year (short-term financing), the China Securities Regulatory Commission and the National Development and Reform Commission expanded the offering rights of enterprises. Subsequently, China's bond market also rapidly developed. Because this financing arrangement is at a relatively low cost and also quite flexible, its scale has been constantly expanding.

22.4.2 Liberalization of the Banking Sector

China's banking system was originally very unitary, and initially, there was only the People's Bank of China, which drew public deposits and had the authority to issue currency. As such, the central bank and commercial bank were one and the same. At the beginning of the market reforms, China created four state-owned specialized banks, namely the Industrial and Commercial Bank of China, the Agricultural Bank of China, the Bank of China, and China Construction Bank. The range of their business was highly regulated and divided, each had a different range, they were kept within their own boundaries, and there was no competition whatsoever. Although they are all commercial banks, nominally speaking however, the size and target of their loans was subject to government intervention, and they often had to undertake policy loans, which are the so-called "stability and solidarity loans". In such an environment, the operational inefficiency of China's banking sector was almost impossible to imagine. So, at that time, China's banking sector had a lot of non-performing loans, with up to 20% at one time, and even Western media outlets would often report that "China's banking sector is already technically bankrupt".

When China began to reform the state-owned banking sector in 1994, the National Development Bank, the Agricultural Development Bank of China, and the Export-Import Bank of China were created to assume the policy loan business which was originally borne by the commercial banks and to appraise the performance of China's banking sector and promote competition. In 1998, China changed the currency control mechanism, abandoned the credit scale controls on banking, implemented asset and liability ratio management, and thus, the right of commercial banks to choose their assets was expanded. This began to chip away at the sphere of influence and barriers to entry which originally fragmented the banking sector. As a prominent example of this trend, the rural Agricultural Bank of China (ABC), which was limited to agricultural business, could compete with the "Western style" Bank of China, which was mainly engaged in the business of foreign exchange, and in the information-oriented, industrialized, modern Chinese megacities there are now a large number of ABC outlets and branches. Of course, the competition in China's banking sector is not only a result of the removal of barriers to specialized banking, but of the rise of many small and medium commercial banks, apart from the four big state-controlled commercial banks, some of which were entirely privately funded. As soon as they entered the banking sector, they were driven by a strong willingness and impulse to expand and had a talent for financial product innovation. The emergence of this competitive force, in turn, promoted a transformation in the operational philosophy and level of services in the originally arrogant national banks. Nowadays, China's banking sector is gradually transitioning into a new stage of opening to private investment.

An important measure of the liberalization of China's banking sector is the reform to the state-owned banking shares, which began at the end of 2003. The government spent 45 billion dollars on the Bank of China and China Construction Bank, with 22.5 billion dollars injected into each of them to replenish their capital. In this fashion, the government also injected a portion of foreign exchange reserves into the Industrial and Commercial Bank of China and the Agricultural Bank of China. Meanwhile, the government also implemented financial restructuring to the state-controlled banks, again stripped them of a large amount of their toxic assets (China removed 1.4 trillion yuan worth of toxic assets in 1999), and improved their balance sheets. Afterwards, many of the banks began to have large foreign commercial banks with a prominent international position as strategic investors in the hopes that the latter could help improve their capacity of products innovation and risks control. Upon the completion of financial restructuring and having attracted strategic investors, the Bank of China, China Construction Bank, the Industrial and Commercial Bank of China, and the Agricultural Bank of China consecutively offered public shares on the Hong Kong Stock Exchange and the Shanghai Stock Exchange. In this way, they became public companies, the stock of which could be held by general investors, and because of this, it makes more sense to call them "state-controlled commercial banks".

22.4.3 Interest Rate Liberalization

For various reasons, China had overlooked the role of the interest rate mechanism. For a relatively long period of time after market reforms, China implemented strict controls over interest rates, and, at that time, because China's financial markets were undeveloped, China had not formed a complete interest rate system. As China's economy continued to become market-oriented, reforms to the interest rate market were added to the agenda.

China's marketization of interest rates began with Treasury bills. In the early 1990s, China began to focus on market reforms of changing the pricing mechanism. In 1992, China implemented Treasury bond underwriting and officially unveiled the marketization of interest rates. In 1996, the interbank interest rates were liberalized, and in 1997, the rates for interbank bond market repos and spot transaction were liberalized. As such, apart from deposit and lending rates which were still subject to controls, all other interest rates were fundamentally marketized.

In 1998, China began its experiments on the marketization of deposit and lending rates, the purpose of which was to improve the risk pricing ability of financial institutions in regard to interest rate, and allow market mechanisms to play the basic role in determining interest rates. China's overall arrangement for the marketization of deposit and lending rates is: "to proceed from foreign currency to domestic currency, from loans to deposits, from long-terms and large amounts to short-terms and small amounts". Since then, the People's Bank of China has continued to adjust the free floating range for the deposit and lending rates of commercial banks. In November 1998, financial institutions could have the interest rate by which they lend to small enterprises float by up to 20% above the benchmark interest rate, and have the rate to medium and large enterprises float up by 10%. In September 1999, the floating range for small enterprises was again expanded to

30%. In 2000, China completely liberalized foreign currency deposit and lending rates so that the foreign currency deposit rates were determined by the market supply and demand. In January 2004, the upper limit on the floating range for the lending rates of commercial banks and urban credit cooperatives was expanded to a level 1.7 times the benchmark rate while the upper limit on the lending rates of rural credit cooperatives was expanded to a level twice the benchmark rate.

Over the process of interest rate marketization and by October 2004, the People's Bank of China had liberalized the upper limit on lending rates and the lower limit on deposit rates, however, upper limit regulations were still implemented on the renminbi lending rates of urban and rural credit cooperatives, was expanded to a level 2.3 times the benchmark rate. The renminbi lending rate of Chinese financial institutions had already transitioned to the stage of upper limit liberalization and lower limit regulations, while deposit rates had reached a stage in which the lower limit was liberalized while the upper limit was regulated. In the fourth quarter of 2008, in order to deal with the adverse effects of the US sub-prime mortgage crisis, the People's Bank of China implemented loose monetary policies and also allowed commercial banks to lend home mortgages at an interest rate that could float 30% below the benchmark lending rate determined by the central bank. In 2011, China's interest rate marketization entered a new stage, in that commercial bank deposit rates could float 10% above the benchmark rate determined by the central bank, while lending rates to enterprises could float down by 20%.

It can be said that in early 2013, the market-oriented reforms to China's interest rate system had achieved great results. The focus of the future marketization of deposit and lending rates is to gradually increase the capacity of commercial banks to determine interest rates and manage risks, establish and improve the People's Bank of China's interest rate adjustment system, further expand the floating range of the lending and deposit rates of financial institutions, and ultimately lift the central bank's direct regulations of the deposit and lending benchmark rates of financial institutions so that the deposit and lending rates can truly be determined by the supply and demand of funds as well as the given risk situation.

22.4.4 Marketization of Exchange Rate Mechanisms and the Reform of Renminbi Convertibility

China originally implemented strict exchange rate controls and a dual exchange rate system. When China implemented a unified exchange rate system in 1994, a managed floating exchange rate system was implemented. However, in the wake of the Asian financial crisis, the renminbi suffered under the considerable pressure of depreciation. In order to avoid the competitive devaluation in the East Asia, China, over the next few years, adopted a dollar peg exchange rate system. However, in 2003, China faced enormous political pressure to appreciate the renminbi, given its accession to the WTO and the low interest rates of the United States and Japan. Additionally, the marketization of the exchange rate mechanism, in itself, was an important component of China's market-oriented economic reforms. Thus, China reformed the renminbi exchange rate system in 2005 and implemented a managed floating exchange rate system in reference to a basket of currencies. Over the next few years, according to the three principles of controllability, stability, and progress, China developed the renminbi derivatives market and also gradually expanded the range of renminbi exchange rate fluctuations which has led to the enhanced flexibility of the currency.

In terms of the convertibility of the renminbi, China implemented current account convertibility in December 1996 and no longer restricts the current international trade payments and transfers, nor does China implement discriminatory currency arrangements or a multiple exchange rate system. However, the progress of renminbi capital convertibility has been slow, as the experiences of many other countries have shown that achieving capital account convertibility or fully liberalized capital accounts prior to the sufficient flexibility of the domestic currency's exchange rate mechanism is an extremely dangerous combination of policies. Although somewhat slow, China's liberalization of capital accounts is still in a systematic manner, and there are asymmetric characteristics.

First of all, compared to the restrictions on capital outflows, there are few restrictions on capital inflows, such as China's efforts to attract foreign direct investment since the market reforms, whereas the restrictions on China's overseas investments are stringent. Secondly, within capital inflows, restrictions are few on direct investment with the primary purpose of physical capital formation, whereas the restrictions on the financial assets of securities investment are more stringent. As a result of China's rapidly expanding foreign exchange reserves, China enhanced its ability to resist the unfavorable exchange rate fluctuations of the renminbi and accelerated the deregulation of capital and financial accounts. Qualified foreign institutional investors (QFII) can invest in a certain amount of Chinese stock or bonds, while qualified domestic institutional investors can also exchange a certain amount of renminbi for a foreign currency to invest in the securities markets of other countries (regions). While China continued to attract foreign direct investment, it also encouraged domestic enterprises and financial institutions to "go global" and directly invest abroad. In accordance with IMF standards, China is currently considered as a country with basic capital account convertibility. However, this alone does not necessarily mean that China has completed the liberalization of its capital accounts. In fact, China, will further liberalize capital accounts in accordance with the principle of "proceeding from capital inflows to outflows, from long-term to short-term, from direct to indirect, and from institutions to individuals". The reform of the renminbi convertibility will increase the usability of the renminbi in international economic activities.

Summary

There are four characteristics which generally exist in the financial system of a developing country: low monetization, duality, generally underdeveloped financial markets, and strict government regulations over the financial system. Financial repression is prevalent in developing countries. The means by which a government represses finance includes special credit institutions, high reserves, interest rate controls, and exchange controls.

In terms of sources of financing, financing within a developing country is primarily endogenous. Because investment is physically inseparable, enterprises in a developing country must go through a relatively long self-accumulation process before they can invest, and in this way, money and capital are complementary in a developing country, in that the higher the investment, the higher the demand for money. To increase the accumulation of money in a developing country, the effective yield on monetary holdings should be increased. An increase in the yield of money will have a tube effect and an asset competition effect on the capital accumulation of internal financing.

In order to increase the rate of savings and capital accumulation in a developing country, the government should promote financial liberalization reforms, lower the rate of inflation, raise real interest rates, and promote the virtuous cycle of savings and growth.

Financial liberalization is when a government reduces administrative interventions in the financial system and allows the financial market to give play to its fundamental role in the allocation of financial resources so as to improve financial efficiency and achieve financial deepening.

Financial liberalization includes components such as banking liberalization, capital market liberalization, interest rate liberalization, and the liberalization of foreign exchange and currency convertibility.

Key Terms

Financial Repression; Financial Deepening; Financial Liberalization; Tube Effect; Asset Competition Effect; Financial Constraint; Currency Convertibility; Cheap Credit

Critical Thinking Questions

1. What are the characteristics of financial systems in developing countries?
2. What are the means of financial repression?
3. Explain why there is complementarity between money and capital in developing countries whose financing is primarily internal.

4. What is financial liberalization? What are the benefits?
5. What does financial liberalization primarily consist of?
6. There are both supporters and opponents to the liberalization of the banking sector. Which are you more inclined to agree with? Why?
7. What should the conditions for currency convertibility be?
8. What is the benefit of capital and financial account convertibility?
9. In 1998, China began to explore the marketization of lending rates. For instance, beginning in November of that year, interest rates on loans issued by financial institutions to small enterprises could float by up to 20% above benchmark lending rates, while the interest rates on loans issued to medium and large enterprises could float by up to 10%. Beginning in September 1999, the interest rates for small and medium enterprises could float by up to 30% above benchmark lending rates, and the interest rates for loans issued to medium and large enterprises could float by up to 10%. In 2002, China began to actively pilot the marketization of deposit and lending rates in eight rural credit cooperatives, giving them greater access to interest rate adjustments, and significantly expanded the lending rate floating range from 50% to 100%, with deposit rates allowed to float upward by a maximum 50%. In 2012, the People's Bank of China again allowed commercial bank deposit rates to float by up to 10% above the stipulated benchmark interest rate. In general, industrial and commercial loans can float downward by 20%. Summarize the relevant content of the "Risk Structure of Interest Rates" and analyze the economic impact of an expansion in the deposit and lending rate fluctuations.
10. When financial liberalization was put into practice, Eastern Europe, the former Soviet Union, and some other countries adopted a strategy of radical liberalization, lifting controls on banking, interest rates, exchange rates, currency convertibility, and capital markets in the early stages of liberalization. China, in turn, adopted a strategy of gradual liberalization, achieving considerable success. Considering what we have learned in Chapter 8, analyze the potential impact on state-owned banks had the government completely lifted the controls on the banking sector during the early stages of liberalization, which would have led to a large scale transfer of deposits out of state-owned banks. In an underdeveloped money market, what role would the central bank play when such state-owned banks face difficulties in resolving this issue? What would be the consequences of the central bank's intervention?

Chapter 23

Financial Crises

Learning Objectives

After studying this chapter, you will be able to:

- Clearly understand the meaning behind a financial crisis and its different varieties
- Clearly understand Fisher's debt-deflation theory
- Understand Minsky's financial instability model
- Understand financial fragility
- Understand the currency crisis model
- Understand several major global financial crises
- Learn the primary methods for preventing a financial crisis

As soon as we talk about a crisis, we associate it with the destruction it causes, just as we associate a crisis of marriage with the destruction it brings to families. Since the 18th century, financial crises have occurred in various ways in different periods and have caused massive destruction to economies and people's lives. Hardly had Asia stepped out from the shadow of the financial crisis of 1997 when it spread to Russia and Argentina, and disaster struck the global financial sector. In order to avoid crises, we have to know what causes them, and then take measures to avoid them.

23.1 What is a Financial Crisis?

Raymond Goldsmith would often say that "perhaps a financial crisis is like a pretty girl, difficult to define but recognizable when seen". So, just as we may describe a pretty girl by her slim figure and stunning looks, we can define a financial crisis according to a certain set of phenomena. A **financial crisis** is a situation in which all or most financial indicators — short-term interest rates, assets prices, exchange rates, and numbers of failed financial institutions — become worse, beyond what society and the economic system can bear. For example, a sharp fall in stock prices can turn a millionaire into a beggar; a sharp rise in interest rates can lead to a sharp fall in bond prices, and institutions that hold them will suffer major losses. All these will cause havoc to the financial system.

Financial crises can be divided into four categories, namely, a currency crisis, a banking crisis, a debt crisis, and a capital market crisis. A currency crisis is a situation in which people lose confidence in a certain country's currency and undersell it, causing the exchange rates of that money to fall sharply within a short period of time. For example, the sharp fall of the exchange rates between the Mexican peso and the US dollar in 1994 and between the Thai baht and the US dollar are classic examples of a currency crisis.

A **banking crisis** is a situation in which, for one reason or another, people lose confidence in banks and rush to withdraw money, causing serious liquidity difficulties in the banking system and widespread bank failures.

A **debt crisis** is a situation in which a country's government cannot pay off its foreign debts as promised, which causes serious losses to financial institutions. There was one such debt crisis in Latin America during the 1980s. In 1982, the Mexican government announced that it could not pay off its international debts that were due that year, which led to an international debt crisis.

A **capital market crisis** is a situation in which people lose confidence in the capital market and hurry to undersell stock and bonds, causing a sharp fall in their prices. For example, in 1929, the Wall Street stock market collapsed, and the Dow Jones Index fell by 80% within a very short period of time. After 1999, the NASDAQ index fell from 6000 points to 1150 points by the end of September 2002.

However, most real-world financial crises belong to none of these four categories, but are the result of a convergence of multiple crises, which become a **systematic financial crisis**. A systematic financial crisis is a situation in which crises occur in major financial sectors, such as banking, exchange rates, and capital markets, causing destructive damage to the real economy. In the Great Crisis of 1929, in addition to a sharp fall in stock prices, over 10,000 banks went bankrupt. The Asian financial crisis of 1997 is a classic example of systematic financial crisis. At that time, exchange rates in Thailand, Indonesia, Malaysia, and South Korea fell sharply, as did the prices of stocks and bonds. Meanwhile, many banks also went bankrupt, and misfortune spread throughout the entire system. In 2008, the US sub-prime mortgage crisis turned into a systematic financial crisis; stock markets and financial institutions all suffered, and people lost confidence in the entire system.

23.2 Financial Fragility and Financial Bubbles

Finance in itself is fragile and often leads to financial crises. **Financial fragility** refers to the fact that the financial system in itself is unstable, and exogenous shocks may cause a financial crisis. Commercial banks, stock markets, and exchange rates are all fragile to a certain degree.

23.2.1 Bank Fragility

When depositors lose confidence in commercial banks, they will rush to the banks to withdraw their money, causing liquidity difficulties, and even bankruptcy. The characteristics of a commercial bank's operation underlie its vulnerability to a deposit run. As an intermediary institution, a commercial bank would take deposits and issue loans, thereby transferring current liabilities to scattered depositors to non-current claims on borrowers, which causes the "maturity mismatch between assets and liabilities" as pointed out in Chapter 8. As for the liabilities of commercial banks, if depositors withdraw money at random, according to the law of large numbers, the capital flow of commercial banks will remain stable. As for assets of commercial banks, if all the assets are held until the date of maturity, and if there is no adverse selection in the issuance of loans and no moral hazards appear, the income of commercial banks will also remain stable. To be brief, if deposits are stable and there is little default risk, commercial banks, by keeping enough liquidity to deal with ordinary deposits, can invest some of their capital into assets with low liquidity but high rates of return.

We know that commercial banks rely on a constant capital inflow from depositors to support their normal operations. This is just like a pool with both a water inlet and outlet. If the diameter of the inlet is longer than that of the outlet, the water in the pool will increase. Otherwise, the water will drain. If non-performing assets increase to a certain amount, depositors will worry about the safety of their principals. If there is any accident which causes depositors to lose their confidence in the bank, they will be on a run to withdraw their money. When this kind of accident happens, the best choice for a depositor is to join the run to withdraw immediately. Because they know that if people begin to withdraw funds, commercial banks must sell their low liquidity assets before the date of maturity to satisfy depositors' needs and thus will suffer a loss, which means that the depositors at the end of the queue will probably have difficulty recovering all of their deposits. As such, even though all the depositors know that the commercial banks are healthy and realize that it is in everybody's best interests if they do not run to withdraw deposits, but they will still join the run for their own benefit. This is the contradiction between individual rationality and collective rationality.

In the arguments above, we assume that the assets of commercial banks are of good quality, only the depositor run forces them to sell assets before the date of maturity, thereby suffering a loss. In reality, more than just a few of the assets of financial institutions are at fault, this then harms the profitability of financial institutions and lowers their ability to pay off loans. In addition, in general cases, it is the worsening of these assets that causes a deposit run.

An important reason as to why commercial bank assets worsen is that commercial banks cannot efficiently select borrowers and supervise them. Imperfect information is the root of inefficient supervision. To select borrowers efficiently, financial institutions must have a thorough understanding of the borrowers' business capacity and the projects they invest in. However, borrowers know more about the risks and profits of their projects than commercial banks do. Therefore, because of asymmetric information, adverse selection often occurs when commercial banks issue loans. That is, commercial banks give loans to borrowers that are more likely to default, and borrowers with good credit are driven out of credit markets. Additionally, because of asymmetric information, it is hard for commercial banks to effectively supervise borrowers after issuing them money, and borrowers, after obtaining money, will most likely invest in risky projects, which is something that commercial banks would not like to see. Once the investments fail, banks will be stuck with non-performing loans, and the quality of their assets will worsen.

In addition to moral hazards and adverse selections in association with the borrowers, commercial banks have their own moral hazards that are harmful to shareholders and depositors. In modern economic systems, commercial banks get "insurance" from the government openly or secretly. Commercial banks believe that once they get into trouble, the government will not leave them stranded. The more serious the crisis, the more likely the government will rescue. For example, in the supervision of banking industry, there are terms such as banks that are "too-big-to-fail" or that are worthy of "regulatory forbearance". **Regulatory forbearance** refers to, situations in which the government, in consideration of financial stability, takes various measures to protect commercial banks in serious financial difficulty from bankruptcy. Therefore, even though a commercial bank realizes that certain loans are risky, if they know that other institutions have been involved in similar operations, they will also follow. Otherwise, they will lose the chance to obtain high returns. As soon as the economy reverses and borrowers cannot pay off these loans, commercial banks will suffer from the suddenly worsened assets.

Systematically speaking, commercial bank managers do not face the same incentives and punishments for their business management, which also leads to inefficient client screening. For risky loans, as soon as they are successful, managers will rake in tremendous rewards; as soon as they fail, the worst thing that could happen to them is that they lose their job. Comparing these two results, commercial bank managers always tend to select projects with high risks, which will generate great profits once successful.

The assets and liabilities structure of commercial banks is another important factor that leads banks to engage in high-risk loans. We know that a commercial bank' equity capital is only a small portion of their total assets, and the net worth of a bank is very small. Thus, the fewer the losses that owners may suffer from poor decisions, the more likely that they will engage in high-risk loans, especially when financial institutions are already in trouble, in which case they will engage in extremely risky investments, hoping to bring themselves back to life, which rarely goes as planned.

In terms of supervision, commercial banks have many advantages over individual depositors when supervising borrowers. However, supervision also comes at a cost, and it is impossible for a contract to cover every detail to supervise thereafter. Thus, the uncertainties in the credit market cannot be solved thoroughly, and commercial banks cannot completely rid themselves of moral hazards and adverse selection.

All in all, the normal operations of commercial banks rely on high-quality assets and stable liabilities. However, given the aforementioned factors that commercial banks face with moral hazards, adverse selections, and liquidity risks, commercial banks are in fact quite fragile.

23.2.2 Financial Market Fragility

In addition to financial institutions, financial markets are also faced with fragility. Financial market fragility refers to when an accident makes people lose their faith, and leads to severe issues in the financial sector, especially when stock prices fall sharply, leading to chaos in the financial sector and the economic system as a whole.

The price of a financial asset is the discounted present value of the cash flow it will generate. However the cash flow is forecast based upon the information that people have. Because of asymmetric information, it is impossible to "foresee" everything in the future. In reality, people are often blind when forecasting the prices of assets which leads to herding in financial asset investments. To be brief, **herding** refers to a phenomenon in which people follow the investment behavior of others. In other words, people will buy when prices rise, and sell when price fall. The so called "buying on tips and selling on bad news" is a classic example of herding.

Another factor that may cause excessive fluctuations in the stock market is the technical characteristics of trade and the market structure. Any technical characteristics that provide convenience to buy low and sell high in a trade system may enlarge the fluctuation in stock markets. Take margin trading for example. Through margin transactions, investors can engage in massive financial transaction, causing frequent changes in market prices. When the price shifts in an unfavorable direction, forced by the margin pressure, these investors have to close out in a hurry, which also causes a sharp fall in stock prices.

The largest stock market fluctuations come in the formation and breakdown of stock market bubbles. A **financial bubble** refers to when the prices of a series of assets go up sharply and continuously. The rise at first will make people expect that the price will rise further, so new buyers are attracted — these people only want to make money through the transaction, and have no interest in the use and profitability of the assets themselves. When the expectations reverse, the prices will fall sharply, which will inevitably lead to a financial crisis. Theoretically, when the price of an asset exceeds the discounted present value of its future cash flow, a financial bubble will occur. For instance, as is analyzed in the dividend discount model of Chapter 9, if the expectations about future dividends are accurate, when the price of a stock exceeds the discounted present value calculated according to the dividend discount model, there will be a financial bubble.

A simple but practical standard to check whether or not there is a bubble is the average price-earnings ratio. When the average price-earnings ratio is too high, there may be a bubble in the stock market. This is because with such a price-earnings ratio, the stock price is much higher than the discounted present value of earnings per share calculated with the current market rate. Then, financial markets will be prosperous. For example, between May 19, 1999 and June, 2001, the Chinese stock price index doubled, and the average price-earnings ratio was 60. Meanwhile, the daily turnover exceeded tens of billions. This led to a bubble in China's stock market. From 2005 to 2007, the same situation appeared when the SSE Composite Index was five times higher than before, and the average price-earnings ratio was 60. Large bubbles existed in prosperity.

However, financial bubbles are unstable, and the prosperity in that period is fragile. In fact, the word "bubble" vividly describes how fast the price and turnover of financial assets rise, and also shows how fragile they are. Even a tiny external force can pop the "bubble". On the eve of the collapse of the bubble, speculation is everywhere and the whole society is enthusiastic about it. People are exhilarant when they talk about stock; everyone, even a fool, seems to be an expert on stock investments. However, the stock market at this time is just like a paper window, which can be easily torn down by unintentional external forces. In *Deflation*, A. Gary Shilling describes it as such: "The story has it that that just before the 1929 crash, Joe Kennedy knew the end was near when he got a stock tip from his shoeshine boy". When the speculation worsens, people start to have doubts, and even a tiny factor may lead to a sharp fall in the stock market. The market will then perform badly for a very long period of time, while the turnover shrinks.

Box 23.1 The Tragedy of Enthusiasm — The Dutch Tulip Bubble

The Dutch Tulip Bubble is one of the most famous bubbles of history. In the early 17th century, where the Netherlands was the world's leader in commerce, the middle class were enthusiastic about tulips, which then led to a bidding war over tulip bulbs.

In 1635, the heyday of the tulip bubble, someone was willing to pay up to 12 hectares of land in the heart of the city in exchange for a special tulip

(*Continued*)

Box 23.1 (*Continued*)

bulb, because there were only two of its kind throughout the Netherlands. Another merchant was willing to pay 4 heads of cattle, 8 pigs, 2 boxes of wine, 4 boxes of beers and 1000 pounds of cheese in exchange for a bulb named "the governor". Some carpenters, peasants, and dustmen also began to invest with a sense of national pride. Foreigners also hopped onto the bandwagon. People were all dreaming about becoming millionaires, even billionaires.

Of course, this didn't last for very long. In 1636, one Dutchman woke up and refused to buy a tulip at the promised price, which caused people to doubt. Then the price fell and stayed down. Many people who had sold everything they owned to snatch up a couple tulips became beggars overnight. Some rich men lost fortunes that had been accumulated generation after generation.

Enthusiasm is the seed of tragedy!

— Richard Zacks: *An Underground Education*
Hainan Publishing House, 2002 Edition

23.3 The Financial Instability Model and How Financial Crisis Begins

23.3.1 Fisher's Debt–Deflation Theory

Fisher is the first economist to put forth a systematic study on the mechanism of financial fragility in a market economy. He analyzed the depressions of 1837 and 1873, and the global economic and financial crisis that began in 1929. He believed that the primary cause of financial crises is a combination of excessive liabilities and deflation. Financial "variations" may lead to "variations" in the real economy. It works generally in the following pattern: when there are some new investment opportunities, such as new inventions, new discoveries, new industries, and new markets, people will have new expected rates of return and will actively borrow. When there is always something new and the capital is also abundant, borrowers will "over-borrow" in pursuit of new profitable opportunities.

When both the creditors and debtors notice that excessive liabilities exist, debtors will have to take measures to sell their assets or borrow less. Credit will then contract, and the economy will falter even though there is an increase in money supply. The velocity of currency circulation will slow down, and prices will fall. The overall fall in commodity prices leads to a decrease in the net value and profitability of corporate assets. Furthermore, more enterprises will go bankrupt, production will decrease, many people will be laid off, and unemployment will increase. Facing this situation, people will lose confidence in the economic outlook and will not be as willing to invest. As a consequence, more money will be left unused, and the velocity of circulation will further decelerate. As investment needs decrease, the fall in commodity prices will further increase the surplus of real money, causing a decrease in nominal interest rates. However, as commodity prices fall faster than nominal interest rates, real interest rates will increase. The chaos in the financial market will then become more serious, more banks will fail and the economy will suffer a financial crisis.

In brief, Fisher's financial instability process is described as follows: new inventions → over-indebtedness → credit contraction → fall in prices, decrease in production, and increase in unemployment → loss of confidence → decrease in investment → fall in nominal interest rates → financial chaos, bank failures, and a financial crisis.

Fisher's model, based on "over-indebtedness" and "monetary deflation", explains "financial instability". Therefore, Fisher's theory is also called the debt-deflation theory.

Major financial crises, such as the American economic recession between 1873 and 1879 and the Great Depression between 1929 and 1933, provide good evidence for Fisher's debt-deflation theory. Take the global depression between 1929 and 1933 as an example. After 1921, the American economy had been driven powerfully by various kinds of "new things", such as the development of the automobile and chemical industries, the construction of highways, improvements in power grids, the development of a modern railway industry, and the resuscitation of real estate. These new inventions caused a serious inflation in financial assets. Asset prices went up sharply, and American loans and investments to foreign countries were active. Many countries in Europe were burdened with heavy short term foreign debt, and the UK adopted a policy of low interest rates and supported the restoration of a new gold standard system. However, bank loans and the supply of money were suddenly cut short, stock prices nosedived in 1929, and many banks went bankrupt.

23.3.2 Minsky's Financial Instability Model

(a) *The Internal Instability of Finance*

In Minsky's analysis of how financial crises occur, he believed that financial instability lies in the economic system itself. This instability arises from "unusual" changes in the economic system. These unusual changes also refer to new inventions and new markets. When there is an unusual change, people begin to believe that a "new era" has come and will have optimistic expectations about the future. Both creditors and debtors will underestimate investment risks, causing enterprises to increase liabilities excessively and actively engage in physical investments and financial investments. As a result, inflation will occur and assets prices will soar. New opportunities to earn profits will lead to the birth of new kinds of financial institutions and financial products, and the financial industry will become more prosperous than ever.

However, what goes up must come down. When the economy is overly prosperous, people will start to worry about whether borrowers are able to pay off their financial debts. This is true especially when easy financing tightens and interest rates rise. Then, assets prices will fall, people will cut back on financial investments to adjust their asset–liability structure, and the economy will begin to falter. In a word, according to Minsky, as people enlarge or lessen the scale of financial transactions all the time and change the structure of financial assets or liabilities (including their asset portfolio), there will be less stability in the entire system, making various connections in the financial industry very unstable.

In his analysis as to the source of financial instability, Minsky emphasizes the importance of cash flow. He believed that the basic structure of people's behavior is shown by "the composition of assets, namely the portfolio (financial portfolio) of all physical assets, financial assets, and financial debts". For example, the business performance of an enterprise is decided not only by the marketability of the products and services it offers and the market dynamics of the non-financial inputs needed for production, but also by its financing situation such as debts, bonds, and stocks, and the selling of the financial products that it holds. The financial transactions which the latter involves are future-oriented and thus uncertain. People's economic activities boil down to asset portfolio under uncertain conditions. Every economic entity chooses their own asset portfolio based on their own judgment as to the future. We cannot tell how subjective an economic entity is. Therefore, with these uncertainties in the choice of portfolios, finance is unstable.

(b) *Three Types of Financing*

Minsky divides financing into three types: hedging, speculative financing, and Ponzi financing. The standard is to compare the repaying cash flow with the expected cash flow, that is the principal and interests cost in a financial debt and the profit the borrowers' real economic behavior generates.

(i) *Hedging*: In this type of financing, the cash to repay debts comes from the cash return on production. Such financing is stable and at little risk. When an enterprise borrows money from a bank to develop new products, it is a form of hedging.

(ii) *Speculative financing*: When an investor uses borrowed money to speculate, it is speculative financing. For example, Wang Xiao'er finds that the stock market has been prosperous as of late, and he expects that stock prices will continue to rise. In order to "take a shot" in the stock market, Wang Xiao'er borrows 500,000 yuan from the bank, with his house as mortgage, to speculate in the stock market. If the stock market performs as expected, Wang Xiao'er can pay the debt with the profit he earns from his transaction; however, if the stock market reverses, Wang Xiao'er will have problems paying his debt.

(iii) *Ponzi financing*: Charles Ponzi is the legendary fraud known as the Financial Wizard. Ponzi financing generally refers to the following: in general, the cash needed to pay off debts is greater than the cash return that production can generate. So, in order to pay off debts, debtors have to borrow more money, namely, "to rob Peter to pay Paul". In Ponzi financing, if there is enough debt cash flow, the situation can be maintained. However, as debt often carries interest, the principal and interests will begin to snowball. Once there is a problem with the cash flow, there will be a crisis.

During booms when financial assets expand, borrowers begin to shift from hedging to speculative financing; during a collapse when financial assets shrink, borrowers shift from hedging to speculative financing, and then to Ponzi financing. One way to check whether finances in an economic system are stable or not is to check the following: the greater the hedging, the healthier; the more Ponzi financing, the unhealthier that the economy has become. Attention is required if speculative financing accounts for a great proportion.

23.3.3 Kindleberger's Theory of the Source of Financial Crises

Kindleberger replenished Minsky's model, and gave the following explanation as to how financial crises occur:

In the first stage, external shocks in the macroeconomic system bring about some "unusual changes". "Unusual changes" refers to external unexpected incidents such as improvements and innovations. These unusual changes give people new profit-making opportunities and change their expectations. Some people will take unusually optimistic measures.

Box 23.2 Ponzi: The Man and His Story

Charles Ponzi (1878–1949) was an Italian immigrant who came to America. He announced that he could take advantage of the chaos in Europe after World War I to make large sums of money. He then bought discounted bills from the International Postal Union from several countries, only to then sell them in America at face value. He promised the public that all of his investments could generate a return of 50% in 45 days. Tempted by high returns, approximately 40,000 Bostonians invested a total of 15 million dollars in Ponzi from 1919 to 1920.

Some of Ponzi's promises were fulfilled, but he used the money from later investors to pay the earlier investors. Only if Ponzi could earn more "investments" than the return he had to pay, he could have fulfilled all of his promises. This is the classical Ponzi scheme.

(*Continued*)

Box 23.2 (*Continued*)

Ponzi was sentenced to five years in prison for what he did. After his release, he did it again, and ended up with a longer prison sentence. In 1934, he was repatriated to Italy but he must have had nerves of steel, for he tried an even more daring attempt: he tried to cheat Mussolini. At last, he got what he deserved: he died in a poor house in Brazil without a single penny.

— Richard Zacks: *An Underground Education*
Hainan Publishing House, 2002 Edition

In the second stage, economic activities reach a peak, misleading people into believing that production and financial investments will continue to expand. Then, more financial transactions occur, which means more bank loans and a greater money supply. Economic prosperity will thus continue for a period of time. This is because, generally speaking, if no borrowers stop borrowing because it is too risky, or no creditors stop lending money because the interest rates are too low, financing activities will go on. Moreover, financial innovations broaden the credit and currency circulation channels, and new products and new deals will continue to appear.

In the third stage, excessive asset transactions and speculative behavior will occur while the scale of financing continues to expand beyond the scale of the real economy. This will result in excessive asset transaction and speculation, bring about an increase in asset price, stimulate further investments, and people will become addicted to the prosperity. Given this context, people will begin to speculate. When there is not enough money to support speculative trades, speculators will use credit transactions or installment payments to enlarge transaction through a leverage effect.

In the fourth stage, the market is extremely prosperous, and people will become extremely enthusiastic in their speculations. Many people will join in on speculative activities because they see other families or enterprises which have made a hefty profit through speculation. Normal and sensible behaviors are replaced by enthusiasm and bubbles.

In the fifth stage, capital demands increase to a great degree, the velocity of money increases, interest rates rise, and enterprises begin to face capital turnover problems. Once assets prices stop rising so fast, speculators will undersell their financial assets, and assets prices will fall sharply. Speculators who are over-engaged in speculations will go bankrupt. Financial institutions will stop issuing loans that are backed by financial assets and will begin to recover loans. Some financial institutions will go bankrupt because they hold too many non-performing assets.

In the sixth stage, if monetary and fiscal authorities have yet to realize that the internal decay of the market economy is to blame for financial instability, and thus fail to take macroeconomic and microeconomic measures, the market will rapidly display reverse operations, finances will shrink, and the economy will be dragged into a financial crisis.

Kindleberger's financial instability process is described as follows: unusual changes → surplus capital → excessive lending → excessive asset transactions, a sharp increase in asset prices → an increase in interest rates, capital and loan recovery → a sharp decrease in asset prices → financial crisis.

It could be said that, whether it be Fisher, Minsky, or Kindleberger, all of these economists emphasize the critical importance of periodic changes in real economy, in changing people's expectations. This point has a great deal of significance when it comes to the prevention of financial crises. However, their analyses concentrate on a closed economy. This can explain a banking crisis, a debt crisis, and a capital market crisis quite well, but it does little to explain the currency crisis of an open economy.

23.4 Currency Crisis Theory

For the last several decades, there have been three different currency crisis theories in the field of Western finance.

23.4.1 The First Generation Currency Crisis Theory

The **first generation currency crisis theory**, also called the standard currency crisis model, first appeared in late 1970s, the foundation of which was laid by Paul Krugman. Krugman believed that a currency crisis is fundamentally caused by the contradiction between expansionary economic policies and an attempt to maintain a fixed exchange rate. The typical circumstances are as follows: The government budget faces a constant fiscal deficit, and to make up for the fiscal deficit, the government issues more currency, to the point where the issuance gets out of control and commodity prices rise. If all else remains equal and the money supply of a certain country is increasing at a rate higher than the international level, then that currency will be under the pressure of depreciation. In this case, if the country wants to maintain its fixed exchange rate, it will have to use foreign reserves to interfere with the foreign exchange markets. If the pressure to depreciate is not serious and only temporary, then it can be dealt with efficiently. If the pressure is serious and lasts for a long time, the foreign reserves of the country's central bank may be used up. When the foreign reserves are about to be used up, some smart speculators will sell out the currency beforehand, causing a sudden shock to the currency. The reserve will then dry up ahead of time and the currency crisis will thus arrive earlier than expected. According to the analysis above, we can see that, in the first generation currency theory, a currency crisis is a product of the budget deficit.

This standard model goes a long way in explaining this reality. First, in reality, many currency crises reflect the contradiction between domestic economic policies and exchange rate policies. The standard model is a brief summary of this contradiction. Second, according to the model, it is not insensible for investors to give up a currency to recover their capital. Market manipulation is not to blame, and, in certain cases, it is a reasonable result given the country's economic status.

23.4.2 The Second Generation Currency Crisis Theory

The **second generation currency crisis theory** begins in the same way as the first generation theory in that it also emphasizes that currency crises are fundamentally caused by the contradiction between domestic economic policies and fixed exchange rate policies. The difference however is that the first generation theory concentrates on fiscal policies, while the second generation concentrates on monetary policies. According to the second generation theory, under a fixed exchange rate policy, if the government adopts expansionary policies, the exchange rate will depreciate significantly and cause a currency crisis. This will then force the government into abandoning the fixed exchange rate policy and adopting a floating exchange rate policy.

Why would the government want the currency to depreciate? The reasons are as follows: (1) The government has debt that is calculated in the domestic currency and wants to reduce it through inflation; if the exchange rate remains unchanged, it would be impossible to achieve this goal. If speculators know the government's motivation, they may start to attack the currency. The French franc crisis in the 1920s is a good example. At that time, international speculators thought that the French government would try to reduce its debts accumulated during World War I, and as such, they attacked the French franc, causing France to abandon its fixed exchange rate policy. (2) There is a serious unemployment problem, and the government wants to solve it through expansionary monetary policies, causing the contradiction between the "internal goals" and "external goals": if it wants to maintain a fixed exchange rate, the expansionary monetary policies will not work efficiently; if expansionary monetary policies have to work, it will be hard to maintain a fixed exchange rate.

If the government is motivated to depreciate because of the domestic economic situation, then why would it maintain a stable exchange rate? One possible reason is that the government thinks that a stable exchange rate is important to international trade and transnational investments. That is to say that, taking external factors into consideration, the government thinks that it is beneficial to maintain a fixed exchange rate. Another reason is that the country has suffered through inflation before, and as such, a stable exchange rate is a certain kind of credit guarantee. In addition, in some countries, the exchange rate is a symbol of national dignity. Or rather, bound by some international treaties, the country has its duty to cooperate on the exchange rate.

The question that remains, however, is why is it that when people lose confidence in the fixed exchange rate itself, it becomes harder to maintain a stable exchange rate? The reason is that if various domestic factors push the currency to depreciate, then it will cost a lot to maintain a fixed exchange rate. For example, foreign creditors may ask for higher interest rates, and debt burdens under current accounts will grow; if the currency does not depreciate at all, foreign capital will stop flowing, making it difficult to maintain the fixed exchange rate. Let us take another example. If most people expect that the exchange rate is going to depreciate, the domestic wages will rise, making domestic industries less competitive compared to other countries. This will cause greater pressure of depreciation in the exchange rate. In addition, if for some reason, a government wants to guard the fixed exchange rate, it may raise short term interest rates, which will worsen the cash flow of the government and enterprises, and furthermore, it will lead to a recession and unemployment. Regardless, the expectation of depreciation itself will change the balance between the pros and cons of maintaining a fixed exchange rate, increase the cost of its maintenance, and force the government to reconsider exchange rate adjustments.

In Krugman's view, if these factors are put together, a theory similar to the standard mode will come into being. Suppose a country is comparing the cost of maintaining and abandoning the current exchange rate. If the former costs are greater, then, even though there is no speculative shock, the currency will still depreciate sometime in the future. Speculators will abandon the currency before the depreciation, causing the depreciation to occur ahead of time. Having realized this, speculators may start to abandon the currency even earlier. Such behavior will cause a crisis, which will lead to the collapse of the fixed exchange rate system before the worsening basic economic factors make it necessary to depreciate. All in all, suppose changes in basic economic factors make it inevitable to abandon the fixed exchange rate and investors get all the information, then the speculative attack will come earlier and will succeed. As for investors, they just want to take advantage of the opportunity for arbitrage: if they do not attack before the crisis, then the profit of depreciation will be taken by other speculators, and they will suffer losses.

It is not hard to see that, in the first generation currency crisis model, a currency crisis is caused directly by the worsening basic economic factors. In the second generation, however, a currency crisis is not directly caused by the worsening basic economic factors, but on the contrary, at least in the view of the government, there are still some basic economic conditions to maintain the exchange rate, and the government is also well prepared to do so. However, because a speculative shock makes it too costly to guard the fixed exchange rate, the government has no choice but to abandon it.

23.4.3 The Third Generation Currency Crisis Theory

From July 1997, a series of financial crises struck Southeast-Asian countries. It just so happened that neither the first nor the second generation currency crisis theory could give a satisfactory explanation as to this crisis. The reasons are as follows: (1) Prior to the crisis, most countries were in good operating conditions: all of the countries had balanced government budgets, none of them adopted irresponsible expansionary credit policies, and above all, inflation rates were low. (2) In 1996, although the economy slowed down and there was overproduction in this region, there were no serious unemployment problems before the crisis. In other words, these countries did not have to abandon fixed exchange rates to adopt expansionary monetary policy and thus improve employment. (3) Before the crisis, capital markets, especially stock and real estate markets had gone through prosperity and recession. (4) During the crisis, financial institutions played a role more important than that of the governments; they borrowed large amounts of short-term debt from international financial markets, and then lent the money to domestic investors. The money was then invested in the real estate and stock markets.

As such, the Asian financial crisis is not attributed to government budget problems as the standard model may suggest, nor does it reflect what the second generation currency crisis model indicates, which would blame it on unreasonable macroeconomic policies. Therefore, some scholars have tried to explain it with new models, and thus **the third generation currency crisis theory** was born.

In emerging market economies, it is very common for governments to provide hidden warrants for loans, and government officials are often connected to financial activities. Therefore, financial institutions believe that if they get into any problems, the government will not leave them stranded. As such, financial institutions will not be as cautious in borrowing money and issuing loans, which will then lead to large investment in high-risk and also highly profitable non-productive industries. This is known as the "excessive borrowing syndrome". In other words, financial institutions will hold onto many high-risk assets. The increase in risky assets will push asset prices up, making the balance sheets of financial institutions look much better than reality. Only if the money chain works well, the process will go on. However, it will not last long after the financial bubble grows beyond that of the real economy. When an external shock occurs, the financial bubble will burst and the entire financial system will suffer. Asset prices will fall, and the risky assets of financial institutions will become enormous non-performing loans in almost an instant. When the crisis becomes serious, the government may be forced to give up hidden warrants, thus weakening the refinancing ability of financial institutions. Then, some institutions will be forced to go bankrupt, and asset prices will further decline. This vicious cycle will eventually lead to the financial crisis.

23.5 Historic Financial Crises

Over the course of history, there have been many financial crises, wreaking havoc on not only developed countries, but on emerging economies as well. Wherever they spread, economies were left utterly battered and bruised, finances suffered enormously, and to many people, the pain was simply unbearable. At this point, we shall briefly introduce several of the major financial crises that have occurred since 1929.

23.5.1 The Great Crisis of 1929 to 1933

The Great Crisis of 1929 to 1933 began with the Wall Street Crash in October 1929. Subsequently, things got out of control, and the Dow Jones fell from its highest point of more than 380 down to about 50 in 1932. The Crash led to a wave of bank failures across America, and banks suffered an unprecedented bank run; the number of banks reduced from more than 25,000 in 1929 to just over 14,700 by 1933. Total assets within the banking system shrunk drastically, the money supply fell, leading to tight credit, which then spiraled the US monetary system out of control, to the point that some small towns and neighborhoods had no choice but to issue their own temporary currency for trading needs.

The stock market crash and bank failures, led to a drastic drop in US industrial production, rising unemployment and a fall in the price of goods. The financial storm soon swept over more regions, and other industrialized countries succumbed to the crisis, suffering the same fate as the United States. Table 23.1 reflects the changes in the primary economic indicators of America, the United Kingdom, France and Germany from 1929 to 1932. As you can see, their industrial production, prices indices, and foreign trade drastically declined. Unemployment rates rose dramatically, and cities were full of the homeless. At that time, the economic

Table 23.1 Changes in the Primary Economic Indicators of America, The United Kingdom, France and Germany from 1929 to 1932

	USA	UK	France	Germany
Industrial Production	−46%	−23%	−24%	−41%
WPI	−32%	−33%	−34%	−29%
Foreign Trade	−70%	−60%	−54%	−61%
Unemployment	+607%	+129%	+214%	+232%

downturn worsened and even President Hoover stopped taking his car and rode a carriage.

This crisis also led to the collapse of the international gold standard, and since then, countries have gradually turned to monetary systems which are not subject to the credit constraints of precious metals. In order to deal with the crisis, the Hoover administration sharply raised tariffs, which then led to the implementation of retaliatory tariffs from such countries as the United Kingdom, France, Italy, and Germany. From 1920 to 1929, the average rate for import tariffs was 13%, however, from 1930 to 1940, the average rate was 16.6%. During those two periods of time, the average rate for French tariffs was 7.1% and 21%, respectively, the average rate for German tariffs was 4.5% and 16.8%, respectively, and the average rate for British tariffs was 9.8% and 23.2%, respectively. The tariff policies of each country were at the expense of others, which only led to a collapse of the international trading system and exacerbated the adverse impact of the crisis on economic activity. In order to take in the lessons of the various countries which "turned a blind eye to others" during the crisis, the General Agreement on Tariffs and Trade (the predecessor to the WTO) and the International Monetary Fund were established after World War II.

After Roosevelt took office in the midst of the crisis, the US government implemented the New Deal to pull the United States out of the crisis as soon as possible. On the financial front, this was mainly reflected in the following ways: First of all, the decoupling of the US dollar–gold relationship, in that the US depreciated the dollars and abandoned the gold standard. In 1933, Roosevelt banned the private hoarding of gold valued greater than 100 dollars and formally abolished the gold standard. In January 1934, the United States passed the Gold Reserve Act which stipulated that the dollar price of gold would change from 20.67 dollars per ounce to 35 dollars per ounce. As such, the United States abandoned the gold standard and replaced it with a flexible system of currency management. Secondly, the government divided banks into investment banks and commercial banks through the Glass–Steagall Act. Third, the government established the Federal Deposit Insurance Corporation to provide a certain amount of deposit insurance to prevent bank runs. Finally, the government implemented interest rate controls (i.e., Regulation Q), so that banks could not publicly pay interest on demand deposit, and a maximum limit was set for the interest rates on savings and time deposits, which means that member banks of the Reserve Board were prohibited from paying interest on their demand deposits (of less than 30 days) and set an interest rate cap on the payments to the aforementioned savings and time deposits. The various systems which the United States established during this crisis had a profound impact on the financial development of America over the next several decades, although, of course, they also foreshadowed the US savings and loan crisis in the early 1980s as well as the sub-prime crisis in the early 21st century.

23.5.2 The Asian Financial Crisis

It had been quite a long time since Asia had suffered from exchange rate volatility, and because of rapid economic growth in East Asian countries and regions, people began to speak of the Four Dragons and Four Tigers. From 1992 to 1995, the annual economic growth rate of Indonesia, Malaysia, Singapore, South Korea, and Thailand exceeded 7%, and from 1994 to 1995, the annual export growth rate of Malaysia, the Philippines, and Thailand exceeded 30%. Also, after the Mexican crisis, capital also quickly shifted to Asia. By 1996, the net private capital inflows to GDP ratio was 5% in South Korea, 6% in Indonesia, 9% in Thailand, and 10% in the Philippines. A significant portion of these capital inflows was in the form of short-term credit obtained foreign banks. One of the most important factors behind the promotion for capital inflows were the low interest rates in major financial centers. Some East Asian countries (regions) borrowed yen and dollars at low interest rates to invest in high-yield Asian securities. This phenomenon is known as a **carry trade**. Meanwhile, Asian currencies were, in fact, pegged to the dollar and interest rate risks for fund inflows were very low. For a long period of time, Asian governments used banks as an instrument for economic development, directly shifting funds to their preferred industries, and in exchange, Asian government were responsible for providing generous public support for these operations. Foreign investors lent to a wide range of Asian banks in the belief that Asian governments would never let them fail. More importantly, prior to the shift to a more flexible exchange rate, these countries had already relaxed controls on capital account transactions. As the East Asian growth model was dependent upon exports, and thus, exchange rate stability, governments were apprehensive about exchange rate fluctuations.

However, as a result of exchange rate controls, these currencies became overvalued, especially the Thai baht. Capital inflows promoted a rise in Thai investments and prices. However, a significant portion of these investments were of poor quality, and investors became increasingly concerned. Foreign banks and individual investors then began to withdraw funds from the Thai market. From mid-1996 onwards, the Bangkok boom began to lose steam, and the baht faced tremendous pressure. In order to maintain the baht exchange rate, the Bank of Thailand sought exchange market intervention, encouraged Thai banks to borrow funds from offshore markets, gave tax breaks, and eased regulations. However, it was not before long that the international reserves at the central bank had dried up. On July 2, the Thai baht was forced to devalue and the government let it float. Because the Philippines relied heavily on capital inflows and was also rigidly pegged to the dollar, the devaluation of the baht placed tremendous pressure on the Philippines. Ten days after the baht began to float, the Philippine peso was also forced to float. The devaluation of the Thai and Philippine currencies soon spread to Indonesia and Malaysia, and these two countries were also quickly forced to let their currencies decline with the baht. Afterwards, Taiwanese authorities let the new Taiwan dollar fall in October. With the gradual devaluation of the currencies of Southeast Asian countries (regions), South Korea was forced to succumb to speculative pressures, the range of volatility for the Korean won expanded from 4.5% to 20% in November, and as a result, the value of the won drastically declined. This caused investors' further concern over other currencies. The Asian financial crisis led to a sharp decrease in the region's output. However, within a year, the fundamental strength of the regional economies led to their innate recovery, and the devaluation of their currencies improved their competitiveness. Insolvent banks received funding and restructuring, which improved their credit. Corporate governance and prudential supervision was also strengthened. Regulations on foreign direct investment were loosened and more flexible exchange rate systems were formally established. Asian countries accumulated large foreign exchange reserves, which serve as a defensive weapon for the economy when the financial sector enters a downturn. Meanwhile, in order to reduce their dependence on international institutions, the **Chiang Mai Initiative** was established as a regional exchange and credit network. Under the Initiative, a foreign exchange repository which ASEAN 10 + 3 countries contribute to, provides financing support for countries which may, in the future, face a massive outflow of capital or a currency devaluation.

23.5.3 The US Subprime Mortgage Crisis

US commercial banks used to issue a certain kind of subprime mortgage, or rather, a home mortgage loan for people with poor personal credit scores, for borrowers who need to use a large proportion of their income to pay off monthly instalment, or a home mortgage loan with a down payment below 20% or even without down payment. In the United States, most mortgages are securitized, in that non-standard mortgages are pooled together and once they are broken down into standardized securities, they are sold to a wide range of investors, including financial institutions. In fact, the securitized product mix in America was becoming increasingly complex, and most people found it difficult to differentiate their risks. Because of the relative ease by which people could obtain subprime mortgages, coupled with the stimulant of low interest rates, borrowing by the US household sector from financial institutions rose sharply. However, because there was no or little down payment, the net worth of the home purchased was completely dependent upon an increase in housing prices. Once prices fell, the net worth of the property quickly was in the red, and moral hazards were more likely to occur with borrowers, and investors who held mortgage-backed securities faced the credit risk of defaulting borrowers. After the Federal Reserve repeatedly raised interest rates from 2004 to 2006, this became the reality. Rising US interest rates led to a general decline in US home prices, which, in turn, led to the negative net worth of radical borrowers of subprime mortgage loans, the general increase in default rates, and the increased losses of financial institutions.

Thus, the subprime crisis of 2007 began. On February 2007, the HSBC Holdings increased 1.8 billion dollars in provisions for the bad debt of US subprime mortgage operations. Afterwards, a domino effect took place among other US subprime mortgage companies, with more than 30 of them forced to close out their business, which then evolved into a systemic crisis. In July 2007, Moody's reduced the credit rating of 399 different subprime mortgage bonds which were valued at a total of 5.2 billion dollars. In August 2007, the American Home Mortgage Corporation filed for bankruptcy protection, and soon afterwards, a number of financial institutions in Europe and Japan announced they were involved in the US subprime mortgage crisis. By early 2008, several major financial institutions, such as Merrill Lynch, Citigroup, UBS, and Bank of America, announced, one after another, huge losses of 2 billion to 10 billion dollars. In March 2008, the fifth largest Wall Street investment bank, Bear Stearns, was acquired by JP Morgan Chase for only 240 million dollars. In September 2008, Lehman Brothers, one of Wall Street's largest five investment banks, also filed for bankruptcy protection. Under the impact of the subprime mortgage crisis, Merrill Lynch was acquired by Bank of America, and Goldman Sachs transformed into a bank holding company. It was an unprecedented reshuffling of the Wall Street financial sphere.

Subprime mortgage delinquencies and huge losses incurred to financial institutions spread to the global stock market. The Dow Jones Index quickly fell from a height of 14,000 points before the crises down to 6000 points, and a market value of more than 60% simply disappeared. The Chinese stock market was no different, and the Shanghai Composite Index fell from a height of 6000 points before the crisis down to less than 1700 points, a market loss of more than 70% — investors suffered heavy losses. During the US subprime mortgage crisis, not a single country's stock market was spared.

Of course, the real economy was also struck by the subprime crisis. US economic growth dropped from 4% before the crisis to −4.1% in the second quarter of 2009, and unemployment rates rose from 4.5% to about 10%. Even though the United States took massive fiscal and monetary measures to stimulate the economy, growth remained low over the next few years while the unemployment rate remained high. European economies were also devastated by the subprime crisis, where the European economic growth rate fell from 4% before the crisis to −5% in 2009. Unemployment climbed, which only added to the financial burden of some European countries. Some countries, such as Iceland, suffered more than others, and the nation was on the brink of bankruptcy according to some analysts. Moreover, the subsequent European sovereign debt crisis was inextricably linked to the US subprime mortgage crisis. Of course, Asian economies also suffered. Take China as an example. Prior to the crisis, China's rate of economic growth was 10%, but by the second quarter of 2009, the rate fell to 6%, forcing the Chinese government to adopt large-scale fiscal and monetary measures to stimulate the growth, which, however, would stock up trouble for stable economic growth in the following years.

23.5.4 The European Sovereign Debt Crisis

The European sovereign debt crisis refers to the inability of several countries in the eurozone to repay government debt or those who faced difficulties in terms of refinancing debt in the absence of third-party assistance. In 1992, EU member states signed the Maastricht Treaty which required that member states be subject to a strictly limited fiscal deficit and government debt in that the fiscal deficit could not exceed 3% of the GDP and that the outstanding government debt to GDP ratio could not exceed 60%. However, in the new century, many member states failed to comply with this treaty and let their fiscal deficits increase significantly. In early 2010, lending parties required that debt-ridden countries, such as Greece, with large fiscal and current account deficits must pay higher interest rates. As a result, governments in these countries found it difficult to refinance their budget deficits, which further led to a decline in economic growth and a large government debt to GDP ratio.

The European sovereign debt crisis struck the countries of Greece, Ireland, Italy, Portugal, and Spain, and as such, these countries have been dubbed the PIIGS, although the crisis also spread to Cyprus later. In the first years of the new century, Greece maintained the fastest economic growth in the eurozone, but this growth was also accompanied by a large structural deficit. In April 2010, the Greek government applied for 45 billion euros in loans from the EU and the IMF to meet their requirements for the rest of the year. Subsequently, the Standard & Poor rating for the Greek government fell to "junk", which led to a drastic rise in the interest rates for Greek government debt and the further deterioration of the Greek government's financial burden. In order to reduce the budget deficit, the Greek government was forced to take contractionary fiscal policies, which led to social unrest.

The Irish crisis is somewhat different from that of Greece in that their sovereign debt crisis is not due to excessive government spending, but rather because of the guarantees it provided for six Irish banks during the subprime crisis. Under the impact of the subprime crisis, the Irish real estate bubble burst, and the Irish banking sector suffered a loss of about 100 billion euros. The real economy plummeted, and unemployment rose from 4% in 2006 to 14% in 2010. While the government had a slight budget surplus in 2007, things worsened markedly in 2008. By 2010, the budget deficit to GDP ratio had risen to 32%, and the Irish government was forced to apply for tens of billions of euros in aid from the EU, the IMF, and other financial institutions. As such, international rating institutions drastically reduced Ireland's debt rating.

In the summer of 2010, Moody's reduced Portugal's sovereign debt rating, which resulted in tremendous pressure on the Portuguese government debt, and finally, in 2011, the Portuguese government was forced to apply for a 78 billion euro rescue package from the EU and IMF. After the government debt rating was reduced to "non-investment grade", the interest rate on Portuguese government debt had risen up to at least 17%.

What happened in Spain was quite similar to that of Ireland. Prior to the crisis, the Spanish government debt to GDP ratio was only 60%, which was lower than Germany's by 20%, and not as high as that of France and America. This is because, prior to the crisis, Spain had also experienced a housing boom, which was an important source of its tax revenue. However, when the bubble burst, the Spanish government also spent a lot of money on relief for its banking sector. Bank bailouts, combined with the economic downturn, led to an increase in the Spanish deficit and the amount of government debt. This caused a reduction in the sovereign debt rating, as well as an increase in interest rates and debt burden. Furthermore, this crisis also spread to Italy and Cyprus, where excessive government debt led to financial market upheavals.

The European sovereign debt crisis aggravated the suffering of European economies which had already been hit hard by the subprime mortgage crisis. The unemployment rate in the eurozone rose from 7.5% in 2008 to more than 12% in 2012. During the subprime mortgage crisis, the economic growth rate in the eurozone had risen, however, in the European sovereign debt crisis of 2010, the rate significantly declined, falling into a −0.9% recession by the fourth quarter of 2012. Of course, the European debt crisis not only affected the eurozone alone, but it also slowed down the US economic recovery process, and greatly affected China's economic performance after 2010. There was a significant decrease in China's economic growth rate and those enterprises which relied on the European market have gradually found themselves in difficulty.

23.6 Preventing Financial Crises

23.6.1 A Sound Macroeconomic Environment

A sound macroeconomic environment and reasonable industrial structure are a necessity for guarding against financial crisis. A sound macroeconomic environment primarily consists of moderate economic growth, low unemployment rates, stable prices, no significant and persistent deficits in balance of payments, balanced government revenue and spending, and a moderate amount of government debt. For instance, excessively high rates of economic growth may lead to overly optimistic expectations, a rapid expansion of credit, and rapidly rising asset prices. Additionally, large deficits and high unemployment rates will result in an excessive growth of the money supply which will lead to inflation. These can bring about hidden pitfalls to the stability of the financial system.

Avoiding over-indebtedness is important for a sound macroeconomic environment. The above-mentioned financial crises, though varying in forms and immediate causes, share the same feature in that over-borrowing had occurred prior to the crisis (in different sectors). For example, the American subprime mortgage crisis was initially manifested in a dramatic increase in the outstanding loan and disposable income in the household sector; the European debt crisis was a direct result of the soaring ratio of outstanding government debt to GDP. Excessively high leverage led to great debt burden, and consequently the financial crisis took place. An important post-crisis trend is deleveraging, thus allowing the debt to return to a more reasonable level.

23.6.2 Establishing a Rational Structure of Corporate Governance

Effective corporate governance structures are the microeconomic foundation for preventing financial crisis. This is because an effective corporate governance structure can prevent the moral hazards and adverse selection of financing to a maximum extent. An effective corporate governance structure consists of incentives for and restraints on corporate management, such as performance rewards as well as punishments for irresponsible behavior, to promote effective management behavior. As such, a rational corporate governance structure will reduce the possibility of a commercial bank taking on non-performing assets, and will also improve the profitability of companies, which will then give investors higher rates of return and contribute to a steady rise in stock prices.

In most cases, if the corporate governance structure is irrational, insider controls will become even more severe and management may use a greater amount of the company's cash and other assets for personal debt management, even directly depositing it in foreign bank accounts or injecting the funds into other companies. When the financial crisis occurred in Asian countries, it was not out of the ordinary for managers to transfer cash and other assets to embezzle the property of other shareholders. In China, due to the irrational corporate governance structure of some listed companies, controlling shareholders take illegal possession of the assets of listed subsidiaries which then results in huge losses in the subsidiaries and stores up great trouble for the stock market. As such, a rational corporate governance structure is the microeconomic foundation for preventing financial crises.

23.6.3 Selecting a Rational Exchange Rate System and Capital Accounts Liberalization

If controls on capital accounts are to be relaxed under an irrational exchange rate system, it may lead to a currency crisis. For instance, the policy mix of a fixed exchange rate system and capital accounts liberalization would be an obvious recipe for disaster. Under a fixed exchange rate system, a country's currency exchange rate will often be overvalued. However, because capital accounts begin to open up,

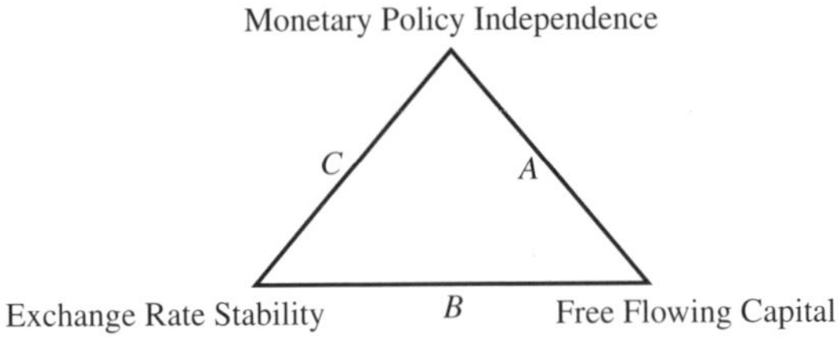

Fig. 23.1 Krugman's Triangle

the country is then vulnerable to speculative attacks. This will lead to a collapse of the fixed exchange rate system and the domestic currency will rapidly depreciate, triggering a currency crisis.

After the Southeast-Asian financial crisis, Krugman proposed the **eternal triangle**, also known as Krugman's Triangle, as depicted in Figure 23.1. Krugman believed that the financial development models of various countries could be summarized with a triangle: A is the selection of the domestic monetary policy independence and the free flow of capital, which was chosen by America and certain Asian countries amidst the financial crisis; B is the selection of a stable exchange rate and the free flow of capital, as under the currency board systems of Hong Kong and several South American countries; C is the selection of monetary policy independence and a stable exchange rate, most representative of which is China. He believed that the reason why America, though having chosen Model A, did not experience a financial crisis was because of its sound and fully-fledged financial system. As for those Asian countries which also opted for this model, the very reason for their financial crises was that none of them had implemented capital controls like China. Controls on capital accounts severed the chances of speculative attacks on domestic currency by speculative capital.

23.6.4 Effective Financial Regulations

The financial sector is one of the economic sectors which are subject to the most government regulation, and effective government regulation can improve the transparency of information, lower moral hazards and reduce adverse selection. Through limitations on the high-risk business activities of financial institutions, governments can also reduce the likelihood of non-performing assets, which will limit the concentration of risk within financial institutions and thereby strengthen the stability of the financial system. Financial regulations limit the financial leverage of borrowers and prevent excessive lending, which is also conducive to sound debtor balance sheets. Since the US subprime mortgage crisis occurred in 2008, major countries around the world have tested more effective financial regulatory systems, such as counter-cyclical macro-prudential regulatory frameworks. As for the content of financial regulations, we will reserve this discussion for the following chapter.

23.6.5 Perfecting the Internal Control System in Financial Institutions

In the prevention of financial crises, the role of financial institutions cannot be ignored. Sound internal controls of financial institutions can be a preventative measure in reducing moral hazards within them. For instance, scientific decision-making can avoid the serious consequences of adverse selection, and strict internal audits may identify potential problems before they become an issue. Additionally, good incentive and restraint mechanisms within financial institutions can improve the prudence of employees in reducing high-risk activities. For instance, a good internal control system within a commercial bank can encourage loan officers to identify less risky potential borrowers but also prevent collusion between borrowers and loan officers in defrauding bank credit. The imperfect internal control system at Barings Bank contributed to its failure, because Leeson, the trader in Singapore, was at free reign to do as he pleased in futures trading. Large financial companies must have a strict internal control system in order to ensure the normal operation of its business. Once this is lost, even small oversights can lead to massive failures, in the same way as a small leak will sink a great ship. Improving the internal control systems of financial institutions is one of the most secure measures for preventing financial crises.

Summary

A financial crisis refers to a situation in which all or most financial indicators become worse, beyond what society and the economic system can bear. There are four types of financial crises: a currency crisis, a banking crisis, a debt crisis, and a capital market crisis. A systematic crisis is when a crisis occurs simultaneously in banks, exchange rates, and capital markets and other such financial sectors, which will then have a devastating effect on the real economy.

Finance in itself is fragile, and this fragility often leads to financial crises. Financial fragility refers to the fact that the financial system in itself is unstable; whether it be commercial banking or the stock market, the financial sectors are fragile.

In theory, there are many explanations as to the instability within finance. Fisher proposed the debt-deflation theory, Minsky proposed the financial instability model, Kindleberger developed his model and proposed a process by which financial crises are formed. Minsky's financial instability model proposed three forms of financing, namely, hedging, speculative financing, and Ponzi financing. When Ponzi financing is no longer possible, a financial crisis will occur.

There are three generational currency crisis theories which have attempted to provide an explanation as to international financial crises. The first generation currency crisis theory focused on the contradiction between fiscal policies and a fixed exchange rate, while the second generation currency crisis theory focused on the contradiction between monetary policies and fixed exchange rates. The third generation currency crisis theory believed that the governments of emerging market economies offer hidden warrants to financial institutions so that these countries suffer from an excessive borrowing syndrome, which results in the dramatic increase in the price of financial assets. Such price rise is not sustainable. Once the price begins to fall, a financial crisis takes place. Financial crises occurred repeatedly in history.

The primary measures for preventing a financial crisis are as follows: a sound macroeconomic environment, a rational, effective corporate governance structure, a rational exchange rate system and the appropriate liberalization of capital accounts, prudent and effective financial regulations, and an improvement in the internal control system of financial institutions.

Key Terms

Currency Crisis; Banking Crisis; Debt Crisis; Systematic Financial Crisis; Ponzi Financing; Debt-Deflation Theory; Financial Bubble; Herding; Financial Fragility; Eternal Triangle; Regulatory Forbearance

Critical Thinking Questions

1. What is a financial crisis? What are the different types of financial crises?
2. Why is finance fragile by nature?
3. What is the main idea behind Fisher's debt-deflation theory?
4. Illustrate the main idea behind Minsky's financial instability model.
5. Illustrate the differences between the three generations of the currency crisis theory.
6. What measures can governments take to prevent financial crises?
7. By abandoning a fixed exchange rate system and transitioning towards a floating exchange rate system, governments can prevent currency crises. Is this true? Why?
8. During the British South Sea Bubble, the great physicist Sir Isaac Newton's initial investment in the South Sea Company had earned him a rate of return of nearly 100%, or approximately 7000 pounds. However, this bout of good luck threw him in over his head, leading to insurmountable losses. At one point, Sir Newton purchased a large volume of their shares, which resulted in a loss of 20,000 pounds. To this end, he could not even bear to hear the name of the South Sea for a great many years. With a sigh, he said that "I can calculate the movements of all celestial bodies, but not the madness of man" How would you comment on Sir Newton's fate in the South Sea Bubble?
9. In 2008, the US subprime mortgage crisis quickly led to the collapse of the small Nordic country of Iceland. Prior to the crisis, the interest rate in Iceland had reached 10%, while the US federal funds rate from 2004 to September 2007 was 1–5.25%. This led to major overseas borrowing by Icelandic banks which they then lent to domestic

enterprises. After the outbreak of the US subprime mortgage crisis, and as foreign creditors demanded the redemption of loans originally granted to Iceland, and the operations of some Icelandic banks in Britain, Germany, and some other countries were frozen. Under the impact of the crisis, the Icelandic currency rapidly depreciated, falling from 1 dollar to 60 krónur in early 2008 to 1 dollar to 130 krónur in October 2008. Meanwhile, the Icelandic banking sector also rapidly fell into liquidity difficulties, the Icelandic stock market crashed, and the price index of Icelandic shares fell by 70% in a single trading day. Given the principles of financial fragility which we learned in this chapter, analyze how exactly the US subprime mortgage crisis would have spread to the Icelandic financial system.

10. As we learned in Chapter 12, the fundamental characteristics of futures trading include margin transactions and the marked to market system. Under a marked to market system, suppose that futures prices veer away from expectations, and as such, the futures exchange requires that traders pay additional margin. However, these traders have no other source of margin, but they are influential traders within the futures market. Analyze, in this case, the influence of this initial decline in the price of futures on the development of the entire market.

Chapter 24

Financial Regulation and Supervision

Learning Objectives

After studying this chapter, you will be able to:

- Understand the need for financial regulation
- Understand the capital adequacy management in the Basel Accord
- Understand the separate and mixed operations of the financial sector
- Clearly understand the primary components of capital market regulation
- Clearly understand the primary components of insurance market regulation
- Understand the standards for an effective financial regulatory system
- Clearly understand the evolutionary trend of the global financial regulatory system

Financial regulation is one of the primary measures for preventing financial crises and a guarantee for fair and equitable financial transactions. Each and every country across the world, even countries like America which are stout advocates for freedom, will subject their financial sector to stringent government regulations. Though the global wave of financial liberalization has done anything but ebb, financial regulation will never weaken or cease to exist. It is only that amidst the wave of financial liberalization, the regulatory methods and system continue to improve with the development of financial instruments and diversification of financial risks.

24.1 Why is There a Need for Financial Regulation?

When a government makes a series of regulations and authorizes corresponding authorities to carry out those regulations to regulate the behavior of financial entities, it is referred to as **financial regulation**. Throughout the world, finance is subject to some of the strictest government regulations. This is true even in America, a firm advocate of liberalization, let alone other countries.

Why is finance subject to such strict supervisions? Externalities and asymmetric information are the main reasons.

24.1.1 Externalities

Externalities are the difference between social cost or benefit and personal cost or earnings of offering a kind of product or service, namely the additive effects an economic entity has on other entities when producing or consuming. The effect can be positive or negative. This positive effect is known as an external economy, while the negative effect is known as an external diseconomy. For example, when someone plays music loudly at home, keeping their neighbors up through the night, then it causes a negative externality for the neighbors; if someone builds a road for himself, but it also is convenient for others, then it is a positive externality. "Where there is a railway, there is money" best describes the positive externality of building a railway which can carry residents from one place to another. Theoretically, people have motivations to get together to eliminate negative externalities. However, as there may be free riders, or the cost of negotiations may be too high, there may be some situations where two is company, three is a crowd. Therefore, the preferred method of removing externalities is through regulations.

In the field of finance, there are also free riders and externalities. For instance, there are free riders in the supervision of managers of public companies as we mentioned before. As a result, scattered shareholders will have no initiative to supervise managers. Negative externalities in the field of finance also appear in that the bankruptcy of one bank may cause other better performing banks to suffer, causing a run on banks, leading to insufficient liquidity among banks and even bankruptcies. In the capital market, a financial fraud case may cause investors to lose confidence in other companies with better finances, leading to a fall in the price of stocks and bonds. The financial scandals of such companies as WorldCom and Enron Corporation will further damage the stock market, leading to lower prices and greater losses. Positive externalities in financial industries are shown in that well-functioning finances will make the economy more stable and generate more benefits for people's lives. Financial regulation is necessary to eliminate negative externalities and generate more positive externalities.

24.1.2 Asymmetric Information

Market failure is, to a large extent, caused by asymmetric information. As pointed out before, asymmetric information means one party does not have the information the other party has, or does not have as much information as the other party does, which may thus put the party in an unfavorable position. Generally, in a transaction, the seller knows much more than the buyer about the goods; in the financial market, the borrower knows better the probability of a project being successful; in the labor market, employees know better about their abilities. Because of asymmetric information, there will be various risks in the market. If people get complete information and handle and analyze it in a rational and reasonable way, there will be no mistakes in their decision-making. For example, consumers will not consciously buy inferior products and creditors will not give loans to borrowers who have bad credit. In the case of perfect information, there will be an optimal allocation of resources. One of the basic assumptions of a perfectly competitive market structure is that all market players have perfect information.

However, perfect information is just an ideal assumption, and information, in reality, is imperfect. Because of asymmetric information, there will be moral hazards and adverse selection. Adverse selection occurs beforehand. For example, a consumer has bought an inferior product. To the consumer, this is an adverse selection beforehand. In financial fields, specifically, the potential risk of bad-performing loans comes from people who actively seek loans. Therefore, people who may cause undesired results to creditors are usually those who want the money most. For instance, speculators or cheaters want to get loans desperately, because they know they will probably not pay them back, or they just do not plan to pay at all. If there is adverse selection, credit resources cannot be allocated efficiently. In addition, once the loan is given, it might become a bad asset to the creditor, which will have a bad influence on the stability of the financial system.

Moral hazards happen after transactions. After creditors lend the money, they will be faced with the risk that debtors might take part in undesired activities. These activities may make it hard for debtors to pay back the loans, and the creditors may suffer a big loss. For instance, debtors get a loan, and because it's not their own money, they may not invest the money in those promised projects, but rather may invest it in some other projects with high risks, but high returns as well; or they may use the borrowed money, which they promised to use, for investments in daily expenditures or speculation (this is quite common among public companies in China. Many companies do not use the money they raise, as stated in the prospectus, after going public. Instead, the money is invested in some high risk projects. There are many cases in which public companies use funds to act as market makers together with some big institutions). Because moral hazards make it possible for debtors to default and thus, lower the expected return for creditors, creditors are less likely to give loans to enterprises. In short, moral hazards also have a negative effect on the financial system.

Asymmetric information and imperfect information also leads to unfair transactions, which are often reflected in stock markets. Investors who get inside information can earn enormous profits, or avoid potential losses. On the other hand, those who do not have inside information may lose the opportunity to make money, or suffer a big loss. Therefore, insider trading will easily cause unfair trade in stock market. In addition to insider trading, there may be price manipulations as well. Price manipulation means institutional investors take advantage of their capital strength to make the price of a financial product move towards the direction that is advantageous for them to make a large profit. Price manipulation is harmful to medium and small investors, and may cause chaos in price signaling, leading to irrational resource allocations.

In terms of the macroeconomy, asymmetric information will make financial risks more transmissible after exposure. Namely, partial disorder in the financial system may lead to chaos in more financial institutions and to a larger extent, spread and worsen the adverse effect of initial exposure, and even cause a systematic financial crisis. When a certain financial institution is in trouble, because of asymmetric information related depositors or investors do not have a clear picture of its real situation. To avoid unnecessary losses, they may immediately adopt a "withdrawal" strategy. There will be deposit runs on banks and underselling of assets in financial markets, causing greater liquidity problems and further declines in the prices of assets. This outbreak will cause serious damage to the macroeconomy, and may even lead to a long-term economic recession.

24.2 Bank Regulation

Financial regulation includes regulation or supervision over entry and exit, business operation, insider trading and price manipulation, and capital adequacy management. In terms of business entities in financial activities, it is divided into regulation on fund raisers, regulation on investors, and regulation on financial institutions.

24.2.1 Entry Regulation

Anyone who wants to run a financial intermediary, whether it be banking, insurance or securities operations, must get permission from the regulatory authority. Running a financial business is much harder than running a supermarket or a grocery store. To run a banking business, it is necessary to meet the requirements of commercial banking laws. There are many objectives for entry regulations, such as preventing disordered competition caused by too many people entering the market, and protecting saver-lenders from potential high-risk entrants. Of course, entry regulations vary from country to country.

24.2.2 Business Regulation and Separate and Mixed Operations

Even though an enterprise has obtained the permission to enter into financial operations, it cannot run the entire financial business. Laws and rules, based on particular historical conditions, usually specify the business scope of each kind of financial institution. For instance, in China, the regulatory authorities used to prohibit financial institutions from running derivative operations such as futures and options, and prohibit banks, securities and insurance companies from diversifying their operations into the other sectors. Furthermore, property insurance companies were not allowed to engage in life insurance at the same time.

An important aspect of business regulation is separate or mixed operations. **Separate operations** are the major part of business regulation for financial institutions. Separate operations refer to when commercial banks, whose main source of capital is deposits, cannot run securities investments, or underwrite and trade in private bonds and stocks; meanwhile, securities investment banks cannot engage in commercial banking such as taking deposits and issuing loans. The Chinese *Commercial Bank Law*, which clearly states that commercial banks shall not engage in securities, trusts and non-self-use estate investments, establishes a separate operational system for China's finance industry.

The first country to establish a separate operational system was the United States. The Great Depression of 1929 to 1933 was the watershed for American finance to shift from free development to overall regulations. In the late 19th century, American heavy industries, such as the rail and steel industries, developed rapidly, leading to a capital concentration and capital flow. The financial industry, especially the securities, continued to grow. On the eve of Wall Street Crash in October 1929, there were more than 20,000 banks in America. At that time, commercial banking and investment banking were mixed, and these banks invested short-term credit capital in risky projects like stock investments. Heavy investment in the stock market brought speculative securities transactions to an unprecedented high. The collapse of stock market prices caused by the Great Depression, however, led to widespread failures of commercial banks involved in stock transactions. The financial crisis caused people to lose confidence in the banking industry, and therefore, the American Congress passed the Glass–Steagall Act in 1933, which states that commercial banks and investment banks shall operate and be managed separately; commercial banks are not allowed to buy stock, loans mortgaged by securities shall not exceed half the value of the securities, and investment banks are not allowed to engage in commercial banking. The act made it clear that commercial banks and investment banks should operate separately, because: (1) the securities operations of commercial banks were the main factor behind the stock market collapse and the Great Depression; (2) the securities operations of commercial banks led to the collapse of the banking system; (3) commercial banks and their securities departments damaged the benefits of their depositors in terms of fund allocation; and (4) there were improper operations in the securities promotion activities of commercial banks.

However, since the 1950s, due to financial innovations, banks have come up with operations that circumvent banking laws. Various financial innovations created new intersections between commercial banking and investment banking, making the separate operations effectively defunct. In April 1999, America passed the Financial Modernization Act, abolishing the Glass–Steagall Act and allowing commercial banks, investment banks and insurance institutions to intersect and mix, thereby establishing the **mixed operational** system. Theoretically, by adopting mixed operations, commercial banks can take full advantage of their resources to realize economies of scale and economies of scope, offering all-around services to their clients.

Mixed operations have become a global trend. However, China still implements a separate operational system, and yet, separate operations are being challenged with the rise of financial holding companies like CITIC Holding and China Everbright Group. In fact, the Chinese government has supported the development of mixed operations: commercial banks are allowed to set up fund management companies, and these banks have monopolized the underwriting of short-term corporate bonds and can sell insurance and funds of other organizations and their own wealth management products.

24.2.3 The Regulation of Bank Capital Adequacy

Equity capital is a powerful tool to fend against moral hazards and opportunistic behavior. Adequate capital is of great importance to ease the conflicts between principals and agents, to reduce the agency costs of financial institutions, and to improve the stability of finances. In addition, the capital of financial institutions can neutralize accidental losses and eliminate instability; it is a temporary cushion for accidental losses. This is because, with all else equal, the greater the initial capital buffer, the less likely that financial institutions will default. Therefore, capital adequacy regulation is a tool for controlling the probability of whether or not a financial institution will go bankrupt.

There is an international standard for regulating bank capital adequacy. In July 1988, the Basel Committee on Banking Supervision drew up *the Agreement on Unifying International Banks' Capital Measurement and Capital Standards*, in short the Basel Accord, which harmonizes the capital adequacy standards of the international banking industry. With the development of international finance, various financial risks appeared. As such, the BCBS has revised the agreement twice. In 2004, it passed the new agreements, the Basel II, which introduced three pillars of banking regulation. They are:

- Minimum Capital Requirement
- Supervisory Review
- Market Discipline

(a) *Minimum Capital Requirements*

Inheriting the regulatory thinking behind the capital adequacy ratio, the capital requirement is the most important pillar. Of course, the new agreement has placed new demands on capital requirements. (1) The first demand is to broaden the scope of risks and emphasize comprehensive risk management. **Comprehensive risk management** refers to the fact that, in addition to credit risk and market risk, it is necessary to take operational risks into consideration. The new accord further sensitizes the credit loss risks capital framework: more capital is required to cope with higher-risk borrowers, while less capital is needed to cope with lower-risk borrowers; attention must be paid to markets risks, including interest rates risk, stock risk, exchange rate risks, commodity risks, and option price risks; attention must also be paid to operational risks, namely, the risk of losses caused by improper or failed internal procedures, staff and systems, or external accidents (such as natural disasters). (2) Methods for calculating risks have been improved, and two ways of risk assessment, the standard approach and internal rating-based approach, have been established. The standard approach calls for external rating institutions to determine the weights of capital risks and calculate the minimum capital requirement; the internal rating-based approach uses the internal rating of banks to determine capital requirements. (3) The scope of capital restrictions was broadened. Corresponding capital restriction approaches were put forward to deal with innovations like the form of financial organization and transaction tools. For example, if a single investment of banks in a non-financial institution exceeds 15% of a bank's total capital, or if the overall investment exceeds the capital of that bank, a corresponding amount should be deducted from the bank's capital; for securitized assets and financial holding companies whose main business is commercial banking, there are new capital requirements, requiring banks to hold adequate minimum capital for various assets.

(b) *Supervisory Review*

The Basel II places a great deal of importance on the supervision of various kinds of internal risks of banks and reinforces the responsibilities of financial regulatory authorities. Regulatory authorities are expected to take the following responsibilities: (1) Fully supervise the adequacy of banking capital. When the capital size is less than the required amount, there should be necessary interference. (2) Foster an internal credit assessment system and encourage banks to adopt risk measurement methods based on an internal credit rating system; perform timely checks on the internal assessment procedures and capital strategies of banks to match the asset level with the risk level. (3) Accelerate the institutionalization process in which commercial banks shall submit complete institutional arrangements on asset classifications and internal risk assessments. As for regulatory methods, the new accord still emphasizes the combination of on-site inspections and off-site reviews.

(c) *Market Discipline*

The Accord emphasizes the role of market in regulating banks, believing market discipline can help banks allocate resources rationally and efficiently and control operational risks. For market discipline to work, it requires that banks make all the necessary public disclosures so that market participants can fully understand banking operations and the methods of risk control and can better distinguish the different banks. It also requires that regulatory authorities supervise the information disclosure itself and assess the bank information disclosure system.

As the US subprime mortgage crisis revealed the many disadvantages of the old regulatory system, the Basel Committee revised the regulatory rules on banking system again, which resulted in the Basel III. As a complement to the Basel II, it is expected to build a more proactive and integrated prudential regulatory system and to enhance the abilities of financial institutions to defend against risks. Regulations on banking capital have been enriched and intensified.

First of all, the Basel III implements stricter capital requirements. To improve its loss absorption capacity, regulatory capital is divided into core tier-1 capital, additional tier-1 capital and tier-2 capital. Core tier-1 capital includes paid-in capital or common stock, capital reserves, surplus reserves, general risk reserves and undistributed earnings. Additional tier-1 capital includes other tier-1 capital instruments and their premiums. Tier-2 capital includes tier-2 capital instruments and their premiums and also excess loan loss reserves, which is the amount of the bank's actual loan loss reserves in excess of expected loss. The specific capital adequacy requirements are no less than 5%, 6% and 8% for core tier-1 capital, additional tier-1 capital and tier-2 capital, respectively; the ratio of common equity that banks hold to risk weighted assets shall be no less than 4.5%.

Secondly, Basel III introduced the framework for **counter-cyclical capital regulation** which requires commercial banks to set aside a mandatory capital conservation buffer (capital reserve) and counter-cyclical capital buffer. The ratio of the mandatory capital conservation buffer to risk weighted assets shall be 2.5%. During periods of high credit growth, regulatory authorities can ask for 0–2.5% more capital, namely, the counter-cyclical capital buffer, which is also included in core tier-1 capital.

Finally, Basel III increased the capital surcharge requirement of systemically important banks. **Systemically important banks** refer to banks which are very big and have wide connections with other banks and financial institutions. The healthiness and stability of systemically important banks has a great influence on the stability of a nation or even the global finance. If systemically important banks get into trouble, there will be disasters throughout the entire financial system and macroeconomy. Therefore, after the subprime mortgage crisis, regulations were strengthened for systemically important banks. These banks face a capital surcharge of 1–2.5%. Under particular circumstances, the ratio can even be as high as 3.5%.

24.2.4 Liquidity and Risk Concentration Regulation

Adequate liquidity is an important indicator to see whether banking institutions are healthy. Insufficient liquidity may cause banks to lose their ability to pay, leading to a crisis of confidence among depositors. Due to the great importance of liquidity for financial institutions, Basel III emphasizes the importance of liquidity risk management for banks. Two important indicators were introduced: the liquidity coverage ratio and the net stable funding ratio. The **liquidity coverage ratio** is the ratio of high quality liquid assets to the net cash outflow for the next 30 days. The liquidity coverage ratio shall be more than 100%, which means banks shall have enough high quality liquid assets to cover the net cash outflow for 30 days. The **net stable funding ratio** is the ratio of stable capital that banks have access to and the amount of stable capital that banks need for its operations. It measures how well the available stable funding of banks can support their on-balance-sheet and off-balance-sheet asset operations. The ratio shall be no less than 100% too. The setting of minimum regulatory standards such as this ratio can help banks support their business with steady capital, and can reduce the risk of maturity mismatch between assets and liabilities. In China, in addition to the indicators of the Basel Accord, there is also another liquidity regulatory standard, the loan-to-deposit ratio, for commercial banks. The loans commercial banks issue shall be no more than 75% of their deposit balance. This ratio requirement forces commercial banks to have secondary reserves like government bonds, so that they can get sufficient liquidity to satisfy the needs of depositors when many depositors withdraw their money. To ensure the liquidity of banks, the ratio of current assets balance to current liabilities balance of commercial banks shall be no less than 25%.

To avoid over-concentration of banking risks which may cause an increase in liquidity risks, banks are typically subject to loan concentration regulation. **Loan concentration** means the ratio of the loan given to an enterprise to the bank's total outstanding loans. The higher the loan concentration, the higher the banking loan risk, and the more damage an enterprise will cause to the bank if the enterprise fails to pay back the loan. Conversely, if loan concentration is low, and loans are scattered among many enterprises, then the credit risk of a single enterprise will not cause much damage to commercial banks. This is consistent with the principle of diversification.

In case commercial banks lose the ability to pay back loans and absorb losses, commercial banks are required to set aside loan loss reserves. A **loan loss reserve** is the money that commercial banks withhold from the profits to make up for possible loan losses. Basel III intensifies regulations on loan loss reserves, and sets up regulatory standards for loan provision ratios and provision coverage ratios. It requires financial institutions to have a minimum provision ratio of 2.5%, and a minimum provision coverage ratio of 150%. Meanwhile, a dynamic adjustment system for the loan loss reserve has also been established. Regulatory authorities will, depending on economic developments and the quality and profit of banking loans, adjust the loan loss reserve requirement from time to time: increasing it moderately when the economy is doing well, and decreasing it on the basis of loan write-off when the economy is turning for the worse; and making appropriate adjustments depending on the loan quality and profitability of individual banks.

24.2.5 Inspections

Regular banking inspections are a good way to check whether a bank meets capital requirements and restrictions on capital holdings and whether it is capable of suppressing moral hazards. The inspection will include a **CAMEL rating**. The CAMEL rating includes: capital adequacy, asset quality, management, earning and liquidity. Regulators can regulate based on such information. If the CAMEL rating of a bank is low, regulators can shut it down because the bank might engage in high-risk investments. Therefore, some moral hazards can be eliminated as well as the problems caused by adverse selection. This is because, if there are few opportunities for risky activities, entrepreneurs who like to take risks would not enter the banking industry.

Inspections on banks can be divided into on-site inspections and off-site reviews. In order to inspect commercial banks on a daily basis, regulatory authorities require banks to hand in financial operation reports on a regular basis, including balance sheet, income statement, and cash flow statement. These are typical examples of **off-site reviews** which are convenient for regulatory authorities to inspect the financial health of commercial banks. Meanwhile, by collecting financial reports on commercial banks, the central bank can get the necessary information to formulate and implement monetary policies.

In case commercial banks hand in fake financial reports, regulatory authorities would also carry out on-site inspections. **On-site inspections** refer to when regulators do not inform the inspected banks beforehand, and instead check the related financial documents and balance sheets themselves to prevent commercial banks from engaging in high-risk investments. Regulatory authorities will punish banks if any errors are found.

24.3 Capital Market Regulation

Capital market regulation covers the following aspects: issuance examinations, information disclosures, insider trading, and price manipulation.

24.3.1 Issuance Examinations

Issuance examinations are aimed at preventing adverse selection. New issues, allotments of shares and further issues will all be examined by the China Securities Regulatory Committee. Generally, not all companies can issue stocks and bonds. Potential public companies shall go through a pre-listing tutorship period before issuing a stock. Only those that have completed the tutorship can issue stocks approved by the China Securities Regulatory Committee.

For issuance examinations, China used to adopt an approval system, although, in 2000, China implemented an authorization system. Under the quota-based approval system, the government decided the amount of stock to be issued and then allocated the total amount among regions and industries. Only companies that were allocated a quota could issue stock. Meanwhile, approval from the China Securities Regulatory Commission was required before a potential listed company could issue stock. In fact, quota controls on the capital market were characteristic of the planned economy in the past.

The approval system and quota controls failed to guarantee the efficiency of capital allocation among industries and regions. As stocks did not have a maturity restriction such as bonds, they seemed to be "free capital" for Chinese enterprises. Therefore, the quota competition was always very fierce. Due to the limited quota, rent-seeking behaviors prevailed, and bribery and bribe-taking became a serious issue. In addition, in order to obtain capital, potential public companies began to present fake financial reports, which posed great danger for China's capital market.

To improve the efficiency of stock issuances, China adopted the authorization system in 2000. Under this system, the government does not set limits on the total amount of stock to be issued every year. Companies can go public only if they meet the requirements.

24.3.2 Information Disclosures

To avoid moral hazards and adverse selection caused by asymmetric information, the government usually requires borrower–spenders to disclose necessary information. Nowadays, you can see notices of public companies in media such as the *China Securities Journal*, the *Shanghai Securities News* and the *Securities Times* every single day. At the beginning of the year and the middle of the year, all public companies publish their financial reports annually or semi-annually. This is the responsibility for information disclosure as required by the regulatory authority.

Petty points out the importance of information disclosure in a humorous way in *A Treatise of Taxes and Contributions*:

> *Credit everywhere, but chiefly in London, being becoming a mere conceit, that a man is responsible or not, without any certain knowledge of his wealth or true estate . . . I should here enlarge upon a paradox, to prove that if every man's estate could be always read in his forehead, our trade would much be advanced thereby, although the poorer ambitious man be commonly the more industrious.*

24.3.3 Insider Trading and Price Manipulation

The financial regulation over insider trading and price manipulation is primarily targeting the capital market and futures market. **Insider trading** refers to getting excess profit through trading in related financial products based on inside information. For example, a public company may reorganize its assets, which then leads to a significant increase in the cash flow of the company. However, the reorganization was not announced to the public, and the managers of the company may have told their relatives and friends about the news, and they subsequently bought large amounts of the company's stock. This is insider trading. **Insider information** refers to unpublished information that might have a great influence on the prices of financial products like stock, bonds, funds, and futures, and it may include information on asset reorganization of a public company, dividend distribution policies, and adjustments to national policies that might affect the financial market. People with knowledge of inside information are insiders, including managers of companies, policy makers, lawyers, accountants involved in asset reorganization, and so on. Prohibitions on insider trading are aimed at ensuring that every investor can take part in financial activities fairly and prevents investors from obtaining improper benefits via inside information. Insider trading is a serious offence in western countries. In the United States, for example, insider trading constitutes a criminal offence and traders will be severely punished.

Price manipulation refers to when investors take advantage of their capital strength to sell or purchase a certain financial product in a large amount so that the price moves towards the direction that is good for them to make a large profit. In China, "market making" in the stock market is a typical form of price manipulation, and classic examples of price manipulation involve Yi'an Tech and China Tech Venture. Yi'an Tech was a public company in Shenzhen, and at the end of 1998, its stock price was less than 5 yuan. However, at the beginning of 2000, the price was 126 yuan. In less than two years, it increased by more than 25 times. However, the sharp rise was not the result of the company's great performance, but was rather the result of joint price manipulation by four investment companies in Guangdong.

Price manipulation is harmful to medium and small investors and can cause an unfair redistribution of social wealth. Moreover, it will disturb the order of financial markets and make it hard for financial markets to function normally. Therefore, to guarantee fair and just transactions, most governments will levy serious punishments on price manipulators.

24.3.4 The Regulation of Financial Market Institutions

Apart from the approval procedures and restrictions on scope of business, regulations on financial market institutions focus more on the control of liquidity and risks. Under the separate operational system, securities companies are not allowed to engage in commercial banking and insurance. For the sake of clients, securities companies shall not divert client margins and securities for other uses and shall not mix agency operations with their proprietary business. To ensure fairness, securities companies shall not take advantage of their status to restrict the operation of a certain client to get rid of competitors. Just like commercial banks, securities companies are regulated on capital and the asset–liability ratio to prevent operational risks.

24.4 The Regulation of Insurance

Regulations of the insurance industry refer to when national authorities, as required by related laws and administrative rules, regulate and supervise insurance companies, insurance agency institutions and their branches registered within the territories of the country. Regulations of insurance focus on fairness and the control of risks, including regulations of insurance clauses and premium, regulations on insurance funding usage, and regulations on insurance protection funds.

24.4.1 The Regulation of Insurance Clauses and Premium

Insurance clauses define the rights and responsibilities of both parties and are an important part of an insurance contract, including the insurance coverage, the insurance period, the exemption from liabilities, compensation, and the methods for settling disputes. As insurance clauses are very technical and professional, ordinary people can hardly understand them. For the sake of the insurants and to ensure the fairness and justice of insurance clauses, in China, clauses of major types of insurance shall be formulated by the China Insurance Regulatory Commission, and clauses of other types of insurance shall be reported to the China Insurance Regulatory Commission. The Commission has the right to define the major types of insurance, which now include business property insurance and motor vehicle insurance, and the major clauses.

24.4.2 The Regulation of Insurance Funding Usage

Insurance funding refers to an insurance company's capital funds, insurance funds, operating funds, various reserves, provident funds, welfare funds, and unappropriated surplus funds. The use of such funds is subject to strict limitations by regulatory authorities, and currently, insurance funds can only be used for bank deposits, the purchase and sale of government bonds, and financial bonds. In addition, they can also be used for investing in the interbank lending market or for investing in funds. However, insurance funds cannot be used to set up securities institutions, for purchasing stock, or for investing in enterprises. This is determined by the separate operations system.

24.4.3 The Regulation of Insurance Protection Funds

Insurance companies are enterprises which specialize in risk, and as such, they accumulate a great deal of risk. Given this fact, insurance companies run the risk of falling into an insolvency crisis. In order to safeguard the interests of the insured, support an insurance company's stable operations, and ensure that the company has a certain degree of debt-serving capacity, an insurance company should set aside a certain amount of insurance protection funds to reduce the losses incurred to those insured in the event of an operating crisis and the influence thereof on society and people's lives. This is no different from requiring commercial banks to hold a deposit reserve and a loan loss reserve.

24.5 Financial Regulatory System: Historic and Future Developments

24.5.1 The Standards of an Effective Financial Regulatory System

A rational, effective financial regulatory system should be forward-looking, efficient, and flexible.

(a) *Forward-looking*

A regulatory system that is forward-looking can estimate the future changes to the form of finances and the structure of transactions, and within such a period of change, the system can maintain efficient regulations, rather than constantly changing policies or regulatory arrangements. Constant changes to regulatory policies lack continuity and stability which will only lead to an increase in the risks within the financial system and is not conducive to stable operations, because policy risks are the most important type of systemic risk within a financial market. Furthermore, this type of risk cannot rationally be predicted. Similarly, there exists a large conversion cost for changing the regulatory arrangements, and such changes will alter the original rules of financial operations and the expectations from the financial market, thereby increasing risks to the financial system. Therefore, regulatory arrangements should be stable. For this purpose, both regulatory policies and structures need to fully consider possible future changes and adaptation of the regulatory system.

(b) *Effective*

The institutional arrangements for financial regulation should allow regulators to achieve their regulatory goals at the lowest possible cost. This also means that the regulatory structure arrangement should not only consider technical feasibility but also consider economic feasibility. For example, under mixed operations, since it is quite difficult and costly for external regulatory authorities to gather information, regulators may consider the possibility of improving the self-discipline mechanism of financial institutions. Another example is also under mixed operations, in that, in order to eliminate the gradually increasing costs that come from potential conflicts of interest, and from the perspective of the cost–benefit effect, as long as the economies of scale and scope of financial institutions and the overall competitiveness of the financial system can significantly increase, it is possible to tolerate a certain degree of the conflict of interest which may do some harm to consumer welfare.

(c) *Flexible*

Financial regulation must be flexible to fully take into account the negative incentives for effective supervision, the competition between different regulatory agencies and regimes from one country to another, the regulatory arbitrage factors, and the ability of the financial regulatory system to adapt to a changing environment.

A proper regulatory system needs to be on guard against lax regulations and excessive tolerance of incompliant financial institutions, and at the same time avoid the side effects associated with stringent and costly controls. For example, as an important part of the United States Federal Insurance Corporation Improvement Act in 1991, the "prompt correction action" provisions divide the process of capitalization into five different levels, and the lower the level of capitalization, the more stringent the controls. This measure has been both incredibly flexible and has saved an enormous amount of regulatory costs.

24.5.2 Separate and Unified Regulation

Separate regulation is aimed at regulating different financial services, for instance, securities regulatory commissions are the regulatory agencies for the securities sector, while insurance regulatory commissions exercise authority over insurance, and banking regulatory commissions exercise authority over commercial banking. **Unified regulation**, on the contrary, subjects all financial operations to the supervision of the same regulatory body.

On the international scale, the financial regulatory system has shifted from unified regulation to separate regulation and then back to unified regulation. In the early development of finances, because the level of development was relatively low, unified regulation prevailed in the world. After the great crisis in the 1930s, the United States took the lead and implemented separate operations, which was an important means for preventing financial risks at that time. Later on, other countries also followed suit. In this way, in order to adapt to the demands of specialization and industry management, some countries implemented separate regulatory regimes accordingly.

After the 1980s, in order to adapt to demands of financial innovations and financial development, some countries focused on unified regulatory standards to reduce the number of overlapping agencies, and as such, the diversified financial regulatory system began to develop towards unification. In Norway, Denmark, Sweden, and other such countries, there was a growing need for a unified system, due to financial innovations and development, particularly the emergence of financial holding groups. As such, these countries successively merged the various financial regulatory bodies into a unified agency which is responsible for banking, securities and insurance regulation. In 1997, the United Kingdom separated the financial regulation role from the Bank of England, and established the Financial Services Authority (FSA) to implement unified financial regulation. Even though various countries began to pay more attention to macro-prudential regulation after the global financial crisis of 2008, this, if anything, only strengthened the growing trend for unified financial regulation. In the following section, we will introduce the framework for macro-prudential regulation which also reflects the new trend for unified regulation.

The transition from separate to unified regulation was primarily motivated by the following reasons: First, the mixing of operations between banking, securities and insurance has weakened the basis for separate regulation, especially with the endless stream of financial innovations which have further blurred the lines between the operations of various financial institutions. Secondly, the business dealings between banking, securities, and insurance are becoming increasingly close, which increases the difficulty of separate regulation. Third, the existence of diversified operations within a holdings company has made separate regulation increasingly inefficient. Finally, financial innovations have resulted in both overlapping and insufficient regulation. For example, under a separate regulatory system, approval of different regulators is required for different financial operations. When the operations of various financial institutions increasingly intersect, the launch of new operations will typically need to go through multiple departments and take a long time before they can be approved. Additionally, the regulation of some new financial services is very much a gray area, which may either result in double regulation or the absence of regulation.

24.5.3 Institutional and Functional Regulation

Corresponding to separate and unified regulation is institutional and functional regulation. **Institutional regulation**, under separate operations, refers to regulation enforced by different authorities for different financial institutions, in that an insurance regulatory commission will supervise insurance institutions, while a securities regulatory commission will supervise securities institutions, and so on. Currently, China implements such an institutional regulatory system (see Figure 24.1).

Institutional regulation is adapted to the separate operations of banking, securities and insurance. Under the separate operations regime, banking, securities, and

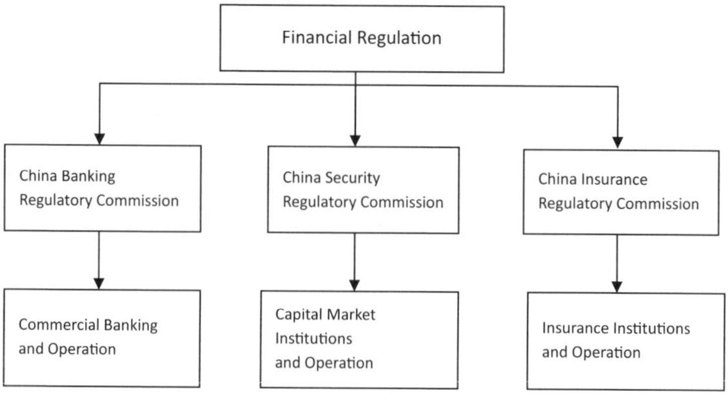

Fig. 24.1 Chinese Institutional Financial Regulatory System

insurance operations cannot intersect, and it is thus feasible for different regulatory bodies to supervise the corresponding financial institutions. However, nowadays, a shift from separate operations to mixed operations has become a global trend, and the distinction between banking, securities, and insurance operations is becoming increasingly blurred. The implementation of institutional regulation may easily create a regulatory gray area. For instance, if a financial institution engages in both commercial banking and securities and insurance at the same time, should the banking regulatory commission, the securities regulatory commission or rather the insurance regulatory commission take precedence? Take the economic activities within the shadow banking system as another example. In this case, it is not just the traditional banking institutions who will participate in a wide range of reforms, a wide variety of other non-banking financial institutions will also create and participate in shadow banking. While providing credit, maturity and liquidity transformation, they also bring about systematic financial risks. Since financial institutions from different sectors extensively engage in shadow banking under an institutional regulatory system, the supervision of shadow banking would also be scattered, easily resulting in a regulatory gray area.

With separate regulation shifting to unified regulation, institutional regulation has also been replaced by functional regulation. **Functional regulation** refers to the situation in which different operations of a financial institution are regulated by specialized management professionals and procedures within a unified regulatory institution. Functional regulation is the new trend for financial regulatory systems under an environment of mixed operations. Figure 24.2 depicts financial regulation under a functional regulatory system. Under a functional regulatory system, the commercial banking of a financial institution is subject to the supervision of a banking regulatory institution, while its securities operations are subject to the supervision of a securities regulatory institution. Similarly, its insurance

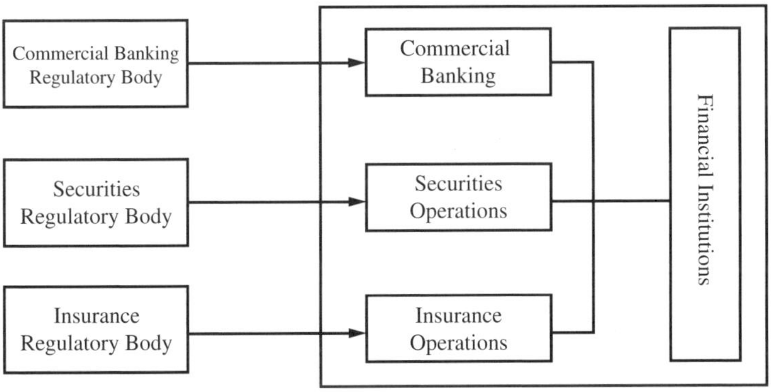

Fig. 24.2 Diagram of Functional Regulation under a Mixed Operational Environment

operations would also be subject to the supervision of an insurance regulatory institution.

Functional regulation has the following characteristics: First, legal authorities are assigned to various regulatory agencies based on the economic functions that they are most familiar with. Second, assigning legal authorities based on economic functions is consistent with the principles of financial regulation. Securities regulations place particular emphasis on openness and transparency; bank regulations focus on the public confidence in banks, and as such, confidentiality is a primary concern of bank regulators. Third, a function-oriented financial regulatory system can greatly reduce the conflicts, overlaps, and gray areas between regulatory functions. However, the biggest drawback to functional regulation is that it will subject a single financial institution to the supervision of multiple regulatory agencies which will virtually increase the cost of financial regulation.

24.5.4 Emphasis on Both Macro-Prudential Regulation and Micro-Prudential Regulation

One of the new trends in financial regulation is that of shifting from purely focusing on the micro-prudential regulation of individual risks of financial institutions to a dual focus on both micro-prudential and macro-prudential regulation. Micro-prudential regulation has two key weaknesses. **Micro-prudential regulation** suppresses the heterogeneous risks of individual financial institutions, with the goal of protecting the interests of depositors or investors, and sets regulatory controls according to the risks of each financial institution. It is generally believed that the health and overall strength of the entire financial system depends on individual institutions, and as long as each one is a well-run financial institution with sound operations, they will be able to promote the stability of the entire financial system. However, the drawback to micro-prudential regulation is that an emphasis on the soundness of individual institutions may lead to over-protection, which may weaken market discipline, and may not ultimately be able to guarantee the safety of these institutions. Another drawback is that this kind of supervision cannot cope with the common risks that financial institutions and financial markets are exposed to, and it is unable to detect rising systemic risks in a timely manner or take appropriate remedial measures. When too much regulatory attention is concentrated on the sound operation of individual financial institutions, the stability of the entire financial system is likely to be ignored.

In the 1970s, the Bank for International Settlements (BIS) recognized the drawbacks of micro-prudential regulation. After the 2008 subprime mortgage crisis, macro-prudential regulation became a very urgent priority on the agenda of financial regulatory reforms, and in different countries and in different forms, a new system of financial regulation was formed, with a dual focus on both micro- and macro-prudential regulation. This so-called macro-prudential regulation refers to prudential control mechanisms set in place based on the systemic probability to curb systemic risks within the financial system and avoid the tremendous impact on the macroeconomy caused by financial instability.

When macro-prudential regulation was put into practice, it looked quite different in different countries. As early as June 2009, the EU decided on the establishment of a financial regulatory system with both macro- and micro-prudential regulation. In 2011, the EU officially launched the European system of financial supervision, which includes the European Systemic Risk Board (ESRB), the European Banking Authority (EBA), the European Securities and Markets Authority (ESMA), and the European Insurance and Occupational Pensions Authority (EIOPA). The ESRB is the core of the system and is responsible for monitoring the EU financial system at the macro level. The other three bodies monitor at a micro level the operations of banking, securities and insurance, respectively. The main duty of the European Systemic Risk Board (ESRB) is to monitor risk, assess risk, warn others about risk, and present policy recommendations. Meanwhile, it also identifies systemic risks and lists them in order. When there are clues as to a significant systemic risk, the ESRB makes early warnings.

With the Dodd–Frank Act, the United States established the Financial Stability Oversight Council (FSOC) in 2010. This council is a cross-sectoral systemic risk management agency, led by the Treasury and joined by the Federal Reserve and other major federal regulatory agencies. The FSOC's main responsibility is to prevent and identify systemic financial risks and maintain financial stability. Additionally, it gives the Federal Reserve the power to monitor systemic risks, and establishes the core position of the Federal Reserve within the American systemic risk management and financial regulatory framework. In order to resolve the "too big to fail" dilemma, the new act allows for the splitting of these large financial institutions in trouble, provides for the new mechanisms for bankruptcy liquidation, sets down adequate risk provisions requirements for large financial institutions, and prohibits the use of taxpayer money for bailout funds. At the same time, the **Volcker Rule** limits the proprietary trading and high-risk derivatives trading of banks, requiring the bank investment in hedge funds and private equity to be no greater than 3% of their tier-1 capital. It also requires that the riskiest derivatives trading operations of a financial institution be split into its subsidiary companies, although it may continue to operate in interest rate swaps, foreign exchange swaps, and gold and silver swaps.

Summary

Financial regulation is the development of a set of rules by the government and the authorization for enforcing these rules by corresponding institutions to regulate the activities of all parties involved in the economic activity. Throughout the world, finance is always subject to the most stringent of government regulations.

Financial regulation is primarily based on the following two reasons: externalities and asymmetric information. The purpose of financial regulation is to ensure the fairness, impartiality and efficiency of financial transactions, reduce financial risks, and prevent financial crises.

The specific content of financial regulation will differ from one financial sector to another. However, all financial sectors are subject to entry regulation, and the regulation of liquidity and risk controls. As for commercial banking, financial regulation primarily includes entry regulation, separate operational regulation, liquidity regulation, risk controls, and capital adequacy regulation. In terms of banking regulation, nowadays, there is an international unified regulatory standard, namely, the Basel Accord. Capital market regulation primarily includes issuance examinations, insider trading and price manipulation, information disclosures, and the regulation of capital market intermediary institutions. Insurance regulation primarily targets insurance clauses, insurance premium, the use of insurance funding, and insurance protection funds.

The Basel Accord determined the unified standard for international bank regulation and stipulated that the capital adequacy ratio of commercial banks cannot be lower than 8%. It also divided commercial bank capital into core capital and supplementary capital, of which core capital cannot be less than 4% of total assets. Also, in the calculation of assets, the risk-weighted approach should be used in order to facilitate the control of commercial bank risks.

An effective financial regulatory system and structure should be forward-looking, flexible, and effective. The main financial regulatory systems are in the form of separate regulation and unified regulation, and institutional and functional regulation. As the global financial industry transitions from separate to mixed operations, accordingly, financial regulatory systems are also transitioning from separate, institutional regulation to unified and functional regulation.

Key Terms

Financial Regulation; Institutional Regulation; Functional Regulation; Insider Information; Insider Trading; Price Manipulation; Basel Accord; Separate Operations; Mixed Operations; CAMEL Rating; Macro-prudential Regulation; Volker Rule; Liquidity Coverage Ratio; Net Stable Funding Ratio

Critical Thinking Questions

1. Why is there a need for financial regulation?
2. What are the primary components of banking regulation?
3. What sort of influence does capital adequacy regulation have on commercial banks?
4. What are the primary components of capital market regulation?

5. What are the primary components of insurance market regulation?
6. What are separate and mixed operations? Discuss the future developments in store for such operations.
7. What are separate regulation and unified regulation? What are their strengths and weaknesses?
8. What are institutional regulation and functional regulation? What are their strengths and weaknesses?
9. Briefly describe the important content of the Basel Accord on capital adequacy regulation as well as the three pillars of the New Basel Capital Accord.
10. Briefly describe macro-prudential regulation.
11. Currently, China implements separate and institutional regulation. If financial holding companies such as China CITIC and China Everbright experience rapid development, how would this impact the current Chinese regulatory system?

Glossary

Acceptance A promise to effect payment.

Accommodation paper Also known as commercial paper, it is a note specially issued for raising capital rather than based on a true commodity transaction.

Adverse selection Due to information asymmetry, individuals or financial institutions lend their surplus capital to higher risk borrowers whom the lenders would have been reluctant to deal with.

Aggregate demand curve A curve that depicts the relationship between different general price levels and aggregate demand.

Aggregate supply curve A curve that depicts the relationship between different general price levels and aggregate supply.

American auction A bidding system in which the bidder with the highest offer wins the bid and the winning bid is its bid price.

American option An option that allows its buyer to exercise on the maturity date or any time prior to the maturity date.

Announcement effect The central bank adjusts rediscount rate to signal possible monetary policy in the future and thereby affect the expectations of commercial banks and the general public.

Annuity A series of equal cash flows or payments.

Asset business The process of capital use of commercial banks.

Asset competition effect When the effective yield of money increases to a certain level, people will hold more money while giving up investment in physical capital.

Asset substitution Domestic residents hold foreign currency-denominated financial assets issued by other countries.

Balance of payments Systematic record of the economic transactions carried out between residents of one country and those of another country within a certain period of time.

Balance of payments deficit Income under the current account and capital and financial account of a country in economic activities with other countries is lower than expenditure under these accounts.

Balance of payments statement A statement reflecting the economic transactions between residents of one country and those of other countries within a certain period.

Balance of payments surplus Income under the current account and capital and financial account of a country in economic activities with other countries is greater than expenditure under these accounts.

Balance of trade The balance between the imports and exports of goods and service.

Balanced fund A fund that diversifies investments in stocks and bonds, with a view to achieving a balance between capital growth and fixed income.

Bank crisis The people who have lost confidence in banks for some reasons withdraw their deposits, leading to the serious liquidity squeeze of banking sector and failure of many banks.

Banker's acceptance draft A note drawn by the payee or payer and honored by the payer's depository bank according to the payer's authorization.

Banking panic Depositors who have lost confidence in banks try to convert their deposits into cash altogether, resulting in serious liquidity squeeze and failure of many banks.

Base currencyBase money Also known as high powered money, it can create via the banking system deposits that are multiple times the original amount under the Fractional Reserve System. It includes cash in circulation and banking reserves.

Basic exchange rate The exchange rate between domestic currency and basic currency.

Benchmark bond Treasury bills with a particularly short term and with no credit risk.

Bill A credit instrument that reflects the debtor–creditor relationship, its transfer and repayment in commodity circulation.

Bill discount A bill holder, who is in need of funds, transfers an unmatured bill to a bank, and the bank would then pay the remaining sum to the bill holder after deducting the interest.

Bill discount market The market available for bill transactions between bill holders and discounting banks.

Bimetallic standard A monetary system that defines both gold and silver as standard money.

Blow-up The change in futures prices is opposite to the original expectation of the trader, and after the marked to market settlement, the trader's margin account has a negative equity.

Bond fund A fund which invests the proceeds raised through the issuance of fund units into corporate bonds or government bonds.

Bond A security that is issued by the user of capital to investors for the purpose of capital raising and for which principal and interest will be repaid within a specified period according to certain conditions.

Borrowed reserves The reserves that a commercial bank creates by borrowing from the central bank or the interbank lending market.

Buying rate The exchange rate used by banks in purchase of foreign exchange.

Call option Also known as a call, it is the right to buy, with a certain amount of option money, an option to purchase a product at a specific price within specified period of time in future, when the option buyer expects that the product's price will go up.

Cambridge Equation Money demand equals a certain proportion of nominal income and is expressed in a formula as following: $M_d = K \cdot P \cdot T$.

CAMEL rating It includes capital adequacy, asset quality, management status, earnings, and liquidity.

Capital adequacy Ratio of capital to assets.

Capital flight Also known as capital refuge, it is an abnormal capital outflow for the purpose of avoiding risks or control of authorities.

Capital market The financial market in which financial instruments have a maturity of one year or more, with the major function to translate savings to investment and promote the formation of material capital.

Capital market crisis The financial phenomenon that the people, who have lost confidence in the capital market, rush to sell out their stocks or bonds, resulting in a sharp decline in the market prices of stocks or bonds.

Central bank bill A bond issued by the People's Bank of China for withdrawing base currencybase money.

Central bank independence The degree to which a central bank is not affected by domestic interest groups when exercising its functions.

Cheap credit A low-interest loan that cannot reflect the market supply and demand condition and the risk profile of fund users.

Check An instrument issued by a drawer, entrusting a bank or any other financial institution qualified for check deposit business to unconditionally pay a specified amount of money to the payee or bearer at sight.

Closed-end fund Securities investment funds which cannot be expanded or downsized during the duration.

Closed-end repo During the effective period of a repo agreement, the bonds held by the bond transferee shall be frozen and shall not be disposed of without authorization.

Commercial acceptance draft A note issued by the payee or payer and honored by the payer enterprise.

Commercial banks Also known as deposit money banks, they are financial enterprises that primarily provide such services as taking deposits, providing loans, conducting transfers and settling accounts for the purpose of profit.

Commercial credit The credit provided by way of deferred payment when enterprises sell goods.

Compensating balance A proportion of a loan that a borrower is required to hold on deposit at the lending bank.

Compound interest Also called "interest on interest", it means that the interest earned on principal in the first interest period will be still calculated in the second period.

Conflict between internal and external equilibrium The conflict between maintaining international payments equilibrium and reducing domestic unemployment or boosting economic growth rate.

Convertible bond The bond which is converted into the ordinary shares of a company in a certain period according to the specified conditions and proportion.

Corporate bond with attached warrant A product combination of bond and warrant, where, in the bond issue, the issuer provides a certain amount of stock warrants to the bond holders, allowing them to subscribe for the company's shares at an agreed price (exercise price) within a specified period.

Corporate bond A credit and debt certificate generally issued by industrial and commercial enterprises, with a certain par value and repayment conditions.

Cost-push inflation Inflation caused by cost rise.

Covered arbitrage While carrying out interest arbitrage activities, one sells foreign exchange in the forward exchange market to avoid the risk of exchange rate fluctuations.

CPI Price index developed on the basis of the consumption of typical families.

Credit allocation The central bank restricts the credit scale of commercial banks in line with the economic situation.

Credit independence The degree to which fiscal deficit depends on the central bank, or the degree to which other variables impact on the base currencybase money.

Credit rationing A bank refuses to grant whole or part of a loan to the borrower, and thus the borrower's fund demand can only be partially satisfied or can not be satisfied at all.

Cross rate Also known as crosses, it refers to the exchange rate between two non-basic currencies based on the basic exchange rate of two currencies.

Currency arbitrage The activity of taking advantage of exchange rate difference between two currencies in different foreign exchange markets at the same time to buy and sell foreign exchange for exchange gains.

Currency board system An exchange rate system in which the law explicitly stipulates that local currency maintains a fixed exchange rate with the convertible currency of another country, and specially restrains the issue of banknotes to guarantee the performance of such a legal obligation.

Currency convertibility Holders of currencies may freely convert one currency into another major international reserve currency according to the market exchange rate.

Currency crisis The circumstances where the people lose confidence in domestic currency and sell off it, thereby resulting in quick depreciation of the currency.

Currency substitution ratio The ratio of increase in foreign currencies held by the people to the increase in domestic currency in current year.

Currency substitution Domestic residents hold foreign currencies as a measure of value, medium of exchange or means of store of value.

Current account Items reflecting the transfer of physical resources between one country and another, including goods, services, income and transfer without compensation.

Darby effect Real interest rate after deducting interest income tax.

Debt crisis The government of a country can not repay its foreign debts as promised, causing huge losses to the financial institutions which lent money to the country.

Debt financing A financing method where the user of capital promises to repay the lender in the future according to certain conditions, mainly including bank loans, bonds, bill financing, and commercial credits.

Debt-for-equity swap A financial asset management company translates the non-performing loans acquired from wholly state-owned commercial banks to the equities of the borrowing enterprises.

Decision lag The interval between the time when the central bank realizes the necessity of adjusting monetary policy and the time when the monetary policy is finally implemented.

Default risk Also known as credit risk, it means the probability that the borrower can not repay principal and interest on schedule.

Deficit debtization To make up fiscal deficits by issuing government bonds.

Deficit monetization To make up fiscal deficits with loans from the central bank.

Defined benefit plan The plan that determines in advance the total amount of pension that an employee will receive after working for a certain number of years.

Defined contribution plan Both employees and the employer shall deposit, on a monthly basis, a certain amount of money in employees' accounts at a certain percentage of their wages.

Deflation The process of a continuous decline in the general price level.

Delegated monitoring Financial intermediaries, on behalf of scattered depositors, monitor the activities of borrowers.

Demand-following financial development Financial development driven by the development of the real economy.

Demand-pull inflation The inflation caused by expansion of total demand.

Dependence on foreign trade The ratio of a country's total imports and exports in a year to its GDP.

Deposit multiplier The number by which the original one-yuan deposits areis multiplied in the deposit creation process, and which equals the reciprocal of the required deposit reserve ratio.

Depository receipt The stock of a company available in the securities market outside the company's home country.

Derivative deposits Deposits created in the commercial bank system by granting loans.

Derivative financial instruments Financial products, including futures and options, which are derived from primary financial instruments, with the main functions to manage the risk exposure arising in connection with the primary instruments.

Direct arbitrage When a difference exists in the exchange rate of the same currency in two different foreign exchange markets, people will purchase this currency in one market *and at the same time* sell *the same currency* in the other *market to* earn a profit.

Direct control monetary policy The central bank controls the money supply or interest rates directly by credit control, so as to attain its monetary policy objectives.

Direct financial transformation mechanism The surplus funds of lender–savers flow to the borrower–spenders via the financial market and a one-to-one relationship exists between the lender–savers and the borrower–spenders.

Direct investment The residents of one country directly establish branches abroad, or purchase enough shares in a foreign enterprise to acquire a certain control right in the enterprise.

Direct quotation The buying rates and selling rates of different delivery periods are directly displayed on the quotation board.

Direct quotation method The exchange rate between two currencies is expressed as the amount of the foreign currency that can be exchanged per unit of the domestic currency.

Discount bond The bond honored for the bond holder at par, but with a market price lower than its par value before maturity.

Discount rate The interest rate used in calculation of present value.

Discretionary monetary policy The monetary authorities or the central bank flexibly selects different monetary policies in line with changing economic situations in different periods, in order to attain its most desired policy objectives.

Disintermediation The phenomenon of substantial outflow of funds from commercial banks due to interest rate control.

Disposable income The balance of gross income deducting income tax.

Distribution The underwriter, as authorized by a company, undertakes the responsibility of issuer to issue and sell bonds or stocks.

Draft A note issued by the drawer, entrusting the payer to unconditionally pay a specified amount of money to the bearer or payee at sight or on the specified date.

Duration The average time that an investor needs to recover its bond investment.

Duration analysis An interest rate risk measurement method taking into account the impact of the average duration of bank assets and liabilities on bank profits.

Dutch auction A bidding system in which the bidder with the highest offer wins the bid but the payment price is the weighted average of the bid prices of all successful bidders.

Economic capital A fictitious capital that is equal to the amount of the unexpected loss of bank risk.

Economic transactions Transfer of economic value from one economic entity to another.

Effect of monetary policy How effectively the central bank attains its ultimate goal by operating monetary policy instruments.

Effective yield The nominal yield minus inflation.

Electronic fund transfer system A system that allows bank customers to go shopping at the chartered merchants of the card issuing banks with debit cards or credit cards, without having to carry cash.

Electronic money Credit money paid and transferred by computer or stored value card.

Endogenous financing Internal financing The user of capital finances its expenditure by its internal accumulation of fund.

Endogenous money supply The central bank can not control money supply independently, and money supply is determined in the operation of economic system.

Equity fund The fund that invests the proceeds raised through the issuance of fund units into corporate stocks.

Eternal triangle Also known as Krugman's triangle, it summarizes the financial development models of various countries as follows: selection of independence of domestic monetary policy and free capital flow, selection of exchange rate stability and free capital flow, and selection of independence of monetary policy and stable exchange rate.

Euromoney The currencies circulated outside the currency issuing countries.

European option An option exercised only at maturity.

Excess reserve Reserve funds held by commercial banks in excess of the required reserves for the purpose of liquidity management.

Exchange Short for foreign exchange.

Exchange rate risk The probability that enterprises or individuals suffer losses as a result of exchange rate changes in the economic activities of holding or using foreign exchange.

Exchange rate system A series of arrangements or provisions made by the monetary authorities of one country with respect to the basic mode of changes in the exchange rates between its domestic currency and foreign currencies.

Exchange rate target zone An exchange rate system of restraining exchange rate fluctuation within a specified range.

Exogenous financing External financing Those short of funds raise capital from those with surplus funds in some ways.

Exogenous money supply The central bank can control money supply independently.

Expectation hypothesis A theory holding that the interest rate of a long-term bond equals the average of short-term interest rates expectations before maturity of the long-term bond.

Expected revenue The weighted average of the expected rates of return on all assets in an asset portfolio.

Expenditure changing policies Macroeconomic policies, including fiscal and monetary policies, which are designed to regulate the balance of payments by changing total domestic expenditure.

Expenditure switching policies The policies, primarily exchange rate policies and direct controls, which are designed to change the relative price of imports and exports and thereby change the demand for them and achieve a balance in international payments.

External mandatory regulation mechanism The government requires that all participants in financial activities must strictly observe relevant laws and regulations.

Fiat money As a commodity, its value is not exactly equal to the value as a currency, and besides it can not used to exchange for commodity money.

Financial assets A general term for the financial instruments with actual price and future valuation as well as specific ownership.

Financial bubble A continuous process which involves abrupt price rise in a series of assets. In the beginning, the price rise will give people the expectation that the price will continue to go up, thereby attracting new buyers. With a reversal in the expectation, the price will plummet and end with a financial crisis.

Financial crisis All or most financial indicators deteriorate too drastically to be tolerable for the socioeconomic system.

Financial deepening The process of optimization of financial structure and constant expansion and improvement of financial functions.

Financial deficit The government's revenue is not enough to cover its expenditure.

Financial development The process of constantly improving and expanding financial functions and thereby boosting financial efficiency and economic growth.

Financial fragility The instability of the financial system.

Financial globalization An economic phenomenon that financial activities are conducted and financial assets and liabilities are operated under the uniform rules in the world, and meanwhile financial risks are globally contagious.

Financial innovation Activities to create new financial instruments, organizations and systems so as to allocate financial resources more reasonably, to increase income or mitigate risks.

Financial instruments Contracts stipulating the debtor–creditor relationship, usually including the amount, conditions and maturity of financial surplus to be transferred from those with surplus funds to those short of funds.

Financial interrelations ratio The ratio of M2 to GDP of a country.

Financial leverage Ratio of debt to equity.

Financial liberalization The government abandons administrative interventions in the financial system, and allows the financial market to give play to its fundamental role in allocation of financial resources.

Financial regulation The government formulates a series of rules and authorizes corresponding institutions to implement these rules so as to regulate the acts of all parties to financial activities.

Financial repression Compulsory administrative interventions in the financial system conducted by the governments of developing countries for specific purposes, making it impossible for the financial system to give play to its role in guiding the reasonable resources allocation by market mechanism.

Financial savings Savings arising from such financial assets as negotiable securities, bank deposits and cash.

Financial structure The ratio between various financial instruments, and assets and number of financial institutions.

Financial transformation mechanism A mechanism to regulate the fund surplus and deficiency by the financial system.

First generation currency crisis theory The theory holding that currency crisis is caused by inconsistency between a large amount of government deficits and fixed exchange rates.

Fiscal policy A macro-economic policy pursued to regulate total demand or total supply by adjustment of government expenditure and taxes.

Fiscal transformation mechanism The government pools the financial surpluses in society and allocates them to the business sectors.

Fisher Effect The relationship between nominal and real interest rates and inflation rate.

Fisher Equation An equation indicating that the product of money supply and velocity of money equals the product of general price level and total output: $M \cdot V = P \cdot T$, and the changes in money supply will lead to a price rise by the same proportion.

Five-tier loan classification approach To divide loans into five categories, i.e., performing, special mention, substandard, doubtful and loss, the last three of which are collectively called non-performing loans.

Fixed exchange rate system The actual exchange rate can only fluctuate within a very narrow band due to the restriction of parity.

Floating exchange rate system The exchange rate system whereby the prevailing exchange rates are not subject to parity but vary with the supply and demand in the foreign exchange market.

Foreign exchange buffer policy Taking advantage of changes in official reserves or temporarily raising foreign capital to offset extra foreign exchange demand or supply.

Foreign exchange market The marketplace for foreign exchange trading.

Foreign exchange reserve Foreign current assets held by the monetary authorities, including bank deposits and treasury bills.

Foreign exchange settlement and sale Export enterprises shall sell foreign exchange earned from exports to designated banks. When an enterprise needs foreign exchange to import goods or equipment, it shall apply for purchasing foreign exchange. As far as a bank is concerned, the former is called foreign exchange settlement, and the latter is called foreign exchange sale.

Foreign exchange speculation Holding long or short positions of foreign exchange based on anticipation for exchange rate changes, in the hope of profiting from fluctuation of exchange rates.

Foreign exchange spot transaction Also called FX spot transaction, it means the transaction in foreign exchange which is delivered within two trading days from the date when the deal is made.

Forward delivery Delivery is completed two trading days after both parties enter into a trade agreement.

Forward discount The forward exchange rate is lower than the spot exchange rate, with a negative forward margin.

Forward exchange rate An exchange rate predetermined by both parties for foreign exchange trade on a specified date in the future.

Forward margin Quote a forward exchange rate certain points higher or lower than the spot exchange rate.

Forward premium The forward exchange rate is higher than the spot exchange rate, with a positive forward margin.

Forward transaction Also known as forward exchange transaction, it is a foreign exchange transaction to be delivered on a specified date in the future according to the forward contract, after both parties conclude a transaction.

Free float An exchange rate system where the monetary authorities do no intervene in the foreign exchange market but let the exchange rate freely float with the change in market supply and demand.

Free reserve The balance of excess reserves of commercial banks less borrowed reserves.

Free rider It means anyone who receives the benefits from other people's economic activities without having to pay for it.

Frictional unemployment Temporary unemployment caused by adjustment of work.

Functional regulation Specific business activities of financial institutions are supervised and reviewed by specialized management experts within a unified regulatory body according to the corresponding management procedures.

Future value The total amount of principal and interest at the end of a certain period in the future, after the interest of a specified amount of initial investment is charged at a compound interest rate.

Gap The gap between the interest rate-sensitive assets and the interest rate-sensitive liabilities.

General price level The general level of prices of all goods and services.

Gibson Paradox The phenomenon that CPI and nominal interest rates change in the same direction.

Global economic imbalance The phenomenon that domestic savings in many developed countries, typically the US, have long been less than investments, thus resulting in huge trade deficits; however, some developing or emerging countries, have exhibited domestic savings greater than investments, and thus have a persistent and significant trade surplus.

GNP deflator The ratio of GNP calculated on the basis of prices of current year to GNP calculated on the basis of fixed prices.

Gold standard A monetary system with gold as the standard money.

Government bond A credit and debt certificate issued by the government, with a certain par value and repayment conditions.

Gresham's law Under the bimetallic standard, arbitrage behavior causes gold or silver, whichever has a market value higher than the official fixed rate, to be removed from circulation.

Gross price method Securities pricing has taken into account the interest accrued in the period of repurchase agreement.

Growth fund A mutual fund mainly aiming at pursuing long-term capital gain.

Guarantee insurance The insurance provided by the insurer for any economic loss incurred by the default of one party to an unsecured loan or sale contract.

Hard currency A currency tending to appreciate in the foreign exchange market.

Hedging Two reverse trading strategies adopted for the same asset, using the profits from the transaction in one direction to make up losses on transaction in the opposite direction.

Herding A phenomenon in which investors in financial assets follow the investment behavior of others.

Hidden inflation The phenomenon that goods are undersupplied and can not be purchased even with money.

Holding period return Rate of return realized during the period of holding a financial instrument.

Housing reserve fund An earmarked fund withheld from staff salaries on a percentage basis to finance their purchase of housing in the future.

Hybrid capital bond A bond with a maturity of no less 15 years and unredeemable within 10 years, which can be used to make up operating losses of commercial banks, suspend claim right or absorb losses, and which ranks below subordinated bond but above equity capital with regard to claim for repayment.

Hybrid fund A mutual fund that invests in stocks and bonds simultaneously.

Immediate annuity A series of equal cash flows generated immediately.

Income effect As raising the interest rate would lead to an increase in future interest income, people only need to deposit a small amount of savings to meet their specific expenditures in the future. Therefore, this will encourage them to increase their current consumption and reduce their savings for the future.

Income fund A mutual fund mainly in pursuit of fixed income.

Income/wealth elasticity of assets Percentage of changes in asset demands caused by every 1% change in income/wealth.

Indirect arbitrage The activity of capitalizing on the exchange rate differences to buy cheap and sell dear the same currency in three different foreign exchange markets so as to earn the rate variance gains.

Indirect financial transformation mechanism A mechanism to channel the funds from economic units with surplus funds to those short of funds via banks and other financial intermediaries, which generally involves two contracts and a risk firewall.

Indirect monetary policy A monetary policy where the central bank influences the reserve funds of commercial banks by market means so as to regulate money supply and market interest rates.

Indirect quotation method A method in which the exchange rate is expressed by one unit of a domestic currency converted into certain units of foreign currencies.

Inflation The process of a continuous rise in the general price level.

Inflation targeting A specific inflation rate explicitly published by the central bank in advance, and the aim of the central bank's monetary policy is to ensure the price rise is maintained within the target range published by the central bank.

Informal finance Sporadic and petty financial activities in which formal financial institutions do not participate.

Information asymmetry One has more information than the other.

Inside information The information that has not been made public but has a significant impact on the prices of stocks, bonds, funds, futures, and other financial products.

Insider control The managers of an enterprise capitalize on their easy access to information in businesss operation to seek their own interests at the cost of the shareholders.

Insider trading The trading activities in which the insiders purchase or sell relevant financial products for extra profits based on inside information.

Institutional regulation Different regulatory authorities regulate and supervise different financial institutions under the separateoperation conditions.

Insurance It refers to the risk management measures whereby an extra fee is paid to avoid huge losses in the future.

Interbank discount A discounting bank transfers the discounted bills to another bank for discounting when it needs funds.

Interbank lending market A market for short-term loans between financial institutions to regulate their temporary positions and meet liquidity needs.

Interbank lending Lending activities conducted to obtain more short-term liabilities and regulate temporary and seasonal needs of funds, rather than making up the deficiencies of reserves or positions.

Interest arbitrage The activity of transferring capital from the country of lower interest rate to the country of higher interest rate to earn the interest spread, when there is difference between the short-term interest rates of the two countries.

Interest rate parity A theory holding that the fluctuation in exchange rate between two currencies depends on the difference between the interest rates of the two countries.

Interest rate risk The probability of loss incurred by fluctuation in market interest rates.

Interest rate The price paid by the borrower to the lender in order to obtain the right to use the latter's funds.

Interest-bearing bond coupon bonds The bonds for which the issuer promises, at the time of issuing bonds, to pay interest at a certain rate and repay principal to the bond holder in the future.

Intermediate target A variable which links the means variable of monetary policy to the ultimate target.

International reserve Assets owned by the monetary authorities of a country for satisfying its need of international payments equilibrium.

Investment savings Save money for more consumptions and income in the future.

IS curve It shows the relationship between interest rates and equilibrium national income when total output equals total demand.

J-curve effect Balance of payments will continue deteriorating in the early period after depreciation of domestic currency, and will gradually improve thereafter.

Laffer curve A curve showing that tax revenue will increase with an increase in tax rates, but beyond a certain degree, increasing tax rates will not raise tax revenue but rather decrease it.

Law of one price Under the free trade condition, the price of the same commodity expressed in the same currency must be the same anywhere, regardless of the place of origin.

Lead underwriter A securities company or an investment bank responsible for organizing other institutions to participate in the underwriting.

Liability business The process that a commercial bank obtains surplus funds from other persons through certain channels.

Liability insurance Insurance coverage designed to protect the insured from the risk of liabilities for civil damages.

Liquidity The ability of an asset to be converted into cash and without loss.

Liquidity premium Rise in the coupon rate of a bond resultinged from mitigation of bond liquidity.

LM curve It shows the relationship between interest rates and national income when money market is in equilibrium.

Loan commitment The commitment that a financial institution signs a contract with an enterprise, promising to grant credit support for the enterprise within a certain period in future as long as the contract conditions remain unchanged.

Loan concentration The proportion of loans granted to an enterprise in the bank's outstanding loans.

Loan loss reserve A part of a commercial bank's income set aside to make up possible loan losses of the bank.

Loan specialization A bank grants most loans to local enterprises or the enterprises of a certain industry.

Luxury goods The assets with an elasticity of demand to income/wealth of more than 1.

M&M theorem Also known as Modigliani–Miller Theorem, it indicates that an enterprise's market value is irrelevant to its financing structure in frictionless markets.

$\boldsymbol{M_0}$ Currency in circulation

M_1 M_0+ Demand deposits

M_2 M_1+ Time deposits + Savings deposits + Other deposits.

Managed floating exchange rate system An exchange rate system which is subject to interventions by the monetary authorities to make exchange rates float in a desirable direction.

Marginal productivity of Capital The added value created by each additional unit of capital input.

Marginal propensity to consume It refers to the increase in consumption expenditure that an additional unit of disposable income brings about.

Marginal propensity to save It refers to the increase in savings that an additional unit of disposable income brings about.

Market segmentation theory A theory holding that the bond markets of different maturities are totally independent and segmented from one another, and the interest rate of each bond is affected only by its own supplydemand dynamics.

Marshall–Lerner condition Only if the sum of the price elasticity of import demand and that of export demand is more than 1, can the international payments be improved through devaluation of domestic currency.

Meade conflict Internal and external conflicts the government's fiscal and monetary policies face under the fixed exchange rate system.

Means variable A monetary policy variable that can be directly controlled by the policy instrument of the central bank.

Menu cost The cost incurred by change of price tags due to price fluctuation.

Missing money The part of money supply growth rate in excess of the sum of the inflation rate and economic growth rate.

Mixed operation A system allowing a financial organization to operate commercial banking, investment banking and insurance business in a mixed way.

Monetary policy The central bank leverages various policy instruments to increase or reduce money supply and thus regulate interest rates and total demands.

Monetary structure Also known as monetary liquidity structure, it is defined as the ratio of the balance of more liquid money to that of less liquid money.

Monetary system Also known as currency system, it is a currency circulation structure and organization form legally defined by the government of a country.

Monetization Increase in the proportion of commodity transactions with money as a medium in the national income and increase in money and other financial assets as a means of wealth storage.

Money creation The process that commercial banks create derivative deposits by granting loans to enterprises.

Money market The financial market with a term of no more than one year, mainly designed to adjust temporary fund surplus and deficit and manage liquidity.

Money multiplier The multiplier by which money supply changes as a result of base currencybase money change.

Money An object that can serve as a measure of value, medium of exchange, store of value and means of payment.

Monthly installment payment A fixed amount payable to a bank on a monthly basis after borrowing money from the bank.

Moral hazard A party short of funds, after receiving an investment, engages in activities that investors would not like them to conduct.

Moral Suasion Also known as window guidance, it means that the central bank informs each bank about its standpoint and leverages its influence so as to implement the monetary policy.

Mutual independence The change in one variable does not relate to the change in another variable.

Natural rate of unemployment The unemployment rate when the labor supply equals the demand in the market or the inflation rate is zero.

Necessities The assets with an elasticity of demand to income/wealth of less than 1.

Negative correlation Two variables change in opposite directions.

Net financial investment The balance of increase in financial assets less increase in financial liabilities in current year.

Net price transaction In a treasury bond transaction, the trading price is separated from the accrued interest of bond and fluctuates in line with market conditions while accrued interest is calculated on a daily basis according to the coupon rate, so as to facilitate bond holders to enjoy the interest accrued during the holding period.

Netting The participants first mutually set off their creditor's rights and debts and then settle the balance thereof (if any).

Nominal exchange rate An exchange rate directly published, used in the social and economic life and reflecting the price relations between the currencies of two countries.

Nominal interest rate The interest rate expressed in nominal currency.

Nominal yield The yield that does not take into account the influence of inflation.

Off-balance-sheet business in the narrow sense It includes loan commitments, guarantee, derivative financial instruments, and investment banking.

Off-balance-sheet business The business that is not reflected in a bank's balance sheet but may affect its operating income and profits.

Off-exchange transaction A general term for various securities trading activities conducted outside the trading hall of a securities exchange.

Off-site review Each commercial bank is required to regularly submit to the banking regulatory authorities financial reports, including balance sheet, income statement and cash flow statement.

On-site inspection Officers of the banking regulatory authorities personally inspect a bank's financial vouchers and assets and liabilities without giving a prior notice.

Open market operation The measures taken by the central bank to purchase or sell marketable securities in the securities market, regulate the banking sector"s reserve funds and further affect the money supply.

Open-end fund An investment fund whose securities may vary in scale throughout the duration of the fund.

Open-end repo A repo transaction mode in which, during the effective period of a repurchase agreement, the repo party may deliberate on change of categories of pledged bonds, or the reverse repo party may dispose of bonds at liberty.

Optimum currency area An independent currency area composed of the regions where economy is open, flows of goods, labor, and capital are free, industrial structures are different but economic growth and inflation rates are close, and economic and monetary policies are comparatively coordinated.

Option A future right to choose that allows an option buyer, after paying a certain amount of premium, to require the option seller to sell or purchase a specific product within a specific period of time in future at the predetermined price.

Ordinary annuity A series of equal cash flows occurring at the end of each period.

OTC transaction The securities trading activities handled over the counters of securities companies or banks.

Own reserve The balance of total reserves of commercial banks less borrowed reserves.

Par bond A coupon bond with par value equal to market price.

Parity The forward and spot exchange rates are equal and the forward margin is zero.

Pegged exchange rate system The exchange rate system adopted by a country whereby a fixed exchange rate is maintained between its local currency and other key currencies, while the exchange rate between its currency and non-key currencies is allowed to fluctuate relative to that between key currencies and non-key currencies.

Permanent income The average income at each period of life.

Perpetuity An annuity that has an infinite term.

Personal insurance It includes life insurance, health insurance, and accidental insurance, with a person's life span and body as the insurance object and a person's subsistence and decease as the condition for benefit payment.

Phillips curve A curve showing the alternative relationship between unemployment rate and inflation rate.

Physical savings Savings in the form of housing, consumer durables, and inventories.

Placement at market value The method of new share issues whereby a number is assigned to each investor according to the market value of shares they will purchase and lots are then cast to decide on the winning number.

Policy bank A non-profit financial institution founded or guaranteed by the government to implement the national industrial policy and regional development policy in light of special financing principles.

Policy independence The degree of autonomy that a central bank has during the formulation and implementation of monetary policy.

Position lending Accommodation of short-term funds among financial institutions in the lending market in order to square positions and supplement required reserves and funds for bill clearing.

Positive correlation One variable changes in the same direction with another.

PPI Price index of enterprise inputs, including purchase of raw materials, which reflects the changes in enterprises" production cost.

Precautionary savings To save as a way of preparing for future uncertainties.

Preferred habit theory A theory holding that the interest rate of a long-term bond equals the average expected interest rate of short-term bonds before the bond becomes due, plus the maturity premium of such bond varying with the demand-supply conditions.

Premium bond A coupon bond with a higher market price than its par value.

Present value A certain amount in the future is converted into the value at present according to a specified interest rate.

Price control The government restricts the range of price rise of various commodities and services.

Price manipulation The trading activity where the investors leverage their capital advantages to buy or sell a large amount of a certain financial product, to make the price of such financial product to change to their advantage and thereby generate exorbitant profits.

Price-earnings ratio The ratio of market price to current earnings per share of stocks.

Primary dealer The commercial bank, securities company, insurance company, trust and investment company, or any other financial institution approved by the People's Bank of China and qualified for trading bonds directly with the People's Bank of China.

Primary dealers in the open market The financial institutions qualified for directly trading bonds with the People's Bank of China by open market operation.

Primary deposit The bank deposit arising from the unspent portion of income.

Primary financial instrument Also known as underlying financial instrument, it is an instrument mainly designed to translate savings to investment or to serve as a certificate for credit-debt settlement.

Primary market Also known as issue market, it is the market for those short of funds to raise capital by issuing various financial instruments.

Primary reserves The required reserves and excess reserves held by commercial banks.

Private placement A financing method of issuing securities to a small number of specific investors.

Promissory note A negotiable instrument signed and issued by the maker promising to pay unconditionally the payee or bearer a specified sum of money at sight.

Propensity to consume The ratio of consumer expenditure to income in the current period.

Propensity to save The proportion of savings in current income.

Property insurance It provides insurance coverage for property and its related interests, and compensates the economic loss incurred by natural disasters or accidents.

Public offering A financing method to raise funds by issuing financial instruments to unspecific public.

Put option Also known as a put, it is the right to buy, with a certain amount of option money, an option to sell a product at a specific price within specified period of time in future, when the option buyer expects that the product's price will go down.

Quasi-money Assets which can not be directly used as a medium of exchange but rather function as a store of value, such as time deposits and savings deposits.

Ratchet effect The effect of short-term consumption in preventing future long-term consumption from dropping.

Rate of return The ratio of return on a financial instrument to the input of capital.

Reaction time lag The time interval from the implementation of monetary policy instruments by the central bank to the change in ultimate goal variables of the monetary policy.

Real bill A bill arising from commodity circulation and used in trade settlement.

Real exchange rate An exchange rate adjusted for the price levels in two countries.

Real interest rate The difference between nominal interest rate and inflation rate, which is measured by the actual goods or services available in the market.

Real time gross settlement Timely settlement of interbank lending transactions one by one.

Recognition lag An interval between the time when the economic situation changes to the time when the central bank has realized the necessity of taking corresponding monetary policy to regulate economic position.

Rediscount A commercial bank transfers unmatured bills to a central bank at a discount when it needs funds.

Rediscount rate The interest rate adopted by a central bank in providing rediscount service for commercial banks.

Refinancing The loans granted by a central bank to commercial banks and other financial institutions.

Regulatory capital The capital calculated as required by the regulatory authorities, including core capital and supplementary capital.

Regulatory forbearance For the sake of financial stability, the government takes various protective measures to prevent commercial banks which face serious financial difficulties from going bankrupt.

Regulatory rule-based monetary policy A monetary policy framework which provides the guidelines for the central bank prior to the formulation and operation of its monetary policy.

Reinsurance Also known as cession, it is a type of insurance where the insurer enters into a contract to transfer the risk it has underwritten to one or several other insured parties so as to lower its exposure to risks.

Relative income hypothesis A theory holding that the propensity to consume depends on the comparison between a person's income and the income of other persons.

Repo A contract promising, at the time of sale of securities, to repurchase these securities from the counterparty at a specified price on a given date in the future.

Repurchase transaction An agreement whereby one party sells treasury bonds to the other party at the price and on the date agreed upon by both parties, and promises to repurchase these treasury bonds from the latter on a specified date in future.

Required reserve The reserve fund that commercial banks are required to hold on deposit with the central bank.

Resale An agreement concluded at the time of purchase of treasury bonds, providing for resale of these bonds at the agreed price on a future date.

Reverse repo While a security is purchased, an agreement is signed simultaneously to sell the same security to the seller at a specified price on a given date in the future.

Ricardian Equivalence Theorem Tax collection and bond issue by the government have the same effect on savings and consumption choices.

Risk The probability of an asset suffering potential losses or the uncertainty of future expected return.

Risk assets The assets with an uncertain rate of return during the period of being traded by investors, and a positive variance/standard deviation of rate of return.

Risk premium Extra compensations provided in order to encourage investors to bear additional risks.

Risk-free assets The assets whose rate of return is foreseeable within the decision range of investors and has a variance/standard deviation of zero.

Savings The part of current income that has not been consumed.

Seasonal unemployment Unemployment caused by seasonal changes.

Second generation currency crisis theory The theory holding that currency crisis is caused by the country's expansionary monetary policy.

Secondary market The financial market available for circulation and transfer of various negotiable financial instruments.

Secondary reserve Marketable securities held by commercial banks which can be sold in the secondary market for the purpose of liquidity management.

Securities investment fund A fund that pools scattered petty funds into a large-scale fund and then invest it in various negotiable securities.

Securities margin ratio Ratio of money that the securities purchasers must pay in cash at the time of purchase.

Securities market overreaction The phenomenon that securities price fluctuates drastically as a result of an event and beyond the expected theoretical level, and then returns to the level that it would have reached by way of reverse correction.

Securitization The process of re-pooling a bank's original non-standardized loan contracts and then subdividing them into standardized financial instruments with the same amount, the same maturity and the same rate of return.

Self-liquidating loan A loan that is based on business activities and gets paid off automatically.

Selling rate The exchange rate used by banks in sale of foreign exchange.

Separate operation Commercial banks, investment banks and insurers are only allowed to operate within their respective business fields.

Separate regulation Financial supervision exercised according to the type of financial activities.

Short-term financing note A negotiable standardized bond issued by a large industrial and commercial enterprise, securities company or any other financial institution, with a term of not more than one year.

Simple interest The interest of principal earned in the first interest period will not be calculated in the second period.

Soft currency A currency tending to depreciate in the foreign exchange market.

Special drawing right (SDR) A book asset allocated by IMF to its member countries according to their quotas, which can be used to repay IMF loans and liquidate the international payment deficits among the governments of member countries.

Speculative demand for money Hold a certain amount of money for speculations at the right time in the future.

Spot bond transaction The bond is traded according to the payment mode specified in the contract, and delivered and settled within a given period to complete the transfer of bond ownership.

Spot delivery Delivery is completed within two trading days after both parties enter into a trade agreement.

Spot exchange rate Also known as spot rate, it represents the exchange rate used in delivery of foreign exchange within two trading days after the transaction is executed between the buyer and the seller.

Standby underwriting The underwriter, who issues relevant financial instruments on behalf of the issuer, shall subscribe for all the remaining instruments if they are unsold within the specified period.

Stock A certificate representing partial ownership of a company.

Structural disequilibrium International payment imbalance caused by the economic structural imbalance of a country.

Subordinated debt Long-term debt of a commercial bank with a fixed term of not less than five years, which, unless bankruptcy or liquidation of the bank, shall not be used to make up the bank's daily operating losses, and which ranks below deposits and other liabilities with regard to claim for repayment.

Substitution effect The higher the interest rates are, the more future consumption will be, and the more likely people are to save.

Supply-leading financial development Financial development driven by financial organizations.

Systematic financial crisis Crisis erupts in all financial fields, including banks, exchange rates and capital markets, and has a frustrating effect on the real economy.

Systematic risk The risk that all the assets in economic system face.

Terms of trade The quantity of imports that can be exchanged for a unit of exports.

Theory of absolute purchasing power parity A theory holding that the exchange rate between the currencies of two countries depends on the price ratio of the same goods of the two countries.

Theory of relative purchasing power parity A theory holding that the fluctuation of exchange rate between two currencies depends on the difference between the inflation rates of two countries.

Third generation currency crisis theory The theory holding that currency crisis is caused by the government's implicit guarantee.

Time lag of monetary policy The time interval between the time when the central bank implements monetary policy as warranted by changes in the economic situation and the time when a change is effected in the ultimate goal variable.

Time value of money It refers to the fact that a certain amount of money today has a higher value than it will in the future.

Tinbergen Norm If a government has *n* economic policy objectives, it needs the same number of independent effective policy instruments, so as to achieve these objectives simultaneously.

Tobin's q The ratio of market value and capital replacement cost of an enterprise.

Trade concentration The ratio of the amount of foreign trade with a certain country or region to the total imports from and exports to the country.

Trade deficit The import value of goods is larger than the export value of goods.

Trade surplus The import value of goods is lower than the export value of goods.

Traditional underwriting The underwriter is fully authorized by the issuer to sell all the currently issued financial instruments to investors.

Transaction demand for money The money held for future transactions in goods and services.

Transmission mechanism of monetary policy The process that the central bank leverages monetary policy instruments to operate indicator variables and thereby attain the ultimate goal of monetary policy.

Treasury bill Negotiable and marketable securities issued by the government for satisfying short-term financing needs.

Triangular debt Chain debt between enterprises.

Tube effect Increasing the actual monetary return will encourage the people to save the more and consume the less and increase endogenous financinginternal financing so as to drive the growth of material capital investment.

Twin deficit The phenomenon that trade deficit and fiscal deficit of the government exist simultaneously.

Two-way quotation A bank quotes buying rate and selling rate simultaneously.

Uncovered arbitrage A pure arbitrage strategy that does not involve selling foreign exchange in the forward exchange market.

Underground transaction The covert transaction in violation of prevailing laws or regulations.

Underwriting syndicate A temporary organization composed of a number of securities companies or investment banks qualified for acceptance to jointly underwrite a stock or bond.

Unified regulation All financial activities are under the supervision of one regulatory body.

Unsystematic risk Specific risk arising from certain enterprises or industries that can be diversified by investment portfolio.

Velocity of money Also known as income velocity or turnover rate of money, it is defined as the frequency of exchange of goods or service for the same unit of money within a given period.

Voluntary unemployment Unemployment when people are able but unwilling to work.

Voting by hand The shareholders participate in the business decisions of a listed company and directly supervise the company.

Voting with feet A shareholder sells out all its shares in a listed company in the secondary market when it is dissatisfied with the operation of the company.

Wage-push inflation Inflation caused by wage rise.

Wealth effect Different propensities to consume and save caused by wealth gap.

Yield to maturity curve The curve that shows the relationship between yield to maturity and remaining period.

Yield to maturity Annual discount rate at which the present value of interest paid in each year of the remaining period of bonds and par value of bonds equal the current market price.

Index

5C and 5P, 192

Absolute Purchasing Power Parity, 434
Acceptance, 242
Actual Future Value, 66
Adverse Selection, 39–47, 605–607, 625–627
After-tax Real Interest Rate, 52, 65
Aggregate Demand, 411, 418–427, 433, 464, 480–484, 486–488, 493, 494, 532, 537
Agricultural Development Bank of China, 146
American auction, 213
American Depositary Receipts, 209
American Options, 301
Annuity, 57–68
A-shares, 208
Asian Financial Crisis, 440, 448, 463, 514, 598, 604, 617, 620, 621, 626
Asset, 4, 8, 16, 17–19, 91
Asset business, 168
Asset Competition Effect, 584
Asset Substitution, 373, 375

Balance of Payments, 161, 431, 437, 441, 442, 448, 449, 453–460, 462–475, 504, 506, 540
Balance of Payments Statement, 454–459, 463
Balanced Fund, 211
Bankers' acceptance bills, 242
Banking Crisis, 179, 604, 614
Banking Panic, 348, 349
Bank-lending Channel, 532
Base Money, 321, 323, 325–341, 343, 345, 352–356
Base money equation, 322
Basel Accord, 509, 570, 636, 639, 650
Basic Rate, 270
bear market, 216
Benchmark bond, 249
Bill discount, 243
Bill discount market, 246
Bill Market, 235, 241, 246
Bill of Exchange, 242, 243
Bills, 119, 241–248, 262
Bimetallic Standard, 14
Bond, 4, 18, 25, 26, 34–39, 72, 76, 84, 92, 93, 95–99, 116–126, 130, 133, 145, 150, 176, 200, 206, 207, 208, 211–215, 219, 220, 248, 249, 252–259, 284, 287–292, 363–375, 384, 390, 392, 397–404, 424, 433, 458, 506, 512, 520, 532, 536, 554, 557, 564, 568, 589, 604, 632, 640–642
Bond Fund, 210
Borrowed Reserve, 189
Borrower–Spenders, 24
BrettonWoods system, 14
Broad Credit Channel, 532
Brokerage, 149, 151, 152
Brokerage Securities Company, 149
B-shares, 208
bull market, 216
Buying Rate, 266, 267

Call Options, 302, 305–307
Cambridge Equation, 361, 362, 379
CAMEL Rating, 640
Capital Flight, 381
Capital Market, 27, 205, 231, 235, 641
Capital Market Instruments, 207, 211
Capital market line (CML), 107
Capital Market Price Index, 215
CAPM model, 105
Central Bank, 156, 157, 180, 182, 502–515, 517–546
Central Bank Bill, 249, 256, 334, 512, 519–521
Central Bank Independence, 539, 544
Cheap Credit, 579
Check, 241, 242
China Bank Regulatory Commission, 159
China Development Bank, 145
China Everbright Holdings, 153
China Insurance Regulatory Commission, 160
China Securities Regulatory Commission, 159
China's State Administration of Foreign Exchange, 161
CITIC Holdings, 153
City commercial banks, 143
Closed-End Fund, 209, 216, 217
Closed-end Repo, 252
Commercial acceptance bills, 242
Commercial Bank, 139, 140–146, 153–155, 157, 158, 167, 635–640
Commercial Credit, 118
Commodity-backed Money, 10
Compensating Balance, 192, 193
Component index, 215
Composite Index, 215
Compound Interest, 50–54
Comprehensive Securities Company, 149
Conflicts between Internal and External Equilibrium, 474, 588
Consumer loans, 114, 118, 119, 116, 169
Consumer Price Index, 19, 409, 410
Convertible bonds, 172, 182, 207
Core capital, 181, 182, 650
Corporate loans, 168
Corporate Pecking Order, 131
Correlation, 101, 102
Cost-push Inflation, 421
Coupon Bond, 218, 219
Covered Interest Arbitrage, 274
Credit assets, 92
Credit Default Swaps, 554
Credit Independence, 539, 540, 543
Credit Rationing, 43, 117, 192, 507, 526, 533
Credit Unions, 155
Credit views, 532
Cross Rate, 270
Currency Board System, 445, 446
Currency Convertibility, 573, 574, 588, 593, 594
Currency Crisis, 375, 604, 614, 615, 617, 626
Currency Mismatch, 277
Currency Ratio, 344–348, 353
Currency Substitution, 373, 375, 376
Currency Swaps, 313
Current Yield, 220

Debt Crisis, 604, 614
Debt Financing, 116, 118–123, 129–132
Debt Instruments, 34, 35
Debt-Deflation Theory, 609, 610
debt-to-equity swap, 153
Decision lag, 538
Defined Benefit Plan, 115
Defined Contribution Plan, 115
Deflation, 52, 81, 95, 195, 241, 355, 410–413, 423–426, 503, 514, 608, 609
Demand-Following Financial Development, 559
Demand-pull Inflation, 241
Deposit Money Banks, 140
Depositary Receipt, 209
Derivative Deposit, 140, 336, 337
Derivative Financial Instruments, 35, 283
Direct Finance, 25
direct financial transformation mechanism, 25

Direct Quotation, 264
Discount, 243–245
Discount Bond, 218, 219
Discount rate, 244
Discretionary Monetary Policies, 541, 543
Disintermediation, 555
Disposable income, 76
Distribution, 212
Diversification, 100–102
Dividend Discount Model, 223
Divorce Effect, 447
Double coincidence of wants, 5
Down-Payment, 193
Duration Analysis, 198, 200
Dutch auction, 213

Economic Capital, 182
Economic Monetization, 558
Electronic Money, 11, 552, 556
Endogenous Financial Development, 560, 561
Equity, 34, 93, 116, 120–125, 131, 132, 180, 184, 185, 191, 208, 370
Equity assets, 92, 93
Equity Capital, 181
Equity Financing, 119–123, 125, 132
Equity Fund, 210
Equity Instruments, 34, 46
Eternal Triangle, 626
Eurocurrency, 555
European Options, 301
European Sovereign Debt Crisis, 502, 570, 622, 623
Excess Reserves, 177, 183, 184, 189, 190, 339
Excess Reserves Ratio, 345, 349, 351
Exchange rate, 264–277
Exchange Rate Risk, 277, 278
Exchange Rate System, 440
Exchange Rate Target Zone System, 446
Exchange-Traded Fund, 210
Expectation Hypothesis, 401, 403, 404
Expected return, 97, 98, 100, 103, 104, 106, 226
Expenditure Change Policy, 467
Expenditure Switching Policy, 467
Export–Import Bank of China, 145
External Financing, 113, 114, 116, 119, 120, 122, 130, 131, 533, 582

Fiat money, 7, 10–12, 15, 16
Financial Accelerator, 532, 533
Financial Asset Management Companies, 152
Financial Assets, 4, 18, 24, 34, 91–95, 608, 610–613
Financial Bubble, 607, 608, 622
Financial Constraint, 82, 591
Financial Deepening, 514, 578, 584–586, 588
Financial Development, 551–553, 556–558, 563, 569
Financial Fragility, 604, 609
Financial Futures, 296
Financial Globalization, 587–592
Financial Holding Companies, 153
Financial Innovation, 18, 30, 31, 35, 153, 182, 356, 552, 554, 555, 631, 635, 645, 646
Financial Instruments, 33–37
Financial Interrelations Ratio, 557–560
Financial Leverage, 120, 130, 131, 626
Financial Liberalization, 561, 562, 573, 574, 584–593
Financial Market, 25, 33, 35, 44
Financial Regulation, 156, 574, 626, 631, 634, 641, 644, 645, 647, 648
Financial Repression, 82, 514, 573, 578, 579, 581, 586
Financial Savings, 72, 73, 80
Financial Structure, 18, 164, 532, 552, 563, 565, 566, 568, 569, 588
Financial Transformation Mechanism, 25, 26
Financing Costs, 123, 506
Financing Structure, 124–126
fiscal deficit, 132, 133
Fiscal Transformation Mechanism, 25
Fisher Equation, 359–362, 364, 377, 380
Five-Tier Loan Classification System, 177

Fixed Exchange Rate System, 440–443, 445, 448, 465, 466, 474, 475, 616, 626
Fixed Income Securities, 35
Floating Exchange Rate System, 440–444, 466, 593, 598, 599
Foreign Currency Options, 310
Foreign Exchange, 262
Foreign Exchange Buffer Policy, 470
Foreign Exchange Market, 262–264, 270, 273–278
Foreign Exchange Speculation, 272
Forward Bond Transaction, 288
Forward Discount, 268
Forward Exchange Settlement and Sale, 291
Forward Margin, 267
Forward Parity, 269
Forward Premium, 268
Forward Rate, 267–270, 272
Forward Speculation, 272
Forward Transactions, 271, 273, 284, 289, 291
Free Floating, 441
Free Reserve, 189
Frictional Unemployment, 503, 504
Full Employment, 355, 360, 361, 449, 474, 503–505
Full-bodied Commodity Money, 9
Functional Regulation, 647, 648
Fund Management Company, 149
Future Value, 52–66
Future Value Interest Factor, 55, 56, 60
Future Value of an Annuity, 58, 64
Futures, 291–311
Futures Brokerage Companies, 151
Futures Exchange, 151

Gap Analysis, 198
General Monetary Policy Instruments, 507, 522
General Price Level, 409–412, 417–422, 544
Gibson Paradox, 394
GNP Deflator, 410
Gold bullion standard, 13
Gold coin standard, 13
Gold exchange standard, 14
Gold Standard, 13
Government bond balance management, 250
Gresham's Law, 15
Growth enterprise markets (GEMs), 206
Growth funds, 210
Guarantee Insurance, 147

Headquarters-Branch Organization Structure, 143
Hedging, 109, 271, 272, 294, 295
Herding, 607
Hidden Inflation, 426
Holding period return, 37, 38
Honeymoon Effect, 447
Housing Reserve Fund, 115
H-shares, 208
Hybrid capital bonds, 172, 181
Hybrid funds, 210
Hyperinflation, 10, 11, 412, 426, 441

Immediate Annuity, 58–60, 65, 66, 68
Income Effect, 85
Income funds, 211
Income/wealth elasticity of assets, 96
Index Fund
Indirect Finance, 25
indirect financial transformation mechanism, 25
Indirect Quotation, 264, 265
Inflation, 9, 11, 17, 19, 38, 51, 52, 65, 66, 85, 95, 133, 195, 271, 347, 357, 394–397, 410, 411–417, 421, 425, 426, 434, 435, 442, 445, 502, 503, 505, 510, 512, 521, 538, 540–544, 581, 583, 585, 587, 594, 610, 615, 617, 624
Inflation Targeting, 542–544
Information Asymmetry, 39, 41, 44, 46, 566, 567
Initial public offerings (IPOs), 211
Insider Control, 41, 122, 625
Insider Information, 641
Insider Trading, 633, 634, 640–642, 650

Institutional Regulation, 646, 647, 665
Insurance, 108, 109, 146
Inter-Bank Discount, 244
Inter-Bank Lending, 236–239
Inter-bank Loans, 188, 238
Interest Arbitrage, 273, 274
Interest Rate Options, 307
Interest Rate Parity, 439, 482, 537
Interest Rate Swap, 201, 311, 314
Intermediate Business, 173
Intermediate Targets of Monetary Policy, 522, 524, 530
Internal Financing, 113–116, 120, 123, 131, 532, 533, 582–584
International Reserves, 165, 449, 458, 464, 594
Investment Banking, 149, 176
Investment Trusts, 155
Irrevocable loan commitment, 175
IS curve, 482–487, 494–497, 528, 529

J-curve effect, 473
joint-stock commercial banks, 142, 143
Junk Bond, 39, 557

Laffer Curve, 133
Law of One Price, 433–435
Lead underwriter, 212
Lender–Savers, 24
Liability business, 170
Liability Insurance, 147
Liquidity, 17–19, 29, 36, 37, 92, 94, 96, 98, 99, 118, 147, 157, 170, 171, 176, 177, 179, 180, 182, 183, 188, 190, 206, 210, 214, 236, 237, 241, 245, 246, 249, 250, 254, 257, 258, 289, 299, 333, 339, 348, 350–356, 362, 368, 392, 394, 398, 505, 510, 515, 518, 521, 524, 527, 553, 604, 605, 607, 638–640, 647, 650
Liquidity Coverage Ratio, 638
Liquidity Effect, 392, 394–397, 406, 536, 537
Liquidity Management, 35, 174, 182–184, 187, 244, 254, 339, 350, 509, 515, 516, 521
Liquidity Preference Theory, 365, 370, 372, 389, 394, 395
Liquidity Premium, 39, 399, 405
Liquidity Risk, 258, 289, 300, 397, 398, 405, 553, 588, 607, 638, 639
Liquidity Shortage, 170, 172
Liquidity Surplus, 170, 172
LM curve, 487, 489, 490, 492–496, 529
Loan, 168
Loan Commitment, 43, 44, 175, 191
Loan Specialization, 192
Loanable Funds Theory, 392
Local government financing vehicle (LGFV), 169
Luxuries, 96, 97

M&M Theorem, 124
$M0$, 17
$M1$ and $M2$, 17
Macro-prudential Regulation, 648, 649
Main board markets, 206
Managed Floating, 441
margin trading, 214
Marginal Propensity to Consume, 77, 78, 388
Marginal Propensity to Save, 77, 78, 86, 388
Market Overreaction, 229
Market Segmentation Theory, 403, 404
Marshall-Lerner Condition, 468, 472, 473, 476
Maturity, 27, 36, 38, 44, 51, 93, 94, 118, 134, 171, 198, 201, 205, 208, 218–220, 243–246, 248, 252, 255, 256, 286, 290, 293, 301, 307, 311, 313, 315, 401–405, 531, 605, 639, 641, 647
Maturity Premium, 404, 405
Meade Conflict, 474
Means of Payment, 7
Medium of Exchange, 7
Micro-Credit Companies, 155
Missing Money, 377
Mixed Operations, 170, 634, 636, 644, 647
Monetary Aggregates, 17, 18, 92, 380, 527
Monetary assets, 92

Monetary Liquidity Structure, 19
Monetary Policy, 157, 158, 235, 239, 249, 391, 417, 424, 425, 441, 449, 474, 502–505
Monetary Policy Instruments, 507, 513, 522, 523, 531
Monetary Policy Transparency, 544, 545
Monetary Structure, 11, 18
Monetary Unit, 11
Money, 4
money creation, 140, 339–341, 354
Money demand, 359, 361–365, 370, 372, 373, 389–393
Money Market, 27, 235, 237, 239, 241, 248, 249, 256
Money Market Fund, 256, 257
Money Multiplier, 341–347, 352, 356
money supply, 10, 13, 15, 18, 140, 157, 158, 172, 249, 321, 332, 341, 343, 345, 352–356, 373, 377–380, 389, 390–396, 425, 441, 442, 464–466, 489, 494, 496, 502, 505–514, 518, 519, 522, 525, 527–529, 532–538, 541, 542, 614, 624
Money veiws, 532
Moral Hazard, 39–45, 521–522, 535, 605–607

NASDAQ, 206, 214
Natural Rate of Unemployment, 416, 417
Necessities, 96, 97
Net Worth, 44, 533, 535–536, 606, 621
Net Financial Investment, 24
Net Price Transactions, 254
Net settlements, 239
Net Stable Funding Ratio, 638, 639
Net Worth, 43–45, 200, 256, 533, 535, 567, 621
Nominal Interest Rate, 50–52, 66
Nominal Return, 38
Non-systematic risks, 99
N-shares, 208

Objectives of Monetary Policy, 158, 502, 524, 531, 539, 544
Off-Balance-Sheet Business, 173
Off-Site Reviews, 640
On-Site Inspections, 640
Open Market Operations, 157, 171, 254, 333, 511–515, 518–521, 532, 535, 545
Open-End Fund, 210, 217
Open-end Repo, 252
Operation Twist, 531
Optimal Currency Area, 448, 449
Options, 110, 284, 301
Ordinary Annuity, 58, 59, 61–64, 66, 68
OTC Market, 214, 215

Par Bond, 219
Pegged Exchange Rate System, 444–446
People's Bank of China (PBOC), 15, 45, 74, 152, 156, 171, 244, 249, 286, 322, 330, 335, 425, 448, 468, 503, 505, 514, 516–521, 540, 541, 592, 595, 597, 598
Permanent Income, 78, 80, 370, 371, 373, 381
Perpetuity, 62, 63, 68
Personal Insurance, 148
Phillips Curve, 415–417
Physical Savings, 72, 73
Policy Assignment Rule, 476
Policy Banks, 144
Policy Independence, 539, 540, 543, 626
Ponzi Financing, 611, 612
Position Lending, 238
Positive Incentive of Contract, 45
Precautionary Savings, 84, 87
Premium Bond, 219
Present Value, 52–56, 59–64, 66, 198, 199, 220, 223, 231
Present Value Interest Factor, 60, 67
Present Value of an Annuity, 59, 61, 63
Price Controls, 423, 426
Price Manipulation, 150, 633, 634, 640–642
price–earnings ratio, 222
Price-to-Book Ratio, 223
Primary Financial Instrument, 35
Primary Market, 29, 206
primary reserve, 171
Principal–Agent, 40, 41

Private banking, 174
Private offering, 122
Producer Price Index, 410
Promissory Note, 241
Propensity to Consume, 76–78, 80, 81, 85
Propensity to Save, 77–80, 84–86
Property Insurance, 147, 148
Proprietary Business, 149
provision coverage, 178
public offering, 122
Purchasing Power Parity, 435, 435
Put Options, 302–307

Qualified Domestic Institutional Investors, 28, 375, 599
Qualified Foreign Institutional Investors, 28, 375, 569, 599
Quantitative Easing, 502, 512, 530, 531
Quasi-Money, 18

Ratchet Effect, 80
Rate of return, 37–40, 94–99, 103–107, 120–123, 128, 129, 131, 257, 258, 350, 398, 482, 583, 584
Real Bill, 243
Real Interest Rate, 50–52
Real Return, 38
Real-time Gross Settlements, 239
Recognition Lag, 538
Rediscount, 243, 244
Rediscount rate, 244
Refinancing, 187
Regulatory Capital, 182
Regulatory Forbearance, 606
Reinsurance, 148
Relative Income Hypothesis, 80
Relative Purchasing Power Parity, 435
Repo, 250–256, 513, 518–521
Repo transactions, 250
required reserves, 183, 184, 339
Reserves, 183
Response Lag, 538
Reverse Repo, 244, 251, 252, 254, 512, 519, 520
Revocable loan commitment, 175
Ricardian Equivalence Theorem, 134
Risk, 29, 34–37, 40, 97
Risk assets, 105
Risk Premium, 39, 106, 130, 249, 397, 398
Risk Structure of Interest Rates, 397
Risk-free assets, 105
RMB/FX Currency Swap, 313
RMB/FX Forward Transaction, 291
RMB/FX Swap, 312
Rule-Based Monetary Policies, 541, 544

Safety, 25, 36, 37, 39, 176, 177, 179–182, 254, 257, 458, 648
Savings, 27, 71, 386–388, 393, 398, 460, 578, 581, 582, 584, 587–589
Seasonal Unemployment, 503, 504
Secondary Market, 29, 33, 35, 44
Secondary Reserve, 171, 184, 186
Securities Company, 148–150
Securities Exchange, 150
Securities Investment Fund, 209, 210
Securitization, 35, 201
Selective Monetary Policy Instruments, 507, 521, 522, 535
Self-Liquidating Loans, 194
Selling Rate, 266, 267
Semi-Strong-Form Efficiency Market, 228
Separate Operations, 170, 634–636, 643, 645–647
Shadow Banking, 552, 647
SHIBOR, 240
short selling, 214
Short-Term Financing Bill, 248, 249
Silver Standard, 14
Simple Interest, 50, 51, 53, 54
Speculative Demand For Money, 364, 365, 369, 488–492
Spot Rate, 267–270
Spot Speculation, 272
Spot transaction, 250, 271
SSE, 180, 215
Standard deviation, 103, 104–107
standby underwriting, 212
State-controlled commercial banks, 141, 142

Stock Exchange, 150
Store of Value, 8
Strong-Form Efficiency Market, 229
Subordinated debt, 172, 181
Subprime Crisis, 622, 623
Substitution Effect, 85
Supplementary capital, 181, 650
Supply-Leading Financial Development, 559, 560
Swap, 311–313
Syndicated loans, 168
Systematic Financial Crisis, 604
Systematic risks, 99, 100

Taylor Rule, 541, 542
Tencent Q coins, 4
Term Structure of Interest Rates, 401
Terms of Trade, 443, 463, 471
The Basel Agreement, 172
The Darby Effect, 52
The Fisher Effect, 51
Third Market, 206
Time Lag of Monetary Policy, 538
Time Value of Money, 49–50
Tinbergen Norm, 474, 476
Traditional underwriting, 211
Transactional Demand for Money, 364, 365
Transmission Mechanisms of Monetary Policy, 531
Treasury bill, 248–250
triangular debt, 118
Trust Assets, 94
Tube Effect, 583

Uncovered Interest Arbitrage, 274
Underground Economy, 349
Underlying Financial Instruments, 35, 283
Underwriting syndicate, 212
Unit of Account, 6

Volker Rule, 649
Voting by Hand, 33
Voting with Feet, 33

Wage-push Inflation, 421
warrant bonds, 208
Weak-Form Efficiency Market, 228
wealth effect, 81
Wealth management, 174
Working capital loan, 168

Yield to Maturity, 38, 220–222, 231, 383
Yield to Maturity, 220, 221
Yield to Maturity Curve, 221